The Gnostic New Testament
And
Jewels From Nag Hammadi

By Joseph Lumpkin

The Gnostic New Testament
And
Jewels From Nag Hammadi

Fifth Estate Blountsville, AL 35031.

First Edition
Cover art by Heidi Milliken
Printed on acid-free paper

Library of Congress Control No: 2017919804

ISBN: 9781936533527

Fifth Estate, 2018

Table of Contents

The History of
The Gospel of Truth

The Gospel of Truth is the crowning jewel of Gnostic scriptures, serving a similar position and function as the book of Romans in the Holy Bible. Gnostic theology and the path of salvation according to that doctrine is laid open like a treasure map for the second century reader, and all seekers who have come after. The wisdom found in the text influenced later Gnostic writing. So rich, deep, and powerful are the spiritual ideas presented in this gospel that they influenced Carl G. Jung's concepts of archetypes in modern psychology, thus proving its continuing relevance over a span of eighteen-hundred years.

The Gospel of Truth is one of the Gnostic found in the Nag Hammadi codices. There were thirteen manuscripts within the discovered collection. Twelve of them made their way into the Coptic Museum in Cairo and were declared national treasures. It exists in two Coptic translations, a Subakhmimic (a late dialect of Coptic standing between Sahidic and Akhmimic) rendition surviving almost in full in the first codex (the "Jung Codex") and a Sahidic (a Coptic dialect of southern Egypt) in fragments in the twelfth manuscript.

A little-known fact is the great father of modern psychology, Carl G. Jung, had great interest in Gnosticism, and went so far as to purchase an ancient codex.

Gilles Quispel is a distinguished professor of Early Christianity who was born in Rotterdam, Holland in 1916. As a young man he obtained a doctorate in literature and the humanities and went on to research and teach about the early Gnostics. He describes his first meeting with Jung in 1944 in Ascona, Switzerland and how he gained the help of Jung and C.A. Meier to retrieve a valuable Gnostic text from the black market. This text had been part of a larger cache of ancient documents found in 1945 buried in a jar in Egypt near Nag Hammadi. Scholars consider these documents extremely valuable as the texts were from around the first century C.E. and contained unknown sayings of Jesus including a book titled, "The Gospel of Truth". The lost text was retrieved and named the Jung Codex.

It may be of interest to note the connection between the ancient Gnostics and modern psychology.

Stephan A. Hoeller wrote, in his article, "C. G. Jung and the Alchemical Renewal," the following:

Jung's "first love" among esoteric systems was Gnosticism. From the earliest days of his scientific career until the time of his death, his dedication to the subject of Gnosticism was relentless. As early as August, 1912, Jung intimated in a letter to Freud that he had an intuition that the essentially feminine-toned archaic wisdom of the Gnostics, symbolically called Sophia, was destined to re-enter modern Western culture by way of depth-psychology. Subsequently, he stated to Barbara Hannah that when he discovered the writings of the ancient Gnostics, "I felt as if I had at last found a circle of friends who understood me."

The circle of ancient friends was a fragile one, however. Very little reliable, first-hand information was available to Jung within which he could have found the world and spirit of such past Gnostic luminaries as Valentinus, Basilides, and others. The fragmentary, and possibly mendacious, accounts of Gnostic teachings and practices appearing in the works of such heresy-hunting church fathers as Irenaeus and Hippolytus were a far cry from the wealth of archetypal lore available to us today in the Nag Hammadi collection. Of primary sources, the remarkable Pistis

Sophia was one of very few available to Jung in translation, and his appreciation of this work was so great that he made a special effort to seek out the translator, the then aged and impecunious George R. S. Mead, in London to convey to him his great gratitude. Jung continued to explore Gnostic lore with great diligence, and his own personal matrix of inner experience became so affinitized to Gnostic imagery that he wrote the only published document of his great transformational crisis, The Seven Sermons to the Dead, using purely Gnostic terminology and mythologems of the system of Basilides.

Throughout all of his devoted study, Jung was disturbed by one principal difficulty: The ancient Gnostic myths and traditions were some seventeen or eighteen hundred years old, and no living link seemed to exist that might join them to Jung's own time. (There is some minimal and obscure evidence indicating that Jung was aware of a few small and secretive Gnostic groups in France and Germany, but their role in constituting such a link did not seem firmly enough established.) As far as Jung could discern, the tradition that might have connected the Gnostics with the present seemed to have been broken. However, his intuition (later justified by painstaking research) disclosed to him that the chief link connecting later ages with the Gnostics was in fact none other than alchemy. While his primary interest at this time was Gnosticism, he was already aware of the relevance of alchemy to his concerns. Referring to his intense inner experiences occurring between 1912 and 1919 he wrote:
"First I had to find evidence for the historical prefiguration of my own inner experiences. That is to say, I had to ask myself, "Where have my particular premises already occurred in history?" If I had not succeeded in finding such evidence, I would never have been able to substantiate my ideas. Therefore, my encounter with alchemy was decisive for me, as it provided me with the historical basis which I hitherto lacked."

In 1926 Jung had a remarkable dream. He felt himself transported back into the seventeenth century, and saw himself as an alchemist, engaged in the opus, or great work of alchemy. Prior to this time, Jung, along with other psychoanalysts, was intrigued and taken aback by the tragic fate of Herbert Silberer, a disciple of Freud, who in 1914 published a work dealing largely with the psychoanalytic implications of alchemy. Silberer, who upon proudly presenting his book to his master Freud, was coldly rebuked by him, became despondent and ended his life by suicide, thus becoming what might be called the first martyr to the cause of a psychological view of alchemy.

Now it all came together, as it were. The Gnostic Sophia was about to begin her triumphal return to the arena of modern thought, and the psychological link connecting her and her modern devotees would be the long despised, but about to be rehabilitated, symbolic discipline of alchemy. The recognition had come. Heralded by a dream, the role of alchemy as the link connecting ancient Gnosticism with modern psychology, as well as Jung's role in reviving this link, became apparent.

As Jung was to recollect later:
"[Alchemy] represented the historical link with Gnosticism, and . . . a continuity therefore existed between past and present. Grounded in the natural philosophy of the Middle Ages, alchemy formed the bridge on the one hand into the past, to Gnosticism, and on the other (hand) into the future, to the modern psychology of the unconscious."

This does not imply that Jung believed one could turn lead into gold, nor did he believe or pursue any other legendary trick of alchemy. To Jung, alchemy seemed to represent the ability to combine the lesser interior elements to produce the gold of the spirit.

According to Marsha West, Carl Jung has been called the "Father of the re-birth of Gnosticism also called Neo-Gnosticism. Dr. Satinover comments, "One of the most powerful modern forms of Gnosticism is without question Jungian psychology, both within or without the Church."
End quote.

Edward Moore wrote, "Carl Jung, drawing upon Gnostic mythical schemas, identified the objectively oriented consciousness with the material or "fleshly" part of humankind — that is, with the part of the human being that is, according to the Gnostics, bound up in the cosmic cycle of generation and decay, and subject to the bonds of fate and time (cf. Apocryphon of John [Codex II] 28:30). The human being who identifies him/herself with the objectively existing world comes to construct a personality, a sense of self, that is, at base, fully dependent upon the ever-changing structures of temporal existence. The resulting lack of any sense of permanence, of autonomy, leads such an individual to experience anxieties of all kinds, and eventually to shun the mysterious and collectively meaningful patterns of human existence in favor of a private and stifling subjective context, in the confines of which life plays itself out in the absence of any reference to a greater plan or scheme. Hopelessness, atheism, and despair, are the results of such an existence. This is not the natural end of the human being, though; for, according to Jung (and the Gnostics) the temporally constructed self is not the true self. The true self is the supreme consciousness existing and persisting beyond all space and time. Jung calls this the pure consciousness or Self, in contradistinction to the "ego consciousness" which is the temporally constructed and maintained form of a discrete existent (cf. C.G. Jung, "Gnostic Symbols of the Self," in The Gnostic Jung 1992, pp. 55-92). This latter form of "worldly" consciousness the Gnostics identified with soul (psukhê), while the pure or true Self they identified with spirit (pneuma) — that is, mind relieved of its temporal contacts and context. This distinction had an important career (role) in

Gnostic thought, and was adopted by St. Paul, most notably in his doctrine of the spiritual resurrection (1 Corinthians 15:44). The psychological or empirical basis of this view, which soon turns into a metaphysical or onto-theological attitude, is the recognized inability of the human mind to achieve its grandest designs while remaining subject to the rigid law and order of a disinterested and aloof cosmos. The spirit-soul distinction (which of course translates into, or perhaps presupposes, the more fundamental mind-body distinction) marks the beginning of a transcendentalist and soteriological attitude toward the cosmos and temporal existence in general."
End Quote

(Author's Note: onto-theological is the theology of being. The term was used by Kant. Kant had distinguished two general types of theology: that which comes from reason and that which comes from revelation. Within the category of reasoned theology, he distinguished two further types, "natural theology" and "transcendental theology". Within natural theology, Kant differentiated between "physico-theology" and an ethical or moral theology. Transcendental theology or reasoned-based theology, he divided into ontotheology and cosmotheology.)

In August 1957, Jung gave a series of filmed interviews for the University of Houston. The following is part of the transcript of the fourth interview with Dr. Richard I. Evans:
"I got more and more respectful of archetypes, and now, by Jove, that thing should be taken into account. That is an enormous factor, very important for our further development and for our well-being. It was, of course, difficult to know where to begin, because it is such an enormously extended field. So the next question I asked myself was, "Now where in the world has anybody been busy with that problem?" And I found nobody had, except a peculiar spiritual movement that went together with the beginnings of Christianity, namely Gnosticism. That was the first

thing, actually, that I saw, that the Gnostics were concerned with the problem of archetypes. They made a peculiar philosophy of it, as everybody makes a peculiar philosophy of it when he comes across it naïvely and doesn't know that the archetypes are structural elements of the unconscious psyche."

The study of Gnosticism by Jung contributed enormously to the field of modern psychology. Here, in the Gospel of Truth, we have a central and clarion work of Gnosticism. Here, in this small work, we have a chance to look into the heart of Gnosticism, and into our own hearts, as we explore this ancient and mystical work.

The Gospel of Truth is not a gospel at all, but a religious discourse, which may wax poetic in places. A gospel is usually seen as a   narrative account of Jesus' birth, death, and resurrection. The orthodox view of the gospel, or good news, is found in the death and resurrection of Jesus and how his death redeems the believer from sin and hell. In the common view of the gospel or good news, it is the sacrifice of Jesus, the perfect and sinless man on our behalf, that re-establishes our right-standing with God. The Gospel of Truth is a Gnostic text and according to the standard Gnostic belief, it is not the death of Jesus that frees us. It is the knowledge he brought with him from the realm of Fullness, also called the Pleroma.

The Gospel of Truth is written in an elegant, Hellenistic style in which the poetry of parallel statements is used to drive home the meaning of the writer's ideas.

The writing is thought to cite or allude to the New Testament Gospels of Matthew and John, as well as 1 and 2 Corinthians, Galatians, Ephesians, Colossians, Hebrews, 1 John, the Book of Revelation, John's Gospel, the Gospel of Thomas Chapters 22 and 28).

In the text, Error is personified and is seen as a Satan like entity. This entity or Power created a fog, such as a mental or spiritual fog, which is ignorance, which keeps us from the truth of the real God.

(Author's Note: 2 Corinthians 4:3-4 3 But if our gospel be hid, it is hid to them that are lost: In whom the god of this world hath blinded the minds of them which believe not, lest the light of the glorious gospel of Christ, who is the image of God, should shine unto them.)

Jesus was sent down by God to remove this ignorance. But Error grew angry at this, and nailed Jesus to a cross. The text also proceeds to describe ignorance as a nightmare and how it is knowledge of the true Father that grants salvation, which constitutes eternal rest.

(Author's note: Matthew 11:27 All things are delivered unto me of my Father: and no man knoweth the Son, but the Father; neither knoweth any man the Father, save the Son, and he to whomsoever the Son will reveal him.)

The world is dark and Jesus is the light that illuminates the path to the Father. In the poetic styling of the gospel, God brings 'fullness' for the 'deficient' and 'inexpressible joy' and the peace that passes all understanding, as discussed in the canonical gospels. Even though the awakened souls still live on earth, they find heavenly joy and rest.

(Author's Note: Ephesians 1:18-19 King James Version (KJV)
 The eyes of your understanding being enlightened; that ye may know what is the hope of his calling, and what the riches of the glory of his inheritance in the saints, And what is the exceeding greatness of his power to us-ward who believe, according to the working of his mighty power...

John 17:14-17 King James Version (KJV) I have given them thy word; and the world hath hated them, because they are not of the world, even as I am not of the world. I pray not that thou shouldest take them out of the world, but that thou shouldest keep them from the evil. They are not of the world, even as I am not of the world. Sanctify them through thy truth: thy word is truth.)

The theology described above is further taught in the parable of the good shepherd. It describes feeding the spiritually hungry and giving rest to those weary of the material world.

Salvation is described as being anointed and becoming perfect or full, lacking nothing and having no deficiency. The text refers to those in ignorance as empty or deficient. The enlightened or saved ones are anointed and they are full jars. Those jars that are empty, the Father fills.

The Father sent the son and the son is the image of the Father. This is the meaning of the phrase, "the name of the Father is the Son". That is to say that the Son is the Logos of the Father

(Author's Note: 1 John 1-2 King James Version (KJV)
That which was from the beginning, which we have heard, which we have seen with our eyes, which we have looked upon, and our hands have handled, of the Word of life; For the life was manifested, and we have seen it, and bear witness, and shew unto you that eternal life, which was with the Father, and was manifested unto us…)

The Gospel of Truth is a Gnostic explanation, elucidating the sum of various other Gnostic gospels that went before. It is one of the earlier writings on the subject of Gnosticism but must have occurred after several of the earliest Gospels were penned and circulated. This puts the dating of the Gospel of Truth around the time of Valentinus, or somewhere around 140-180 C.E.

Valentinus may have written this work. To say the least, his influence can be seen in the text. Valentinus is considered by some to be the father of the Christian Gnostic faith. He first taught at Alexandria and then in Rome. He established the largest Gnostic movement around A.D. 160. This movement was founded on an elaborate mythology and a system of sexual duality of male and female interplay, both in its deities and its savior.

Tertullian stated that between 135 A.D. and 160 A.D. Valentinus, a prominent Gnostic, had great influence in the Christian church. Valentinus ascended in church hierarchy and became a candidate for the office of bishop of Rome, the office that quickly evolved into that of Pope. He lost the election by a narrow margin. Even though Valentinus was outspoken about his Gnostic slant on Christianity, he was a respected member of the Christian community until his death and was probably a practicing bishop in a church of lesser status than the one in Rome.

The main platform of Gnosticism was the ability of its followers to transcend the material world through the possession of privileged and directly imparted knowledge. Following this doctrine, Valentinus claimed to have been instructed by a direct disciple of one of Jesus' apostles, a man by the name of Theodas.

G.R.S. Mead considered Valentinus to be the father of modern Gnosticism. His vision of the faith is summarized by G.R.S. Mead in the book "Fragments of a Faith Forgotten."

"The Gnosis in his hands is trying to embrace everything, even the most dogmatic formulation of the traditions of the Master. The great popular movement and its incomprehensibilities were recognized by Valentinus as an integral part of the mighty outpouring; he labored to weave all together, external and internal, into one piece, devoted his life to the task, and doubtless only at his death perceived that for that age he was attempting the impossible. None but the very few could ever appreciate the ideal of the man, much less understand it. "(Fragments of a Faith Forgotten, p. 297)

The mainline or orthodox Christian church had sought to eliminate Gnosticism and destroy all Gnostic documents. There were times in early church history that Gnostics were hunted down and killed for heresy, but these texts were saved and sealed by Gnostics as they attempted to preserve some of their most holy books, and thus they came to us with some of the texts still intact.

The translation of the Nag Hammadi library was completed in the 1970's and the information contained in the cache' would turn Christianity on its head by revealing an unknown history of Christianity and a fight for control of doctrine and the faith. Among the Gnostic works are scriptures such as the Gospel of Thomas, the Gospel of Philip, and many others. Gnosticism is an undeniable part of the history of Christianity. By both influence and opposition, it has helped shape what we now know as the Christian faith.

The text of the Gospel of Truth was first discovered in the last part of the month of December in 1945. It was found among 52 other Gnostic Christian texts contained in 13 codices or scrolls. The discovery was made by two peasant Egyptian brothers as they dug for fertilizer near their home. While digging in the rich soil around the Jabal al-Ɉārif caves near present-day Hamra Dom in Upper Egypt, they found several papyri in a large earthenware vessel. The find of these codices came to be known as the Nag Hammadi library because of their proximity to the Egyptian town of Nag Hammadi, which was the nearest major settlement.

The brothers wanted to make money by selling the manuscripts, but when they brought some of the scrolls home their mother burned several of the manuscripts. One source indicates she burned them as kindling, while another source claims she was superstitious and worried that the writing might be dangerous.

News of the discovery appeared gradually as the brothers tried to sell certain scrolls. The full significance of the new find was not immediately apparent until sometime after the initial discovery. As more of the scrolls were examined it was revealed that the find included a large number of primary Gnostic Gospels, some of which had never been seen before.

In 1946, the brothers became involved in a feud, and left the manuscripts with a Coptic priest. In October of that year a codex, now called codex III, was sold to the Coptic Museum in Old Cairo. The resident Coptologist and religious historian Jean Doresse realized the significance of the artifact and published the first reference to it in 1948.

With the death of Jesus placed around 33 C.E., the Christian church was still very young at the time of the writing of The Gospel of Truth. The church was attempting to fix or codify its doctrines and canon. The author of this manuscript seemed to be acquainted with the New Testament books of Paul, John, and Hebrews, and alludes to them in the text. There are also references to many of the New Testament books and no obvious citations from the Old Testament. This is likely due to the fact that Gnostic believed that the Old Testament God was a false and flawed God and the cause of the existence of pain, suffering, and disease in the world. It was the New Testament God of love and mercy that Jesus came to reveal.

In Gnostic Christian theology, God revealed himself to man through his Word/Logos and his Son. These are not the same "entities" but are within the same person. Jesus, the man of flesh, was born to interface with mortal men but the true power from above is the Logos, who is the son of the All, the true God, He Who Is. This makes Jesus the perfect guide, teacher, and example for men.

Unlike the belief and doctrine that became orthodox Christianity, to Gnostics it was knowledge that freed us from ignorance and thus the entrapment in the sin or illusion of this world. It was knowledge that brought about understanding and through understanding and applying this knowledge there was faith.

Ignorance is sin and error. Knowledge is the good news.
Jesus did not come to save us from our sins but to awaken us out of a dream state caused by living in this false world. The error of living in ignorance and the error of believing in the god of this world is our sin. Knowledge takes away this sin. Jesus brought the revelation that enables us to understand the concept of the true God, beyond this realm and our sonship in Him. Jesus came to teach us that we were not created to live in this world, but to be the sons and daughters of God. We are not of this world but simply passers by.

Like Jesus himself, the awakened or enlightened ones begin to see themselves as a body, soul, spirit combined but not the same. Our bodies continue to live and function on this material realm, but our spirit reaches higher and higher. Passing out of this realm, seeking unity with the true God.

"The Gospel of Truth describes three stages on the way of salvation: first, the stage of receiving divine ideas from the Logos and then applying them to purify our lower nature; second, the stage of acting as if the Logos were in charge of our lives, even though many illusions still remain in us; and third, the stage of rest, in which our lower nature is restful because our illusions are

largely absent, permitting the Logos to act through us."
(Lansdowne, p41)

The idea that Gnosis could come from one's own correct understanding took the "church" and its leaders out of the equation of salvation. There was no need of a priest or church to bring salvation through its teachings or baptisms. This threatened the emerging church and its hierarchy. As the orthodox or mainstream church grew and took power it would begin to hunt down and kill Gnostics.

History is written by the victors. With Gnosticism declared heresy and Gnostics persecuted and killed, the church set about to eliminate all traces of the old faith. They failed. With the discovery of the Nag Hammadi codices we have rediscovered the broad and rich history of Gnosticism.

To understand the text of The Gospel of Truth better, we need a basic knowledge of Gnostic theology, specifically Valentinian Gnosticism.

Valentinian Gnosticism

Gilles Quispel states that for Valentinus, a Gnostic teacher of the second century, Christ is "the Paraclete from the Unknown who reveals…the discovery of the Self, which is the divine spark within you."

The heart of the human problem for the Gnostic is ignorance, sometimes called "sleep," "intoxication," "deficiency", "lack" or "blindness." But Jesus redeems man from such ignorance.

Stephan Hoeller says that in the Valentinian system "there is no need whatsoever for guilt, for repentance from so-called sin, neither is there a need for a blind belief in vicarious salvation by way of the death of Jesus." Rather, Jesus is savior in the sense of being a "spiritual maker of wholeness" who cures us of our sickness of ignorance.

According to Valentinus, the seeker awakens through knowledge or Gnosis. This secret Gnosis provides the key that is essential for a complete understanding of Jesus' message. The Valentinus doctrine states, "The scriptures are ambiguous and the truth cannot be extracted from them by those who are ignorant of tradition." (Irenaeus Against Heresies 3:2:1). (Irenaeus was arguing against Valentinus and Gnosticism in his book.) One must be spiritually mature to comprehend the full meaning of the scriptures.

1 Corinthians 2:14 New International Version (NIV)
The person without the Spirit does not accept the things that come from the Spirit of God but considers them foolishness, and cannot understand them because they are discerned only through the Spirit.

According to the Valentinian tradition, Paul and the other apostles revealed these teachings only to those who were 'spiritually mature'. This is the transmission of Gnosis from master to student.

1 Corinthians 2:4-6 New International Version (NIV)
4 My message and my preaching were not with wise and persuasive words, but with a demonstration of the Spirit's power,
5 so that your faith might not rest on human wisdom, but on God's power.
6 We do, however, speak a message of wisdom among the mature, but not the wisdom of this age or of the rulers of this age, who are coming to nothing.

Valentinians believed that God could never be directly observed or experienced. Neither could God be fully understood, directly known, described or explained. He is eternal. He is the origin of all things.

The Godhead manifests itself through a process of unfolding wherein various parts or qualities were manifested, all the while maintaining its unity. In certain instances, the expressions of God in turn had expressions, such as the Christ Spirit or Son, which was an expression or emanation, that in turn had expressions or emanations, like circles within circles.

Valentinians believed that God is androgynous and contained within God is a male-female dyad. We see this in the fact that the Hebrew word for the Spirit of God was Ruak (Ruach). The word and the spirit (Ruak) were presented in female form. It was through the constraint of language, as the translations went from Hebrew to Greek and from Greek to Latin, that the feminine gender of the Spirit was lost. However, in the beginning she "Brooded" over the waters.

Genesis 1:1-2 Amplified Bible (AMP)
1 In the beginning God (Elohim) created [by forming from nothing] the heavens and the earth. 2 The earth was formless and void or a waste and emptiness, and darkness was upon the face of the deep [primeval ocean that covered the unformed earth]. The Spirit of God was moving (hovering, brooding) over the face of the waters.

In the literal reading, it can be seen that God provides the universe with both male and female energies of form and substance. The feminine aspect of the deity is called Wisdom, Mercy, Silence, Grace and Thought. Silence is God's primordial state of tranquility and self-awareness. She is also the active creative thought that gives substance to the powers or states of being, such as "Aeons". The first feminine energy of God is called the Divine Thought.

In some Gnostic systems she is called, Barbelo, the mother of all that is. There are differences concerning the Holy Spirit between various Gnostic groups. Some have the Spirit as a function of Barbelo, while others say it is through Sophia. The variations may depend on where and how the spirit is introduced. For example, according to Valentinus, Sophia gives the spiritual seed to those who hear the true word of "He Who Is".

The masculine aspect of God is Depth, Power, Law, and Order. He is also called Ineffable, the All, Unity, and First Father. Depth is the most profound aspect of God. It is all-encompassing and can never be fully understood. He is essentially passive, yet when moved to action by his feminine energy, Thought, he gives the universe form. It was through the union of the masculine force of the All and Divine Thought that the Christ Spirit was brought forth.

Aeons are beings produce by an emanation of energy, like a fire produces light and heat. In many Gnostic systems, the various emanations of God, who is also known by such names as the One, the Monad, The All, and Depth emanated Aeons such as "Sophia" (wisdom) and Christos (Christ, the Anointed One). In turn, Sophia and Christ also have emanations and thus produced Aeons, Archons, and angels. To the mind of the modern Christian Aeons may be thought of as angles, although there are differences.

In different Gnostic systems, these emanations are differently named, classified, and described, but the emanation theory itself is common to all forms of Gnosticism.

The origin of the universe is described as a process of emanation from the Godhead. As a fire does not intend to emanate light, but does so simply because of its nature, so does God emanates and produces. The male and female aspects of the Father, acting in conjunction, manifested themselves in the Son. Thus, the Son is produced by the All alone, since the All has both male and female energies. The Son is depicted by Valentinians as a male-female dyad.

After the Son came into being, he manifested himself in twenty-six spiritual entities or Aeons arranged into male-female pairs. Together they constitute the Fullness (pleroma) of the Godhead.

The Aeons who are manifested by the Son are conceived as having psychological autonomy. They lie within God or the sphere where God resides but are separated from him by a boundary. As a result, they do not know the one who brought them into being. The Aeons sensed that they were incomplete and long to know their origin.

According to Valentinus, all Powers and Aeons were made in pairs. All had a consort that balanced and perfected them. Sophia's consort was Christ. We see this idea in the Catholic and Orthodox Bibles and the book of Wisdom, contained in the

Apocrypha.

The Book of Wisdom uses personification. The Hebrew word chakmah, like its Greek (sophia) and Latin (sapientia) equivalents, is a noun with feminine gender.

"I will tell you what wisdom is and how she came to be, and I will hide no secrets from you, but I will trace her course from the beginning of creation, and make knowledge of her clear, and I will not pass by the truth" (Wisdom 6:22).

"With you is wisdom, she who knows your works and was present when you made the world; she understands what is pleasing in your sight and what is right according to your commandments" (Wisdom 9:9).

Wisdom is called the "fashioner of all things" (Wisdom 7:22).

She has a spirit that is intelligent, holy, unique, subtle, mobile, clear, unpolluted, distinct, invulnerable, loving the good, keen, irresistible, humane, steadfast, sure, and free from anxiety (Wisdom 7:22–23).

Even in Proverbs 1–9 Wisdom is spoken of as a woman.

Sophia (Wisdom), the youngest of the Aeons, yearned to know the All, the parent of all beings. She attempted to know and understand him. Some stories have her capturing a divine creative spark from God and using it by herself, without her consort. As a result, she became separated from her consort. According to several Gnostic stories, the consort of Sophia was Christ himself. Being separated from him she fell into a state of deficiency and suffering. In such a state, her creation was deficient and monstrous. He is called the Demiurge, the half-maker, and the craftsman.

Sophia's fall into ignorance produced three creations. The first is "Illusion". This is the belief the material world is all there is. But there is always a deeper feeling there is something else lying beyond. Illusion is characterized by a material existence and suffering. The personification of this state is the Devil.

The second creation of the fallen Sophia is the Soul. It originated as ignorance began to give way to knowledge. It is personified as the Craftsman or Demiurge who formed the material world. He is a creative force but is deficient and is usually seen as ignorant of his position, ignorant of the All, and lacking Gnosis.

The third creation is the "Spiritual Seed", which is born from her knowledge (gnosis) and is personified in the fallen Sophia herself.

Through the power of Limit, Sophia was divided into two parts. Her higher part was returned to her consort in the pleroma but her lower part was separated from the Fullness into a lower realm along with the deficiency and suffering. This lower realm is the material or physical world.

Valentinians envisioned the universe as series of spheres within spheres. The smallest and center sphere is the physical world or the deficiency, where the fallen or lower Sophia was exiled and where man resides. Enclosing this is a larger sphere of the Fullness (pleroma) where the Aeons are. The Aeons are enclosed within the Son, as his sphere is with the Father and encompasses all things. The largest sphere is where the Son resides with the Father (Depth and Silence).

There is a boundary or limit between God and the pleroma. There is a second boundary or limit between the pleroma and the material world. Just as the pleroma is a product of the Godhead and lies within it, so the realm of deficiency, which is the material world, is a product of the pleroma and is contained in a sphere lying within the sphere of the pleroma. The deficiency arose as result of ignorance and it will only be escaped or dissolved through knowledge (gnosis).

In Gnosticism "Limit" is a power or creation. Limit is the name of the personification of the power to divide and cut off. Where the word "Limit or Boundary" are used, it can be an actual creation with the active ability to cleave, cut, separate, or contain.

Error, like Limit, is the personification of ignorance and the acts that follow from it. Error is similar to the Devil.

Through mediation on the Son, which is the knowledge of the true Father of All and how all beings were created and connected, the Aeons within the pleroma were given rest. All twenty-six of the Aeons then joined together in celebration were spontaneously integrated back into the personality of the Son. The fully integrated Son is called the Savior. Even though the Son is seen as having both male and female energies, he is destined to be the male partner or bridegroom of the fallen Sophia. He is surrounded by angels who were brought forth in honor of the Aeons.

The fallen Sophia remained in ignorance, trapped in the fallen material sphere. She continued to suffer the emotional pain of grief, fear, and confusion. Because of her confusion and ignorance, she was unable to distinguish what was real and what was illusion. In her pain, she began to call out for help. She sought the light and she began to plead for help. Her consort responded. The Savior, and his assisting and attending angels descended through the Limit to her. Through his knowledge (gnosis) of the eternal realm, he freed the fallen part of Sophia from her illusion and suffering.

Sophia rejoiced because of her Savior and consort and his angels.

In her joy she produced spiritual substances or spiritual seeds in his image (some stories have her producing spiritual seeds in the images of the savior and his angels, others have her producing spiritual seeds only in the image of the savior). This spiritual substance or seeds are the spirits present in every Christian who collectively make up the spiritual Church. As the Savior is the bridegroom of Sophia, in the end times his emanations, the angels, will be the bridegrooms of the spiritual seeds, which are the Christians making up the spiritual church.

In the act of salvation, it is Sophia who sows a spiritual seed in all who hear the message of Jesus. Those who accept and gain Gnosis are spiritual Christians.

Despite the fact that the fallen Sophia was no longer ignorant, the ignorance was not fully dissipated. The spiritual seeds were immature and needed training. For this purpose, the creation of the material world was necessary. The fallen Sophia and the Savior secretly influenced the Demiurge to create the material world in the image of the Fullness. The Demiurge is ignorant of his mother and the All. He thinks that he acts alone and is the only creative force, but he unconsciously acts as her agent.

The Demiurge created the material world and human beings. The Demiurge created the Archons as his helpers. The Deminurge and the Archons are responsible for the material/physical world and its systems. Valentinians believed that in addition to a physical body, people were composed of a demonic part (chous / dirt, dust), a rational soul (psyche / mind), and a spiritual seed (pneuma / spirit).

Because the Demiurge is the deficient, corrupt, and a cruel creator of this world, Gnostic theology has answered many nagging questions, such as why there is suffering, why is there disease, and why do bad things happen to good people.

Human beings were divided into three categories, depending on which of the three natures they exhibited. Valentinus believed that the children of Adam and Eve metaphorically represented the three categories of humans. Cain represented the carnal (choic) Abel represented the animate (psychic), and Seth represented the spiritual (pneumatic).

The ultimate pinnacle of world history came in the ministry of Jesus. Jesus is the physical manifestation of the Son or Savior. Prior to his coming, the true God was unknown. Jesus came to bring knowledge (gnosis) to a suffering humanity that was desperately seeking the true God.

This is why the Old Testament God and New Testament God are so different. The Old Testament God, the Demiurge, was vengeful, wrathful, jealous and cruel, and the New Testament God, who Jesus was sent to reveal to us, is sweet, loving, kind and merciful.

By knowledge, the spiritual seed and their consorts or counterpart, the angels are joined. This union was foreshadowed by the reuniting of Sophia and Christ.

In Valentinian Gnosticism there is a distinction between the human Jesus and the divine Jesus. The human Jesus is the son of Mary and Joseph. By grace his body was constructed of the same substance as Sophia and her spiritual seed. When Jesus was thirty years old, he was baptized by John and as he went down into the water God sent the "Spirit of the Thought of the Father" in the form of a dove and it descended on him and he was born of the virgin spirit. According to Valentinus, this is the true "virgin birth" and resurrection from the dead.

Jesus taught the people in parables, so that only the matured and spiritually awake would understand. He revealed the full and plain truth about the fall of Sophia and the coming restoration of the Fullness only to his closest followers. According to Valentinus, Mary Magdalene was a member of this inner circle. She is seen as an image of the lower Sophia and is described as Jesus' consort in the Gospel of Philip.

The divine Jesus experienced all of the emotions of human beings including grief, fear and confusion in the Garden of Gethsemane but only the body suffered. The son of Mary and Joseph was crucified but the spiritual Jesus did not physically suffer death, for before the body suffered and died the spiritual Jesus ascended.

Jesus has shed his body and is now a spiritual being. He is "He Who Is". The spirit left the body before the torment began and the divine Jesus was not harmed or hurt. His death held no great meaning for Gnostic since it was his teaching and not his death that freed people and pointed their way to heaven. This divergence from the view of the crucifixion held by the orthodox church turned the church against Gnostics and in time led to the murder of thousands of Gnostics by the church, culminating in the Cathar massacre. The Cathars were a Gnostic Christian community living in southern France, between the 12th and 13th centuries. In 1209 the crusaders came, sent by the Pope. The order was to kill every Gnostic in the area. Arnaud-Amaury, the Cistercian abbot-commander, is supposed to have been asked how to tell Cathars from Catholics. His reply, recalled by Caesarius of Heisterbach, a fellow Cistercian, thirty years later was "Caedite eos. Novit enim Dominus qui sunt eius" – "Kill them all, the Lord will recognize His own". The doors of the church of St Mary Magdalene were broken down and the refugees dragged out and slaughtered. At least 7,000 innocent men, women and children were killed there by Catholic forces. In the town Gnostic and Catholics were living together. There was no way to distinguish between the two Christian sects. All were killed. Thousands were mutilated and murdered. Prisoners were blinded, dragged behind horses, and used for target practice. The permanent population of the town at that time was then probably no more than 5,000, but local refugees seeking shelter within the city walls could conceivably have increased the number to 20,000.

Following the crucifixion Jesus appeared and taught his disciples about the Father for eighteen months. After his ascension, he appeared in visions. This is how Paul and Valentinus experienced Jesus.

People who receive the knowledge of Jesus' teaching receive a spiritual seed from Sophia that will bear fruit by awakening them from their stupor to a mystical knowledge (gnosis). They recognize their own spiritual nature. With or because of this knowledge they are joined with their angel consorts who accompanies the Savior. This is the true resurrection of the dead. It is the spirit that was dead and now resurrected. Resurrections does not take place after death. It must be experienced in the living present.

First, the person spiritually ascends above the realm of the Demiurge and this material world to join with their consort angel, Sophia and the Savior in the higher realm of the Fullness or pleroma. Then, rejoicing with all of the saved, the person is joined with their angel and enters the Fullness. The person continues to have a physical existence in the material world but they are an awakened spirit and are in the world but not of it. They come to understand this physical existence is an illusion to keep men enslaved and asleep. From ignorance, deficiency and spiritual slumber, to knowledge, awakening, and spiritual ascent – this is the Gnostic's idea of the death and resurrection.

The Translation of the Gospel of Truth

The translation presented here is not a word-for-word translation. Too much is lost in that approach. Language structure, cultural differences, and the esoteric nature of the Gnostic belief system all present issues to the modern reader. The translation here represents an attempt to communicate to the reader each complete thought of the author in the clearest form possible. Even in such an approach there are places where author's notes are inserted to clarify certain passages.

The Gospel of Truth

The gospel of truth gives joy to those who received it from the Father of truth. It is the gift of knowing him, which is imparted by the power of the Word (Logos), who has come from the Fullness (Pleroma). It is He who was in the thought and the mind of the Father. He is called "Savior," because that is what he must do for the redemption of those who have not known the Father. The gospel is named for the hope which is revealed and culminates in discovery of those who seek him, just as the realm of All sought him from whom it had originated.

(Author's Note: Logos was within the All. The realm originated from the Logos and thus sought him.
1 John 1:1-4 King James Version: That which was from the beginning, which we have heard, which we have seen with our eyes, which we have looked upon, and our hands have handled, of the Word of life; (For the life was manifested, and we have seen it, and bear witness, and shew unto you that eternal life, which was with the Father, and was manifested unto us;) That which we have seen and heard declare we unto you, that ye also may have fellowship with us: and truly our fellowship is with the Father, and with his Son Jesus Christ. And these things write we unto you, that your joy may be full.)

Understand – He had been within the All, and the All is without limit, and cannot be understood, and is beyond any thought.

Ignorance of the Father caused terror and fear. And terror became dense like a fog so that no one was able to see. Because of this, Error became strong. Error worked on the material substance in vain, because it did not know the truth. It took on (material /

bodily) form while it was preparing a false truth that was beautiful and powerful.

This presented no humiliation for Him who cannot be understood and is without limit. The terror, forgetfulness, and material lies are nothing compared to the established truth, for it is unchanging, undisturbed, and its beauty is absolute.

For this reason, it is not necessary to take Error too seriously. It has no root. It resides in a fog and does not know the Father. It is busy preparing ways to bring about great forgetfulness and fear in order to trick those of the middle and to make them captive.

(Author's Note: the phrase, "those of the middle", is used to describe members of mankind who have not awakened and spiritually ascended.)

The forgetfulness caused by Error was not made known. It did not become light in the presence of the Father. Forgetfulness did not exist with the Father, although it came into existence because of him.

(Author's Note: Forgetfulness was caused by the error of thinking this material world and its creator was all there is. It caused a fog to fall on the minds of mankind because of the deception of the Demiurge.

What exists in the All is knowledge, which was made known so that forgetfulness might be destroyed and the Father might be known. Forgetfulness exists because they did not know the Father, but if they come to know the Father, forgetfulness will cease from that moment forward.

That is the gospel pertaining to the one they seek. The All has revealed this as the hidden mystery, which is Jesus the Christ. It is

34

made known to the perfected ones through the mercies of the Father.

Through Jesus the All enlightened those in darkness due to forgetfulness. He enlightened them and gave them a path. The path is the truth which he taught them.

For this reason, Error was angry with him, so it persecuted and interfered and caused him tumult. Error tried to make him powerless.

He was nailed to a cross. He became a fruit of the knowledge of the Father. He did not destroy those who ate of it. Instead, to those who ate He brought discovery and the truth made them joyous.

(Author's Note: This is a reference to the tree of knowledge of good and evil in the garden of Eden. To the Gnostics, the fruit and thus the knowledge, is a good thing since knowledge frees us from the illusion. Jesus became the fruit of the Father, which brought the ultimate knowledge of the All.)

Those who obtained the fruit found that He was in them and they were in Him, that unlimited one we can never understand, that perfect Father who made everything. In Him is the realm of All but the realm of All lacks Him because He keeps Himself and His perfection in Himself and He had not given it to the all.

(1 Corinthians 15:20-26: But now is Christ risen from the dead, and become the firstfruits of them that slept. For since by man came death, by man came also the resurrection of the dead. For as in Adam all die, even so in Christ shall all be made alive. But every man in his own order: Christ the firstfruits; afterward they that are Christ's at his coming. Then cometh the end, when he shall have delivered up the kingdom to God, even the Father; when he shall have put down all rule and all authority and power. For he must

reign, till he hath put all enemies under his feet. The last enemy that shall be destroyed is death.)

The Father was not jealous. What jealousy can there be between him and his members (limbs)? Even if the Aeon had obtained their own perfection, they would not have been able to approach the perfection of the Father. He retains their perfection within himself and grants it to them as a way to return to Him. With the perfection comes a unique knowledge.

He is the one who set the everything in order and in whom everything exists. It is Him that everything lacks. Some have no knowledge of Him. He desires that they know him and that they love him. For what is it that everything lacked, if not the knowledge of the Father?

(Author's Note: An alternative reading of the above paragraph may be: He is the one who set the realm of All in order and in whom the realm of All exists but it is He whom the realm of All lacks. Some have no knowledge of Him. He desires that they know him and that they love him. For what is it that the realm of the All lacked, if not the knowledge of the Father?)

He became a guide, quiet and at rest. In the middle of a school He came and He spoke the Word, as a teacher. Those who thought themselves to be wise came to test him. But he disgraced them like they were fools. They hated him because he revealed that they were not wise men. After all these (fools) came the little children, who are those who have the knowledge of the Father (to whom His knowledge belongs). When they became strong they were taught the appearance and features of the Father's face. They came to know Him and they were known by Him. They were glorified by Him and they gave Him glory. The living book of the Living ones is manifest in their hearts. This is the book which was written in the thought and in the mind of the Father. Before the foundation of the All, it has been kept in that part of Him we can never understand. This is the book no one can take or steal. It was reserved for him who will take it and be slain.

(Author's Note: Revelation 20:12 - And I saw the dead, small and great, stand before God; and the books were opened: and another book was opened, which is [the book] of life: and the dead were judged out of those things which were written in the books, according to their works.
Revelation 3:5 - He that overcometh, the same shall be clothed in white raiment; and I will not blot out his name out of the book of life, but I will confess his name before my Father, and before his angels.)

Of those who believed in salvation, no one could manifest as long as that book had not appeared. Jesus, who is faithful and compassionate, knew that his death meant life for many, and so he endured his suffering with patience until he could take that book.

(Author's Note: Revelation 5:1-5 King James Version (KJV)
And I saw in the right hand of him that sat on the throne a book written within and on the backside, sealed with seven seals. And I saw a strong angel proclaiming with a loud voice, Who is worthy to open the book, and to loose the seals thereof? And no man in heaven, nor in earth, neither under the earth, was able to open the book, neither to look thereon. And I wept much, because no man was found worthy to open and to read the book, neither to look thereon. And one of the elders saith unto me, Weep not: behold, the Lion of the tribe of Judah, the Root of David, hath prevailed to open the book, and to loose the seven seals thereof.)

The book can be compared to a will which has not yet been opened. The fortune of the deceased master of the house is hidden in the unopened will. The All was hidden, invisible, in Himself alone, known only to Himself. For this reason, Jesus appeared. He took ownership of the book and when he was nailed to a cross he affixed the command of the Father upon the cross.

This is the great teaching! Although he is clothed in eternal life, he humbled himself, even unto death. Then He took off and threw away these perishable rags and he clothed himself in incorruptibility, which no one could possibly take from him.

(Philippians 2:5-10 King James Version: Let this mind be in you, which was also in Christ Jesus: Who, being in the form of God, thought it not robbery to be equal with God: But made himself of no reputation, and took upon him the form of a servant, and was made in the likeness of men: And being found in fashion as a man, he humbled himself, and became obedient unto death, even the death of the cross. Wherefore God also hath highly exalted him, and given him a name which is above every name.)

Having entered the empty space of fear, he passed in the midst of those who were stripped by forgetfulness. He was both knowledge and perfection, and he was proclaiming the things that are in the heart of the Father. In doing this, He became wisdom to those who would receive the teaching.

But those who are to be taught are the living who are inscribed in the book of the living. They learn of themselves and receive instructions from the Father as they turn to him again. Since the perfection of the All is in the Father, it is necessary for the All to ascend to him again.

Therefore, if one has knowledge, he receives what is his and he draws it to himself. He who is ignorant, is lacking (knowledge). This great deficiency he lacks is that which would make him perfect.

(Author's Note: This specific doctrine, of learning from oneself, plumbing the depths of the spirit, finding the divine spark with each of us, and that divine spark leading us back to its origin (God) places the organized church and clergy in a position of little consequence to personal salvation. This placed the emerging orthodoxy and Gnostics on a collision course.)

Since the perfection of the All is in the Father, it is necessary for the All to ascend to him again so that he can receive those who are His. He selected and recorded them first and prepared them so they who came from him could be given to him.

(Author's Note: In the centuries-old debate between foreknowledge and predestination, this statement falls on the side of predestination.)

Those whose name he knew first were called last, so that the one who has knowledge is he whose name the Father announced. He whose name is not spoken is he who is ignorant. It is obvious. How can anyone hear if his name is not called? He who continues in ignorance is a creature of forgetfulness and he will perish along with it. If this was not true, then why do these wretched ones have no name, why have they not been called?

Therefore, if a person has knowledge, he is from above. If he is called, he hears, he responds, he knows what he is called, and then he turns to Him who called him and he ascends to Him. Since he has knowledge, he does the will of Him who called him. He wants to please Him and (in doing so) he finds rest.

He receives a certain name. He who has knowledge knows where he came from and where he is going. He is like a person who was drunk, and when he becomes sober he comes to himself and sets about to make right what is his (recover that which is his own).

He has recovered many from Error. He has gone before them to their places they were in when they departed and erred. They erred because of the depth of Him who surrounds every place but He is surrounded by nothing. It was a great wonder that they were in the Father without knowing him and that they were able come out of their place by themselves, since they were not able to understand or know him even though they were in Him. It would not be so if His will had not emanated from him. For he revealed His knowledge, in which all its emanations concurred. The knowledge of the living book which He revealed to the Aeons at last as His letters, and it showed them that these are not vowels sounds nor sounds of consonants, so that someone could read them and place some foolish meaning on them. But instead they are the true letters (letters of truth). And they can be pronounced only by those who know. Each letter is a complete truth (thought) like a complete book. They are letters written by the hand of the One (He who is unified). The Father wrote them so that by means of his letters the Aeons might come to know the Father.

While his wisdom mediates on the Logos (Word), his teaching speaks it, and his knowledge reveals it. His patience and mercy are a crown upon it. His joy concurs with it and his glory exalts it. It has revealed his image. It has received his rest. Around it His love manifested in bodily form. His faithfulness embraced it. This is how the Word (Logos) of the Father goes forth into the All. It is the fruit of his heart and expression of his will. It supports the All and by its choice it takes the form of the All, purifying them, and causing them to return to the Father and to the Mother who is Jesus of the greatest sweetness.

The Father opens his bosom. His bosom is the Holy Spirit. The Holy Spirit reveals part of him that was hidden, which is his son. In this way, through the compassion of the Father, the Aeons may know him and stop their weary searching for the Father. Then they may know rest and they will finally rest in him.

After he had filled that which was deficient he did away with its form. The form of it is the world. That is where he served. It is the place of emptiness, envy and strife. But where there is unity, there is perfection and completeness.

Deficiency came into being because they did not know the Father. From the instant they know the father deficiency (incompleteness, emptiness) will cease to exist. As one's ignorance disappears with knowledge, and as darkness disappears with light, so incompleteness vanishes when there is completeness. Now, all their works lie scattered about but in an instant form will no longer be manifest but it will dissolve, being fused together with Unity (All). In time Unity will make the place complete. Within Unity each person will understand himself. Through knowledge he will purify himself of his diversity and multiplicity (fragmented thoughts) and come into Unity, consuming matter within himself like fire, consuming darkness by light, consuming death by life.

Now, if these things have happened to each one of us, it is only right that we should think about the All and make the house holy and silent for Unity. Like people who have moved out of a house and have some cracked bowls they usually destroy them. This way the householder does not lose (what may be placed in the broken bowls), but he is glad because in place of the broken bowls there are perfect ones. This is the judgement from above and it judges every person like a two-edged sword that cuts on both sides. When the Word (Logos) appears, and is in the heart of those who pronounce it, it does not only become a sound but it become a body. And there is a great disturbance among the bowls, for some were emptied, others filled: some were used, others were removed; some were whole, and others were broken. Every place was shaken and disturbed, for they became disordered and unstable. Error was confused and did not know what to do. It was afraid and it grieved. It became frantic because it knew nothing.

Knowledge is the end of Error and when Knowledge approaches with all its emanations, Error is empty and there is nothing in it. When Error was gone, Truth appeared and all its emanations recognized it. They all greeted the Father with complete power they join with the Father. For each one loves truth because truth is the mouth of the Father and His tongue is the Holy Spirit. He who is joined to Truth is connected to the mouth of the Father by His tongue he shall receive the Holy Spirit. This is the manifestation of the Father and He reveals it to his Aeons.

He revealed His hidden self and He explained it. For who is it that exists if it is not the Father alone? Everywhere are his emanations. They knew that they had come from him like children from a mature man. Each one the Father beget knew that they had not yet received form nor had they received a name. Even though they were within Him, when they receive form by his knowledge, they still do not know him. But the Father is perfect. He knows every place within himself. He manifests anyone whom he desires by giving them a form and by giving them a name. He gives them a name and causes them to come into existence. Yet, before they exist they were ignorant of the one who created them.

I am not saying that they who have not come into existence amount to nothing. But they who wish to come into existence are in Him and they will exist when He pleases. They are like an event which is destined to happen.

He knows what will happen before it is revealed. He knows what he will produce before it is manifest. The fruit which has not yet been produced does not know anything, nor is it yet anything. So, it is that every place (everything) that is in the Father comes from the pre-existent one, who has established it from nonexistence.

This is why he who does not exist at all, will never come to exist.

What is it that he wants him to think? It is this: "I am like shadows and phantoms of the night." When morning's light comes, he knows that the things he feared were nothing.

This is why they were ignorant of the Father. He was the one they did not see. Since there had been terror and confusion and doubt and lack of commitment and division. These were the many illusions which were concocted by him as he went on and they were all because on emptiness and ignorance. It was as if they fell into a deep sleep and found themselves the prey in some nightmare. Or in their dream they were running to find a place to hide, or they were too weak to fight off the unknown thing that chased them. Or they were trying to strike out at something, or they themselves were being beaten. Or they were falling from some high place, or they fly into the air but they had no wings. Other times, they could dream that people were trying to kill them, even though no one was actually chasing them. Or, they were covered in blood and trying to murder someone close to them.
For those who are so disturbed and are experiencing these confusions, the instant they awake, they see it was actually nothing because dreams are nothing.

It is this way for those who cast ignorance aside as if it were only sleep and they do not consider it to be anything. They do not consider anything in it to be something that is real. They put it out of their minds like one would a bad dream at night, but they consider knowledge of the Father to be like the dawn. This is how each one that has awakened has acted, as if he were asleep when he was ignorant, but he has awakened into understanding. The man who comes to himself and awakens is happy. He who has opened the eyes of the blind is blessed.

And the Spirit ran to him and hurried to awaken him. Having reached out a hand to the one lying flat on the ground who had never stood before, but the Spirit raised him up to be steady on his feet. He gave them the means of understanding the knowledge of the Father and the revelation of his son. For when they saw him and listened to him, he permitted them to taste and smell and to touch the beloved son.

He appeared to instruct them about the Father, the unlimited one who could not be understood. He inspired (breathed into them) them with that which is in the thought, while doing his will.

(Author's Note: To be in- spired is to be breathed into. This may reference John 20:22: And when he had said this, he breathed on them, and saith unto them, Receive ye the Holy Ghost.)

Many received the light and turned to him. But men of the material world were alien to him and they did not recognize him or comprehend his appearance. He came in the form of flesh and nothing obscured his path because the incorruptible is irresistible (it cannot be restrained by this world). While he was teaching new things, he was speaking what was in the heart of the Father. He preached the Word without fault.

Light spoke through his mouth, and his voice produced life. He gave them thought, understanding, mercy, and salvation. And the Spirit of strength which came from the infinite sweetness of the Father.

He caused punishment and torture to stop leading astray those who were actually in need of mercy, for they were led astray from him and placed in chains because of Error. But he utterly destroyed them who lead some astray and he confounded them with knowledge. He became both a path for those who went astray and knowledge for those who were ignorant. He was the discovery for those who were searching, and he was a support for those who were unsure. He was purity for those who were defiled.

He is the shepherd who left behind the ninety-nine sheep which had not gotten lost and he searched for that one which was strayed away. He rejoiced when he had found it. For ninety-nine is a number held in the left hand.

(Author's Note: New International Version Luke 15:4 "Suppose one of you has a hundred sheep and loses one of them. Doesn't he leave the ninety-nine in the open country and go after the lost sheep until he finds it? The left hand represents a weaker side, servant, lacking, subservient, unfilled. The right side represents power, control, strength, fullness.)

The moment he finds the one, the complete number is passed into the right hand. So it is with him who lacks the one. The entire right hand draws out that which is deficient and takes it from the left side and transfers it to the right hand. In this way, the number becomes one hundred. This number is the sign of the Father.

(Author's Note: According to W.E. Filmer in his book, "God Counts", in the Bible, 100 represents the children of promise. According to "Numbers in Scripture" by Tony Warren, 100 represents fullness and totality.)

Even on the Sabbath he worked to free the sheep which he found fallen into the pit. He saved the life of that sheep by pulling it up from the pit so that you might thoroughly understand and feel what that Sabbath really is. The Sabbath is the day in which is it is not fitting that salvation should be idle. We say it is a heavenly day which has no night and the sun never sets because it is perfect. Be sure that is your heart and you are that perfect day, and in you the light is perfect and it does not fade.

Speak to those who seek concerning the truth and speak of knowledge to those who have committed sin in their error. Make firm and stable the feet of those who stumble. Give your hand to the sick. Feed the hungry. Give assurance to those who are troubled. (Give rest to the weary.) Encourage men to love. Awaken men and make those who sleep stand. For you are the understanding which draws them. If the strong follow this path, they will become stronger.

Pay attention to yourselves. Do not concern yourself with other things. Do not pick back up what you banished from yourselves. Do not return to what you have dismissed. Do not return to your vomit and eat it. Do not be like a moth or a worm or eat like they eat. Do not go back to what you have already shaken off. Do not be a house for the devil after you have already destroyed him. Do not support or strengthen (those who may be) obstacles for you. That is unthinkable and deserves condemnation.

Remember, the lawless one amounts to nothing. He harms himself more than the law. A person does the devil's works because he is a lawless person. But a righteous person does his works among other people. Do the Father's will because you are from him.

The Father is sweet and his will is good. He knows what is yours, and makes it so you will find rest in them. If you are children of the Father you will be known by your fruits and you will have his scent because you were born from the grace of his countenance.

The Father loved his fragrance; and made it appear in every place. And he gives his aroma to the light when his scent is mixed with matter. He causes it to exceed every form and sound. Here no nose can detect the smell of the aroma, but the Spirit possesses the sense of smell and it is drawn to itself and it basks in the fragrance of the Father.

He returns the fragrance to the place it came from because the first aroma had grown cold. It had become a form of the mind, resembling frozen water which when one sees it the would think it is as hard as earth, but if a warm breath is breathed on it, it melts. When the fragrance is frozen there are divisions (cracked pieces). But God came and destroyed the division when he sent the warm Fullness (Pleroma) of love, so that the cold would never return. Then came Unity of perfect Thought.

This is the word of the Gospel for finding the Fullness (Pleroma). It is for those who await the salvation that comes from on high. While they await what they hope for, hope itself is waiting. It will be time for the Pleroma to come when their likeness is light and they have no shadow.

The deficiency of matter did not come because of the limitlessness of the Father, but he came at the time of the deficiency. It was a surprise that the incorruptible One came in this way. But the depth of the Father is increasing, and the Error of thought is not with him. It is as if something has falling down that is easily set up right again. When one finds He who has come to him (to set him up right again) he will turn back (from being fallen). This turning back is called "repentance".

For this reason, incorruption has breathed forth and it pursues the sinner so that he can find rest. What remains for those of the light which are living in the deficiency is forgiveness, and this is the Word from the Fullness (Pleroma). For the physician wants to hurry to the place where there is sickness. The sick man is lacking and he does not hide himself but he reveals what he lacks because the physician possesses what he lacks. A diminishing occurred in the place where there is no grace. One who deficiency takes hold of becomes weak and lacking. Deficiency has no Grace. The Fullness has no deficiency and this is the same way the deficiency is filled by the Pleroma, which has emptied itself so that it may fill the one who is lacking and he may receive Grace. And he discovered the light of truth which rose upon him and it was unchanging.

This is why they who have been troubled speak about Christ when they are together, so that they may be brought back and he may anoint them with the ointment of mercy from the Father, for he will have mercy on them. Those whom he has anointed are made complete (perfect). It is the full vessel that He customarily anoints. And when the anointing is complete, the vessel is emptied, and the as the ointment is used a deficiency is left. After that, a breath draws it only through the power which it has. But the one who lacks nothing has no seal broken nor anything poured out of them, but those who are the deficient are filled again by the perfect Father. He is good. He knows his plantings because he is the one who has planted them in his Paradise, which is his place of rest.

This is the perfection in the thought of the Father and these are the words of his meditation. Each one of his words is the work of his will alone, and it reveals his Word (Logos). Since they were in the depth of his Thoughts, the Word (Logos), who was the first to come forth, caused them to appear, along with the mind which speaks the only Word in the grace of silence. It was called "Thought," since they were in Him before it became manifest. It happened at the moment that it was the first to come forth and it was pleasing to the will of him who desired it. It is the will that the Father rests in and in it he is pleased.

Nothing happens without him, and without the will of the Father nothing is done. But his will cannot be understood. His will is his sign and no one can fathom it, even if they focus only on it they could not possibly grasp it. But that which he desires takes place at the moment he wills it, even if no one likes it, it is the will of

God. You see, the Father knows the beginning and the end of all things. And when their end arrives, he will question them himself directly. The end is the knowledge of Father who is hidden. From Him the beginning he formed everything and everything will return to him. For they were made manifest for His joy and for the glory of his name.

And the name of the Father is the Son. It is he who, in the beginning, gave a name to him who came forth from him who is himself, and he begot him as a son. He gave him his name which belonged to him. He is the Father and everything which exists is around him. He has the name and he is the son. It is possible for him to be seen, but the name remains invisible. The name alone is the mystery of the invisible and through the Father`s action it fills the ears completely. The Father's, name is not spoken, but it is revealed through the son.

This is why the name is great. Who, then, is able to utter his great name except him alone to whom the name belongs and the sons of the name for the Father resides in them and they in turn rest in his name, since the Father has no beginning (He was not born)?

It is he alone who engendered for himself a name in the beginning before he created the Aeons, so that the name of the Father should be over their heads as lord.

(Alternate rendering: The Father is neither male nor female and the Father alone created Himself a name before he created the Aeons so that His name may be placed over them as their lord.)

It is, the true name, which is made true by his command and by his power it is made perfect. For the name is not drawn from any word, list, or book, nor is his name given as a title, but His name is invisible. He alone gave the name to himself, because he alone knew it and only He had the ability to give himself a name. For he who does not exist has no name. Why give a name to someone who did not exist? But He exists with his name and he alone knows it. Father gave a name to Him only. The Son is the name of the Father. He did not, keep it hidden or make it a secret, but he manifested the son. The name is the Father's, just as the name of the Father is the Son. Where would compassion find a name but in the Father? And there is no compassion found outside of the Father.

Doubtless one neighbor will say to another, "Who would give a name to someone who existed before himself, as if, children did not receive their name from one of those who begot them?"

Above all, then, it is right for us to ponder this point over: What is the real and true name? The name came from the Father and it is His name. He did not get the name from someone else who was born before, like others have done. This is the name of power. There is no one else to whom he has given it. It has remained unnamed, unspeakable, and it cannot be described. It remained thus until the moment he who is perfect pronounced it. It was he alone who was able to pronounce and see his name.

It pleased him that his son he loved should be his pronounced name. He who came from the depth spoke about his secrets, because he knew that the Father was absolute goodness and had no evil in Him. For this reason, He sent a unique one to speak about his place of rest from which he came, and that he might glorify the Fullness (Pleroma), and the greatness of his name and the sweetness of the Father.

Just as everyone wants to talk about the place they are from, and how their region nourished them and how they wish to go back home, He will hurry to return home once again because he tasted the things of place, and he was nourished and grew. And his own place of rest is his Pleroma (Fullness). All the emanations from the

Father, make up the Fullness, and all his emanations are rooted in the one who caused them to grow from himself. He appointed Limit and assigned them a path. Then they came into existence one by one, individually, and they had their own thought and will. And that place about which they think is their root. And their thought lifts them up to the heights where the Father is. When they reach His head, they rest, and they remain there near to it so that they say that they have experienced his face with a kiss. But these of this kind were not manifest, because they are not exalted. But they do not deprive the Father of glory. They never thought of him as small, or bitter, or angry, but they know He is absolutely good, never upset, always sweet, and he knowing everything before it came into existence. He has no need of a teacher.

This is the way of those who possess immeasurable greatness from above. They yearn for that unique and perfect one who is there for them. They do not descend to the place of the dead (Hades). They do not have envy or groaning, or death in them. But they rest in him who is rest. They no longer weary themselves searching for truth. But, they are the truth because the Father is in them, and they are in the Father. The Father is completely good and they are perfected by Him and they will never leave him. They lack for nothing, and they are given rest and are refreshed by the Spirit. And they heed their root and he who will find his root will refresh themselves and he will never lose his soul. This is the place of the blessed; this is their dwelling.

The rest of the people will know that this place does not suit me, for after I have been in the place of rest there is nowhere else to be. But I shall be in Him and I will devote myself to the Father of the All and the true brothers at all times. We are those upon whom the love of the Father is poured out, and among them and in Him nothing is lacking. It is they who appear in truth since they are in that true and eternal life and they speak of the light, which is perfect and it is filled with the seed of the Father. It is in his heart and in the his Fullness (Pleroma). His Spirit rejoices and glorifies him because the Father is good and the Spirit is in Him. And his children are perfect and worthy of his name, because he is their Father. And He loves the Children of this kind.

Introduction to the Gospel of Thomas

In the winter of 1945, in Upper Egypt, an Arab peasants were gathering fertilizer and topsoil for his crops. While digging in the soft dirt they came across a large earthen vessel. Inside were scrolls containing hitherto unseen books.

The scrolls were discovered near the site of the ancient town of Chenoboskion, at the base of a mountain named Gebel et-Tarif, near Hamra-Dum, in the vicinity of Nag 'Hammadi, about sixty miles from Luxor in Egypt. The texts were written in the Coptic language and preserved on papyrus sheets. The lettering style dated them as having been penned around the third or fourth century A.D. The Gospel of Thomas is the longest of the volumes consisting of 114 verses. Recent study indicates that the original work of Thomas, of which the scrolls are copies, may predate the four canonical gospels of Matthew, Mark, Luke, and John. The origin of The Gospel of Thomas is now thought to be from the first or second century A.D.

The word Coptic is an Arabic corruption of the Greek word Aigyptos, which in turn comes from the word Hikaptah, one of the names of the city of Memphis, the first capital of ancient Egypt.

There has never been a Coptic state or government per se, however the word has been used to generally define a culture and language present in the area of Egypt.

The known history of the Copts starts with King Mina the first King, who united the northern and southern kingdoms of Egypt circa 3050 B.C. The ancient Egyptian civilization under the rule of the Pharaohs lasted over 3000 years. Saint Mina (named after the king) is one of the major Coptic saints. He was martyred in 309 A.D.

The culture has come to be recognized as one containing a distinctive art, architecture, and even a certain Christian church system.

The Coptic Church is based on the teachings of St. Mark, who introduced the region to Christianity in the first century A.D. The Copts take pride in the monastic flavor of their church and the fact that the Gospel of Mark is thought to be the oldest of the Gospels. Now, lying before a peasant boy was a scroll written in the ancient Coptic tongue; The Gospel of Thomas, possibly older than and certainly quite different from any other Gospel.

The peasant boy who found the treasure of the Gospel of Thomas stood to be rewarded greatly. This could have been the discovery of a lifetime for his family, but the boy had no idea what he had. He took the scrolls home, where his mother burned some as kindling. Others were sold to the black market antique dealers in Cairo. It would be years until they found their way into the hands of a scholar.

Part of the thirteenth codex was smuggled from Egypt to America. In 1955 whispers of the existence of the codex had reached the ears of Gilles Quispel, a professor of religion and history in the Netherlands. The race was on to find and translate the scrolls.

The introduction of the collected sayings of Jesus refers to the writer as Didymus (Jude) Thomas. This is the same Thomas who doubted Jesus and was then told to place his hand within the breach in the side of the Savior. In the Gospel of St. John, he is referred to as Didymus, which means twin in Greek. In Aramaic, the name Jude (or Judas) also carries the sense of twin. The use of this title led some in the apocryphal tradition to believe that he was the twin brother and confidant of Jesus. However, when applied to Jesus himself, the literal meaning of twin must be rejected by orthodox Christianity as well as anyone adhering to the doctrine of the virgin birth of the only begotten Son of God. The title is likely meant to signify that Thomas was a close confidant of Jesus, or more simply, he was part of a set of twins and in no way related to Jesus.

Ancient church historians mention that Thomas preached to the Parthians in Persia and it is said he was buried in Edessa. Fourth century chronicles attribute the evangelization of India (Asia-Minor or Central Asia) to Thomas.

The text, which some believe predates the four gospels, has a very Taoist, Zen-like, or Eastern flavor. Since it is widely held that the four gospels of Matthew, Mark, Luke, and John have a common reference in the basic text of Mark, it stands to reason that all follow the same general history, insights, and language. Since scholars believe that the Gospel of Thomas predates the four main gospels, it can be assumed it was written outside the influences common to the other gospels.

The Gospel of Thomas is actually not a gospel at all. It contains no narrative but is instead a collection of sayings, which are said to be from Jesus himself as written (quoted) by Thomas. Although the codex found in Egypt is dated to the fourth century, most biblical scholars place the actual construction of the text of Thomas at about 70 – 150 A.D.

The gospel was often mentioned in early Christian literature, but no copy was thought to have survived until the discovery of the Coptic manuscript. Since then, part of the Oxyrynchus papyri have been identified as older Greek fragments of Thomas. The papyri were discovered in 1898 in the rubbish heaps of Oxyrhynchus, Egypt. This discovery yielded over thirty-five manuscript fragments for the New Testament. They have been dated to about 60 A.D. As a point of reference, a fragment of papyrus from the Dead Sea Scrolls had been dated to before 68 A.D.

There are marked differences between the Greek and Coptic texts, as we will see.

The debate on the date of Thomas centers in part on whether Thomas is dependent upon the canonical gospels, or is derived from an earlier document that was simply a collection of sayings. Many of the passages in Thomas appear to be more authentic versions of the synoptic parables, and many have parallels in Mark and Luke. This has caused a division of thought wherein some believe Thomas used common sources also used by Mark and Luke. Others believe Thomas was written independently after witnessing the same events.

If Thomas wrote his gospel first, without input from Mark, and from the standpoint of Eastern exposure as a result of his sojourn into India, it could explain the mystical quality of the text. It could also explain the striking differences in the recorded quotes of Jesus as memories were influenced by exposure to Asian culture.

There is some speculation that the sayings found in Thomas could be more accurate to the original intent and wording of Jesus than the other gospels. This may seem counter-intuitive until we realize that Christianity itself is an Eastern religion, albeit Middle-Eastern. Although, as it spread west the faith went through many changes to westernize or Romanize it...Jesus was both mystical and Middle-Eastern. The Gospel of Thomas may not have seen as much "dilution" by Western society.

The Gospel of Thomas was most likely composed in Syria, where tradition holds the church of Edessa was founded by Judas

Thomas, The Twin (Didymos). The gospel may well be the earliest written tradition in the Syriac church

The Gospel of Thomas is sometimes called a Gnostic Gospel, although it seems more likely Thomas was adopted by the Gnostic community and interpreted in the light of their beliefs.

The term Gnostic is derived from gnosis, which in Greek means knowledge. Gnostics believed that knowledge is formed or found from a personal encounter with God brought about by inward or intuitive insight. It is this knowledge that brings salvation. The Gnostics believed they were privy to a secret knowledge about the divine. It is their focus on knowledge that leads to their name. The roots of the Gnosticism pre-date Christianity. Similarities exist to the wisdom and knowledge cults found in Egypt. The belief system seems to have spread and found a suitable home in the mystical side of the Christian faith.

There are numerous references to the Gnostics in second century literature. Their form of Christianity was considered heresy by the early church fathers. The intense resistance to the Gnostic belief system seems to be based in two areas. First, there was a general Gnostic belief that we were all gods, with heaven contained within us. Jesus, according to the Gnostics, was here to show us our potential to become as he was; a son or daughter of god, for God is both father and mother, male and female. These beliefs ran contrary to the newly developing orthodoxy. The second line of resistance was political. This resistance developed later and would have come from the fact that a faith based on a personal encounter flew in the face of the developing church political structure that placed priests and church as the keepers of heaven's gate with salvation through them alone.

It is from the writings condemning the group that we glean most of our information about the Gnostics. They are alluded to in the Bible in 1 Tm 1:4 and 1 Tm 6:20, and possibly the entirety of Jude, as the writers of the Bible defended their theology against that of the Gnostics.

The Coptic and Greek translations of The Gospel of Thomas presented herein are the result of a gestalt brought about by contrasting and comparing all of the foremost translations, where the best phrasing was chosen to follow the intent and meaning of the text.

Because there are differences between the Coptic manuscript and the Greek fragments of Thomas, each verse will have the following format for the reader to view; The Coptic text will be presented first, since we have the entire Gospel in this language. The Greek text will come next. If there is not a second rendition of the verse the reader may assume there was no Greek fragment found for that verse or the Greek version of the verse was identical to the Coptic version. Lastly, obvious parallels found in the Bible are listed.

Let us keep in mind that some of the differences between the translations of the Greek and Coptic may be attributed in part to the choice of word or phrase of those translating. It is the differences in overall meaning of verses between Coptic and Greek on which we should focus.

In the document to follow, the Gospel of Thomas will appear as a bold text. If there are other relevant but divergent interpretations of phrases in Thomas, they are included in parenthesis. Any parallels of text or meaning that appear in the Bible are placed below the verse in italicized text. Author's notes are in regular text. In this way the reader can easily identify which body of work is being referenced and observe how they fit together.

Since the deeper meanings within Thomas are both in metaphor and in plain, understandable language, it is hoped that each time the words are read some new insight and treasure can be taken from them. As we change our perspective, we see the meaning of each verse differently. As one turns a single jewel to view each facet, we should study the Gospel of Thomas in the same way.

The Gospel Of Thomas

These are the secret sayings which the living Jesus has spoken and Judas who is also Thomas (the twin) (Didymos Judas Thomas) wrote. (Living, after the resurrection.)

1. And he said: Whoever finds the interpretation of these sayings will not taste death.

1. He said to them: Whoever discovers the interpretation of these words shall never taste death.
John 8:51 Very truly I tell you, whoever keeps my word will never see death.

2. Jesus said: Let he who seeks not stop seeking until he finds, and when he finds he will be troubled, and when he has been troubled he will marvel (be astonished) and he will reign over all and in reigning, he will find rest.

2. Jesus said: Let he who seeks not stop until he finds, and when he finds he shall wonder and in wondering he shall reign, and in reigning he shall find rest.

3. Jesus said: If those who lead you say to you: Look, the Kingdom is in the sky, then the birds of the sky would enter before you. If they say to you: It is in the sea, then the fish of the sea would enter ahead you. But the Kingdom of God exists within you and it exists outside of you. Those who come to know (recognize) themselves will find it, and when you come to know yourselves you will become known and you will realize that you are the children of the Living Father. Yet if you do not come to know yourselves then you will dwell in poverty and it will be you who are that poverty.

3. Jesus said, If those who lead you say, "See, the Kingdom is in the sky," then the birds of the sky will precede you. If they say to you, "It is under the earth," then the fish of the sea will precede you. Rather, the Kingdom of God is inside of you, and it is outside of you.

Those who come to know themselves will find it; and when you come to know yourselves, you will understand that it is you who are the sons of the living Father. But if you will not know yourselves, you dwell in poverty and it is you who are that poverty.

Luke 17:20 And when he was demanded of by the Pharisees, when the kingdom of God should come, he answered them and said, The kingdom of God cometh not with observation: Neither shall they say, Lo here! Lo there! For, behold, the kingdom of God is within you.

4. Jesus said: The person of old age will not hesitate to ask a little child of seven days about the place of life, and he will live. For many who are first will become last, (and the last will be first). And they will become one and the same.

4. Jesus said: Let the old man who has lived many days not hesitate to ask the child of seven days about the place of life; then he will live. For many that are first will be last, and last will be first, and they will become a single one.

Mark 9:35-37 He sat down, called the twelve, and said to them: Whoever wants to be first must be last of all and servant of all. Then he took a little child and put it among them, and taking it in his arms, he said to them: Whoever welcomes one such child in my name welcomes me, and whoever welcomes me welcomes not me but the one who sent me.

5. Jesus said: Recognize what is in front of your face, and what has been hidden from you will be revealed to you. For there is nothing hidden which will not be revealed (become manifest), and nothing buried that will not be raised.

5.   Jesus said: Know what is in front of your face and what is hidden from you will be revealed to you.
For there is nothing hidden that will not be revealed.

Mark 4:22 For there is nothing hid, except to be made manifest; nor is anything secret, except it come to light.

Luke 12:2 Nothing is covered up that will not be revealed, or hidden that will not be known.
Matthew 10:26 So have no fear of them; for nothing is covered up that will not be uncovered, and nothing secret that will not become known.

6. His Disciples asked Him, they said to him: How do you want us to fast, and how will we pray? And how will we be charitable (give alms), and what laws of diet will we maintain?

Jesus said: Do not lie, and do not practice what you hate, for everything is in the plain sight of Heaven. For there is nothing concealed that will not become manifest, and there is nothing covered that will not be exposed.

6.   His disciples asked him, "How do you want us to fast? And how shall we pray? And how shall we give alms? And what kind of diet shall we follow?"
Jesus said, don't lie, and don't do what you hate to do, for all things are revealed before the truth. For there is nothing hidden which shall not be revealed.

Luke 11:1 He was praying in a certain place, and after he had finished, one of his disciples said to him, Lord, teach us to pray, as John taught his disciples.

7. Jesus said: Blessed is the lion that the man will eat, for the lion will become the man. Cursed is the man that the lion shall eat, and still the lion will become man.

Mathew 26:23-30 He who dipped his hand with me in the dish, the same will betray me. The Son of Man goes, even as it is written of him, but woe to that man through whom the Son of Man is betrayed! It would be better for that man if he had not been born. Judas, who betrayed him, answered, "It isn't me, is it, Rabbi?" He said to him, You said it. As they were eating, Jesus took bread, gave thanks for it, and broke it. He gave to the disciples, and said, Take, eat; this is my body. He took the cup, gave thanks, and gave to them, saying: All of you drink it, for this is my blood of the new covenant, which is poured out for many for the remission of sins. But I tell you that I will not drink of this fruit of the vine from now on, until that day when I drink it anew with you in my Father's Kingdom. When they had sung a hymn, they went out to the Mount of Olives.

8. And he said: The Kingdom of Heaven is like a wise fisherman who casts his net into the sea. He drew it up from the sea full of small fish. Among them he found a fine large fish. That wise fisherman threw all the small fish back into the sea and chose the large fish without hesitation. Whoever has ears to hear, let him hear!

Matthew 13:47-48 Again, the kingdom of heaven is like a net that was thrown into the sea and caught fish of every kind; when it was full, they drew it ashore, sat down, and put the good into baskets but threw out the bad.

9. Jesus said: Now, the sower came forth. He filled his hand and threw (the seeds). Some fell upon the road and the birds came and gathered them up. Others fell on the stone and they did not take deep enough roots in the soil, and so did not produce grain. Others fell among the thorns and they choked the seed, and the

worm ate them. Others fell upon the good earth and it produced good fruit up toward the sky, it bore 60 fold and 120 fold.

Matthew 13:3-8 And he told them many things in parables, saying: Listen! A sower went out to sow. And as he sowed, some seeds fell on the path, and the birds came and ate them up. Other seeds fell on rocky ground, where they did not have much soil, and they sprang up quickly, since they had no depth of soil. But when the sun rose, they were scorched; and since they had no root, they withered away. Other seeds fell among thorns, and the thorns grew up and choked them. Other seeds fell on good soil and brought forth grain, some a hundred fold, some sixty, some thirty.

Mark 4:2-9 And he taught them many things in parables, and in his teaching he said to them: Behold! A sower went out to sow. And as he sowed, some seed fell along the path, and the birds came and devoured it. Other seed fell on rocky ground, where it had not much soil, and immediately it sprang up, since it had no depth of soil; and when the sun rose it was scorched, and since it had no root it withered away. Other seed fell among thorns and the thorns grew up and choked it, and it yielded no grain. And other seeds fell into good soil and brought forth grain, growing up and increasing and yielding thirty fold and sixty fold and a hundred fold. And he said, He who has ears to hear, let him hear.

Luke 8:4-8 And when a great crowd came together and people from town after town came to him, he said in a parable: A sower went out to sow his seed; and as he sowed, some fell along the path, and was trodden under foot, and the birds of the air devoured it. And some fell on the rock; and as it grew up, it withered away, because it had no moisture. And some fell among thorns; and the thorns grew with it and choked it. And some fell into good soil and grew, and yielded a hundred fold. As he said this, he called out, He who has ears to hear, let him hear.

10. Jesus said: I have cast fire upon the world, and as you see, I guard it until it is ablaze.

Luke 12:49 I came to bring fire to the earth, and how I wish it were already kindled.

11. Jesus said: This sky will pass away, and the one above it

will pass away. The dead are not alive, and the living will not die. In the days when you consumed what is dead, you made it alive. When you come into the Light, what will you do? On the day when you were united (one), you became separated (two). When you have become separated (two), what will you do?

Matthew 24:35 Heaven and earth will pass away, but my words will not pass away.

12. The Disciples said to Jesus: We know that you will go away from us. Who is it that will be our teacher?

Jesus said to them: Wherever you are (in the place that you have come), you will go to James the Righteous, for whose sake Heaven and Earth were made (came into being).

13. Jesus said to his Disciples: Compare me to others, and tell me who I am like. Simon Peter said to him: You are like a righteous messenger (angel) of God. Matthew said to him: You are like a (wise) philosopher (of the heart). Thomas said to him: Teacher, my mouth is not capable of saying who you are like!

Jesus said: I'm not your teacher, now that you have drunk; you have become drunk from the bubbling spring that I have tended (measured out). And he took him, and withdrew and spoke three words to him: ahyh ashr ahyh (I am who I am).

Now when Thomas returned to his comrades, they inquired of him: What did Jesus say to you? Thomas said to them: If I tell you even one of the words which he spoke to me, you will take up stones and throw them at me, and fire will come from the stones to consume you.

Mark 8:27-30 Jesus went on with his disciples to the villages of Caesarea Philippi; and on the way he asked his disciples, Who do people say that I am? And they answered him, John the Baptist; and others, Elijah; and still others, one of the prophets. He asked them, But who do you say that I am? Peter answered him, You are the Messiah. And he sternly ordered them not to tell anyone about him.

14. Jesus said to them: If you fast, you will give rise to transgression (sin) for yourselves. And if you pray, you will be condemned. And if you give alms, you will cause harm (evil) to your spirits. And when you go into the countryside, if they take you in (receive you) then eat what they set before you and heal the sick among them. For what goes into your mouth will not defile you, but rather what comes out of your mouth, that is what will defile you.

Luke 10:8-9 Whenever you enter a town and its people welcome you, eat what is set before you; Cure the sick who are there, and say to them, The kingdom of God has come near to you.

Mark 7:15 There is nothing outside a person that by going in can defile, but the things that come out are what defile.

Matthew 15:11 It is not what goes into the mouth that defiles a man, but what comes out of the mouth, this defiles a man.

Romans 14:14 I know and am persuaded in the Lord Jesus that nothing is unclean in itself; but it is unclean for any one who thinks it unclean.

15. Jesus said: When you see him who was not born of woman, bow yourselves down upon your faces and worship him for he is your Father.

Galatians 4:3-5 Even so we, when we were children, were in bondage under the elements of the world: But when the fullness of the time was come, God sent forth his Son, made of a woman, made under the law, To redeem them that were under the law, that we might receive the adoption of sons.

16. Jesus said: People think perhaps I have come to spread

peace upon the world. They do not know that I have come to cast dissention (conflict) upon the earth; fire, sword, war. For there will be five in a house. Three will be against two and two against three, the father against the son and the son against the father. And they will stand alone.

Matthew 10:34-36 Do not think that I have come to bring peace to the earth; I have not come to bring peace, but a sword. For I have come to set a man against his father, and a daughter against her mother, and a daughter-in-law against her mother-in-law; and one's foes will be members of one's own household.

Luke 12:51-53 Do you think that I have come to give peace on earth? No, I tell you, but rather division; for henceforth in one house there will be five divided, three against two and two against three; they will be divided, father against son and son against father, mother against daughter and daughter against her mother, mother-in-law against her daughter-in-law and daughter-in-law against her mother-in-law.

17. Jesus said: I will give to you what eye has not seen, what ear has not heard, what hand has not touched, and what has not occurred to the mind of man.
1 Cor 2:9 But, as it is written, What no eye has seen, nor ear heard, nor the human heart conceived, what God has prepared for those who love him.

18. The Disciples said to Jesus: Tell us how our end will come. Jesus said: Have you already discovered the beginning (origin), so that you inquire about the end? Where the beginning (origin) is, there the end will be. Blessed be he who will take his place in the beginning (stand at the origin) for he will know the end, and he will not experience death.

19. Jesus said: Blessed is he who came into being before he came into being. If you become my Disciples and heed my sayings, these stones will serve you. For there are five trees in paradise for you, which are undisturbed in summer and in winter and their leaves do not fall. Whoever knows them will not experience death.

20. The Disciples said to Jesus: Tell us what the Kingdom of Heaven is like. He said to them: It is like a mustard seed, smaller than all other seeds and yet when it falls on the tilled earth, it produces a great plant and becomes shelter for the birds of the sky.

Mark 4:30-32 He also said, With what can we compare the kingdom of God, or what parable will we use for it? It is like a mustard seed, which, when sown upon the ground, is the smallest of all the seeds on earth; yet when it is sown it grows up and becomes the greatest of all shrubs, and puts forth large branches, so that the birds of the air can make nests in its shade.

Matthew 13:31-32 The kingdom of heaven is like a grain of mustard seed which a man took and sowed in his field; it is the smallest of all seeds, but when it has grown it is the greatest of shrubs and becomes a tree, so that the birds of the air come and make nests in its branches.

Luke 13.18-19 He said therefore, What is the kingdom of God like? And to what shall I compare it? It is like a grain of mustard seed which a man took and sowed in his garden; and it grew and became a tree, and the birds of the air made nests in its branches.

21. Mary said to Jesus: Who are your Disciples like? He said: They are like little children who are living in a field that is not theirs. When the owners of the field come, they will say: Let us have our field! It is as if they were naked in front of them (They undress in front of them in order to let them have what is theirs) and they give back the field. Therefore I say, if the owner of the house knows that the thief is coming, he will be alert before he arrives and will not allow him to dig through into the house to carry away his belongings. You, must be on guard and beware of the world (system). Prepare yourself (arm yourself) with great strength or the bandits will find a way to reach you, for the problems you expect will come. Let there be among you a person of understanding (awareness). When the crop ripened, he came quickly with his sickle in his hand to reap. Whoever has ears to hear, let him hear!

Matthew 24:43 But understand this: if the owner of the house had known in what part of the night the thief was coming, he would have stayed awake and would not have let his house be broken into.

Mark 4:26-29 He also said, The kingdom of God is as if someone would scatter seed on the ground, and would sleep and rise night and day, and the seed would sprout and grow, he does not know how. The earth produces of itself, first the stalk, then the head, then the full grain in the head. But when the grain is ripe, at once he goes in with his sickle, because the harvest has come.

Luke 12:39-40 But know this, that if the householder had known at what hour the thief was coming, he would not have left his house to be broken into. You also must be ready; for the Son of man is coming at an unexpected hour.

22. Jesus saw little children who were being suckled. He said to his Disciples: These little children who are being suckled are like those who enter the Kingdom.

They said to him: Should we become like little children in order to enter the Kingdom?

Jesus said to them: When you make the two one, and you make the inside as the outside and the outside as the inside, when you make the above as the below, and if you make the male and the female one and the same (united male and female) so that the man will not be masculine (male) and the female be not feminine (female), when you establish an eye in the place of an eye and a hand in the place of a hand and a foot in the place of a foot and an likeness (image) in the place of a likeness (an

image), then will you enter the Kingdom.

Luke 18:16 But Jesus called for them and said, Let the little children come to me, and do not stop them; for it is to such as these that the kingdom of God belongs. Truly I tell you, whoever does not receive the kingdom of God as a little child will never enter it.

Mark 9:43-48 If your hand causes you to stumble, cut it off; it is better for you to enter life maimed than to have two hands and to go to hell, to the unquenchable fire. And if your foot causes you to stumble, cut it off; it is better for you to enter life lame than to have two feet and to be thrown into hell. And if your eye causes you to stumble, tear it out; it is better for you to enter the kingdom of God with one eye than to have two eyes and to be thrown into hell, where the worm never dies, and the fire is never quenched.
Matthew 18:3-5 And said, Verily, I say unto you, unless you turn and become like children, you will never enter the kingdom of heaven. Whoever humbles himself like this child, he is the greatest in the kingdom of heaven. Whoever receives one such child in my name receives me;
Matthew 5:29-30 If your right eye causes you to sin, pluck it out and throw it away; it is better that you lose one of your members than that your whole body be thrown into hell. And if your right hand causes you to sin, cut it off and throw it away; it is better that you lose one of your members than that your whole body go into hell.

23. Jesus said: I will choose you, one out of a thousand and two out of ten thousand and they will stand as a single one.

Matthew 20:16 So the last shall be first, and the first last: for many be called, but few chosen.

24. His Disciples said: Show us the place where you are (your place), for it is necessary for us to seek it.
He said to them: Whoever has ears, let him hear! Within a man of light there is light, and he illumines the entire world. If he does not shine, he is darkness (there is darkness).

John13:36 Simon Peter said to him, Lord, where are you going? Jesus answered, Where I am going, you cannot follow me now; but you will follow afterward.

Matthew 6:22-23 The eye is the lamp of the body. So, if your eye is healthy, your whole body will be full of light; but if your eye is unhealthy, your whole body will be full of darkness. If then the light in you is darkness, how great is the darkness!

Luke 11:34-36 Your eye is the lamp of your body; when your eye is sound, your whole body is full of light; but when it is not sound, your body is full of darkness. Therefore be careful lest the light in you be darkness. If then your whole body is full of light, having no part dark, it will be wholly bright, as when a lamp with its rays gives you light.

Note:

Early philosophers thought that light was transmitted from the eye and bounced back, allowing the person to sense the world at large. Ancient myths tell of Aphrodite constructing the human eye out of the four elements (earth, wind, fire, and water). The eye was held together by love. She kindled the fire of the soul and used it to project from the eyes so that it would act like a lantern, transmitting the light, thus allowing us to see.

Euclid, (330 BC to 260BC) speculated about the speed of light being instantaneous since you close your eyes, then open them again, even the distant objects appear immediately.

25. Jesus said: Love your friend (Brother) as your soul; protect him as you would the pupil of your own eye.

Romans 12:9-11 Let love be without dissimulation. Abhor that which is evil; cleave to that which is good. Be kindly affectioned one to another with brotherly love; in honour preferring one another; Not slothful in business; fervent in spirit; serving the Lord;

26. Jesus said: You see the speck in your brother's eye but the beam that is in your own eye you do not see. When you remove

the beam out of your own eye, then will you see clearly to remove the speck out of your brother's eye.

26.   Jesus said, You see the splinter in your brother's eye, but you don't see the log in your own eye. When you take the log out of your own eye, then you will see well enough to remove the splinter from your brother's eye.

Matthew 7:3-5 Why do you see the speck in your neighbor's eye, but do not notice the log in your own eye? Or how can you say to your neighbor, Let me take the speck out of your eye, while the log is in your own eye? You hypocrite, first take the log out of your own eye, and then you will see clearly to take the speck out of your neighbor's eye.

Luke 6:41-42 Why do you see the speck that is in your brother's eye, but do not notice the log that is in your own eye? Or how can you say to your brother, Brother, let me take out the speck that is in your eye, when you yourself do not see the log that is in your own eye? You hypocrite, first take the log out of your own eye, and then you will see clearly to take out the speck that is in your brother's eye.

27. Jesus said: Unless you fast from the world (system), you will not find the Kingdom of God. Unless you keep the Sabbath (entire week) as Sabbath, you will not see the Father.

27.   Jesus said: Unless you fast (abstain) from the world, you shall in no way find the Kingdom of God; and unless you observe the Sabbath as a Sabbath, you shall not see the Father.

28. Jesus said: I stood in the midst of the world. In the flesh I appeared to them. I found them all drunk; I found none thirsty among them. My soul grieved for the sons of men, for they are blind in their hearts and do not see that they came into the world empty they are destined (determined) to leave the world empty. However, now they are drunk. When they have shaken off their wine, then they will repent (change their ways).

28.   Jesus said: I took my stand in the midst of the world, and they saw me in the flesh, and I found they were all drunk, and I found none of them were thirsty. And my soul grieved over the souls of men because they are blind in their hearts. They do not see that they came into the world empty and they are determined to leave the world empty. However, now they are drunk. When they have shaken off their wine, then they will change their ways.

29. Jesus said: If the flesh came into being because of spirit, it is a marvel, but if spirit came into being because of the body, it would be a marvel of marvels. I marvel indeed at how great wealth has taken up residence in this poverty.

30. Jesus said: Where there are three gods, they are gods (Where there are three gods they are without god). Where there is only one, I say that I am with him. Lift the stone and there you will find me, Split the wood and there am I.

30.   Jesus said: Where three are together they are not without God, and when there is one alone, I say, I am with him.

Note:
 Many believe pages of the manuscript were misplaced and verses 30 and 77 should run together as a single verse.

77. Jesus said: I-Am the Light who is over all things, I-Am the All. From me all came forth and to me all return (The All came from me and the All has come to me). Split wood, there am I. Lift up the stone and there you will find me.

Matthew 18:20 For where two or three are gathered in my name, I am there among them.

31. Jesus said: No prophet is accepted in his own village, no physician heals those who know him.

31.   Jesus said: A prophet is not accepted in his own country, neither can a doctor cure those that know him.

Mark 6:4 Then Jesus said to them, Prophets are not without honor, except in their hometown, and among their own kin, and in their own house.

Matthew 13:57 And they took offense at him. But Jesus said to them: A prophet is not without honor save in his own country and in his own house.

Luke 4:24 And he said, Truly, I say to you, no prophet is acceptable in his own country.

John 4:43-44 After the two days he departed to Galilee. For Jesus himself testified that a prophet has no honor in his own country.

32. Jesus said: A city being built (and established) upon a high mountain and fortified cannot fall nor can it be hidden.

32. Jesus said: A city built on a high hilltop and fortified can neither fall nor be hidden.

Matthew 5:14 You are the light of the world. A city built on a hill cannot be hid.

33. Jesus said: What you will hear in your ear preach from your rooftops. For no one lights a lamp and sets it under a basket nor puts it in a hidden place, but rather it is placed on a lamp stand so that everyone who comes and goes will see its light.

33. Jesus said: What you hear with one ear preach from your rooftops. For no one lights a lamp and sets it under a basket or

hides, but rather it is placed on a lamp stand so that everyone who comes and goes will see its light.

Matthew 10:27 What I say to you in the dark, tell in the light; and what you hear whispered, proclaim from the housetops.

Luke 8:16 No one after lighting a lamp hides it under a jar, or puts it under a bed, but puts it on a lamp stand, so that those who enter may see the light.

Matthew 5:15 Nor do men light a lamp and put it under a bushel, but on a stand, and it gives light to all in the house.

Mark 4:21 And he said to them, Is a lamp brought in to be put under a bushel, or under a bed, and not on a stand?

Luke 11:33 No one after lighting a lamp puts it in a cellar or under a bushel, but on a stand, that those who enter may see the light.

34. Jesus said: If a blind person leads a blind person, both fall into a pit.

Matthew 15:14 Let them alone; they are blind guides of the blind. And if one blind person guides another, both will fall into a pit.

Luke 6:39 He also told them a parable: Can a blind man lead a blind man? Will they not both fall into a pit?

35. Jesus said: It is impossible for anyone to enter the house of a strong man to take it by force unless he binds his hands, then he will be able to loot his house.

Matthew 12:29 Or how can one enter a strong man's house and plunder his goods, unless he first binds the strong man? Then indeed he may plunder his house.

Luke 11:21-22 When a strong man, fully armed, guards his own palace, his goods are in peace; but when one stronger than he assails him and overcomes him, he takes away his armor in which he trusted, and divides his spoil.

Mark 3:27 But no one can enter a strong man's house and plunder his property without first tying up the strong man; then indeed the house can be plundered.

36. Jesus said: Do not worry from morning to evening nor from evening to morning about the food that you will eat nor about what clothes you will wear. You are much superior to the Lilies which neither card nor spin. When you have no clothing, what do you wear? Who can add time to your life (increase your stature)? He himself will give to you your garment.

Matthew 6:25-31 Therefore I tell you, do not worry about your life, what you will eat or what you will drink, or about your body, what you will wear. Is not life more than food, and the body more than clothing? Look at the birds of the air; they neither sow nor reap nor gather into barns, and yet your heavenly Father feeds them. Are you not of more value than they? And can any of you by worrying add a single hour to your span of life? And why do you worry about clothing? Consider the lilies of the field, how they grow; they neither toil nor spin, yet I tell you, even Solomon in all his glory was not clothed like one of these. But if God so clothes the grass of the field, which is alive today and tomorrow is thrown into the oven, will he not much more clothe you--you of little faith? Therefore do not worry, saying, What will we eat? or What will we drink? or What will we wear?

Luke 12:22-23 And he said to his disciples, Therefore I tell you, do not be anxious about your life, what you shall eat, nor about your body, what you shall put on. For life is more than food, and the body more than clothing.

37. His Disciples said: When will you appear to us, and when will we see you?

Jesus said: When you take off your garments without being ashamed, and place your garments under your feet and tread on them as the little children do, then will you see the Son of the Living-One, and you will not be afraid.

37 His disciples said to him, when will you be visible to us, and

when shall we be able to see you?

He said, when you strip naked without being ashamed and place your garments under your feet and tread on them as the little children do, then will you see the Son of the Living-One, and you will not be afraid.

38. Jesus said: Many times have you yearned to hear these sayings which I speak to you, and you have no one else from whom to hear them. There will be days when you will seek me but you will not find me.

39. Jesus said: The Pharisees and the Scribes have received the keys of knowledge, but they have hidden them. They did not go in, nor did they permit those who wished to enter to do so. However, you be as wise (astute) as serpents and innocent as doves.

39. Jesus said: The Pharisees and the Scribes have stolen the keys of heaven, but they have hidden them. They have entered in, but they did not permit those who wished to enter to do so. However, you be as wise as serpents and innocent as doves.
Luke 11:52 Woe to you lawyers! For you have taken away the key of knowledge; you did not enter yourselves, and you hindered those who were entering.
Matthew 10:16 See, I am sending you out like sheep into the midst of wolves; so be wise as serpents and innocent as doves.
Matthew 23.13 But woe unto you, scribes and Pharisees, hypocrites! because you shut the kingdom of heaven against men; for you neither enter yourselves, nor allow those who would enter to go in.

40. Jesus said: A grapevine has been planted outside the (vineyard of the) Father, and since it is not viable (supported) it

will be pulled up by its roots and destroyed.
Matthew 15:13 He answered, Every plant that my heavenly Father has not planted will be uprooted.

41. Jesus said: Whoever has (it) in his hand, to him will (more) be given. And whoever does not have, from him will be taken even the small amount which he has.
Matthew 25:29 For to all those who have, more will be given, and they will have an abundance; but from those who have nothing, even what they have will be taken away.
Luke 19:26 I tell you, that to every one who has will more be given; but from him who has not, even what he has will be taken away.

42. Jesus said: Become passers-by.

43. His Disciples said to him: Who are you, that you said these things to us?

Jesus said to them: You do not recognize who I am from what I said to you, but rather you have become like the Jews who either love the tree and hate its fruit, or love the fruit and hate the tree.

John 8:25 They said to him, Who are you? Jesus said to them, Why do I speak to you at all?
Matthew 7:16-20 You will know them by their fruits. Are grapes gathered from thorns, or figs from thistles? In the same way, every good tree bears good fruit, but the bad tree bears bad fruit. A good tree cannot bear bad fruit, nor can a bad tree bear good fruit. Every tree that does not bear good fruit is cut down and thrown into the fire. Thus you will know them by their fruits.

44. Jesus said: Whoever blasphemes against the Father, it will be forgiven him. And whoever blasphemes against the Son, it will be forgiven him. Yet whoever blasphemes against the Holy Spirit, it will not be forgiven him neither on earth nor in heaven.

Mark 3:28-29 Truly I tell you, people will be forgiven for their sins and whatever blasphemies they utter; but whoever blasphemes against the Holy Spirit can never have forgiveness, but is guilty of an eternal sin.
Matthew 12:31-32 Therefore I tell you, every sin and blasphemy will be forgiven men, but the blasphemy against the Spirit will not be forgiven. And whoever says a word against the Son of man will be forgiven; but whoever speaks against the Holy Spirit will not be forgiven, either in this age or in the age to come.
Luke 12:10 And every one who speaks a word against the Son of man will be forgiven him; but he who blasphemes against the Holy Spirit will not be forgiven.

45. Jesus said: Grapes are not harvested from thorns, nor are figs gathered from thistles, for they do not give fruit. A good person brings forth goodness out of his storehouse. A bad person brings forth evil out of his evil storehouse which is in his heart, and he speaks evil, for out of the abundance of the heart he brings forth evil.

Luke 6:43-45 For no good tree bears bad fruit, nor again does a bad tree bear good fruit; for each tree is known by its own fruit. For figs are not gathered from thorns, nor are grapes picked from a bramble bush. The good man out of the good treasure of his heart produces good, and the evil man out of his evil treasure produces evil; for out of the abundance of the heart his mouth speaks.

46. Jesus said: From Adam until John the Baptist there is none born of women who surpasses John the Baptist, so that his eyes should not be downcast (lowered). Yet I have said that whoever among you becomes like a child will know the Kingdom, and he will be greater than John.

Matthew 11:11 Truly I tell you, among those born of women no one has arisen greater than John the Baptist; yet the least in the kingdom of heaven is greater than he.

Luke 7:28 I tell you, among those born of women none is greater than John; yet he who is least in the kingdom of God is greater than he.

Matthew 18:2-4 He called a child, whom he put among them, and said, Truly I tell you, unless you change and become like children, you will never enter the kingdom of heaven. Whoever becomes humble like this child is the greatest in the kingdom of heaven.

47. Jesus said: It is impossible for a man to mount two horses or to draw two bows, and a servant cannot serve two masters, otherwise he will honor the one and disrespect the other. No man drinks vintage wine and immediately desires to drink new wine, and they do not put new wine into old wineskins or they would burst, and they do not put vintage wine into new wineskins or it would spoil (sour). They do not sew an old patch on a new garment because that would cause a split.

Matthew 6:24 No one can serve two masters; for a slave will either hate the one and love the other, or be devoted to the one and despise the other. You cannot serve God and wealth.

Matthew 9:16-17 No one sews a piece of cloth, not yet shrunk, on an old cloak, for the patch pulls away from the cloak, and a worse tear is made. Neither is new wine put into old wineskins; otherwise, the skins burst, and the wine is spilled, and the skins are destroyed; but new wine is put into fresh wineskins, and so both are preserved.

Mark 2:21-22 No one sews a piece of unshrunk cloth on an old garment; if he does, the patch tears away from it, the new from the old, and a worse tear is made. And no one puts new wine into old wineskins; if he does, the wine will burst the skins, and the wine is lost, and so are the skins; but new wine is for fresh skins.

Luke 5:36-39 He told them a parable also: No one tears a piece from a new garment and puts it upon an old garment; if he does, he will tear the new, and the piece from the new will not match the old. And no one puts new wine into old wineskins; if he does, the new wine will burst the skins and it will be spilled, and the skins will be destroyed. But new wine must be put into fresh wineskins. And no one after drinking old wine desires new; for he says, "The old is good."

48. Jesus said: If two make peace with each other in this one house, they will say to the mountain: Be moved! and it will be moved.

Matthew 18:19 Again, truly I tell you, if two of you agree on earth about anything you ask, it will be done for you by my Father in heaven.

Mark 11:23-24 Truly I tell you, if you say to this mountain, Be taken up and thrown into the sea, and if you do not doubt in your heart, but believe that what you say will come to pass, it will be done for you. So I tell you, whatever you ask for in prayer, believe that you have received it, and it will be yours.

Matthew 17:20 He said to them, Because of your little faith. For truly, I say to you, if you have faith as a grain of mustard seed, you will say to this mountain, Move from here to there, and it will move; and nothing will be impossible to you.

49. Jesus said: Blessed is the solitary and chosen, for you will find the Kingdom. You have come from it, and unto it you will return.

Matthew 5:1-3 And seeing the multitudes, he went up into a mountain: and when he was set, his disciples came unto him: And he opened his mouth, and taught them, saying, Blessed are the poor in spirit: for theirs is the kingdom of heaven.

John 20:28-30 And Thomas answered and said unto him, My LORD and my God. Jesus saith unto him, Thomas, because thou hast seen me, thou hast believed: blessed are they that have not seen, and yet have believed. And many other signs truly did Jesus in the presence of his disciples, which are not written in this book:

50. Jesus said: If they say to you: From where do you come? Say to them: We have come from the Light, the place where the Light

came into existence of its own accord and he stood and appeared in their image. If they say to you: Is it you? (Who are you?), say: We are his Sons and we are the chosen of the Living Father. If they ask you: What is the sign of your Father in you? Say to them: It is movement with rest (peace in the midst of motion or chaos).

51. His Disciples said to him: When will the rest of the dead occur, and when will the New World come? He said to them: That which you look for has already come, but you do not recognize it.

52. His Disciples said to him: Twenty-four prophets preached in Israel, and they all spoke of (in) you. He said to them: You have ignored the Living-One who is in your presence and you have spoken only of the dead.

53. His Disciples said to him: Is circumcision beneficial or not? He said to them: If it were beneficial, their father would beget them already circumcised from their mother. However, the true spiritual circumcision has become entirely beneficial.

Jeremiah 4:3-5 For thus saith the LORD to the men of Judah and Jerusalem, Break up your fallow ground, and sow not among thorns. Circumcise yourselves to the LORD, and take away the foreskins of your heart, ye men of Judah and inhabitants of Jerusalem: lest my fury come forth like fire, and burn that none can quench it, because of the evil of your doings. Declare ye in Judah, and publish in Jerusalem; and say, Blow ye the trumpet in the land: cry, gather together, and say, Assemble yourselves, and let us go into the defenced cities.

54. Jesus said: Blessed be the poor, for yours is the Kingdom of the Heaven.

Matthew 6:20 Then he looked up at his disciples and said: Blessed are
you who are poor, for yours is the kingdom of God.
Luke 6:20 And he lifted up his eyes on his disciples, and said: Blessed are
you poor, for yours is the kingdom of God.
Matthew 5:3 Blessed are the poor in spirit, for theirs is the kingdom of
heaven.

55. Jesus said: Whoever does not hate his father and his mother will not be able to become my Disciple. And whoever does not hate his brothers and his sisters and does not take up his own cross in my way, will not become worthy of me.

Luke 14:26-27 If any one comes to me and does not hate his own father
and mother and wife and children and brothers and sisters, yes, and even
his own life, he cannot be my disciple. Whoever does not bear his own
cross and come after me, cannot be my disciple.
John 17:11-21 And now I am no more in the world, but these are in the
world, and I come to thee. Holy Father, keep through thine own name
those whom thou hast given me, that they may be one, as we are. While I
was with them in the world, I kept them in thy name: those that thou
gavest me I have kept, and none of them is lost, but the son of perdition;
that the scripture might be fulfilled. And now come I to thee; and these
things I speak in the world, that they might have my joy fulfilled in
themselves. I have given them thy word; and the world hath hated them,
because they are not of the world, even as I am not of the world. I pray
not that thou shouldest take them out of the world, but that thou
shouldest keep them from the evil. They are not of the world, even as I am
not of the world. Sanctify them through thy truth: thy word is truth. As
thou hast sent me into the world, even so have I also sent them into the
world. And for their sakes I sanctify myself, that they also might be
sanctified through the truth. Neither pray I for these alone, but for them
also which shall believe on me through their word; That they all may be
one; as thou, Father, art in me, and I in thee, that they also may be one in
us: that the world may believe that thou hast sent me.

56. Jesus said: Whoever has come to understand the world (system) has found a corpse, and whoever has found a corpse, is superior to the world (of him the system is not worthy).

Hebrews 11:37-40 They were stoned, they were sawn asunder, were tempted, were slain with the sword: they wandered about in sheepskins and goatskins; being destitute, afflicted, tormented; (Of whom the world was not worthy:) they wandered in deserts, and in mountains, and in dens and caves of the earth. And these all, having obtained a good report through faith, received not the promise: God having provided some better thing for us, that they without us should not be made perfect.

57. Jesus said: The Kingdom of the Father is like a person who has good seed. His enemy came by night and sowed a weed among the good seed. The man did not permit them to pull up the weed, he said to them: perhaps you will intend to pull up the weed and you pull up the wheat along with it. But, on the day of harvest the weeds will be very visible and then they will pull them and burn them.

Matthew 13:24-30 He put before them another parable: The kingdom of heaven may be compared to someone who sowed good seed in his field; but while everybody was asleep, an enemy came and sowed weeds among the wheat, and then went away. So when the plants came up and bore grain, then the weeds appeared as well. And the slaves of the householder came and said to him, Master, did you not sow good seed in your field? Where, then, did these weeds come from? He answered, An enemy has done this. The slaves said to him, Then do you want us to go and gather them? But he replied, No; for in gathering the weeds you would uproot the wheat along with them. Let both of them grow together until the harvest; and at harvest time I will tell the reapers, Collect the weeds first and bind them in bundles to be burned, but gather the wheat into my barn.

58. Jesus said: Blessed is the person who has suffered, for he has found life. (Blessed is he who has suffered to find life and found life).
Matthew 11:28 Come to me, all you that are weary and are carrying heavy burdens, and I will give you rest.

59. Jesus said: Look to the Living-One while you are alive, otherwise, you might die and seek to see him and will be unable to find him.
John 7:34 You will search for me, but you will not find me; and where I am, you cannot come.
John 13:33 Little children, I am with you only a little longer. You will look for me; and as I said to the Jews so now I say to you, Where I am going, you cannot come.

60. They saw a Samaritan carrying a lamb, on his way to Judea. Jesus said to them: Why does he take the lamb with him? They said to him: So that he may kill it and eat it. He said to them: While it is alive he will not eat it, but only after he kills it and it becomes a corpse. They said: How could he do otherwise? He said to them: Look for a place of rest for yourselves, otherwise, you might become corpses and be eaten.

61. Jesus said: Two will rest on a bed and one will die and the other will live. Salome said: Who are you, man? As if sent by someone, you laid upon my bed and you ate from my table. Jesus said to her: I-Am he who is from that which is whole (the undivided). I have been given the things of my Father. Salome said: I'm your Disciple. Jesus said to her: Thus, I say that whenever someone is one (undivided)
he will be filled with light, yet whenever he is divided (chooses) he will be filled with darkness.

Luke 17:34 I tell you, on that night there will be two in one bed; one will be taken and the other left.

62. Jesus said: I tell my mysteries to those who are worthy of my mysteries. Do not let your right hand know what your left hand is doing.

Mark 4:11 And he said to them, To you has been given the secret of the kingdom of God, but for those outside, everything comes in parables.
Matthew 6:3 But when you give alms, do not let your left hand know what your right hand is doing.
Luke 8:10 He said, To you it has been given to know the secrets of the kingdom of God; but for others they are in parables, so that seeing they may not see, and hearing they may not understand.
Matthew 13:10-11 Then the disciples came and said to him, Why do you speak to them in parables? And he answered them, To you it has been given to know the secrets of the kingdom of heaven, but to them it has not been given.

63. Jesus said: There was a wealthy person who had much money, and he said: I will use my money so that I may sow and reap and replant, to fill my storehouses with grain so that I lack nothing. This was his intention (is what he thought in his heart) but that same night he died. Whoever has ears, let him hear!
Luke 12:21 Then he told them a parable: The land of a rich man produced abundantly. And he thought to himself, What should I do, for I have no place to store my crops? Then he said, I will do this: I will pull down my barns and build larger ones, and there I will store all my grain and my goods. And I will say to my soul, Soul, you have ample goods laid up for many years; relax, eat, drink, be merry. But God said to him, You fool! This very night your life is being demanded of you. And the things you have prepared, whose will they be? So it is with those who store up treasures for themselves but are not rich toward God.

64. Jesus said: A person had houseguests, and when he had prepared the banquet in their honor he sent his servant to invite the guests. He went to the first, he said to him: My master invites you. He replied: I have to do business with some merchants. They are coming to see me this evening. I will go to place my orders with them. I ask to be excused from the banquet. He went to another, he said to him: My master has invited you. He replied to him: I have just bought a house and they require me for a day. I will have no spare time. He came to another, he said to him: My master invites you. He replied to him: My friend is getting married and I must arrange a banquet for him. I will not be able to come. I ask to be excused from the banquet. He went to another, he said to him: My master invites you. He replied to him: I have bought a farm. I go to receive the rent. I will not be able to come. I ask to be excused. The servant returned, he said to his master: Those whom you have invited to the banquet have excused themselves. The master said to his servant: Go out to the roads, bring those whom you find so that they may feast. And he said: Businessmen and merchants will not enter the places of my Father.

Luke 14:16-24 Then Jesus said to him:, Someone gave a great dinner and invited many. At the time for the dinner he sent his slave to say to those who had been invited, Come; for everything is ready now. But they all alike began to make excuses. The first said to him, I have bought a piece of land, and I must go out and see it; please accept my regrets. Another said, I have bought five yoke of oxen, and I am going to try them out; please accept my regrets. Another said, I have just been married, and therefore I cannot come. So the slave returned and reported this to his master. Then the owner of the house became angry and said to his slave, Go out at once into the streets and lanes of the town and bring in the poor, the crippled, the blind, and the lame. And the slave said, Sir, what you ordered has been done, and there is still room. Then the master said to the slave, Go out into the roads and lanes, and compel people to come in, so that my house may be filled. For I tell you, none of those who were invited will taste my dinner.

Matthew 19:23 Then Jesus said to his disciples, Truly I tell you, it will be hard for a rich person to enter the kingdom of heaven.

Matthew 22:1-14 And Jesus answered and spake unto them again by parables, and said, The kingdom of heaven is like unto a certain king, which made a marriage for his son, and sent his servants to call those who were invited to the marriage feast; but they would not come. Again he sent other servants, saying, Tell those who are invited, Behold, I have made ready my dinner, my oxen and my fat calves are killed, and everything is ready; come to the marriage feast. But they made light of it and went off, one to his farm, another to his business, while the rest seized his servants, treated them shamefully, and killed them. The king was angry, and he sent his troops and destroyed those murderers and burned their city. Then he said to his servants, The wedding is ready, but those invited were not worthy. Go therefore to the thoroughfares, and invite to the marriage feast as many as you find. And those servants went out into the streets and gathered all whom they found, both bad and good; so the wedding hall was filled with guests. But when the king came in to look at the guests, he saw there a man who had no wedding garment; and he said to him, Friend, how did you get in here without a wedding garment? And he was speechless. Then the king said to the attendants, Bind him hand and foot, and cast him into the outer darkness; there men will weep and gnash their teeth. For many are called, but few are chosen.

65. He said: A kind person who owned a vineyard leased it to tenants so that they would work it and he would receive the fruit from them. He sent his servant so that the tenants would give to him the fruit of the vineyard. They seized his servant and beat him nearly to death. The servant went, he told his master what had happened. His master said: Perhaps they did not recognize him. So, he sent another servant. The tenants beat him also. Then the owner sent his son. He said: Perhaps they will respect my son. Since the tenants knew that he was the heir to the vineyard, they seized him and killed him. Whoever has ears, let him hear!

Matthew 21:33-39 Listen to another parable. There was a landowner who planted a vineyard, put a fence around it, dug a wine press in it, and built a watchtower. Then he leased it to tenants and went to another country. When the harvest time had come, he sent his slaves to the tenants to collect his produce. But the tenants seized his slaves and beat one, killed another, and stoned another. Again he sent other slaves, more than the first; and they treated them in the same way. Finally he sent his son to them, saying, They will respect my son. But when the tenants saw the son, they said to themselves, This is the heir; come, let us kill him and get his inheritance. So they seized him, threw him out of the vineyard, and killed him.

Mark 12:1-9 And he began to speak to them in parables. A man planted a vineyard, and set a hedge around it, and dug a pit for the wine press, and built a tower, and let it out to tenants, and went into another country. When the time came, he sent a servant to the tenants, to get from them some of the fruit of the vineyard. And they took him and beat him, and sent him away empty-handed. Again he sent to them another servant, and they wounded him in the head, and treated him shamefully. And he sent another, and him they killed; and so with many others, some they beat and some they killed. He had still one other, a beloved son; finally he sent him to them, saying, They will respect my son. But those tenants said to one another, This is the heir; come, let us kill him, and the inheritance will be ours. And they took him and killed him, and cast him out of the vineyard. What will the owner of the vineyard do? He will come and destroy the tenants, and give the vineyard to others.

Luke 20:9-16 And he began to tell the people this parable: A man planted a vineyard, and let it out to tenants, and went into another country for a long while. When the time came, he sent a servant to the tenants, that they should give him some of the fruit of the vineyard; but the tenants beat him, and sent him away empty-handed. And he sent another servant; him also they beat and treated shamefully, and sent him away empty-handed. And he sent yet a third; this one they wounded and cast out. 13 Then the owner of the vineyard said, What shall I do? I will send my beloved son; it may be they will respect him. 14 But when the tenants saw him, they said to themselves, This is the heir; let us kill him, that the inheritance may be ours. 15 And they cast him out of the vineyard and killed him. What then will the owner of the vineyard do to them? 16 He will come and destroy those tenants, and give the vineyard to others. When they heard this, they said, God forbid!

66. Jesus said: Show me the stone which the builders have rejected. It is that one that is the cornerstone (keystone).

Matthew 21:42 Jesus said to them, Have you never read in the scriptures: The very stone which the builders rejected has become the head of the corner; this was the Lord's doing, and it is marvelous in our eyes?

Mark 12:10-11 Have you not read this scripture: The very stone which the builders rejected has become the head of the corner; this was the Lord's doing, and it is marvelous in our eyes?

Luke 20:17 But he looked at them and said, What then does this text mean: The stone that the builders rejected has become the cornerstone?

67. Jesus said: Those who know everything but themselves, lack everything. (whoever knows the all and still feels a personal lacking, he is completely deficient).

Jeremiah 17:5- 10 Thus saith the LORD; Cursed be the man that trusteth in man, and maketh flesh his arm, and whose heart departeth from the LORD. For he shall be like the heath in the desert, and shall not see when good cometh; but shall inhabit the parched places in the wilderness, in a salt land and not inhabited. Blessed is the man that trusteth in the LORD, and whose hope the LORD is. For he shall be as a tree planted by the waters, and that spreadeth out her roots by the river, and shall not see when heat cometh, but her leaf shall be green; and shall not be careful in the year of drought, neither shall cease from yielding fruit. The heart is deceitful above all things, and desperately wicked: who can know it? I the LORD search the heart, I try the reins, even to give every man according to his ways, and according to the fruit of his doings.

68. Jesus said: Blessed are you when you are hated and

persecuted, but they themselves will find no reason why you have been persecuted.

Matthew 5:11 Blessed are you when people revile you and persecute you and utter all kinds of evil against you falsely on my account.

Luke 6:22 Blessed are you when men hate you, and when they exclude you and revile you, and cast out your name as evil, on account of the Son of man!

69. Jesus said: Blessed are those who have been persecuted in their heart these are they who have come to know the Father in truth. Jesus said: Blessed are the hungry, for the stomach of him who desires to be filled will be filled.

Matthew 5:8 Blessed are the pure in heart, for they will see God.

Luke 6:21 Blessed are you who are hungry now, for you will be filled.

70. Jesus said: If you bring forth what is within you, it will save you. If you do not have it within you to bring forth, that which you lack will destroy you.

71. Jesus said: I will destroy this house, and no one will be able to build it again.

Mark 14:58 We heard him say, I will destroy this temple that is made with hands, and in three days I will build another, not made with hands.

72. A person said to him: Tell my brothers to divide the possessions of my father with me. He said to him: Oh man, who made me a divider? He turned to his Disciples, he said to them: I'm not a divider, am I?

Luke 12:13-15 Someone in the crowd said to him, Teacher, tell my brother to divide the family inheritance with me. But he said to him,

Friend, who set me to be a judge or arbitrator over you? And he said to them, Take care! Be on your guard against all kinds of greed; for one's life does not consist in the abundance of possessions.

73. Jesus said: The harvest is indeed plentiful, but the workers are few. Ask the Lord to send workers for the harvest.

Matthew 9:37-38 Then he said to his disciples, The harvest is plentiful, but the laborers are few; therefore ask the Lord of the harvest to send out laborers into his harvest.

74. He said: Lord, there are many around the well, yet there is nothing in the well. How is it that many are around the well and no one goes into it?

75. Jesus said: There are many standing at the door, but only those who are alone are the ones who will enter into the Bridal Chamber.

Matthew 25:1-8 Then shall the kingdom of heaven be likened unto ten virgins, which took their lamps, and went forth to meet the bridegroom. And five of them were wise, and five were foolish. They that were foolish took their lamps, and took no oil with them: But the wise took oil in their vessels with their lamps. While the bridegroom tarried, they all slumbered and slept. And at midnight there was a cry made, Behold, the bridegroom cometh; go ye out to meet him. Then all those virgins arose, and trimmed their lamps. And the foolish said unto the wise, Give us of your oil; for our lamps are gone out.

76. Jesus said: The Kingdom of the Father is like a rich merchant who found a pearl. The merchant was prudent. He sold his fortune and bought the one pearl for himself. You also, seek for his treasure which does not fail, which endures where no moth can come near to eat it nor worm to devour it.

Matthew 13:45-46 Again, the kingdom of heaven is like a merchant in search of fine pearls; on finding one pearl of great value, he went and sold all that he had and bought it.

Matthew 6:19-20 Do not store up for yourselves treasures on earth, where moth and rust consume and where thieves break in and steal; but store up for yourselves treasures in heaven, where neither moth nor rust consumes and where thieves do not break in and steal.

77. Jesus said: I-Am the Light who is over all things, I-Am the All. From me all came forth and to me all return (The All came from me and the All has come to me). Split wood, there am I. Lift up the stone and there you will find me.

Note:
Many scholars believe the order of verses 30 and 77 were misplaced and these two verses should be connected as one verse.

30. Jesus said: Where there are three gods, they are gods (Where there are three gods they are without god). Where there is only one, I say that I am with him. Lift the stone and there you will find me, Split the wood and there am I.

John 8:12 Again Jesus spoke to them, saying, I am the light of the world. Whoever follows me will never walk in darkness but will have the light of life.

John 1:3 All things came into being through him, and without him not one thing came into being.

78. Jesus said: Why did you come out to the wilderness; to see a reed shaken by the wind? And to see a person dressed in fine (soft – plush) garments like your rulers and your dignitaries? They are clothed in plush garments, and they are not able to recognize (understand) the truth.

Matthew 11:7-9 As they went away, Jesus began to speak to the crowds about John: What did you go out into the wilderness to look at? A reed shaken by the wind? What then did you go out to see? Someone dressed in soft robes? Look, those who wear soft robes are in royal palaces. What then did you go out to see? A prophet? Yes, I tell you, and more than a prophet.

79. A woman from the multitude said to him: Blessed is the womb which bore you, and the breasts which nursed you! He said to her: Blessed are those who have heard the word (meaning) of the Father and have truly kept it. For there will be days when you will say: Blessed be the womb which has not conceived and the breasts which have not nursed.

Luke 11:27-28 While he was saying this, a woman in the crowd raised her voice and said to him, Blessed is the womb that bore you and the breasts that nursed you! But he said, Blessed rather are those who hear the word of God and obey it!

Luke 23:29 For the days are surely coming when they will say, Blessed are the barren, and the wombs that never bore, and the breasts that never nursed.

80. Jesus said: Whoever has come to understand (recognize) the world (world system) has found the body (corpse), and whoever has found the body (corpse), of him the world (world system) is not worthy.

Hebrews 11:37-40 They were stoned, they were sawn asunder, were tempted, were slain with the sword: they wandered about in sheepskins and goatskins; being destitute, afflicted, tormented; (Of whom the world was not worthy:) they wandered in deserts, and in mountains, and in dens and caves of the earth. And these all, having obtained a good report through faith, received not the promise: God having provided some better thing for us, that they without us should not be made perfect.

81. Jesus said: Whoever has become rich should reign, and let whoever has power renounce it.

82. Jesus said: Whoever is close to me is close to the fire, and whoever is far from me is far from the Kingdom.
John 14:6-9 Jesus saith unto him, I am the way, the truth, and the life: no man cometh unto the Father, but by me. If ye had known me, ye should have known my Father also: and from henceforth ye know him, and have seen him. Philip saith unto him, Lord, show us the Father, and it sufficeth us. Jesus saith unto him, Have I been so long time with you, and yet hast thou not known me, Philip? he that hath seen me hath seen the Father;

83. Jesus said: Images are visible to man but the light which is within them is hidden. The light of the father will be revealed, but he (his image) is hidden in the light.

84. Jesus said: When you see your reflection, you rejoice. Yet when you perceive your images which have come into being before you, which neither die nor can be seen, how much will you have to bear?

85. Jesus said: Adam came into existence from a great power and a great wealth, and yet he was not worthy of you. For if he had been worthy, he would not have tasted death.

86. Jesus said: The foxes have their dens and the birds have their nests, yet the Son of Man has no place to lay his head for rest.
Matthew 8:20 And Jesus said to him, Foxes have holes, and birds of the air have nests; but the Son of Man has nowhere to lay his head.

87. Jesus said: Wretched is the body which depends upon another body, and wretched is the soul which depends on these two (upon their being together).

88. Jesus said: The angels and the prophets will come to you, and what they will give you belongs to you. And you will give them what you have, and say among yourselves: When will they come to take (receive) what belongs to them?

89. Jesus said: Why do you wash the outside of your cup? Do you not understand (mind) that He who creates the inside is also He who creates the outside?

Luke 11:39-40 Then the Lord said to him, Now you Pharisees clean the outside of the cup and of the dish, but inside you are full of greed and wickedness. You fools! Did not the one who made the outside make the inside also?

90. Jesus said: Come unto me, for my yoke is comfortable (natural) and my lordship is gentle — and you will find rest for yourselves.

Matthew 11:28-30 Come to me, all you that are weary and are carrying heavy burdens, and I will give you rest. Take my yoke upon you, and learn from me; for I am gentle and humble in heart, and you will find rest for your souls. For my yoke is easy, and my burden is light.

Acts 15:5-17 But there rose up certain of the sect of the Pharisees which believed, saying, That it was needful to circumcise them, and to command them to keep the law of Moses. And the apostles and elders came together for to consider of this matter. And when there had been much disputing, Peter rose up, and said unto them, Men and brethren, ye know how that a good while ago God made choice among us, that the Gentiles by my mouth should hear the word of the gospel, and believe. And God, which knoweth the hearts, bare them witness, giving them the Holy Ghost, even as he did unto us; And put no difference between us and them, purifying their hearts by faith. Now therefore why tempt ye God, to put a yoke upon the neck of the disciples, which neither our fathers nor we were able to bear? But we believe that through the grace of the LORD Jesus Christ we shall be saved, even as they. Then all the multitude kept silence, and gave audience to Barnabas and Paul, declaring what miracles and wonders God had wrought among the Gentiles by them. And after they had held their peace, James answered, saying, Men and brethren, hearken unto me: Simeon hath declared how God at the first did visit the Gentiles, to take out of them a people for his name. And to this agree the words of the prophets; as it is written, After this I will return, and will build again the tabernacle of David, which is fallen down; and I will build again the ruins thereof, and I will set it up: That the residue of men might seek after the Lord, and all the Gentiles, upon whom my name is called, saith the Lord, who doeth all these things.

91. They said to him: Tell us who you are, so that we may believe in you. He said to them: You examine the face of the sky and of the earth, yet you do not recognize Him who is here with you, and you do not know how to seek in (to inquire of Him at) this moment (you do not know how to take advantage of this opportunity).

John 9:36 He answered, And who is he, sir? Tell me, so that I may believe in him.
Luke 12:54-56 He also said to the crowds, When you see a cloud rising in the west, you immediately say, It is going to rain; and so it happens. And when you see the south wind blowing, you say, There will be scorching heat; and it happens. You hypocrites! You know how to interpret the appearance of earth and sky, but why do you not know how to interpret the present time?

92. Jesus said: Seek and you will find. But in the past I did not answer the questions you asked. Now I wish to tell them to you, but you do not ask about (no longer seek) them.

Matthew 7:7 Ask, and it will be given you; search, and you will find; knock, and the door will be opened for you.

93. Jesus said: Do not give what is sacred to the dogs, lest they throw it on the dung heap. Do not cast the pearls to the swine, lest they cause it to become dung (mud).

Matthew 7:6 Do not give what is holy to dogs; and do not throw your pearls before swine, or they will trample them under foot and turn and maul you.

94. Jesus said: Whoever seeks will find. And whoever knocks, it will be opened to him.
Matthew 7:8 For everyone who asks receives, and everyone who searches finds, and for everyone who knocks, the door will be opened.

95. Jesus said: If you have money, do not lend at interest, but rather give it to those from whom you will not be repaid.
Luke 6:34-35 If you lend to those from whom you hope to receive, what credit is that to you? Even sinners lend to sinners, to receive as much again. But love your enemies, do good, and lend, expecting nothing in return. Your reward will be great, and you will be children of the Most High; for he is kind to the ungrateful and the wicked.

96. Jesus said: The Kingdom of the Father is like a woman who has taken a little yeast and hidden it in dough. She produced large loaves of it. Whoever has ears, let him hear!

Matthew 13:33 He told them another parable: The kingdom of heaven is like yeast that a woman took and mixed in with three measures of flour until all of it was leavened.

97. Jesus said: The Kingdom of the Father is like a woman who was carrying a jar full of grain. While she was walking on a road far from home, the handle of the jar broke and the grain poured out behind her onto the road. She did not know it. She had noticed no problem. When she arrived in her house, she set the jar down and found it empty.

98. Jesus said: The Kingdom of the Father is like someone who wished to slay a prominent person. While still in his own house he drew his sword and thrust it into the wall in order to test whether his hand would be strong enough. Then he slew the prominent person.

99. His Disciples said to him: Your brethren and your mother are standing outside. He said to them: Those here who do my Father's desires are my Brethren and my Mother. It is they who will enter the Kingdom of my Father.

Matthew 12:46-50 While he was still speaking to the crowds, his mother and his brothers were standing outside, wanting to speak to him. Someone told him, Look, your mother and your brothers are standing outside, wanting to speak to you. But to the one who had told him this, Jesus replied, Who is my mother, and who are my brothers? And pointing to his disciples, he said, Here are my mother and my brothers! For whoever does the will of my Father in heaven is my brother and sister and mother.

100. They showed Jesus a gold coin, and said to him: The agents of Caesar extort taxes from us. He said to them: Give the things of Caesar to Caesar, give the things of God to God, and give to me what is mine.

Mark 12:14-17 Is it lawful to pay taxes to the emperor, or not? Should we pay them, or should we not? But knowing their hypocrisy, he said to them, Why are you putting me to the test? Bring me a denarius and let me see it. And they brought one. Then he said to them, Whose head is this, and whose title? They answered, The emperor's. Jesus said to them,

Give to the emperor the things that are the emperor's, and to God the
things that are God's. And they were utterly amazed at him.

**101. Jesus said: Whoever does not hate his father and his
mother, as I do, will not be able to become my Disciple. And
whoever does not love his father and his mother, as I do, will
not be able to become my disciple. For my mother bore me, yet
my true Mother gave me the life.**
*Matthew 10:37 Whoever loves father or mother more than me is not
worthy of me; and whoever loves son or daughter more than me is not
worthy of me.*

**102. Jesus said: Damn these Pharisees. They are like a dog
sleeping in the feed trough of oxen. For neither does he eat, nor
does he allow the oxen to eat.**

*Matthew 2:13 But woe unto you, scribes and Pharisees, hypocrites!
because you shut the kingdom of heaven against men; for you neither
enter yourselves, nor allow those who would enter to go in.*

**103. Jesus said: Blessed (happy) is the person who knows at
what place of the house the bandits may break in, so that he can
rise and collect his things and prepare himself before they enter.**
*Matthew 24:43 But understand this: if the owner of the house had known
in what part of the night the thief was coming, he would have stayed
awake and would not have let his house be broken into.*

**104. They said to him: Come, let us pray today and let us fast.
Jesus said: What sin have I committed? How have I been
overcome (undone)? When the Bridegroom comes forth from the
bridal chamber, then let them fast and let them pray.**

105. Jesus said: Whoever acknowledges (comes to know) father and mother, will be called the son of a whore.

106. Jesus said: When you make the two one, you will become Sons of Man (children of Adam), and when you say to the mountain: Move! It will move.

Mark 11:23 Truly I tell you, if you say to this mountain, Be taken up and thrown into the sea, and if you do not doubt in your heart, but believe that what you say will come to pass, it will be done for you.

107. Jesus said: The Kingdom is like a shepherd who has a hundred sheep. The largest one of them went astray. He left the ninety-nine and sought for the one until he found it. Having searched until he was weary, he said to that sheep: I desire you more than the ninety-nine.

Matthew 18:12-13 What do you think? If a shepherd has a hundred sheep, and one of them has gone astray, does he not leave the ninety-nine on the mountains and go in search of the one that went astray? And if he finds it, truly I tell you, he rejoices over it more than over the ninety-nine that never went astray.

108. Jesus said: Whoever drinks from my mouth will become like me. I will become him, and the secrets will be revealed to him. (The mouth is the gateway to the soul.)

109. Jesus said: The Kingdom is like a person who had a treasure hidden in his field and knew nothing of it. After he died, he bequeathed it to his son. The son accepted the field knowing nothing of the treasure. He sold it. Then the person who bought it came and plowed it. He found the treasure. He began to lend money at interest to whomever he wished.

Matthew 13:44 The kingdom of heaven is like treasure hidden in a field, which someone found and hid; then in his joy he goes and sells all that he has and buys that field.

110. Jesus said: Whoever has found the world (system) and becomes wealthy (enriched by it), let him renounce the world (system).

Mark 10:21-23 Then Jesus beholding him loved him, and said unto him, One thing thou lackest: go thy way, sell whatsoever thou hast, and give to the poor, and thou shalt have treasure in heaven: and come, take up the cross, and follow me. And he was sad at that saying, and went away grieved: for he had great possessions. And Jesus looked round about, and saith unto his disciples, How hardly shall they that have riches enter into the kingdom of God!

111. Jesus said: Heaven and earth will roll up (collapse and disappear) before you, but he who lives within the Living-One will neither see nor fear death. For, Jesus said: Whoever finds himself, of him the world is not worthy.

112. Jesus said: Damned is the flesh which depends upon the soul. Damned is the soul which depends upon the flesh.

113. His Disciples said to him: When will the Kingdom come? Jesus said: It will not come by expectation (because you watch or wait for it). They will not say: Look here! or: Look there! But the Kingdom of the Father is spread upon the earth, and people do not realize it.

Luke 17:20 And when he was demanded of by the Pharisees, when the kingdom of God should come, he answered them and said, The kingdom of God cometh not with observation: Neither shall they say, Lo-Here! Lo-There! For, behold, the kingdom of God is within you.

(Saying 114 was written later and was added to the original text.)

114. Simon Peter said to them: Send Mary away from us, for women are not worthy of this life. Jesus said: See, I will draw her into me so that I make her male, in order that she herself will become a living spirit like you males. For every female who becomes male will enter the Kingdom of the Heavens.

Epilog

Having read the words of Thomas, what can we now say? Are these the words of Jesus? Is this a true catalog of the sayings, insights, and wisdom of the living Christ? Is Thomas simply conveying to us his memories of what he heard from Jesus when he walked the earth and taught the people? If these sayings are true they force us to reexamine modern, orthodox Christianity.

In the words of Jesus we find a plea, a command, to reach inside and reveal our true self. In discovering and knowing ourselves on the deepest level we will understand the kingdom of Heaven is within us – it has always been. We will know ourselves for what we are; the sons and daughters of the living God.

Jesus warns against organized religion. He steers us away from priests who steal the keys of the kingdom, keeping the truth from the people. Heaven is not above us, nor below us, nor in the hands of others, and not in any institution. God is in you and around you and there heaven must be also.

It is no wonder that the Gospel of Thomas was suppressed by the early church. As the church struggled to consolidate its authority and power, the enemy would have been individual, spiritual advancement independent of ritual and rule. Yet, that is the essence of what the Protestant church calls salvation, if all other rituals and man-made rules were abandoned. It is the awakening caused by a personal encounter with truth itself – God, and when you are awake, fully awake, you can never fall asleep to the truth again. But the church has fallen asleep again and again, from reformation to reformation. Always, the body politic of the church struggles to suppress or even kill those rebels that have in some way awakened to the truth.

If you have ever felt as if there was more to existence than you could see, that there was another world just behind the curtain of your mind, that just out of reach was the full truth, Jesus' words will echo within you and lead you into light.

What is the essential wisdom within The Gospel of Thomas? Simply this; the search for self is the most difficult and troubling journey anyone could ever attempt, but it is also the only path with lasting spiritual results. If you can find what is real and honest within you, and if you have the courage to bring it forth, you will gain peace and strength and freedom forever. To deny your selfishness is to refuse to overcome it. To deny your blindness is to be held hostage by it. To ignore the longing in your heart for God is to die without knowing Him. Worst of all, to refuse to bring forth the true and holy part of you is to be destroyed by it as it sours and turns rancid within you, unborn and unseen. In this state we are neither true to God nor ourselves. We are lost and destined to suffer.

If we understand the Gospel we understand the clear and elegant truth. God is in us and outside of us, impossible to miss, undeniable to those who seek, and irresistible in His grace. He is the forgiving and loving father who awaits our return. A child knows the way and old men may realize they have lost the way, but the masses become so involved in the "world system" the way to God is forgotten or ignored.

"What must we do to be saved?" has been the same question posed for thousands of years. Jesus' answer in The Gospel of Thomas is shockingly simple. "Become passers by" and " bring forth what is within you".   What does this mean? Become detached. Don't allow the world to posses you, but instead view it as though you are watching from a distance. Separate yourself from feelings based in a world that is temporary and meaningless. Instead, focus on what is real within you. Find that part of you that is part of Him. Keep it, let it gestate, and give birth to it in your words, deeds, and thoughts. Reject all else.

How will you know it is done? What is the sign of your father in you? It is peace in the midst of motion. It is movement and rest. Whether the motion is external chaos or it is the emotions of anger or fear, there is peace and rest in your spirit. As Jesus commanded the storm, "peace, be still", He also commands us when he says, "Peace, peace I give to you. My peace I give to you, not as the world gives it, but as I alone can give it". But first, we must understand and obey.

Whoever finds the interpretation of these sayings will not taste death.

Let he who seeks not stop seeking until he finds, and when he finds he will be troubled, and when he has been troubled he will marvel (be astonished) and he will reign over all and in reigning, he will find rest.

If those who lead you say to you: Look, the Kingdom is in the sky, then the birds of the sky would enter before you. If they say to you: It is in the sea, then the fish of the sea would enter ahead of you. But the Kingdom of God exists within you and it exists outside of you. Those who come to know (recognize) themselves will find it, and when you come to know yourselves you will become known and you will realize that you are the children of the Living Father. Yet if you do not come to know

yourselves then you will dwell in poverty and it will be you who are that poverty.

Recognize what is in front of your face, and what has been hidden from you will be revealed to you. For there is nothing hidden which will not be revealed (become manifest), and nothing buried that will not be raised.

I will give to you what eye has not seen, what ear has not heard, what hand has not touched, and what has not occurred to the mind of man.

Unless you fast from the world (system), you will not find the Kingdom of God.

I stood in the midst of the world. In the flesh I appeared to them. I found them all drunk; I found none thirsty among them. My soul grieved for the sons of men, for they are blind in their hearts and do not see that they came into the world empty and they are destined (determined) to leave the world empty. However, now they are drunk. When they have shaken off their wine, then they will repent (change their ways).

Many times have you yearned to hear these sayings which I speak to you, and you have no one else from whom to hear them. There will be days when you will seek me but you will not find me.

Become passers-by.

Blessed is the solitary and chosen, for you will find the Kingdom. You have come from it, and unto it you will return.
If they said to you: From where do you come? Say to them: We have come from the Light, the place where the Light came into existence of its own accord and he stood and appeared in their

image. If they say to you: Is it you? (Who are you?), say: We are his Sons and we are the chosen of the Living Father. If they ask you: What is the sign of your Father in you? Say to them: It is movement with rest.

Those who know everything but themselves, lack everything. (whoever knows the all and still feels a personal lacking, he is completely deficient).

If you bring forth what is within you, it will save you. If you do not have it within you to bring forth, that which you lack will destroy you.

"I-Am" the Light who is over all things, "I-Am" the All. From me all came forth and to me all return (The All came from me and the All has come to me). Split wood, there am I. Lift up the stone and there you will find me.

Whoever is close to me is close to the fire, and whoever is far from me is far from the Kingdom.

Whoever drinks from my mouth will become like me. I will become him, and the secrets will be revealed to him.

Heaven and earth will roll up before you, but he who lives within the Living-One will neither see nor fear death. Whoever finds himself, of him the world is not worthy.
(The mouth of the master feeds the soul. It is the gateway to the soul, thus his word is a soul-to-soul communication.)

Introduction to The Gospel Of Barnabas

The New Testament identifies a 1st Century Jew named Joseph, a Levitical priest from the Mediterranean island of Cyprus, a follower of Jesus. His nicknamed was Barnabas or "son of encouragement". It is this same Barnabas who is held up as the author of the Gospel of Barnabas. The church in Jerusalem sent Barnabas to Antioch to investigate the stories of Gentiles becoming Christians, and later the Holy Spirit would send Barnabas and the apostle Paul out from Antioch on a missionary journey. (Acts, chapters 4 through 13 verify these facts.)

The Gospel of Barnabas is a book depicting the life of Jesus, supposedly written by a man claiming to be Jesus' disciple called Barnabas. Two manuscripts are known to have existed, both dated to the late 16th or early 17th century and written respectively in Italian and in Spanish. The Spanish manuscript is now lost. The text now only exists in a partial 18th-century transcript. The Gospel of Barnabas in the Italian manuscript has 222 chapters, which makes it longer than the four biblical gospels put together. The majority of the book is devoted to an account of Jesus' ministry. Much of it harmonized well with gospel accounts but there is divergence, which is similar to the Islamic interpretation of Christian origins and contradicts the New Testament teachings. The Gospel of Barnabas was relatively unknown until recently when Muslims began publishing the text claiming it was the oldest or most authentic gospel. It is neither.

The first mention of a text called the Gospel of Barnabas occurs around the 6th or 7th century, coinciding with the beginning time of Islam. The first actual manuscript was seen around 1700.

Prince Eugene's Italian manuscript had been presented to him in

1713 by John Frederick Cramer and was later transferred to the Austrian National Library in Vienna in 1738. Attempts to find the origins on the manuscript was a dead end and researchers reported no success in tracking and identifying previous owners, or in finding a corresponding manuscript listed in any Amsterdam catalogue or inventory. Linguistic forms trace back to only the 1500's and actually shows sentence and wording forms similar to Dante'. Later a Spanish manuscript was reported, which was different. The Spanish version was lost but later re-discovered in Sydney Australia.

Aside from the missing 80 chapters, there are differences in the chapter divisions between the Italian and Spanish texts; and also between the Sydney transcript and the Spanish passages quoted by Dr. White in English. The Italian and Spanish chapters agree for the prologue and up to chapter 116. Chapter 117 in the Italian version is split into Chapters 117 and 118 in the Spanish; and then Chapters 118 and 119 in the Italian correspond with 119 in the Spanish.

Some of the later versions of The Gospel of Barnabas seem to have been influenced by Islam. The development of Islam was heavily influenced by the Ebionite Christian sect and it appears Barnabas follows that same Ebionite doctrine. The text of this Gospel is considered by the majority of academics, including Christians and some Muslims, to be late and pseudepigraphical. However, some academics suggest that it may contain some remnants of an earlier, apocryphal work, which was perhaps Gnostic, Ebionite or Diatessaronic. The text was then further redacted to bring it more in line with Islamic doctrine.

The Gospel of Barnabas is anti-Pauline and anti-Trinitarian. Jesus is described as a prophet and not the son of God. Paul is called "the deceived". The Gospel of Barnabas states that Jesus escaped crucifixion by being raised alive to heaven while Judas Iscariot the traitor was crucified in his place. The belief that Jesus is a prophet of God and was raised alive without being crucified conforms to Islamic teachings in which Jesus is a major prophet and he did not die on the cross but was taken alive by angels to God (Allah).

Other passages conflict with the teachings of the Koran. In the account of the Nativity, Mary is said to have given birth to Jesus without pain. In Jesus' ministry he permits the drinking of wine and enjoins monogamy. In the Gospel of Barnabas hell is only be for those who commit the seven deadly sins (Barnabas: 4-44/135). Anyone who refuses to be circumcised will not enter paradise (Barnabas 17/23). There is an interesting statement that God has a soul (Barnabas 6/82). The Gospel indicates the existence of 9 heavens (Barnabas 3/105).

The Gospel of Barnabas may be an attempted synthesis of elements from both Christianity and Islam. If that is the case it would make sense of this confusing book.

The Gospel of Barnabas

This Translation of the Gospel of Barnabas is based on the Lonsdale and Laura Ragg translation, London, 1907.

Opening-
True Gospel of Jesus, called Christ, a new prophet sent by God to the world: according to the description of Barnabas his apostle.

Barnabas, apostle of Jesus the Nazarene, called Christ, to all them that dwell upon the earth who desire peace and consolation. Dearly beloved the great and wonderful God has during these past days visited us by his prophet Jesus Christ in great mercy of teaching and miracles, by reason whereof many, being deceived of Satan, under presence of piety, are preaching most impious doctrine, calling Jesus son of God, repudiating the circumcision ordained of God for ever, and permitting every unclean meat: among whom also Paul has been deceived, whereof I speak not without grief, for which cause I am writing that truth which I have seen and heard, in the intercourse that I have had with Jesus, in order that you may be saved, and not be deceived of Satan and perish in the judgment of God. Therefore beware of every one that preaches unto you new doctrine contrary to that which I write, that you may be saved eternally. The great God be with you and guard you from Satan and from every evil. Amen.

Chapter 1 The angel Gabriel visits Virgin Mary concerning the birth of Jesus.

In these last years a virgin called Mary, of the lineage of David, of the tribe of Judah, was visited by the angel Gabriel from God. This virgin, living in all holiness without any offense, being blameless, and abiding in prayer with fastings, being one day alone, there entered into her chamber the angel Gabriel, and he saluted her, saying: 'God be with thee, O Mary'.

The virgin was affrighted at the appearance of the angel, but the angel comforted her, saying: 'Fear not, Mary, for you have found favor with God, who has chosen thee to be mother of a prophet, whom he will send to the people of Israel in order that they may walk in his laws with truth of heart.'

The virgin answered: 'Now how shall I bring forth sons, seeing I know not a man?' The angel answered: 'O Mary, God who made man without a man is able to generate in thee man with- out a man, because with him nothing is impossible.'

Mary answered: 'I know that God is almighty, therefore his will be done.' The angel answered: 'Now be conceived in thee the prophet, whom you shall name Jesus: and you shall keep him from wine and from strong drink and from every unclean meat, because the child is an holy one of God.' Mary bowed herself with humility, saying:

'Behold the handmaid of God, be it done according to your word.' The angel departed, and the virgin glorified God, saying: 'Know, O my soul, the greatness of God, and exult, my spirit, in God my Savior, for he has regarded the lowliness of his handmaiden, insomuch that I shall be called blessed by all the nations, for he that is mighty has made me great, and blessed be his holy name. For his mercy extends from generation to generation of them that fear him. Mighty has he made his hand, and he has scattered the proud in the imagination of his heart. He has put down the mighty from their seat, and has exalted the humble. Him who has been hungry has he filled with good things, and the rich he has sent empty away. For he keeps in memory the promises made to Abraham and to his son for ever'.

Chapter 2   The warning of the angel Gabriel given to Joseph concerning the conception of the Virgin Mary.

Mary having known the will of God, fearing the people, lest they should take offense at her being great with child, and should stone her as guilty of fornication, chose a companion of her own lineage, a man by name called Joseph, of blameless life: for he as a righteous man feared God and served him with fastings and prayers, living by the works of his hands, for he was a carpenter.

Such a man the virgin knowing, chose him for her companion and revealed to him the divine counsel.

Joseph being a righteous man, when he perceived that Mary was great with child, was minded to put her away because he feared God. Behold, whilst he slept, he was rebuked by the angel of God, saying 'O Joseph, why art you minded to put away Mary your wife? Know that whatsoever has been wrought in her has all been done by the will of God. The virgin shall bring forth a son, whom you shall call by the name Jesus, whom you shall keep from wine and strong drink and from every unclean meat, because he is an holy one of God from his mother's womb. He is a prophet of God sent unto the people of Israel, in order that he may convert Judah to his heart, and that Israel may walk in the law of the Lord, as it is written in the law of Moses. He shall come with great power, which God shall give him, and shall work great miracles, whereby many shall be saved'. Joseph, arising from sleep, gave thanks to God, and abode with Mary all his life, serving God with all sincerity.

Chapter 3 Wonderful birth of Jesus, and appearance of angels praising God.

There reigned at that time in Judaea Herod, by decree of Caesar Augustus, and Pilate was governor in the priesthood of Annas and Caiaphas. Wherefore, by decree of Augustus, all the world was enrolled, wherefore each one went to his own country, and they presented themselves by their own tribes to be enrolled. Joseph accordingly departed from Nazareth, a city of Galilee, with Mary his wife, great with child, to go to Bethlehem (for that it was his city, he being of the lineage of David), in order that he might be enrolled according to the decree of Caesar. Joseph having arrived at Bethlehem, for that the city was small, and great the multitude of them that were strangers there, he found no place, wherefore he took lodging outside the city in a lodging made for a shepherds' shelter. While Joseph abode there the days were fulfilled for Mary to bring forth.

The virgin was surrounded by a light exceeding bright, and

brought forth her son without pain, whom she took in her arms, and wrapping him in swaddling-clothes, laid him in the manger, because there was no room in the inn. There came with gladness a great multitude of angels to the inn, blessing God and announcing peace to them that fear God. Mary and Joseph praised the Lord for the birth of Jesus, and with greatest joy nurtured him.

Chapter 4 Angels announced to the shepherds the birth of Jesus, and they, after having found him, announce him.

At that time the shepherds were watching over their flock, as is their custom. And, behold, they were surrounded by an exceeding bright light, out of which appeared to them an angel, who blessed God. The shepherds were filled with fear by reason of the sudden light and the appearance of the angel, whereupon the angel of the Lord comforted them, saying:

'Behold, I announce to you a great joy, for there is born in the city of David a child who is a prophet of the Lord, who brings great salvation to the house of Israel. The child you shall find in the manger, with his mother, who blesseth God.'

And when he had said this there came a great multitude of angels blessing God, announcing peace to them that have good will. When the angels were departed, the shepherds spoke among themselves, saying: 'Let us go even unto Bethlehem, and see the word which God by his angel has announced to us.' There came many shepherds to Bethlehem seeking the new-born babe. and they found outside the city the child that was born. according to the word of the angel. lying in the manger.

They therefore made obeisance to him, and gave to the mother that which they had, announcing to her what they had heard and seen. Mary therefore kept all these things in her heart, and Joseph [likewise], giving thanks to God. The shepherds returned to their flock, announcing to everyone how great a thing they had seen. And so the whole hill-country of Judaea was filled with fear, and every man laid up this word in his heart, saying: 'What, think we, shall this child be?'

Chapter 5   Circumcision of Jesus

When the eight days were fulfilled according to the law of the Lord, as it is written in the book of Moses, they took the child and carried him to the temple to circumcise him. And so they circumcised the child, and gave him the name Jesus, as the angel of the Lord had said before he was conceived in the womb. Mary and Joseph perceived that the child must needs be for the salvation and ruin of many. Wherefore they feared God, and kept the child with fear of God.

Chapter 6   Three Magi are led by a star in the east to Judaea, and, finding Jesus, make obeisance to him and gifts.

In the reign of Herod, king of Judaea, when Jesus was born, three magi in the parts of the east were observing the stars of heaven. Whereupon appeared to them a star of great brightness, wherefore having concluded among themselves, they came to Judaea, guided by the star, which went before them, and having arrived at Jerusalem they asked where was born the King of the Jews. And when Herod heard this he was affrighted, and all the city was troubled. Herod therefore called together the priests and the scribes, saying: 'Where should Christ be born?' They answered that he should be born in Bethlehem, for thus it is written by the prophet:

'And you, Bethlehem, art not little among the princes of Judah: for out of thee shall come forth a leader, who shall lead my people Israel.'

Herod accordingly called together the magi and asked them concerning their coming: who answered that they had seen a star in the east, which had guided them thither, wherefore they wished with gifts to worship this new King manifested by his star. Then said Herod: 'Go to Bethlehem and search out with all diligence concerning the child, and when you have found him, come and tell it to me, because I also would fain come and worship him.' And this he spoke deceitfully.

Chapter 7 The visitation of Jesus by magi, and their return to their own country, with the warning of Jesus given to them in a

dream.

The magi therefore departed out of Jerusalem, and lo, the star which appeared to them in the east went before them. Seeing the star the magi were filled with gladness. And so having come to Bethlehem, outside the city, they saw the star standing still above the inn where Jesus was born. The magi therefore went thither, and entering the dwelling found the child with his mother, and bending down they did obeisance to him. And the magi presented unto him spices, with silver and gold, recounting to the virgin all that they had seen. Whereupon, while sleeping, they were warned by the child not to go to Herod: so departing by another way they returned to their own home, announcing all that they had seen in Judaea.

Chapter 8   Jesus is carried in flight to Egypt, and Herod massacres the innocent children.

Herod seeing that the magi did not return, believed himself mocked of them, whereupon he determined to put to death the child that was born. But behold while Joseph was sleeping there appeared to him the angel of the Lord, saying: 'Arise up quickly, and take the child with his mother and go into Egypt for Herod wills to slay him'. Joseph arose with great fear, and took Mary with the child, and they went into Egypt, and there they abode until the death of Herod: who, believing himself derided of the magi, sent his soldiers to slay all the new-born children in Bethlehem. The soldiers therefore came and slew all the children that were there, as Herod had commanded them. Whereby were fulfilled the words of the prophet, saying: 'Lamentation and great weeping are there in Ramah; Rachel laments for her sons, but consolation is not given her because they are not.'

Chapter 9 Jesus, having returned to Judaea, holds a wondrous disputation with doctors, having come to the age of twelve years.

When Herod was dead, behold the angel of the Lord appeared in a dream to Joseph, saying: 'Return into Judaea, for they are dead that willed the death of the child.' Joseph therefore took the child with Mary (he having come to the age of seven years), and came to Judaea, whence, hearing that Archelaus, son of Herod, was reigning in Judaea, he went into Galilee, fearing to remain in Judaea, and they went to dwell at Nazareth. The child grew in grace and

wisdom before God and before men.

Jesus, having come to the age of twelve years, went up with Mary and Joseph to Jerusalem, to worship there according to the law of the Lord written in the book of Moses. When their prayers were ended they departed, having lost Jesus, because they thought that he was returned home with their kinsfolk. Mary therefore returned with Joseph to Jerusalem, seeking Jesus among kinsfolk and neighbors. The third day they found the child in the temple, in the midst of the doctors, disputing with them concerning the law. And every one was amazed at his questions and answers, saying: "How can there be such doctrine in him, seeing he is so small and has not learned to read?'

Mary reproved him, saying: 'Son, what have you done to us? Behold I and your father have sought thee for three days sorrowing.' Jesus answered: 'Know you not that the service of God ought to come before father and mother?' Jesus then went down with his mother and Joseph to Nazareth, and was subject to them with humility and reverence.

Chapter 10

Jesus having come to the age of thirty years, as he himself said unto me, went up to

Mount Olives with his mother to gather olives. Then at midday as he was praying, when he came to these words: 'Lord, with mercy . . ,' he was surrounded by an exceeding bright light and by an infinite multitude of angels, who were saying: 'Blessed be God.' The angel Gabriel presented to him as it were a shining mirror, a book, which descended into the heart of Jesus, in which he had knowledge of what God has done and what He has said and what God wills insomuch that everything was laid bare and open to him, as he said unto me: 'Believe, Barnabas, that I know every prophet with every prophecy, insomuch that whatever I say the whole bath come forth from that book.'

Jesus, having received this vision, and knowing that he was a prophet sent to the house of Israel, revealed all to Mary his mother, telling her that he needs must suffer great persecution for the honor of God, and that he could not any longer abide with her to serve her. Whereupon, having heard this, Mary answered: 'Son. ere you west born all was announced to me, wherefore blessed be the holy name of God. Jesus departed therefore that day from his mother to attend to his prophetic office.

Chapter 11 Jesus Miraculously heals a leper, and goes into Jerusalem.

Jesus descending from the mountain to come into Jerusalem, met a leper, who by divine inspiration knew Jesus to be a prophet. Therefore with tears he prayed him, saying, 'Jesus, you son of David, have mercy on me.' Jesus answered: 'What wilt you, brother, that I should do unto thee?'

The leper answered: 'Lord, give me health.'

Jesus reproved him, saying: 'You art foolish, pray to God who created thee, and he will give thee health, for I am a man, as you art.'

The leper answered: 'I know that you, Lord, art a man, but an holy one of the Lord. Wherefore pray you to God, and he will give me health.'

Then Jesus, sighing, said: 'Lord God Almighty, for the love of your holy prophets give health to this sick man.' Then, having said this, he said, touching the sick man with his hands in the name of God: 'O brother, receive your health!' And when he had said this the leprosy was cleansed, insomuch that the flesh of the leper was left unto him like that of a child. Seeing which namely, that he was healed, the leper with a loud voice cried out: 'Come hither, Israel, to receive the prophet whom God sends unto thee'. Jesus prayed him, saying: 'Brother, hold your peace and say nothing,' but the more he prayed him the more he cried out, saying: 'Behold the prophet! behold the holy one of God!' At which words many that were going out of Jerusalem ran back, and entered with Jesus into Jerusalem, recounting that which God through Jesus had done unto the leper.

Chapter 12 First sermon of Jesus delivered to the people: wonderful in doctrine concerning the name of God.

The whole city of Jerusalem was moved by these words, wherefore they all ran together to the temple to see Jesus, who had entered therein to pray, so that they could scarce be contained there. Therefore the priests besought Jesus, saying: 'This people desires to see thee and hear thee, therefore ascend to the pinnacle, and if God give thee a word speak it in the name of the Lord.' Then ascended Jesus to the place whence the scribes were wont to speak. And having beckoned with the hand for silence, he opened his mouth, saying: 'Blessed be the holy name of God, who of his goodness and mercy willed to create his creatures that they might glorify him. Blessed be the holy name of God, who created the splendor of all the saints and prophets before all things to send him for the salvation of the world, as he spoke by his servant David, saying: "Before Lucifer in the brightness of the saints I created thee." Blessed be the holy name of God, who created the angels that they might serve him. And blessed be God, who punished and reprobated Satan and his followers, who would not reverence him whom God wills to be reverenced. Blessed be the holy name of God, who created man out of the clay of the earth, and set him over his works. Blessed be the holy name of God, who drove man out of paradise for having transgressed his holy precept. Blessed be the holy name of God, who with mercy looked upon the tears of Adam and Eve, first parents of the human race. Blessed be the holy name of God who just punished Cain the fratricide, sent the deluge upon the earth. burned up three wicked cities, scourged Egypt, overwhelmed Pharaoh in the Red Sea, scattered the enemies of his people, chastised the unbelievers and punished the impenitent. Blessed be the holy name of God, who with mercy looked upon his creatures, and therefore sent them his holy prophets, that they might walk in truth and righteousness before him, who delivered his servants from every evil, and gave them this land, as he promised to our father Abraham and to his son for ever. Then by his servant Moses he gave us his holy law, that Satan should not deceive us: and he exalted us above all other peoples.

'But, brethren, what do we to-day, that we be not punished for our sins?'

And then Jesus with greatest vehemence rebuked the people for that they had forgotten the word of God, and gave themselves only to vanity, he rebuked the priests for their negligence in God's service and for their worldly greed; he rebuked the scribes because they preached vain doctrine, and forsook the law of God; he rebuked the doctors because they made the law of God of none effect through their traditions. And in such wise did Jesus speak to the people, that all wept, from the least to the greatest, crying mercy, and beseeching Jesus that he would pray of them, save only their priests and leaders, who on that day conceived hatred against Jesus for having thus spoken against the priests, scribes, and doctors. And they meditated upon his death, but for fear of the people, who had received him as a prophet of God, they spoke no word.

Jesus raised his hands to the Lord God and prayed, and the people weeping said: 'So be it, O Lord, so be it.' The prayer being ended, Jesus descended from the temple, and that day he departed from Jerusalem, with many that followed him. And the priests spoke evil of Jesus among themselves.

Chapter 13   The remarkable fear of Jesus and his prayer, and the wonderful comfort of the angel Gabriel.

Some days having passed, Jesus having in spirit perceived the desire of the priests, ascended the Mount of Olives to pray. And having passed the whole night in prayer, in the morning Jesus praying said: 'O Lord, I know that the scribes hate me, and the priests are minded to kill me, your servant; therefore, Lord God almighty and merciful, in mercy hear the prayers of the servant, and save me from their snares, for you art my salvation. You know, Lord, that I your servant seek thee alone, O Lord, and speak your word, for your word is truth, which endures for ever.'

When Jesus had spoken these words, behold there came to him the angel Gabriel, saying: 'Fear not, O Jesus, for a thousand thousand who dwell above the heaven guard your garments, and you shall not die till everything be fulfilled, and the world shall be near its end.'

Jesus fell with his face to the ground, saying: 'O great Lord God, how great is your mercy upon me, and what shall I give thee, Lord, for all that you have granted me?' The angel Gabriel answered: 'Arise, Jesus, and remember

Abraham, who being willing to make sacrifice to God of his only-begotten son Ishmael, to fulfill the word of God, and the knife not being able to cut his son, at my word offered in sacrifice a sheep. Even so therefore shall you do, O Jesus, servant of God.

Jesus answered: 'Willingly, but where shall I find the lamb, seeing I have no money, and it is not lawful to steal it?' Thereupon the angel Gabriel showed unto him a sheep, which Jesus offered in sacrifice, praising and blessing God, who is glorious for ever.

Chapter 14 After the fast of forty days, Jesus chooses twelve apostles.

Jesus descended from the mount, and passed alone by night to the farther side of Jordan, and fasted forty days and forty nights, not eating anything day nor night, making continual supplication to the Lord for the salvation of his people to whom God had sent him. And when the forty days were passed he was an hungered. Then appeared Satan unto him, and tempted him in many words, but Jesus drove him away by the power of words of God. Satan having departed, the angels came and ministered unto Jesus that whereof he had need.

Jesus, having returned to the region of Jerusalem, was found again of the people with exceeding great joy, and they prayed him that he would abide with them, for his words were not as those of the scribes, but were with power, for they touched the heart.

Jesus, seeing that great was the multitude of them that returned to their heart for to walk in the law of God, went up into the mountain, and abode all night in prayer, and when day was come he descended from the mountain, and chose twelve, whom he called apostles, among whom is Judas, who was slain upon the cross. Their names are: Andrew and Peter his brother, fishermen, Barnabas, who wrote this, with Matthew the publican, who sat at the receipt of custom, John and James, sons of Zebedee, Thaddaeus and Judas, Bartholomew and Philip, James, and Judas Iscariot the traitor. To these he always revealed the divine secrets, but the Iscariot Judas he made his dispenser of that which was given in alms, but he stole the tenth part of everything.

Chapter 15 Miracle wrought by Jesus at the marriage, turning the water into wine.

When the feast of tabernacles was nigh, a certain rich man invited Jesus with his disciples and his mother to a marriage. Jesus therefore went, and as they were feasting the wine ran short. His mother accosted Jesus, saying: 'They have no wine.' Jesus answered: 'What is that to me, mother mine?' His mother commanded the servants that whatever Jesus should command them they should obey. There were there six vessels for water according to the custom of Israel to purify themselves for prayer. Jesus said: 'Fill these vessels with water.' The servants did so. Jesus said unto them: 'In the name of God, give to drink unto them that are feasting.' The servants thereupon bare unto the master of the ceremonies, who rebuked the attendants saying: 'O worthless servants why have you kept the better wine till now?' For he knew nothing of all that
Jesus had done.

The servants answered: 'O sir, there is here a holy man of God, for he has made of water, wine.' The master of the ceremonies thought that the servants were drunken, but they that were sitting near to Jesus, having seen the whole matter, rose from the table and paid him reverence, saying: 'Verily you art an holy one of God, a true prophet sent to us from God!'

Then his disciples believed on him, and many returned to their heart, saying: 'Praised be God, who has mercy upon Israel, and visits the house of Judah with love, and blessed be his holy name.'

Chapter 16 Wonderful teaching giving by Jesus to his apostles concerning conversion from the evil life.

One day Jesus called together his disciples and went up on to the mountain, and when he had sat down there his disciples came near unto him, and he opened his mouth and taught them, saying: 'Great are the benefits which God bath bestowed on us wherefore it is necessary that we should serve him with truth of heart. And forasmuch as new wine is put into new vessels, even so ought you to become new men, if you will contain the new doctrine that shall come out of my mouth. Verily I say unto you, that even as a man cannot see with his eyes the heaven and the earth at one and the same time, so it is impossible to love God and the world.

'No man can in any wise serve two masters that are at enmity one with the other: for if the one shall love you, the other will hate you. Even so I tell you in truth that you cannot serve God and the world for the world lies in falsehood, covetousness, and malignity. Ye cannot therefore find rest in the world, but rather persecution and loss. Wherefore serve God and despise the world, for from me you shall find rest for your souls, Hear my words for I speak unto you in truth.

'Verily, blessed are they that mourn this earthly life, for they shall be comforted.

'Blessed are the poor who truly hate the delights of the world, for they shall abound in the delights of the kingdom of God.

'Verily, blessed are they that eat at the table of God, for the angels shall minister unto them.

'Ye are journeying as pilgrims. Doth the pilgrim encumber himself with palaces and fields and other earthly matters upon the way? Assuredly not: but he bears things light and prized for their usefulness and convenience upon the road. This now should be an example unto you, and if you desire another example I will give it you, in order that you may do all that I tell you.

'Weigh not down your hearts with earthly desires, saying: "Who shall clothe us?" or "Who shall give us to eat?" But behold the flowers and the trees, with the birds, which God our Lord clothed and nourished with greater glory than all the glory of Solomon. And he is able to nourish you, even God who created you and called you to his service, who for forty years caused the manna to fall from heaven for his people Israel in the wilderness, and did not suffer their clothing to wax old or perish, they being six hundred and forty thousand men, besides women and children. Verily I say unto you, that heaven and earth shall fail, yet shall not fail his mercy unto them that fear him. But the rich of the world in their prosperity are hungry and perish. There was a rich man whose incomings increased, and he said, "What shall I do, O my soul? I will pull down my barns because they are small, and I will build new and greater ones: therefore you shall triumph my soul!" Oh, wretched ban! for that night he died. He ought to have been mindful of the poor, and to have made himself friends with the alms of unrighteous riches of this world, for they bring treasures in the kingdom of heaven.

'Tell me, I pray you, if you should give your money into the bank to a publican, and he should give unto you tenfold and twentyfold, would you not give to such a man everything that you had? But I say unto you, verily, that whatsoever you shall give and shall forsake for love of God, you receive it back an hundred-fold, and life everlasting. See then how much you ought to be content to serve God.

Chapter 17   In this chapter is clearly perceived the unbelief of Christians, and the true faith of Mumin.

When Jesus had said this, Philip answered: 'We are content to serve God, but we desire, however, to know God, for Isaiah the prophet said: "Verily you art a hidden God," and God said to Moses his servant: "I am that which I am."

Jesus answered: 'Philip, God is a good without which there is naught good, God is a being without which there is naught that is, God is a life without which there is naught that lives, so great that he fills all and is everywhere. He alone has no equal. He has had no beginning, nor will he ever have an end, but to everything has he given a beginning, and to everything shall he give an end. He has no father nor mother, he has no sons. nor brethren. nor companions. And because God has no body, therefore he eats not, sleeps not, dies not, walks not, moves not, but abides eternally without human similitude, for that he is incorporeal, uncompounded, immaterial, of the most simple substance. He is so good that he loves goodness only; he is so just that when he punishes or pardons it cannot be gainsaid. In short, I say unto thee, Philip, that here on earth you canst not see him nor know him perfectly, but in his kingdom you shall see him for ever: wherein consists all our happiness and glory.'

Philip answered: 'Master, what say you? It is surely written in Isaiah that God is our father; how, then, has he no sons?'

Jesus answered: 'There are written in the prophets many parables, wherefore you ought not to attend to the letter, but to the sense. For all the prophets, that are one hundred and forty-four thousand, whom God has sent into the world, have spoken darkly. But after me shall come the Splendor of all the prophets and holy ones, and shall shed light upon the darkness of all that the prophets have said, because he is the messenger of God' And having said this, Jesus sighed and said: 'Have mercy on Israel, O Lord God, and look with pity upon Abraham and upon his seed, in order that they may serve thee with truth of heart.

His disciples answered: 'So be it, O Lord our God!'

Jesus said: 'Verily I say unto you, the scribes and doctors have made void the law of God with their false prophecies, contrary to the prophecies of the true prophets of God: wherefore God is wrath with the house of Israel and with this faithless generation.'

His disciples wept at these words, and said: 'Have mercy, O God, have mercy upon the temple and upon the holy city, and give it not into contempt of the nations that they despise not your holy covenant.' Jesus answered: 'So be it, Lord God of our fathers.'

Chapter 18 Here is shown forth the persecution of the servants

of God by the world, and God's protection saving them.

Having said this, Jesus said: 'Ye have not chosen me, but I have chosen you, that you may be my disciples. If then the world shall hate you, you shall be truly my disciples, for the world has been ever an enemy of servants of God. Remember [the] holy prophets that have been slain by the world, even as in the time of Elijah ten thousand prophets were slain by Jezebel, insomuch that scarcely did poor Elijah escape, and seven thousand sons of prophets who were hidden by the captain of Ahab's host. Oh, unrighteous world, that know not God! Fear not therefore you, for the hairs of your head are numbered so that they shall not perish. Behold the sparrows and other

birds, whereof falls not one feather without the will of God. Shall God, then, have more care of the birds than of man, for whose sake he has created everything. Is there any man, perchance, who cares more for his shoes than for his own son? Assuredly not. Now how much less ought you to think that God would abandon you, while taking care of the birds! And why speak I of the birds? A leaf of a tree falls not without the will of God.

'Believe me, because I tell you the truth, that the world will greatly fear you if you shall observe my words. For if it feared not to have its wickedness revealed it would not hate you, but it fears to be revealed, therefore it will hate you and persecute you. If you shall see your words scorned by the world lay it not to heart, but consider how that God is greater than you, who is in such wise scorned by the world that his wisdom is counted madness If God endures the world with patience, wherefore will you lay it to heart, O dust and clay of the earth? In your patience you shall possess your soul. Therefore if one shall give you a blow on one side of the face, offer him the other that he may smite it. Render not evil for evil, for so do all the worst animals, but render good for evil, and pray God for them that hate you. Fire is not extinguished with fire, but rather with water; even so I say unto you that you shall not overcome evil with evil, but rather with good. Behold God, who causes the sun to come upon the good and evil, and likewise the rain. Sought you to do good to all, for it is written in the law: "Be you holy, for I your God am holy, be you pure, for I am pure, and be you perfect, for I am perfect." Verily I say unto you that the servant studies to please his master, and so he puts not on any garment that is displeasing to his master. Your garments are your will and your love. Beware, then, not to will or to love a thing that is displeasing to God, our Lord. Be you sure that God hates the pomp and lusts of the world, and therefore hate you the world.'

Chapter 19 Jesus foretells his betrayal, and, descending from the mountain, heals ten lepers.

When Jesus had said this, Peter answered: 'O teacher, behold we have felt all to follow thee, what shall become of us?' Jesus answered: 'Verily you in the day of judgment shall sit beside me, giving testimony against the twelve tribes of Israel.' And having said this Jesus sighed, saying: 'O Lord, what thing is this? for I have chosen twelve, and one of them is a devil.'

The disciples were sore grieved at this word, whereupon he who writes secretly questioned Jesus with tears, saying: 'O master, will Satan deceive me, and shall I then become reprobate?'

Jesus answered: "Be not sore grieved, Barnabas, for those whom God has chosen before the creation of the world shall not perish. Rejoice, for your name is written in the book of life.' Jesus comforted his disciples, saying: 'Fear not, for he who shall hate me is not grieved at my saying, because in him is not the divine feeling.' At his words the chosen were comforted. Jesus made his prayers, and his disciples said: 'Amen, so be it, Lord God almighty and merciful.' Having finished his devotions, Jesus came down from the mountain with his disciples, and met ten lepers, who from afar off cried out: 'Jesus, son of David, have mercy on us!' Jesus called them near to him, and said unto them: 'What will you of me, O brethren?' They all cried out: 'Give us health!' Jesus answered: 'Ah, wretched that you are, have you so lost your reason for that you say: "Give us health?" See you not me to be a man like yourselves. Call unto our God that has created you: and he that is almighty and merciful will heal you. With tears the lepers answered: 'We know that you art man like us, but yet an holy one of God and a prophet of the Lord, wherefore pray you to God, and he will heal us.

Thereupon the disciples prayed Jesus, saying: 'Lord, have mercy upon them.' Then groaned Jesus and prayed to God, saying: 'Lord God almighty and merciful, have mercy and hearken to the words of your servant: and for love of Abraham our father and for your holy covenant have mercy on the request of these men, and grant them health.' Whereupon Jesus, having said this, turned himself to the lepers and said: 'Go and show yourselves to the priests according to the law of God.'

The lepers departed and on the way were cleansed. Whereupon one of them. seeing that he was healed, returned to find Jesus, and he was an Ishmaelite. And having found Jesus he bowed himself, doing reverence unto him, and saying: 'Verily you art an holy one of God' and with thanks he prayed him that he would receive him for servant. Jesus answered: 'Ten have been cleansed, where are the nine?' And he said to him that was cleansed: 'I am not come to be served, but to serve: wherefore go to shine home, and recount how much God has done in thee, in order that they may know that the promises made to Abraham and his son, with the kingdom of God, are drawing nigh.' The cleansed leper departed, and having arrived in his own neighborhood recounted how much God through Jesus had wrought in him.

Chapter 20 Miracle on the sea wrought by Jesus, and Jesus declares where the prophet is received.

Jesus went to the sea of Galilee, and having embarked in a ship sailed to his city of Nazareth, whereupon there was a great tempest in the sea, insomuch that the ship was nigh unto sinking. And Jesus was sleeping upon the prow of the ship. Then drew near to him his disciples, and awoke him, saying: 'O master, save thyself, for we perish!' They were encompassed with very great fear, by reason of the great wind that was contrary and the roaring of the sea. Jesus arose, and raising his eyes to heaven, said: 'O

Elohim Sabaoth, have mercy upon your servants.' Then, when Jesus had said this, suddenly the wind ceased, and the sea became calm. Wherefore the
seamen feared, saying: 'And who is this, that the sea and the wind obey him?"

Having arrived at the city of Nazareth the seamen spread through the city all that Jesus had wrought, whereupon the house where Jesus was, was surrounded by as many as dwelt in the city. And the scribes and doctors having presented themselves unto him said: 'We have heard how much you have wrought in the sea and in Judaea: give us therefore some sign here in your own country.' Jesus answered: 'This faithless generation seek a sign, but it shall not be given them, because no prophet is received in his own country. In the time of Elijah there were many widows in Judaea, but he was not sent to be nourished save unto a widow of Sidon. Many were the lepers in the time of Elisha in Judaea, nevertheless only Naaman the Syrian was cleansed.'

Then were the citizens enraged and seized him and carried him on to the top of a precipice to cast him down. But Jesus walking through the midst of them, departed from them.

Chapter 21   Jesus heals a demoniac, and the swine are cast into the sea. Afterwards he heals the daughter of the Canaanites.

Jesus went up to Capernaum, and as he drew near to the city behold there came out of the tombs one that was possessed of a devil, and in such wise that no chain could hold him, and he did great harm to the man.

The demons cried out through his mouth, saying: 'O holy one of God, why art you come before the time to trouble us?' And they prayed him that he would not cast them forth.

Jesus asked them how many they were. They answered: 'Six thousand six hundred and sixty-six.' When the disciples heard this they were affrighted, and prayed Jesus that he would depart.

Then said Jesus: 'Where is your faith? It is necessary that the demon should depart, and not I.' The demons therefore cried: 'We will come out, but permit us to enter into those swine.' There were feeding there, near to the sea, about ten thousand swine belonging to the Canaanites. Thereupon Jesus said: 'Depart, and enter into the swine.' With a roar the demons entered into the swine, and cast them headlong into the sea. Then fled into the city they that fed the swine, and recounted all that had been brought to pass by Jesus.

Accordingly the men of the city came forth and found Jesus and the man that was healed. The men were filled with fear and prayed Jesus that he would depart out of their borders. Jesus accordingly departed from them and went up into the parts of Tyre and Sidon.

And lo! a woman of Canaan with her two sons, who had come forth out of her own country to find Jesus. Having therefore seen him come with his disciples, she cried out: 'Jesus, son of David, have mercy on my daughter, who is tormented of the devil! Jesus did not answer even a single word, because they were of the uncircumcised people. The disciples were moved to pity, and said: 'O master, have pity on them! Behold how much they cry out and weep!'

Jesus answered: 'I am not sent but unto the people of Israel.' Then the woman, with her sons, went before Jesus, weeping and saying: 'O son of David, have mercy on me!' Jesus answered: 'It is not good to take the bread from the children's hands and give it to the dogs.' And this said Jesus by reason of their uncleanness, because they were of the un- circumcised people.

The woman answered: 'O Lord, the dogs eat the crumbs that fall from their masters' table.' Then was Jesus seized with admiration at the words of the woman, and said: 'O woman, great is your faith.' And having raised his hands to heaven he prayed to God, and then he said: 'O woman, your daughter is freed, go your way in peace.' The woman departed, and returning to her home found her daughter, who was blessing God.' Wherefore the woman said: 'Verily there is none other God than the God of Israel.' Whereupon all her kinsfolk joined themselves unto the law of [God], according to the law written in the book of Moses.

Chapter 22   Miserable condition of the uncircumcised in that a dog is better than they.

The disciples questioned Jesus on that day, saying: 'O master, why didst you make such answer to the woman, saying that they were dogs?'

Jesus answered: 'Verily I say unto you that a dog is better than an uncircumcised man.' Then were the disciples sorrowful, saying: 'Hard are these words, and who shall be able to receive them?'

Jesus answered: "If you consider, O foolish ones, what the dog doth, that has no reason, for the service of his master, you will find my saying to be true. Tell me, doth the dog guard the house of his master, and expose his life against the robber? Yea, assuredly. But what receives he? Many blows and injuries with little bread, and he always shows to his master a joyful countenance. Is this true?'

'True it is, O master,' answered the disciples.

Then said Jesus: 'Consider now how much God has given to man, and you shall see how unrighteous he is in not observing the covenant of God made with Abraham his servant. Remember that which David said to Saul king of Israel, against Goliath the Philistine: "My lord," said David, "while your servant was keeping your servant's flock there came the wolf, the bear, and the lion and seized your servant's sheep: whereupon your servant went and slew them, rescuing the sheep. And what is this uncircumcised one but like unto them ? Therefore will your servant go in the name of the Lord God of Israel, and will slay this unclean one that blasphemes the holy people of God."

Then said the disciples: 'Tell us O master for what reason man must needs be circumcised?"

Jesus answered: 'Let it suffice you that God has commanded it to Abraham. saying: "Abraham, circumcise your foreskin and that of all your house, for this is a covenant between me and thee for ever."

Chapter 23 Orgin of Circumcision, and covenant of God with Abraham, and damnation of the uncircumcised.

And having said this, Jesus sat nigh unto the mountain which they looked upon. And his disciples came to his side to listen to his words. Then said Jesus: 'Adam the first man having eaten, by fraud of Satan, the food forbidden of God in paradise, his flesh rebelled against the spirit, whereupon he swore, saying: "By God, I will cut thee!"

And having broken a piece of rock, he seized his flesh to cut it with the sharp edge of the stone: whereupon he was rebuked by the angel Gabriel. And he answered: "I have sworn by God to cut it, I will never be a liar!"

'Then the angel showed him the superfluity of his flesh, and that he cut off. And hence, just as every man takes flesh from the flesh of Adam, so is he bound to observe all that Adam promised with an oath. This did Adam observe in his sons, and from generation to generation came down the obligation of circumcision. But in the time of Abraham there were but few circumcised upon the earth, because that idolatry was multiplied up the earth. Whereupon God told to Abraham the fact concerning circumcision, and made this covenant, saying: "The soul that shall not have his flesh circumcised, I will scatter him from among my people for ever." '

The disciples trembled with fear at these words of Jesus, for with vehemence of spirit he spoke. Then said Jesus: Leave fear to him that has not circumcised his foreskin, for he is deprived of paradise. And having said this, Jesus spoke again, saying: 'The spirit in many is ready in the service of God, but the flesh is weak. The man therefore that fears God ought to consider what the flesh is, and where it had its origin, and whereto it shall be reduced. Of the clay of the earth created God flesh, and into it he breathed the breath of life, with an inbreathing therein. And therefore when the flesh shall hinder the service of God it ought to be spurned like clay and trampled on, forasmuch as he that hates his soul in this world shall keep it in life eternal.

'What the flesh is at this present its desires make manifest -that it is a harsh enemy of all good: for it alone desires sin.

'Ought then man for the sake of satisfying one of his enemies to leave off pleasing God, his creator? Consider you this. All the saints and prophets have been enemies of their flesh for service of God: wherefore readily and with gladness they went to their death, so as not to offend against the law of God given by Moses his servant, and go and serve the false and lying gods.

'Remember Elijah, who fled through desert places of the mountains, eating only grass, clad in goats' skin. Ah, how many days he supped not! Ah, how much cold he endured! Ah, how many showers drenched him, and [that] for the space of seven years, wherein endured that fierce persecution of the unclean Jezebel!

Remember Elisha, who ate barley-bread, and wore the Coarsest raiment. Verily I say unto you that they, not fearing to spurn the flesh, were feared with great terror by the king and princes. This should suffice for the spurning of the flesh, O men. But if you will gaze at the sepulchers, you shall know what the flesh is.'

Chapter 24 Natable example how one ought to flee from banqueting and feasting.

Having said this, Jesus wept, saying: 'Woe to those who are servants to their flesh, for they are sure not to have any good in the other life, but only torments for their sins. I tell you that there was a rich glutton who paid no heed to aught but gluttony, and so every day held a splendid feast. There stood at his gate a poor man by name Lazarus, who was full of wounds, and was fain to have those crumbs that fell from the glutton's table. But no one gave them to him, nay, all mocked him. Only the dogs had pity on him, for they licked his wounds. It came to pass that the poor man died, and the angels carried him to the arms of Abraham our father. The rich man also died, and the devils carried him to the arms of Satan, whereupon, undergoing the greatest torment, he lifted up his eyes and from afar saw Lazarus in the arms of Abraham. Then cried the rich man: "O father Abraham, have mercy on me, and send Lazarus, who upon his fingers may bring me a drop of water to cool my tongue, which is tormented in this flame."

'Abraham answered: "Son, remember that you receive your good in the other life and Lazarus his evil, wherefore now you shall be in torment, and Lazarus in consolation."

'The rich man cried out again, saying: "O father Abraham, in my house there are three brethren of mine. Therefore send Lazarus to announce to them how much I am suffering, in order that they may repent and not come hither."

'Abraham answered: "They have Moses and the prophets, let them hear them."

'The rich man answered: "Nay, father Abraham, but if one dead shall arise they will believe."

'Abraham answered: "Whoso believeth not Moses and the prophets will not believe even the dead if they should arise.

'See then whether the poor are blessed,' said Jesus, 'who have patience, and only desire that which is necessary, hating the flesh. O wretched they, who bear others to the burial, to give their flesh for food of worms, and do not learn the truth. So far from it that they live here like immortals, for they build great houses and purchase great revenues and live in pride.'

Chapter 25 How one ought to despise the flesh, and how one ought to live in the world.

Then said he who writes: 'O master, true are your words and therefore have we forsaken all to follow thee. Tell us, then how we ought to hate our flesh: for to kill oneself is not lawful, and living we needs must give it its livelihood.'

Jesus answered: 'Keep your flesh like a horse, and you shall live securely. For unto a horse food is given by measure, and labor without measure, and the bridle is put on him that he may walk at your will, he is tied up that he may not annoy any one, he is kept in a poor place, and beaten when he is not obedient: so do you, then, O Barnabas, and you shall live always with God.

'And be not offended at my words, for David the prophet did the same thing, as he confesses , saying: "I am as an horse before thee: and am always by thee."

'Now tell me, whether is poorer he who is content with little, or he who desires much?   Verily I say unto you, that if the world had but a sound mind no one would amass anything for himself, but all would be in common. But in this is known its madness, that the more it amasses the more it desires, And much as it amasses, for the fleshly repose of others doth it amass the same. Therefore let one single robe suffice for you, cast away your purse, carry no wallet, no sandals on your feet, and do not think, saying: "What shall happen to us ?" but have thought to do the will of God, and he will provide for your need, insomuch that nothing shall be lacking unto you.

'Verily I say unto you. that the amassing much in this life gives sure witness of not having anything to receive in the other. For he that has Jerusalem for his native country builds not houses in Samaria, for that there is enmity between there cities. Understand you?'

'Yea, answered the disciples.

Chapter 26   How one ought to love God. And in this chapter is contained the wonderful contention of Abraham with his father.
Then Jesus said: "There was a man on a journey who, as he was walking, discovered a treasure in a field that was to be sold for five pieces of money. Straightway the man, when he knew this, sold his cloak to buy that field. Is that credible?" The disciples answered: "He who would not believe this is mad."

Thereupon Jesus said: "You will be mad if you do not give your senses to God to buy your soul in which resides the treasure of love, for love is an incomparable treasure. For he that loves God has God for his own, and whoever has God has everything." Peter answered: "O master, how can one love God with true love? Tell us."

Jesus replied: "Truly I say to you that he who shall not hate his father and his mother, and his own life, and children and wife for love of God, such is not worthy to be loved of God." Peter answered: "O master, it is written in the Law of God in the Book of Moses: Honor your father, that you may live long upon the earth.

And further he says: Cursed be the son that obeys not his father and his mother" God commanded that such a disobedient son should be stoned by the wrath of the people before the gate of the city. [Why] do you bid us to hate father and mother?"

Jesus replied: "Every word of mine is true, because it is not mine, but God's, who has sent me to the House of Israel. Therefore I say to you that all that which you possess God has bestowed it upon you: and so, what is more precious, the gift or the giver? When your father and your mother with every other thing is a stumbling block to you in the service of God, abandon them as enemies. Did not God say to Abraham: Go forth from the house of your father and of your kindred, and come to dwell in the land which I will give to you and to your seed? Why did God say this, except that the father of Abraham was an image-maker, who made and worshipped false gods? [For this reason] there was enmity between them, such that the father wished to burn his son." Peter answered: "Your words are true. I pray you tell us how Abraham mocked his father."

Jesus replied: "Abraham was seven years old when he began to seek God. So one day he said to his father: 'Father, what made man?' The foolish father answered: 'Man [made man]; for I made you, and my father made me.' Abraham answered: 'Father, it is not so; for I have heard an old man weeping and saying: 'O my God, why have you not given me children?" His father replied: 'It is true, my son, that God helps man to make man, but he does not put his hands to [the task]; it is only necessary that man come to pray to his God and to give him lambs and sheep, and his God will help him.' Abraham answered: 'How many gods are there, father?' The old man replied: 'They are infinite in number, my son.'

Then Abraham said: 'O father, what shall I do if I serve one god and another [god] wishes me evil because I do not serve him? In any case discord will come between them, and so war will arise among the gods. And if, perhaps, the god that wills me evil shall slay my own god, what shall I do? It is certain that he will slay me also. The old man, laughing, answered: "O son, have no fear, for no god makes war upon another god; no, in the great temple there are a thousand gods with the great god Baal; and I am now near seventy years old, and yet never have I seen that one god has smitten another god. And assuredly all men do not serve one god, but one man one, and another."

Abraham answered: "So, then, they have peace among themselves?" His father said: "They have." Then said Abraham: "O father, what be the gods like?" The old man answered: "Fool, every day I make a god, which I sell to others to buy bread, and you know not what the gods are like!" And then at that moment he was making an idol. "This," said he, "is of palm wood, that one is of olive, that little one is of ivory: see how fine it is! Does it not seem as though it were alive? Assuredly, it lacks but breath!" Abraham answered: "And so, father, the gods are without breath? Then how do they give breath? And being without life, how give they life? It is certain, father, that these are not God." The old man was wroth at these words, saying: "If you were of age to understand, I would break your head with this axe: But hold your peace, because you have not understanding!" Abraham answered: "Father, if the gods help to make man, how can it be that man should make the gods? And if the gods are made of wood, it is a great sin to burn wood. But tell me, father, how is it that, when you have made so many gods, the gods have not helped you to make so many other children that you should become the most powerful man in the world?"

The father was beside himself, hearing his son speak so; the son went on: "Father, was the world for some time without men?" Yes," answered the old man, "and why?" "Because," said Abraham, "I should like to know who made the first God." "Now go out of my house!" said the old man, "and leave me to make this god quickly, and speak no words to me; for, when you are hungry you desire bread and not words." Abraham said: "A fine god, truly, that you cut him as you will, and he defends not himself!" Then the old man was angry, and said: "All the world says that it is a god, and you, mad fellow, say that it is not. By my gods, if you were a man I could kill you!" And having said this, he gave blows and kicks to Abraham, and chased him from the house."

Chapter 27   In this chapter is clearly seen how improper is laughter in men: also the prudence of Abraham.

The disciples laughed over the madness of the old man, and stood amazed at the prudence of Abraham. But Jesus reproved them, saying: "You have forgotten the words of the prophet, who says: Present laughter is a herald of weeping to come, and further, You shall not go where is laughter, but sit where they weep, because this life passes in miseries." Then Jesus said, "In the time of Moses, know you not that for laughing and mocking at others God turned into hideous beasts many men of Egypt? Beware that in anywise you laugh not at any one, for you shall surely weep [for it]."

The disciples answered: "We laughed over the madness of the old man." Then Jesus said: "Truly I say to you, every like loves his like, and therein finds pleasure. Therefore, if you were not mad you would not laugh at madness. They answered: "My God have mercy on us. Jesus said: "So be it."

Then said Philip: "O master, how came it to pass that Abraham's father wished to burn his son?" Jesus answered: "One day, Abraham having come to the age of twelve years, his father said to him: "Tomorrow is the festival of all the gods, therefore we shall go to the great temple and bear a present to my god, great Baal. And you shall choose for yourself a god, for you are of age to have a god."

Abraham answered with guile: "Willingly, O my father." And so betimes in the morning they went before every one else to the temple. But Abraham bare beneath his tunic an axe hidden. Whereupon, having entered into the temple, as the crowd increased Abraham hid himself behind an idol in a dark part of the temple. His father, when he departed, believed that Abraham had gone home before him, wherefore he did not stay to seek him.

Chapter 28

When every one had departed from the temple, the priests closed the temple and went away. Then Abraham took the axe and cut off the feet of all the idols, except the great god Baal. At its feet he placed the axe, amid the ruins which the statues made, for they, through being old and composed of pieces, fell in pieces. Thereupon, Abraham, going forth from the temple, seen by certain men, who suspected him of having gone to thieve something from the temple. So they laid hold on him, and having arrived at the temple, when they saw their gods so broken in pieces, they cried out with lamentation: "Come quickly, O men, and let us slay him who has slain our gods!" There ran together there about ten thousand men, with the priests, and questioned Abraham of the reason why he had destroyed their gods. Abraham answered: "You are foolish! Shall then a man slay God? It is the great God that has slain them. See you not that axe which he has near his feet? Certain it is that he desires no fellows." Then arrived there the father of Abraham, who, mindful of the many discourses of Abraham against their gods, and recognizing the axe wherewith Abraham had broken in pieces the idols, cried out: "It has been this traitor of a son of mine, who has slain our gods! for this axe is mine." And he recounted to them all that had passed between him and his son. Accordingly the men collected a great quantity of wood, and having bound Abraham's hands and feet put him upon the wood, and put fire underneath.

'Lo! God, through his angel, commanded the fire that it should not burn Abraham his servant. The fire blazed up with great fury, and burned about two thousand men of those who had condemned Abraham to death. Abraham truly found himself free, being carried by the angel of God near to the house of his father, without seeing who carried him, and thus Abraham escaped death."

Chapter 29

Then Philip said: "Great is the mercy of God upon whoever loves him. Tell us, O master, how Abraham came to [have] the knowledge of God." Jesus answered: "Having arrived near to the house of his father, Abraham feared to go into the house; so he removed [himself] some distance from the house and sat under a palm tree, where, being by himself, he said: "There must be a God who has life and power more than man, since he makes man, and man without God could not make man."

Thereupon, looking round upon the stars, the moon, and the sun, he thought that they had been God. But after considering their variableness with their movements, he said: "It must be [necessarily] that God does not move and that clouds do not hide him [as they hide the planets], otherwise men would be reduced to nothing." Remaining thus in suspense, he heard himself called by name, "Abraham!" And so, turning round and not seeing any one on any side, he said: "I am sure I heard myself called by name, 'Abraham. " Then, two other times in a similar manner, he heard himself called by name, "Abraham!"

He answered: "What calls me?" Then he heard [the voice] say: "I am the angel of God, Gabriel." Abraham was filled with fear; but the angel comforted him, saying: "Do not fear, Abraham, for you are friend of God When you broke in pieces the gods of men, you were chosen [by] the God of the angels and prophets such that you are written in the Book of Life." Then said Abraham: "What should I do [so as] to serve the God of the angels and holy prophets?" The angel answered: "Go to that fount and wash yourself, for God wishes to speak with you."

Abraham answered: "How should I wash myself?" Then the angel appeared to him as a beautiful youth, and washed himself in the fount, saying: "Do the same as this, O Abraham." When Abraham had washed himself, the angel said: "Go up that mountain, for God wills to speak to you there." Abraham ascended the mountain as the angel [had instructed him], and having sat down upon his knees he said to himself: "When will the God of the angels speak to me?" He heard himself called with a gentle voice: "Abraham!" Abraham answered him: "Who calls me?" The voice answered: "I am your God, O Abraham."

Abraham, filled with fear, bent his face to earth, saying: "How shall your servant who is dust and ashes hearken to you!" Then said God: "Fear not, but rise up, for I have chosen you as my servant, and I will bless you and make you increase into a great people. Therefore go forth from the house of your father and of your kindred, and come to dwell in the land which I will give to you and to your seed."

Abraham answered: "I will do everything, Lord, but guard me [so] that no other god may harm me." Then God spoke, saying: "I am God alone, and there is none other god but me. I strike down, and make whole; I slay, and give life; I lead down to hell, and I bring out thereof, and no-one is able to deliver himself out of my hands." Then God gave him the covenant of circumcision, and so our father Abraham knew God." And having said this, Jesus lifted up his hands, saying: "To you be honor and glory, O God. So be it!"

Chapter 30

Jesus went to Jerusalem, near to the Senofegia, a feast of our nation . The scribes and Pharisees having perceived this, took counsel to catch him in his talk. Whereupon, there came to him a doctor, saying: "Master, what must I do to have eternal life?" Jesus answered: "How is it written in the Law?" The tempter answered, saying: "Love the Lord your God, and your neighbor. You shall love your God above all things, with all your heart and your mind, and your neighbor as yourself." Jesus answered: "You have answered well: therefore go and do you so, I say, and you shall have eternal life." He said to him: "And who is my neighbor?" Jesus answered, lifting up his eyes: "A man was going down from Jerusalem to go to Jericho, a city rebuilt under a curse. This man on the road was seized by robbers, wounded and stripped, whereupon they departed, leaving him half dead. It chanced that a priest passed by that place, and he, seeing the wounded man, passed on without greeting him. In like manner passed a Levite, without saying a word. It chanced that there passed [also] a Samaritan, who, seeing the wounded man, was moved to compassion, and alighted from his horse, and took the wounded man and washed his wounds with wine, and anointed them with ointment, and binding up his wounds for him and comforting him, he set him upon his own horse.

Whereupon, having arrived in the evening at the inn, he gave him into the charge of the host. And when he had risen on the morrow, he said: "Take care of this man, and I will pay you all." And having presented four gold pieces to the sick man for the host, he said: "Be of good cheer, for I will speedily return and conduct you to my own home." "Tell me," said Jesus, "which of these was the neighbor?" The doctor answered: "He who showed mercy." Then Jesus said: "You have answered rightly, therefore go and do you likewise." The doctor departed in confusion.

Chapter 31

Then drew near to Jesus the priests, and said: "Master, is it lawful to give tribute to Caesar?" Jesus turned round to Judas, and said: "Have you any money?" And taking a penny in his hand, Jesus turned himself to the priests, and said to them: "This penny has an image: tell me, whose image is it?" They answered: "Caesar's". "Give therefore," said Jesus, "that which is Caesar's to Caesar, and that which is God's give it to God." Then they departed in confusion.

And behold there drew near a centurion, saying: "Lord, my son is sick, have mercy on my old age!" Jesus answered: "The Lord God of Israel have mercy on you!" The man was departing; and Jesus said: "Wait for me, for I will come to your house, to make prayer over your son." The centurion answered: "Lord, I am not worthy that you, a prophet of God, should come to my house, sufficient to me is the word that you have spoken for the healing of my son, for your God has made you lord over every sickness, even as his angel said to me in my sleep."

Then Jesus marveled greatly, and turning to the crowd, he said: "Behold this stranger, for he has more faith than all that I have found in Israel." And turning to the centurion, he said: "Go in peace, because God, for the great faith that he has given you, has granted health to your son." The centurion went his way, and on the road he met his servants, who announced to him how his son was healed. The man answered: "At what hour did the fever leave him?" They said: "Yesterday, at the sixth hour, the heat departed from him."

The man knew that when Jesus said: "The Lord God of Israel have mercy on you," his son received his health. *Whereupon the man believed in our God, and having entered into his house, he brake in pieces all his own gods, saying: "There is only the God of Israel, the true and living God." Therefore said he: "None shall eat of my bread that does not worship the God of Israel."

Chapter 32

One skilled in the Law invited Jesus to supper, in order to tempt him. Jesus came thither with his disciples, and many scribes, to tempt him, waited for him in the house. Whereupon, the disciples sat down to table without washing their hands. The scribes called Jesus, saying: "Wherefore do not your disciples observe the traditions of our elders, in not washing their hands before they eat bread?" Jesus answered: "And I ask you, for what cause have you annulled the precept of God to observe your traditions? You say to the sons of poor fathers: "Offer and make vows to the Temple." And they make vows of that little wherewith they ought to support their fathers. And when their fathers wish to take money, the sons cry out: "This money is consecrated to God", whereby the fathers suffer. O false scribes, hypocrites, does God use this money? Assuredly not, for God eats not, as he says by his servant David the prophet: Shall I then eat the flesh of bulls and drink the blood of sheep? Render to me the sacrifice of praise, and offer to me your vows; for if I should be hungry I will not ask aught of you, seeing that all things are in my hands, and the abundance of paradise is with me. Hypocrites! you do this to fill your purse, and therefore you tithe rue and mint.

Oh miserable ones! for to others you show the most clear way, by which you will not go. 'You scribes and doctors lay upon the shoulders of others weights of unbearable weight, but you yourselves the while are not willing to move them with one of your fingers. Truly I say to you, that every evil has entered into

143

the world under the pretext of the elders. Tell me, who made idolatry to enter into the world, if not the usage of the elders? For there was a king who exceedingly loved his father, whose name was Baal.

Whereupon, when the father was dead, his son for his own consolation, caused to be made an image like to his father, and set it up in the market-place of the city. And he made a decree that every one who approached that statue within a space of fifteen cubits should be safe, and no one any account should do him hurt. Hence the malefactors, by reason of the benefit they received therefrom, began to offer to the statue roses and flowers, and in a short time the offerings were changed into money and food, insomuch that they called it god, to honor it. Which thing from custom was transformed into a law, insomuch that the idol of Baal spread through all the world;

and how much does God lament this by the prophet Isaiah, saying: "Truly this people worships me in vain, for they have annulled my Law given to them by my servant Moses, and follow the traditions of their elders.

Truly I say to you, that to eat bread with unclean hands defiles not a man, because that which enters into the man defiles not the man, but that which comes out of the man defiles the man." Thereupon, said one of the scribes: "If I shall eat pork, or other unclean meats, will they not defile my conscience?" Jesus answered: "Disobedience will not enter into the man, but will come out of the man, from his heart, and therefore will he be defiled when he shall eat forbidden food."

Then said one of the doctors: "Master, you have spoken much against idolatry as though the people of Israel had idols, and so you have done us wrong." Jesus answered: "I know well that in Israel today there are not statues of wood, but there are statues of flesh." Then answered all the scribes in wrath: "And so we are idolaters?" Jesus answered: "Truly I say to you, the precept says not "You shall worship", but "You shall love the Lord your God with all your soul, and with all your heart, and with all your mind." Is this true?" said Jesus. "It is true" answered every one.

Chapter 33

Then Jesus said: "Truly all that which a man loves, for which he leaves everything else but that, is his god. And so the fornicator has for his image the harlot, the glutton and drunkard has for image his own flesh, and the covetous has for his image silver and gold, and so likewise every other sinner." Then said he who had invited him: "Master, which is the greatest sin?"

Jesus answered: "Which is the greatest ruin of a house?" Every one was silent, when Jesus with his finger pointed to the foundation, and said: "If the foundation give way, immediately the house falls in ruin, in such wise that it is necessary to build it up anew: but if every other part give way it can be repaired. Even so then say I to you, that idolatry is the greatest sin, because it deprives a man entirely of faith, and consequently of God, so that he can have no spiritual affection. But every other sin leaves to man the hope of obtaining mercy: and therefore I say that idolatry is the greatest sin." All stood amazed at the speaking of Jesus, for they perceived that it could not in any wise be assailed.

Then Jesus continued: "Remember that which God spoke and which Moses and Joshua wrote in the Law, and you shall see how grave is this sin. God said, speaking to Israel: "You shall not make to yourself any image of those things which are in heaven nor of those things which are under the heaven, nor shall you make it of those things which are above the earth, nor of those which are under the earth; nor of those which are above the water, nor of those which are under the water. For I am your God, strong and jealous, who will take vengeance for this sin upon the fathers and upon their children even to the fourth generation."

Remember how, when our people had made the calf, and when they had worshipped it, by commandment of God Joshua and the tribe of Levi took the sword and slew of them one hundred and twenty thousand of those that did not crave mercy of God. Oh, terrible judgment of God upon the idolaters!"

Chapter 34

There stood before the door one who had his right hand shrunken in such fashion that he could not use it. Whereupon Jesus, having lift up his heart to God, prayed, and then said: "In order that you may know that my words are true, I say, "In the name of God, man, stretch out your infirm hand!" He stretched it out whole, as if it had never had anything wrong with it.

Then with fear of God they began to eat. And having eaten somewhat, Jesus said again: "Truly I say to you, that it were better to burn a city than to leave an evil custom. For on account of such is God wroth with the princes and kings of the earth, to whom God has given the sword to destroy iniquities."

Afterwards said Jesus: "When you are invited, remember not to set yourself in the highest place, in order that if a greater friend of the host come the host say not to you: "Arise and sit lower down!' which were a shame to you. But go and sit in the meanest place, in order that he who invited you may come and say: "Arise, friend, and come and sit here, above!" For then shall you have great honor: for every one that exalts himself shall be humbled, and he that humbles himself shall be exalted.

'Truly I say to you, that Satan became not reprobate for any other sin than for his pride. Even as says the prophet Isaiah;, reproaching him with these words: "How are you fallen from heaven, O Lucifer, that were the beauty of the angels, and did shine like the dawn: truly to earth is fallen your pride!"

'Truly I say to you, that if a man knew his miseries, he would always weep here on earth and account himself most mean, beyond every other thing. For no other cause did the first man with his wife weep for a hundred years without ceasing, craving mercy of God. For they knew truly where they had fallen through their pride."

And having said this, Jesus gave thanks; and that day it was published through Jerusalem how great things Jesus had said, with the miracle he had wrought, insomuch that the people gave thanks to God blessing his holy name.

But the scribes and priests, having understood that he spoke against the traditions of the elders, were kindled with greater hatred. And like Pharaoh they hardened their heart: wherefore they sought occasion to slay him, but found it not.

Chapter 35

Jesus departed from Jerusalem, and went to the desert beyond Jordan: and his disciples that were seated round him said to Jesus: "O master, tell us how Satan fell through pride, for we have understood that he fell through disobedience, and because he always tempts man to do evil."

Jesus answered: "God having created a mass of earth, and having left it for twenty-five thousand years without doing aught else; Satan, who was as it were priest and head of the angels, by the great understanding that he possessed, knew that God of that mass of earth was to take one hundred and forty and four thousand signed with the mark of prophecy, and the Messenger of God, the soul of which messenger he had created sixty thousand years before aught else;. Therefore, being indignant, he instigated the angels, saying: "Look you, one day God shall will that this earth be revered by us. Wherefore consider that we are spirit, and therefore it is not fitting so to do." Many therefore forsook God. Whereupon said God, one day when all the angels were assembled: "Let each one that holds me for his lord straightway do reverence to this earth."

They that loved God bowed themselves, but Satan, with them that were of his mind, said: "O Lord, we are spirit, and therefore it is not just that we should do reverence to this clay;." Having said this, Satan became horrid and of fearsome look, and his followers became hideous; because for their rebellion God took away from them the beauty wherewith he had endued them in creating them. Whereat the holy angels, when, lifting their heads, they saw how terrible a monster Satan had become, and his followers, cast down their face to earth in fear. Then said Satan: "O Lord, you have unjustly made me hideous, but I am content thereat, because I desire to annul all that you shall do. And the other devils said: "Calf him not Lord, O Lucifer, for you are Lord."

Then said God to the followers of Satan: "Repent you, and recognize me as God, your creator." They answered: "We repent of having done you any reverence, for that you are not just, but Satan is just. Then said God: "Depart from me, O you cursed, for I have no mercy on you." And in his departing Satan spat up that mass of earth, and that spittle the angel Gabriel lifted up with some earth, so that therefore now man has the navel in his belly."

Chapter 36

The disciples stood in great amazement at the rebellion of the angels. Then Jesus said: "Truly I say to you, that he who makes not prayer is more wicked than Satan, and shall suffer greater torments. Because Satan had, before his fall, no example of fearing, nor did God so much as send him any prophet to invite him to repentance: but man now that all the prophets are come except the Messenger of God who shall come after me, because so God wills, and that I may prepare his way and man, I say, albeit he have infinite examples of the justice of God, lives carelessly without any fear, as though there were no God. Even as of such spoke the prophet David; "The fool has said in his heart, there is no God. Therefore are they corrupt and become abominable, without one of them doing good."

Make prayer unceasingly, O my disciples' 'in order that you may receive. For he who seeks finds, and he who knocks, to him it is opened, and he who asks receives. And in your prayer do not look to much speaking, for God looks on the heart; as he said through Solomon, "O my servant, give me your heart." Truly I say to you, as God lives, the hypocrites make much prayer in every part of the city in order to be seen and held for saints by the multitude: but their heart is full of wickedness, and therefore they do not mean that which they ask. It is needful that you mean your prayer if you will that God receive it. Now tell me: who would go to speak to the Roman governor to Herod, except he first have made up his mind to whom he is going, and what he is going to do? Assuredly none. And if man does so in order to speak with man, what ought man to do in order to speak with God, and ask of him mercy for his sins, while thanking him for all that he has given him?

Truly I say to you, that very few make true prayer, and therefore Satan has power over them, because God wills not those who honor him with their lips: who in the Temple ask [with] their lips for mercy, and their heart cries out for justice. Even as he says to Isaiah the prophet, saying: "Take away this people that is irksome to me, because with their lips they honor me, but their heart is far from me." Truly I say to you, that he that goes to make prayer without consideration mocks God.

Now who would go to speak to Herod with his back towards him, and before him speak well of Pilate the governor, whom he hates to the death? Assuredly none. Yet no less does the man who goes to make prayer and prepares not himself. He turns his back to God and his face to Satan, and speaks well of him. For in his heart is the love of iniquity, whereof he has not repented. If one, having injured you, should with his lips say to you, "Forgive me,' and with his hands should strike you a blow, how would you forgive him? Even so shall God have mercy on those who with their lips say: "Lord, have mercy on us," and with their heart love iniquity and think on fresh sins."

Chapter 37

The disciples wept at the 'words of Jesus and besought him, saying: "Lord, teach us to make prayer." Jesus answered: "Consider what you would do if the Roman governor seized you to put you to death, and that same do you when you go to make prayer. And let your words be these:

"O Lord our God, hallowed be your holy name, your kingdom come in us, your will be done always, and as it is done in heaven so be it done in earth; give us the bread for every day, and forgive us our sins, as we forgive them that sin against us, and suffer us not to fall into temptations, but deliver us from evil, for you are alone our God, to whom pertains glory and honor for ever."

Chapter 38

Then answered John: "Master let us wash ourselves as God

commanded by Moses." * Jesus said: "Do you think that I have come to destroy the Law and the prophets? Truly I say to you, as God lives, I have not come to destroy it, but rather to observe it. For every prophet has observed the Law of God and all that God by the other prophets has spoken. As God lives, in whose presence my soul stands, no one that breaks one least precept can be pleasing to God, but shall be least in the kingdom of God, for he shall have no part there. Moreover I say to you, that one syllable of the Law of God cannot be broken without the. gravest sin. But I do you to wit that it is necessary to observe that which God says by Isaiah the prophet, with these words: "Wash you and be clean, take away your thoughts from my eyes. 'Truly I say to you, that all the water of the sea will not wash him who with his heart loves iniquities.

And furthermore I say to you, that no one will make prayer pleasing to God if he be not washed, but will burden his soul with sin like to idolatry. 'Believe me, in sooth, that if man should make prayer to God as is fitting, he would obtain all that he should ask. Remember Moses the servant of God, who with his prayer scourged Egypt, opened the Red Sea, and there drowned Pharaoh and his host. Remember Joshua, who made the sun stand still, Samuel, who smote with fear the innumerable host of the Philistines, Elijah, who made the fire to rain from heaven, Elisha raised a dead man, and so many other holy prophets, who by prayer obtained all that they asked. But those men truly did not seek their own in their matters, but sought only God and his honor."

Chapter 39

Then said John: "Well have you spoken, O master, but we lack to know how man sinned through pride." Jesus answered: "When God has expelled Satan, and the angel Gabriel had purified that mass of earth whereon Satan spat, God created everything that lives, both of the animals that fly and of them that walk and swim, and he adorned the world with all that it has. One day Satan approached to the gates of paradise, and, seeing the horses eating

grass, he announced to them that if that mass of earth should
receive a soul there would be for them grievous labor; and that
therefore it would be to their advantage to trample that piece of
earth in such wise that it should be no more good for anything.
The horses aroused themselves and impetuously set themselves to
run over that piece of earth which lay among lilies and roses,.
Whereupon God gave spirit to that unclean portion of earth upon
which lay the spittle of Satan, which Gabriel had taken up from
the mass; and raised up the dog, who, barking, filled the horses
with fear, and they fled. Then God gave his soul to man, while all
the holy angels sang: "Blessed be your holy name, O God our
Lord." "Adam, having sprung upon his feet, saw in the air a
writing that shone like the sun;, which said: "There is only one
God, and Muhammad is the Messenger of God."
Whereupon Adam opened his mouth and said: "I thank you, O
Lord my God, that you have deigned to create me, but tell me. I
pray you, what means the message of these words: "Muhammad
is Messenger of God. Have there been other men before me?"
'Then said God: "Be you welcome, O my servant Adam. . I tell you
that you are the first man whom I have created. And he whom
you have seen [mentioned] is your son, who shall come into the
world many years hence, and shall be my Messenger, for whom I
have created all things; who shall give light to the world when he
shall come; whose soul was set in a celestial splendor sixty
thousand years before I made any thing."
Adam besought God, saying: "Lord, grant me this writing upon
the nails of the fingers of my hands." Then God gave to the first
man upon his thumbs that writing; upon the thumb-nail of the
right hand it said: "There is only one God," and upon the thumb-
nail of the left it said: "Muhammad is Messenger of God." Then
with fatherly affection the first man kissed those words, and
rubbed his eyes, and said: "Blessed be that day when you shall
come to the world."
Seeing the man alone, God said: "It is not well that he should
remain alone." Wherefore he made him to sleep, and took a rib

from near his heart, filling the place with flesh. * Of that rib made he Eve, and gave her to Adam for his wife. He set the twain of them as lords of Paradise, to whom he said: "Behold I give to you every fruit to eat, except the apples and the corn" whereof he said: "Beware that in no wise you eat of these fruits, for you shall become unclean, insomuch that I shall not suffer. You to remain here, but shall drive you forth, and you shall suffer great miseries."

Chapter 40

When Satan had knowledge of this he became mad with indignation, and so he drew near to the gate of paradise where a horrid serpent with legs like a camel, and nails on his feet [that] cut like a razor on every side, stood on guard. The enemy said to him: 'Let me to enter into paradise.'

The serpent answered: 'How shall I let you enter [since] God has commanded me to cast you out?' Satan answered: 'You see how much God loves you; he has set you outside of paradise to keep guard over a lump of clay, which is man! If you bring me into paradise I will make you so terrible that every one shall flee you, and so you shall go and stay at your pleasure.' Then the serpent said: 'And how shall I set you within [paradise]?'

Satan said, 'You are great: therefore, open your mouth, and I will enter into your belly, and so [when] you enter into paradise [you] shall place me near to those two lumps of clay that are newly walking upon the earth.' Then the serpent did so, and placed Satan near Eve, for Adam, her husband, was sleeping. Satan presented himself before the woman like a beauteous angel, and said to her: 'Why do you not eat of those apples and corn?' Eve answered: 'Our God has said to us that [if we] eat [them] we shall be unclean, and he will drive us from paradise.'

Satan answered: 'He does not speak the truth! You must know that God is wicked and envious, and suffers no equals, but keeps every one as a slave. [This is] why he has said this [to you], in order that you may not become equal to him. But if you and your companion do according to my counsel, you shall eat of those

fruits as [you eat] of the other [fruits], and you shall not remain
subject to others but like God you shall know good and evil, and
you shall do whatever you please, because you shall be equal to
God.'

Then Eve took and ate of those [fruits], and when her husband
awoke she told [him everything] that Satan had said, and he took
and ate the fruit [when] his wife offered them to him. But, as the
food was going down, he remembered the words of God, and,
wishing to stop the food, he put his hand into his throat, where
every man has the mark.

Chapter 41

Then both of them knew that they were naked, and, being
ashamed, they took fig leaves and made a clothing for their secret
parts. When midday was passed, God appeared to them, and
called Adam, saying: 'Adam, where are you?' He answered: 'Lord,
I hid myself from your presence because my wife and I are naked,
and so we are ashamed to present ourselves before you.' Then
God said: 'And who has robbed you of your innocence, unless you
have eaten the fruit
[that makes you] unclean, and will not be able to abide [any]
longer in paradise?'

Adam answered: 'O Lord, the wife whom you have given me
[urged] me to eat [it] and so I have eaten it.' Then God said to the
woman: 'Why did you give [this] food to your husband?' Eve
answered: 'Satan deceived me, and so I ate [the fruit].' 'And how
did that reprobate enter into [the garden]?' said God. Eve
answered: 'A serpent that stands at the northern gate brought him
near to me.'

Then God said to Adam: 'Because you have [listened to] your wife
and have eaten the fruit, cursed be the earth in your works, it shall
bring forth brambles and thorns for you, and you shall eat bread
by the sweat of your face. Remember that you are earth, and to
earth you return.' And he spoke to Eve, saying: 'And you who did
[listen] to Satan, and gave the food to your husband, shall abide
under the dominion of man, who shall keep you as a slave, and

you shall bear children with travail.'

And having called the serpent, God called the angel Michael, who holds the sword of God, [and] said: 'First drive this wicked serpent forth from paradise, and when outside cut off his legs: for if he wants to walk, he must trail his body upon the earth.'

Afterwards God called Satan, who came laughing, and he said to him: 'Because you, reprobate, have deceived [Adam and Eve] and have made them unclean, I will that every uncleanness [from] them and [from] all their children - [of which] they shall be truly penitent and shall serve me - in going forth from their body shall enter through your mouth, and so shall you be satiated with uncleanness.'

Satan then gave a horrible roar, and said: 'Since you will to make me [continually] worse, I will make me that which I shall be able!' Then said God: 'Depart, cursed one, from my presence!' Then Satan departed, and God said to Adam [and] Eve, who were both weeping: 'Go forth from paradise, and do penance, and do not let your hope fail, for I will send your son so that your seed shall lift the dominion of Satan from off the human race: for I will give all things to he who shall come, my Messenger.'

God hid himself [from Adam and Eve], and the angel Michael drove them forth from paradise. Then, Adam, turning around, saw written above the gate, There is only one God, and Muhammad is Messenger of God. Weeping, he said: 'May it be pleasing to God, O my son, that you come quickly and draw us out of misery.' And thus," said Jesus, "Satan and Adam sinned through pride, the one by despising man, the other by wishing to make himself equal with God."

Chapter 42

Then the disciples wept after this discourse, and Jesus was weeping, when they saw many who came to find him, for the chiefs of the priests took counsel among themselves to catch him in his talk. Wherefore they sent the Levites and some of the scribes to question him, saying: "Who are you?"

Jesus confessed, and said the truth: "I am not the Messiah." They

said: "Are you Elijah or Jeremiah, or any of the ancient prophets?"
Jesus answered: "No." Then said they: "Who are you? Say, in order
that we may give testimony to those who sent us." Then Jesus
said: "I am a voice that cries through all Judea, and cries: "Prepare
you the way for the messenger of the Lord," even as it is written in
Esaias."

They said: "If you be not the Messiah nor Elijah, or any prophet,
wherefore do you preach new doctrine, and make yourself of
more account than the Messiah?" Jesus answered: "The miracles
which God works by my hands show that I speak that which God
wills, nor indeed do I make myself to be accounted as him of
whom you speak. For I am not worthy to unloose the ties of the
hosen or the ratchets of the shoes of the Messenger of God whom
you call "Messiah," who was made before me, and shall come after
me, and shall bring the words of truth, so that his faith shall have
no end."

The Levites and scribes departed in confusion, and recounted all
to the chiefs of the priests, who said: "He has the devil on his back
who recounts all to him." Then Jesus said to his disciples: "Truly I
say to you, that the chiefs and the elders of our people seek
occasion against me." Then said Peter: "Therefore go not you any
more into Jerusalem." Therefore said Jesus to him: "You are
foolish, and know not what you say, for it is necessary that I
should suffer many persecutions, because so have suffered all the
prophets and holy one of God. But fear not, for there be that are
with us and there be that are against us."

And having said this, Jesus departed and went to the mount
Tabor, and there ascended with him Peter and James, and John,
his brother, with him who writes this. Whereupon there shone a
great light above him, and his garments became white like snow
and his face glistened as the sun, and lo! there came Moses and
Elijah, speaking with Jesus concerning all that needs must come
upon our race and upon the holy city.

Peter spoke, saying: "Lord, it is good to be here. Therefore, if you
will, we will make here three tabernacles, one for you and one for

Moses and the other for Elijah." And while he spoke they were covered with a white cloud, and they heard a voice saying: "Behold my servant, in whom I am well pleased, hear you him." The disciples were filled with fear, and fell with their face upon the earth as dead. Jesus went down and raised up his disciples, saying: "Fear not, for God loves you, and has done this in order that you may believe on my words."

Chapter 43

Jesus went down to the eight disciples who were awaiting him below. And the four narrated to the eight all that they had seen: and so there departed that day from their heart all doubt of Jesus, save [from] Judas Iscariot, who believed nothing. Jesus seated himself at the foot of the mountain, and they ate of the wild fruits, because they had not bread. Then said Andrew: "You have told us many things of the Messiah, therefore of your kindness tell us clearly all." And in like

manner the other disciples besought him.

Accordingly Jesus said: "Everyone that works works for an end in which he finds satisfaction. Wherefore I say to you that God, truly because he is perfect, has not need of satisfaction, seeing that he has satisfaction himself. And so, willing to work, he created before all things the soul of his Messenger, for whom he determined to create the whole, in order that the creatures should find joy and blessedness in God, whence his Messenger should take delight in all his creatures, which he has appointed to be his slaves. And wherefore is this, so save because thus he has willed?

Truly I say to you, that every prophet when he is come has borne to one nation only the mark of the mercy of God. And so their words were not extended save to that people to which they were sent. But the Messenger of God, when he shall come, God shall give to him as it were the seal of his hand, insomuch that he shall carry salvation and mercy to all the nations of the world that shall receive his doctrine. He shall come with power upon the ungodly, and shall destroy idolatry, insomuch that he shall make Satan confounded, for so promised God to Abraham, saying: "Behold, in your seed I will bless all the tribes of the earth; and as you have broken in pieces the idols, O Abraham, even so shall your seed do.""

James answered: "O master, tell us in whom this promise was made, for the Jews say "in Isaac," and the Ishmaelites say "in Ishmael." Jesus answered: David, whose son was he, and of what lineage?" James answered: "Of Isaac, for Isaac was father of Jacob, and Jacob was father of Judah, of whose lineage is David."

Then Jesus said: "And the Messenger of God when he shall come, of what lineage will he be?" The disciples answered: "Of David." Whereupon Jesus said: "You deceive yourselves, for David in spirit calls him lord, saying thus: God said to my lord, sit you on my right hand until I make your enemies your footstool. God shall send forth your rod which shall have lordship in the midst of your enemies. If the Messenger of God whom you call Messiah were son of David, how should David call him lord? Believe me, for truly I say to you, that the promise was made in Ishmael, not in Isaac."

Chapter 44

The disciples said: "O master, it is written in the Book of Moses, that the promise was made in Isaac." Jesus answered with a groan: "It is so written, but Moses did not write it, nor Joshua, but rather our rabbis, who do not fear God! Truly I say to you, that if you consider the words of the angel Gabriel, you shall discover the malice of our scribes and doctors. For the angel said: "Abraham, all the world shall know how God loves you, but how shall the world know the love that you bear to God? Assuredly it is necessary that you do something for love of God." Abraham answered: 'Behold the servant of God, ready to do all that which God shall will.'

Then spoke God, saying to Abraham: "Take your son, your firstborn Ishmael, and come up the mountain to sacrifice him." How is Isaac firstborn, if when Isaac was born Ishmael was seven years old? Then said the disciples: "Clear is the deception of our doctors: therefore tell us you the truth, because we know that you are sent from God." Then answered Jesus: "Truly I say to you, that Satan ever seeks to annul the laws of God; and therefore he with his followers, hypocrites and evil-doers, the former with false doctrine, the latter with lewd living, to day have contaminated almost all things, so that scarcely is the truth found. Woe to the hypocrites! for the praises of this world shall turn for them into insults and torments in hell.

"I therefore say to you that the Messenger of God is a splendor that shall give gladness to nearly all that God has made, for he is adorned with the spirit of understanding and of counsel, the spirit of wisdom and might, the spirit of fear and love, the spirit of prudence and temperance, he is adorned with the spirit of charity and mercy, the spirit of justice and Piety, the spirit of gentleness and patience, which he has received from God three times more than he has given to all his creatures.

O blessed time, when he shall come to the world! Believe me that I have seen him and have done. him reverence, even as every prophet has seen him: seeing that of his spirit God gives to them prophecy. And when I saw him my soul was filled with consolation, saying: "O Muhammad, God be with you, and may he make me worthy to untie, your shoelatchet, for obtaining this I shall be a great prophet and holy one of God." And having said this, Jesus rendered his thanks to God.

Chapter 45

Then came the angel Gabriel to Jesus, and spoke to him in such wise that we also heard his voice, which said: "Arise, and go to Jerusalem!" Accordingly Jesus departed and went up to Jerusalem. And on the sabbath day he entered into the Temple, and began to teach the people. Whereupon the people ran together to the Temple with the high priest and priests, who drew near to Jesus, saying: "O master, it has been said to us that you say evil of us therefore beware lest

some evil befall you." Jesus answered: "Truly I say to you, that I speak evil of the hypocrites therefore if you be hypocrites I speak against you." They answered: "Who is a hypocrite? Tell us plainly."

Jesus said: "Truly I say to you, that he who does a good thing in order that men may see him, even he is a hypocrite, forasmuch as his work penetrates not the heart which men cannot see, and so leaves therein every unclean thought and every filthy lust. Know you who is hypocrite? He who with his tongue serves God, but with his heart serves men. O wretched man! for dying he loses all his reward. For on this matter says the prophet David: "Put not your confidence in princes, [nor] in the children of men, in whom is no salvation, for at death their thoughts perish": no, before death they find themselves deprived of reward, for "man is," as said Job the prophet of

God, "unstable, so that he never continues in one stay." So that if today he praises you, tomorrow he will abuse you, and if today he wills to reward you, tomorrow he will be fain to despoil you. Woe, then, to the hypocrites, because their reward is vain. As God lives, in whose presence I stand, the hypocrite is a robber and commits sacrilege, inasmuch as he makes use of the Law to appear good, and thieves the honor of God, to whom alone pertains praise and honor for ever.

Furthermore I say to you, that the hypocrite has not faith, forasmuch as if he believed that God sees all and with terrible judgment would punish wickedness, he would purify his heart, which, because he has not faith, he keeps full of iniquity. Truly I say to you, that the hypocrite is as a sepulcher, that [on the outside] is white, but within is full of corruption and worms. So then if you, O priests, do the service of God because God has created you and asks it of you, I speak not against you, for you are servants of God, but if you do all for gain, and so buy and sell in the Temple as in a market-place, not regarding that the Temple of God is a house of prayer and not of merchandise, which you convert into a cave of robbers: if you do all to please men, and have put God out of your mind, then cry I against you that you are sons of the devil, and not sons of Abraham, who left his father's house for love of God, and was willing to slay his own son. Woe to you, priests and doctors, if you be such, for God will take away from you the priesthood!"

Chapter 46

Again spoke Jesus, saying: "I set before you an example. There was a householder who planted a vineyard, and made a hedge for it in order that it should not be trampled down of beasts. And in the midst of it he built a press for the wine, and thereupon let it out to husbandman. Whereupon, when the time was come to collect the wine he sent his servants, whom when the husbandman saw, they stoned some and burned some, and others they ripped open with a knife. And this they did many times. Tell me, what will the lord of the vineyard do to the husbandmen" Every one answered: "In evil wise will he make them to perish, and his vineyard will he give to other husbandman." Therefore said Jesus: "Know you not that the vineyard is the House of Israel, and the husbandman are the people of Judah and Jerusalem? Woe to you, for God is wroth with you, having ripped open so many prophets of God, so that at the time of Ahab there was not found one to bury the holy ones of God!" And when he had said this the chief priests wished to seize him, but they feared the common people, which magnified him.

Then Jesus, seeing a woman who from her birth had remained with her head bent toward the ground, said: "Raise your head, O woman, in the name of our God, in order that these may know that I speak truth, and that he wills that I announce it." Then the woman raised herself up whole, magnifying God. The chief of the priests cried out, saying: "This man is not sent of God, seeing he keeps not the sabbath, for today he has healed an infirm person." Jesus answered: "Now tell me, is it not lawful to speak on the sabbath day, and to make prayer for the salvation of others? And who is there among you who, if on the sabbath his ass or his ox fell into the ditch, would not pull him out on the sabbath? Assuredly none. And shall I then have broken the sabbath day by having given health to a daughter of Israel? Surely, here is known your hypocrisy! Oh, how many are there today that fear the smiting of a straw in another's eye, while a beam is ready to cut off their own head! Oh, how many there are that fear an ant, but flinch not of an elephant!" And having said this, he went forth from the Temple. But the priests chafed with rage among themselves, because they were not able to seize him and to work their will upon him, even as their fathers have done against the holy ones of God.

Chapter 47

Jesus went down, in the second year of his prophetic ministry, from Jerusalem, and went to Nain. Whereupon, as he drew near to the gate of the city, the citizens were bearing to the sepulcher the only son of his mother, a widow, over whom every one was weeping. Whereupon, when Jesus had arrived, the men understood how that Jesus, a prophet of Galilee, was come: and so they set themselves to beseech him for the dead man, that he being a prophet should raise him up, which also his disciples did. Then Jesus feared greatly, and turning himself to God, said: "Take me from the world, O Lord, for the world is mad, and they well near call me God!". And having said this, he wept.

Then came the angel Gabriel, and said: "O Jesus, fear not, for God has given you power over every infirmity, insomuch that all that you shall grant in the name of God shall be entirely accomplished." Hereupon Jesus gave a sigh, saying: "Thy will be done, Lord God almighty and merciful. And having said this, he drew near to the mother of the dead, and with pity said to her: "Woman, weep not." And having taken the hand of the dead , he said: "I say to you, young man, in the name of God arise up healed!" Then the boy revived, whereupon all were filled with fear, saying: "God has raised up a great prophet amongst us, and he has visited his people."

Chapter 48

At that time the army of the Romans was in Judea, our country being subject to them for the sins of our forefathers. Now it was the custom of the Romans to call god and to worship him that did any new thing of benefit to the common people. And so [some] of these soldiers finding themselves in Nain, they rebuked now one, now another, saying: "One of your gods has visited you, and you make no account of it. Assuredly if our gods should visit us we would give them all

that we have. And you see how much we fear our gods, since to their images we give the best of all we have."

Satan did so instigate this manner of speaking that he aroused no small sedition among the people of Nain." But Jesus did not tarry in Nain, but turned to go into Capernaum. The discord of Nain was such that some said: "He is our God who has visited us", others said: "God is invisible, so that none has seen him, not even Moses, his servant, therefore it is not God, but rather his son." Others said: "He is not God, nor son of God, for God has not a body to beget anything, but he is a great prophet of God." And so did Satan instigate that, in the third year of the prophetic ministry of Jesus, great ruin to our people was like to arise therefrom. Jesus went into Capernaum: whereupon the citizens, when they knew him, assembled together all the sick folk they had, and placed them in front of the porch of the house where Jesus was lodging with his disciples. And having called Jesus forth, they besought him for the health of them. Then Jesus laid his hands upon each of them, saying: "God of Israel, by your holy name, give health to this sick person." Whereupon each one was healed. On the sabbath Jesus entered into the synagogue, and all the people ran there together to hear him speak.

Chapter 49

The scribe that day read the psalm of David, where says David: When I shall find a time, I will judge uprightly. Then, after the reading of the prophets, arose Jesus, and made sign of silence with his hands, and opening his mouth he spoke thus: "Brethren, you have heard the words spoken by David the prophet, our father, that when he should have found a time he would judge uprightly. I tell you in truth that many judge, in which judgment they fall for no other reason than

because they judge that which is not meet for them, and that which is meet for them they judge before the time. Wherefore the God of our fathers cries to us by his prophet David, saying: Justly judge, O sons of men.

Miserable therefore are those who set themselves at street corners, and do nothing but judge all those who pass by, saying: "That one is fair, this one is ugly, that one is good, this one is bad." Woe to them, because they lift the scepter of his judgment from the hand of God, who says: "I am witness and judge, and my honor I will give to none.'" Truly I tell you that these testify of that which they have not seen nor really heard, and judge without having been constituted judges. Therefore are they abominable on the earth before the eyes of God, who will pass tremendous judgment upon them in the last day.

Woe to you, woe to you who speak good of the evil, and call the evil good, for you condemn as a malefactor God, who is the author of good, and justify as good Satan, who is the origin of all evil. Consider what punishment you shall have, and that it is horrible to fall into the judgment of God, which shall be then upon those who justify the wicked for money, and judge not the cause of the orphans and widows. Truly I say to you, that the devils shall tremble at the judgment of such, so terrible shall it be. You man who are set as a judge, regard no other thing, neither kinsfolk nor friends, neither honor nor gain, but look solely with fear of God to the truth, which you shall seek with greatest diligence, because it will secure you in the judgment of God. But I warn you that without mercy shall he be judged who judges without mercy".

Chapter 50

Tell me, O man, you that judge another man, do you not know that all men had their

origin in the same clay? Do you not know that none is good save God alone? wherefore every man is a liar and a sinner. Believe me man, that if you judge others of a fault your own heart has whereof to be judged. Oh, how dangerous it is to judge! oh, how many have perished by their false judgment! Satan judged man to be more vile than himself therefore he rebelled against God, his creator: whereof he is impenitent, as I have knowledge by speaking with him. Our first parents judged the speech of Satan to be good, therefore they were cast out of paradise, and condemned all their progeny. Truly I say to you, as God lives in whose presence I stand, false judgment is the father of all sins. Forasmuch as none sins without will, and none wills that which he does not know. Woe, therefore, to the sinner who with the judgment judges sin worthy and goodness unworthy, who on that account rejects goodness and chooses sin. Assuredly he shall bear an intolerable punishment when God shall come to judge the world.

Oh, how many have perished through false judgment, and how many have been near to perishing! Pharaoh judged Moses and the people of Israel to be impious, Saul judged David to be worthy of death, Ahab judged Elijah, Nebuchadnezzar the three children who would not worship their lying gods. The two elders judged Susanna, and all the idolatrous princes judged the prophets. Oh, tremendous judgment of God! the judge perishes, the judged is saved. And wherefore this, O man, if not because [in] rashness they falsely judge the innocent?

How nearly then the good approached to ruin by judging falsely, is shown by the brethren of Joseph, who sold him to the Egyptians, by Aaron and Miriam, sister of Moses, who judged their brother. Three friends of Job judged the innocent friend of God, Job. David judged Mephibosheth and Uriah. Cyrus judged Daniel to be meat for the lions and many others, the which were near to their ruin for this. Therefore I say to you, Judge not and you shall not be judged."

And then, Jesus having finished his speech, many forthwith were converted to repentance, bewailing their sins, and they would fain have forsaken all to go with him. But Jesus said: "Remain in your homes, and forsake sin and serve God with fear, and thus shall you be saved, because I am not come to receive service, but rather to serve." And having said thus, he went out of the synagogue and the city, and retired into the desert to pray, because he loved solitude greatly.

Chapter 51

When he had prayed to the Lord, his disciples came to him and said: "O master, two things we would know; one is how you talked with Satan, who nevertheless you say is impenitent; the other is, how God shall come to judge in the day of judgment.' Jesus replied: "Truly I say to you I had compassion on Satan, knowing his fall, and I had compassion on mankind whom he tempts to sin. Therefore I prayed and fasted to our God, who spoke to me by his angel Gabriel: "What seek you, O Jesus, and what is your request?" I answered: "Lord, you know of what evil Satan is the cause, and that through his temptations many perish; he is your creature, Lord, whom you did create, therefore, Lord, have mercy upon him." God answered: "Jesus, behold I will pardon him. Only cause him to say, "Lord, my God, I have sinned, have mercy upon me," and I will pardon him and restore him to his first state." 'I rejoiced greatly," said Jesus, when I heard this, believing that I had made this peace. Therefore I called Satan, who came, saying: "What must I do for you, O Jesus?" I answered: "You shall do it for yourself, O Satan, for I love not your services, but for your good have I called you."

Satan replied: "If you desire not my services neither desire I yours, for I am nobler than you, therefore you are not worthy to serve me you who are clay, while I am spirit." "Let us leave this," I said, "and tell me if it were not well you should return to your first beauty and your first state. You must know that the angel Michael must needs on the day of judgment strike you with the sword of God one hundred thousand times, and each blow will give you the pain of ten hells." Satan replied: "We shall see in that day who can do most; certainly I shall have on my side many angels and most potent idolaters who will trouble God, and he shall know how great a mistake he made to banish me for the sake of a vile [piece of] clay." Then I said: "O Satan, you are infirm in mind, and know not what you say."

Then Satan, in a derisive manner wagged his head, saying: "Come now, let us make up this peace between me and God, and what must be done say you, O Jesus, since you are sound in mind." I answered: "Two words only need be spoken." Satan replied: "What words?" I answered: "These: I have sinned, have mercy on me." Then Satan said: "Now willingly will I make this peace if God will say these words to me." "Now depart from me," I said, "O cursed one, for you are the wicked author of all injustice and sin, but God is just and without any sin." Satan departed shrieking, and said: "It is not so, O Jesus, but you tell a lie to please God." Now consider," said Jesus to his disciples, "how he will find mercy. They answered: "Never, Lord, because he is impenitent. Speak to us now of the judgment of God."

Chapter 52

The judgment day of God will be so dreadful that, truly I say to you, the reprobates would sooner choose ten hells than go to hear God speak in wrath against them against whom all things created will witness. Truly I say to you, that not alone shall the reprobates fear, but the saints and the elect of God, so that Abraham shall not trust in his righteousness, and Job shall have no confidence in his innocence. And what say I? Even the Messenger of God shall fear, for that God, to make known his majesty, shall deprive his Messenger of memory, so that he shall have no remembrance how that God has given him all things. Truly I say to you that, speaking from the heart, I tremble because by the world I shall be called God, and for this I shall have to render an account.

As God lives, in whose presence my soul stands, I am a mortal man as other men are, for although God has placed me as prophet over the House of Israel for the health of the feeble and the correction of sinners, I am the servant of God, and of this you are witness, how I speak against those wicked men who after my departure from the world shall annul the truth of my gospel by the operation of Satan. But I shall return towards the end, and with me shall come Enoch and Elijah, and we will testify against the wicked, whose end shall be accursed."

And having thus spoken, Jesus shed tears, whereat his disciples wept aloud, and lifted their voices, saying: "Pardon O Lord God, and have mercy on your innocent servant." Jesus answered: "Amen, Amen."

Chapter 53

"Before that day shall come," said Jesus, "great destruction shall come upon the world, for there shall be war so cruel and pitiless that the father shall slay the son, and the son shall slay the father by reason of the factions of peoples. Wherefore the cities shall be annihilated, and the country shall become desert. Such pestilences shall come that none shall be found to bear the dead to burial, so that they shall be left as food for beasts. To those who remain upon the earth God shall send such scarcity that bread shall be valued above gold, and they shall eat all manner of unclean things. O miserable age, in which scarce any one shall be heard to say: "I have sinned, have mercy on me, O God", but with horrible voices they shall blaspheme him who is glorious and blessed for ever.

After this, as that day draws near, for fifteen days, shall come every day a horrible sign over the inhabitants of the earth. The first day the sun shall run its course in heaven without light, but black as the dye of cloth, and it shall give groans, as a father who groans for a son near to death. The second day the moon shall be turned into blood, and blood shall come upon the earth like dew. The third day the stars shall be seen to fight among themselves like an army of enemies. The fourth day the stones and rocks shall dash against each other as cruel enemies. The fifth day every plant and herb shall weep blood. The sixth day the sea shall rise without leaving its place to the height of one hundred and fifty cubits, and shall stand all day like a wall. The seventh day it shall on the contrary sink so low as scarcely to be seen. The eighth day the birds and the animals of the earth and of the water shall gather themselves close together, and shall give forth roars and cries. The ninth day there shall be a hailstorm so horrible that it shall kill [such] that scarcely the tenth part of the living shall escape. The tenth day shall come such horrible lightning and thunder [such] that the third part of the mountains shall be split and scorched. The eleventh day every river shall run backwards, and shall run blood and not water. The twelfth day every created thing shall groan and cry. The thirteenth day the heaven shall be rolled up like a book, and it shall rain fire, so that every living thing shall die. The fourteenth day there shall be an earthquake so horrible that the tops of the mountains shall fly through the air like birds, and all the earth shall become a plain. The fifteenth day the holy angels shall die, and God alone shall remain alive, to whom be honor and glory." And having said this, Jesus smote his face with both his hands, and then smote the ground with his head. And having raised his head, he said: "Cursed be every one who shall insert into my sayings that I am the son of God." At these words the disciples fell down as dead, whereupon Jesus lifted them up, saying: 'Let us fear God now, if we would not be affrighted in that day.'

Chapter 54

When these signs be passed, there shall be darkness over the world forty years, God alone being alive, to whom be honor and glory forever. When the forty years have passed, God shall give life to his Messenger, who shall rise again like the sun, but resplendent as a thousand suns. He shall sit, and shall not speak, for he shall be as it were beside himself. God shall raise again the four angels favored of God, who shall seek the Messenger of God, and, having found him, shall
station themselves on the four sides of the place to keep watch upon him. Next shall God give life to all the angels, who shall come like bees circling round the Messenger of God. Next shall God give life to all his prophets, who, following Adam, shall go every one to kiss the hand of the Messenger of God, committing themselves to his protection. Next shall God give life to all the elect, who shall cry out: "O Muhammad be mindful of us!" At whose cries pity shall awake in the
Messenger of God, and he shall consider what he ought to do,

fearing for their salvation.

Next shall God give life to every created thing and they shall return to their former existence, but every one shall besides possess the power of speech. Next shall God give life to all the reprobates, at whose resurrection, by reason of their hideousness, all the creatures of God shall be afraid, and shall cry: "Let not your mercy forsake us, O Lord our God." After this shall God cause Satan to be raised up, at whose aspect every creature shall be as dead, for fear of the horrid form of his appearance. May it please God," said Jesus, "that I behold not that monster on that day. The Messenger of God alone shall not be affrighted by such shapes, because he shall fear God only.

"Then the angel, at the sound of whose trumpet all shall be raised, shall sound his trumpet again, saying: "Come to the judgment, O creatures, for your Creator wills to judge you." Then shall appear in the midst of heaven over the valley of Jehoshaphat; a glittering throne over which shall come a white cloud, whereupon the angels shall cry out: "Blessed be you our God, who has created us and saved us from the fall of Satan." Then the Messenger of God shall fear, for that he shall perceive that none has loved God as he should. For he who would get in change a piece of gold must have sixty mites, wherefore, if he have but one mite he cannot change it. But if the Messenger of God shall fear, what shall the ungodly do who are full of wickedness?"

Chapter 55

The Messenger of God shall go to collect all the prophets, to whom he shall speak praying them to go with him to pray God for the faithful. And every one shall excuse himself for fear, nor, as God lives, would I go there, knowing what I know. Then God, seeing this, shall remind his Messenger how he created all things for love of him, and so his fear shall leave him, and he shall go near to the throne with love and reverence, while the angels sing: "Blessed be your holy name O God, our God."

And when he has drawn near to the throne, God shall open [his mind] to his Messenger, even as a friend to a friend when for a

169

long while they have not met. The first to speak shall be the Messenger of God, who shall say: "I adore and love you, O my God, and with all my heart and soul I give you thanks for that you did vouchsafe to create me to be your servant, and made all for love of me, so that I might love you for all things and in all things and above all things, therefore let all your creatures praise you, O my God." Then God shall say: "We give you thanks, O Lord, and bless your holy name." Truly I say to you, the demons and reprobates with Satan shall then weep so that more water shall flow from the eyes of one of them than is in the river of Jordan. Yet shall they not see God "And God shall speak to his Messenger, saying: "You are welcome, O my faithful servant, therefore ask what you will, for you shall obtain all." The Messenger of God shall answer. "O Lord, I remember that when you did create me, you said that you had willed to make for love of me the world and paradise, and angels and men, that they might glorify you by me your servant. Therefore, Lord God, merciful and just. I pray you that you recollect your promise made to your servant."

And God shall make answer even as a friend who jests with a friend, and shall say: 'Have you witnesses of this, my friend Muhammad?' And with reverence he shall say: "Yes, Lord." Then God shall answer: "Go, call them, O Gabriel," The angel Gabriel shall come to the Messenger of God, and shall say: "Lord who are your 'witnesses?" The Messenger of God shall answer: "They are Adam, Abraham, Ishmael, Moses, David, and Jesus son of Mary?" "Then shall the angel departs and he shall call the aforesaid witnesses, who with fear shall go thither. And when they are present God shall say to them: Remember you that which my Messenger affirms?" They shall reply: "What thing, O Lord?" God shall say: "That I have made all things for love of him, so that all things might praise me by him."

Then every one of them shall answer: "There are with us three witnesses better than we are, O Lord." And God shall reply: "Who are these three witnesses?" Then Moses shall say: "The book that you gave to me is the first"; and David shall say: "The book that

170

you gave to me is the second"; and he who speaks to you shall say: "Lord the whole world, deceived by Satan, that I was your son and your fellow, but the book that you gave me said truly that I am your servant; and that book confesses that which your Messenger affirms." Then shall the Messenger of God speak, and shall say: "Thus says the book that you gave me O Lord." And when the Messenger of God has said this, God shall speak, saying: All that I have now done, I have done in order that every one should know how much I love you." And when he has thus spoken, God shall give to his Messenger a book, in which are written all the names of the elect of God. Wherefore every creature shall do reverence to God, saying: "To you alone O God, be glory and honor, because you have given us to your Messenger.

Chapter 56

God shall open the book in the hand of his Messenger, and his Messenger reading therein shall call all the angels and prophets and all the elect, and on the forehead of each one shall be written the mark of the Messenger of God. And in the book shall be written the glory of paradise.

Then shall each pass to the right hand of God, next to whom shall sit the Messenger of God. and the prophets shall sit near him, and the saints shall sit near the prophets, and the blessed near the saints, and the angel shall then sound the trumpet, and shall call Satan to judgment.

Chapter 57

Then that miserable one shall come, and with greatest contumely shall be accused of every creature. Wherefore God shall call the angel Michael, who shall strike him one hundred thousand times with the sword of God. He shall strike Satan, and every stroke is heavy as ten hells, and he shall be the first to be cast into the abyss. The angel shall call his followers, and they shall in like manner be abused and accused. Wherefore the angel Michael, by commission from God, shall strike some a hundred times, some fifty, some twenty, some ten, some five. And then shall they descend into the abyss, because God shall say to them: "Hell is your dwelling-place, O cursed ones."

After that shall be called to judgment all the unbelievers and reprobates, against whom shall first arise all creatures inferior to man, testifying before God how they have served these men, and how the same have outraged God and his creatures. And the prophets every one shall arise, testifying against them, wherefore they shall be condemned by God to infernal flames. Truly I say to you, that no idle lord or thought shall pass unpunished in that tremendous day. Truly I say to you, that the hair-shirt shall shine like the sun, and every louse a man shall have borne for love of God shall be turned into pearl. O, thrice and four times blessed are the poor, who in true poverty shall have served God from the heart, for in this world are they destitute of worldly cares, and shall therefore be freed from many sins, and in that day they shall not have to render an account of how they have spent the riches of the world, but they shall be rewarded for their patience and their poverty. Truly I say to you, that if the world knew his it would choose the hair-shirt sooner than purple, lice sooner than gold, fasts sooner than feasts.

When all have been examined, God shall say to his Messenger: "Behold, O my friend, their wickedness, how great it has been, for I their creator did employ all created things in their service and in all things have they dishonored me. It is most just, therefore, that I have no mercy on them." The Messenger of God shall answer:, "It is true, Lord, our glorious God, not one of your friends and servants could ask you to have mercy on them, no, I your servant before all ask justice against them."

And he having said these words, all the angels and prophets, with all the elect of God no, why say I the elect? truly I say to you, that spiders and flies, stones and sand shall cry out against the impious, and shall demand justice. Then shall God cause to return to earth every living soul inferior to man, and. he shall send the impious to hell. Who, in going, shall see again that earth, to which dogs and horses and other vile animals shall be reduced. Wherefore shall they say: "O Lord God, cause us also to return to that earth." But that which they ask shall not be granted to them."

Chapter 58

While Jesus was speaking the disciples wept bitterly. And Jesus wept many tears. Then after he had wept, John spoke: "O master, we desire to know two things. The one is, how it is possible that the Messenger of God, who is full of mercy and pity, should have no pity on reprobates that day, seeing that they are of the same clay as himself? The other is, how is it to be understood that the sword of Michael is [as] heavy as ten hells? Is there more than one hell?"

Jesus replied: "Have you not heard what David the prophet says, how the just shall laugh at the destruction of sinners, and shall deride him with these words, saying: I saw the man who put his hope in his strength and his riches, and forgot God. Truly, therefore, I say to you, that Abraham shall deride his father, and Adam [shall deride] all reprobate men: and this shall be because the elect shall rise again so perfect and united to God that they shall not conceive in their minds the smallest] thought against his justice. Each of them shall demand justice, and above all the Messenger of God. As God lives, in whose presence I stand, though now I weep for pity of mankind, on that day I shall demand justice without mercy against those who despise my words, and most of all against those who defile my gospel.

Chapter 59

Hell is one, O my disciples, and in it the damned shall suffer punishment eternally. Yet has it seven rooms or regions, one deeper than the other, and he who goes to the deep shall suffer greater punishment. Yet my words [are] true concerning the sword of the angel Michael, for he that commits but one sin merits hell, and he that commits two sins merits two hells. Therefore in one hell the reprobates shall feel punishment as though they were in ten, or in a hundred or in a

thousand; and the omnipotent God, through his power and by reason of his justice, shall cause Satan to suffer as though he were in ten hundred thousand hells, and the rest each one according to his wickedness."

Then Peter answered: "O master, truly the justice of God is great, and today this discourse has made you sad, therefore, we pray you, rest, and tomorrow tell us what hell is like." Jesus answered: "O Peter, you tell me to rest; O Peter, you do not know what you say, [or] else you would not have spoken thus.

Truly I say to you, that rest in this present life is the poison of piety and the fire which consumes every good work. Have you forgotten how Solomon, God's prophet, with all the prophets, has reproved sloth? It is true that he says: The idle will not work the soil for fear of the cold, therefore in summer shall he beg. [And for this reason] he said: All that your hand can do, do it without rest. And what says Job, the most innocent friend of God: As the bird is born to fly, man is born to work. Truly I say to you, I hate rest above all things."

Chapter 60

Hell is one, and is contrary to paradise, as winter is contrary to summer, and cold to heat. Therefore, he who would describe the misery of hell must have seen the paradise of God's delights. O place accursed by God's justice for the malediction of the faithless and reprobate, of which Job, the friend of God, said: There is no order there, but everlasting fear! And Isaiah the prophet, against the reprobate, says: Their flame shall not be quenched nor their worm die.

And David our father, weeping said: Then lightning and bolts and brimstone and great tempest shall rain upon them." O miserable sinners, how loathsome delicate meats, costly raiment, soft couches, and [the] concord of sweet song shall seem to them! How sick shall raging hunger, burning flames, scorching cinders, and cruel torments with bitter weeping make them!"

And then Jesus uttered a lamentable groan, saying: "Truly, it is better never to have been formed than to suffer such cruel torments, for imagine a man suffering torments in every part of his body, who has no one to show him compassion, but is mocked by everyone; tell me, would not this be great pain?" The disciples

174

answered: "The greatest."

Then Jesus said: "This is a delight [in comparison] to hell. For I tell you in truth, that if God should place in one balance all the pain which all men have suffered in this world and shall suffer till the Day of Judgment, and in the other [balance] one single hour of the pain of hell, the reprobates would without doubt choose the worldly tribulations, for the worldly [tribulations] come from the hand of man, but the others from the hand of devils, who are utterly without compassion.

O what cruel fire they shall give to miserable sinners! O what bitter cold, which yet shall not temper their flames! What gnashing of teeth and sobbing and weeping! For the Jordan has less water than the tears which shall flow from their eyes every moment. Their tongues shall curse all created things, with their. father and mother, and their Creator, who is blessed for ever."

Chapter 61

Having said this, Jesus washed himself, with his disciples, according to the Law of God written in the Book of Moses, and then they prayed. And the disciples, seeing [Jesus] sad did not speak at all to him that day, but each stood terror-struck at his words. Then Jesus, opening his mouth after the evening [prayer], said: * "What father of a family, if he knew that a thief meant to break into his house, would sleep? None surely, for he would watch and stand prepared to slay the thief. Do you not know then that Satan is as a roaring lion that goes about seeking whom he may devour. Thus he seeks to make man sin. Truly I say to you, that if man would act as the merchant he should have no fear in that day, because he would be well prepared.

There was a man who gave money to his neighbors that they might trade with it, and the profit should be divided in a just proportion. And some traded well, so that they doubled the money. But some used the money in the service of the enemy of him who gave them the money, speaking evil of him. Tell me now, when the neighbor shall call the debtors to account how shall the matter go? Assuredly he will reward those who traded well, but against the others his anger shall vent itself in reproaches. And then he will punish them according to the Law. As God lives, in whose presence my soul stands, the neighbor is God, who has given to man all that he has, with life itself, so that, [man] living well in this world, God may have praise, and man the glory of paradise. For those who live well double their money by their example, because sinners, seeing their example, are converted to repentance, wherefore men who live well shall be rewarded with a great reward. But wicked sinners, who by their sins halve what God has given them, by their lives spent in the service of Satan the enemy of God, blaspheming God and giving offence to others tell me what shall be their punishment?" "It shall be without measure," said the disciples.

Chapter 62

Then Jesus said: "He who would live well should take example from the merchant who locks up his shop, and selling guards it day and night with great diligence. And again the things which he buys he is fain to make a profit, for if he perceives that he will lose thereby he will not sell, no, not to his own brother. Thus then should you do, for in truth your soul is a merchant, and the body is the shop: wherefore what it receives from outside, through the senses, is bought and sold by it. And the money is love. See then that with your love you do not sell nor buy the small thought by which d work be all for you cannot profit. But let thought, speech, and love of God, for so shall you find safety in that day.

Truly I say to you, that many make ablutions and go to pray, many fast and give alms, many study and preach to others, whose end is abominable before God, because they cleanse the body and not the heart, they cry with the mouth not with the heart, they abstain from meats, and fill themselves with sins; they give to others things not good for them, in order that they may be held good; they study that they may know to speak, not to work; they preach to others against that which they do themselves, and thus are condemned by their own tongue. As God lives, these do not know God with their hearts; for if they knew him they would love

176

him; and since whatsoever a man has he has received it from God, even so should he spend all for the love of God."

Chapter 63

After certain days Jesus passed near to a city of the Samaritans, and they would not let him enter the city, nor would they sell bread to his disciples. Wherefore said James and John: "Master, may it please you that we pray God that he send down fire from heaven upon these people?"

Jesus answered: "You know not by what spirit you are led, that you so speak. *Remember that God determined to destroy Nineveh because he did not find one who feared God in that city; the which was so wicked that God, having called Jonah; the prophet to send him to that city, he would fain for fear of the people have fled to Tarsus;, wherefore God caused him to be cast into the sea, and received by a fish and cast up near to Nineveh. And he preaching there, that people was converted to repentance, so that God had mercy on them.

Woe to them that call for vengeance; for on themselves it shall come, seeing that every man has in himself cause for the vengeance of God. Now tell me, have you created this city with this people? O madmen that you are, assuredly no. For all creatures united together could not create a single new fly from nothing, and this it is to create. If the blessed God who has created this city now sustains it, why desire you to destroy it? Why did you not say: "May it please you, master, that we pray to the Lord our God that this people may be converted to penitence?"

Assuredly this is the proper act of a disciple of mine, to pray to God for those who do evil. Thus did Abel when his brother Cain, accursed of God, slew him.

Thus did Abraham for Pharaoh, who took from him his wife, and whom therefore, the angel of God did not slay, but only struck with infirmity. Thus did Zechariah when, by decree of the impious king, he was slain in the Temple. Thus did Jeremiah, Isaiah, Ezekiel, Daniel, and David, with all the friends of God and holy prophets. Tell me, if a brother were stricken with frenzy,

177

would you slay him because he spoke evil and struck those who came near him? Assuredly you would not do so, but rather would you endeavor to restore his health with medicines suitable to his infirmity."

Chapter 64

"As God lives, in whose presence my soul stands, a sinner is of infirm mind when he persecutes a man. For tell me, is there anyone who would break his head for the sake of tearing the cloak of his enemy? Now how can he be of sane mind who separates himself from God, the head of his soul, in order that he may injure the body of his enemy?

"Tell me, O man, who is your enemy? Assuredly your body, and every one who praises you. Wherefore if you were of sane mind you would kiss the hand of those who revile you, and present gifts to those who persecute you and strike you much; because, O man because the more that for your sins you are reviled and persecuted in this life the less shall you be in the day of judgment. But tell me, O man, if the saints and prophets of God have been persecuted and defamed by the

world even though they were innocent, what shall be da one to you, O sinner? and if they endured all with patience, praying for their persecutors, what should you do, O man, who are worthy of hell?

Tell me, O my disciples, do you not know that Shimei cursed the servant of God, David the prophet, and threw stones at him? Now what said David to those who would fain have killed Shimei?

"What is it to you, O Joab, that you would kill Shimei? let him curse me, for this is the will of God, who will turn this curse into a blessing." And thus it was, for God saw the patience of David and delivered him from the persecution of his own son, Absalom. Assuredly not a leaf stirs without the will of God. Wherefore, when you are in tribulation do not think of how much you have borne, nor of him who afflicts you; but consider how much for your sins you are worthy to receive at the hand of the devils of hell. You are angry with this city because it would not receive us, nor sell bread to us. Tell me, are these people your slaves? have you given them this city? have you given them their corn? or have you helped them to reap it? Assuredly no, for you are strangers in this land, and poor men. What thing is this then that you say?" The two disciples answered: "Lord, we have sinned, may God have mercy on us." And Jesus answered: "So be it."

Chapter 65

The Passover drew near, so Jesus, with his disciples, went up to Jerusalem. And he went to the pool called Probatica. And the bath was so called because every day the angel of God troubled the water, and whoever first entered the water after its movement was cured of every kind of infirmity. For this reason a great number of sick persons remained beside the pool, which had five porticoes. And Jesus saw there an impotent man, who had been there thirty-eight years sick with a grievous infirmity. So Jesus, knowing this by divine inspiration, had compassion on the sick man, and said to him: "Do you want to be made whole?" The impotent man answered: "Sir, when the angel troubles the waters I do not have anyone to put me into it, but while I am coming [to the water] another steps down before me and enters." Then Jesus lifted up his eyes to heaven and said: "Lord our God, God of our fathers, have mercy upon this impotent man." And having said this, Jesus said: "In God's name, brother, be whole, rise and take up your bed."

Then the impotent man arose, praising God, and carried his bed upon his shoulders, and went to his house praising God. Those who saw him cried: "It is the Sabbath day, it is not lawful for you to carry your bed." He answered: "He that made [me] whole said to me, 'Pick up your bed, and go your way to your home.'" Then asked they him: "Who is he?" He answered: "I do not know his name."

So among themselves they said: "It must have been Jesus the Nazarene." Others said: "No, for [Jesus the Nazarene] is a holy one of God, whereas he who has done this thing is a wicked man, for he causes the sabbath to be broken." And Jesus went into the

Temple, and a great multitude drew near to him to hear his words [for which reason] the priests were consumed with envy.

Chapter 66

One of them came to him, saying: "Good master, you teach well and truly, tell me therefore, what reward shall God give us in paradise?" Jesus answered: "You call me good, and do not know that God alone is good, even as Job, the friend of God, said: A child of a day old is not clean, yes, even the angels are not faultless in God's presence. Moreover he said: The flesh attracts sin, and sucks up iniquity even as a sponge sucks up water. The priest was silent, being confounded. And Jesus said: "Truly I say to you, nothing is more perilous than speech. For so said Solomon: Life and death are in the power of the tongue. "

And he turned to his disciples, and said: "Beware of those who bless you, because they deceive you. With the tongue Satan blessed our first parents, but the outcome of his words was miserable. So did the sages of Egypt bless Pharaoh. So did Goliath bless the Philistines. So did four hundred false prophets bless Ahab, but false were their praises, so that the praised one perished with the praisers. Wherefore not without cause did God say by Isaiah the prophet: O My people, those that bless you deceive you. Woe to you, scribes and Pharisees! Woe to you, priests and Levites! because you have corrupted the sacrifice of the Lord, so that those who come to sacrifice believe that God eats cooked flesh [in the manner of] a man.

Chapter 67

For you say to them: 'Bring your sheep and bulls and lambs to the Temple of your God, and do not eat it all, but give to your God a share of that which he has given you'; and you do not tell them of the origin of sacrifice, that it is for a witness of the life granted to the son of our father Abraham, so that the faith and obedience of our father Abraham, with the promises made to him by God and the blessing given to him, should never be forgotten. But God says by Ezekiel the prophet: Remove from me these your sacrifices, your victims are abominable to me.

For the time draws near when that shall be done of which our God spoke by Hosea the prophet, saying: I will call chosen the people not chosen. And as he says in Ezekiel the prophet: God shall make a new covenant with his people, not according to the covenant which he gave to your fathers, which they did nott and he shall take from them a heart of stone, and give them a new heart" : and all this shall be because you do not walk now in his Law. And you have the key and do not open: rather you block the road for those who would walk in it." The priest was departing to report everything to the high priest, who stood near the sanctuary, but Jesus said: "Stay, for I will answer your question."

Chapter 68

You ask me to tell you what God will give us in paradise. Truly I say to you that those who think of the wages do not love the master. A shepherd who has a flock of sheep, when he sees the wolf coming, prepares to defend them, contrariwise, the hireling when he sees the wolf leaves the sheep and flees. As God lives, in whose presence I stand, if the God of our fathers were your God you would not have thought of saying: "What will God give me?" But you would have said, as did David his prophet: What shall I give to God for all that he has given to me?

"I will speak to you by a parable that you may understand. There was a king who found by the wayside a man stripped by thieves,, who had wounded him to death. And he had compassion on him, and commanded his slaves to bear that man to the city and tend him, and this they did with all diligence. And the king conceived a great love for the sick man, so that he gave him his own daughter in marriage, and made him his heir. Now assuredly this king was most merciful; but the man beat the slaves, despised the medicines, abused his wife, spoke evil of the king, and caused his vassals to rebel against him. And when the king required any service, he was wont to say: "What will the king give me as reward?" Now when the king heard this, what did he do to so impious a man?" They all replied: "Woe to him, for the king deprived him of all, and cruelly punished him."

Then Jesus said: "O priests, and scribes, and Pharisees, and you high-priest that hear my voice, I proclaim to you what God has said to you by his prophet Isaiah: "I have nourished slaves and exalted them, but they have despised me." "The king is our God, who found Israel in this world full of miseries, and gave him therefore to his servants Joseph, Moses and Aaron, who tended him. And our God conceived such love for him that for the sake of the people of Israel he smote Egypt, drowned Pharaoh, and discomfited an hundred and twenty kings of the Canaanites and Madianites, he gave him his laws, making him heir of all that [land] wherein our people dwells.

"But how does Israel bear himself? How many prophets has he slain, how many prophecies has he contaminated, how has he violated the Law of God: how many for that cause have departed from God and gone to serve idols, through your offence, O priests! And how do you dishonor God with your manner of life! And now you ask me: "What will God give us in paradise?" You ought to have asked me: What will be the punishment that God will give you in hell, and then what you ought to do for true penitence in order that God may have mercy on you: for this I can tell you, and to this end am I sent to you."

Chapter 69

As God lives, in whose presence I stand, you will not receive adulation from me, but truth. Wherefore I say to you, repent and turn to God even as our fathers did after sinning, and harden not your heart. The priests were consumed with rage at this speech, but for fear of the common people they spoke not a word.

And Jesus continued, saying: "O doctors, O scribes, O Pharisees, O priests, tell me. You desire horses like knights, but you desire not to go forth to war: you desire fair clothing like women, but you desire not to spin and nurture children; you desire the fruits of the field, and you desire not to cultivate the Earth; you desire the fishes of the sea, but you desire not to go a fishing; you desire honor as citizens, but you desire not the burden of the republic; and you desire tithes and first fruits as priests, but you desire not to serve God in truth. What then shall God do with you, seeing you desire here every good without any evil? Truly I say to you that God will give you a place where you will have every evil without any good."

And when Jesus had said this, there was brought to him a demoniac who could not speak nor see, and was deprived of hearing. Whereupon Jesus, seeing their faith, raised his eyes to heaven and said: "Lord God of our fathers, have mercy on this sick man and give him health, in order that this people may know that you have sent me."

And having said this Jesus commanded the spirit to depart, saying: "In the power of the name of God our Lord, depart, evil one, from the man. The spirit departed and the dumb man spoke, and saw with his eyes. Whereupon every one was filled with fear, but the scribes said: "In the power of Beelzebub, prince of the demons, he casts out the demons."

Then Jesus said: "Every kingdom divided against itself destroys itself, and house falls upon house. If in the power of Satan, Satan be cast out, how shall his kingdom stand? And if your sons cast out Satan with the scripture that Solomon the prophet gave them, they testify that I cast out Satan in the power of God. As God lives, blasphemy against the Holy Spirit is without remission in this and in the other world, because the wicked man of his own will reprobates himself, knowing the reprobation."

And having said this Jesus went out of the Temple. And the common people magnified him, for they brought all the sick folk whom they could gather together, and Jesus having made prayer gave to all their health: whereupon on that day in Jerusalem the Roman soldiery, by the working of Satan, began to stir up the common people, saying that Jesus was the God of Israel, who was come to visit his people.

Chapter 70

Jesus departed from Jerusalem after the Passover, and entered into the borders of Caesarea Philippi. Whereupon, the angel Gabriel having told him of the sedition which was beginning among the common people, he asked his disciples, saying: "What do men say of me?" They said: "Some say that you are Elijah, others Jeremiah, and others one of the old prophets." Jesus answered: "And you, what say you that I am?" Peter answered: "You are Christ, son of God."

Then was Jesus angry, and with anger rebuked him, saying: "Be gone and depart from me, because you are the devil and seek to cause me offences And he threatened the eleven, saying: "Woe to you if you believe this, for I have won from God a great curse against those who believe this." And he was fain to cast away Peter, whereupon the eleven besought Jesus for him, who cast him not away, but again rebuked him saying: "Beware that never again you say such words, because God would reprobate you!" Peter wept and said: "Lord, I have spoken foolishly, beseech God that he pardon me."

Then Jesus said: "If our God willed not to show himself to Moses his servant, nor to Elijah whom he so loved, nor to any prophet, will you think that God should show himself to this faithless generation? But know you not that God has created all things of nothing with one single word, and all men have had their origin out of a piece of clay? Now, how shall God have likeness to man? Woe to those who suffer themselves to be deceived of Satan!" And having said this, Jesus besought God for Peter, the eleven and Peter weeping, and saying: "So be it, so be it, O blessed Lord our God." Afterwards Jesus departed and went into Galilee, in order that this vain opinion which the common folk began to hold concerning him might be extinguished.

Chapter 71

Jesus having arrived in his own country, it was spread through all the region of Galilee how that Jesus the prophet was come to Nazareth. Whereupon with diligence sought they the sick and brought them to him, beseeching him that he would touch them with his hands. And so great was the multitude that a certain rich man, sick of the palsy, not being able to get himself carried through the door, had himself carried up to the roof of the house in which Jesus was, and having caused the roof to be uncovered, had himself let down by sheets in front of Jesus. Jesus stood for a moment in hesitation, and then he said: "Fear not, brother, for your sins are forgiven you." Every one was offended hearing this, and they said: "And who is this who forgives sins?"

Then Jesus said: "As God lives, I am not able to forgive sins, nor is any man, but God alone forgives. But as servant of God I can beseech him for the sins of others: and so I have besought him for this sick man, and I am sure that God has heard my prayer. Wherefore, that you may know the truth, I say to this sick man: "In the name of the God of our fathers, the God of Abraham and his sons, rise up healed!"" And when Jesus had said this the sick man rose up healed, and glorified God.

Then the common people besought Jesus that he would beseech God for the sick who stood outside. Whereupon Jesus went out to them, and, having lifted up his hands, said: "Lord God of hosts, the living God, the true God, the holy God, that never will die, having mercy upon them!" Whereupon every one answered: "Amen.". And this having been said, Jesus laid his hands upon the sick folk, and they all received their health. Thereupon they magnified God, saying: "God has visited us by his prophet, and a great prophet has God sent to us."

Chapter 72

At night Jesus spoke in secret with his disciples, saying: "Truly I say to you that Satan desires to sift you as wheat, but I have besought God for you, and there shall not perish of you save he that lays snares for me." And this he said of Judas, because the angel Gabriel said to him how that Judas had hand with the priests, and reported to them all that Jesus spoke.

With tears drew near to Jesus he who writes this saying: "O master, tell me, who is he that should betray you?" Jesus answered, saying: "O Barnabas, this is not the hour for you to know him, but soon will be wicked one reveal himself, because I shall depart from the world." Then wept the apostles, saying: "O master, wherefore will you forsake us? It is much better that we should die than be forsaken of you!"

Jesus answered: "Let not your heart be troubled, neither be you fearful: for I have not created you, but God our creator who has created you will protect you. As for me, I am now come to the world to prepare the way for the Messenger of God, who shall bring salvation to the world. But beware that you be not deceived, for many false prophets shall come, who shall take my words and contaminate my gospel."

Then said Andrew: "Master tell us some sign, that we may know him." Jesus answered: "He will not come in your time, but will come some years after you, when my gospel shall be annulled, insomuch that there shall be scarcely thirty faithful. At that time God will have mercy on the world, and so he will send his Messenger, over whose head will rest a white cloud, whereby he shall be known of one elect of God, and shall be by him manifested to the world. He shall come with great power against the ungodly, and shall destroy idolatry upon the earth. And it rejoices me because that through him our God shall be known and glorified, and I shall be known to be true, and he will execute vengeance against those who shall say that I am more than man. Truly I say to you that the moon shall minister sleep to him in his boyhood, and when he shall be grown up he shall take her in his hands. Let the world beware of casting him out because he shall slay the idolaters, for many more were slain by Moses, the servant of God, and Joshua, who spared not the cities which they burnt, and slew the children, for to an old wound one applies fire. "He shall come with truth more clear than that of all the prophets, and shall reprove him who use the world amiss. The towers of the city of our father shall greet one another for joy: and so when idolatry shall be seen to fall to the ground and confess me a man like other men, truly I say to you the Messenger of God shall be come."

Chapter 73

"Truly I say to you, that if Satan shall try whether you be friends of God; because no one assails his own cities if Satan should have his will over you he would suffer you to glide at your own pleasure, but because he knows that you be enemies to him he will do every violence to make you perish. But fear not you, for he will be against you as a dog that is chained, because God has heard my prayer." John answered: "O master, not only for us, but for them that shall

believe the gospel, tell us how the ancient tempter lays wait for man."

Jesus answered: "In four ways tempts that wicked one. The first is when he tempts by himself, with thoughts. The second is when he tempts with words and deeds by means of his servants; the third is when he tempts with false doctrine; the fourth is when he tempts with false visions. Now how cautious ought men to be, and all the more according as he has in his favor the flesh of man, which loves sin as he who has fever loves water. Truly I say to you, that if a man fear God he shall have victory over all, as says David his prophet: "God shall give his angels charge over you, who shall keep your ways, so that the devil shall not cause you to stumble. A thousand shall fall on your left hand, and ten thousand on your right hand, so that they shall not come near you."

"Furthermore, our God with great love promised to us by the same David to keep us, saying: "I give to you understanding, which shall teach you, and in your ways wherein you shall walk I will cause My eye to rest upon you." "But what shall I say? He has said by Isaiah: "Can a mother forget the child of her womb? But I say to you, that when she forget, I will not forget you." "Tell me, then, who shall fear Satan, having for guard the angels and for protection the living God? Nevertheless, it is necessary, as says the prophet Solomon, that "You, my son, that are come to fear the Lord, prepare your soul for temptations." Truly I say to you, that a man ought to do as the banker who examines money, examining his thoughts, that he sin not against God his creator."

Chapter 74

There have been and are in the world men who hold not thought for sin [and] who are in the greatest error. Tell me, how [did] Satan sin? It is certain that he sinned in the thought he was more worthy than man. Solomon sinned in thinking to invite all the creatures of God to a feast, [so] a fish corrected him by eating all that he had prepared. Not without cause, our father David says, that to ascend in one's heart sets one in the valley of tears. And why does God cry by his prophet Isaiah, saying: Take away your evil thoughts from my eyes? And to what purpose [does] Solomon say, With all your keeping, keep your heart?"

As God lives, in whose presence my soul stands, all [scripture speaks] against the evil thoughts with which sin is committed, for without thinking it is not possible to sin. Now tell me, when the husbandman plants the vineyard does he set the plants deep? Assuredly yes. Satan does [the same]. In planting sin [he] does not stop at the eye or the ear, but passes into the heart, which is God's dwelling, as Moses his servant, [said]: I will dwell in them, in order that they may walk in my Law.

Now tell me, if Herod the king gave you a house to keep in which he desired to dwell, would you let Pilate, his enemy, enter there or place his goods in it? Surely not. Then how much less ought you let Satan enter into your heart, or place his thoughts [in your heart]. Our God has given you your heart to keep, which is his dwelling.

Observe, therefore, [how] the banker considers [his] money. [He considers] whether the image of Caesar is right, whether the silver is good or false, and whether it is of due weight. He turns it over much in his hand. Ah, mad world! How prudent you are in your business; in the last day you will reprove and judge the servants of God of negligence and carelessness, for without doubt your servants are more prudent than the servants of God. Tell me, now, who is he who examines a thought as the banker a silver coin? No one."

Chapter 75

Then said James: "O master, how is the examination of a thought like to [that of] a coin?" Jesus answered: "The good silver in the thought is piety, because every impious thought comes of the devil. The right image is the example of the holy ones and

188

prophets, which we ought to follow, and the weight of the thought is the love of God by which all ought to be done. Whereupon the enemy will bring there impious thoughts against your neighbor, [thoughts] conformed to the world, to corrupt the flesh, [thoughts] of earthly love to corrupt the love of God." Bartholomew answered: "O master, what ought we to do to think little, in order that we may not !fall into temptation?" Jesus answered: "Two things are necessary for you. The first is to exercise yourselves much, and the second is to talk little: for idleness is a sink wherein is gathered every unclean thought, and too much talking is a sponge which picks up iniquities. It is, therefore, necessary not only your working should hold the body occupied, but also that the soul be occupied with prayer. For it needs never to cease from prayer.

"I tell you for an example: There was a man who paid ill, wherefore none that knew him would go to till his fields. Whereupon he, like a wicked man, said: 'I will go to the market-place to find idle ones who are doing nothing, and will therefore come to till my vines.' This man went forth from his house, and found many strangers who were standing in idleness, and had no money. To them he spoke, and led them to his vineyard. But truly none that knew him and had work for his hands went thither. He is Satan, that one who pays ill, for he gives labor, and man receives for it the eternal fires in his service. Wherefore he has gone forth from paradise, and goes in search of laborers. Assuredly he sets to his labors those who stand in idleness whoever they be, but much more those who do not know him. It is not in any wise enough for any one to know evil in order to escape it, but it is a duty to work at good in order to overcome it."

Chapter 76

I tell you for an example. There was a man who had three vineyards, which he let out to three husbandman. Because the first knew not how to cultivate the vineyard the vineyard brought forth only leaves. The second taught the third how the vines ought to be cultivated, and he most excellently hearkened to his words;

and he cultivated his, as he told him, insomuch that the vineyard of the third bore much. But the second left his vineyard uncultivated, spending his time solely in talking. When the time was come for paying the rent to the lord of the vineyard, the first said: "Lord, I know not how your vineyard ought to be cultivated: therefore I have not received any fruit this year." The lord answered: "O fool, do you dwell alone in the world, that you has not asked counsel of my second vinedresser, who knows well how to cultivate the land? Certain it is that you shall pay me."

And having said this he condemned him to work in prison until he should pay his lord; who moved with pity at his simplicity liberated him, saying: "Be gone, for I will not that you work longer at my vineyard, it is enough for you that I give you your debt." The second came, to whom the lord said: "Welcome, my vinedresser! Where are the fruits that you owe me? Assuredly, since you know well how to prune the vines, the vineyard that I let out to you must needs have borne much fruit." The second answered: "O lord, your vineyard is backward because I have not pruned the wood nor worked up the soil, but the vineyard has not borne fruit, so I cannot pay you." Whereupon the lord called the third and with wonder said: "You said to me that this man, to whom I let out the second vineyard, taught you perfectly to cultivate the vineyard which I let out to you. How then can it be that the vineyard I let out to him should not have borne fruit, seeing it is all one soil."

The third answered: "Lord, the vines are not cultivated by talking only, but he needs must sweat a shirt every day who wills to make it bring forth its fruit. And how shall your vineyard of your vinedresser bear fruit, O lord, if he does nothing but waste the time in talking? Sure it is, O lord, that if he had put into practice his own words, [while] I who cannot talk so much have given you the rent for two years, he would have given you the rent of the vineyard for five years." The lord was wroth, and said with scorn to the vinedresser, "And so you have wrought a great work in not cutting away the wood and leveling the vineyard, wherefore there is owing to you a great reward!" And having called his servants he had him beaten without any mercy. And then he put him into prison under the keeping of a cruel servant who beat him every day, and never was willing to set him free for prayers of his friends."

Chapter 77

Truly I say to you, that on the day of judgment many shall say to God: "Lord, we have preached and taught by your Law." Against them even the stones shall cry out, saying: "When you preached to others, with your own tongue you condemned yourselves, O workers of iniquity." "As God lives," said Jesus, "he who knows the truth and works the contrary shall be punished with such grievous penalty that Satan shall almost have compassion on him. Tell me, now has our God given us the Law for knowing or for working? Truly I say to you, that all knowledge has for end that wisdom which works all it knows. "Tell me, if one were sitting at table and with his eyes beheld delicate meats, but with his hands should choose unclean things and eat those, would not he be mad?" "Yes, assuredly," said the disciples.

Then Jesus said: "O mad beyond all madmen are you, O man, that with your understanding know heaven, and with your hands choose earth; with your understanding know God, and with your affection desire the world; with your understanding know the delights of paradise, and with your works choose the miseries of hell. Brave soldier, that leaves the sword and carries the scabbard to fight! Now, know you not that he who walks by night desires light, not only to see the light, but rather to see the good road, in order that he may pass safely to the inn?

O miserable world, to be a thousand times despised and abhorred! since our God by his holy prophets has ever willed to grant it to know the way to go to his country and his rest: but you, wicked one, not only wiliest not to go, but, which is worse, have despised the light! True is the proverb of the camel, that it likes not clear water to drink, because it desires not to see its own ugly face. So does the ungodly who works ill, for he hates the light lest his evil works should be known. But he who receives wisdom, and not only works not well, but, which is worse, employs it for evil, is like to him who should use the gifts as instruments to slay the giver."

Chapter 78

Truly I say to you, that God had not compassion on the fall of Satan, but yet [had compassion on the fall of Adam. And let this suffice you to know the unhappy condition of him who knows good and does evil." Then said Andrew: "O master, it is a good thing to leave learning aside, so as not to fall into such condition." Jesus answered: "If the world is good without the sun, man without eyes, and the soul without understanding, then is it good not to know. Truly I say to you, that bread is not so good for the temporal life as is learning for the eternal life. Know you not that it is a precept of God to learn? For thus says God: Ask of your elders, and they shall teach you. And of the Law says God: See that my precept be before your eyes, and when you sit down, and when you walk, and at all times meditate thereon. Whether, then, it is good not to learn, you may now know. Oh, unhappy he who despises wisdom, for he is sure to lose eternal life."

James answered: "O master, we know that Job learned not from a master, nor Abraham, nevertheless they became holy ones and prophets." Jesus answered: "Truly I say to you, that he who is of the bridegroom's house does not need to be invited to the marriage, because he dwells in the house where the marriage is held, but they that are far from the house. Now know you not that the prophets of God are in the house of God's grace and mercy, and so have the Law of God manifest in them: as David our father says on this matter: The Law of his God is in his heart, therefore his path shall not be dug up.

Truly I say to you that our God in creating man not only created him righteous, but inserted in his heart a light that should show to him that it is fitting to serve God. Wherefore, even if this light be darkened after sin, yet is it not extinguished. For every nation has this desire to serve God, though they have lost God and serve false and lying gods. Accordingly it is necessary that a man be taught of the prophets of God, for they have clear the light to teach the way to go to paradise, our country, by serving God well: just as it is necessary that he who has his eyes diseased should be guided and helped."

Chapter 79

James answered: "And how shall the prophets teach us if they are dead, and how shall he be taught who has not knowledge of the prophets?" Jesus answered: "Their doctrine is written down, so that it ought to be studied, for [the writing] is to you for a prophet. Truly, truly, I say to you that he who despises the prophecy despises not only the prophet, but despises also God who has sent the prophet. But concerning such as know not the prophet, as are the nations, I tell you that if there shall live in those regions any man who lives as his heart shall show him, not doing to others that which he would not receive from others, and giving to his neighbor that which he would receive from others, such a man shall not be forsaken of the mercy of God.

Wherefore at death, if not sooner, God will show him and give him his Law with mercy. Perhaps you think that God has given the Law for love of the Law? Assuredly this is not true, but rather has God given his Law in order that man might work good for love of God. And so if God shall find a man who for love of him works good, shall he perhaps despise him? No, surely, but rather will he love him more than those to whom he has given the Law. I tell you for an example: There was a man who had great possessions, and in his territory he had desert land that only bore unfruitful things. And so, as he was walking out one day through such desert land, he found among such unfruitful plants a plant that had delicate fruits. Whereupon this man said: "Now how does this plant here bear these so delicate fruits? Assuredly I will not that it be cut down and put on the fire with the rest." And having called his servants he made them dig it up and set it in his garden. Even so, I tell you, that our God shall preserve from the flames of hell those who work righteousness, wheresoever they be."

Chapter 80

"Tell me, where dwelt Job but in Uz among idolaters? And at the
time of the flood, how writes Moses? Tell me. He says: "Noah
truly found grace before God." Our father Abraham had a father
without faith, for he made and worshipped false idols. Lot abode
among the most wicked men on earth. Daniel as a child, with
Ananias, Azarias, and Misael, were taken captive by
Nebuchadnezzar in such wise that they were but two years old
when they were taken; and they were nurtured among the
multitude of idolatrous servants. As God lives, even as the fire
burns dry things and converts them into fire, making no
difference between olive and cypress and palm, even so our God
has mercy on every one that works righteously, making no
difference between Jew, Scythian, Greek, or Ishmaelite.
But let not your heart stop there, O James, because where God has
sent the prophet it is necessary entirely to deny your own
judgment and to follow the prophet, and not to say: 'Why says he
thus? Why does he thus forbid and command?' But say: 'Thus
God wills. Thus God commands.' Now what said God to Moses
when Israel despised Moses? They have not despised you, but
they have despised me. Truly I say to you, that man ought to
spend all the time of his life not in learning how to speak or to
read, but in learning how to work well. Now tell me, who is that
servant of Herod who would not study to please him by serving
him with all diligence? Woe to the world that studies only to
please a body that is clay and dung, and studies not but forgets
the service of God who has made all things, who is blessed for
evermore."

Chapter 81

Tell me, would it have been a great sin of the priests if when they
were carrying the ark of the testimony of God they had let it fall to
the ground? The disciples trembled hearing this, for they knew
that God slew Uzzah for having wrongly touched the ark of God.
And they said: "Most grievous would be such a sin." Then Jesus

said: "As God lives, it is a greater sin to forget the word of God, wherewith he made all things, whereby he offers you eternal life." And having said this Jesus made prayer, and after the prayer he said: "Tomorrow we needs must pass into Samaria, for so has said to me the holy angel of God."

Early on the morning of a certain day, Jesus arrived near the well which Jacob made and gave to Joseph his son. Whereupon Jesus being wearied with the journey, sent his disciples to the city to buy food. And so he sat himself down by the well, upon the stone of the well. And, lo, a woman of Samaria comes to the well to draw water. Jesus says to the woman: "Give me to drink." The woman answered: "Now, are you not ashamed that you, being an Hebrew, ask drink of me which am a Samaritan woman?" Jesus answered: "O woman, if you knew who he is that asks you for drink, perhaps you would have asked of him for drink." The woman answered: "Now how should you give me to drink, seeing you have no vessel to draw the water, nor rope, and the well is deep?"

Jesus answered: "O woman, whoever drinks of the water of this well, thirst comes to him again, but whosoever drinks of the water that I give has thirst no more, but to them that have thirst give they to drink, insomuch that they come to eternal life." Then said the woman: "O Lord, give me of this your water." Jesus answered: "Go call your husband, and to both of you I will give to drink." The woman said: "I have no husband." Jesus answered: "Well have you said the truth, for you have had five husbands, and he whom you now have is not your husband."

The woman was confounded hearing this, and said: "Lord, hereby perceive I that you are a prophet, therefore tell me, I pray: the Hebrews make prayer on mount Sion in the Temple built by Solomon in Jerusalem, and say that there and nowhere else [men] find grace and mercy of God. And our people worship on these mountains, and say that only on the mountains of Samaria ought worship to be made. Who are the true worshippers?"

Chapter 82

Then Jesus gave a sigh and wept, saying: "Woe to you, Judea, for you glory, saying: "The Temple of the Lord, the Temple of the Lord," and live as though there were no God, given over wholly to the pleasures and gains of the world, for this woman in the day of judgment shall condemn you to hell, for this woman seeks to know how to find grace and mercy before God."

And turning to the woman he said: "O woman, you Samaritans worship that which you know not, but we Hebrews worship that which we know. Truly, I say to you, that God is spirit and truth, and so in spirit and in truth must he be worshipped. For the promise of God was made in Jerusalem, in the Temple of Solomon, and not elsewhere. But believe me, a time will come that God will give his mercy in another city, and in every place it will be possible to worship him in truth. And God in every place will have accepted true prayer with mercy.

The woman answered: "We look for the Messiah, when he comes he will teach us." Jesus answered: "Know you, woman, that the Messiah must come?" *She answered: "Yes, Lord." Then Jesus rejoiced, and said: "So far as I see, O woman, you are faithful: know therefore that in the faith of the Messiah shall be saved every one that is elect of God, therefore it is necessary that you know the coming of the Messiah." The woman said: "O Lord, perhaps you are the Messiah." Jesus answered: "I am indeed sent to the House of Israel as a prophet of salvation, but after me shall come the Messiah, sent of God to all the world, for whom God has made the world.

And then through all the world will God be worshipped, and mercy received, insomuch that the year of jubilee, which now comes every hundred years, shall by the Messiah be reduced to every year in every place." Then the woman left her waterpot and ran to the city to announce all that she had heard from Jesus.

Chapter 83

Whilst the woman was talking with Jesus came his disciples, and marveled that Jesus was speaking so with a woman. Yet no one said to him: "Why speak you thus with a Samaritan woman?"

Whereupon, when the woman was departed, they said: "Master, come and eat." Jesus answered: "I must eat other food." Then said the disciples one to another: "Perhaps some wayfarer has spoken with Jesus and has gone to find him food." And they questioned him who writes this, saying: "Has there been any one here, O Barnabas, who might have brought food to the master?" Then answered he who writes: "There has not been here any other than the woman whom you saw, who brought this empty vessel to fill it with water." Then the disciples stood amazed, awaiting the issue of the words of Jesus. Whereupon Jesus said: "You know not that the true food is to do the will of God, because it is not bread that sustains man and gives him life, but rather the word of God, by his will. And so for this reason the holy angels eat not, but live nourished only by the will of God. And thus we, Moses and Elijah and yet another, have been forty days and forty nights; without any food."

And lifting up his eyes, Jesus said: "How far off is the harvest?" The disciples answered: "Three months." Jesus said: "Look now, how the mountain is white with corn, truly I say to you, that today there is a great harvest to be reaped." And then he pointed to the multitude who had come to see him. For the woman having entered into the city had moved all the city, saying: "O men, come and see a new prophet sent of God to the House of Israel", and she recounted to them all that she had heard from Jesus. When they were come thither they besought Jesus to abide with them, and he entered into the city and abode there two days, healing all the sick, and teaching concerning the kingdom of God. Then said the citizens to the woman: "We believe more in his words and miracles than we do in what you said, for he is indeed a holy one of God, a prophet sent for the salvation of those that shall believe on him."

After the prayer of midnight, the disciples came near to Jesus, and he said to them: "This night shall be in the time of the Messiah, Messenger of God, the jubilee every year that now comes every hundred years. Therefore I will not that we sleep, but let us make prayer, bowing our head a hundred times, doing reverence to our God, mighty and merciful, who is blessed for evermore, and therefore each time let us say: "I confess you our God alone, that has not had beginning, nor shall ever have end; for by your mercy gave you to all things their beginning, and by your justice you shall give to all an end; that has no likeness among men, because in your infinite goodness you are not subject to motion nor to any accident. Have mercy on us, for you have created us, and we are the works of your hand.""

Chapter 84

Having made the prayer, Jesus said: "Let us give thanks to God because he has given to us this night great mercy; for that he has made to come back the time that needs must pass in the night, in that we have made prayer in union with the Messenger of God. And I have heard his voice." The disciples rejoiced greatly at hearing this, and said: "Master, teach us some precepts this night." Then Jesus said: "Have you ever seen dung mixed with balsam?" They answered: "No, Lord, for no one is so mad as to do this thing."

"Now I tell you that there be in the world greater madmen, said Jesus, "because with the service of God they mingle the service of the world. So much so that many of blameless life have been deceived of Satan, and while praying have mingled with their prayer worldly business, whereupon they have become at that time abominable in the sight of God. Tell me, when you wash yourselves for prayer, do you take care that no unclean thing touch you? Yes, assuredly. But what do you when you are making prayer? You wash your soul from sins through the mercy of God. Would you be willing then, while you are making prayer, to speak of worldly things? Take care not to do so, for every worldly word becomes dung of the devil upon the soul of him that speaks." Then the disciples trembled, because he spoke with vehemence of spirit, and they said: "O master, what shall we do if when we are making prayer a friend shall come to speak to us?" Jesus answered: "Suffer him to wait, and finish the prayer."

Bartholomew said;: "But what if he shall be offended and go his way, when he see that we speak not with him?" Jesus answered: "If he shall be offended, believe me he will not be a friend of yours nor a believer, but rather an unbeliever and a companion of Satan. Tell me, if you went to speak with a stable boy of Herod;, and found him speaking into Herod's ears, would you be offended if he made you to wait?' No, assuredly, but you would be comforted at seeing your friend in favor with the king. Is this true?" said Jesus.

The disciples answered: "It is most true." Then Jesus said: "Truly I say to you, that every one when he prays speaks with God. Is it then right that you should leave speaking with God in order to speak with man? Is it right that your friend should for this cause be offended, because you have more reverence for God than for him? Believe me that if he shall be offended when you make him wait, he is a good servant of the evil. For this desires the devil, that God should be forsaken for man. As God lives, in every good work he that fears God ought to separate himself from the works of the world, so as not to corrupt the good work."

Chapter 85

"When a man works ill or talks ill, if one go to correct him, and hinder such work, what does such an one?" said Jesus. The disciples answered: "He does well, because he serves God, who always seeks to hinder evil, even as the sun that always seeks to chase away the darkness." Jesus said: "And I tell you on the contrary that when one works well or, speaks well, whosoever seeks to hinder him, under pretext of aught that is not better, he serves the devil, no, he even becomes his companion. For the devil attends to nothing else but to hinder every good thing. "But what shall I say to you now? I will say to you as said Solomon, the prophet, holy one, and friend of God: "Of a thousand whom you know, one be your friend."

Then said Matthew: "Then shall we not be able to love any one." Jesus answered: "Truly I say to you, that it is not lawful for you to hate anything save only sin: insomuch that you cannot hate even

Satan as creature of God, but rather as enemy of God. Know you wherefore? I will tell you; because he is a creature of God, and all that God has created is good and perfect. Accordingly, whoever hates the creature hates also the creator. But the friend is a singular thing, that is not easily found, but is easily lost. For the friend will not suffer contradiction against him whom he supremely loves. Beware, be you cautious, and choose not for friend one who loves not him whom you love. Know you what friend means? Friend means nothing but physician of the soul; And so, just as one rarely finds a good physician who knows the sicknesses and understands to apply the medicines thereto, so also are friends rare who know the faults and understand how to guide to good. But herein is an evil, that there are many who have friends that feign not to see the faults of their friend, others excuse them, others defend them under earthly pretext, and, what is worse, there are friends who invite and aid their friend to err, whose end shall be like to their villainy. Beware that you receive not such men for friends, for that in truth they are enemies and slayers of the soul.

Chapter 86

"Let your friend be such that, even as he wills to correct you, so he may receive correction; and even as he wills that you should leave all things for love of God, even so again it may content him that you forsake him for the service of God. "But tell me, if a man know not how to love God how shall he know how to love himself; and how shall he know how to love others, not knowing how to love himself? Assuredly this is impossible. Therefore when you choose you one for friend (for truly he is supremely poor who has no friend at all), see that you consider first, not his fine lineage, not his fine family, not his fine house, not his fine clothing, not his fine person, nor yet his fine words, for you shall be easily deceived.

But look how he fears God, how he despises earthly things, how he loves good works, and above all how he hates his own flesh, and so shall you easily find the true friend: if he above all things shall fear God, and shall despise the vanities of the world; if he shall be always occupied in good works, and shall hate his own body as a cruel enemy. Nor yet shall you love such a friend in such wise that your love stay in him, for [so] shall you be an idolater. But love him as a gift that God has given you, for so shall God adorn [him] with greater favor. Truly I say to you, that he who has found a true friend has found one of the delights of paradise; no, such is the key of paradise."

Thaddaeus answered: "But if perhaps a man shall have a friend who is not such as you have said, O master? What ought he to do? Ought he to forsake him?" Jesus answered: "He ought to do as the mariner does with the ship, who sails it so long as he perceives it to be profitable, but when he sees it to be a loss forsakes it. So shall you do with your friend that is worse than you: in those things wherein he is an offence to you, leave him if you would not be left of the mercy of God."

Chapter 87

"Woe to the world because of offences. It needs must be that the offence come, because all the world lies in wickedness. But yet woe to that man through whom the offence comes. It were better for the man if he should have a millstone about his neck and should be sunk in the depths of the sea than that he should offend his neighbor. If your eye be an offence to you, pluck it out. For it is better that you go with one eye only into paradise than with both of them into hell. If your hand or your foot offend you, do likewise; for it is better that you go into the kingdom of heaven with one foot or with one hand, than with two hands and two feet go into hell."

Simon, called Peter: said "Lord, how must I do this? Certain it is that in a short time I shall be dismembered." Jesus answered: "O Peter, put off fleshly prudence and straightway you shall find the truth. For he that teaches you is your eye, and he that helps you to work is your foot, and he that ministers aught to you is your hand. Wherefore when such are to you an occasion of sin leave them; for it is better for you to go into paradise ignorant, with few

works, and poor, than to go into hell wise, with great works, and
rich. Everything that may hinder you from serving God, cast it
from you as a man casts away everything that hinders his sight."
And having said this, Jesus called Peter close to him, and said to
him: * "If your brother shall sin against you, go and correct him. If
he amend, rejoice, for you have gained your brother; but if he
shall not amend go and call afresh two witnesses and correct him
afresh; and if he shall not amend, go and tell it to the church; and
if he shall not then amend, count him for an unbeliever, and
therefore you shall not dwell under the same roof whereunder he
dwells, you shall not eat at the same table whereat he sits, and you
shall not speak with him; insomuch that if you know where he
sets his foot in walking you shall not set your foot there."

Chapter 88

"But beware that you hold not yourself for better; rather shall you
say thus: "Peter, Peter, if God helped you not with his grace you
would be worse than he." Peter answered: "How must I correct
him?" Jesus answered: "In the way that you yourself would fain be
corrected And as you would fain be borne with, so bear with
others. Believe me, Peter, for truly I say to you that every time you
shall correct your brother with mercy you shall receive mercy of
God, and your words shall bear some fruit; but if you shall do it
with rigor, you shall be rigorously punished by the justice of God,
and shall bear no fruit.

Tell me, Peter: Those earthen pots wherein the poor cook their
food they wash them, perhaps, with stones and iron hammers?
No, assuredly; but rather with hot water. Vessels are broken in
pieces with iron, things of wood are burned with fire; but man is
amended with mercy. Wherefore, when you shall correct your
brother you shall say to yourself: "If God help me not, I shall do
tomorrow worse than all that he has done today." Peter answered:
"How many times must I forgive my brother, O master?" Jesus
answered: "As many times as you would fain be forgiven by him."
Peter said: "Seven times a day?" Jesus answered: "Not only seven,
but seventy times seven you shall forgive him every day; for he

that forgives, to him shall it be forgiven, and he that condemns shall be condemned." Then said he who writes this: "Woe to princes! for they shall go to hell" Jesus reproved him, saying: "You are become foolish, O Barnabas. in that you have spoken thus. Truly I say to you, that the bath is not so necessary for the body, the bit for the horse, and the tiller for the ship, as the prince is necessary for the state. And for what cause did God give Moses, Joshua, Samuel, David, and Solomon, and so many others who passed judgment? To such has God given the sword for the extirpation of iniquity."

Then said he who writes this: "Now, how ought judgment to be given, condemning and pardoning?" Jesus answered: "Not every one is a judge: for to the judge alone it appertains to condemn others, O Barnabas. And the judge ought to condemn the guilty, even as the father commands a putrefied member to be cut off from his son, in order that the whole body may not become putrefied."

Chapter 89

Peter said: "How long must I wait for my brother to repent?" Jesus answered: "So long as you would be waited for." Peter answered: "Not every one will understand this; wherefore speak to us more plainly." Jesus answered: "Wait for your brother as long as God waits for him." "Neither will they understand this," said Peter. Jesus answered: "Wait for him so long as he has time to repent." Then was Peter sad, and the others also, because they understood not the meaning. Whereupon Jesus answered: "If you had sound understanding, and knew that you yourselves were sinners, you would not think ever to cut off your heart from mercy to the sinner. And so I tell you plainly, that the sinner ought to be waited for that he may repent, so long as he has a soul beneath his teeth to breathe. For so does our God wait for him, the mighty and merciful. God said not: "In that hour that the sinner shall fast, do alms, make prayer, and go on pilgrimage, I will forgive him." Wherefore this have many accomplished, and are damned eternally. But he said: "In that hour that the sinner shall bewail his sins, I for my part will not remember any more his iniquities." Do you understand?" said Jesus.

The disciples answered: "Part we understand, and part not." Jesus said: "Which is the part that you understand not?" They answered: "That many who have made prayer with fastings are damned." Then Jesus said: "Truly I say to you, that the hypocrites and the Gentiles make more prayers, more alms, and more fasts than do the friends of God. But because they have not faith, they are not able to repent for love of God, and so they are damned." Then said John: "Teach us, for love of God, of the faith." Jesus answered: "It is time that we say the prayer of the dawn." Whereupon they arose, and having washed themselves made prayer to our God, who is blessed for evermore.

Chapter 90

When the prayer was done, his disciples again drew near to Jesus, and he opened his mouth and said: Draw near, John, for today will I speak to you of all that you have asked. Faith is a seal whereby God seals his elect: which seal he gave to his Messenger, at whose hands every one that is elect has received the faith. For even as God is one, so is the faith one. Wherefore God, having created before all things his Messenger, gave to him before aught else the faith which is as it were a likeness of God and of all that God has done and said. And so the faithful by faith sees all things, better than one sees with his eyes; because the eyes can err; no they do almost always err; but faith errs never, for it has for foundation God and his word. Believe me that by faith are saved all the elect of God. And it is certain that without faith it is impossible for any one to please God.

Wherefore Satan seeks not to bring to nothing fastings and prayer, alms and pilgrimages, no rather he incites unbelievers thereto, for he takes pleasure in seeing man work without receiving pay. But he takes pains with all diligence to bring faith to nothing, wherefore faith ought especially to be guarded with diligence, and the safest course will be to abandon the "Wherefore," seeing that the "Wherefore" drove men out of Paradise and changed Satan from a most beautiful angel into a horrible devil."

Then said John: "Now, how shall we abandon the "Wherefore,"
seeing that it is the gate of knowledge?" Jesus answered: "No,
rather the "Wherefore" is the gate of hell." Thereupon John kept
silence, when Jesus added: "When you know that God has said a
thing, who are you, O man, that you should say, "Wherefore have
you so said, O God: wherefore have you so done?" Shall the
earthen vessel, perhaps, say to its maker: "Wherefore have you
made me to hold water and not to contain balsam?" Truly I say to
you, it is necessary against every temptation to strengthen
yourself with this word, saying "God has so said"; "So has God
done"; "God so wills"; for so doing you shall live safely."

Chapter 91

At this time there was a great disturbance throughout Judea
because of Jesus. The Roman soldiery, through the operation of
Satan, [had] stirred up the Hebrews, saying that Jesus was God
come to visit them. So great [was the] sedition [that] arose, that
near the Forty Days all Judea was in arms, such that the son was
against the father, and the brother against the brother. Some said
that Jesus was God come to the world; others said: 'No, but he is a
son of God'; and others said: 'No, for God has no human
similitude, and therefore does not beget sons; but Jesus of
Nazareth is a prophet of God.' This [sedition] arose because of the
great miracles which Jesus did.

To quiet the people, it was necessary that the high-priest should
ride in procession, clothed in his priestly robes, with the holy
name of God, the teta gramaton (the four letters that make up the
name Jehovah or Yahweh) , on his forehead, and the governor
Pilate, and Herod rode in a similar manner. Then, three armies
assembled in Mizpeh, each one of two hundred thousand men
that bare sword. Herod spoke to them, but they were not
quietened. Then the governor and the high-priest spoke, saying:
"Brothers, this war [has been] aroused by the work of Satan, for
Jesus is alive, and we ought to resort to him, and ask him to give
testimony of himself, and then believe him, according to his

word."

So at this everyone was quieted; and having laid down their arms they all embraced one another, saying to one another: 'Forgive me, brother!' *On that day, therefore, every one laid this in his heart, to believe [whatever] Jesus said. The governor and the high-priest offered great rewards to whoever should come [forward and] announce where Jesus was to be found.

Chapter 92

At this time, by the word of the holy angel, we, [had] gone to Mount Sinai with Jesus. There Jesus [and] his disciples kept the forty days.

When this was past, Jesus drew near to the river Jordan, to go to Jerusalem. And he was seen by one of them who believed Jesus to be God. Then, crying with great gladness [over and over] "Our God comes!" he reached the city [and] moved the whole city saying: Our God comes, O Jerusalem; prepare you to receive him! And he testified that he had seen Jesus near to [the] Jordan.

Then everyone, small and great, went out from the city to see Jesus, so that the city was left empty, for the women [carried] their children in their arms, and forgot to take food to eat. When they [saw] this, the governor and the high-priest rode forth and sent a messenger to Herod, who [also] rode forth to find Jesus, in order to quiet the sedition of the people. For two days they sought him in the wilderness near to [the] Jordan, and the third day they found him, near the hour of midday, when he (with his disciples) was purifying himself for prayer, according to the Book of Moses. Jesus marveled greatly, seeing the multitude which covered the ground with people, and [he] said to his disciples: "Perhaps Satan has raised sedition in Judea. May it please God to take away from Satan the dominion which he has over sinners." And when he had said this, the crowd drew near, and when they knew him they began to cry out: "Welcome to you, O our God!" and they began to do him reverence, as to God. Jesus gave a great groan and said: "Get from before me, O madmen, for I fear [that] the earth shall open and devour me with you for your abominable words!" At this the people were filled with terror and began to weep.

Chapter 93

Then Jesus, having lifted his hand in token of silence, said: "Truly you have erred greatly, O Israelites, in calling me, a man, your God. And I fear that God may for this give heavy plague upon the holy city, handing it over in servitude to strangers;. O a thousand times accursed Satan, that has moved you to this!"

And having said this, Jesus smote his face with both his hands, whereupon arose such a noise of weeping that none could hear what Jesus was saying. Whereupon once more he lifted up his hand in token of silence;, and the people being quieted from their weeping, he spoke once more: "

I confess before heaven, and I call to witness everything that dwells upon the earth, that I am a stranger to all that you have said; seeing that I am man, born of mortal woman, subject to the judgment of God, suffering the miseries of eating and sleeping, of cold and heat, like other men. Whereupon when God shall come to judge, my words like a sword shall pierce each one [of them] that believe me to be more than man." And having said this, Jesus saw a great multitude of horsemen, whereby he perceived that there were coming the governor with Herod and the high-priest. Then Jesus said: "Perhaps they also are become mad."

When the governor arrived there, with Herod and the priest, every one dismounted, and they made a circle round about Jesus, insomuch that the soldiery could not keep back the people that were desirous to hear Jesus speaking with the priest. Jesus drew near to the priest with reverence, but he was wishful to bow himself down and worship Jesus, when Jesus cried out: "Beware of that which you do, priest of the living God! Sin not against our God!"

The priest answered: "Now is Judea so greatly moved over your signs and your teaching that they cry out that you are God; wherefore, constrained by the people, I am come here with the Roman governor and king Herod. We pray you therefore from our heart, that you will be content to remove the sedition which is arisen on your account. For some say you are God, some say you are son of God, and some say you are a prophet."

Jesus answered: "And you, O high priest of God, why have you not quieted this sedition? Are you also perhaps, gone out of your mind? Have the prophecies, with the Law of God, so passed into oblivion, O wretched Judea, deceived of Satan!"

Chapter 94

And having said this, Jesus said again: "I confess before heaven, and call to witness everything that dwells upon the earth, that I am a stranger to all that men have said of me, to wit, that I am more than man. For I am a man, born of a woman, subject to the judgment of God; that live here like as other men, subject to the common miseries. As God lives, in whose presence my soul stands, you have greatly sinned, O priest, in saying what you have said. May it please God that there come not upon the holy city great vengeance for this sin." Then said the priest: "May God pardon us, and do you pray for us. Then said the governor and Herod: "Sir, it is impossible that man should do that which you do; wherefore we understand not that which you say.

Jesus answered: "That which you say is true, for God works good in man, even as Satan works evil. For man is like a shop, wherein whoever enters with his consent works and sells therein. But tell me, O governor, and you O king, you say this because you are strangers to our Law: for if you read the testament and covenant of our God you would see that Moses with a rod made the water turn into blood, the dust into fleas, the dew into tempest, and the light into darkness. He made the frogs and mice to come into Egypt;, which covered the ground, he slew the first-born, and opened the sea, wherein he drowned Pharaoh;. Of these things I have wrought none.

And of Moses, every one confesses that he is a dead man at this present. Joshua made the sun to stand still, and opened the Jordan, which I have not yet done. And of Joshua every one confesses that he is a dead man at this present. Elijah made fire to come visibly down from heaven, and rain, which I have not done.

And of Elijah every one confesses that he is a man. And [in like manner] very many other prophets, holy men, friends of God, who in the power of God have wrought things which cannot be grasped by the minds of those who know not our God, almighty and merciful, who is blessed for evermore."

Chapter 95

Accordingly the governor and the priest and the king prayed Jesus that in order to quiet the people he should mount up into a lofty place and speak to the people. Then went up Jesus on to one of the twelve stones which Joshua made the twelve tribes take up from the midst of Jordan;, when all Israel passed over there dry shod; and he said with a loud voice: "Let our priest go up into a high place whence he may confirm my words." Thereupon the priest went up thither; to whom Jesus said distinctly, so that everyone might hear: "It is written in the testament and covenant of the living God that our God has no beginning, neither shall he ever have an end." The priest answered: "Even so is it written therein."

Jesus said: "It is written there that our God by his word alone has created all things." "Even so it is," said the priest. Jesus said: "It is written there that God is invisible and hidden from the mind of man, seeing he is incorporeal and uncomposed, without variableness." "So is it, truly" said the priest. Jesus said: "It is written there how that the heaven of heavens cannot contain him, seeing that our God is infinite." "So said Solomon the prophet," said the priest, "O Jesus." Jesus said: "It is written there that God has no need, forasmuch as he eats not, sleeps not,; and suffers not from any deficiency." "So is it," said the priest.

Jesus said: "It is written there that our God is everywhere, and that there is not any other god but he, who strikes down and makes whole, and does all that pleases him." "So is it written," replied the priest. Then Jesus, having lifted up his hands, said: "Lord our God, this is my faith wherewith I shall come to your judgment: in testimony against every one that shall believe the contrary."

And turning himself towards the people, he said: "Repent, for from all that of which the priest has said that it is written in the Book of Moses, the covenant of God for ever, you may perceive your sin; for. that I am a visible man and a morsel of clay that walks upon the earth, mortal as are other men. And I have had a beginning, and shall have an end, and [am] such that I cannot create a fly over again."

Thereupon the people raised their voices weeping, and said: "We have sinned, Lord our God, against you; have mercy upon us. And they prayed Jesus, every one, that he would pray for the safety of the holy city, that our God in his anger should not give it over to be trodden down of the nations. Thereupon Jesus, having lifted up his hands, prayed for the holy city and for the people of God, every one crying: "So be it," "Amen."

Chapter 96

When the prayer was ended, the priest said with a loud voice: "Stay, Jesus, for we need to know who you are, for the quieting of our nation." Jesus answered: "I am Jesus, son of Mary, of the seed of David, a man that is mortal and fears God, and I seek that to God be given honor and glory."

The priest answered: "In the Book of Moses it is written that our God must send us the Messiah, who shall come to announce to us that which God wills, and shall bring to the world the mercy of God. Therefore I pray you tell us the truth, are you the Messiah of God whom we expect?"

Jesus answered: "It is true that God has so promised, but indeed I am not he, for he is made before me, and shall come after me." The priest answered: "By your words and signs at any rate we believe you to be a prophet and an holy one of God, wherefore I pray you in the name of all Judea and Israel that you for love of God should tell us in what wise the Messiah will come.

Chapter 97

Jesus answered: "As God lives, in whose presence my soul stands, I am not the Messiah whom all the tribes of the earth expect, even as God promised to our father Abraham, saying: "In your seed will I bless all the tribes of the earth." But when God shall take me away from the world, Satan will raise again this accursed sedition, by making the impious believe that I am God and son of God, whence my words and my doctrine shall be contaminated, insomuch that scarcely shall there remain thirty faithful ones: whereupon God will have mercy upon the world, and will send his Messenger for whom he has made all things who shall come from the south with power, and shall destroy the idols with the idolaters who shall take away the dominion from Satan which he has over men. He shall bring with him the mercy of God for salvation of them that shall believe in him, and blessed is he who shall believe his words.

"Unworthy though I am to untie his hosen, I have received grace and mercy from God to see him." Then answered the priest, with the governor and the king, saying: "Distress not yourself, O Jesus, holy one of God, because in our time shall not this sedition be any more, seeing that we will write to the sacred Roman senate in such wise that by imperial decree none shall any more call you God or son of God." Then Jesus said: "With your words I am not consoled, because where you hope for light darkness shall come; but my consolation is in the coming of the Messenger, who shall destroy every false opinion of me, and his faith shall spread and shall take hold of the whole world, for so has God promised to Abraham our father. And that which gives me consolation is that his faith shall have no end, but shall be kept inviolate by God."

The priest answered: "After the coming of the Messenger of God shall other prophets come?" Jesus answered: "There shall not come after him true prophets sent by God, but there shall come a great number of false prophets, whereat I sorrow. For Satan shall raise them up by the just judgment of God, and they shall hide themselves under the pretext of my gospel." Herod answered: "How is it a just judgment of God that such impious men should come?"

Jesus answered: "It is just that he who will not believe in the truth to his salvation should believe in a lie to his damnation. Wherefore I say to you, that the world has ever despised the true prophets and loved the false, as can be seen in the time of Micaiah and Jeremiah. For every like loves his like."

Then said the priest: "How shall the Messiah be called, and what sign shall reveal his coming?" Jesus answered: "The name of the Messiah is admirable, for God himself gave him the name when he had created his soul, and placed it in a celestial splendor. God said: "Wait Muhammad; for your sake I will to create paradise, the world, and a great multitude of creatures, whereof I make you a present, insomuch that whoever shall bless you shall be blessed, and whoever shall curse you shall be accursed. When I shall send you into the world I shall send you as my Messenger of salvation, and your word shall be true, insomuch that heaven and earth shall fail, but your faith shall never fail." Muhammad is his blessed name." Then the crowd lifted up their voices, saying: "O God send us your Messenger: O Muhammad, come quickly for the salvation of the world!"

Chapter 98

And having said this, the multitude departed with the priest and the governor with Herod, having great disputations concerning Jesus and concerning his doctrine. Whereupon the priest prayed the governor to write to Rome to the senate the whole matter; which thing the governor did; wherefore the senate had compassion on Israel, and decreed that on pain of death none should call Jesus the Nazarene, prophet of the Jews, either God or son of God. Which decree was posted up in the Temple, engraved upon copper.

When the greater part of the crowd had departed, there remained about five thousand men, without women and children who being wearied by the journey, having been two days without bread, for that through longing to see Jesus they had forgotten to bring any, whereupon they ate raw herbs therefore they were not able to depart like the others. Then Jesus, when he perceived this, had pity on them, and said to Philip: "Where shall we find bread for them that they perish not of hunger?" Philip answered: "Lord, two hundred pieces of gold could not buy so much bread that each one should taste a little." Then said Andrew: "There is here a child which has five loaves and two fishes, but what will it be among so many?"

Jesus answered: "Make the multitude sit down" And they sat down upon the grass by fifties and by forties. Thereupon said Jesus: "In the name of God!" And he took the bread, and prayed to God and then brake the bread, which he gave to the disciples, and the disciples gave it to the multitude; and so did they with the fishes. Every one ate and every one was satisfied. Then Jesus said: "Gather up that which is over." So the disciples gathered those fragments, and filled twelve baskets.

Thereupon every one put his hand to his eyes, saying: "Am I awake, or do I dream?" And they remained, every one, for the space of an hour. as it were beside themselves by reason of the great miracle. Afterwards Jesus, when he had given thanks to God, dismissed them, but there were seventy-two men that willed not to leave him; wherefore Jesus, perceiving their faith, chose them for disciples.

Chapter 99

Jesus, having withdrawn into a hollow part of the desert in Tiro near to Jordan, called together the seventy-two with the twelve, and, when he had seated himself upon a stone, made them to sit near him. And he opened his mouth with a sigh and said: "This day have we seen a great wickedness in Judea and in Israel such that my heart trembles within my breast for fear of God. Truly I say to you, that God is jealous for his honor, and loves Israel as a lover. You know that when a youth loves a lady, and she does not love him, but another, he is moved to indignation and slays his rival. Even so, I tell you, does God: for, when Israel has loved anything such that he forgets God, God has brought such a thing to nothing.

Now what thing is more dear to God here on earth than the priesthood and the holy Temple? Nevertheless, in the time of Jeremiah the prophet, when the people had forgotten God, and boasted only of the Temple, for that there was none like it in all the world, God raised up his wrath by Nebuchadnezzar, king of Babylon, and with an army caused him to take the holy city and burn it with the sacred Temple, such that the sacred things which the prophets of God trembled to touch were trodden under foot by infidels full of wickedness.

Abraham loved his son Ishmael a little more than was right, so in order to kill that evil love out of the heart of Abraham, God commanded that he should slay his son: which he would have done had the knife cut. * David loved Absalom vehemently, and therefore God brought it to pass that the son rebelled against his father and was suspended by his hair and slain by Joab. O fearful judgment of God, that Absalom loved his hair above all things, and this was turned into a rope to hang him!

Innocent Job came near to loving his seven sons and three daughters [too much], when God gave him into the hand of Satan, who not only deprived him of his sons and his riches in one day, but also struck him with grievous sickness, such that worms came out of his flesh for the next seven years. Our father Jacob loved Joseph more than his other sons, so God caused him to be sold, and caused Jacob to be deceived by these same sons, such that he believed that the beasts had devoured his son, and so lived in mourning for ten years.

Chapter 100

As God lives, brothers, I fear that God will be angered against me. Therefore you must go through Judea and Israel, preaching the truth to the twelve tribes, that they may be undeceived." The disciples answered with fear, weeping: "We will do whatever you bid us [to do]."

Then Jesus said: "Let us make prayer and fast for three days, and from henceforth every evening when the first star shall appear, when prayer is made to God, let us make prayer three times, asking him for mercy three times: because the sin of Israel is three times more grievous than other sins." "So be it," answered the disciples.

When the third day was ended, on the morning of the fourth day,

Jesus called together all the disciples and apostles and said to them: "Barnabas and John will stay with me: you others are to go through all the region of Samaria and Judea and Israel, preaching penitence: because the axe is laid near to the tree, to cut it down. And make prayer over the sick, because God has given me authority over every sickness."

Then he who writes said: "O Master, if your disciples be asked how they ought to show penitence, what shall they answer?" Jesus answered: "When a man loses a purse does he turn back only his eye, to see it? or his hand, to take it? or his tongue, to ask? No, but he turns his whole body back and employs every power of his soul to find it. Is this true?" Then he who writes answered : "It is most true."

Chapter 101

Then Jesus said: "Penitence is a reversing of the evil life: for every sense must be turned around to the contrary of that which it wrought while sinning. Instead of delight must be mourning; for laughter, weeping; for reveling, fasts; for sleeping, vigils; for leisure, activity; for lust, chastity; let storytelling be turned into prayer and avarice into almsgiving." Then he who writes answered: "But if they are asked, how are we to mourn, how are we to weep, how are we to fast, how are we to show activity, how are we to remain chaste, how are we to make prayer and do alms; what answer shall they give? And how shall they do penance properly if they do not know how to repent."

Jesus answered: "You have asked [a good question], O Barnabas, and I wish to answer all fully if it is pleasing to God. So today I will speak to you of penitence generally, and that which I say to one I say to all. Know then that penitence more than anything [else] must be done for pure love of God; otherwise it will be vain to repent. I will speak to you by a similitude. Every building, if its foundation be removed, falls into ruin: is this true?" "It is true," answered the disciples.

Then Jesus said: "The foundation of our salvation is God, without whom there is no salvation. When man has sinned, he has lost the foundation of his salvation; so it is necessary to begin from the foundation. Tell me, if your slaves had offended you, and you knew that they did not grieve at having offended you, but grieved at having lost their reward, would you forgive them? Certainly not. I tell you that this is what God will do to those who repent for having lost paradise. Satan, the enemy of all good, has great remorse for having lost paradise and gained hell. Yet he will he never find mercy. Do you know why? Because he does not love God; no, he hates his Creator.

Chapter 102

Truly I say to you, that every animal according to its own nature, if it loses that which it desires, mourns for the lost good. Accordingly, the sinner who will be truly penitent must have [a] great desire to punish in himself that which he has done in opposition to his Creator: [to the extent that] when he prays he dare not to crave paradise from God, or that God [will] free him from hell, but in confusion of mind, prostrate before God, he says in his prayer:

'Behold the guilty one, O Lord, who has offended You without any cause at the very time when he ought to have been serving You. Here he seeks that what he has done may be punished by Your hand, and not by the hand of Satan, Your enemy; in order that the ungodly may not rejoice over your creatures. Chastise, punish as it pleases you, O Lord, for you will never give me so much torment as this wicked one deserves.'

The sinner, holding to this manner of [penitence], will find mercy with God in proportion to [the extent that] he craves justice. Assuredly, [the] laughter of a sinner is an abominable sacrilege since this world is rightly called by our father David a vale of tears.

There was a king who adopted one of his slaves as [his] son [and] he made him lord of all that he possessed. Now it happened that by the deceit of a wicked man the wretched one fell under the displeasure of the king, so that he suffered great miseries, not only in his substance, but in being despised, and being deprived of all that he won each day by working. Do you think that such a man would laugh for any time?" "No," answered the disciples, "for if the king should have known it he would have had him slain, seeing him laugh at the king's displeasure. But it is probable that he would weep day and night."

Then Jesus wept saying: "Woe to the world, for it is sure of eternal torment. O wretched mankind, that God has chosen you as a son, granting you paradise, at which you, O wretched one, by the operation of Satan, did fall under the displeasure of God, and was cast out of paradise and condemned to the unclean world, where you receive all things with toil and every good work is taken from you by continual sinning. And the world simply laughs, and, what is worse, he that is the greatest sinner laughs more than the rest! It will be, therefore, as you have said: that God will give the sentence of eternal death upon the sinner who laughs at his sins and does not weep."

Chapter 103

The weeping of the sinner ought to be like that of a father who weeps over his son [who is] near to death. O madness of man, that weeps over the body from which the soul is departed, and [yet] does not weep over the soul from which the mercy of God has departed because of sin! Tell me, if the mariner, when his ship has been wrecked by a storm, could recover all that he had lost by weeping, what would he do? It is certain that he would weep bitterly. But I say to you truly, that in every thing [for which] a man weeps, he sins, except when he weeps for his sin. For every misery that comes to man comes to him from God for his salvation, so that he should rejoice [when it befalls him]. But sin comes from the devil for the damnation of man, and [yet] man is not sad about that. Surely here you can perceive that man seeks loss and not profit."

Bartholomew said: "Lord, what shall he do who cannot weep because his heart is a stranger to weeping? " Jesus answered: "Not all those who shed tears weep, O Bartholomew. As God lives, there are found men from whose eyes no tear has ever fallen, and

217

they have wept more than a thousand of those who [do] shed tears. The weeping of a sinner is a consumption of earthly affection by vehemence of sorrow.

Just as the sunshine preserves from putrefaction what is placed uppermost, even so this consumption preserves the soul from sin. If God should grant as many tears to the true penitent as the sea has waters he would desire far more: and so that desire consumes that little drop that he would shed, as a blazing furnace consumes a drop of water. But they who readily burst into weeping are like the horse that goes faster the more lightly he is laden.

Chapter 104

'Truly there are men who have both the inward affection and the outward tears. But he who is thus, will be a Jeremiah. In weeping, God measures more the sorrow than the tears.' Then said John: "O master, how does man lose in weeping over things other than sin?" Jesus answered: 'If Herod; should give you a mantle to keep for him, and afterwards should take it away from you, would you have reason to weep?'

"No," said John. Then Jesus said: 'Now has man less reason to weep when he loses aught, or has not that which he would; for all comes from the hand of God. Accordingly, shall not God have power to dispose at his pleasure of his own things, O foolish man? For you have of your own, sin alone; and for that ought you to weep, and not for aught else.'

Matthew said: "O master, you have confessed before all Judea that God has no similitude like man, and now you have said that man receives from the hand of God; accordingly, since God has hands he has a similitude with man." Jesus answered: 'You are in error, O Matthew, and many have so erred, not knowing the sense of the words. For man ought to consider not the outward [form] of the words, but the sense; seeing that human speech is as it were an interpreter between us and God. Now knew you not, that when God willed to speak to our fathers on mount Sinai, our fathers cried out: "Speak you to us, O Moses, and let not God speak to us, lest we die"? And what said God by Isaiah the prophet, but that, so far as the heaven is distant from the earth, even so are the ways of God distant from the ways of men, and the thoughts of God from the thoughts of men?

Chapter 105

'God is so immeasurable that I tremble to describe him. But it is necessary that I make to you a proposition. I tell you, then, that the heavens are nine and that they are distant from one another even as the first heaven is distant from the earth, which is distant from the earth five hundred years' journey. Wherefore the earth is distant from the highest heaven four thousand and five hundred years' journey. I tell you, accordingly, that [the earth] is in proportion to the first heaven as the point of a needle and the first heaven in like manner is in proportion to the second as a point, and similarly all the heavens are inferior each one to the next. But all the size of the earth with that of all the heavens is in proportion to paradise as a point, no, as a grain of sand. Is this greatness immeasurable?'

The disciples answered: 'Yes, surely.'

Then Jesus said: 'As God lives, in whose presence my soul stands, the universe before God is small as a grain of sand, and God is as many times greater [than it] as it would take grains of sand to fill all the heavens and paradise, and more. Now consider you if God has any proportion with man, who is a little piece of clay that stands upon the earth. Beware, then, that you take the sense and not the bare words, if you wish to have eternal life.' The disciples answered: 'God alone can know himself, and truly it is as said Isaiah the prophet: "He is hidden from human senses."

Jesus answered: 'So is it true; wherefore, when we are in paradise we shall know God, as here one knows the sea from a drop of salt water. Returning to my discourse, I tell you that for sin alone one ought to weep, because by sinning man forsakes his Creator. But how shall he weep who attends at reveling and feasts? He will weep even as ice will give fire! You needs must turn reveling into fasts if you will have lordship over your senses, because even so has our God lordship. Thaddaeus said: 'So then, God has sense over which to have lordship.'

Jesus answered: 'Go you back to saying, "God has this," "God is such"? Tell me, has man sense?' 'Yes,' answered the disciples. Jesus said: 'Can a man be found who has life in him, yet in him sense works not?' 'No,' said the disciples. 'You deceive yourselves,' said Jesus, 'for he that is blind, deaf, dumb, and mutilated-where is his sense? And when a man is in a swoon?' Then were the disciples perplexed; when Jesus said: 'Three things there are that make up man: that is, the soul and the sense and the flesh, each one of itself separate. Our God created the soul and the body as you have heard, but you have not yet heard how he created the sense. Therefore to-morrow, if God please, I will tell you all.' And having said this Jesus gave thanks to God, and prayed for the salvation of our people, every one of us saying: 'Amen.'

Chapter 106

When he had finished the prayer of dawn, Jesus sat down under a palm tree, and thither his disciples drew near to him. Then Jesus said: 'As God lives, in whose presence stands my soul, many are deceived concerning our life. For so closely are the soul and the sense joined together, that the more part of men affirm the soul and the sense to be one and the same thing, dividing it by operation and not by essence, calling it the sensitive, vegetative, and intellectual soul. But truly I say to you, the soul is one, which thinks and lives. O foolish ones, where will they find the intellectual soul without life? Assuredly, never. But life without senses will readily be found, as is seen in the unconscious when the sense leaves him.' Thaddaeus answered: "O master, when the sense leaves the life, a man does not have life."

Jesus answered: "This is not true, because man is deprived of life when the soul departs; because the soul returns not any more to the body, save by miracle. But sense departs by reason of fear that it receives, or by reason of great sorrow that the soul has. For the sense has God created for pleasure, and by that alone it lives, even as the body lives by food and the soul lives by knowledge and love. This sense is now rebellious against the soul, through

220

indignation that it has at being deprived of the pleasure of paradise through sin. Wherefore there is the greatest need to nourish it with spiritual pleasure for him who wills not that it should live of carnal pleasure. Understand you? Truly I say to you, that God having created it condemned it to hell and to intolerable snow and ice; because it said that it was God; but when he deprived it of nourishment, taking away its food from it, it confessed that it was a slave of God and the work of his hands. And now tell me, how does sense work in the ungodly? Assuredly, it is as God in them: seeing that they follow sense, forsaking reason and the Law of God. Whereupon they become abominable, and work not any good."

Chapter 107

'And so the first thing that follows sorrow for sin is fasting. For he that sees that a certain food makes him sick, for that he fears death, after sorrowing that he has eaten it, forsaken it, so as not to make himself sick. So ought the sinner to do. Perceiving that pleasure has made him to sin against God his creator by following sense in these good things of the world, let him sorrow at having done so, because it deprives him of God, his life, and gives him the eternal death of hell. But because man while living has need to take these good things of the world, fasting is needful here. So let him proceed to mortify sense and to know God for his lord. And when he sees the sense abhor fastings, let him put before it the condition of hell, where no pleasure at all but infinite sorrow is received; let him put before it the delights of paradise, that are so great that a grain of one of the delights of paradise is greater than all those of the world. For so will it easily be quieted; for that it is better to be content with little in order to receive much, than to be unbridled in little and be deprived of all and abide in torment. 'You ought to remember the rich feaster in order to fast well. For he, wishing here on earth to fare deliciously every day, was deprived eternally of a single drop of water: while Lazarus, being content with crumbs here on earth, shall live eternally in full abundance of the delights of paradise. But let the penitent be cautious; for that Satan seeks to annul every good work, and more in the penitent than in others, for that the penitent has rebelled against him, and from being his faithful slave has turned into a rebellious foe. Whereupon Satan will seek to cause that he shall not fast in any wise, under pretext of sickness, and when this shall not avail he will invite him to an extreme fast, in order that he may fall sick and afterwards live deliciously. And if he succeed not in this, he will seek to make him set his fast simply upon bodily food, in order that he may be like to himself, who never eats but always sins.

As God lives, it is abominable to deprive the body of food and fill the soul with pride, despising them that fast not, and holding oneself better than they. Tell me, will the sick man boast of the diet that is imposed on him by the physician, and call them mad who are not put on diet? Assuredly not. But he will sorrow for the sickness by reason of which he needs must be put upon diet. Even so I say to you, that the penitent ought not to boast in his fast, and despise them that fast not; but he ought to sorrow for the sin by reason whereof he fasts. Nor should the penitent that fasts procure delicate food, but he should content himself with coarse food. Now will a man give delicate food to the dog that bites and to the horse that kicks? No, surely, but rather the contrary. And let this suffice you concerning fasting.'

Chapter 108

Hearken, then, to what I shall say to you concerning watching. For just as there are two kinds of sleeping, viz. that of the body and that of the soul, even so must you be careful in watching that while the body watches the soul sleep not. For this would be a most grievous error. Tell me, in parable: there is a man who whilst walking strikes himself against a rock, and in order to avoid striking it the more with his foot, he strikes with his head what is the state of such a man?' "Miserable," answered the disciples, "for such a man is frenzied."

Then Jesus said: "Well have you answered, for truly I say to you that he who watches with the body and sleeps with the soul is frenzied. As the spiritual infirmity is more grievous than the corporeal, even so is it more difficult to cure. Wherefore, shall such a wretched one boast of not sleeping with the body, which is the foot of the life, while he perceives not his misery that he sleeps with the soul, which is the head of the life? The sleep of the soul is forgetfulness of God and of his fearful judgment. The soul, then, that watches is that which in everything and in every place perceives God, and in everything and through everything and above everything gives thanks to his majesty, knowing that always at every moment it receives grace and mercy from God. Wherefore in fear of his majesty there always resounds in its ear that angelic utterance "Creatures, come to judgment, for your Creator wills to judge you." For it abides habitually ever in the service of God. * Tell me, whether do you desire the more: to see by the light of a star or by the light of the sun?" Andrew answered: "By the light of the sun; for by the light of the star we cannot see the neighboring mountains, and by the light of the sun we see the tiniest grain of sand. Wherefore we walk with fear by the light of the star, but by the light of the sun we go securely."

Chapter 109

Jesus answered: "Even so I tell you that you ought to watch with the soul by the sun of justice [which is] our God, and not to boast yourselves of the watching of the body. It is most true, therefore, that bodily sleep is to be avoided as much as is possible, but [to avoid it] altogether is impossible, the sense and the flesh being weighed down with food and the mind with business. Wherefore let him that will sleep little avoid too much business and much food. As God lives, in whose presence stands my soul, it is lawful to sleep somewhat every night, but it is never lawful to forget God and his fearful judgment: and the sleep of the soul is such oblivion."

Then answered he who writes: "O master, how can we always have God in memory? Assuredly, it seems to us impossible. Jesus said, with a sigh: "This is the greatest misery that man can suffer, O Barnabas. For man cannot here upon earth have God his creator always in memory; saving them that are holy, for they always have God in memory, because they have in them the light of the grace of God, so that they cannot forget God. But tell me, have you seen them that work quarried stones, how by their constant practice they have so learned to strike that they speak with others and all the time are striking the iron tool that works the stone without looking at the iron, and yet they do not strike their hands? Now do you likewise.

Desire to be holy if you wish to overcome entirely this misery of forgetfulness. Sure it is that water cleaves the hardest rocks with a single drop striking there for a long period. Do you know why you have not overcome this misery? Because you have not perceived that it is sin. I tell you then that it is an error, when a prince gives you a present, O man, that you should shut your eyes and turn your back upon him. Even so do they err who forget God, for at all times man receives from God gifts and mercy."

Chapter 110

Now tell me, does our God at all times grant you [his bounty]? Yes, assuredly; for unceasingly he ministers to you the breath whereby you live. Truly, truly, I say to you, every time that your body receives breath your heart ought to say: "God be thanked!"'

Then said John: "it is most true what you say, O master; teach us therefore the way to attain to this blessed condition."

Jesus answered: "Truly I say to you, one cannot attain to such condition by human powers, but rather by the mercy of God our Lord. It is true indeed that man ought to desire the good in order that God may give it him. Tell me, when you are at table do you take those meats which you would not so much as look at? No, assuredly. Even so I say to you that you shall not receive that which you will not desire. God is able, if you desire holiness, to make you holy in less time than the twinkling of an eye, but in order that man may be sensible of the gift and the giver our God wills that we should wait and ask.

Have you seen them that practice shooting at a mark? Assuredly they shoot many times in vain. Howbeit, they never wish to shoot in vain, but are always in hope to hit the mark. Now do you this, you who ever desire to have our God in remembrance, and when you forget, mourn; for God shall give you grace to attain to all that I have said. Fasting and spiritual watching are so united one with the other that, if one break the watch, straightway the fast is broken. For in sinning a man breaks the fast of the soul, and forgets God. So is it that watching and fasting as regards the soul are always necessary for us and for all men. For to none is it lawful to sin.

But the fasting of the body and its watching, believe me, they are not possible at all times, nor for all persons. For there are sick and aged folk, women with child, men that are put upon diet, children, and others that are of weak complexion. For indeed everyone, even as he clothes himself according to his proper measure, so should choose his [manner of] fasting. For just as the garments of a child are not suitable for a man of thirty years, even so the watching and fastings of one are not suitable for another."

Chapter 111

'But beware that Satan will use all his strength [to bring it to pass] that you [shall] watch during the night, and afterward be sleeping when by commandment of God you ought to be praying and listening to the word of God. Tell me, would it please you if a friend of yours should eat the meat and give you the bones?" Peter answered: "No, master, for such an one ought not to be called friend, but a mocker."

Jesus answered with a sigh: "You have well said the truth, O Peter, for truly every one that watches with the body more than is necessary, sleeping, or having his head weighed down with slumber when he should be praying or listening to the words of God, such a wretch mocks God his creator, and so is guilty of such a sin. Moreover, he is a robber, seeing that he steals the time that he ought to give to God, and spends it when, and as much as, pleases him.

In a vessel of the best wine a man gave his enemies to drink so long as the wine was at its best, but when the wine came down to the dregs he gave to his lord to drink. What, think you, will the master do to his servant when he shall know all, and the servant be before him? Assuredly, he will beat him and slay him in righteous indignation according to the laws of the world. And now what shall God do to the man that spends the best of his time in business, and the worst in prayer and study of the Law? Woe to the world, because with this and with greater sin is its heart weighed down! Accordingly, when I said to you that laughter should be turned into weeping, feasts into fasting, and sleep into watching, I compassed in three words all that you have heard that here on earth one ought always to weep, and that weeping should be from the heart, because God our creator is offended; that you ought to fast in order to have lordship over the sense, and to watch in order not to sin; and that bodily weeping and bodily fasting and watching should be taken according to the constitution of each one."

Chapter 112

Having said this, Jesus said: "You needs must seek of the fruits of the field the wherewithal to sustain our life, for it is now eight days that we have eaten no bread. Wherefore I will pray to our God, and will await you with Barnabas."

So all the disciples and apostles departed by fours and by sixes and went their way according to the word of Jesus. There remained with Jesus he who writes; whereupon Jesus, weeping, said: "O Barnabas, it is necessary that I should reveal to you great secrets, which, after that I shall be departed from the world, you shall reveal to it." Then answered he that writes, weeping, and said: "Suffer me to weep, O master, and other men also, for that we are sinners. And you, that are an holy one and prophet of God, it is not fitting for you to weep so much."

Jesus answered: "Believe me, Barnabas that I cannot weep as much as I ought. For if men had not called me God, I should have seen God here as he will be seen in paradise, and should have been safe not to fear the day of judgment. But God knows that I am innocent, because never have I harbored thought to be held more than a poor slave. No, I tell you that if I had not been called God I should have been carried into paradise when I shall depart from the world, whereas now I shall not go thither until the judgment. Now you see if I have cause to weep.

Know, O Barnabas, that for this I must have great persecution, and shall be sold by one of my disciples for thirty pieces of money. Whereupon I am sure that he who shall sell me shall be slain in my name, for that God shall take me up from the earth, and shall change the appearance of the traitor so that every one shall believe him to be me; nevertheless, when he dies an evil death, I shall abide in that dishonor for a long time in the world. But when Muhammad shall come, the sacred Messenger of God, that infamy shall be taken away. And this shall God do because I have confessed the truth of the Messiah who shall give me this reward, that I shall be known to be alive and to be a stranger to that death of infamy."

Then answered he that writes: "O master, tell me who is that wretch, for I fain would choke him to death." "Hold your peace," answered Jesus, "for so God wills, and he cannot do otherwise but see you that when my mother is afflicted at such an event you tell her the truth, in order that she may be comforted." Then answered he who writes: "All this will I do, O master, if God please."

Chapter 113

When the disciples were come they brought pine-cones, and by the will of God they found a good quantity of dates. So after the midday prayer they ate with Jesus. Whereupon the apostles and disciples, seeing him that writes of sad countenance, feared that Jesus needs must quickly depart from the world. Whereupon Jesus consoled them, saying: "Fear not, for my hour is not yet come that I should depart from you. I shall abide with you still for a little while. Therefore must I teach you now, in order that you may go, as I have said, through all Israel to preach penitence; in order that God may have mercy upon the sin of Israel. Let every one therefore beware of sloth, and much more he that does penance; because every tree that bears not good fruit shall be cut down and cast into the fire.

There was a citizen who had a vineyard, and in the midst thereof had a garden, which had a fine fig-tree; whereon for three years when the owner came he found no fruit, and seeing every other tree bare fruit there he said to his vinedresser: "Cut down this bad tree, for it cumbers the ground." The vinedresser answered: "Not so, my lord, for it is a beautiful tree." "Hold your peace," said the owner, "for I care not for useless beauties. You should know that the palm and the balsam are nobler than the fig. But I had planted in the courtyard of my house a plant of palm and one of balsam, which I had surrounded with costly walls, but when these bare no fruit, but leaves which heaped themselves up and putrefied the ground in front of the house, I caused them both to be removed. And how shall I pardon a fig-tree far from the house, which cumbers my garden and my vineyard where every other tree bears fruit? Assuredly I will not suffer it any longer."

Then said the vinedresser: "Lord, the soil is too rich. Wait, therefore, one year more, for I will prune the fig-plant's branches, and take away from it the richness of the soil, putting in poor soil with stones, and so shall it bear fruit." The owner answered: "Now go and do so; for I will wait, and the fig-plant shall bear fruit." Understand you this parable?" The disciples answered: "No, Lord, therefore explain it to us."

Chapter 114

Jesus answered: "Truly I say to you, the owner is God, and the vinedresser is his Law. God, then, had in paradise the palm and the balsam; for Satan is the palm and the first man the balsam. Then did he cast out because they bare not fruit of good works, but uttered ungodly words that were the condemnation of many angels and many men. Now that God has man in the world, in the midst of his creatures that serve God, all of them, according to his precept: and man, I say, bearing no fruit, God would cut him down and commit him to hell, seeing he pardoned not the angel and the first man, punishing the angel eternally, and the man for a time.

Whereupon the Law of God says that man has too much good in this life, and so it is necessary that he should suffer tribulation and be deprived of earthly goods, in order that he may do good works. Therefore our God waits for man to be penitent. Truly I say to you, that our God has condemned man to work, so that, as said Job, the friend and prophet of God: "As the bird is born to fly and the fish to swim, even so is man born to work." So also David our father, a prophet of God, says: Eating the labors of our hands we shall be blessed, and it shall be well with us. Wherefore let every one work, according to his quality. Now tell me, if David our father and Solomon his son worked with their hands, what ought the sinner to do?"

Said John: "Master, to work is a fitting thing, but this ought the poor to do." Jesus answered: "Yes, for they cannot do otherwise. But know you not that good, to be good, must be free from necessity? Thus the sun and the other planets are strengthened by the precepts of God so that they cannot do otherwise, wherefore they shall have no merit. Tell me, when God gave the precept to work, he said not: "A poor man shall live of the sweat of his face"? And Job did not say that: "As a bird is born to fly, so a poor man is born to work"? But God said to man: "In the sweat of your countenance shall you eat bread," and Job that "Man is born to work." Therefore [only] he who is not man is free from this precept. Assuredly for no other reason are all things costly, but that there are a great multitude of idle folk: if these were to labor, some attending the ground and some at fishing the water, there would be the greatest plenty in the world. And of the lack thereof it will be necessary to render an account in the dreadful day of judgment.

Chapter 115

Let man say somewhat to me. What has he brought into the world, by reason of which he would live in idleness? Certain it is that he was born naked, and incapable of anything. Hence, of all that he has found, he is not the owner, but the dispenser. And he will have to render an account thereof in that dreadful day.

The abominable lust, that makes man like the brute beasts, ought greatly to be feared; for the enemy is of one's own household, so that it is not possible to go into any place where your enemy may not come. Ah, how many have perished through lust! Through lust came the deluge, insomuch that the world perished before the mercy of God and so that there were saved only Noah and eighty-three human persons. For lust God overwhelmed three wicked cities whence escaped only Lot and his two children. For lust the tribe of Benjamin was all but extinguished. And I tell you truly that if I should narrate to you how many have perished through lust, the space of five days would not suffice." James answered: "O Master, what signifies lust?"

Jesus answered: "Lust is an unbridled desire of love, which, not being directed by reason, bursts the bounds of man's intellect and affections; so that the man, not knowing himself, loves that which he ought to hate. Believe me, when a man loves a thing, not because God has given him such thing, but as its owner, he is a fornicator; for that the soul, which ought to abide in union with God its creator, he has united with the creature. And so God laments by Isaiah the prophet, saying: You have committed fornication with many lovers; nevertheless, return to me and I will receive you.

As God lives in whose presence my soul stands, if there were not internal lust within the heart of man, he would not fall into the external; for if the root be removed the tree dies speedily. Let a man content himself therefore with the wife whom his creator has given him, and let him forget every other woman." Andrew answered: "How shall a man forget the women if he live in the city where there are so many of them?" Jesus replied: "O Andrew, certain it is he who lives in the city, it will do him harm; seeing that the city is a sponge that draws in every iniquity.

Chapter 116

It suits a man to live in the city, even as the soldier lives when he has enemies around the fortress, defending himself against every assault and always fearing treachery on the part of the citizens.

saying that I could make myself lord of all Judea, if I confessed myself to be God, and that I am mad to wish to live in poverty among desert places, and not abide continually among princes in delicate living. Oh hapless man, that prizes the light that is common to flies and ants and despises the light that is common only to angels and prophets and holy friends of God!

If, then, the eye shall not be guarded, O Andrew, I tell you that it is impossible not to fall headlong into lust. Wherefore Jeremiah the prophet, weeping vehemently, said truly: "My eye is a thief that robs my soul." For therefore did David our father pray with greatest longing to God our Lord that he would turn away his eyes in order that he might not behold vanity. For truly everything which has an end is vain. Tell me, then, if one had two pence to buy bread, would he spend it to buy smoke? Assuredly not, seeing that smoke does hurt to the eyes and gives no sustenance to the body. Even so then let man do, for with the outward sight of his eyes and the inward sight of his mind he should seek to know God his creator and the good pleasure of his will, and should not make the creature his end, which causes him to lose the creator.

Chapter 119

For truly every time that a man beholds a thing and forgets God who has made it for man, he has sinned. For if a friend of yours should give you somewhat to keep in memory of him, and you should sell it and forget your friend, you have offended against your friend. Even so does man; for when he beholds the creature and has not in memory the creator, who for love of man has created it, he sins against God his creator by ingratitude.

He therefore who shall behold women and shall forget God who for the good of man created woman, he will love her and desire her. And to such degree will this lust of his break forth, that he will love everything like to the thing loved: so that hence comes that sin of which it is a shame to have memory. If, then, man shall put a bridle upon his eyes, he shall be lord of the sense, which cannot desire that which is not presented to it. For so shall the flesh be subject to the spirit. Because as the ship cannot move without wind, so the flesh without the sense cannot sin.

That thereafter it would be necessary for the penitent to turn story-telling into prayer, reason itself shows, even if it were not also a precept of God. For in every idle word man sins, and our God blots out sin by reason of prayer. For that prayer is the advocate of the soul; prayer is the medicine of the soul; prayer is the defense of the heart; prayer is the weapon of faith, prayer, is the bridle of sense; prayer is the salt of the flesh that suffers it not to be corrupted by sin. I tell you that prayer is the hands of our life, whereby the man that prays shall defend himself in the day of judgment: for he shall keep his soul from sin here on earth, and shall preserve his heart that it be not touched by evil desires; offending Satan because he shall keep his sense within the Law of God, and his flesh shall walk in righteousness;, receiving from God all that he shall ask.

As God lives, in whose presence we are, a man without prayer can no more be a man of good works than a dumb man can plead his cause to a blind one; than fistula can be healed without unguent; a man defend himself without movement; or attack another without weapons, sail without rudder, or preserve dead flesh without salt. For truly he who has no hand cannot receive. If man could change dung into gold and clay into sugar, what would he do?

Then, Jesus being silent, the disciples answered: "No one would exercise himself in any way other than in making gold and sugar." Then Jesus said: "Now why does not man change foolish story-telling into prayer? Is time, perhaps, given him by God that he may offend God? For what prince would give a city to his subject in order that the latter might make war upon him? As God lives, if man knew after what manner the soul is transformed by vain talking he would sooner bite off his tongue with his teeth than talk. O wretched world! for today men do not assemble together for prayer, but in the porches of the Temple and in the very Temple itself Satan has there the sacrifice of vain talk, and that which is worse of things which I cannot talk of without shame.

Chapter 120

The fruit of vain talking is this, that it weakens the intellect in such wise that it is not ready to receive the truth; even as a horse accustomed to carry but one ounce of cotton flock cannot carry an hundred pounds of stone. But what is worse is the man who spends his time in jests. When he is fain to pray, Satan will put into his memory those same jests, insomuch that when he ought to weep over his sins to provoke God to mercy and to win forgiveness for his sins, by laughing he provokes God to anger who will chastise him, and cast him out.

Woe, therefore, to them that jest and talk vainly! But if our God has in abomination them that jest and talk vainly, how will he hold them that murmur and slander their neighbor, and in what plight will they be who deal with sinning as with a business supremely necessary? Oh impure world, I cannot conceive how grievously you will be punished by God! He, then, who would do penance, he, I say, must give out his words at the price of gold. His disciples answered: "Now who will buy a man's words at the price of gold? Assuredly no one. And how shall he do penance? It is certain that he will become covetous!" Jesus answered: "You have your heart so heavy that I am not able to lift it up. Hence in every word it is necessary that I should tell you the meaning. But give thanks to God, who has given you grace to know the mysteries of God. I do not say that the penitent should sell his talking, but I say that when he talks he should think that he is casting forth gold. For indeed, so doing, even as gold is spent on necessary things, so he will talk [only] when it is necessary to talk. And just as no one spends gold on a thing which shall cause hurt to his body, so let him not talk of a thing that may cause hurt to his soul.

Chapter 121

When the governor has arrested a prisoner whom he examines while the notary writes down [the case], tell me, how does such a man talk?" The disciples answered: "He talks with fear and to the point, so as not to give suspicion of himself, and he is careful not to say anything that may displease the governor, but seeks to speak somewhat whereby he may be set free." Then answered Jesus: "This ought the penitent to do, then, in order not to lose his soul. For that God has given two angels to every man for notaries, the one writing the good, the other the evil that the man does. If then a man would receive mercy let him measure his talking more than gold is measured.

Chapter 122

As for avarice, that must be changed into almsgiving. truly I say to you, that even as the plummet has for its end the centre, so the avaricious has hell for his end, for it is impossible for the avaricious to possess any good in paradise. Know you wherefore? for I will tell you. As God lives, in whose presence my soul stands, the avaricious, even though he be silent with his tongue, by his works says: "There is no other God than I." Inasmuch as all that he has he is fain to spend at his own pleasure, not regarding his beginning or his end, that he is born naked, and dying leaves all. Now tell me if Herod should give you a garden to keep, and you were fain to bear yourselves as owners, not sending any fruit to Herod, and when Herod sent for fruit you drove away his messengers, tell me, would you be making yourselves kings over that garden? Assuredly you. Now I tell you that even so the avaricious man makes himself god over his riches which God has given him.

Avarice is a thirst of the sense, which having lost God through sin because it lives by pleasure, and being unable to delight itself in God, who is hidden from it, surrounds itself with temporal things which it holds as its good and it grows the stronger the more it sees itself deprived of God. And so the conversion of the sinner is from God, who gives the grace to repent. As said our father David: This change comes from the right hand of God." It is necessary that I should tell you of what sort man is, if you would know how penitence ought to be done. And so today let us render thanks to God, who has given us the grace to communicate his will by my word."

Whereupon he lifted up his hands and prayed, saying: "Lord God almighty and merciful, who in mercy has created us, giving us the rank of men, your servants, with the faith of your true Messenger, we thank you for all your benefits and would fain adore you only all the days of our life, bewailing our sins praying and giving alms, fasting and studying your word, instructing those that are ignorant of your will, suffering from the world for love of you, and giving up our life to the death to serve you. Do you, O Lord, save us from Satan, from the flesh and from the world, even as you save your elect for love of your own self and for love of your Messenger for whom you did create us, and for love of all your holy ones and prophets." The disciples ever answered: "So be it, so be it, Lord, so be it, O our merciful God."

Chapter 123

When it was day, Friday morning, early, Jesus, after the prayer, assembled his disciples and said to them: "Let us sit down for even as on this day God created man of the clay of the earth even so will I tell you what a thing is man, if God please." When all were seated, Jesus said again: "Our God, to show to his creatures his goodness and mercy and his omnipotence, with his liberality and justice, made a composition of four things contrary the one to the other, and united them in one final object, which is man and this is earth, air, water, and fire in order that each one might temper its opposite.

And he made of these four things a vessel, which is man's body, of flesh, bones, blood, marrow, and skin, with nerves and veins, and with all his inward parts wherein God placed the soul and the sense, as two hands of this life: giving for lodgement to the sense every part of the body, for it diffused itself there like oil. And to the soul gave he for lodgement the heart, where, united with the sense, it should rule the whole life.

God, having thus created man, put into him a light which is called reason, which was to unite the flesh, the sense, and the soul in a single end to work for the service of God. Whereupon, he placing this work in paradise, and the reason being seduced of the sense by the operation of Satan, the flesh lost its rest, the sense lost the delight whereby it lives, and the soul lost its beauty. Man having come to such a plight, the sense, which finds not repose in labor, but seeks delight, not being curbed by reason, follows the light which the eyes show it whence, the eyes not being able to see aught but vanity, it deceives itself, and so, choosing earthly things, sins.

Thus it is necessary that by the mercy of God man's reason be enlightened afresh, to know good from evil and [to distinguish] the true delight: knowing which, the sinner is converted to penitence. Wherefore I say to you truly, that if God our Lord enlighten not the heart of man, the reasoning of men are of no avail." John answered: "Then to what end serves the speech of men?"

Jesus replied "Man as man avails nothing to convert man to penitence but man as a means which God uses converts man so that seeing God works by a secret fashion in man for man's salvation, one ought to listen to every man, in order that among all may be received him in whom God speaks to us." James answered: "O Master, if perhaps there shall come a false prophet and lying teacher pretending to instruct us, what ought we to do?

Chapter 124

Jesus answered in parable: "A man goes to fish with a net, and therein he catches many fishes, but those that are bad he throws away.' A man went forth to sow, but only the grain that falls on good ground bears seed.' Even so ought you to do, listening to all and receiving only the truth, seeing that the truth alone bears fruit to eternal life."

Then answered Andrew: "Now how shall the truth be known?"

Jesus answered: "Everything that conforms to the Book of Moses, that receive you for true seeing that God is one, the truth is one whence it follows that the doctrine is one and the meaning of the doctrine is one and therefore the faith is one. Truly I say to you that if the truth had not been erased from the Book of Moses, God would not have given to David our father the second. And if the book of David had not been contaminated, God would not have committed the Gospel to me seeing that the Lord our God is unchangeable, and has spoken but one message to all men. Wherefore, when the Messenger of God shall come, he shall come to cleanse away all wherewith the ungodly have contaminated my book."

Then answered he who writes: "O Master, what shall a man do when the Law shall be found contaminated and the false prophet shall speak?" Jesus answered: "Great is your question, O Barnabas wherefore I tell you that in such a time few are saved, seeing that men do not consider their end, which is God. As God lives, in whose presence my soul stands, every doctrine that shall turn man aside from his end, which is God, is most evil doctrine. Wherefore there are three things that you shall consider in doctrine namely, love towards God, pity towards one's neighbor, and hatred towards yourself, who had offended God, and offends him every day. Wherefore every doctrine that is contrary to these three heads do you avoid, because it is most evil.

Chapter 125

I will return now to avarice: and I tell you that when the sense would fain acquire a thing or tenaciously keep it, reason must say: "Such a thing will have its end." It is certain that if it will have an end it is madness to love it. Wherefore it is good (a duty) for one to love and to keep that which will not have an end. Let avarice then be changed into alms, distributing rightly what [a man] has acquired wrongly.

And let him see to it that what the right hand shall give the left hand shall not know'. Because the hypocrites when they do alms desire to be seen and praised of the world. But truly they are vain, seeing that for whom a man works from him does he receive his wages. If, then, a man would receive anything of God, it is good (a duty) for him to serve God.

And see that when you do alms, you consider that you are giving to God all that [you give] for love of God. Wherefore be not slow to give, and give of the best of that which you have, for love of God. Tell me, desire you to receive of God anything that is bad? Certainly not, O dust and ashes! Then how have you faith in you if you shall give anything bad for love of God?

It were better to give nothing than to give a bad thing for in not giving you shall have some excuse according to the world: but in giving a worthless thing, and keeping the best for yourselves, what shall be the excuse? And this is all that I have to say to you concerning penitence." Barnabas answered: "How long ought penitence to last?" Jesus replied: "As long as a man is in a state of sin he ought always to repent and do penance for it. Wherefore as human life always sins, so ought it always to do penance; unless you would make more account of your shoes than of your soul, since every time that your shoes are burst you mend them."

Chapter 126

Jesus having called together his disciples, sent them forth by two and two through the region of Israel, saying: "Go and preach even as you have heard." Then they bowed themselves and he laid his hand upon their heads, saying: "In the name of God, give health to the sick, cast out the demons, and undeceive Israel concerning me, telling them that which I said before the high priest."

They departed therefore, all of them save him who writes, with James and John and they went through all Judea, preaching penitence even as Jesus had told them, healing every sort of sickness, insomuch that in Israel were confirmed the words of Jesus that God is one and Jesus is prophet of God, when they saw such a multitude do that which Jesus did concerning the healing of the sick.

But the sons of the devil found another way to persecute Jesus, and these were the priests and the scribes. Whereupon they began to say that Jesus aspired to the monarchy over Israel. But they feared the common people, wherefore they plotted against Jesus secretly.

Having passed throughout Judea the disciples returned to Jesus, who received them as a father receives his sons, saying: "Tell me,

how has wrought the Lord our God? Surely I have seen Satan fall
under your feet and you trample upon him even as the
vinedresser treads the grapes!" The disciples answered: "O Master,
we have healed numberless sick persons, and cast out many
demons which tormented men."

Jesus said: "God forgive you, O brethren, because you have sinned
in saying "We have healed,' seeing it is God that has done all."
Then said they: "We have talked foolishly wherefore, teach us
how to speak." Jesus answered: "In every good work say 'God has
wrought' and in every bad one say 'I have sinned." "So will we
do," said the disciples to him.

Then Jesus said: "Now what says Israel, having seen God do by
the hands of so many men that which God has done by my
hands?" The disciples answered: "They say that there is one God
alone and that you are God's prophet." Jesus answered with joyful
countenance: "Blessed be the holy name of God, who has not
despised the desire of me his servant!" And when he had said this
they retired to rest.

Chapter 127

Jesus departed from the desert and entered into Jerusalem
whereupon all the people ran to the Temple to see him. So after
the reading of the psalms Jesus mounted up on the pinnacle
where the scribe used to mount, and, having beckoned for silence
with his hand, he said : "Blessed be the holy name of God, O
brethren, who has created us of the clay of the earth, and not of
flaming spirit. For when we sin we find mercy before God, which
Satan will never find, because through his pride he is incorrigible,
saying that he is always noble, for that he is flaming spirit.

Have you heard, brethren, that which our father David says of our
God, that he remembers that we are dust and that our spirit goes
and returns not again, wherefore he has had mercy upon us?
Blessed are they that know these words, for they will not sin
against their Lord eternally, seeing that after the sin they repent,
wherefore their sin abides not. Woe to them that extol themselves,
for they shall be humbled to the burning coals of hell. Tell me,

brethren, what is the cause for self-exaltation? Is there, perhaps, any good here upon earth? No, assuredly, for as says Solomon, the prophet of God: "Everything that is under the sun is vanity." But if the things of the world do not give us cause to extol ourselves in our heart, much less does our life give us cause for it is burdened with many miseries, since all the creatures inferior to man fight against us. O, how many have been slain by the burning heat of summer, how many have been slain by the frost and cold of winter; how many have been slain by lightning and by hail; how many have been drowned in the sea by the fury of winds; how many have died of pestilence, of famine, or because they have been devoured of wild beasts, bitten of serpents, choked by food!

O hapless man, who extols himself having so much to weigh him down, being laid wait for by all the creatures in every place! But what shall I say of the flesh and the sense that desire only iniquity of the world, that offers nothing but sin of the wicked, who, serving Satan, persecute whosoever would live according to the Law of God? Certain it is, brethren, that if man, as says our father David, with his eyes should consider eternity, he would not sin. To extol oneself in one's heart is but to lock up the pity and mercy of God, that he pardon not. For our father David says that our God remembers that we are but dust and that our spirit goes and returns not again. Whoever extols himself, then, denies that he is dust, and hence, not knowing his need, he asks not help, and so angers God his helper. As God lives, in whose presence my soul stands, God would pardon Satan if Satan should know his own misery, and ask mercy of his Creator, who is blessed for evermore.

Chapter 128

Accordingly, brethren, I, a man, dust and clay, that walk upon the earth, say to you: Do penance and know your sins. I say, brethren, that Satan, by means of the Roman soldiery, deceived you when you said that I was God. Wherefore, beware that you believe them not, seeing they are fallen under the curse of God, serving the false and lying gods even as our father David invokes a curse

242

upon them, saying: The gods of the nations are silver and gold, the work of their

hands that have eyes and see not, have ears and hear not, have noses and smell not, have a mouth and eat not, have a tongue and speak not, have hands and touch not, have feet and walk not. Wherefore said David our father, praying our living God, Like to them be they that make them and they that trust in them.

O pride unheard of, this pride of man, who being created by God out of earth forgets his condition and would fain make God at his own pleasure! Wherein he silently mocks God, as though he should say: There is no use in serving God. For so do their works show. To this did Satan desire to reduce you, O brethren, in making you believe me to be God because, I not being able to create a fly, and being passable and mortal, I can give you nothing of use, seeing that I myself have need of everything. How, then, could I help you in all things, as it is proper to God to do? Shall we, then, who have for our God the great God who has created the universe with his word, mock at the Gentiles and their gods? There were two men who came up here into the Temple to pray: the one was a Pharisee and the other a publican. The Pharisee drew near to the sanctuary, and praying with his face uplifted said: "I give you thanks, O Lord my God, because I am not as other men, sinners, who do every wickedness, and particularly as this publican, for I fast twice in the week and give tithes of all I possess.' The publican remained afar off, bowed down to the earth, and beating his breast he said with bent head: 'Lord, I am not worthy to look upon the heaven nor upon your sanctuary, for I have sinned much; have mercy upon me!' Truly I say to you, the publican went down from the Temple in better case than the Pharisee, for that our God justified him, forgiving him his sin. But the Pharisee went down in worse case than the publican, because our God rejected him, having his works in abomination.

Chapter 129

Shall the axe, perhaps, boast itself at having cut down the forest where a man has made a garden? No, assuredly, for the man has done all, yes and [made] the axe, with his hands. And you, O man, shall you boast yourself of having done anything that is good, seeing our God created you of clay and works in you all good that is wrought? And why do you despise your neighbor? Do you not know that if God had not preserved you from Satan you would be worse than Satan?

Do you not know that one single sin changed the fair angel into the most repulsive demon? And that the most perfect man that has come into the world, which was Adam, it changed into a wretched being, subjecting him to what we suffer, together with all his offspring? What decree, then, have you, in virtue whereof you may live at your own pleasure without any fear? Woe to you, O clay, for because you have exalted yourself above God who created you you shall be abased beneath the feet of Satan who lays wait for you."

And having said this, Jesus prayed, lifting up his hands to the Lord, and the people said: "So be it! So be it!" When he had finished his prayer he descended from the pinnacle. Whereupon there were brought to him many sick folk whom he made whole, and he departed from the Temple. Thereupon Simon, a leper whom Jesus had cleansed, invited him to eat bread. The priests and scribes, who hated Jesus, reported to the Roman soldiers that which Jesus had said against their gods. For indeed they were seeking how to kill him, but found it not, because they feared the people.

Jesus, having entered the house of Simon, sat down to the table. And while he was eating, behold a woman named Mary, a public sinner, entered into the house, and flung herself upon the ground behind Jesus' feet, and washed them with her tears, anointed them with precious ointment, and wiped them with the hairs of her head. Simon was scandalized, with all that sat at meat, and they said in their hearts: "If this man were a prophet he would know who and of what sort is this woman, and would not suffer her to touch him." Then Jesus said: "Simon, I have a thing to say to you." Simon answered: "Speak, O Master, for I desire your word."

244

Chapter 130

Jesus said: "There was a man who had two debtors. The one owed to his creditor fifty pence, the other five hundred. Whereupon, when neither of them had wherewithal to pay, the owner, moved with compassion, forgave the debt to each. Which of them would love his creditor most?" Simon answered: "He to whom was forgiven the greater debt." Jesus said: "You have well said; I say to you, therefore, behold this woman and yourself, for you were both debtors to God, the one for leprosy of the body, the other for leprosy of the soul, which is sin. God our Lord, moved with compassion through my prayers, has willed to heal your body and her soul.

You, therefore, love me little, because you have received little as a gift. And so, when I entered your house you did not kiss me nor anoint my head. But this woman, lo! straightway on entering your house she placed herself at my feet, which she has washed with her tears and anointed with precious ointment. Wherefore truly I say to you, many sins are forgiven her, because she has loved much." And turning to the woman he said: "Go your way in peace, for the Lord our God has pardoned your sins, but see you sin no more. Your faith has saved you."

Chapter 131

His disciples drew near to Jesus after the nightly prayer, and said: "O Master, how must we do to escape pride?" Jesus answered: "Have you seen a poor man invited to a prince's house to eat bread?" John answered: "I have eaten bread in Herod's house. For before I knew you I went to fish, and used to sell the fish to the family of Herod. Whereupon, one day when he was feasting, I having brought thither a fine fish, he made me stay and eat there." Then Jesus said: "Now how did you eat bread with infidels? God pardon you, O John! But tell me, how did you bear yourself at the table? Did you seek to have the most honorable place? Did you ask for the most delicate food? Did you speak when you were not questioned at the table? Did you account yourself more worthy than the others to sit at table?"

John answered: "As God lives, I did not dare to lift up my eyes, seeing myself, a poor fisherman, ill-clad, sitting among the king's barons. Whereupon, when the king gave me a little piece of flesh, I thought that the world had fallen upon my head, for the greatness of the favor that the king did to me. And truly I say that, if the king had been of our Law, I should have been fain to serve him all the days of my life." Jesus cried out: "Hold your peace, John, for I fear lest God should cast us into the abyss, even like Abiram, for our pride!"

The disciples trembled with fear at the words of Jesus, when he said again: "Let us fear God, that He cast us not into the abyss for our pride. O brethren, have you heard of John what is done in the house of a prince? Woe to the men that come into the world, for as they live in pride they shall die in contempt and shall go into confusion. For this world is a house where God feasts men, wherein have eaten all the holy ones and prophets of God. And truly I say to you, everything that a man receives, he receives it from God. Wherefore man ought to bear himself with deepest humility, knowing his own vileness and the greatness of God, with the great bounty by which he nourishes us. Therefore it is not lawful for man to say: 'Ah, why is this done and this said in the world?' but rather to account himself, as in truth he is, unworthy to stand in the world at God's board. As God lives, in whose presence my soul stands, there is nothing so small received here in the world from [the hand of] God, but that in return man ought to spend his life for love of God.

As God lives, you sinned not, O John, in eating with Herod, for it was of God's disposition you did so, in order that you might be our teacher and [the teacher] of every one that fears God. So do," said Jesus to his disciples, "that you may live in the world as John lived in the house of Herod when he ate bread with him, for so shall you be in truth free from all pride."

Chapter 132

Jesus walking along the sea of Galilee was surrounded by a great multitude of folk, wherefore he went into a little boat which lay a little off from the shore by itself, and anchored so near the land that the voice of Jesus might be heard. Whereupon they all drew near to the sea, and sitting down awaited his word. He then opened his mouth and said:

"Behold, the sower went out to sow, whereupon as he sowed some of the seed fell upon the road, and this was trodden under foot of men and eaten up of birds, some fell upon the stones, whereupon when it sprang up, because it had no moisture, it was burnt up by the sun, some fell in the hedges, whereupon when it grew up the thorns chocked the seed and some fell on good ground, whereupon it. bare fruit, even to thirty, sixty, and an one hundredfold."

Again Jesus said: "Behold, the father of a family sowed good seed in his field: whereupon, as the servants of the good man slept, the enemy of the man their master came and sowed tares over the good seed. Whereupon, when the corn sprang up, there was seen sprung up among the corn a great quantity of tares. The servants came to their master and said: "O Sir, did you not sow good seed in your field? Wherefore then is there sprung up therein a great quantity of tares?" The master answered: 'Good seed did I sow, but while men slept the enemy of man came and sowed tares over the corn.'

Said the servants: "Will you that we go and pull up the tares from among the corn?" The master answered: "Do not so, for you would pull up the corn therewith, but wait till the time of harvest comes. For then shall you go and pull up the tares from among the corn and cast them into the fire to be burned, but the corn you shall put into my granary.' "

Again Jesus said: "There went forth many men to sell figs. But when they arrived at the market-place, behold, men sought not good figs but fair leaves. Therefore the men were not able to sell their figs. And seeing this, an evil citizen said: 'Surely I may become rich.' Whereupon he called together his two sons and [said]: 'Go you and gather a great quantity of leaves with bad figs.' And these they sold for their weight in gold, for the men were mightily pleased with leaves. Whereupon the men, eating the figs, became sick with a grievous sickness."

Again Jesus said: "Behold a citizen has a fountain, from which all the neighboring citizens take water to wash off their uncleanness; but the citizen suffers his own clothes to putrefy."

Again Jesus said: "There went forth two men to sell apples. The one chose to sell the peel of the apple for its weight in gold, not caring for the substance of the apples. The other desired to give the apples away, receiving only a little bread for his journey. But men bought the peel of the apples for its weight in gold, not caring for him who was fain to give them, no even despising him." And thus on that day Jesus spoke to the crowd in parables. Then having dismissed them, he went with his disciples to Nain, where he had raised to life the widow's son, who, with his mother, received him into his house and ministered to him.

Chapter 133

His disciples drew near to Jesus and asked him, saying: "O Master, tell us the meaning of the parables which you spoke to the people." Jesus answered: "The hour of prayer draws near, wherefore when the evening prayer is ended I will tell you the meaning of the parables." When the prayer was ended, the disciples came near to Jesus and he said to them: 'The man who sows seed upon the road, upon the stones, upon the thorns, upon the good ground, is he who teaches the word of God, which falls upon a great number of men.

It falls upon the road when it comes to the ears of sailors and merchants, who by reason of the long journeys which they make, and the variety of nations with whom they have dealings, have the word of God removed from their memory by Satan. It falls upon the stones when it comes to the ears of courtiers, for by reason of the great anxiety these have to serve the body of a prince the word of God to does not sink into them. Wherefore, albeit they have some memory thereof, as soon as they have any tribulation the word of God goes out of their memory: for, seeing they serve not God, they cannot hope for help from God.

It falls among the thorns when it comes to the ears of them that love their own life, whereupon, though the word of God grow upon them, when carnal desires grow up they choke the good seed of the word of God, for carnal comforts cause [men] to forsake the word of God. That which falls on good ground is when the word of God comes to the ears of him who fears God, whereupon it brings forth fruit of eternal life. Truly I say to you, that in every condition when man fears God the word of God will bear fruit in him.

'Of that father of a family, I tell you truly that he is God our Lord, father of all things, for that he has created all things. But he is not a father after the manner of nature, for that he is incapable of motion, without which generation is impossible. It is, then, our God, whose is this world, and the field where he sows is mankind, and the seed is the word of God. So when the teachers are negligent in preaching the word of God, through being occupied in the business of the world, Satan sows error in the heart of men, whence are come countless sects of wicked doctrine.

'The holy ones and prophets cry: "O Sir, gave you not, then, good doctrine to men? Wherefore, then, be there so many errors?" God answers: 'I have given good doctrine to men, but while men have been given up to vanity Satan has sowed errors to bring to nothing my Law.' The holy ones say: 'O Sir, we will disperse these errors by destroying men."

God answers: 'Do not so, for the faithful are so closely joined to the infidels by kinship that the faithful will be lost with the infidel. But wait until the Judgment, for at that time shall the infidels be gathered by my angels and shall be cast out with Satan into hell, while the good faithful ones shall come to my kingdom.' Surely, many infidel fathers shall beget faithful sons, for whose sake God waits for the world to repent.

Chapter 134

They that bear good figs are the true teachers who preach good doctrine, but the world, which takes pleasure in lies, seeks from the teachers leaves of fine words and flattery. The which seeing,

Satan joins himself with the flesh and the sense, and brings a large supply of leaves; that is, a quantity of earthly things, in which he covers up sin, which receiving, man becomes sick and ready for eternal death. The citizen who has the water and gives his water to others to wash off their uncleanness, but suffers his own garments to become putrefied, is the teacher who to others preaches penitence and himself abides still in sin. O wretched man, because not the angels but his own tongue writes upon the air the punishment that is fitting for him!

If one had the tongue of an elephant, and the rest of his body were as small as an ant, would not this thing be monstrous? Yes, surely. Now I say to you, truly, that he is more monstrous who preaches penitence to others, but himself repents not of his sins. Those two men that sell apples are the one, he who preaches for love of God, wherefore he flatters none, but' preaches in truth, seeking only a poor man's livelihood. As God lives, in whose presence my soul stands, such a man is not received by the world, but rather despised. But he who sells the peel for its weight in gold, and gives the apple away, he it is who preaches to please men: and, so flattering the world, he ruins the soul that follows his flattery. Ah! how many have perished for this cause!' Then answered he who writes and said: "How should one listen to the word of God, and how should one know him that preaches for love of God?"

Jesus answered: "He that preaches should be listened to as though God were speaking when he preaches good doctrine; because God is speaking through his mouth. But he that reproves not sins, having respect of persons, flattering particular men, should be avoided as an horrible serpent, for in truth he poisons the human ear." Understand you? Truly I say to you, even as a wounded man has no need of fine bandages to bind up his wounds, but rather of a good ointment, so also has a sinner no need of fine words, but rather of good reproofs, in order that he may cease to sin.'

Chapter 135

Then said Peter: "O Master, tell us how the lost shall be tormented, and how long they shall be in hell, in order that man may flee from sin." Jesus answered: 'O Peter, it is a great thing that you have asked, nevertheless, if God please, I will answer you. Know you, therefore, that hell is one, yet has seven centers one below another. Hence, even as sin is of seven kinds, for as seven gates of hell has Satan generated it: so are there seven punishments therein.

For the proud, that is the loftiest in heart, shall be plunged into the lowest centre, passing through all the centers above it, and suffering in them all the pains that are therein. And as here he seeks to be higher than God, in wishing to do after his own manner, contrary to that which God commands, and not wishing to recognize anyone above him: even so there shall he be put under the feet of Satan and his devils, who shall trample him down as the grapes are trampled when wine is made, and he shall be ever derided and scorned of devils.

'The envious, who here chaffs at the good of his neighbor and rejoices at his misfortune, shall go down to the sixth Centre, and there shall be chafed by the fangs of a great number of infernal serpents. And it shall seem to him that all things in hell rejoice at his torment, and mourn that he be not gone down to the seventh centre. For although the damned are incapable of any joy, yet the justice of God shall cause that it shall so seem to the wretched envious man, as when one seems in a dream to be spurned by some one and feels torment thereby even so shall be the object set before the wretched envious man. For where there is no gladness at all it shall seem to him that every one rejoices at his misfortune, and mourns that he has no worse.

The covetous shall go down to the fifth Centre, where he shall suffer extreme poverty, as the rich feast suffered. And the demons, for greater torment, shall offer him that which he desires, and when he shall have it in his hands other devils with violence shall snatch it from his hands with these words: "Remember that you would not give for love of God; so God wills not that you now receive. Oh unhappy man! Now shall he find himself in that condition when he shall remember past abundance and behold

251

the penury of the present, and that with the goods that then he may not have he could have acquired eternal delights!

To the fourth centre shall go the lustful, where they that have transformed the way given them by God shall be as corn that is cooked in the burning dung of the devil. And there shall they be embraced by horrible infernal serpents. And they that shall have sinned with harlots, all these acts of impurity shall be transformed for them into union with the infernal furies, which are demons like women, whose hair is serpents, whose eyes are flaming sulfur, whose mouth is poisonous, whose tongue is gull whose body is all girt with barbed hooks like those wherewith they catch the silly fish, whose claws are like those of gryphons, whose nails are razors, the nature of whose generative organs is fire. Now with these shall all the lustful enjoy the infernal embers which shall be their bed.

To the third centre shall go down the slothful who will not work now. Here are built cities and immense palaces, which as soon as they are finished must needs be pulled down straightway, because a single stone is not placed aright. And these enormous stones are laid upon the shoulders of the slothful, who has not his hands free to cool his body as he walks and to ease the burden, seeing that sloth has taken away the power of his arms. and his legs are fettered with infernal serpents. And, what is worse, behind him are the demons, who push him, and make him fall to earth many times beneath the weight, nor does any help him to lift it up: no, it being too much to lift, a double amount is laid upon him.

To the second centre shall go down the gluttonous. Now here there is dearth of food, to such a degree that there shall be nothing to eat but live scorpions and live serpents, which give such torment that it would be better never to have been born than to eat such food. There are offered to them indeed by the demons, in appearance, delicate meats, but for that they have their hands and feet bound with fetters of fire, they cannot put out a hand on the occasion when the meat appears to them. But what is worse, those

252

very scorpions which he eats that they may devour his belly, not being able to come forth speedily, rend the secret parts of the glutton. And when they are come forth foul and unclean, filthy as they are, they are eaten over again.

The wrathful goes down to the first centre, where he is insulted by all the devils and by as many of the damned as go down lower than he. They spurn him and smite him, making him lie down upon the road where they pass, planting their feet upon his throat. Yet is he not able to defend himself, for that he has his hands and feet bound. And what is worse, he is not able to give vent to his wrath by insulting others, seeing that his tongue is fastened by a hook, like that which he uses who sells flesh. In this accursed place shall there be a general punishment, common to all the centers, like the mixture of various grains make a loaf. For fire, ice, thunderstorms, lightning,

sulfur, heat, cold, wind, frenzy, terror, shall all be united by the justice of God, and in such wise that the cold shall not temper, the heat nor the fire the ice, but each shall give torment to the wretched sinner.

Chapter 136

In this accursed spot shall abide the infidels for evermore: insomuch that if the world were filled with grains of millet, and a single bird once in a hundred years should take away a single grain to empty the world if when it should be empty the infidels were to go into paradise, they would rest delighted. But there is not this hope, because their torment cannot have an end, seeing that they were not willing for the love of God to put an end to their sin. But the faithful shall have comfort, because their torment shall have an end.' The disciples were affrighted, hearing this, and said: 'So then the faithful must go into hell?'

Jesus answered: 'Every one, be he who he may, must go into hell. It is true, however, that the holy ones and prophets of God shall go there to behold, not suffering any punishment and the righteous, only suffering fear. And what shall I say? I tell you that thither shall come [even] the Messenger of God, to behold the justice of God. Thereupon hell shall tremble at his presence. And because he has human flesh, all those that have human flesh and shall be under punishment, so long as the Messenger of God shall abide to behold hell, so long shall they abide without punishment. But he shall abide there [only] so long as it takes to shut and open the eyes. And this shall God do in order that every creature may know that he has received benefit from the Messenger of God. When he shall go there all the devils shall shriek, and seek to hide themselves beneath the burning embers, saying one to another: "Fly, fly, for here comes Muhammad, our enemy!" Hearing which, Satan shall smite himself upon the face with both his hands, and screaming shall say: "You are more noble than I, in my despite, and this is unjustly done!" As for the faithful, who are in seventy-two grades, those of the two last grades, who shall have had the faith without good works, the one being sad at good works, and the other delighting in evil, they shall abide in hell seventy thousand years.

After those years shall the angel Gabriel come into hell, and shall hear them say: "O Muhammad, where are your promises made to us, saying that those who have your faith shall not abide in hell for evermore?" Then the angel of God shall return to paradise, and having approached with reverence the Messenger of God shall narrate to him what he has heard. Then shall his Messenger speak to God and say: "Lord, my God, remember the promise made to me your servant, concerning them that have received my faith, that they shall not abide for evermore in hell." God shall answer: "Ask what you will, O my friend, for I will give you all that you ask."

Chapter 137

Then shall the Messenger of God say: "O Lord, there are of the faithful who have been in hell seventy thousand years. Where, O Lord, is your mercy? I pray you, Lord, to free them from those bitter punishments."

Then shall God command the four favorite angels of God that they go to hell and take out every one that has the faith of his

Messenger, and lead him into paradise. And this they shall do. And such shall be the advantage of the faith of God's Messenger, that those that shall have believed in him, even though they have not done any good works, seeing they died in this faith, shall go into paradise after the punishment of which I have spoken.'

Chapter 138

When morning was come, early, all the men of the city, with the women and children, came to the house where Jesus was with his disciples, and sought him saying: "Sir, have mercy upon us, because this year the worms have eaten the corn, and we shall not receive any bread this year in our land." 2. Jesus answered: "O what fear is yours! Do you not know that Elijah, the servant of God, while the persecution of Ahab continued for three years, did not see bread, nourishing himself only with herbs and wild fruits? David our father, the prophet of God, ate wild fruits and herbs for two years, [while] being persecuted [by] Saul, [and] twice only did he eat bread." 3. The men answered: "Sir, they were prophets of God, nourished with spiritual delight, and therefore they endured well; but how shall these little ones fare?" and they showed him the multitude of their children. Then Jesus had compassion on their misery, and said: "How long is it until harvest?" They answered: "Twenty days." 4. Then Jesus said: "See that for these twenty days we give ourselves to fasting and prayer; for God will have mercy upon you. Truly I say to you, God has caused this dearth because here began the madness of men and the sin of Israel when they said that I was God, or Son of God." 5. When they had fasted for nineteen days, on the morning of the twentieth day, they beheld the fields and hills covered with ripe corn. They ran to Jesus, and recounted everything to him. And when he had heard it Jesus gave thanks to God, and said: "Go, brethren, gather the bread which God has given." They gathered so much corn that they did not know where to store it, and this thing was cause of plenty in Israel.

The citizens took council to set up Jesus as their king knowing which he fled from them and the disciples strove fifteen days to find him.

Chapter 139

Jesus was found by him who writes, and by James with John. And they, weeping, said: "O Master, why did you flee from us? We have sought you mourning; yes, all the disciples seek you weeping." Jesus answered: "I fled because I knew that a host of devils is preparing for me that which in a short time you shall see. For, the chief priests with the elders of the people shall rise against me and [they] shall wrest authority to kill me from the Roman governor, because they shall fear that I wish to usurp kingship over Israel. Moreover, I shall be sold and betrayed by one of my disciples, as Joseph was sold into Egypt. 2. But the just God shall make him fall, as says the prophet David: He shall make him fall into the pit who spreads a snare for his neighbor. For God shall save me from their hands, and shall take me out of the world."

The three disciples were afraid, but Jesus comforted them saying: "Do not be afraid, for none of you shall betray me." [And the three disciples] received some consolation [from this].

The day following there came, two by two, thirty-six of Jesus' disciples, and he abode in Damascus awaiting the others. And they mourned every one, for they knew that Jesus must depart from the world. Wherefore he opened his mouth and said: "He who walks without knowing where he goes is surely unhappy, but more unhappy is he who is able and knows how to reach a good hostelry, yet desires and wills to abide on the miry road, in the rain, and in peril of robbers.

Tell me, brethren, is this world our native country? Surely not, seeing that the first man was cast out into the world into exile and there he suffers the punishment of his error. [Is there] an exile who does not aspire to return to his own rich country when he finds himself in poverty? Assuredly reason denies it, but experience proves it, because the lovers of the world will not think upon death. No, when one speaks to them [of death] they will not [heed] his speech.

Chapter 140

Believe, O men, that I [have] come into the world with a privilege which no man has had, nor will even the Messenger of God have it, seeing that our God did not create man to set him in the world, but rather to place him in paradise. It is certain that he who has no hope of receiving anything from the Romans, because they are of a law that is foreign to him, is not willing to leave his own country with all that he has, never to return, and go to live in Rome. And much less would he do so when he found himself to have offended Caesar. Even so I tell you truly, and Solomon, God's prophet, cries with me: O death, how bitter is the remembrance of you to them that have rest in their riches! 2. I do not say this because I have to die now, for I am sure that I shall live even near to the end of the world. But I will speak to you of this [matter] in order that you may learn to die. As God lives, everything that is done amiss, even once, shows that to work a thing well it is necessary to exercise oneself in that [thing]. Have you seen the soldiers, how in time of peace they exercise themselves with one another as if they were at war? How shall a man who has not learned to die well die a good death? 3. The death of the holy is precious in the sight of the Lord, said the prophet David. Do you know why [such a death is precious]? I will tell you. It is because, even as all rare things are precious, so the death of them that die well, being rare, is precious in the sight of God our creator. Whenever a man begins anything, not only is he [aiming] to finish [it], but he takes pains that his design may have a good conclusion. 4. O miserable man, that prizes his [clothes] more than himself, for when he cuts the cloth he measures it carefully before he cuts it; and when it is cut he sews it with care. But his life - which is born to die, since [only he] who is not born does not die - [why] will men not measure their life by death? 5. Have you seen them that build [and] how they lay every stone with the foundation in view, measuring if it is straight [so] that the wall will not fall down? O wretched man! for the building of his life will fall with great ruin because he does not look not to the foundation of death!

Chapter 141

Tell me: when a man is born, how is he born? Surely, he is born naked. And when he is laid dead beneath the ground, what advantage has he? A mean linen cloth in which he is wound: and this is the reward which the world gives him. If the means in every work must be proportionate to the beginning and the end in order that the work is brought to a good end, what end shall the man have who desires earthly riches? He shall die, as says David, prophet of God: "The sinner shall die a most evil death."

If a man sewing cloth should thread beams instead of thread in the needle, how would the work attain [its end]? Surely he would work in vain, and be despised of his neighbors. Now man sees not that he is doing this continually when he gathered earthly goods. For death is the needle, wherein the beams of earthly goods cannot be threaded. Nevertheless in his madness he strives continually to make the work succeed, but in vain.

And whoever believes not this at my word, let him gaze upon the tombs, for there shall he find the truth. He who would fain become wise beyond all others in the fear of God, let him study the book of the tomb, for there shall he find the true doctrine for his salvation. For he will know to beware of the world, the flesh, and the sense, when he sees that man's flesh is reserved to be food of worms. Tell me, if there were a road which was of such condition that walking in the midst thereof a man should go safely, but walking on the edges he would break his head, what would you say if you saw men opposing one another, and striving in emulation to get nearest to the edge and kill themselves? What amazement would be yours! Assuredly you would say: "They are mad and frenzied, and if they are not frenzied they are desperate." 'Even so is it true,' answered the disciples.

Then Jesus wept and said: 'Even so, truly, are the lovers of the world. For if they lived according to reason, which holds a middle place in man, they would follow the Law of God, and would be saved from eternal death. But because they follow the flesh and the world they are frenzied, and cruel enemies of their own selves, striving to live more arrogantly and more lasciviously than one another.'

Chapter 142

Judas, the traitor, when he saw that Jesus was fled, lost the hope of becoming powerful in the world, for he carried Jesus' purse, wherein was kept all that was given him for love of God. He hoped that Jesus would become king of Israel, and so he himself would be a powerful man. Wherefore, having lost this hope, he said within himself: 'If this man were a prophet, he would know that I steal his money, and so he would lose patience and cast me out of his service, knowing that I believe not in him. And if he were a wise man he would not flee from the honor that God wills to give him. Wherefore it will be better that I make arrangement with the chief priests and with the scribes and Pharisees, and see how to give him up into their hands, for so shall I be able to obtain something good.'

Whereupon, having made his resolution, he gave notice to the scribes and Pharisees how the matter had passed in Nain. And they took counsel with the high priest, saying: 'What shall we do if this man become king? Surely we shall fare badly, because he is fain to reform the worship of God after the ancient custom, for he cannot away with our traditions. Now how shall we fare under the sovereignty of such a man? Surely we shall all perish with our children: for being cast out of our office we shall have to beg our bread.

We now, praised be God, have a king and a governor that are alien to our Law, who care not for our Law, even as we care not for theirs. And so we are able to do whatsoever we list, for, even though we sin, our God is so merciful that he is appeased with sacrifice and fasting. But if this man become king he will not be appeased unless he shall see the worship of God according as Moses wrote, and what is worse, he says that the Messiah shall not come of the seed of David (as one of his chief disciples has told us), but says that he shall come of the seed of Ishmael, and that the promise was made in Ishmael and not in Isaac.

259

What then shall the fruit be if this man be suffered to live? Assuredly the Ishmaelites shall come into repute with the Romans, and they shall give them our country in possession, and so shall Israel again be subjected to slavery as it was aforetime.' Wherefore, having heard the proposal, the high priest gave answer that he must needs treat with Herod and with the governor, 'because the people are so inclined towards him that without the soldiery we shall not be able to do anything, and may it please God that with the soldiery we may accomplish this business.' Wherefore, having taken counsel among themselves, they plotted to seize him by night, when the governor and Herod should agree thereto.

Chapter 143

Then all the disciples came to Damascus, by the will of God. And on that day Judas the traitor, more than any other, made show of having suffered grief at Jesus' absence, at which Jesus said: "Let every one beware of him who without occasion labors to give you tokens of love." And God took away our understanding, that we might not know to what end he said this. After the coming of all the disciples, Jesus said: "Let us return into Galilee, for the angel of God has said to me that I must go there."

So one sabbath morning, Jesus came to Nazareth. When the citizens recognized Jesus, everyone desired to see him. A publican named Zacchaeus, who was of small stature, not being able to see Jesus because of the great multitude, climbed to the top of a sycamore, and there waited for Jesus to pass that place when he went to the synagogue. Jesus then, having come to that place, lifted up his eyes and said: "Come down, Zacchaeus, for today I will abide in your house." The man came down and received him with gladness, making a splendid feast.

The Pharisees murmured, saying to Jesus' disciples: "Why [has] your master gone in to eat with publicans and sinners?" Jesus answered: "Why does the physician [enter] into a house? Tell me, and I will tell you why I am come in here." They answered: "To heal the sick." "You say the truth," said Jesus, "for [those who are] whole have no need of medicine, only the sick.

Chapter 144

As God lives, in whose presence my soul stands, God sends his prophets and servants into the world in order that sinners may repent, and he sends [them] not for the sake of the righteous, because they had no need of repentance, even as he that is clean has no need of the bath. But truly I say to you, if you were true Pharisees you would be glad that I should have gone in to sinners for their salvation. Tell me, do you know your origin and how the world began to receive

Pharisees? I will tell you, seeing that you do not know it, so hearken to my words.

Enoch, a friend of God, who walked with God in truth, making no account of the world, was translated into paradise; and there he abides until the Judgment (for when the end of the world draws near he shall return to help the world with Elijah and one other). And so men, having knowledge of this, through desire of paradise, began to seek God their creator. For 'Pharisee' strictly means 'seeks God' in the language of Canaan, for there did this name begin [as a] way of deriding good men, since the Canaanites were given up to idolatry, which is the worship of human hands. Whereupon the Canaanites, beholding those of our people that were separated from the world to serve God, when they saw such an one, said in derision 'Pharisee!' that is, 'He seeks God', as much as to say: 'O madman, you have no statues of idols and adore the wind, look to your fate and come and serve our gods.' Truly I say to you," said Jesus, "all the saints and prophets of God have been Pharisees not in name, as you are, but in very deed. For in all their acts they sought God their creator, and for love of God they forsook cities and their own goods, selling [their goods] and giving to the poor for love of God."

Chapter 145

As God lives, in the time of Elijah, friend and prophet of God, there were twelve mountains inhabited by seventeen thousand Pharisees, and so it was that [even] in so great a number there was not found a single reprobate, but all were elect of God. But now, when Israel has more than a hundred thousand Pharisees, may it please God that out of every thousand there be one elect!"

The Pharisees answered in indignation: "So then we are all reprobate, and you hold our religion in reprobation!" Jesus answered: "I do not hold the religion of the true Pharisees in reprobation but in approbation and for that I am ready to die. But come, let us see if you are [true] Pharisees. Elijah, the friend of God, at the prayer of his disciple Elisha, wrote a little book in which he included all human wisdom with the Law of God our Lord."

The Pharisees were confounded when they heard the name of the book of Elijah, because they knew that, through their traditions, no one observed such doctrine. They [claimed they had] to depart under pretext of business to be done. Then Jesus said: "If you were [true] Pharisees you would forsake all other business to attend to this, for the Pharisee seeks God alone." So they tarried in confusion to listen to Jesus, who said again.:

"Elijah, servant of God" (for so begins the little Book), "to all them that desire to walk with God their creator, writes this:

Whoever desires to learn much, they (sic) fear God little, because he who fears God is content to know only that which God wills. They that seek fair words do not seek God, who does nothing but reprove our sins.

They that desire to seek God, let them shut fast the doors and windows of their house, for the master does not suffer himself to be found outside his house [in a place] where he is not loved. Therefore guard your senses and guard your heart, because God is not found outside of us, in this world in which he is hated.

They that wish to do good works, let them attend to their own selves, for [there is no profit] in gaining the whole world and losing one's own soul.

They that wish to teach others, let them live better than others, because nothing can be learned from him who knows less than ourselves. How shall the sinner amend his life when he hears one worse than he teaching him?

They that seek God, let him (sic) flee the conversation of men, because Moses being alone upon Mount Sinai found him and spoke with God, as does a friend who speaks with a friend.

They that seek God, shall come forth [to where] there are men of the world only once in [every] thirty days for in respect of the business of him that seeks God works for two years can be done in one day.

When he walks, let him not look save at his own feet.

When he speaks, let him not speak save that which is necessary.

When they eat, let them rise from the table still hungry, thinking every day not to attain to the next; spending their time as one draws his breath.

Let one garment, of the skin of beasts, suffice.

Let the lump of earth sleep on the naked earth [and] for every night let two hours of sleep suffice.

Let him hate no one save himself, condemn no one save himself.

In prayer, let them stand in such fear as if they were at the Judgment to come.

Now do this in the service of God, with the Law that God has given you through Moses, for in this way you shall find God [so] that in every time and place you shall feel that you are in God and God [is] in you."

This is the little book of Elijah, O Pharisees. Again I say to you that if you were [true] Pharisees you would have had joy that I [have] entered in here, because God has mercy upon sinners."

Chapter 146

Then Zacchaeus said: "Sir, behold I will give, for love of God, fourfold all that I have received by usury." Then Jesus said: "This day has salvation come to this house. Truly, truly, many publicans, harlots, and sinners shall go into the kingdom of God, and they that account themselves righteous shall go into eternal flames." Hearing this, the Pharisees departed in indignation.

Then Jesus said to them that were converted to repentance, and to his disciples: "* There was a father who had two sons, and the

263

younger said: 'Father, give me my portion of goods', and his father gave it [to] him. And he, having received his portion, departed and went into a far country, where he wasted all his substance with harlots, living luxuriously. After this there arose a mighty famine in that country, such that the wretched man went to serve a citizen, who set him to feed swine in his property. And while feeding them he assuaged his hunger in company with the swine, eating acorns.

But when he came to himself he said: 'Oh, how many in my father's house [are] feasting in abundance, and I perish here with hunger! I will arise, therefore, and will go to my father, and will say to him: 'Father, I have sinned in heaven against you, do with me as you do to one of your servants.' The poor man went, and it came to pass that his father saw him coming from afar off, and was moved to compassion over him. So he went forth to meet him, and having come up to him he embraced him and kissed him.

The son bowed himself down, saying: 'Father, I have sinned in heaven against you, do to me as to one of your servants, for I am not worthy to be called your son.' The father answered: 'Son, do not say so, for you are my son, and I will not suffer you to be in the condition of my slave.' And he called his servants and said: 'Bring new robes here and clothe my son, and give him new [garments], give him the ring on his finger, and kill the fatted calf and we will make merry. For [this] son [of mine] was dead but has now come to life again; he was lost and now is found.'

Chapter 147

While they were making merry in the house, the elder son came home, and hearing that they were making merry within, he marveled and called one of the servants, asking him why they were making merry in this way. The servant answered him: 'Your brother [has] come [home] and your father has killed the fatted calf, and they are feasting.' The elder son was greatly angered when he heard this, and would not go into the house. Therefore his father came out to him and said to him: 'Son, your brother [has] come. Come therefore and rejoice with him.'

The [elder] son answered with indignation: 'I have always served you with good service, and you never gave me a lamb to eat with my friends. But as for this worthless fellow that departed from you, wasting all his portion with harlots, now that he is come you have killed the fatted calf!" The father answered: 'Son, you are always with me and everything is yours, but this one was dead and is alive again, was lost and now is found, [that is why] we must rejoice.' The elder son was more angry, and said: 'You can go and triumph [but] I will not eat at the table of fornicators." And he departed from his father without receiving even a piece of money. As God lives," said Jesus, "even so is there rejoicing among the angels of God over one sinner that repents."

And when they had eaten he departed for he [was going] to Judea. The disciples said: "Master, do not go to Judea, for we know that the Pharisees have taken counsel with the high priest against you." Jesus answered: "I knew it before they did it, but I do not fear, for they cannot do anything contrary to the will of God. Let them do all that they desire, for I do not fear them but [rather] fear God.

Chapter 148

'Tell me now: the Pharisees of today, are they [really] Pharisees? are they servants of God? Surely not! Yes, and I say to you truly, that there is nothing worse here upon earth than [when] a man covers himself with [the] profession and garb of religion [in order] to cover his wickedness. I will tell you one single example of the Pharisees of old time, in order that you may know the present ones. After the departure of Elijah, because of the great persecution by idolaters, that holy congregation of Pharisees was dispersed. For in that same time of Elijah more than ten thousand prophets who were true Pharisees were slain in one year.

Two Pharisees went into the mountains to dwell there, and one [of them] abode fifteen years knowing nothing of his neighbor, although they were but one hour's journey apart. See then if they were inquisitive! It came to pass that there arose a drought on those mountains, and so both set themselves to search for water, and so they found each other. The more aged [one] said - for it was their custom that the eldest should speak before every other, and they held it a great sin for a young man to speak before an old one - the elder, therefore, said: 'Where do you dwell, brother?' He answered, pointing out the dwelling with his finger: 'I dwell here' (for they were near to the dwelling of the younger.)

The elder said: 'How long [have] you dwelt here, brother?' The younger answered: 'Fifteen years.' The elder said: 'Perhaps you came [here] when Ahab slew the servants of God?' 'Even so,' replied the younger. The elder said: 'O brother, do you know who is now king of Israel?' The younger answered: 'It is God that is King of Israel, for the idolaters are not kings but persecutors of Israel.' 'It is true,' said the elder, "but I meant to say, who is it that now persecutes Israel?'

The younger answered: 'The sins of Israel persecute Israel, because, if they had not sinned, [God] would not have raised the idolatrous princes up against Israel.' Then the elder said: 'Who is that infidel prince whom God has sent for the chastisement of Israel?' The younger answered: 'How should I know, seeing [that for] these fifteen years I have not seen any man except you, and I do not know how to read so no letters are sent to me?' The elder said: '[But] how new are your sheepskins! Who has given them to you, if you have not seen any man?'

Chapter 149

The younger answered: 'He who kept the raiment of the people of Israel good for forty years in the wilderness has kept my skins even as you see [them].' Then the elder perceived that the younger was more perfect than he, for every year he had had dealings with men. So, in order that he might have [the benefit of] his conversation, he said: 'Brother, you do not know how to read, [but] I know how to read, and I have in my house the psalms of David. Come, then, that I may give you a reading each day and make plain to you what David says.' The younger answered: 'Let us go now.'

The elder said: 'O brother, it is now two days since I have drunk water, therefore let us seek a little water.' The younger replied: 'O brother, it is now two months since I have drunk water. Let us go, therefore, and see what God says by his prophet David: the Lord is able to give us water.' [And so] they returned to the dwellings of the elder, at the door of which they found a spring of fresh water. The elder said: 'O brother, you are a holy one of God, God has given this spring for your sake.'

The younger answered: 'O brother, you say this in humility, but it is certain that if God had done this for my sake he would have made a spring close to my dwelling [so] that I should not [have to] depart [in search of it]. For I confess to you that I sinned against you. When you said that for two days you did not drink [and that] you sought water, and I had been for two months without drinking, I felt an exaltation within me, as though I were better than you.' Then the elder said: 'O brother, you said the truth, therefore you did not sin.'

The younger said: 'O brother, you have forgotten what our father Elijah said, that he who seeks God ought to condemn himself alone. Surely he did not write it that we might [only] know it, but rather that we might observe it.' The more aged [of the two], perceiving the truth and righteousness of his companion, said: 'It is true, and our God has pardoned you.' And having said this he took the Psalms, and read that which our father David says: I will set a watch over my mouth that my tongue decline not to words of iniquity, excusing with excuse my sin. And here the aged man made a discourse upon the tongue, and the younger departed. [After this] there were fifteen more years before they found one another, because the younger changed his dwelling.

Accordingly, when he had found him again, the elder [Pharisee] said: 'O brother, why have you not returned to any dwelling?' The younger answered: 'Because I have not yet learned well what you said to me.' Then the elder said: 'How can this be, seeing [that] fifteen years have past?' The younger replied: 'As for the words, I learned them in a single hour and have never forgotten them, but I have not yet observed them. To what purpose is it, then, to learn too much, and not to observe it? Our God does not seek that our intellect should be good, but rather our heart. So, on the Day of Judgment, he will not ask us what we have learned, but what we have done.'

Chapter 150

'The elder answered: "O brother, say not so, for you despise knowledge, which our God wills to be prized." The younger replied: "Now, how shall I speak now so as not to fall into sin: for your word is true, and mine also. I say, then, that they who know the commandments of God written in the Law ought to observe those [first] if they would afterwards learn more. And all that a man learns, let it be observe it, and not [merely] to know it." Said the elder: "O brother, tell me, with whom have you spoken, that you know you have not learned all that I said?"

'The younger answered: "O brother, I speak with myself. Every day I place myself before the judgment of God, to give account of myself. And ever do I feel within myself one that excuses my faults." 'Said the elder: "O brother, what faults have you, who are perfect ? The younger answered: "O brother, say not so, for that I stand between two great faults: the one is that I do not know myself to be the greatest of sinners, the other that I do not desire to do penance for it more than other men." 'The elder answered: "Now, how should you know yourself to be the greatest of sinners, if you are the most perfect [of men]?"

'The younger replied: "The first word that my master said to me when I took the habit of a Pharisee was this: that I ought to consider the goodness of others and my own iniquity for if I should do so I should perceive myself to be the greatest of sinners. 'Said the elder: "O brother, whose goodness or whose faults consider you on these mountains, seeing there are no men here?" The younger answered: "I ought to consider the obedience of the sun and the planets, for they serve their Creator better than I. But them I condemn, either because they give not light as I desire, or because their heat is too great, or there is too much or too little rain upon the ground."

'Whereupon, hearing this, the elder said: "Brother, where have you learned this doctrine, for I am now ninety years old, for seventy-five years whereof I have been a Pharisee?" The younger answered: "O brother, you say this in humility, for you are a holy one of God. Yet I answer you that God our creator looks not on time, but looks on the heart: wherefore David, being fifteen years old, younger than six other his brethren, was chosen king of Israel, and became a prophet of God our Lord."

Chapter 151

'This man was a true Pharisee,' said Jesus to his disciples, and may it please God that we be able on the day of judgment to have him for our friend.'

Jesus then embarked on a ship, and the disciples were sorry that they had forgotten to bring bread. Jesus rebuked them, saying: "Beware of the leaven of the Pharisees of our day, for a little leaven mars a mass of meal." Then said the disciples one to another: 'Now what leaven have we, if we have not even any bread?' * Then Jesus said: 'O men of little faith, have you then forgotten what God wrought in Nain, where there was no sign of corn? And how many ate and were satisfied with five loaves and two fishes? The leaven of the Pharisee is want of faith in God, and thought of self, which has corrupted not only the Pharisees of this day, but has corrupted Israel.

For the simple folk, not knowing how to read, do that which they see the Pharisees do, because they hold them for holy ones. Know you what is the true Pharisee? He is the oil of human nature. For even as oil rests at the top of every liquor, so the goodness of the true Pharisee rests at the top of all human goodness. He is a living book, which God gives to the world, for everything that he says and does is according to the Law of God. Wherefore, who does as he does observes the Law of God. The true Pharisee is salt that suffers not human flesh to be putrefied by sin, for every one who sees him is brought to repentance. He is a light that lightens the pilgrims' way, for every one that considers his poverty with his penitence perceives that in this world we ought not to shut up our heart. But he that makes the oil rancid, corrupts the book, putrefies the salt, extinguishes the light - this man is a false Pharisee. If, therefore, you would not perish, beware that you do not as does the Pharisee today.?

Chapter 152

Jesus having come to Jerusalem, and having entered one sabbath day into the Temple, the soldiers drew near to tempt him and take him, and they said: "Master, is it lawful to wage war?" Jesus answered: "Our faith tells us that our life is a continual warfare upon the earth." Said the soldiers: "So would you convert us to your faith, and wish that we should forsake the multitude of gods (for Rome alone has twenty-eight thousand gods that are seen) and should follow your God who is one only and for that he cannot be seen, it is not known where he is, and perhaps he is but vanity."

Jesus answered: "If I had created you, as our God has created you, I would seek to convert you." They answered: "Now how has your God created us, seeing it is not known where he is? Show us your God, and we will become Jews." Then Jesus said: "If you had eyes to see him I would show him to you, but since you are blind, I cannot show you him." The soldiers answered: "Surely, the honor which this people pays you must have taken away your understanding. For every one of us has two eyes in his head, and you say we are blind."

Jesus answered: "The carnal eyes can only see things gross and external: you therefore will only be able to see your gods of wood and silver and gold that cannot do anything. But we of Judah have spiritual eyesight which are the fear and the faith of our God, wherefore we can see our God in every place." The soldiers answered: "Beware how you speak, for if you pour contempt on our gods we will give you into the hand of Herod, who will take vengeance for our gods, who are omnipotent."

Jesus answered: "If they are omnipotent as you say, pardon me, for I will worship them." The soldiers rejoiced at hearing this, and began to extol their idols. Then Jesus said: "[In this matter] we need not words but deeds cause therefore that your gods create one fly, and I will worship them." The soldiers were dismayed at hearing this, and knew not what to say, wherefore Jesus said: "Assuredly, seeing they make not a single fly afresh, I will not for them forsake that God who has created everything with a single word, whose name alone affrights armies." The soldiers answered: "Now let us see this, for we are fain to take you," and they were fain to stretch forth their hands against Jesus.

Then Jesus said: "Adonai Sabaoth!" Whereupon straightway the soldiers were rolled out of the Temple as one rolls casks of wood when they are washed to refill them with wine, insomuch that now their head and now their feet struck the ground, and that without any one touching them. And they were so affrighted and fled in such wise that they were never more seen in Judea.

Chapter 153

The priests and Pharisees murmured among themselves and said: "He has the wisdom of Baal and Ashtaroth, and so in the power of Satan has he done this." Jesus opened his mouth and said: "Our God commanded that we should not steal our neighbor's goods. But this single precept has been so violated and abused that it has filled the world with sin, and such [sin] as shall never be remitted as other sins are remitted: seeing that for every other sin, if a man bewail it and commit it no more, and fast with prayer and almsgiving, our God, mighty and merciful, forgives. But this sin is of such a kind that it shall never be remitted,, except that which is wrongly taken be restored.

Then said a scribe: 'O master, how has robbery filled all the world with sin? Assuredly now, by the grace of God, there are but few robbers, and they cannot show themselves but they are immediately hanged by the soldiery.' Jesus answered: 'Whoso knows not the goods, they (sic) cannot know the robbers. No, I say to you truly that many rob who know not what they do, and therefore their sin is greater than that of the others, for the disease that is not known is not healed.' Then the Pharisees drew near to Jesus and said: 'O master, since you alone in Israel know the truth, teach you us.'

Jesus answered: 'I say not that I alone in Israel know the truth, for this word "alone" appertains to God alone and not to others. For he is the truth, who alone knows the truth. Wherefore, I should say so I should be a greater robber, for I should be stealing the honor of God. And in saying that I alone knew God I should be falling into greater ignorance than all. You, therefore, committed a grievous sin in saying that I alone know the truth. And I tell you that, if you said this to tempt me, your sin is greater still.'

Then Jesus, seeing that all held their peace, said again: 'Though I be not alone in Israel knowing the truth, I alone will speak, wherefore hearken to me, since you have asked me. All things created belong to the Creator, in such wise that nothing can lay claim to anything. Thus soul, sense, flesh, time, goods, and honor, all are God's possessions, so that if a man receive them not as God wills he becomes a robber. And in like manner, if he spend them contrary to that which God wills, he is likewise a robber. I say, therefore, to you that, as God lives, in whose presence my soul stands, when you take time, saying: "Tomorrow I will do thus, I will say such a thing, I will go to such a place," and not saying: "If God will," you are robbers: And you are greater robbers when you spend the better part of your time in pleasing yourselves and not in pleasing God, and spend the worse part in God's service: then are you robbers indeed. Whoever commits sin, be he of what fashion he will, is a robber, for he steals time and the soul and his own life, which ought to serve God, and gives it to Satan, the enemy of God.'

Chapter 154

'The man, therefore, who has honor, and life, and goods - when his possessions are stolen, the robber shall be hanged when his life is taken, the murderer shall be beheaded. And this is just, for God has so commanded. But when a neighbor's honor is taken away, why is not the robber crucified? Are goods, forsooth, better than honor? Has God, perhaps, commanded that he who takes goods shall be punished and he that takes life with goods shall be punished, but he that takes away honor shall go free? Surely not, for by reason of their murmuring our fathers entered not into the land of promise, but only their children. And for this sin the serpents slew about seventy thousand of our people.

As God lives, in whose presence my soul stands, he that steals honor is worthy of greater punishment than he that robs a man of goods and of life. And he that hearkens to the murmurer is likewise guilty, for the one receives Satan on his tongue and the other in his ears." The Pharisees were consumed [with rage] at hearing this, because they were not able to condemn his speech. Then there drew near to Jesus a doctor, and said to him: 'Good master, tell me, wherefore God did not grant corn and fruit to our fathers? Knowing that they must needs fall, surely he should have allowed them corn, or not have suffered men to see it.'

Jesus answered: 'Man, you call me good, but you err, for God alone is good. And much more do you err in asking why God has not done according to your brain. Yet I will answer you all. I tell you, then, that God our creator in his working conforms not himself to us, wherefore it is not lawful for the creature to seek his own way and convenience, but rather the honor of God his creator, in order that the creature may depend on the Creator and not the Creator on the creature. As God lives, in whose presence my soul stands, if God had granted everything to man, man would not have known himself to be God's servant, and so he would have accounted himself lord of paradise. Wherefore the Creator, who is blessed for evermore, forbade him the food, in order that man might remain subject to him.

And truly I say to you, that whoever has the light of his eyes clear sees everything clear, and draws light even out of darkness itself, but the blind does not so. Wherefore I say that, if man had not sinned, neither I nor you would have known the mercy of God and his righteousness. And if God had made man incapable of sin he would have been equal to God in that matter, wherefore the blessed God created man good and righteous, but free to do that which he pleases in regard to his own life and salvation or damnation.' The doctor was astounded when he heard this, and departed in confusion.

Chapter 155

Then the high-priest called two old priests secretly and sent them to Jesus, who was gone out of the Temple, and was sitting in Solomon's porch, waiting to pray the midday prayer. And near him he had his disciples with a great multitude of people. The priests drew near to Jesus and said: 'Master, wherefore did man eat corn and fruit? Did God will that he should eat it, or no?' And this they said tempting him, for if he said: 'God willed it,' they would answer: 'Why did he forbid it?' and if he said: 'God willed it not,' they would say: 'Then man has more power than God, since he works contrary to the will of God.'

Jesus answered: 'Your question is like a road over a mountain, which has a precipice on the right hand and on the left: but I will walk in the middle.' When they heard this the priests were confounded, perceiving that he knew their heart. Then Jesus said: 'Every man, for that he has need, works everything for his own use. But God, who has no need of anything, wrought according to his good pleasure. Wherefore in creating man he created him free in order that he might know that God had no need of him, as does a King, who to display his riches, and in order that his slaves may love him more, gives freedom to his slaves.

God, then, created man free in order that he might love his Creator much the more and might know his bounty. For although God is omnipotent, not having need of man, having created him by his omnipotence, he left him free by his bounty, in such wise that he could resist evil and do good. For although God had power to hinder sin, he would not contradict his own bounty (for God has no contradiction) in order that, his omnipotence and bounty having wrought in man, he should not contradict sin in man, I say, in order that in man might work the mercy of God and his righteousness. And in token that I speak the truth, I tell you that the high-priest has sent you to tempt me, and this is the fruit of his priesthood.' The old men departed and recounted all to the high-priest, who said: 'This fellow has the devil at his back, who recounts everything to him, for he aspires to the kingship over Israel, but God will see to that.'

Chapter 156

When he had made the midday prayer, Jesus, as he went out of the Temple, found one blind from his mother's womb. His disciples asked him saying: "Master, who sinned in this man, his father or his mother, that he was born blind?' Jesus answered: "Neither his father nor his mother sinned in him, but God created him so, for a testimony of the Gospel. And having called the blind man up to him he spat on the ground and made clay and placed it upon the eyes of the blind man and said to him: 'Go to the pool of Siloam and wash you!'

The blind man went, and having washed received light, whereupon, as he returned home, many who met him said: 'If this man were blind I should say for certain that it was he who was wont to sit at the beautiful gate of the Temple.' Others said: 'It is he, but how has he received light?' And they accosted him saying: 'Are you the blind man that was wont to sit at the beautiful gate of the Temple?' He answered: 'I am he and wherefore?' They said: 'Now how did you receive your sight?'

He answered:, 'A man made clay, spitting on the ground, and this clay he placed upon my eyes and said to me: "Go and wash you in the pool of Siloam." I went and washed, and now I see: blessed be the God of Israel!' When the man born blind was come again to the beautiful gate of the Temple, all Jerusalem was filled with the matter. Wherefore he was brought to the chief of the priests, who was conferring with the priests and the Pharisees against Jesus. The high priest asked him, saying: 'Man, wast you born blind?' 'Yes,' he replied. 'Now give glory of God,' said the high-priest, 'and tell us what prophet has appeared to you in a dream and given you light. Was it our father Abraham, or Moses the servant of God, or some other prophet? For others could not do such a thing.

The man born blind replied: 'Neither Abraham nor Moses, nor any prophet have I seen in a dream and been healed by him, but as I sat at the gate of the Temple a man made me come near to him and, having made clay of earth with his spittle, put some of that clay upon my eyes and sent me to the pool of Siloam to wash, whereupon I went, and washed me, and returned with the light of my eyes.' The high-priest asked him the name of that man. The man born blind answered: 'He told me not his name, but a man who saw him called me and said: "Go and wash you as that man has said, for he is Jesus the Nazarene, a prophet and an holy one of the God of Israel."' Then said the high-priest: 'Did he heal you perhaps today, that is, the Sabbath?' The blind man answered: 'Today he healed me.' Said the high-priest: 'Behold now, how that this fellow is a sinner, seeing he keeps not the Sabbath!'

Chapter 157

The blind man answered: 'Whether he is a sinner I know not but this I know, that whereas I was blind, he has enlightened me.' The Pharisees did not believe this, so they said to the high priest: 'Send for his father and mother, for they will tell us the truth.' They sent, therefore, for the father and mother of the blind man, and when they were come the high-priest questioned them saying: 'Is this man your son?' They answered: 'He is truly our son.' Then said the high-priest: 'He says that he was born blind, and now he sees how has this thing befallen?'

The father and mother of the man born blind replied: 'Truly he was born blind, but how he may have received the light, we know not he is of age, ask him and he will tell you the truth.' Thereupon they were dismissed, and the high-priest said again to the man born blind: 'Give glory to God, and speak the truth.' (Now the father and mother of the blind man were afraid to speak, because a decree had gone forth from the Roman senate that no man might contend for Jesus, the prophet of the Jews, under pain of death: this decree had the governor obtained wherefore they said: 'He is of age, ask him.')

The high-priest, then, said to the man born blind: 'Give glory to God and speak the truth, for we know this man, whom you say to have healed you, that he is a sinner.' The man born blind answered: 'Whether he be a sinner, I know not, but this I know, that I saw not and he has enlightened me. Surely, from the beginning of the world to this hour, there has never yet been enlightened one who was born blind, and God would not hearken to sinners.' Said the Pharisees: 'Now what did he when he enlightened you?' Then the man born blind marveled at their unbelief, and said: 'I have told you, and wherefore ask you me again? Would you also become his disciples?'

The high-priest then reviled him saying: 'You were altogether born in sin, and would you teach us? Be gone, and become you disciple of such a man! for we are disciples of Moses, and we know that God has spoken to Moses, but as for this man, we know not whence he is.' And they cast him out of the synagogue and Temple, forbidding him to make prayer with the clean among Israel.

Chapter 158

The man born blind went to find Jesus, who comforted him saying: 'At no time have you been so blessed as you are now, for you are blest of our God who spoke through David, our father and his prophet, against the friends of the world, saying: "They curse and I bless"; and by Micah the prophet he said: "I curse your blessing." For earth is not so contrary to air, water to fire, light to darkness, cold to heat, or love to hate, as is the will that God has contrary to the will of the world.'

The disciples accordingly asked him, saying: 'Lord, great are your words, tell us, therefore, the meaning, for as yet we understand not." Jesus answered: "When you shall know the world, you shall see that I have spoken the truth, and so shall you know the truth in every prophet. Know you, then, that there be three kinds of worlds comprehended in a single name the one stands for the heavens and the earth, with water, air and fire, and all the things that are inferior to man. Now this world in all things follows the will of God, for, as says David, prophet of God: "God has given them a precept which they transgress not."

The second stands for all men, even as the "house of such an one" stands not for the walls, but for the family. Now this world, again, loves God, because by nature they long after God, forasmuch as according to nature every one longs after God, even though they err in seeking God. And know you wherefore all long after God? Because they long every one after an infinite good without any evil, and this is God alone. Therefore the merciful God has sent his prophets to this world for its salvation.

'The third world is men's fallen condition of sinning, which has transformed itself into a law contrary to God, the creator of the world. This makes man become like to the demons, God's enemies. And this world our God hates so sore that if the prophets had loved this world what think you? - assuredly God would have taken from them their prophecy. And what shall I say As God lives, in whose presence my soul stands, when the Messenger of God shall come to the world, if he should conceive love towards this evil world, assuredly God would take away from him all that he gave him when he created him, and would make him reprobate: so greatly is God contrary to this world."

Chapter 159

The disciples answered: "O master, exceeding great are your words, therefore have mercy upon us, for we understand them not." Jesus said: "Think you perhaps that God has created his Messenger to be a rival, who should be fain to make himself equal with God? Assuredly not, but rather as his good slave, who should not will that which his Lord wills not. You are not able to understand this because you know not what a thing is sin. Wherefore hearken to my words. Truly, truly, I say to you, sin cannot arise in man save as a contradiction of God, seeing that only is sin which God wills not: insomuch that all that God wills is most alien from sin.

Accordingly, if our high-priests and priests, with the Pharisees, persecuted me because the people of Israel has called me God, they would be doing a thing pleasing to God, and God would reward them, but because they persecute me for a contrary reason, since they will not have me say the truth, how they have contaminated the Book of Moses; and that of David, prophets and friends of God, by their traditions, and therefore hate me and desire my death therefore God has them in abomination. Tell me, Moses slew men and Ahab slew men, is this in each case murder? Assuredly not, for Moses slew the men to destroy idolatry and to preserve the worship of the true God, but Ahab slew the men to destroy the worship of the true God and to preserve idolatry. Wherefore to Moses the slaying of men was converted into sacrifice, while to Ahab it was converted into sacrilege: insomuch that one and the same work produced these two contrary effects. "As God lives, in whose presence my soul stands, if Satan had spoken to the angels in order to see how they loved God, he would not have been rejected of God, but because he sought to turn them away from God, therefore is he reprobate." Then answered he who writes : "How, then, is to be understood that which was said in Micaiah the prophet, concerning the lie which God ordained to be spoken by the mouth of false prophets, as is written in the book of the kings of Israel?" Jesus answered: "O Barnabas, recite briefly all that befell, that we may see the truth clearly."

Chapter 160

Then said he who writes: "Daniel the prophet, describing the history of the kings of Israel and their tyrants, writes thus: "The king of Israel joined himself with the king of Judah to fight against the sons of Belial (that is, reprobates) who were the Ammonites. Now Jehoshaphat, king of Judah, and Ahab, king of Israel, being seated both on a throne in Samaria, there stood before them four hundred false prophets, who said to the king of Israel: "Go up against the Ammonites, for God will give them into your hands, and you shall scatter Ammon."

Then said Jehoshaphat: "Is there here any prophet of the God of our fathers?" Ahab answered: "There is one only, and he is evil, for

279

he always predicts evil concerning me, and him I hold in prison."
And this he said, to wit, "there is only one," because as many as
were found had been slain by decree of Ahab, so that the
prophets, even as you have said, O Master, were fled to the
mountain tops where men dwelt not. Then said Jehoshaphat:
"Send for him here, and let us see what he says." Ahab therefore
commanded that Micaiah be sent for hither, who came with fetters
on his feet, and his face bewildered like a man that lives between
life and death. Ahab asked him, saying: "Speak, Micaiah, in the
name of God. Shall we go up against the Ammonites? Will God
give their cities into our hands?"

Micaiah answered: "Go up, go up, for prosperously shall you go
up, and still more prosperously come down!" Then the false
prophets praised Micaiah as a true prophet of God, and broke off
the fetters from his feet. Jehoshaphat, who feared our God, and
had never bowed his knees before the idols, asked Micaiah,
saying: "For the love of the God of our fathers, speak the truth, as
you have seen the issue of this war." Micaiah answered: "O
Jehoshaphat, I fear your face where. fore I tell you that I have seen
the people of Israel as sheep without a shepherd." Then Ahab,
smiling, said to Jehoshaphat: "I told you that this fellow predicts
only evil, but you did not believe it..

Then said they both: "Now how know you this, O Micaiah?"
"Micaiah answered: "I thought there assembled a council of the
angels in the presence of God, and I heard God say thus: "Who
will deceive Ahab that he may go up against Ammon and be
slain?" Whereupon one said one thing and another said another.
Then came an angel and said: "Lord, I will fight against Ahab, and
will go to his false prophets and will put the lie into their mouth,
and so shall he go up and be slain." And hearing this, God said:
"Now go and do so, for you shall prevail". Then were the false
prophets enraged, and their chief smote Micaiah's cheek, saying:
"O reprobate of God, when did the angel of truth depart from us
and come to you? Tell us, when came to us the angel that brought
the lie?"

'Micaiah answered: "You shall know when you shall flee from house to house for fear of being slain, having deceived your king." Then Ahab was wroth, and said: "Seize Micaiah, and the fetters which he had upon his feet place on his neck, and keep him on barley bread and water until my return, for now I know not what death I would inflict on him"., They went up, then, and according to the word of Micaiah the matter befell. For the king of the Ammonites said to his servants: "See that you fight not against the king of Judah, nor against the princes of Israel, but slay the king of Israel, Ahab, my enemy."' Then Jesus said: "Stop there, Barnabas for it is enough for our purpose."

Chapter 161

"Have you heard all?" said Jesus. The disciples answered: "Yes, Lord." Whereupon Jesus said: "Lying is indeed a sin, but murder is a greater, because the lie is a sin that appertains to him that speaks, but the murder, while it appertains to him that commits it, is such that it destroys also the dearest thing that God has here upon earth, that is, man. And lying can be remedied by saying the contrary of that which has been said, whereas murder has no remedy, seeing it is not possible to give life again to the dead. Tell me, then, did Moses the servant of God sin in slaying all whom he slew?"

The disciples answered: "God forbid, God forbid that Moses should have sinned in obeying God who commanded him!" Then Jesus said: "And I say, God forbid that that angel should have sinned who deceived Ahab's false prophets with the lie, for even as God receives the slaughter of men as sacrifice, so received he the lie for praise. Truly, truly, I say to you, that even as the child errs which causes its shoes to be made by the measure of a giant, even so errs he who would subject God to the law, as he himself as man is subject to the law. When, therefore, you shall believe that only to be sin which God wills not, you will find the truth, even as I have told you. Wherefore, because God is not composite nor changeable, so also is he unable to will and not will a single thing, for so would he have contradiction in himself, and consequently pain, and would not be infinitely blessed."

Philip answered: 'But how is that saying of the prophet Amos to be understood, that "there is not evil in the city that God has not done?" Jesus answered: 'Now here see, Philip, how great is the danger of resting in the letter, as do the Pharisees, who have invented for themselves the "predestination of God in the elect," in such wise that they come to say in fact that God is unrighteous, a deceiver and a liar and a hater of judgment (which shall fall upon them).

Wherefore I say that here Amos the prophet of God speaks of the evil which the world calls evil: for if he had used the language of the righteous he would not have been understood by the world. For all tribulations are good, either for that they purge the evil that we have done, or are good because they restrain us from doing evil, or are good because they make man to know the condition of this life, in order that we may love and long for life eternal. Accordingly, had the prophet Amos said: "There is no good in the city but what God has wrought it," he had given occasion for despair to the afflicted, as they beheld themselves in tribulation and sinners living in prosperity. And, what is worse, many, believing Satan to have such sovereignty over man, would have feared Satan and done him service, so as not to suffer tribulation. Amos therefore did as does the Roman interpreter, who considers not his words [as one] speaking in the presence of the high-priest, but consider the will and the business of the Jew that knows not to speak the Hebrew tongue.

Chapter 162

If Amos had said: "There is no good in the city but what God has done it," as God lives, in whose presence my soul stands, he would have made a grievous error, for the world holds nothing good save the iniquities and sins that are done in the way of vanity. Whereupon men would have wrought much more iniquitously, believing that there is not any sin or wickedness which God has not done, at hearing whereof the earth trembles." And when Jesus had said this, straightway there arose a great earthquake, in so much that every one fell as dead. Jesus raised them up, saying: 'Now see if I have told you the truth. Let this, then, suffice you, that Amos, when he said that "God has done evil in the city talking with the world," spoke of tribulations, which sinners alone call evil. Let us come now to predestination, of which you desire to know, and whereof I will speak to you near Jordan on the other side, tomorrow, if God will.'

Chapter 163

Jesus went into the wilderness beyond Jordan with his disciples, and when the midday prayer was done he sat down near to a palm-tree, and under the shadow of the palm-tree his disciples sat down. Then Jesus said: 'So secret is predestination, O brethren, that I say to you, truly, only to one man shall it be clearly known. He it is whom the nations look for, to whom the secrets of God are so clear that, when he comes into the world, blessed shall they be that shall listen to his words, because God shall overshadow them with his mercy even as this palm-tree overshadows us. Yes, even as this tree protects us from the burning heat of the sun, even so the mercy of God will protect from Satan them that believe in that man.'

The disciples answered, "O Master, who shall that man be of whom you speak, who shall come into the world?" Jesus answered with joy of heart: 'He is Muhammad, Messenger of God, and when he comes into the world, even as the rain makes the earth to bear fruit when for a long time it has not rained, even so shall he be occasion of good works among men, through the abundant mercy which he shall bring. For he is a white cloud full of the mercy of God, which mercy God shall sprinkle upon the faithful like rain.'

Chapter 164

I will accordingly tell you now [what] little God has granted me to know concerning this same predestination. The Pharisees say that everything has been so predestined that he who is elect cannot become reprobate, and he who is reprobate cannot by any means become elect, and that, even as God has predestined well-doing as the road by which the elect shall walk to salvation, even so has he predestined sin as the road by which the reprobate shall walk into damnation. Cursed be the tongue that said this, with the hand that wrote it, for this is the faith of Satan. Wherefore one may know of what manner are the Pharisees of the present day, for they are faithful servants of Satan.

What can predestination mean but an absolute will to give an end to a thing [of which] one has the means in hand? for without the means one cannot destine an end. How, then, shall he who not only lacks stone and money to spend, but has not even so much land as to place one foot upon, destine to build a house? Surely, none [could do so]. No more, then, I tell you, is predestination, taking away the free will that God has given to man of his pure bounty, the Law of God. Surely it is not predestination but abomination we shall be establishing.

That man is free the Book of Moses shows, where, when our God gave the Law upon Mount Sinai, he spoke thus: My commandment is not in the heaven that you should excuse yourself, saying: Now, who shall go to bring us the commandment of God? and who perhaps shall give us strength to observe it? Neither is it beyond the sea, that in like manner you should excuse yourself. But my commandment is near to your heart, that when you will you may observe it..

Tell me, if King Herod should command an old man to become young and a sick man that he should become whole, and when they did not [do] it should cause them to be killed, would this be just? The disciples answered: "If Herod gave this command, he would be most unjust and impious."

Then Jesus, sighing, said: "These are the fruits of human traditions, O brethren, for in saying that God has predestinated the reprobate such that he cannot become elect they blaspheme God as impious and unjust. For he commands the sinner not to sin, and when he sins to repent, while such predestination takes away from the sinner the power not to sin, and entirely deprives him of repentance."

284

Chapter 165

But hear what says God by Joel the prophet: "As I live, [says] your God, I will not the death of a sinner, but I seek that he should be converted to penitence." Will God then predestinate that which he [does] not will? Consider that which God says, and that which the Pharisees of this present time say. Further, God says by the prophet Isaiah: "I have called, and you would not hearken to me." And how much God has called, hear how he says by the same prophet: All the day have I spread out my hands to a people that believe me not, but contradict me."

And our Pharisees, when they say that the reprobate cannot become elect, what [do] they say, then, but that God mocks men even as he would mock a blind man who should show him something white, and as he would mock a deaf man who should speak into his ears? And that the elect can be reprobated, consider what our God says by Ezekiel the prophet: "As I live, says God, if the righteous shall forsake his righteousness and shall do abominations, he shall perish, and I will not remember any more any of his righteousness, for trusting therein it shall forsake him before me and it shall not save him." And of the calling of the reprobate, what says God by the prophet Hosea but this: I will call a people not elect, I will call them elect." God is true, and cannot tell a lie: for God being truth speaks truth. But the Pharisees of this present time with their doctrine contradict God altogether.

Chapter 166

Andrew replied: "But how is that to be understood which God said to Moses, that he will have mercy on whom he wills to have mercy and will harden whom he wills to harden." Jesus answered: "God says this in order that man may not believe that he is saved by his own virtue, but may perceive that life and the mercy of God have been granted him by God of his bounty. And he says it in order that men may shun the opinion that there be other gods than he.

If, therefore, he hardened Pharaoh he did it because he had afflicted our people and essayed to bring it to nothing by destroying all the male children in Israel: whereby Moses was near to losing his life. Accordingly, I say to you truly, that predestination has for its foundation the Law of God and human free will. Yes, and even if God could save the whole world so that none should perish he would not will to do so lest thus he should deprive man of freedom, which he preserves to him in order to do despite to Satan, in order that this [lump of] clay, scorned of the spirit, even though it shall sin as the spirit did, may have power to repent and go to dwell in that place whence the spirit was cast out. Our God wills, I say, to pursue with his mercy man's free will, and wills not to forsake the creature with his omnipotence. And so on the day of judgment none will be able to make any excuse for their sins, seeing that it will then be manifest to them how much God has done for their conversion, and how often he has called them to repentance.

Chapter 167

Accordingly, if your mind will not rest content in this, and you be fain to say again: "Why so?" I will disclose to you a wherefore." It is this. Tell me, wherefore cannot a [single] stone rest on the top of the water, yet the whole earth rests on the top of the water? Tell me, why is it that, while water extinguishes fire, and earth flees from air, so that none can unite earth, air, water, and fire in harmony, nevertheless they are united in man and are preserved harmoniously?

If, then, you know not this no, all men, as men, cannot know it how shall they understand that God created the universe out of nothing with a single word? How shall they understand the eternity of God? Assuredly they shall by no means be able to understand this, because, man being finite and composite with the body, which, as says the prophet Solomon, being corruptible, presses down the soul, and the works of God being proportionate to God, how shall they be able to comprehend them?

Isaiah, prophet of God, seeing [it to be] thus, exclaimed, saying: Truly you are a hidden God! And of the Messenger of God, how God has created him, he says: His generation, who shall narrate?

And of the working of God he says: Who has been his counselor? Wherefore God says to human nature: Even as the heaven is exalted above the earth, so are my ways exalted above your ways and my thoughts above your thoughts. Therefore I say to you, the manner of predestination is not manifest to men, albeit the fact is true, as I have told you. Ought man then, because he cannot find out the mode, to deny the fact? Assuredly, I have never yet seen any one refuse health, though the manner of it be not understood. For I know not even now how God by my touch heals the sick."

Chapter 168

Then said the disciples: "Truly God speaks in you, for never has man spoken as you speak." Jesus answered: "Believe me when God chose me to send me to the House of Israel, he gave me a book like to a clear mirror, which came down into my heart in such wise that all that I speak comes forth from that book. And when that book shall have finished coming forth from my mouth, I shall be taken up from the world." Peter answered: "O master, is that which you now speak written in that book?" Jesus replied: "All that I say for the knowledge of God and the service of God, for the knowledge of man and for the salvation of mankind all this comes forth from that book, which is my gospel." Said Peter: "Is there written therein the glory of paradise?"

Chapter 169

Jesus answered: ."Hearken, and I will tell you of what manner is paradise, and how the holy and the faithful shall abide there without end, for this is one of the greatest blessings of paradise seeing that everything, however great, if it have an end, becomes small, yes nothing. 'Paradise is the home where God stores his delights, which are so great that the ground which is trodden by the feet of the holy and blessed ones is so precious that one drachma of it is more precious than a thousand worlds.

These delights were seen by our, father, David, prophet of God, for God showed them to him, seeing he caused him to behold the glories of paradise: whereupon, when he returned to himself, he closed his eyes with both his hands, and weeping said: "Look not any more upon this world, O my eyes, for all is vain, and there is no good!". Of these delights said Isaiah ,the prophet: "The eyes of man have not seen, his ears have not heard, nor has the human heart conceived, that which God has prepared for them that love him." Know you wherefore they have not seen, heard, conceived such delights? It is because while they live here below they are not worthy to behold

such things. Wherefore, albeit our father David truly saw them, I tell you that he saw them not with human eyes, for God took his soul to himself, and thus, united with God, he saw them with light divine. As God lives, in whose presence my soul stands, seeing that the delights of paradise are infinite and man is finite, man cannot contain them, even as a little earthen jar cannot contain the sea.

Behold, then, how beautiful is the world in summer-time, when all things bear fruit! The very peasant, intoxicated with gladness by reason of the harvest that is come, makes the valleys and mountains resound with his singing, for that he loves his labors supremely. Now lift up even so your heart to paradise, where all things are fruitful with fruits proportionate to him who has cultivated it. As God lives, this is sufficient for the knowledge of paradise, forasmuch as God has created paradise for the home of his own delights. Now think you that immeasurable goodness would not have things immeasurably good? Or that immeasurable beauty would not have things immeasurably beautiful? Beware, for you err greatly if you think he have them not.

Chapter 170

God says thus to the man who shall faithfully serve him: "I know your works, that you work for me. As I live eternally, your love shall not exceed my bounty. Because you serve me as God your creator, knowing yourself to be my work, and ask nothing of me save grace and mercy to serve me faithfully, because you set no end to my service, seeing you desire to serve me eternally: even so will I do, for I will reward you as if you were God, my equal. For

288

not only will I place in your hands the abundance of paradise, but I will give you myself as a gift, so that, even as you are fain to be my servant for ever, even so will I make your wages forever."'

Chapter 171

What think you," said Jesus to his disciples, "of paradise? Is there a mind that could comprehend such riches and delights? Man must needs have a knowledge as great as God's if he would know what God wills to give to his servants. Have you seen, when Herod makes a present to one of his favorite barons, in what sort he presents it?" John answered: "I have seen it twice, and assuredly the tenth part of that which he gives would be sufficient for a poor man." Jesus said: "But if a poor man shall be presented to Herod what will he give to him" John answered: "One or two mites."
Now let this be your book wherein to study the knowledge of paradise," [said Jesus]: "because all that God has given to man in this present world for his body is as though Herod should give a mite to a poor man, but what God will give to the body and soul in paradise is as though Herod should give all that he has, yes and his own life, to one of his servants."

Chapter 172

God says thus to him that loves him, and serves him faithfully: "Go and consider the sands of the sea, O my servant, how many they are. Wherefore, if the sea should give you one single grain of sand, would it appear small to you? Assuredly, yes. As I, your creator, live, all that I have given in this world to all the princes and kings of the earth is less than a grain of sand that the sea would give you, in comparison of that which I will give you in my paradise."

Chapter 173

'Consider, then," said Jesus, "the abundance of paradise. For if God has given to man in this world an ounce of welling, in paradise he will give him ten hundred thousand loads. Consider the quantity of fruits that are in this world, the quantity of food, the quantity of flowers, and the quantity of things that minister to man. As God lives, in whose presence my soul stands, as the sea has still sand over and above when one receives a grain thereof, even so will the quality and

quantity of figs [in paradise] excel the sort of figs we eat here. And in like manner every other thing in paradise. But furthermore, I say to you that truly, as a mountain of gold and pearls is more precious than the shadow of an ant, even so are the delights of paradise more precious than all the delights of the princes of the world which they have had and shall have even to the judgment of God when the world shall have an end."

Peter answered: "Shall, then, our body which we now have go into paradise?" Jesus answered: "Beware, Peter; lest you become a Sadducee, for the Sadducees say that the flesh shall not rise again, and that there be no angels. 'Wherefore their body and soul are deprived of entrance into paradise, and they are deprived of all ministry of angels in this world. Have you perhaps forgotten Job, prophet and friend of God, how he says: "I know that my God lives, and in the last day I shall rise again in my flesh, and with my eyes I shall see God my Savior"?

But believe me, this flesh of ours shall be so purified that it shall not possess a single property of those which now it has, seeing that it shall be purged of every evil desire, and God shall reduce it to such a condition as was Adam's before he sinned. Two men serve one master in one and the same work. The one alone sees the work, and gives orders to the second, and the second performs all that the first commands. Seems it just to you, I say, that the master should reward only him who sees and commands, and should cast out of his house him who wearied himself in the work? Surely not.

How then shall the justice of God bear this? The soul and the body with sense of man serve God: the soul only sees and commands the service, because the soul, eating no bread, fasts not, [the soul] walks not, feels not cold and heat, falls not sick, and is not slain, because the soul is immortal: it suffers not any of those corporal pains which the body suffers at the instance of the elements. Is it, then, just, I say, that the soul alone should go into paradise, and not the body, which has wearied itself so much in serving God?" Peter answered: "O master, the body, having caused the soul to sin, ought not to be placed in paradise. Jesus answered: "Now how shall the body sin without the soul? Assuredly it is impossible. Therefore, in taking away God's mercy from the body, you condemns the soul to hell."

Chapter 174

As God lives, in whose presence my soul stands, our God promises his mercy to the sinner, saying: "In that hour that the sinner shall lament his sin, by myself, I will not remember his iniquities for ever." Now what should eat the meats of paradise, if the body go not thither? The soul? Surely not, seeing it is spirit." Peter answered: "So then, the blessed shall eat in paradise, but how shall the meat be voided without uncleanness?"

Jesus answered: "Now what blessedness shall the body have if it eat not nor drink? Assuredly it is fitting to give glory in proportion to the thing glorified. But you err, Peter, in thinking that such meat should be voided in uncleanness, because this body at the present time eats corruptible meats, and thus it is that putrefaction comes forth: but in paradise the body shall be incorruptible, impassible, and immortal, and free from every misery and the meats, which are without any defect, shall not generate any putrefaction.

Chapter 175

God says this in Isaiah the prophet, pouring contempt on the reprobate: My servants shall sit at my table in my house and shall feast joyfully, with gladness and with the sound of harps and organs, and I will not suffer them to have need of anything. But you that are my enemies shall be cast away from me, where you shall die in misery, while every servant of mine despises you..

Chapter 176

To what does it serve to say, "They shall feast"?' said Jesus to his disciples. 'Surely God speaks plain. But to what purpose are the four rivers of precious liquor in paradise, with so many fruits? Assuredly, God eats not, the angels eat not, the soul eats not, the sense eats not, but rather the flesh, which is our body. Wherefore the glory of paradise is for the body the meats, and for the soul and the sense God and the conversation of angels and blessed spirits. That glory shall be better revealed by the Messenger of God, who (seeing God has created all things for love of him) knows all things better than any other creature.'

Said Bartholomew: 'O master, shall the glory of paradise be equal for every man? If it be equal, it shall not be just, and if it be not equal the lesser will envy the greater.' Jesus answered: 'It will not be equal, for that God is just, and everyone shall be content, because there is no envy there. Tell me, Bartholomew, there is a master who has many servants, and he clothes all of those his servants in the same cloth. Do then the boys, who are clothed in the garments of boys, mourn because they have not the apparel of grown men? Surely, on the contrary, if the elders desired to put on them their larger garments they would be wroth, because, the garments not being of their size, they would think themselves mocked. Now, Bartholomew, lift your heart to God in paradise, and you shall see that all one glory, although it shall be more to one and less to another, shall not produce ought of envy.'

Chapter 177

Then said he who writes : 'O master, has paradise light from the sun as this world has?' Jesus answered: 'Thus has God said to me, O Barnabas: 'The world wherein you men that are sinners dwell has the sun and the moon and the stars that adorn it, for your benefit and your gladness, for this have I created. " Think you, then, that the house where my faithful dwell shall not be better? Assuredly, you err, so thinking: for I, your God, am the sun of paradise; and my Messenger is the moon, who from me receives all and the stars are my prophets which have preached to you my will. Wherefore my faithful, even as they received my word from my prophets [here] , shall in like manner obtain delight and gladness through them in the paradise of my delights."

Chapter 178

And let this suffice you,' said Jesus, 'for the knowledge of paradise.' Whereupon Bartholomew said again: 'O master, have patience with me if I ask you one word.' Jesus answered: 'Say that which you desire.' Said Bartholomew: 'Paradise is surely great: for, seeing there be in it such great goods, it needs must be great.' Jesus answered: 'Paradise is so great that no man can measure it. Truly I say to you that the heavens are nine, among which are set the planets, that are distant one from another five hundred years' journey for a man: and the earth in like manner is distant from the first heaven five hundred years' journey.

But stop you at the measuring of the first heaven, which is by so much greater than the whole earth as the whole earth is greater than a grain of sand. So also the second heaven is greater than the first, and the third than the second, and so on, up to the last heaven, each one is likewise greater than the next. And truly I say to you that paradise is greater than all the earth and all the heavens [together], even as all the earth is greater than a grain of sand.' Then said Peter: 'O master, paradise must needs be greater than God, because God is seen within it.' Jesus answered: 'Hold your peace, Peter, for you unwittingly blaspheme.'

Chapter 179

Then the angel Gabriel came to Jesus and showed him a mirror shining like the sun, in which he beheld these words written: 'As I live eternally, even as paradise is greater than all the heavens and the earth, and as the whole earth is greater than a grain of sand, even so am I greater than paradise and as many times more as the sea has grains of sand, as there are drops of water upon the sea, as there are [blades of] grass upon the ground, as there are leaves upon the trees, as there are skins upon the beasts and as many times more as the grains of sand that would go to fill the heavens and paradise and more.'

Then Jesus said: "Let us do reverence to our God, who is blessed for evermore." They bowed their heads a hundred times and prostrated themselves to earth upon their face in prayer. When the prayer was done, Jesus called Peter and told him and all the disciples what he had seen. And to Peter he said: "Your soul, which is greater than all the earth, sees through one eye the sun which is a thousand times greater than all the earth." "It is true," said Peter. Then Jesus said: "Even so, through [the eye of] paradise, shall you see God our Creator." And having said this, Jesus gave thanks to God our Lord, praying for the House of Israel and for the holy city. And everyone answered: "So be it, Lord."

Chapter 180

One day, Jesus being in Solomon's porch, a scribe, one of them that made discourse to the people, drew near to him and said to him: "O master, I have many times made discourse to this people, in my mind there is a passage of scripture which I am not. able to understand." Jesus answered: "And what is it?" The scribe said: "That which God said to Abraham your father, I will be your great reward. Now how could man merit [such reward]?"

Then Jesus rejoiced in spirit, and said: "Assuredly you are not far from the kingdom of God! Listen to me, for I will tell you the meaning of such teaching. God being infinite, and man finite, man cannot merit God and is this [the reason for] your doubt, brother?" The scribe answered, weeping: "Lord, you know my heart. Speak, therefore, for my soul desires to hear your voice." Then Jesus said: "As God lives, man cannot merit [even] a little breath which he receives every moment."

The scribe was beside himself, hearing this, and the disciples marveled as well, because they remembered that which Jesus said, that whatever they gave for love of God, they should receive a hundredfold [in return]. Then he said: "If someone should lend you a hundred pieces of gold, and you should spend those pieces, could you say to that man: 'I give you a decayed vine-leaf, therefore give me your house, for I merit it'?" The scribe answered: "No, Lord, for he should first pay that which he owed, and then, if he wished for anything, he should give him good things, but what good is a corrupted leaf ?"

Chapter 181

Jesus answered: "You have spoken well, O brother, so tell me, Who created man out of nothing? Surely it was God, who also gave [man] the whole world for his benefit. But man by sinning has spent it all, for because of sin the world is turned against man, and man in his misery has nothing to give to God but works corrupted by sin. For, sinning every day, he makes his own work corrupt, as Isaiah the prophet says: Our righteousness are as a menstruation cloth.

How, then, shall man have merit, seeing he is unable to give satisfaction? Is it, perhaps, that man does not sin? It is certain that our God says by his prophet David: Seven times a day falls the righteous. How then falls the unrighteous? And if our righteousness are corrupt, how abominable are our unrighteousness! As God lives, there is nothing that a man should shun more than this saying: 'I merit.' Brother, let a man know the works of his hands, and he will straightway see his merit. Every good thing that comes out of a man, truly, man does not do it, but God works it in him, for his being is of God who created him. That which man does is to contradict God his creator and to commit sin, [and so] he merits not reward, but torment.

Chapter 182

'Not only has God created man, as I say, but he created him perfect. He has given him the whole world; after the departure from paradise he has given him two angels to guard him, he has sent him the prophets, he has granted him the Law, he has granted him the faith, every moment he delivers him from Satan, he is fain to give him paradise no more, God wills to give himself to man. Consider, then, the debt, if it is great! [a debt] to cancel which you would need to have created man of yourselves out of nothing, to have created as many prophets as God has sent, with a world and a paradise, no, more, with a God great and good as is our God, and to give it ne all to God. So would the debt be cancelled and there would remain to you only the obligation to give thanks to God. But since you are not able to create a single fly, and seeing there is but one God who is lord of all things, how shall you be able to cancel your debt? Assuredly, if a man should lend you an hundred pieces of gold, you would be obliged to restore an hundred pieces of gold.

Accordingly, the sense of this, O brother, is that God, being lord of paradise and of everything, can say that which pleases him, and give whatsoever pleases him. Wherefore, when he said to Abraham: "I will be your great reward," Abraham could not say: "God is my reward," but "God is my gift and my debt." So when you discourse to the people, O brother, you ought thus to explain this passage: that God will give to man such and such things if man works well. When God shall speak to you, O man, and shall say: "O my servant, you have wrought well for love of me, what reward seek you from me, your God?" answer you: "Lord, seeing I am the work of your hands, it is not fitting that there should be in me sin, which Satan loves. Therefore, Lord, for your own glory, have mercy upon' the works of your hands.

And if God say: "I have pardoned you, and now I would fain reward you", answer you: "Lord, I merit punishment for what I have done, and for what you have done you merit to be glorified. Punish, Lord, in me what I have done, and save that which you have wrought." And if God say: "What punishment seems to you fitting for your sin?" do you answer, "As much, O Lord, as all the reprobate shall suffer." And if God say: "Wherefore seek you so great punish. men, O my faithful servant?" answer you: "Because every one of them, if they had received from you as much as I have received, would have served you more faithfully than I [have done]." And if God say: "When will you receive this punishment, and for how long a time?" answer you: "Now, and without end." As God lives, in whose presence my soul stands, such a man would be more pleasing to God than all his holy angels. For God loves true humility, and hates pride.'

Then the scribe gave thanks to Jesus, and said to him, 'Lord, let us go to the house of your servant, for your servant will give meat to you and to your disciples.' Jesus answered: 'I will come thither when you will promise to call me "Brother" and not "Lord," and shall say you are my brother, and not my servant.' The man promised, and Jesus went to his house.

Chapter 183

While they sat at meat the scribe said: 'O master, you said that God loves true humility. Tell us therefore what is humility, and how it can be true and false.' [Jesus replied:] "Truly I say to you that he who becomes not as a little child shall not enter into the kingdom of heaven." Every one was amazed at hearing this, and they said one to another: 'Now how shall he become a little child who is thirty or forty years old? Surely, this is a hard saying.' Jesus answered: 'As God lives, in whose presence my soul stands, my words are true. I said to you that [a man] has need to become as a little child: for this is true humility. For if you ask a little child: "Who has made your garments?" he will answer: "My father." If you ask him whose is the house where he lives, he will say: "My father's." If you shall say: "Who gives you to eat?" he will reply: "My father." If you shall say: "Who has taught you to walk and to speak?" he will answer, "My father." But if you shall say: "Who has broken your forehead, for that you have your forehead so bound up?" he will answer: "I fell down, and so did I break my head." If you shall say: "Now why did you fall down?" he will answer: "See you not that I am little, so that I have not the strength to walk and run like a grown man? so my father must needs take me by the hand if I would walk firmly. But in order that I might learn to walk well, my father left me for a little space, and I, wishing to run, fell down." If you shall say: "And what said your father?" he will answer: "Now why did you not walk quite slowly? See that in future you leave not my side."

Chapter 184

Tell me, is this true?' said Jesus. The disciples and the scribe answered: 'It is most true.' Then Jesus said: 'He who in truth of heart recognizes God as the author of all good, and himself as the author of sin, shall be truly humble. But whoever shall speak with the tongue as the child speaks, and shall contradict [the same] in act, assuredly he has false humility and true pride. For pride is then at its height when it makes use of humble things, that it be not reprehended and spurned of men.

True humility is a lowliness of the soul whereby man knows himself in truth, but false humility is a mist from hell which so darkens the understanding of the soul that what a man ought to ascribe to himself, he ascribes to God, and what he ought to ascribe to God, he ascribes to himself. Thus, the man of false humility will say that he is a grievous sinner, but when one tells him that he is a sinner he will wax wroth against him, and will persecute him. The man of false humility will say that God has given him all that he has, but that he on his part has not slumbered, but done good works. And these Pharisees of this present time, brethren, tell me how they walk.'

The scribe answered, weeping: "O master, the Pharisees of the present time have the garments and the name of Pharisees, but in their heart and their works they are Canaanites. And would to God they usurped not such a name, for then would they not deceive the simple! O ancient time, how cruelly have you dealt with us, that have taken away from us the true Pharisees and left us the false!'

Chapter 185

Jesus answered: 'Brother, it is not time that has done this, but rather the wicked world. For in every time it is possible to serve God in truth, but by companying with the world, that is with the evil manners in each time, men become bad. Now know you not that Gehazi, servant of Elisha the prophet, lying, and shaming his master, took the money and the raiment of Naaman the Syrian? And yet Elisha had a great number of Pharisees to whom God made him to prophesy.

Truly I say to you that men are so inclined to evil working, and so much does the world excite them thereto, and work Satan entice them to evil, that the Pharisees of the present day avoid every good work and every holy example: and the example of Gehazi is sufficient for them to be reprobated of God. 'The scribe answered: "It is most true", whereupon Jesus said: "I would that you would narrate to me the example of Haggai and Hosea, both prophets of God, in order that we may behold the true Pharisee." The scribe answered: "O master, what shall I say? Surely many believe it not, although it is written by Daniel the prophet, but in obedience to you I will narrate the truth.

Haggai was fifteen years old when, having sold his patrimony and given it to the poor, he went forth from Anathoth to serve Obadiah the prophet. Now the aged Obadiah, who knew the humility of Haggai, used him as a book wherewith to teach his disciples. Wherefore he oftentimes presented him raiment and delicate food, but Haggai ever sent back the messenger, saying: "Go, return to the house, for you have made a mistake. Shall Obadiah send me such things? Surely not: for he knows that I am good for nothing, and only commit sins.

And Obadiah, when he had anything bad, used to give it to the one next to Haggai, in order that he might see it. Thereupon Haggai. when he saw it, would say to himself: "Now, behold, Obadiah has certainly forgotten you, for this thing is suited to me alone, because I am worse than all. And there is nothing so vile but that, receiving it from Obadiah, by whose hands God grants it to me, it were a treasure."

Chapter 186

When Obadiah desired to teach any one how to pray, he would call Haggai and say: "Recite here your prayer so that every one may hear your words." Then Haggai would say: "Lord God of Israel, with mercy look upon your servant, who calls upon you, for that you have created him. Righteous Lord God, remember your righteousness and punish the sins of your servant, in order that I may not pollute your work. Lord my God, I cannot ask you for the delights that you grant to your faithful servants, because I do nothing but sins. Wherefore, Lord, when you would give an infirmity to one of your servants, remember me your servant, for your own glory." And when Haggai did so,' said the scribe, 'God so loved him that to every one who in his time stood by him God gave, [the gift of] prophecy. And nothing did Haggai ask in prayer that God withheld.'

Chapter 187

The good scribe wept as he said this, as the sailor weeps when he sees his ship broken up. And he said: "Hosea, when he went to serve God, was prince over the tribe of Naphtali, and aged fourteen years. And so, having sold his patrimony and given it to the poor, he went to be disciple of Haggai. Hosea was so inflamed with charity that concerning all that was asked of him he would say: 'This has God given me for you, O brother, accept it, therefore!' For which cause he was soon left with two garments only namely, a tunic of sackcloth and a mantle of skins. He sold, I say, his patrimony and gave it to the poor, because otherwise no one would be suffered to be called a Pharisee.

Hosea had the Book of Moses, which he read with greatest earnestness. Now one day Haggai said to him: "Hosea, who has taken away from you all that you had?" He answered: "The Book of Moses." It happened that a disciple of a neighboring prophet wanted to go to Jerusalem, but did not have a mantle. Wherefore, having heard of the charity of Hosea, he went to find him, and said to him: 'Brother, I would want to go to Jerusalem to perform a sacrifice to our God, but I have not a mantle, wherefore I know not what to do.'

When he heard this, Hosea said: 'Pardon me, brother, for I have committed a great sin against you: because God has given me a mantle in order that I might give it to you, and I had forgotten. Now therefore accept it, and pray to God for me.' The man, believing this, accepted Hosea's mantle and departed. And when Hosea went to the house of Haggai, Haggai said: 'Who has taken away your mantle?' Hosea replied: 'The Book of Moses.' Haggai was much pleased at hearing this, because he perceived the goodness of Hosea.

It happened that a poor man was stripped by robbers and left naked. Whereupon Hosea, seeing him, stripped off his own tunic and gave it to him that was naked, himself being left with a little piece of goat-skin over the privy parts. Wherefore, as he came not to see Haggai, the good Haggai thought that Hosea was sick. So he went with two disciples to find him: and they found him

wrapped in palm-leaves. Then said Haggai: 'Tell me now, why
have you not been to visit me?' Hosea answered: "The Book of
Moses has taken away my tunic, and I feared to come thither
without a tunic." Whereupon Haggai gave him another tunic.
It happened that a young man, seeing Hosea read the Book of
Moses, wept, and said: 'I also would learn to read if I had a book.'
Hearing which, Hosea gave him the book, saying: 'Brother, this
book is yours, for God gave it me in order that I should give it to
one who, weeping, should desire a book.' The man believed him,
and accepted the book.

Chapter 188

There was a disciple of Haggai near to Hosea, and he, wishing to
see if his own book was well written, went to visit Hosea, and said
to him: "Brother, take your book and let us see if it is even as mine.
" Hosea answered: "It has been taken away from me." " Who has
taken it from you?" said the disciple. Hosea answered: "The Book
of Moses," Hearing which, the other went to Haggai, and said to
him: "Hosea has gone mad, for he says that the Book of Moses has
taken away from him the Book of Moses." Haggai answered:
"Would to God, O brother, that I were mad in like manner, and
that all mad folk were like to Hosea!"
Now the Syrian robbers, having raided the land of Judea, seized
the son of a poor widow, who dwelt hard by Mount Carmel,
where the prophets and Pharisees abode. It chanced, accordingly,
that Hosea having gone to cut wood met the woman, who was
weeping. Thereupon he straightway began to weep, for whenever
he saw any one laugh he laughed, and whenever he saw any one
weep he wept. Hosea then asked the woman touching the reason
of her weeping, and she told him all.
Then said Hosea: 'Come, sister, for God wills to give you your
son." And they went both of them to Hebron, where Hosea sold
himself, and gave the money to the widow;, who, not knowing
how he had gotten that money, accepted it, and redeemed her son.
He who had bought Hosea took him to Jerusalem, where he had
an abode, not knowing Hosea. Haggai, seeing that Hosea was not

to be found, remained afflicted thereat. Whereupon the angel of God told him how he had been taken as a slave to Jerusalem. The good Haggai, when he heard this, wept for the absence of Hosea as a mother weeps for the absence of her son. And having called two disciples he went to Jerusalem. And by the will of God, in the entrance of the city he met Hosea, who was laden with bread to carry it to the laborers in his master's vineyard.

Having recognized him, Haggai said: "Son, how is it that you have forsaken your old father, who seeks you mourning?" Hosea answered: "Father, I have been sold." Then said Haggai in wrath: "Who is that bad fellow who has sold you?" Hosea answered: "God forgive you, O my father, for he who has sold me is so good that if he were not in the world no one would become holy." 'Who, then, is he?" said Haggai. 'Hosea answered: "O my father, it was the Book of Moses." Then the good Haggai remained as it were beside himself, and said: "Would to God, my son, that the Book of Moses would sell me also with all my children, even as it has sold you!"

And Haggai went with Hosea to the house of his master, who when he saw Haggai said: "Blessed be our God, who has sent his prophet to my house", and he ran to kiss his hand. Then said Haggai: "Brother, kiss the hand of your slave whom you have bought, for he is better than I." And he narrated to him all that had passed, whereupon the master gave Hosea his freedom. 'And that is all that you desired, O Master,' [said the scribe].

Chapter 189

Then Jesus said: "This is true, because I am assured of it by God. Therefore, that every one may know that this is the truth, in the name of God let the sun stand still, and not move for twelve hours!" And so it came to pass, to the great terror of all Jerusalem and Judea.

And Jesus said to the scribe: "O brother, what seek you to learn from me, seeing you have such knowledge? As God lives, this is sufficient for man's salvation, inasmuch as the humility of Haggai, with the charity of Hosea, fulfils all the Law and all the prophets.

Tell me, brother, when you came to question me in the Temple, did you think, perhaps. that God had sent me to destroy the Law and the prophets? It is certain that God will not do this, seeing he is unchangeable, and therefore that which God ordained as man's way of salvation, this has he caused all the prophets to say.

As God lives, in whose presence my soul stands, if the Book of Moses with the book of our father David had not been corrupted by the human traditions of false Pharisees and doctors, God would not have given his word to me. And why speak I of the Book of Moses and the book of David? Every prophecy have they corrupted, in so much that today a thing is not sought because God has commanded it, but men look whether the doctors say it, and the Pharisees observe it, as though God were in error, and men could not err.

Woe, therefore, to his faithless generation, for upon them shall come the blood of every prophet and righteous man, with the blood of Zechariah son of Berachiah, whom they slew between the Temple and the altar! What prophet have they not persecuted? What righteous man have they suffered to die a natural death? Scarcely one! And they seek now to slay me. They boast themselves to be children of Abraham, and to possess the beautiful Temple. As God lives, they are children of Satan, and therefore they do his will: therefore the Temple, with the holy city, shall go to ruin, in so much that there shall not remain of the Temple one stone upon another.'

Chapter 190

'Tell me, brother, you that are a doctor learned in the Law in whom was the promise of the Messiah made to our father Abraham? In Isaac or in Ishmael." The scribe answered: 'O master, I fear to tell you this, because of the penalty of death.' Then Jesus said: 'Brother, I am grieved that I came to eat bread in your house, since you love this present life more than God your creator, and for this cause you fear to lose your life, but fear not to lose the faith and the life eternal,

which is lost when the tongue speaks contrary to that which the heart knows of the Law of God. Then the good scribe wept, and said: "O master, if I had known how to bear fruit, I should have preached many things which I have left unsaid lest sedition should be roused among the people."

Jesus answered: "You should respect neither the people, nor all the world, nor all the holy ones, nor all the angels, when it should cause offence to God. Wherefore let the whole [world] perish rather than offend God your creator, and preserve it not with sin. For sin destroys and preserves not, and God is mighty to create as many worlds as there are sands in the sea, and more."

Chapter 191

The scribe then said: "Pardon me, O master, for I have sinned." Jesus said: "God pardon you. for against him have you sinned." Whereupon said the scribe: I have seen an old book, written by the hand of Moses and Joshua ;(he who made the sun stand still, as you have done), servants and prophets of God, which book is the true Book of Moses. Therein is written that Ishmael is the father of Messiah, and Isaac the father of the messenger of the Messiah. And thus says the book, that Moses said: "Lord God of Israel, mighty and merciful, manifest to your servant the splendor of your glory."

Whereupon God showed him his Messenger in the arms of Ishmael, and Ishmael in the arms of Abraham. Near to Ishmael stood Isaac, in whose arms was a child, who with his finger pointed to the Messenger of God, saying: "This is he for whom God has created all things." Whereupon Moses cried out with joy: "O Ishmael, you have in your arms all the world, and paradise! Be mindful of me, God's servant, that I may find grace in God's sight by means of your son, for whom God has made all."

Chapter 192

In that Book it is not found that God eats the flesh of cattle or sheep, in that Book it is not found that God has locked up his mercy in Israel alone, but rather that God has mercy on every man that seeks God his creator in truth. All of this book I was not able to read, because the high priest, in whose library I was, forbade me, saying that an Ishmaelite had written it.'

Then Jesus said: "See that you never again keep back the truth, because in the faith of the Messiah God shall give salvation to men, and without it shall none be saved." And there did Jesus end his discourse. Whereupon, as they sat at meat, lo! Mary, who wept at the feet of Jesus, entered into the house of Nicodemus (for that was the name of the scribe), and weeping placed herself at the feet of Jesus, saying: 'Lord, your servant, who through you has found mercy with God, has a sister, and a brother who now lies sick in peril of death.'

Jesus answered: 'Where is your house? Tell me, for I will come to pray God for his health.' Mary answered: 'Bethany is [the home] of my brother and my sister, for my own house is Magdala: my brother, therefore, is in Bethany.' Jesus said to the woman: 'Go you straightway to your brother's house, and there await me, for I will come to heal him. And fear you not, for he shall not die.' The woman departed, and having gone to Bethany found that her brother had died that day, wherefore they laid him in the sepulcher of their fathers.

Chapter 193

Jesus abode two days in the house of Nicodemus, and the third day he departed for Bethany, and when he was near to the town he sent two of his disciples before him, to announce to Mary his coming. She ran out of the town, and when she had found Jesus. said, weeping: 'Lord, you said that my brother would not die, and now he has been buried four days. Would to God you had come before I called you, for then he had not died!'

Jesus answered: 'Thy brother is not dead, but sleeps, therefore I come to awake him.' Mary answered, weeping: 'Lord, from such a sleep he shall be awakened on the day of judgment by the angel of God sounding his trumpet.' Jesus answered: 'Mary, believe me that he shall rise before [that day], because God has given me power over his sleep, and truly I say to you he is not dead, for he alone is dead who dies without finding mercy with God.' Mary returned quickly to announce to her sister Martha the coming of Jesus.

Now there were assembled at the death of Lazarus a great number of Jews from Jerusalem, and many scribes and Pharisees. Martha, having heard from her sister Mary of the coming of Jesus, arose in haste and ran outside, whereupon the multitude of Jews, scribes, and Pharisees followed her to comfort her, because they supposed she was going to the sepulcher to weep over her brother. When therefore she arrived at the place where Jesus had spoken to Mary, Martha weeping said: 'Lord, would to God you had been here, for then my brother had not died!' Mary then came up weeping, whereupon Jesus shed tears, and sighing said: 'Where have you laid him?' They answered: 'Come and see.'

The Pharisees said among themselves: 'Now this man, who raised the son of the widow at Nain, why did he suffer this man to die, having said that he should not die?' Jesus having come to the sepulcher, where every one was weeping, said: 'Weep not, for Lazarus sleeps, and I am come to awake him.' The Pharisees said among themselves: 'Would to God that you did so sleep!' Then Jesus said: 'My hour is not yet come, but when it shall come I shall sleep in like manner, and shall be speedily awakened.' Then Jesus said again: 'Take away the stone from the sepulcher.' Said Martha: 'Lord, he stinks, for he has been dead four days.' Jesus said: 'Why then am I come hither, Martha? Believe you not in me that I shall awaken him?' Martha answered: 'I know that you are the holy one of God, who has sent you into this world.'

Then Jesus lifted up his hands to heaven, and said: ' God of our fathers, God of Abraham, God of Ishmael, and Lord of Isaac, have mercy upon the affliction of these women, and give glory to your holy name.' And when every one had answered 'Amen,' Jesus said with a loud voice: 'Lazarus, come forth!' Whereupon he that was dead arose, and Jesus said to his disciples: 'Loose him.' For he was bound in the grave-clothes with the napkin over his face, even as our fathers were accustomed to bury [their dead].

A great multitude of the Jews and some of the Pharisees believed in Jesus, because the miracle was great. Those that remained in their unbelief departed and went to Jerusalem and announced to the chief of the priests the resurrection of Lazarus, and how that many were become Nazarenes, for so they called them who were brought to penitence through the word of God which Jesus preached.

Chapter 194

The scribes and Pharisees took counsel with the high priest to slay Lazarus, for many renounced their traditions and believed in the word of Jesus, because the miracle of Lazarus was a great one, seeing that Lazarus had conversation with men, and ate and drank. But because he was powerful, having a following in Jerusalem, and possessing with his sister Magdala and Bethany, they knew not what to do.

Jesus entered into Bethany, into the house of Lazarus, and Martha, with Mary, ministered to him. *Mary, sitting one day at the feet of Jesus, was listening to his words, whereupon Martha said to Jesus: 'Lord, see you not that my sister takes no care for you, and provides not that which you must eat and your disciples?' Jesus answered: 'Martha, Martha, do you take thought for that which you should do, for Mary has chosen a part which shall not be taken away from her for ever.

Jesus, sitting at table with a great multitude that believed in him, spoke, saying: 'Brethren, I have but little time to remain with you, for the time is at hand that I must depart from the world. Wherefore I bring to your mind the words of God spoken to Ezekiel the prophet, saying: "As I, your God, live eternally, the soul that sins, it shall die, but if the sinner shall repent he shall not die but live." Wherefore the present death is not death, but rather the end of a long death: even as the body when separated from the sense in a swoon, though it have the soul within it, has no other advantage over the dead and buried save this, that the buried [body] awaits God to raise it again, but the unconscious waits for the sense to return. Behold, then, the present life that it is death, through having no perception of God.

Chapter 195

'They that shall believe in me shall not die eternally, for through my word they shall perceive God within them, and therefore shall work out their salvation. What is death but an act which nature does by commandment of God? As it would be if one held a bird tied, and held the cord in his hand, when the head wills the bird to fly away, what does it? Assuredly it commands naturally the hand to open, and so straightway the bird flies away. "Our soul," as says the prophet David,

"is as a sparrow freed from the snare of the fowler," when man abides under the protection of God. And our life is like a cord whereby nature holds the soul bound to the body and the sense of man. When therefore God wills, and commands nature to open, the life is broken and the soul escapes in the hands of the angels whom God has ordained to receive souls.

Let not, then, friends weep when their friend is dead, for our God has so willed. But let him weep without ceasing when he sins, for [so] the soul dies, seeing it separates itself from God, the true Life. If the body is horrible without its union with the soul, much more frightful is the soul without union with God, who with his grace and mercy beautifies and quickens it.' And having said this Jesus gave thanks to God, whereupon Lazarus said: 'Lord, this house belongs to God my creator, with all that he has given into my keeping, for the service of the poor. Wherefore, since you are poor, and have a great number of disciples, come you to dwell here when you please, and as much as you please, for the servant of God will minister to you as much as shall be needful, for love of God.'

Chapter 196

Jesus rejoiced when he heard this, and said: 'See now how good a thing it is to die! Lazarus has died once only, and has learned such doctrine as is not known to the wise men in the world that have grown old among books! Would to God that every man might die once only and return to the world, like Lazarus, in order that men might learn to live.' John answered: 'O master, is it permitted to me to speak a word?'

'Speak a thousand,' answered Jesus, 'for just as a man is bound to dispense his goods in the service of God, so also is he bound to dispense doctrine: and so much the more is he bound [so to do) inasmuch as the world has power to raise up a soul to penitence, whereas goods cannot bring back life to the dead. Wherefore he is a murderer who has power to help a poor man and when he helps him not the poor man dies of hunger; but a more grievous murderer is he who could by the word of God convert the sinner to penitence, and converts him not, but stands, as says God, "like a dumb dog." Against such says God: "The soul of the sinner that shall perish because you have hidden my word, I will require it at your hands, O unfaithful servant."

In what condition, then, are now the scribes and Pharisees who have the key and will not enter, no hinder them who would fain enter, into eternal life? 'You ask me, O John, permission to speak one word, having listened to an hundred thousand words of mine. Truly I say to you, I am bound to listen to you ten times for every one that you have listened to me. And he who will not listen to another, every time that he shall speak he shall sin, seeing that we ought to do to others that which we desire for ourselves, and not do to others that which we do not desire to receive.' Then said John: 'O master, why has not God granted this to men, that they should die once and return as Lazarus has done, in order that they might learn to know themselves and their creator?'

Chapter 197

Jesus answered: 'Tell me, John, there was an householder who gave a perfect axe to one of his servants in order that he might cut down the wood which obstructed the view of his house. But the laborer forgot the axe, and said: "If the master would give me an old axe I should easily cut down the wood." Tell me, John, what said the master? Assuredly he was wroth, and took the old axe and struck him on the head, saying: Fool and knave! I gave you an axe wherewith you might cut down the wood without toil, and seek you this axe, wherewith one must work with great toil, and all that is cut is wasted and good for nothing? I desire you to cut down the wood in such wise that your work shall be good." Is this true?'

John answered: 'It is most true.' [Then Jesus said:] 'As I live eternally,' said God, 'I have given a good axe to every man, which is the sight of the burial of one dead. Whoso wield well this axe remove the wood of sin from their heart without pain, wherefore they receive my grace and mercy, giving them merit of eternal life for their good works. But he who forgets that he is mortal, though time after time he see others die, and says. "If I should see the other life, I would do good works," my fury shall be upon him, and I will so smite him with death that he shall never more receive any good.' 'O John,' said Jesus, 'how great is the advantage of him who from the fall of others learns to stand on his feet!'

Chapter 198

Then said Lazarus: 'Master, truly I say to you, I cannot conceive the penalty of which he is worthy who time after time sees the dead borne to the tomb and fears not God our creator. Such an one for the things of this world, which he ought entirely to forsake, offends his creator who has given him all.'

Then Jesus said to his disciples: 'You call me Master, and you do well, seeing that God teaches you by my mouth. But how will you call Lazarus? Truly he is here master of all the masters that teach doctrine in this world. I indeed have taught you how you ought to live well, but Lazarus will teach you how to die well. As God lives, he has received the gift of prophecy, listen therefore to his words, which are truth. And so much the more ought you to listen to him, as good living is vain if one die badly.'

Said Lazarus: 'O master, I thank you that you make the truth to be prized, therefore will God give the great merit.' Then said he who writes this: 'O master how speaks Lazarus the truth in saying to you "You shall have merit," whereas you said to Nicodemus that man merits nothing but punishment? Shall you accordingly be punished of God?' Jesus answered: 'May it please God that I receive punish. men of God in this World, because I have not

310

served him so faithfully as I was bound to do.

But God has so loved me, by his mercy, that every punishment is withdrawn from me, in so much that I shall only be tormented in another person. For punishment was fitting for me, for that men have called me God, but since I have confessed, not only that I am not God, as is the truth, but have confessed also that I am not the Messiah, therefore God has taken away the punishment from me, and will cause a wicked one to suffer it in my name, so that the shame alone shall be mine. wherefore I say to you, my Barnabas, that when a man speaks of what God shall give to his neighbor let him say that his neighbor merits it: but let him look to it that, when he speaks of

what God shall give to himself , he say: God will give me." And let him look to it that he say not, I have merit, because God is pleased to grant his mercy to his servants when they confess that they merit hell for their sins.

Chapter 199

God is so rich in mercy that the water of a thousand seas, if so many were to be found, could not quench a spark of the flames of hell, yet a single tear of one who mourns at having offended God quenches the whole of hell, by the great mercy wherewith God feeds and sustains him. God, therefore, to confound Satan and to display his own bounty, wills to call merit in the presence of his mercy every good work of his faithful servant, and wills him so to speak of his neighbor. But of himself a man must beware of saying: "I have merit", for he would be condemned.'

Chapter 200

Jesus then turned to Lazarus, and said: 'Brother, I must needs for a short time abide in the world, wherefore when I shall be near to your house I will not ever go elsewhere, because you will minister to me, not for love of me, but for love of God.' It was near to the Passover of the Jews, [so] Jesus said to his disciples: "Let us go to Jerusalem to eat the paschal lamb." And he sent Peter and John to the city, saying: "You shall find an ass near the gate of the city with a colt: loose her and bring her here, for I must ride [on her] into Jerusalem. And if any one ask you saying, "Why [do] you loose her?" say to them: "The Master has need [of her]," and they will permit you to bring her."

The disciples went, and found all that Jesus had told them, and accordingly they brought the ass and the colt. The disciples [then] placed their mantles upon the colt, and Jesus rode [on her]. And it came to pass that, when the men of Jerusalem heard that Jesus of Nazareth was coming, the men went forth with their children eager to see Jesus, bearing in their hands branches of palm and olive, singing: 'Blessed be he that comes to us in the name of God, hosanna son of David!'

Jesus having come into the city, the men spread out their garments under the feet of the ass, singing: "Blessed be he that comes to us in the name of the Lord God, hosanna, son of David!" The Pharisees rebuked Jesus, saying: 'See you not what these say? Cause them to hold their peace!' Then Jesus said: 'As God lives, in whose presence my soul stands, if men should hold their peace, the stones would cry out against the unbelief of malignant sinners.' And when Jesus had said this all the stones of Jerusalem cried out with a great noise: 'Blessed be he who comes to us in the name of the Lord God!' Nevertheless the Pharisees remained still in their unbelief, and, having assembled themselves together, took counsel to catch him in his talk.

Chapter 201

Jesus having entered into the Temple, the scribes and Pharisees brought to him a woman taken in adultery. They said among themselves: 'If he save her, it is contrary to the Law of Moses, and so we have him as guilty, and if he condemn her it is contrary to his own doctrine, for he preaches mercy.' Wherefore they came to Jesus and said: 'Master, we have found this woman in adultery. Moses commanded that [such] should be stoned: what then say you?'

Thereupon Jesus stooped down and with his finger made a mirror on the ground wherein every one saw his own iniquities. They still pressed for the answer, Jesus lifted up himself As and, pointing to the mirror with his finger, said: 'He that is without sin among you, let him be first to stone her.' And again he stooped down, shaping the mirror. The men, seeing this, went out one by one, beginning from the eldest, for they were ashamed to see their abominations.

Jesus having lifted up himself, and seeing no one but the woman, said: 'Woman, where are they that condemned you?' The woman answered, weeping: 'Lord, they are departed; and if you will pardon me as God lives, I will sin no more.' Then Jesus said: 'Blessed be God! Go your way in peace and sin no more, for God has not sent me to condemn you.'

Then, the scribes and Pharisees being assembled, Jesus said to them: 'Tell me: if one of you had an hundred sheep, and should lose one of them, would you not go to seek it, leaving the ninety and nine? And when you found it, would you not lay it upon your shoulders and, having called together your neighbors, say to them: "Rejoice with me, for I have found the sheep which I had lost"? Assuredly you would do so. Now tell me, shall our God love less man, for whom he has made the world? As God lives, even so there is joy in the presence of the angels of God over one sinner that repents, because sinners make known God's mercy.'

Chapter 202

'Tell me, by whom is the physician more loved: by them that have never had any sickness, or by them whom the physician has healed of grievous sickness?' Said the Pharisees to him: 'And how shall he that is whole love the physician? assuredly he will love him only for that he is not sick, and not having knowledge of sickness he will love the physician but little.'

Then with vehemence of spirit Jesus spoke, saying: 'As God lives, your own tongues condemn your pride, inasmuch as our God is loved more by the sinner that repents, knowing the great mercy of God upon him, than by the righteous. For the righteous has not knowledge of the mercy of God. Wherefore there is more rejoicing in the presence of the angels of God over one sinner that repents than over ninety and nine righteous persons. Where are the righteous in our time? As God lives, in whose presence my soul stands, great is the number of the righteous unrighteous, their condition being like to that of Satan.'

The scribes and Pharisees answered: 'We are sinners, wherefore God will have mercy on us.' And this they said tempting him, for the scribes and Pharisees count it the greatest insult to be called sinners. Then Jesus said: 'I fear that you be righteous unrighteous. For if you have sinned and deny your sin, calling yourselves righteous, you are unrighteous, and if in your heart you hold yourselves righteous, and with your tongue you say that you are sinners, then are you doubly righteous unrighteous.'

Accordingly the scribes and Pharisees hearing this were confounded and departed, leaving Jesus with his disciples in peace, and they went into the house of Simon the leper, whose leprosy he [had] cleansed. The citizens had gathered together the sick to the house of Simon and prayed Jesus for the healing of the sick. Then Jesus, knowing that his hour was near, said: 'Call the sick, as many as there be, because God is mighty and merciful to heal them.' They answered: 'We know not that there be any other sick folk here in Jerusalem.'

Jesus weeping answered: 'O Jerusalem, O Israel, I weep over you, for you know not your visitation, because I would fain have gathered you to the love of God your creator, as a hen gathers her chickens under her wings, and you would not! Wherefore God says thus to you

Chapter 203

O city, hard-hearted and perverse of mind, I have sent to you my servant, to the end that he may convert you to your heart, and you may repent, but you, O city of confusion, have forgotten all that I did upon Egypt and upon Pharaoh for love of you, O Israel. Many times weep you that my servant may heal your body of sickness, and you seek to slay my servant because he seeks to heal your soul of sin.

Shall you, then, alone remain unpunished by me? Shall you, then, live eternally? And shall your pride deliver you from my hands?

Assuredly not. For I will bring princes with they shall surround you with might, an army against you, and in such wise will I give you over into their hands that your pride shall fall down into hell. I will not pardon the old men or the widows, I will not pardon the children, but I will give you all to famine, the sword, and derision and the Temple, whereon I have looked with mercy, I will make desolate with the city, insomuch that you shall be for a fable, a derision, and a proverb among the nations. So is my wrath abiding upon you, and my indignation sleeps not."

Chapter 204

Having said this, Jesus said again: 'Know you not that there be other sick folk? As God lives, they be fewer in Jerusalem that have their soul sound than they that be sick in body. And in order that you may know the truth, I say to you, O sick folk, in the name of God, let your sickness depart from you! And when he had said this, immediately they were healed.

The men wept when they heard of the wrath of God upon Jerusalem, and prayed for mercy, when Jesus said: '"If Jerusalem shall weep for her sins and do penance, walking in my ways, said God, "I will not remember her iniquities any more, and I will not do to her any of the evil which I have said. But Jerusalem weeps for her ruin and not for her dishonoring of me, wherewith she has blasphemed my name among the nations. Therefore is my fury kindled much more. As I live eternally, if Job, Abraham, Samuel, David, and Daniel my servants, with Moses, should pray for this people, my wrath upon Jerusalem will not be appeased."' And having said this, Jesus retired into the house, while every one remained in fear.

Chapter 205

While Jesus was supping with his disciples in the house of Simon the leper, behold Mary the sister of Lazarus entered into the house, and having broken a vessel, poured ointment over the head and garment of Jesus. Seeing this, Judas the traitor was fain to hinder Mary from doing such a work, saying: "Go and sell the ointment and bring the money that I may give it to the poor.' Jesus said: 'Why hinder you her? Let her be, for the poor you shall have always with you, but me you shall not have always.'

Judas answered: 'O master, this ointment might be sold for three hundred pieces of money now see how many poor folk would be helped.' Jesus answered: 'O Judas, I know your heart: have patience, therefore, and I will give you all.' Every one ate with fear, and the disciples were sorrowful, because they knew that Jesus must soon depart from them. But Judas was indignant, because he knew that he was losing thirty pieces of money for the ointment not sold, seeing he stole the tenth part of all that was given to Jesus.

He went to find the high priest, who assembled in a council of priests, scribes, and Pharisees, to whom Judas spoke, saying: 'What will you give me, and I will betray into your hands Jesus, who would fain make himself king of Israel?' *They answered: 'Now how will you give him into our hand?' Judas said: 'When I shall know that he goes outside the city to pray I will tell you, and will conduct you to the place where he shall be found, for to seize him in the city will be impossible without a sedition.' The high priest answered: 'If you will give him into our hand we will give the thirty pieces of gold and you shall see how well I will treat you.'

Chapter 206

When day was come, Jesus went up to the Temple with a great multitude of people. Whereupon the high priest drew near, saying: 'Tell me, O Jesus, have you forgotten all that you did confess, that you are not God, nor son of God, nor even the Messiah?' Jesus answered: 'No, surely, I have not forgotten, for this is my confession which I shall bear before the judgment seat of God on the day of judgment. For all that is written in the Book of Moses is most true, inasmuch as God our creator is [God] alone, and I am God's servant and desire to serve God's Messenger whom you call Messiah.'

Said the high priest: 'Then what boots it to come to the Temple with so great a multitude of people? Seek you, perhaps, to make yourself king of Israel? Beware lest some danger befall you!' Jesus answered: 'If I sought my own glory and desired my portion in this world, I had not fled when the people of Nain would fain have made me king. Believe me, truly, that I seek not anything in this world.' Then said the high priest: 'We want to know a thing concerning the Messiah.' And then the priests, scribes, and Pharisees made a circle round about Jesus.

Jesus answered: 'What is that thing which you seek to know about the Messiah? Perhaps it is the lie? Assuredly I will not tell you the lie. For if I had said the lie I had been adored by you, and by the scribes [and] Pharisees with all Israel: but because I tell you the truth you hate me and seek to kill me.' Said the high priest: 'Now we know that you have the devil at your back, for you are a Samaritan, and have not respect to the priest of God.'

Chapter 207

Jesus answered: 'As God lives, I have not the devil at my back, but I seek to cast out the devil. Wherefore, for this cause the devil stirs up the world against me, because I am not of this world, but I seek that God may be glorified, who has sent me into the world.

Hearken therefore to me, and I will tell you who has the devil at his back. As God lives, in whose presence my soul stands, he who works after the will of the devil, he has the devil at his back, who has put on him the bridle of his will and rules him at his pleasure, making him to run into every iniquity.

Even as a garment changes its name when it changes its owner, although it is all the same cloth: so also men, albeit they are all of one material, are different by reason of the works of him who works in the man. 'If I (as I know) have sinned, wherefore do you not rebuke me as a brother, instead of hating me as an enemy? Truly the members of a body support one another when they are united with the head, and they that are cut off from the head give it no support. For the hands of one body do not feel the pain of another body's feet, but that of the body in which they are united. As God lives, in whose presence my soul stands, he who fears and loves God his Creator has the feeling of mercy over them [over]

317

whom God his head has mercy: and seeing that God wills not the death of the sinner, but waits for each one to repent, if you were of that body wherein I am incorporate, as God lives, you would help me to work according to my head.

Chapter 208

If I work iniquity, reprove me, and God will love you, because you shall be doing his will, but if none can reprove me of sin it is a sign that you are not sons of Abraham as you call yourselves, nor are you incorporate with that head wherein Abraham was incorporate. As God lives, so greatly did Abraham love God, that he not only brake in pieces the false idols and forsook his father and mother, but was willing to slay his own son in obedience to God.

The high priest answered: "This I ask of you, and I do not seek to slay you, wherefore tell us: Who was this son of Abraham?" Jesus answered: "The zeal of your honor, O God, inflames me, and I cannot hold my peace. Truly I say, the son of Abraham was Ishmael, from whom must be descended the Messiah promised to Abraham, that in him should all the tribes of the earth be blessed." Then was the high priest wroth, hearing this, and cried out: "Let us stone this impious fellow, for he is an Ishmaelite, and has spoken blasphemy against Moses and against the Law of God." Whereupon every scribe and Pharisee, with the elders of the people, took up stones to stone Jesus, who vanished from their eyes and went out of the Temple. And then, through the great desire that they had to slay Jesus, blinded with fury and hatred, they struck one another in such wise that there died a thousand men, and they polluted the holy Temple. The disciples and believers, who saw Jesus go out of the Temple (for from them he was not hidden), followed him to the house of Simon.

Thereupon Nicodemus came thither and counseled Jesus to go out of Jerusalem beyond the brook Cedron, saying: 'Lord, I have a garden with a house beyond the brook Cedron, I pray you, therefore, go thither with some of your disciples, to tarry there until this hatred of our priests be past, for I will minister to you

318

what is necessary. And the multitude of disciples leave you here in the house of Simon and in my house, for God will provide for all.' And this Jesus did, desiring only to have with him the twelve first called apostles.

Chapter 209

At this time, while the Virgin Mary, mother of Jesus, was standing in prayer, the angel Gabriel visited her and narrated to her the persecution of her son, saying: "Fear not, Mary, for God will protect him from the world." Mary, weeping, departed from Nazareth, and came to Jerusalem to the house of Mary Salome, her sister, seeking her son.

But since he had secretly retired beyond the brook Cedron she was not able to see him any more in this world, except after the deed of shame, for [then] the angel Gabriel, with the angels Michael, Rafael, and Uriel, by [the] command of God, brought him to her.

Chapter 210

When the confusion in the Temple ceased by the departure of Jesus, the high priest ascended on high, and having beckoned for silence with his hands he said:, 'Brethren, what do we? See you not that he has deceived the whole world with his diabolical art? Now, how did he vanish, if he be not a magician? Assuredly, if he were an holy one and a prophet, he would not blaspheme against God and against Moses [his] servant, and against the Messiah, who is the hope of Israel. And what shall I say? He has blasphemed all our priesthood, wherefore truly I say to you, if he be not removed from the world Israel will be polluted, and our God will give us to the nations. Behold now, how by reason of him this holy Temple has been polluted.'

And in such wise did the high priest speak at many forsook Jesus, wherefore the secret persecution was converted into an open one, insomuch that the high priest went in person to Herod, and to the Roman governor, accusing Jesus that he desired to make himself king of Israel, and of this they had false witnesses.

Thereupon was held a general council against Jesus, forasmuch as the decree of the Romans made them afraid. For so it was that twice the Roman Senate had sent a decree concerning Jesus: in one decree it was forbidden, on pain of death, that any one should call Jesus of Nazareth, the prophet of the Jews, either God or Son of God, in the other it forbade, under capital sentence, that any one should contend concerning Jesus of Nazareth, prophet of the Jews. Wherefore, for this cause, there was a great division among them. Some desired that they should write again to Rome against Jesus; others said that they should leave Jesus alone, regardless of what he said, as of a fool, others adduced the great miracles that he wrought.

The high priest therefore spoke that under pain of anathema none should speak a word in defense of Jesus; and he spoke to Herod, and to the governor, saying 'In any case we have an ill venture in our hands, for if we slay this sinner we have acted contrary to the decree of Caesar, and, if we suffer him to live and he make himself king, how will the matter go?' Then Herod arose and threatened the governor, saying: 'Beware lest through your favoring of that man this country be rebellious: for I will accuse you before Caesar as a rebel.'

Then the governor feared the Senate and made friends with Herod (for before this they had hated one another to death), and they joined together for the death of Jesus, and said to the high priest: 'Whenever you shall know where the malefactor is, send to us, for we will give you soldiers.' This was done to fulfill the prophecy of David who had foretold of Jesus, prophet of Israel, saying: The princes and kings of the earth are united against the holy one of Israel, because he announces the salvation of the world. Thereupon, on that day, there was a general search for Jesus throughout Jerusalem.

Chapter 211

Jesus, being in the house of Nicodemus beyond the brook Cedron, comforted his disciples, saying: 'The hour is near that I must depart from the world, console yourselves and be not sad, seeing that where I go I shall not feel any tribulation. 'Now, shall you be my friends if you be sad at my welfare? No, assuredly, but rather enemies. When the world shall rejoice, be you sad, because the rejoicing of the world is turned into weeping, but your sadness shall be turned into joy and your joy shall no one take from you: for the rejoicing that the heart feels in God its creator not the whole world can take away. See that you forget not the words which God has spoken to you by my mouth. Be you my witnesses against every one that shall corrupt the witness that I have witnessed with my gospel against the world, and against the lovers of the world.

Chapter 212

Then lifting up his hands to the Lord, he prayed, saying: 'Lord our God, God of Abraham, God of Ishmael and Isaac, God of our fathers, have mercy upon them that you have given me, and save them from the world. I say not, take them from the world, because it is necessary that they shall bear witness against them that shall corrupt my gospel. But I pray you to keep them from evil, that on the day of your judgment they may come with me to bear witness against the world and against the House of Israel that has corrupted your testament.

Lord God, mighty and jealous, that take vengeance upon idolatry against the sons of idolatrous fathers even to the fourth generation, do you curse eternally every one that shall corrupt my gospel that you gave me, when they write that I am your son. For I, clay and dust, am servant of your servants, and never have I thought myself to be your good servant, for I cannot give you aught in return for that which you have given me, for all things are yours.

Lord God, the merciful, that shows mercy to a thousand generations upon them that fear you, have mercy upon them which believe my words that you have given me. For even as you are true God, so your word which I have spoken is true, for it is yours, seeing I have ever spoken as one that reads, who cannot read save that which is written in the book that he reads: even so have I spoken that which you have given me.

'Lord God the Savior, save them whom you have given me, in order that Satan may not be able to do aught against them, and save not only them, but every one that shall believe in them. Lord, bountiful and rich in mercy, grant to your servant to be in the congregation of your Messenger, on the Day of Judgment: and not me only, but every one whom you have given me, with all them that shall believe on me through their preaching. And this do, Lord, for your own sake, that Satan boast not himself against you, Lord.

'Lord God, who by your providence provides all things necessary for your people Israel, be mindful of all the tribes of the earth, which you have promised to bless by your Messenger, for whom you did create the world. Have mercy on the world and send speedily your Messenger, that Satan your enemy may lose his empire.' And having said this, Jesus said three times: 'So be it, Lord, great and merciful!' And they answered, weeping: 'So be it," all save Judas, for he believed nothing.

Chapter 213

The day having come for eating the lamb, Nicodemus sent the lamb secretly to the garden for Jesus and his disciples, announcing all that had been decreed by Herod with the governor and the high priest. Whereupon Jesus rejoiced in spirit, saying: 'Blessed be your holy name, O Lord, because you have not separated me from the number of your servants that have been persecuted by the world and slain. I thank you, my God, because I have fulfilled your work.' And turning to Judas, he said to him: 'Friend, wherefore do you tarry? My time is near, wherefore go and do that which you must do."

The disciples thought that Jesus was sending Judas to buy something for the day of the Passover;: but Jesus knew that Judas was betraying him, wherefore, desiring to depart from the world, he so spoke. Judas answered: 'Lord, suffer me to eat, and I will go.' 'Let us eat,' said Jesus, 'for I have greatly desired to eat this lamb before I am parted from you.'

And having arisen, he took a towel and girded his loins, and having put water in a basin, he set himself to wash his disciples' feet. Beginning from Judas, Jesus came to Peter. Said Peter, 'Lord, would you wash my feet?' Jesus answered: 'That which I do you know not now, but you shall know hereafter.' Peter answered: 'You shall never wash my feet. Then Jesus rose up, and said: 'Neither shall you come in my company on the day of judgment.' Peter answered: 'Wash not only my feet, Lord, but my hands and my head.'

When the disciples were washed and were seated at table to eat, Jesus said: 'I have washed you, yet are you not all clean, for as much as all the water of the sea will not wash him that believes me not.' This said Jesus, because he knew who was betraying him. The disciples were sad at these words, when Jesus said again: 'Truly I say to you, that one of you shall betray me, insomuch that I shall be sold like a sheep, but woe to him, for he shall fulfill all that our father David said of such an one, that "he shall fall into the pit which he had prepared for others." '

Whereupon the disciples looked one upon another, saying with sorrow: 'Who shall be the traitor?' Judas then said: 'Shall it be I, O Master?' Jesus answered: 'You have told me who it shall be that shall betray me.' And the eleven apostles heard it not. When the lamb was eaten, the devil came upon the back of Judas, and he went forth from the house, Jesus saying to him again: 'Do quickly that which you must do.'

Chapter 214

Having gone forth from the house, Jesus retired into the garden to pray, according as his custom was to pray, bowing his knees an hundred times and prostrating himself upon his face. Judas, accordingly, knowing the place where Jesus was with his disciples, went to the high priest, and said: "If you will give me what was promised, this night will I give into your hand Jesus whom you seek, for he is alone with eleven companions." The high priest answered: "How much do you seek?" Judas said, "Thirty pieces of gold."

Then straightway the high priest counted to him the money, and sent a Pharisee to the governor to fetch soldiers, and to Herod, and they gave a legion of them, because they feared the people, wherefore they took their arms, and with torches and lanterns upon staves went out of Jerusalem.

Chapter 215

When the soldiers with Judas drew near to the place where Jesus was, Jesus heard the approach of many people, wherefore in fear he withdrew into the house. And the eleven were sleeping. Then God, seeing the danger of his servant, commanded Gabriel, Michael, Rafael, and Uriel, his ministers, to take Jesus out of the world. The holy angels came and took Jesus out by the window that looks toward the South. They bare him and placed him in the third heaven in the company of angels blessing God for evermore.

Chapter 216

Judas entered impetuously before all into the chamber whence Jesus had been taken up. And the disciples were sleeping. Whereupon the wonderful God acted wonderfully, insomuch that Judas was so changed in speech and in face to be like Jesus that we believed him to be Jesus. And he, having awakened us, was seeking where the Master was. Whereupon we marveled, and answered: 'You, Lord, are our master, have you now forgotten us?'

And he, smiling, said: 'Now are you foolish, that know not me to be Judas Iscariot!' And as he was saying this the soldiery entered, and laid their hands upon Judas, because he was in every way like to Jesus. We having heard Judas' saying, and seeing the multitude of soldiers, fled as beside ourselves. And John, who was wrapped in a linen cloth, awoke and fled, and when a soldier seized him by the linen cloth he left the linen cloth and fled naked. For God heard the prayer of Jesus, and saved the eleven from evil.

Chapter 217

The soldiers took Judas and bound him, not without derision. For he truthfully denied that he was Jesus, and the soldiers, mocking him, said: 'Sir, fear not, for we are come to make you king of Israel, and we have bound you because we know that you do refuse the kingdom.' Judas answered: 'Now have you lost your senses! You are come to take Jesus of Nazareth, with arms and lanterns as [against] a robber, and you have bound me that have guided you, to make me king!'

Then the soldiers lost their patience, and with blows and kicks they began to flout Judas, and they led him with fury into Jerusalem. John and Peter followed the soldiers afar off and they affirmed to him who writes that they saw all the examination that was made of Judas by the high priest, and by the council of the Pharisees, who were assembled to put Jesus to death. Whereupon Judas spoke many words of madness, insomuch that every one was filled with laughter, believing that he was really Jesus, and that for fear of death he was feigning madness. Whereupon the scribes bound his eyes with a bandage, and mocking him said: 'Jesus, prophet of the Nazarenes ,(for so they called them who believed in Jesus), 'tell us, who was it that smote you?' And they buffeted him and spat in his face.

When it was morning there assembled the great council of scribes and elders of the people; and the high priest with the Pharisees sought false witness against Judas, believing him to be Jesus: and they found not that which they sought. And why say I that the chief priests believed Judas to be Jesus? No all the disciples, with him who writes, believed it, and more, the poor Virgin mother of Jesus, with his kinsfolk and friends, believed it, insomuch that the sorrow of every one was incredible.

As God lives, he who writes forgot all that Jesus had said: how that he should be taken up from the world, and that he should suffer in a third person, and that he should not die until near the end of the world. Wherefore he went with the mother of Jesus and with John to the cross. The high priest caused Judas to be brought before him bound, and asked him of his disciples and his doctrine. Whereupon Judas, as though beside himself, answered nothing to the point. The high priest then adjured him by the living God of Israel that he would tell him the truth.

Judas answered: 'I have told you that I am Judas Iscariot, who promised to give into your hands Jesus the Nazarene, and you, by what are I know not, are beside yourselves, for you will have it by every means that I am Jesus.' The high priest answered: 'O perverse seducer, you have deceived all Israel, beginning from Galilee, even to Jerusalem here, with your doctrine and false miracles: and now think you to flee the merited punishment that befits you by feigning to be mad?

As God lives,' you shall not escape it!' And having said this he commanded his servants to smite him with buffetings and kicks, so that his understanding might come back into his head. The derision which he then suffered at the hands of the high priest's servants is past belief. For they zealously devised new inventions to give pleasure to the council. So they attired him as a juggler, and so treated him with hands and feet that it would have moved the very Canaanites to compassion if they had beheld that sight. But the chief priests and Pharisees and elders of the people had their hearts so exasperated against Jesus that, believing Judas to be really Jesus, they took delight in seeing him so treated.

Afterwards they led him bound to the governor, who secretly loved Jesus. Whereupon he, thinking that Judas was Jesus, made him enter into his chamber, and spoke to him, asking him for what cause the chief priests and the people had given him into his hands. Judas answered: 'If I tell you the truth, you will not believe me, for perhaps you are deceived as the (chief) priests and the Pharisees are deceived.'

The governor answered (thinking that he wished to speak concerning the Law): 'Now know you not that I am not a Jew? but the (chief) priests and the elders of your people have given you into my hand, wherefore tell us the truth, wherefore I may do what is just. For I have power to set you free and to put you to death.' Judas answered: 'Sir, believe me, if you put me to death, you shall do a great wrong, for you shall slay an innocent person, seeing that I am Judas Iscariot, and not Jesus, who is a magician, and by his are has so transformed me.'

When he heard this the governor marveled greatly, so that he sought to set him at liberty. The governor therefore went out, and smiling said: 'In the one case, at least, this man is not worthy of death, but rather of compassion.' 'This man says,' said the governor, 'that he is not Jesus, but a certain Judas who guided the soldiery to take Jesus, and he says that Jesus the Galilean has by his are magic so transformed him. Wherefore, if this be true, it were a great wrong to kill him, seeing that he were innocent. But if he is Jesus and denies that he is, assuredly he has lost his understanding, and it were impious to slay a madman.'

Then the chief priests and elders of the people, with the scribes and Pharisees, cried out with shouts, saying: 'He is Jesus of Nazareth, for we know him, for if he were not the malefactor we would not have given him into your hands. Nor is he mad, but rather malignant, for with this device he seeks to escape from our hands, and the sedition that he would stir up if he should escape would be worse than the former.' Pilate (of such was the governor's name), in order to rid himself of such a case, said: 'He is a Galilean, and Herod is king of Galilee: wherefore it pertains not to me to judge such a case, so take you him to Herod.' Accordingly they led Judas to Herod, who of a long time had desired that Jesus should go to his house. But Jesus had never been willing to go to his house, because Herod was a Gentile, and adored the false and lying gods, living after the manner of the unclean Gentiles. Now when Judas had been led thither, Herod asked him of many things, to which Judas gave answers not to the purpose, denying that he was Jesus. Then Herod mocked him, with all his court, and caused him to be clad in white as the fools are clad, and sent him back to Pilate, saying to him, 'Do not fail in justice to the people of Israel!' * And this Herod wrote, because the chief priests and scribes and the Pharisees had given him a good quantity of money. The governor having heard that this was so from a servant of Herod, in order that he also might gain some money, feigned that he desired to set Judas at liberty. Whereupon he caused him to be scourged by his slaves, who were paid by the scribes to slay him under the scourges. But God, who had decreed the issue, reserved Judas for the cross, in order that he might suffer that horrible death to which he had sold another. He did not suffer Judas to die under the scourges, notwithstanding that the soldiers scourged him so grievously that his body rained blood. Thereupon, in mockery they clad him in an old purple garment, saying: 'It is fitting to our new king to clothe him and crown him': so they gathered thorns and made a crown, like those of gold and precious stones which kings wear on their heads. And this crown of thorns they placed upon Judas' head, putting in his hand a reed for scepter, and they made him sit in a high place.

And the soldiers came before him, bowing down in mockery, saluting him as King of the Jews. And they held out their hands to receive gifts, such as new kings are accustomed to give; and receiving nothing they smote Judas, saying: 'Now, how are you crowned, foolish king, if you will not pay your soldiers and servants?' *The chief priests with the scribes and Pharisees, seeing that Judas died not by the scourges, and fearing lest Pilate should set him at liberty, made a gift of money to the governor, who having received it gave Judas to the scribes and Pharisees as guilty to death. Whereupon they condemned two robbers with him to the death of the cross.

So they led him to Mount Calvary, where they used to hang malefactors, and there they crucified him naked, for the greater ignominy. *Judas truly did nothing else but cry out: 'God, why have you forsaken me, seeing the malefactor has escaped and I die unjustly?' *Truly I say that the voice, the face, and the person of Judas were so like to Jesus, that his disciples and believers entirely believed that he was Jesus, wherefore some departed from the doctrine of Jesus, believing that Jesus had been a false prophet, and that by art magic he had done the miracles which he did: for Jesus had said that he should not die till near the end of the world, for that at that time he should be taken away from the world.

But they that stood firm in the doctrine of Jesus were so encompassed with sorrow, seeing him die who was entirely like to

Jesus, that they remembered not what Jesus had said. And so in company with the mother of Jesus they went to Mount Calvary, and were not only present at the death of Judas, weeping continually, but by means of Nicodemus and Joseph of Abarimathia they obtained from the governor the body of Judas to bury it. Whereupon, they took him down from the cross with such weeping as assuredly no one would believe, and buried him in the new sepulcher of Joseph, having wrapped him up in an hundred pounds of precious ointments.

Chapter 218

Then returned each man to his house. He who writes, with John and James his brother, went with the mother of Jesus to Nazareth. Those disciples who did not fear God went by night [and] stole the body of Judas and hid it, spreading a report that Jesus was risen again, whence great confusion arose. The high priest then commanded, under pain of anathema, that no one should talk of Jesus of Nazareth. And so there arose a great persecution, and many were stoned and many beaten, and many banished from the land, because they could not hold their peace on such a matter. The news reached Nazareth how that Jesus, their fellow citizen, having died on the cross was risen again. Whereupon, he that writes prayed the mother of Jesus that she would be pleased to leave off weeping, because her son was risen again. Hearing this, the Virgin Mary, weeping, said: 'Let us go to Jerusalem to find my son. I shall die content when I have seen him.'

Chapter 219

The Virgin returned to Jerusalem with him who writes, and James and John, on that day on which the decree of the high priest went forth. Whereupon, the Virgin, who feared God, albeit she knew the decree of the high priest to be unjust, commanded those who dwelt with her to forget her son. Then how each one was affected! God who discerns the heart of men knows that between grief at the death of Judas whom we believed to be Jesus our master, and the desire to see him risen again, we, with the mother of Jesus, were consumed.

329

So the angels that were guardians of Mary ascended to the third heaven, where Jesus was in the company of angels, and recounted all to him. Wherefore Jesus prayed God that he would give him power to see his mother and his disciples. Then the merciful God commanded his four favorite angels, who are Michael, Gabriel, Rafael, and Uriel, to bear Jesus into his mother's house, and there keep watch over him for three days continually, suffering him only to be seen by them that believed in his doctrine.

Jesus came, surrounded with splendor, to the room where abode Mary the Virgin with her two sisters, and Martha and Mary Magdalen, and Lazarus, and him who writes, and John and James and Peter. Whereupon, through fear they fell as dead. And Jesus lifted up his mother and the others from the ground, saying: 'Fear not, for I am Jesus, and weep not, for I am alive and not dead.' They remained every one for a long time beside himself at the presence of Jesus, for they altogether believed that Jesus was dead. Then the Virgin, weeping, said: 'Tell me, my son, wherefore God, having given you power to raise the dead. suffered you to die, to the shame of your kinsfolk and friends, and to the shame of your doctrine? For every one that loves you has been as dead.'

Chapter 220

Jesus replied, embracing his mother: 'Believe me, mother, for truly I say to you that I have not been dead at all, for God has reserved me till near the end of the world.' And having said this he prayed the four angels that they would manifest themselves, and give testimony how the matter had passed.

Thereupon the angels manifested themselves like four shining suns, insomuch that through fear every one again fell down as dead. Then Jesus gave four linen cloths to the angels that they might cover themselves, in order that they might be seen and heard to speak by his mother and her companions. And having lifted up each one, he comforted them, saying: 'These are the ministers of God: Gabriel, who announces God's secrets; Michael, who fights against God's enemies, Rafael, who receives the souls of them that die, and Uriel, who will call every one to the judgment of God at the last day. Then the four angels narrated to the Virgin how God had sent for Jesus, and had transformed Judas, that he might suffer the punishment to which he had sold another.

Then said he who writes: 'O Master, is it lawful for me to question you now, as it was lawful for me when you dwelt with us?' Jesus answered: 'Ask what you please, Barnabas, and I will answer you.' Then said he who writes: 'O Master, seeing that God is merciful, wherefore has he so tormented us, making us to believe that you were dead? and your mother has so wept for you that she has been near to death; and you, who are an holy one of God, on you has God suffered to fall the calumny that you were slain amongst robbers on the Mount Calvary?'

Jesus answered: 'Believe me, Barnabas, that every sin, however small it be, God punishes with great punishment, seeing that God is offended at sin. Wherefore, since my mother and my faithful disciples that were with me loved me a little with earthly love, the righteous God has willed to punish this love with the present grief, in order that it may not be punished in the flames of hell. And though I have been innocent in the world, since men have called me "God," and "Son of God," God, in order that I be not mocked of the demons on the day of judgment, has willed that I be mocked of men in this world by the death of Judas, making all men to believe that I died upon the cross. And this mocking shall continue until the advent of Muhammad, the Messenger of God, who, when he shall come, shall reveal this deception to those who believe in God's Law. Having thus spoken, Jesus said: 'You are just, O Lord our God, because to you only belongs honor and glory without end.'

Chapter 221

Jesus turned himself to him who writes, and said: "Barnabas, see that by all means you write my gospel concerning all that has happened through my dwelling in the world. And write in a similar manner that which has befallen Judas, in order that the faithful may be undeceived, and every one may believe the truth."

331

Then answered he who writes: "I will do so, if God wills, O Master, but I do not know what happened to Judas, for I did not see it."

Jesus answered: "Here are John and Peter who saw everything, and they will tell you all that has passed." And then Jesus commanded us to call his faithful disciples [so] that they might see him. So James and John called together the seven disciples with Nicodemus and Joseph, and many others of the seventy-two, and they ate with Jesus.

The third day Jesus said: "Go to the Mount of Olives with my mother, for there I will ascend again to heaven, and you will see who shall bear me up." So they all went there except twenty-five of the seventy-two disciples, who for fear had fled to Damascus. And as they all stood in prayer, at midday Jesus came with a great multitude of angels who were praising God: and the splendor of his face made them greatly afraid and they fell with their faces to the ground. But Jesus lifted them up, comforting them, and saying: "Do not be afraid, I am your master."

And he reproved many who believed that he had died and risen again, saying: "Do you hold me and God for liars? I said to you that God has granted to me to live almost to the end of the world. Truly I say to you, I did not die, it was Judas the traitor. Beware, for Satan will make every effort to deceive you. Be my witnesses in Israel, and throughout the world, of all things that you have heard and seen."

And having said this, he prayed God for the salvation of the faithful, and the conversion of sinners and [then], his prayer ended, he embraced his mother, saying: "Peace be to you, my mother. Rest in God who created you and me." And having said this, he turned to his disciples, saying: "May God's grace and mercy be with you." Then before their eyes the four angels carried him up into heaven.

Chapter 222

After Jesus had departed, the disciples scattered through the different parts of Israel and of the world, and the truth, hated of

Satan, was persecuted, as it always is, by falsehood. For certain evil men, pretending to be disciples, preached that Jesus died and rose not again. Others preached that he really died, but rose again. Others preached, and yet preach, that Jesus is the Son of God, among whom is Paul deceived. But we - as much as I have written - we preach to those that fear God, that they may be saved in the last day of God's Judgment. Amen.

END OF THE GOSPEL OF BARNABAS

Introduction to the Gospel of Peter

In the valley of the Upper Nile, on the bank of the river, is the town of Akhmim, once called Panopolis. In ancient times Panoplis was the capital of the district. In the town stood remnants of a monastery. The ruins of the temple marked the intellectual life of ancient days. On the lands of the monastery was a graveyard wherein were interred the monks and priests who served there long ago.

In 1868 a French archeologist and his team were excavating this same cemetery in Egypt when they came upon a certain tomb from the eighth century. In the tomb was a monk, reclining peacefully with hands folded on his breast. His reverent hands clasped a small book, which he believed to be sacred, holy, and inspired. The book was an anthology containing three books the monk held most precious. One of these texts was the Gospel of Peter.

Six years later a translation was published in the Memoirs of the French Archeological Mission at Cairo. It was then that scholars realized a discovery of importance had been made. A portion of The Gospel According to Peter had been restored to the Christian community after having been lost over a thousand years.

Rev. D. H. Stanton, in The Journal of Theological Studies states, "The conclusion with which we are confronted is that the Gospel of Peter once held a place of honor comparable to that assigned to the four Gospels, perhaps even higher than some of them".

The text recovered was fragmentary. It begins in the middle of a sentence and ends in the middle of a sentence. The first sentence reads:

"...none of the Jews wished to wash their hands so Pilate stood up... "

This line is of great importance since it shows Pilate gave the Jews in attendance a chance to be free of the bloodshed which was about to take place, but none wished to abstain. The Book of Peter indicates the Jews held a high degree of culpability for the death of Jesus. In this Gospel it was the Jewish king Herod who ordered the death of Jesus. However, none of these differences were the reason for the Gospel of Peter to be rejected from canon.

The decision to set aside the Gospel of Peter from consideration of inclusion in the list of canon texts was a single line, which could have been interpreted a number of ways. The line read:
"They brought forth two evildoers and crucified the Lord between them, but he was silent as if he felt no pain."

Since the emerging orthodoxy was fighting what they considered to be a heretical belief that the Lord did not actually come in the flesh but was a spirit disguised as a man, they were very sensitive to any statement that could be construed as a way of bolstering the belief that Jesus was only a spirit. The idea that Jesus was not flesh and blood or that he was a spirit maintaining an illusion of being a man by covering himself (itself) with what was termed a " fleshly or bodily shell" came to have the theological term, "docetic". Since the text stated Jesus remained silent "as if he felt no pain" it could be construed to mean he did not have a body or he was a spirit which did not feel pain. The text was said to have a docetic tone and thus was rejected by the church fathers.

That is not to say the feared interpretation was what the Gospel of Peter was trying to convey. The author of Peter may well have been alluding to an Old Testament passage.

Isaiah 53:7 Holman Christian Standard Bible
He was oppressed and afflicted, yet He did not open His mouth. Like a

lamb led to the slaughter and like a sheep silent before her shearers, He did not open His mouth.

The true intent did not matter. Those in power, now referred to as the orthodox church, were much too concerned about leaving the smallest crack where heresy might slip in. Since the Gospel of Peter seems to suggest that Jesus was assumed into heaven directly from the cross, it added to the Gospel's label of docetic. Ignoring the Old Testament passages and pointing to the possible heretical interpretation, they banned the Gospel of Peter just to be safe.

As we examine what the church fathers and modern scholars have to say about the Gospel of Peter we will encounter repetition, as they seem to split into two camps. Although there are repetitive views, each has something to add and thus it is worth knowing what each man says in his own words.

The church father, Eusebius records the negative opinion expressed by Bishop Serapion of Antioch after he had read a copy of this apocryphal gospel:

"... most of it is indeed in accordance with the true teaching of the Savior, but some things are additions to that teaching, which items also we place below for your benefit."
Unfortunately, Eusebius, to whom we are indebted for a copy of this part of Serapion's letter, did not quote the specific points which the bishop found objectionable.

F.F. Bruce sums up the situation quite well.
F. F. Bruce writes in Jesus and Christian Origins Outside the New Testament, p. 93:

"The docetic note in this narrative appears in the statement that Jesus, while being crucified, 'remained silent, as though he felt no pain', and in the account of his death. It carefully avoids saying that he died, preferring to say that he 'was taken up', as though he - or at least his soul or spiritual self - was 'assumed' direct from the cross to the presence of God. (We shall see an echo of this idea in the Qur'an.) Then the cry of dereliction is reproduced in a form which suggests that, at that moment, his divine power left the bodily shell in which it had taken up temporary residence."

F. F. Bruce continues (op. cit.):

Here Bruce is referring to the last words of Jesus according to the Gospel of Peter. "My Power. My Power. Why have you forsaken me?"

The canon Gospels tell us Jesus acknowledged the time his spirit would leave his body by saying, "Father, into your hands I commit my spirit." But the church fathers believed this portrayed a natural death whereas the events in the Gospel of Peter do not because it never says he died or "gave up the ghost." A fine line is being drawn.

Ryan Turner, in the publication, "Christian Apologetics and Research Ministry" states:

"Prior to the discovery of the Akhmîm fragment in 1886-87, scholars knew very little about the Gospel of Peter. Their first main source was Eusebius of Caesarea (c. A.D. 260-340), the well-known early church historian, who noted that the Gospel of Peter was among the church's rejected writings and had heretical roots. The second main source for the Gospel of Peter is a letter by Serapion, a bishop in Antioch (in office A.D. 199-211), titled "Concerning What is Known as the Gospel of Peter." Bishop Serapion notes that the Gospel of Peter had docetic overtones and advised that church leaders not read it to their congregations. From Bishop Serapion's statements we know that the Gospel of Peter was written sometime in the second century, but we are left with little knowledge of its actual contents from Serapion's statements alone.

There is some debate among scholars regarding whether the Akhmîm fragment actually is a Gnostic document. There are two possible Gnostic examples. One describes the crucifixion of Jesus and states, "But he held his peace, as though having no pain." This may reflect the Gnostic view of Docetism which viewed Jesus as not possessing a physical body. This would explain Jesus' lack of pain on the cross. The other describes Jesus' death cry on the cross as, "My power, my power, thou hast forsaken me." Some scholars see this as a reference to "...a docetic version of the cry of dereliction which results from the departure of the divine power from Jesus' bodily shell." However, some scholars dispute these references as referring to full blown Gnosticism or Gnostic teachings at all.

Although many scholars dismiss the Gospel of Peter as having little theological impact, some scholars disagree. These place The Gospel of Peter solidly in the stream of development of the Passion narrative.

Ron Cameron argues that the Gospel of Peter is independent of the canonical four (The Other Gospels, pp. 77-8):

"Identification of the sources of the Gospel of Peter is a matter of considerable debate. However, the language used to portray the passion provides a clue to the use of sources, the character of the tradition, and the date of composition. Analysis reveals that the passion narrative of the Gospel of Peter has been composed on the basis of references to the Jewish scriptures. The Gospel of Peter thus stands squarely in the tradition of exegetical interpretation of the Bible. Its sources of the passion narrative is oral tradition, understood in the light of scripture, interpreted within the wisdom movement. This accords with what we know of the confessions of the earliest believers in Jesus: in the beginning, belief in the suffering, death, burial, and resurrection of Jesus was simply the conviction that all this took place "according to the scriptures" (I Cor. 15:3-5). In utilizing scriptural references to compose the work, the Gospel of Peter shows no knowledge of the special material distinctive to each of the four gospels now in the New Testament. The developed apologetic technique typical of the Gospel of Matthew and of Justin (a church writer who lived in the middle of the second century), which seeks to demonstrate a correspondence between so-called prophetic "predictions" in the scriptures and their "fulfillments" in the fate of Jesus, is lacking. The use of quotation formulas to introduce scriptural citations is also absent.

All of this suggests that the Gospel of Peter is an independent witness of gospel traditions. Its earliest possible date of composition would be in the middle of the first century, when passion narratives first began to be compiled. The latest possible date would be in the second half of the second century, shortly before this gospel was used by the Christians at Rhossus and the copy discovered at Oxyrhynchus was made. It is well known that the passion narrative which Mark used originally circulated independently of his gospel. The Gospel of John demonstrates that different versions of this early passion narrative were in circulation. It is possible that the Gospel of Peter used a source similar to that preserved independently in Mark and John. The basic stories underlying the accounts of the epiphany and the empty tomb are critically discrete and probably very old. In fact, these stories are closely related to certain legendary accounts and apologetic fragments that intrude into the gospel of the New Testament (Matt. 27:51-54, 62-66; 28:2-4; Mark 9:2-8 and parallels).
"

Thus it is pointed out that the Passion Narrative contained within Mark was at one time independent of Mark and was added to the Gospel afterward to give us what we now view as the complete Gospel of Mark. The Passion Story within Mark differs from that in The Gospel of John. Based on this information, it can be seen that there were several stories of the crucifixion, death, burial, resurrection and subsequent appearances of Jesus developing at about the same time. The Gospel of Peter contains one of these various storylines.

There are other parts of the Gospel of Peter which diverge from the other Gospels. Peter records the exoneration of Pilate, the Roman procurator, telling us it was the Jews who demanded Jesus' death and Pilate who tried to restrain them. He then offered any of the Jews in the crowd the ability to abstain from the killing by symbolically washing their hands of the matter. When on one took the opportunity, Pilate himself got up and washed his hands, denouncing the action which was about to take place against his wishes. This is but a small and insignificant difference from Matthew 27:24 in which Pilate proclaims his innocence of the murder.

Matthew 27:24 When Pilate saw that he was getting nowhere, but that instead an uproar was starting, he took water and washed his hands in front of the crowd. "I am innocent of this man's blood," he said. "It is your responsibility!"

What makes this scripture of interest is that scholars believe it was inserted into Matthew's Gospel at a later date when ant-Semitism was on the rise. It was believed to have been placed in The Gospel of Peter for the same reason. These alterations, and the accompanying anti-Jewish tone are additions to these primitive narratives, influenced by a situation in which the Jesus movement was beginning to define itself in opposition to, or separation from other Jewish communities.

In setting itself apart from traditional Judaism, the Christian movement began to define itself as separate and correct. Within this framework of thought there will usually be an intentional diminishing or demonizing of the other group. Thus began the first wave of Christian anti-Jewish thought and behavior.

Approval of the content of the narrative with its complete exoneration of Pilate from all responsibility for the crucifixion of Jesus is seen in the fact that Pilate would later obtain canonization in the Coptic Church.

When Pilate refuses to be held accountable for the trial, which he signifies by washing his hands Herod Antipas takes over from him, assuming the responsibility of the crucifixion that he declined to accept in Luke's narrative.

It must be noted here that Herod was the Jewish king of the time and place around which Jesus was being called by the people, "King of the Jews." Herod would have much to lose by leaving the claim of the people unanswered.

Roman soldiers play no part in the crucifixion. They did not appear until commanded by Pilate to stand guard at the tomb of Jesus. The Jewish authorities requested this duty. The scriptures tell of this action as a deterrent to anyone wishing to steal the body from the tomb and claim Jesus had risen as prophesied. Throughout the texts the villains are the Jews, or at least the Jewish authority represented by Herod and led by the chief priests and the scribes. It is the priests and scribes who condemn Jesus to death and abuse him. They then divide his clothing among themselves.

In The Death of the Messiah, Raymond Brown maintains that the Gospel of Peter is dependent on the canonical gospels by oral remembrance of the gospels spoken in churches. The opinion that the Gospel of Peter is dependent upon the canonical gospels directly is also a common one.

Other scholars have suggested that the Gospel of Peter was

dependent upon a number of sources, but it is quite possible that the document was written before the four gospels of the New Testament and may have served as a source for their respective authors. This opinion is not held by the majority, who believe it was Mark that served as a template to the Gospels of Matthew and Luke, although it is possible for both camps to be correct if Mark used Peter as a source. If the date usually assigned to the writing of Peter is correct the theory of Peter coming before the four Gospels of the New Testament could not be correct unless there is an old version, or an oral tradition containing the Gospel of Peter.

The Gospel of Peter was probably composed in the second half of the first century, most likely in western Syria. As such, it is the oldest extant writing produced and circulated under the authority of the apostle Peter.

There is a large body of evidence that the earliest Christians, such as the first Apostles, led by James and excluding Paul, who never met the incarnate Jesus, did not believe that Jesus was a sin sacrifice. They believed he was the messiah, and following the Jewish concept of a messiah, he was blessed and anointed by God, just a King David and others were. He communed with God, spoke to God, and taught the people about God's plans, but he was not God. James and the other apostles believed Jesus kept the law perfectly and that is what he meant when he said, "I come to fulfill the law..." That is to completely follow the law. It was Paul who began to change the religion of Jesus, the Jewish religion, into the religion of Jesus, the Christian religion. Following this teaching, the Christian community began to form the passion narrative.

The creation of a passion and resurrection narrative was the product of a community of believers who understood the ultimate activity of God to have taken place in their own time, when the powers of unrighteousness and death were conquered by God's definitive act of raising the dead. Accordingly, the fate of Jesus is interpreted, in the hindsight of scripture, as God's vindication of the suffering righteous one.

J.D. Crossan is most famous for his reconstruction of a Cross Gospel preserved in the Gospel of Peter. He believed the Gospel of Peter served as the basis for the passion narrative in all four canonical gospels. Crossan has set forward this thesis briefly in his book, Four Other Gospels, as well as in his book The Cross that Spoke.

Koester has criticized this hypothesis for several reasons: "The Gospel of Peter has been preserved mostly in one late manuscript, making certainty about the text difficult; Crossan seems to underestimate the role of oral tradition and assigns all the gospel materials to earlier noncanonical sources; finally, appearance stories cannot have been present in the passion narrative because they are independent of each other in the canonical gospels." (Ancient Christian Gospels, pp. 219-20). Koester continues by saying (op. cit., p.240):
"The Gospel of Peter, as a whole, is not dependent upon any of the canonical gospels. It is a composition which is analogous to the Gospels of Mark and John. All three writings, independently of each other, use an older passion narrative which is based upon an exegetical tradition that was still alive when these gospels were composed, and to which the Gospel of Matthew also had access. All five gospels under consideration, Mark, John, and Peter, as well as Matthew and Luke, concluded their gospels with narratives of the appearances of Jesus on the basis of different epiphany stories that were told in different contexts. However, fragments of the epiphany story of Jesus being raised from the tomb, which the Gospel of Peter has preserved in its entirety, were employed in different literary contexts in the Gospels of Mark and Matthew."

As previously stated, the present fragment was discovered in 1868 in a tomb at Akhmimin Egypt. The manuscript of The Gospel of Peter was found in a little book containing a portion of the Book of Enoch in Greek. The Book of Enoch is a book, which is canon to the Ethiopic Christian church. The book of Enoch, also called First Enoch, can be obtained through Fifth Estate Publishing. The fragment of Peter on the Passion and another, a description of Heaven and Hell, which is probably a second fragment of the Gospel, or a piece of the Apocalypse of Peter.

Writers of the end of the second century quote the Gospel of Peter. It has been argued that Justin Martyr used it soon after the middle of the second century. Evidence to this is not compelling. The earliest dates set the writing to around 150 A.D.

To sum up the information provided by various scholars and sources: Some believe it was written independently of the four canonical Gospels. Some believe it uses the four Gospels as its construct. The Gospel of Peter is the earliest non-canonical account of the Passion that exists. Some of the passages can be construed as being not wholly orthodox. It gives way to doubt regarding the reality of the Lord's sufferings, and by consequence it brings doubt on the fact that Jesus was fully and completely corporeal. Serapion of Antioch and other church fathers believed it to have a docetic character.

Following the death of Jesus there were many Christian theologies vying for dominance in the early church. Those who held one belief may reject texts which taught other doctrines. Other Christian sects may have accepted books rejected by the first sect because it conformed to the theology taught by their sect.

The reason we have the canon which exists today is that those who held a particular set of beliefs espoused by what we now call the New Testament won the political and social battle and became the dominate sect. Once a sect became dominant it could call itself orthodox and label all other beliefs heretical. Canon was set by the dominant sect based on several factors: It must be of apostolic origin, as decided by the sect. That is to say, the leaders must agree that it was written by an apostle or those who served them, such as Luke; It must conform to the doctrine of the sect; It should be accepted and circulated by the majority of churches. In this light, the Gospel of Peter was set aside by most orthodox Christians due to what some interpreted as a docetic tone. But obviously not all agreed. Some learned Christians held on to the text and viewed it as sacred, even into the eighth century, as attested by the silent hands of a dead monk in a tomb in Egypt.

Having covered the history and theology of the book, let us now look at the text of the Gospel of Peter.

The translation presented herein is an updated and modernized version based on the work M.R. James as published in The Apocryphal New Testament. The work was published in Oxford by Clarendon Press in 1924. Language and sentence structure have been brought up to date. Meanings and translations have been updated based on information gathered since the text was first translated. Commentary has been added and appears in italicized font. Words in parentheses have been inserted for the sake of clarification.

The Gospel of Peter

1 ...but of the Jews no man washed his hands. Herod did not wash his hands nor did any of his judges. Pilate, seeing they would not wash, stood up (and washed his hands). 2 And then Herod the king commanded that the Lord should be given to them. And Herod said to them, "All that I commanded you to do to him, do.

3 Now, Joseph the friend of Pilate and of the Lord was standing near, and he saw that they were about to crucify him (Jesus), so Joseph came to Pilate and begged to be given the body of Jesus for burial. So Pilate sent to Herod, asking for his body. 5 Herod replied: Brother Pilate, even if no one had asked for him, we were going to bury him, because the Sabbath would dawn (begin); for it is written in the law that the sun should not set upon one that has been slain (murdered).

The phrasing that the Sabbath "dawns" is an odd choice of words considering the fact that the Sabbath begins on Friday evening at sunset and ends on Saturday night with the appearance of three stars. All Jewish days begin at sunset. This is based on the wording of the Creation story in Genesis 1. At the end of the description of each day, we find the phrase: "And there was evening, and there was morning of the first day..." Since evening is mentioned first, the ancient rabbis deduced that evening is first of the beginning of the day. Thus the day "dawns" at sundown.

6 And Herod presented the Lord to the people before the first day of (or on the day before the) unleavened bread, which was their feast. And they took the Lord and pushed him as they ran, and said: Let us hale the Son of God, seeing that now we have control of him (authority over him). 7 And they put a purple robe on him

and made him sit upon the seat of judgment, saying: O you King of Israel, give us righteous judgment. 8 And one of them brought a crown of thorns and set it upon the Lord's head. 9 And others stood by and spit in his eyes, and others struck his cheeks; and others stabbed him with sticks, and some of them whipped him, shouting, "This is how we honor you – This is what you are worth to us, the son of God."

10 And they brought two criminals and crucified the Lord between them. 11 But he kept silence, like someone who felt no pain.

This statement, "But he kept silent, like someone who felt no pain," was one of the lines in this small book that the church fathers believed to be open to docetic interpretation, thus disallowing the book from being considered as canon.

And when they had set the cross upright, they wrote on it, "This is the King of Israel." 12 And they laid out his garments before him, and divided them among themselves and gambled (cast the lot) for them.

The practice of casting lots is mentioned 70 times in the Old Testament and seven times in the New Testament. In spite of the many references to casting lots, little is known about the actual lots themselves. They could have been sticks of various lengths, flat stones like coins, or some kind of dice; but their exact nature is unknown. The closest modern practices to casting lots are flipping a coin, rolling dice, or choosing the longest stick from those held in a person's closed fist.

13 But one of those criminals shamed them, saying: We have suffered like this for the evils we have done, but this man which has become the savior of men, how has he injured (any of) you? 14 And they were enraged with him, and commanded that his legs should not be broken, that so he might die in torment.

347

*Breaking the legs of a criminal was an act of mercy since it would
shorten the time of punishment because his death would come quicker.
The crucified person would have to push up on his feet, which were
staked to the pole, in order to fill his lungs and breathe a single breath.
Breaking the legs meant he could not push himself up and would
suffocate sooner and die.*

15 Now it was noon but darkness covered all of Judaea: and the
people were afraid and in anguish, thinking the sun had set
because he (Jesus) was still alive, because it is written that the sun
should not set upon him that had been killed (murdered). 16 And
one of them said: Give him gall with vinegar to drink, and they
mixed it and gave it to him to drink. 17 In this way they fulfilled
all things and completed placing their sins upon their own heads.
18 And many went about with lamps, thinking it was night and
some fell down. 18 And the Lord cried out aloud saying: My
power, my power, you have forsaken me. And when he had so
said, he was taken up.

*Deuteronomy 21: 22"If a man has committed a sin worthy of death and
he is put to death, and you hang him on a tree, 23 his corpse shall not
hang all night on the tree, but you shall surely bury him on the same day
(for he who is hanged is accursed of God), so that you do not defile your
land which the LORD your God gives you as an inheritance.*

*Instead of crying aloud, "My God, My God, why have you forsaken
me?" the Gospel of Peter has Jesus crying out, "My power, my power,
you have forsaken me." An old Syriac translation has Jesus' last words
being:*
 *"At the ninth hour Jesus cried out with a
great voice and said, "O helper, O helper,
why have you forsaken me"*
This could also be interpreted as "My power, My Power...
This could be seen as contributing to a theology that saw Jesus as a vessel

or shell containing a great spirit, which was assumed into heaven before the body died.

According to the bible, Jesus' last words on the cross are "My God, My God, why have you forsaken Me" or as Younan said "why have you spared me", but as the words have more than one meaning and they were being passed from one language to another, (remember, Jesus spoke Aramaic and the New Testament was written in Greek, and then copied and translated into other tongues), we can read in other Bible translations:"eli eli lema sabachtani" as well as "eloi eloi lama sabaktani". It also exists in the reading of the Peshitta as " eil eil lmana shvaqtan" and even a Hebrew reading (D 05 Codex): "elei elei lama zaphtanei" (both in Matthew and Mark). How "my God" became "my power"? Simply because 'el means God/god but also power as we can see it in Genesis.

EL, ELOAH: God "mighty, strong, prominent" (Genesis 7:1; Isaiah 9:6) – etymologically, El appears to mean "power," as in "I have the power to harm you" (Genesis 31:29). El is associated with other qualities, such as integrity (Numbers 23:19), jealousy (Deuteronomy 5:9), and compassion (Nehemiah 9:31), but the root idea of might remains. The scribe reading "eli" understood my power instead of my God.

20 And in the same hour the veil of the temple of Jerusalem was ripped in two.
21 And then they pulled the nails out of the hands of the Lord and laid him on the ground. Then the entire earth was shaken, and a great fear fell upon every one.

22 Then the sun began to shine and (the position of the sun indicated) it was the ninth hour. 23 And the Jews celebrated, and they gave his body to Joseph to bury it, because he had witnessed all the good things Jesus had done. 24 And he took the Lord and washed him and wrapped him in linen and brought him unto his own sepulcher, which is called the Garden of Joseph.

*Generally speaking, hours were reckoned from sunrise, so the ninth hour
of the day would be about nine hours after sunrise. Depending on the
time of year, that is usually around 3PM.*

*In this period of time bodies of the dead were placed in a sepulcher, which
was a small cave carved out of the stone of a hill. After the body
decomposed the bones were collected and placed in an ossuary, which was
a chest or box, made to serve as the final resting place of human skeletal
remains.*

25 Then the Jews and the elders and the priests realized what an
evil thing they had done they began to lament and say, "We
greatly regret our sin and now judgment and the end of Jerusalem
draws near."

26 But I (Peter) with my fellows were grieving, and our minds
were wounded. We hid ourselves because they sought for us as
criminals, and we were even considering setting the temple on
fire. 27 And beside all these things we were fasting, and we sat
mourning and weeping night and day until the Sabbath.

28 But the scribes and Pharisees and elders gathered together
because they had heard that all the people were murmuring and
beating their breasts and saying, "He must have been very
righteous because all these signs have come to pass." 29 And the
elders were afraid and came to Pilate, begging him and saying, 30
"Give us soldiers so that we (or they) may watch his sepulcher for
three days, otherwise his disciples will come and steal him away
and the people will believe that he is risen from the dead, and do
us harm.

*The belief at the time of Jesus was that the spirit remained earth bound
and close to the body for three days. At the end of the third day after
death the spirit departed and went to its resting place, according to deeds
of the person. There was a chance the spirit could return to the body
within the three day period. This belief could have been fostered by the*

fact that there was no way of detecting suppressed heartbeats and occasionally a person might not have been dead and would revive.

31 And Pilate gave them Petronius the centurion with soldiers to watch the sepulcher; and the elders and scribes came with them to the tomb. 32 Then they rolled a large stone to set it at the front of the tomb as a door and they sealed it with plaster and they placed seven seals on the door (to detect intrusion). Then they placed the centurion and the soldiers together in front of the tomb. 33 And they (the scribes and Pharisees) pitched a tent there and kept watch.

34 Early in the morning at sunrise on the Sabbath, a multitude from Jerusalem and the surrounding area arrived to see the sepulcher that had been sealed.

35 Now the night when the Lord's Day began, the soldiers were keeping guard in pairs on every watch. Then there was heard a great sound in the heaven. 36 And they saw the heaven open up and two young men descend from the opening and they had a (were shining with) a bright light. And they came near the sepulcher. 37 And the stone, which had been placed on the door, rolled away by itself and went back to the side, and the sepulcher was opened.

38 Both men entered in. When the soldiers saw these things they woke the centurion and the elders (because they were also there keeping watch). 39 But while they were telling them the things which they had seen, they saw again three men come out of the sepulcher. The two men were supporting another man. 40 And a cross was following them. 41 And they saw that the heads of the two men reached up to heaven, the man supported by them exceeded the heavens. 42 And they heard a voice out of the heavens saying, "Have you preached to them that sleep?" And an answer was heard from the cross, saying, "Yes."

43 All the men discussed these things with one another and decided to report what had transpired to Pilate. But while they were still there the heavens opened again, and a man descended and entered the tomb. 45 Then the centurion and those who were with him saw this they hurried off by night to inform Pilate and they left the sepulcher where they were supposed to be keeping watch, and told everyone they encountered what they had seen, and they were terrified, saying, " It is true, he was the son of God."

46 Pilate answered them and said, "I am clean of the blood of the Son of God, but to do these things seemed good to you."
47 Then all they came seeking Pilate and begging him to command the centurion and the soldiers to tell nothing they had seen. 48 They said it is better for us to incur this, the greatest of sin, before God than to fall into the hands of the people and to be stoned by the Jews. 49 Therefore Pilate commanded the centurion and the soldiers to say nothing.

50 Now early on the Lord's day Mary Magdalene, a disciple of the Lord, was afraid of the Jews because they were very angry. She had not gone to the sepulcher of the Lord to perform those things which women are accustomed to do to the dead who were loved by them.

It was usually up to the women to perform the ritual bathing. The body was to be bathed, and wrapped in linen with aloes and myrrh. In accordance with Jewish burial practices of the first century C.E. Jesus' disciples would have taken his body, bought a great quantity of myrrh and aloes, "and wound it in linen clothes with the spices, as the manner of the Jews is to bury" (John 19:40). There was a delay in completing the preparation of the body for burial because of the Sabbath (Mark 16:1; Luke 23:56). Luke (7:11–17) gives a vivid picture of the simple funeral of the poor; the body of a young man of Nain is borne out of the city on a

pallet, clothed but without coffin, followed by the weeping mother and
"much people of the city." The problem with the text here is that Joseph
had already performed the ritual of cleaning, anointing, and wrapping
the body with myrrh and aloes. The women must have been there to
mourn, grieve and to bring symbolic gifts.

51 So she took with her women who were her friends. 52 And
they came to the tomb where he was laid. And they feared the
Jews would see them, and they said, "Even if we were not able to
weep and lament him on that day when he was crucified, let us
now do so at his tomb." 53 "But who will roll away the stone for
us that is placed in the doorway of the tomb so that we may enter
and sit beside him and perform that which is due? The stone is
large, and we fear that some man might see us. But if we cannot
perform these things, let us lay the items we bring down at the
door as a memorial to him, and we will weep and lament until we
come back to our house."

55 And they went and found the sepulcher open. As they
approached it they looked in and saw a young man sitting in the
middle of the sepulcher. He was beautiful and he was clothed in
very bright raiment. 56 He said to them, "Why have you come
here? Whom do you seek? Is it him that was crucified? He is risen
and has departed, but if you do not believe me, look in and see the
place where he was laid. He is not here, for he is risen and is
departed back from where he was sent. 57 Then the women
became afraid and they fled.

58 Now it was the last day of unleavened bread, and many were
coming out of the city and returning to their own homes because
the feast was at an end. 59 But we, the twelve disciples of the
Lord, were weeping and were sorrowful, and each one grieved
over what had happened. 60 So each man departed to his own
house. But I, Simon Peter, and my brother Andrew, took our nets
and went to the sea, and there was with us Levi the son of

Alphaeus, whom the Lord…

Here, the text ends abruptly.

History of The Apocryphon of John

The Apocryphon, or "Secrets" of John forms the cornerstone of Gnostic mythology and cosmology. In this text we are introduced to the major entities of creation and lordship. We learn how the universe, including earth and man, came into being. The origin of evil, the creator god, and the material world are explained in detail. The story seems to be a mixture of various belief systems, including Chrithat of Plato, who seems to have borrowed freely from the format of Greek mythology, and Christianity. The story is loosely based on Genesis chapters 1 through 13 as a timeline.

The basic text of the Apocryphon of John existed in some form before 185 C.E. when A book called the Apocryphon of John was referred to by Irenaeus in his book, Against Heresies (Adversus Haereses), written in that year. Irenaeus reported about the Gnostic texts saying that teachers in 2nd century Christian communities were writing their own books to gain converts. He calls these books, "an indescribable number of secret and illegitimate writings, which they themselves have forged, to bewilder the minds of foolish people, who are ignorant of the true scriptures" (A.H. 1.20.1)

The Apocryphon of John continued to be circulated, expanded and embellished for the next seven hundred years. The document was reportedly in use during the eighth century by the Audians of Mesopotamia. Part of the mythology revealed in the Apocryphon of Jonh is also present in the Gnostic book, The Sophia (Wisdom) of Jesus as well as other Gnostic texts.

The specific document that so angered Irenaeus was lost and remained so until 1945, when a library of papyrus codices from the 4th century were found at Nag Hammadi in Egypt. The Apocryphon of John was among the texts,

Four versions have been found thus far. These are comprised

of a long version, of which we have two identical Coptic manuscripts. A short version is also Coptic but differs from the others by eliminating certain details. A third, shorter Coptic manuscript had been found that differs slightly from the first shorter manuscript in style and vocabulary. A fragment has been found that shows some minor differences which distinguish it from the other.

Which, if any, of these texts are original have not been determined, however, it is the longer version that is presented here. This version was chosen because it contained more details and offered an overall cohesion of thought. This could be due to additions and embellishments sown through the shorter, less detailed versions.

Since we have already covered the general idea behind Gnostic mythology it need not be repeated her. However, a chart showing the main characters and their position on the divine family tree might serve us well. It is shown below.

Simplified Cast Of Characters

"Divine All", "Spirit" or "Father"
|
Divine Thought or Barbelo

_____

|

Fore-   Indestruct-   Fore-   Eternal   Truth
knowledge   ability   thought   Life

_____

|
|
Christ, Self-created one, Perfect man
|
Sophia or wisdom
|
Elohim and Yaldaboth (who is also known as Yahweh)
|
|
Man and the material universe

The Apocryphon of John

The teaching of the savior, that will reveal the mysteries of things hidden which he taught John, his disciple, in silence.
On the day when John, the brother of James, the sons of Zebedee, had come to the temple, a Pharisee named Arimanius came up to him and said, "Where is your master whom you followed?" He said to him, He has gone back to the place he came from. The Pharisee said to him, This Nazarene deceived all of you with his deception. He filled your ears with lies, and closed your hearts and turned you all away from your fathers' traditions.

When I, John, heard these things I walked away from the temple into the desert. I grieved greatly in my heart, saying, How was the savior appointed, and why was he sent to the world by his Father, and who is his Father who sent him, and to which kingdom shall we go? What did he mean when he said to us, 'This kingdom which you will go to is an imperishable kingdom, but he did not teach us what kind it is.

Then, while I was meditating on these things, I saw the heavens open and the whole creation below heaven was shining and the world shook. I was afraid, and then I saw in the light a young man who stood by me. As I was looking at him he became like an old man. And he changed his visage again and become like a servant. There were not many beings in front of me, but there was a single being with many forms composed of light, and they could be seen through each other, and there were three forms within the one being.
He said to me, John, John, why do you doubt, and why are you afraid? (Mat. 28:17) Do you understand this image, do you not? Do not be afraid! I am the one who is with all of you always. I am the Father and the Mother, and I am the Son. I am the undefiled

358

and incorruptible one. I have come to teach you what is and what was and what will be, so that you may know the things visible and invisible, and to teach you concerning the upright, immutable (unshakable / unwavering) race of the perfect Man. Now, therefore, lift up your face, that you may receive the things that I shall teach you today, and may tell them to your fellow spirits who are from the upright, immutable (unwavering/ unshakable) race of the perfect Man. (Eph.4:13)

And I asked if I might understand it, and he said to me, The One God is a king with nothing above it. It is he who exists as God and Father of everything, the invisible One who rules over everything, who exists as incorruptible, which is in the pure light that no eye can look upon.
He is the invisible Spirit. It is not correct to think of him as a god, or anything similar. He is more than god, since there is nothing above him, for no one is above him. He does not exist within anything inferior to him, because everything exists within him. He has establishes himself. He is eternal, self-sufficient, and self-sustaining. He is complete perfection. He did not lack anything to be complete and he is continually perfect in light. He is unlimited, since there was no one before him to limit him. He is unknowable, since there exists no one prior to him to comprehend him. He is immeasurable, since there was no one before him to measure him. He is invisible, since no one has seen him. He is eternal, since he exists always. He is an enigma, since no one was able to apprehend him or explain him. He is unnamable, since there is no one came before him to give him a name.

He is One, immeasurable light, which is pure, holy and immaculate. He is too sacred to speak of, being perfect and incorruptible. He is beyond perfection, blessedness, and divinity, because he is vastly superior to them all. He is not corporeal nor is he incorporeal. He is One and cannot be qualified or quantified, for no one can know him. He is not one among other beings;

instead, he is far superior to all. He is so superior to all things that his essence is not part of the kingdoms, nor is he part of time. He who is a kingdom was created beforehand. Time does not matter to him, since he does not receive anything from another, for it would be received on loan. He who comes first needs nothing from anyone. Such a one expectantly beholds himself in his own light. He is majestic perfection. He is pure, immeasurable mind. He is a kingdom that gives the kingdoms their kingdom. He is life that gives life. He is the blessed One that blesses. He is knowledge and he gives knowledge. He is goodness that gives goodness. He is mercy and redemption and he bestows mercy. He is grace that gives grace. He does not give because he has these things but he gives the immeasurable, incomprehensible light from which all things flow.

How am I to speak with you about him? His kingdom is indestructible, at peace and existing in silence, at rest before everything was. He is the head of all the kingdoms (kingdoms), and he gives them strength in his goodness. For we know not the things that are unspeakably sacred, and we do not understand that which cannot be measured, except for him who was created from him, namely from the Father. It is he alone who told it to us.

He who beholds himself in the light which surrounds him and comes from him is the spring of the water of life. It is he who sustains the entire kingdom in every way, and it is he who gazes upon the image which he sees in the spring of the Spirit. It is he who puts his desire in the liquid light which is in the spring of the pure liquid light which surrounds him.
The Father's thought performed a deed and she was created from it. It is she who had appeared before him in the shining of his light. This is the first power which was before all of them and which was created from his mind. She is the Thought of the All and her light shines like his light. It is the perfect power which is the visage of the invisible. She is the pure, undefiled Spirit who is

perfect. She is the first power, the glory of Barbelo, the perfect glory of the kingdom (kingdoms), the glory revealed. She glorified the pure, undefiled Spirit and it was she who praised him, because thanks to him she had come forth. She is the first thought, his image; she became the womb of everything, for it is she who preceded them all. She is the Mother-Father, the first man, the Holy Spirit, the threefold male, the triple power, the androgynous one with three names, and the eternal kingdom among the invisible ones, and the first to come forth.

She asked the invisible, pure, undefiled Spirit, Barbelo, to give her Foreknowledge, and the Spirit agreed. And when he had agreed, the Foreknowledge was created, and it stood by the Thought; it originates from the thought of the invisible, pure, undefiled Spirit. It glorified him and his perfect power, Barbelo. It was for it was because of her that it had been created.

And she asked again to grant her indestructibility, and he agreed. When he had agreed, indestructibility was created, and it stood by the Divine Thought and the Foreknowledge. It glorified the invisible One and Barbelo, the one because of whom they had been created.

And Barbelo asked to grant her Eternal Life. And the invisible Spirit agreed. And when he had agreed, Eternal Life was created, and they attended and glorified the invisible Spirit and Barbelo, the one because of whom they had been created.

And she asked again to grant her truth. And the invisible Spirit agreed. And when he had agreed, Truth was created, and they attended and glorified the invisible, excellent Spirit and his Barbelo, the one because of whom they had been created.

This is the five-fold creation of the kingdom of the Father, which is the first man and the image of the invisible Spirit, which came from Barbelo, who was the divine Thought; Forethought, Foreknowledge, Indestructibility, Eternal life, and Truth.

This is the androgynous five-fold being of the kingdom, which is the ten types of kingdoms, which is the Father.

(Five, being both male and female, or neither male nor female, become ten)

And he looked at Barbelo with his pure light which surrounds the
invisible Spirit, and his sparks, and she was impregnated by him.
And a spark of light produced a light resembling his blessedness
but it did not equal his greatness. This was the only-begotten child
of the Mother-Father which had come forth. It is the only
offspring and the only begotten of the Father, the pure Light.
And the invisible, pure, undefiled Spirit rejoiced over the light
which was created, that which was produced by the first power of
his Thought, which is Barbelo. And he poured his goodness over
it until it became perfect and did not lack in any goodness,
because he had anointed the child with the goodness of the
invisible Spirit. It was his child and the child was there with him
and he poured upon the child an anointing. And immediately
when the child had received the Spirit, it glorified the Holy Spirit
and the perfect Divine Thought, because the child owed these its
existence.
And it asked to be given Mind as a fellow worker, and he agreed
gladly. And when the invisible Spirit had agreed, the Mind was
created, and it attended the anointed one (Christ), glorifying him
and Barbelo. And all these were created in silence.

And Mind wanted to initiate and action through the word of the
invisible Spirit. Thus, his will became an action and it appeared
with the mind; and the light glorified it. And the word followed
the will. It was because of the word that Christ, the divine self-
created one, created everything. And Eternal Life and his will and
Mind and Foreknowledge attended and glorified the invisible
Spirit and Barbelo, because of whom they had been created.

And the Holy Spirit perfected and matured the divine Self-created
one, and brought the son, together with Barbelo, so that he might
present himself to the mighty and invisible, pure, undefiled Spirit
as the divine Self-created one, the Christ (the anointed one) who

loudly proclaimed honor to the spirit. He was created through Forethought. And the invisible, pure, undefiled Spirit placed the divine Self-created one of truth over everything. And he caused every authority to be subject to him and to Truth, which is in him, so that he may know the name of the "All," whose name is exalted above every name. That name will only be spoken to those who are worthy of it.

From the light, which is the Christ, there is incorruptibleness and through the gift of the Spirit four lights shone from the divine Self-created one. He wished that they might be with him. And the three are will, thought, and life. And the four powers are Understanding, Grace, Perception, and Thoughtfulness.

And Grace belongs to the everlasting realm of the luminary Harmozel, which is the first angel. And there are three other kingdoms with this everlasting kingdom: Grace, Truth, and Form. And the second luminary is Oriel, who has authority over the second everlasting realm. And there are three other kingdoms with him: Conception, Perception, and Memory. And the third luminary is Daveithai, who has authority over the third everlasting realm. And there are three other kingdoms with him: Understanding, Love, and Idea. And the fourth luminary, Eleleth , was given authority over the fourth everlasting realm. And there are three other kingdoms with him: Perfection, Peace, and Wisdom (Sophia). These are the four luminaries which serve the divine Self-created one. These are the twelve kingdoms which serve the child of god, the Self-created one, the Christ. They serve him through the will and the grace of the invisible Spirit. The twelve kingdoms belong to the child of the Self-created one. All things were established by the will of the Holy Spirit through the Self-created one.

From the Foreknowledge of the perfect mind, through the

expression of the will of the invisible Spirit and the will of the Self-created one, the perfect Man came into being. He was the first revelation and the truth. The pure, undefiled Spirit called him "Adam, The Stranger" (not of the earthly realm, but belonging to the divine realm). The spirit placed him over the first realm with the mighty one, the Self-created one, the Christ, by the authority of the first luminary, Harmozel; and with him are his powers. And the invisible one gave Adam The Stranger an invincible spiritual power. And Adam The Stranger spoke, glorifying and praising the invisible Spirit, saying, "It is because of you that everything has been created and therefore, everything will return to you. I shall praise and glorify you and the Self-created one and all the realms, the three: the Father, the Mother, and the Son, who make up the perfect power."

And Adam The Stranger placed his son Seth over the second realm in which the second luminary Oriel is present. And in the third realm the children of Seth were established over the third luminary, Daveithai. And the souls of the saints were lodged there. In the fourth realm the souls are kept of those who do not know the Pleroma and who did not repent at once. These are they who persisted for a while and repented afterwards; they are in the area of the fourth luminary, Eleleth. They are those which glorify the invisible Spirit.

And the Sophia of the eternal realm manifested a thought from herself through the invisible Spirit and Foreknowledge. She wanted to produce a likeness of herself out of herself without the consent of the Spirit, but he had not approved. She attempted this act without her male consort, and without his permission. She had no male approval thus, she had not found her agreement. She had considered this without the consent of the Spirit and the knowledge of her compliment, but she brought forth her creation anyway. Because of the invincible power she possessed her thought did not remain idle, and something came out of her which was imperfect and different from her appearance because she had produced it without her compliment. It did not look like its mother because it has another form.

As she beheld the results of her desire, it changed into a form of a lion-faced serpent. Its eyes were like fire-like lightning which flashed. When she saw it she cast it away from her and threw it outside the realm so that none of the immortal ones might see it, for she had created it in ignorance. She surrounded it with a brightly glowing cloud and she put a throne in the middle of the cloud that no one might see it except the Holy Spirit who is called the mother of all that lives. And she called his name Yaldaboth.

This is the first Archon who took great power from his mother. And he left her and moved away from the realm in which he was born. He became strong and created for himself other kingdoms with a flame of glowing fire which still existed. And he mated with his own mindless ego that he had with him (he masturbated / or he was like is mother and did the same act of creation by himself) and brought into existence authorities for himself.

The name of the first one is Athoth, whom the generations call the reaper.
The second one is Harmas, who is the eye of envy.
The third one is Kalila-Oumbri.
The fourth one is Yabel.
The fifth one is Adonaiou, who is called Sabaoth (fool or chaos).
The sixth one is Cain, whom the generations of humans call the sun.
The seventh is Abel.
The eighth is Abrisene.
The ninth is Yobel.
The tenth is Armoupieel.
The eleventh is Melceir-Adonein.
The twelfth is Belias, it is he who is over the depth of Hades.

(These could be the 12 stations of the zodiac.)

 There he placed seven kings corresponding to the sections of heaven to reign over the seven heavens and he placed five to reign over the depth of the abyss. (There were 7 known planets at the time of writing.) And he shared his fire with them, but he did not relinquish any power of the light which he had taken from his mother, for he is ignorant darkness.

And when light is added to darkness, it made the darkness bright. When darkness is added to light, it dims the light and it became neither light nor dark, but it became like dusk.

Now the Archon who is like the gloaming (gloom) has three names. The first name is Yaldaboth (fool / son of chaos), the second is Saklas, and the third is Samael. And he is evil in the arrogance and thoughtlessness that is in him. For he said, "I am God and there is no other God beside me" (Isaiah chapters 45 and 46). He said this because he did not know where his strength originated, nor from where he himself had come.

And the Archons created seven powers for themselves, and the powers created for themselves six angels for each one until they became 365 angels (the number of days in the solar year). And these are the bodies belonging with the names:
The first is Athoth, a he has a sheep's face;
The second is Eloaiou, he has a donkey's face;
The third is Astaphaios, he has a hyena's face;
The fourth is Yao, he has a snake face with seven heads;
The fifth is Sabaoth, he has a dragon's face;
The sixth is Adonin, he had a ape face;
The seventh is Sabbede (or Sabbadaios), he has a face that shone like fire.
This is the nature of seven types within the week.

But Yaldaboth had a plethora of faces, more than all of them, so that he could exhibit any face he wished to any of them, when he is in the midst of seraphim (seraphim plural of seraph. Seraphim are a class or type of angel of which, according to this text, Yaldaboth seems to be the head). He shared his fire with them and became their lord. He called himself God because of the power of the glory (brightness) he possessed that was taken from his mother's light. He rebelled against the place from which he came.

And he united the seven powers of his thoughts with the authorities that were with him. And when he spoke it became (happened).

And he named each power beginning with the highest:
The first is goodness with the first authority, Athoth;
The second is Foreknowledge with the second power, Eloaio; The third is divinity with the third one, Astraphaio);
The fourth is lordship with the fourth power, Yao;
The fifth is kingdom with the fifth one, Sabaoth;
The sixth is envy with the sixth one, Adonein;
The seventh is understanding with the seventh one, Sabbateon.
And these each has a kingdom (sphere on influence) within the realm (kingdom of heaven).
They were given names according to the glory belonging to heaven for the powers of their destructiveness. And there was power in the names given to them by their creator. But the names they were given according to the glory of heaven would mean their loss of power and their destruction. Thus they have two names.

He (Yaldaboth) created all things and structured things after the model of the first kingdom created so that he might create things in an incorruptible manner. It was not because he had ever seen the indestructible ones, but the power in him, which he had taken from his mother, produced in him the image of the order of the universe. And when he saw the creation surrounding him the innumerable amount of angels around him that had come from him, he said to them, "I am a jealous God, and there is no other God beside me." (Exodus 20:3) But by announcing this he had let the angels who were with him know that there is another God. If there were no other god, why would he be jealous?

Then the mother began to move here and there. She realized she has lost part of herself when the brightness of her light dimmed. And she became darker because her partner had not consorted with her.

I (John) said, Lord, what does it mean that she moved here and there? The lord smiled and said, "Do not think happened the way that Moses said it did 'above the waters'." (Genesis 1:2) No, it did not, but when she had seen the wickedness which had happened, and the fact her son had stolen from her, she repented. In the darkness of ignorance began to forget and to be ashamed. She did not dare to go back there, but she was restless. This restlessness was the moving here and there.

And the prideful one stole power from his mother. For he was ignorant and thought that there was no other in existence except his mother. When he saw innumerable angels he had created he exalted himself above them. When the mother recognized that the cloak (body) of darkness was imperfect, and she knew that her partner had not consorted with her, she repented and wept greatly. The entire pleroma heard the prayer of her repentance, and they praised the invisible, pure, undefiled Spirit on her behalf. And the Spirit agreed and when he agreed the Holy Spirit anointed her from the entire pleroma. For her consort did not come to her alone, but he brought to her through the pleroma that which was needed to restore what she was lacking. And she was allowed to ascend, not to her own kingdom but to the kingdom above her son, that she could remain in the ninth (heaven /

kingdom) until she restored what she lacked in herself.

And a voice called from the highest kingdom of heaven: "The Man exists and the son of Man." And the head Archon, Yaldaboth, heard it and thought that the voice had come from his mother. He did not know whence it came. He taught them, the holy and perfect Mother-Father, the complete Foreknowledge, the image of the invisible one who is the Father of the all things and through whom everything came into being, the first Man. He is the one who revealed his image in human form.

And the whole kingdom of the first (head) Archon quaked, and the foundations of the abyss shook. And the underside of waters, which are above material world, were illuminated by the appearance of his image which had been revealed. When all the authorities and the head Archon looked, they saw the whole region of the underside (of the waters) that was illuminated. And through the light they saw the form of the image (reflected) in the water.

And he (Yaldaboth) said to the authorities him, "Come, let us make a man using the image of God as a template to our likeness, that his image may become a light for us." And they created by the means of their various powers matching the features which were given to them. And each authority supplied a feature in the form of the image which Yaldaboth had seen in its natural form. He created a being according to the likeness of the first, perfect Man. And they said, "Let us call him Adam (man), that his name may be a power of light for us."

And the powers began to create.
The first one, Goodness, created a bone essence; and the second, Foreknowledge, created a sinew essence; the third, Divinity, created a flesh essence; and the fourth, the Lordship, created a marrow essence; the fifth, Kingdom created a blood essence; the

sixth, Envy, created a skin essence; the seventh, Understanding, created a hair essence. And the multitude of the angels were with him and they received from the powers the seven elements of the natural (form) so they could create the proportions of the limbs and the proportion of the buttocks and correct functioning of each of the parts together.

The first one began to create the head. Eteraphaope-Abron created his head; Meniggesstroeth created the brain; Asterechme created the right eye; Thaspomocha, the left eye; Yeronumos, the right ear; Bissoum, the left ear; Akioreim, the nose; Banen-Ephroum, the lips; Amen, the teeth; Ibikan, the molars; Basiliademe, the tonsils; Achcha, the uvula; Adaban, the neck; Chaaman, the vertebrae; Dearcho, the throat; Tebar, the right shoulder; the left shoulder; Mniarcon, the right elbow; the left elbow; Abitrion, the right underarm; Evanthen, the left underarm; Krys, the right hand; Beluai, the left hand; Treneu, the fingers of the right hand; Balbel, the fingers of the left hand; Kriman, the nails of the hands; Astrops, the right breast; Barroph, the left breast; Baoum, the right shoulder joint; Ararim, the left shoulder joint; Areche, the belly; Phthave, the navel; Senaphim, the abdomen; Arachethopi, the right ribs; Zabedo, the left ribs; Barias, the right hip; Phnouth the left hip; Abenlenarchei, the marrow; Chnoumeninorin, the bones; Gesole, the stomach; Agromauna, the heart; Bano, the lungs; Sostrapal, the liver; Anesimalar, the spleen; Thopithro, the intestines; Biblo, the kidneys; Roeror, the sinews; Taphreo, the spine of the body; Ipouspoboba, the veins; Bineborin, the arteries; Atoimenpsephei, theirs are the breaths which are in all the limbs; Entholleia, all the flesh; Bedouk, the right buttock; Arabeei, the penis; Eilo, the testicles; Sorma, the genitals; Gorma-Kaiochlabar, the right thigh; Nebrith, the left thigh; Pserem, the kidneys of the right leg; Asaklas, the left kidney; Ormaoth, the right leg; Emenun, the left leg; Knyx, the right shin-bone; Tupelon, the left shin-bone; Achiel, the right knee; Phnene, the left knee; Phiouthrom, the right foot; Boabel, its toes; Trachoun, the left foot;

Phikna, its toes; Miamai, the nails of the feet; Labernioum.
And those who were appointed over all of these are: Zathoth,
Armas, Kalila, Jabel, (Sabaoth, Cain, Abel). And those who are
particularly active in the limbs are the head Diolimodraza, the
neck Yammeax, the right shoulder Yakouib, the left shoulder
Verton, the right hand Oudidi, the left one Arbao, the fingers of
the right hand Lampno, the fingers of the left hand Leekaphar, the
right breast Barbar, the left breast Imae, the chest Pisandriaptes,
the right shoulder joint Koade, the left shoulder joint Odeor, the
right ribs Asphixix, the left ribs Synogchouta, the belly Arouph,
the womb Sabalo, the right thigh Charcharb, the left thigh
Chthaon, all the genitals Bathinoth, the right leg Choux, the left
leg Charcha, the right shin-bone Aroer, the left shin-bone
Toechtha, the right knee Aol, the left knee Charaner, the right foot
Bastan, its toes Archentechtha, the left foot Marephnounth, its toes
Abrana.

Seven have power over all of these: Michael, Ouriel, Asmenedas,
Saphasatoel, Aarmouriam, Richram, Amiorps. And the ones who
are in charge of the senses are Archendekta; and he who is in
charge of the receptions is Deitharbathas; and he who is in charge
over the imagination is Oummaa; and he who is over creativity
Aachiaram, and he who is over the whole impulse Riaramnacho.

The origin of the demons that are in the entire body is known to
be these four: heat, cold, wetness, and dryness. And the mother of
all of them is the material creation. And he who rules over the
heat is Phloxopha; and he who rules over the cold is Oroorrothos;
and he who rules over what is dry is Erimacho; and he who rules
over the wetness is Athuro. And the mother of all of these is
Onorthochrasaei, who stands in with them without limits, and she
covorts with all of them. She is truly material and they are
sustained by her.

The four ruling demons are: Ephememphi, who is attached to

pleasure,

Yoko, who is attached to desire,

Nenentophni, who is attached to grief,

Blaomen, who is attached to fear,

and the mother of them all is Aesthesis-Ouch-Epi-Ptoe.

And from the four demons passions was created. And grief spawned envy, jealousy, distress, trouble, pain, callousness, anxiety, mourning, and more. Pleasure spawned wickedness, vanity, pride, and similar things. Desire spawned anger, wrath, and bitterness, and driving passion, the inability to be satisfied, and similar things. Fear spawned dread, subservience, agony, and shame. These are both good and evil, but the understanding of their nature is attributed to Anaro, who is over the material soul. It belongs with the seven senses, which are controlled by Ouch-Epi-Ptoe.

This is the number of the angels: together they are 365. They all worked on it from limb to limb, until the physical (material) body was completed by them. Now there are other ones in charge over the remaining passions whom I did not mention to you. But if you wish to know them, it is written in the book of Zoroaster. And all the angels and demons worked until they had constructed (fashioned) the physical body. And their creation was completely devoid of activity and was motionless for a long time.

And when the mother (Sophia) wanted to recapture the power which was taken from her by the head Archon, she prayed to the Mother-Father of the All, who is most merciful. He sent a holy decree containing the five lights down to the place where the angels of the head Archon reside. They advised him (Yaldaboth) that he should bring forth the power of the mother. And they said to Yaldaboth, "Blow some of your spirit into his face and his body will arise." And he blew the spirit power of the mother into his (Adam's) face. (Genesis 2:7) Yaldaboth did not know to do this because he existed in ignorance. And the power of the mother

372

went out of Yaldaboth into Adam's physical body, which they had fashioned after the image of the one who exists from the beginning. The body moved and gained strength, and it was enlightened.

And in that instant the other powers became jealous, although he (Adam) had been created through all of them. They were jealous because they had given Adam their power and now he was more intelligent than those who had made him, and his mind was greater than that of the head Archon. And when they recognized that he was enlightened, and that he could think better than they, and that he was free of evil, they took him and threw him into the lowest material realm.

But the blessed One, the Mother-Father, the giving and gracious One, had mercy on the power of the mother which had been transmitted from the head Archon because he did not want the Archons to gain power over the material body again. Therefore, he sent, a helper to Adam through his giving Spirit and his great compassion. The enlighted Afterthought which comes out of him is called "Life" (Zoe means life and is the name of Eve in certain Greek texts and the Septuagint). And she assists the whole creature, by working with him and restoring him to his fullness and by teaching him about the descent (flaws) of his seed and by teaching him about the way of ascent (to go upward again), which is based on the way he came down. (Rom. 8:22)

And the enlightened Afterthought was hidden within Adam so that the Archons would not know she was there, but that the Afterthought might restore (correct) what was lacking of the mother.

And the man was revealed because of the shadow of light in him. And his thinking was higher to all those who had made him. When they looked up and realized that his thinking was superior.

And they conspired with the entire force of Archons and angels. They took fire and earth and water as a mixture and added the four fiery winds. And they worked them together and caused a great noise. And they brought Adam into the shadow of death so that that they might re-make him from earth, water, fire and the spirit (wind) which make up matter. This was the ignorance of their darkness and desire, and their lying (false) spirit. This is the tomb of the re-formed body that the thieves had clothed Adam in. It contained the bonds of forgetfulness and cause him to become a mortal entity. He is the first one who came down, and the first to be separated (from the Divine All). Now, it is up to the Afterthought of the light which was in him to awaken his thinking.

And the Archons took him and placed him in paradise. And they said to him, "Eat at your leisure," (Genesis 2:16) for their pleasure is bitter and their beauty is twisted. Their pleasure is entrapment and their trees lack any holiness and their fruit is deadly poison and their promise is death. And the tree of their life they had placed in the center of paradise (Genesis 2:9).

And I (Jesus) shall teach all of you the mystery of their life. It is the plan that they made together, which is made from the template of their spirit. The root of this tree is bitter and its branches are death, its shadow is hate. Its leaves are a trap, and its blossom is the ointment of evil. Its fruit is death and its seed is desire. It sprouts (blooms) in darkness. Those who taste it dwell in Hades, and they rest in darkness.
But what they call "the tree of knowledge of good and evil" is the Afterthought of the light. They stationed themselves in front of it so that Adam might not understand his fullness and recognize his nakedness and be ashamed. But it was I (Jesus) who made them decide what they ate.

And to I said to the savior, Lord, wasn't it the serpent that instructed Adam to eat? The savior smiled and said, The serpent instructed them to eat because of it's evil desire to produced sexual lust and destruction so that Adam would be useful to him. Adam knew that he was disobedient to Yaldaboth because the light of the Afterthought lived in him and made him stronger and more accurate in his thinking than the head Archon. Yaldaboth wanted to harvest the power that he himself had given Adam. And he caused Adam to forget.

And I said to the savior, "What is this forgetfulness?" He said, "It is not how Moses wrote and it is not how you have heard. He wrote in his first book, 'He put him to sleep' (Genesis 2:21), but that was how Adam perceived it. For also he said through the prophet, 'I will make their minds heavy, that they may not perceive nor understand.' (Isaiah 6:10)."

The Afterthought of the light hid herself in Adam. The head Archon wanted to bring her out through his rib but the Afterthought of the light cannot be apprehended. Although darkness pursued her, it did not catch her. Yaldaboth brought out part of Adam's power and he created another and formed a woman, using the template of the Afterthought which he had seen. The power he had taken from the Adam was formed into the female. This is what happened and not as Moses said, 'She was formed from the bone of his rib.' (Genesis 2:21)

Adam saw the woman beside him. In that instant the enlightened Afterthought appeared. She lifted the veil which occluded his mind. Adam sobered from the drunkenness of darkness and recognized his counterpart (compliment / agreement) , and he said, 'This is indeed bone of my bones and flesh of my flesh.' (Genesis 2:23) Therefore the man will leave his father and his mother, and he will cleave to his wife, and they will both be one flesh. (Genesis 2:24) For his partner will be sent to him and he will leave his father and his mother .

Our sister Sophia is the one who came down innocently in order to reclaim what she has lost. That is why she was called Life, because she is the mother of the living, by the Foreknowledge of the sovereignty of heaven. Through her they that live have tasted the perfect Knowledge. I (Jesus) appeared in the form of an eagle on the tree of knowledge, which is the Afterthought from the Foreknowledge of the pure light. I did this so that I might teach them and wake them from them the deep sleep. For they were both in a fallen state, and they recognized they were naked. The Afterthought appeared to them in the form of light and she awakened their minds.

When Yaldaboth noticed that they fled from him, he cursed the earth he has made. He found the woman as she was preparing herself for her husband. He was lord over her, though he did not know the mystery was instated through the holy plan, so they were afraid to rebel against Yaldaboth. And he demonstrated to his angels the ignorance in him by casting them out of paradise, and he clothed them in darkening blackness.

And the head Archon saw the virgin standing beside Adam, and that the enlightened Afterthought of life had appeared in her Yaldaboth was ignorant. But when the Foreknowledge of All noticed it, she sent agents and they quickly stole the life (Zoe) out of Eve.

Then, the head Archon seduced her and he conceived two sons in her. The first is Eloim and the second is Yahweh. Eloim has a face like a bear and Yahweh has a face like a cat. The one is righteous but the other is unjust. (Yahweh is related to the New Testament and is considered a more just and kind God. Eloim is related to the Old Testament and is considered a jealous, revengeful, wrathful God.) He set Yahweh over fire and wind, and he set Eloim over water and earth. And he name them Cain and Abel in an attempt to deceive.

Sexual intercourse continues to this very day because of the head Archon. He instilled sexual desire in the woman who belongs to Adam. And Adam, through intercourse caused bodies to be replicated, and Yaldaboth breathed into them with his fraudulent spirit.

And he set the two Archons (Elohim and Yehweh) over principal elements, so that they might rule over the tomb (body). When Adam recognized the image of his own Foreknowledge, he begot the image of the son of man (Jesus) and he called him Seth, according to the fashion of the divine race living in the ethereal kingdoms. The mother (Sophia) sent her spirit also. It was in her image and a was a replica of those who are in the pleroma. In this way she will prepare a dwelling place for the kingdoms to come.

Yaldaboth made them drink water of forgetfulness that he had made so that they might not remember from where they came. The seed remained with man for a while to assist him so that when the Spirit comes out from the holy kingdoms, he may raise up and heal him of his lack so the whole pleroma may again become holy and complete.

And I said to the savior, Lord, will all the souls be led safely into the pure light? He answered me and said, "Great things have arisen in your mind, and it is difficult to explain them to anyone except those from the race that cannot be moved. These are they on whom the Spirit of life will descend and with whom will be with the Power. They will be saved and become complete, perfect and worthy of greatness. They will be purified from all wickedness and evil actions. Then they will have no other care other than the incorruption, on which they shall focus their attention from here on, without anger or envy or jealousy or desire and greed for anything. They are affected by nothing except existing in the flesh, which they bear while looking expectantly for the time when they will be met by those who will receive them (their body). Such ones are worthy of the (incorruptible) imperishable, eternal life and the calling. They endure everything and bear up under everything, that they may finish the good fight (wrestling contest) and inherit eternal life. (Cor. 13:7)

I said to him, Lord, will the souls of those who did not do these works (things) but on whom the power and Spirit descended, be rejected? He answered and said to me, "If the Spirit descended upon them, they will certainly be saved, and they will be changed. The power will descend on every man, for without it no one could stand. And after they are born, when the Spirit of life grows in them and the power comes and strengthens that soul, no one can be led astray with evil deeds, but those on whom the false spirit falls are drawn astray by him.

I said, Lord, where will the souls go when they shed their flesh? And he laughed (smiled) and said to me, "The soul in which the power will become stronger than the false spirit is strong and she (the soul) turns and runs from evil and through the intervention of the incorruptible one, she is saved taken up to the kingdoms and will rest there.

And I said, "Lord, what about those who do not know to whom they belong, where will their souls go?" And he said to me, "Those, the spoiled (double-minded) spirit has gained strength while they went astray and that casts a burden on the soul and draws her towards the deeds of evil, and he throws her down into forgetfulness. After she comes out of the body, it is handed over to the authorities that came into being through the Archon. They bind her with chains and cast her into prison, and hound her until she is set free from the forgetfulness and acquires knowledge. If she becomes perfected she is saved.

And I said, Lord, how can the soul become young again and return to its mother's womb or into (another) man? (This is a question regarding reincarnation.) He was glad when I asked him this, and he said to me, "You are blessed because you have understood!" That soul is made to follow another, since the Spirit of life is in it. It is saved through that soul. It is not forced into another flesh (body) again.

And I said, Lord, "Where will the souls go form those who gained knowledge but afterward turned away?" Then he said to me, "They will go to the place where the angels of misery (abject poverty) go. This is the place where there is no repentance (escape). There they will be kept with those who have blasphemed the spirit. They will be tortured and punished forever and ever. (Heb 6:4-8 and Heb 12:17-31)

I said, "Lord, from where did the false (evil) spirit come?" Then he said to me, "The Mother-Father, who is the gracious and holy of Spirit, the One who is merciful and who has compassion for all, the Afterthought of the Foreknowledge of light raised up the child of the perfect race and their thought was the eternal light of man.

When the head Archon realized that these people were exalted above him and their minds were stronger than him he wanted to capture their thought. He did not know that their minds were stronger and that he would not be able to capture their thoughts.

He made a plan with his agents, his powers, and they raped (committed adultery together (all of them) with) Sophia, and unbearable imprisonment (bitter fate) was born through them, which is the last unbreakable bondage. It is the kind that is unpredictable fate. This fate is harder and stronger than the gods, angels and demons and all the generations until this day together have seen. It imprisoned all through periods, seasons, and times. From that fate every sin, unrighteousness, blasphemy, forgetfulness, and ignorance and every oppressive command, and carnal sins and fear emerged. From this the whole creation was blinded, so that they may not know the God who is above them all. And because of the chain of forgetfulness, their sins were hidden from them. They are bound with measures, seasons, and time since fate is lord over everything.

When the head Archon repented for everything which had been created through him, he sought to cause a flood to destroy the works of man (Genesis 6:6). But the great light, the Foreknowledge, told Noah, and Noah announced it to all the children, the sons of men. But those who were estranged from him did not listen to him. It is not as Moses said, "They hid themselves in an ark" (Genesis 7: 7), but they hid in a certain place. Noah hid and also many other people from the immutable race. They went to a certain place and hid in a shining, glowing (enlightened) cloud. Noah understood his authority because she who is part of the light was with him. She enlightened them because the head Archon darkened the entire earth.

And he planned with his agents to send his emissaries (angels) to the daughters of men so that they might take some (as wives) for themselves and raise offspring (children) for their personal enjoyment. At first they had no success so they came together again and laid a plan. They made a false spirit (like themselves), but who looked like the Spirit which had come down to them. In this way they could defile souls through it.

And the emissaries (angels) transformed themselves into the image of the husbands of the women (the daughters of men). They filled them with the spirit of darkness, which was an evil concoction they had made for them. They brought gold and silver and a gift and copper and iron and metal and all kinds of things to the angels. And they led those who followed them away into great turmoil with their lies. The people grew old without enjoying life.

They died before finding truth and without knowing the God of truth. This way the entire creation was enslaved forever, from the beginning of the world until now.

And they took wives and produced children of darkness born in the image of their spirit. To this day, they closed their minds, and they hardened their hearts through the intractability of the false spirit.

I, the perfect Aeon of the All, changed myself into my own child (seed), for I existed first and have traveled every path. I am the fullness of the light. I am the remembrance of the pleroma. I sojourned to the kingdom of darkness and endured so I could I entered into the midst of this prison. The foundations of chaos shook. I disguised myself from the wicked ones, and they did not recognize me.

I returned for the second time, and I journeyed here and there. I was created from those who belong to the light, and I am that light, the perfect Aeon. I entered into the midst of darkness and depths of Hades to accomplish my task. And the foundations of chaos shook so hard they could have fallen down and killed those in chaos. I sought to root them in light so that they might not be destroyed before the time was complete.

Still for a third time I went - I am the light which exists in the light, I am the remembrance of the perfect Aeon. I entered into the midst of darkness and the depths of Hades. I filled my face with light so I could perfect (complete) their kingdom. I came into the midst of their prison, which is the prison of the body (flesh). I announced, "He who hears, let him wake up from the deep sleep." And he wept and shed tears. He wiped away bitter tears from himself and he said, "Who is it that calls my name, and from where has this hope come to me, while I am in the chains of the prison?" And I said, 'I am the perfect Aeon of the pure light; I am

381

the thought of the pure, undefiled Spirit, who raised you up to the place of honor. Stand and remember that it is you who heard and sought your own beginnings, which is I, the merciful one. Guard yourself against the angels of bitter providence and the demons of chaos and all those who seek to entrap you Guard against of the deep sleep and the cage of Hades.

And I stood him up and sealed him in the light of the water with five seals so that death might not have power over him ever again. Now I shall go ascend to the perfect kingdom. I have told you all I have to say. And I have said everything to you that you might write it down and give them secretly to your fellow spirits. It is the mystery of the immutable race.

And the savior gave these things to John so that he might write them down and keep them intact. And he said to him, Cursed is everyone who will trade these things for a gift or for food or for water or clothing or anything. These things were presented to him in a mystery, and immediately he disappeared from him. And he went to his fellow disciples and told them what the savior had told him.
Jesus Christ, Amen.

Introduction To
The First Apocalypse of James

The First Apocalypse of James was written in the Coptic language around the second half of the third century CE. It is regarded as part of the New Testament apocrypha. The text was first discovered in the last part of the month of December in 1945. It was found among 52 other Gnostic Christian texts contained in 13 codices or scrolls. The discovery was made by two peasant Egyptian brothers as they dug for fertilizer near their home. While digging in the rich soil around the Jabal al-Ṭārif caves near present-day Hamra Dom in Upper Egypt, they found several papyri in a large earthenware vessel. The find of these codices came to be known as the Nag Hammadi library because of their proximity to the Egyptian town of Nag Hammadi, which was the nearest major settlement.

The brothers wanted to make money by selling the manuscripts, but when they brought some of the scrolls home their mother burned several of the manuscripts. One source indicates she burned them as kindling, while another source claims she was superstitious and worried that the writing might be dangerous.

News of the discovery appeared gradually as the brothers tried to sell certain scrolls. The full significance of the new find was not immediately apparent until sometime after the initial discovery. As more of the scrolls were examined it was revealed that the find included a large number of primary Gnostic Gospels, some of which had never been seen before.

In 1946, the brothers became involved in a feud, and left the manuscripts with a Coptic priest. In October of that year a codex, now called codex lll, was sold to the Coptic Museum in Old Cairo.

The resident Coptologist and religious historian Jean Doresse realized the significance of the artifact and published the first reference to it in 1948.

After Egypt's political revolution in 1952, these texts were handed to the Coptic Museum in Cairo where they were declared national property.

The Apocalypse of James, found within the collection of discovered scrolls, seems to be founded on Valentinian Gnosticism, although it does seem to have element of Sethian Gnosticism also. The name, Adonaios comes up in the text. He is an offspring of Yaldaboth, the Demiurge and is one of the twelve Powers created or spawned by Yaldaboth. Adonaios is mentioned in The Second Treatise of the Great Seth.

One the great Gnostic schools was the Hellenistic or Alexandrian School. The system absorbed the philosophy and concepts of the Greeks, and the Semitic nomenclature was replaced by Greek names. The cosmology and myth had grown out of proportion and appear to our eyes to be unwieldy. Yet, this school produced two great thinkers, Basilides and Valentinus. Though born at Antioch, in Syria, Basilides founded his school in Alexandria around the year A.D. 130, where it survived for several centuries.

Epiphanius (ca. 390) wrote that he learned through word of mouth that Valentinus was born in Phrebonis in the Nile Delta, and thus was a native of Paralia in Egypt. His sources were not confirmed as reliable and the information is speculative. Valentinus received his Greek education in nearby Alexandria, an important and metropolitan center of early Christianity. There he may have heard the Christian philosopher Basilides. Valentinus was familiar with Hellenistic Middle Platonism and the culture of Hellenized Jews like the great Alexandrian Jewish allegorist and philosopher Philo.

Valentinus first taught at Alexandria and then in Rome. He established the largest Gnostic movement around A.D. 160. This movement was founded on an elaborate mythology and a system of sexual duality of male and female interplay, both in its deities and its savior.

Tertullian stated that between 135 A.D. and 160 A.D. Valentinus, a prominent Gnostic, had great influence in the Christian church. Valentinus ascended in church hierarchy and became a candidate for the office of bishop of Rome, the office that quickly evolved into that of Pope. He lost the election by a narrow margin. Even though Valentinus was outspoken about his Gnostic slant on Christianity, he was a respected member of the Christian community until his death and was probably a practicing bishop in a church of lesser status than the one in Rome.

The main platform of Gnosticism was the ability of its followers to transcend the material world through the possession of privileged and directly imparted knowledge. Following this doctrine, Valentinus claimed to have been instructed by a direct disciple of one of Jesus' apostles, a man by the name of Theodas.

Valentinus is considered by many to be the father of modern Gnosticism. His vision of the faith is summarized by G.R.S. Mead in the book "Fragments of a Faith Forgotten."

"The Gnosis in his hands is trying to embrace everything, even the most dogmatic formulation of the traditions of the Master. The great popular movement and its incomprehensibilities were recognized by Valentinus as an integral part of the mighty outpouring; he laboured to weave all together, external and internal, into one piece, devoted his life to the task, and doubtless only at his death perceived that for that age he was attempting the impossible. None but the very few could ever appreciate the ideal of the man, much less understand it. "(Fragments of a Faith Forgotten, p. 297)

The mainline or orthodox Christian church had sought to eliminate Gnosticism and destroy all Gnostic documents. There were times in early church history that Gnostics were hunted down and killed for heresy, but these texts were saved and sealed by Gnostics as they attempted to preserve some of their most holy books, and thus they came to us with some of the texts still intact.

The translation of the Nag Hammadi library was completed in the 1970's and the information contained in the cache' would turn Christianity on its head by revealing an unknown history of Christianity and a fight for control of doctrine and the faith. Among the Gnostic works are scriptures such as the Gospel of Thomas, the Gospel of Philip, the Gospel of Truth, and many others. Gnosticism is an undeniable part of the history of Christianity. By both influence and opposition, it has helped shape what we now know as the Christian faith.

The First Apocalypse of James is reasonably well preserved and fairly legible, but there are fragments missing, as the codex was brittle and pieces were broken away from the scroll. The Apocalypse of James should not be confused with the Apocryphon of James, which is a completely different text and was found in the Codex Jung. Another copy of the Apocalypse of James has recently been found in the Codex Tchacos, where it is simply titled 'James'. A Greek copy of the text, dating to the fifth century CE, was discovered in 2017 at Oxford University by Geoffrey Smith and Brent Landau, religious studies scholars at the University of Texas at Austin. It is thought this copy was used in a school environment to teach students to read and write. This is because each word in the document was broken into syllables with a dot mid-line between each syllable. This approach broke each word into smaller parts so the student could read each syllable separately and more easily construct each word.

As the title implies, the text reports to have been written by James, one of the most influential leaders of the early church. The 1st century theologian, Clement of Rome, wrote that James was called the "bishop of bishops, who ruled Jerusalem, the Holy Church of the Hebrews, and all the Churches everywhere." According to this James was over the early Christian Church, which at that time consisted mostly of Jewish converts, although Paul's influence and the coming pagan converts were on the horizon.

The Apocalypse of James is a revelation dialogue between Jesus and James, the man the Lord calls "Brother". In the manuscript, Jesus clarifies the title by explaining that James is a brother in a purely spiritual sense. Jesus identifies his place and essence by saying, "I am an alien, a son of the Father's race". This separates the "race" of the Lord from the human "race" of man and means their very substance is somehow different.

In the text, James knows of the upcoming events of the Lord's suffering and death. The knowledge, along with James' inability to change the upcoming events engenders anxiety and questions. The Lord's gives James secret knowledge in the form of teachings and explanation. This gnosis or knowledge places the Apocalypse of James in the realm of Valentinian Gnosticism.

Gilles Quispel states that for Valentinus, a Gnostic teacher of the second century, Christ is "the Paraclete from the Unknown who reveals…the discovery of the Self, which is the divine spark within you."

The heart of the human problem for the Gnostic is ignorance, sometimes called "sleep," "intoxication," or "blindness." But Jesus redeems man from such ignorance. Stephan Hoeller says that in the Valentinian system "there is no need whatsoever for guilt, for repentance from so-called sin, neither is there a need for a blind belief in vicarious salvation by way of the death of Jesus." Rather, Jesus is savior in the sense of being a "spiritual maker of wholeness" who cures us of our sickness of ignorance.

According to Valentinus, the seeker awakens through knowledge or Gnosis. This secret Gnosis provides the key that is essential for a complete understanding of Jesus' message. The Valentinus doctrine states, "The scriptures are ambiguous and the truth cannot be extracted from them by those who are ignorant of tradition." (Irenaeus Against Heresies 3:2:1). One must be spiritually mature to comprehend the full meaning of the scriptures.

1 Corinthians 2:14New International Version (NIV)
The person without the Spirit does not accept the things that come from the Spirit of God but considers them foolishness, and cannot understand them because they are discerned only through the Spirit.

 According to the Valentinian tradition, Paul and the other apostles revealed these teachings only to those who were 'spiritually mature'. This is the transmission of Gnosis from master to student.

1 Corinthians 2:4-6 New International Version (NIV)
4 My message and my preaching were not with wise and persuasive words, but with a demonstration of the Spirit's power, 5 so that your faith might not rest on human wisdom, but on God's power.
6 We do, however, speak a message of wisdom among the mature, but not the wisdom of this age or of the rulers of this age, who are coming to nothing.

Valentinians believed that God could never be directly observed or experienced. Neither could God be fully understood, directly known, described or explained. He is eternal. He is the origin of all things.

The Godhead manifests itself through a process of unfolding wherein various parts or qualities were manifested, all the while maintaining its unity. In certain instances, the expressions of God in turn had expressions, such as the Christ Spirit or Son, which was an expression or emanation, which in turn had expressions or emanations, like circles within circles.

Valentinians believed that God is androgynous and contained within God was as a male-female dyad. We see this in the fact that the Hebrew word for the Spirit of God was Ruak (Ruach). The word and the spirit (Ruak) were presented in female form. It was through the constraint of language, as the translations went from Hebrew to Greek and from Greek to Latin, that the feminine gender of the Spirit was lost. However, in the beginning she "Brooded" over the waters.

Genesis 1:1-2 Amplified Bible (AMP)
1 In the beginning God (Elohim) created [by forming from nothing] the heavens and the earth. 2 The earth was formless and void or a waste and emptiness, and darkness was upon the face of the deep [primeval ocean that covered the unformed earth]. The Spirit of God was moving (hovering, brooding) over the face of the waters.

In the literal reading, it can be seen that God provides the universe with both male and female energies of form and substance. The feminine aspect of the deity is called Wisdom, Mercy, Silence, Grace and Thought. Silence is God's primordial state of tranquility and self-awareness She is also the active creative thought that gives substance to the powers or states of being, such as "Aeons". The first feminie energy of God is called the Divine Thought.

In some Gnostic systems she is called, Barbelo, the mother of all that is. There are differences concerning the Holy Spirit between various Gnostic groups. Some have the Spirit as a function of Barbelo, while others say it is through Sophia. The variations may depend on where and how the spirit is introduced. For example, according to Valentinus, Sophia gives the spiritual seed to those who hear the true word of He Who Is.

The masculine aspect of God is Depth, Power, Law, and Order. He is also called Ineffable, the All, and First Father. Depth is the most profound aspect of God. It is all-encompassing and can never be fully understood. He is essentially passive, yet when moved to action by his feminine energy, Thought, he gives the universe form. It was through the union of the masculine force of the ALL and Divine Thought that the Christ Spirit was brought forth.

Aeons are beings produced by an emanation of energy, like a fire produces light and heat. In many Gnostic systems, the various emanations of God, who is also known by such names as the One, the Monad, The All, and Depth emanated Aeons such as "Sophia" (wisdom) and Christos (Christ, the Anointed One). In turn, Sophia and Christ also have emanations and thus produced Aeons, Archons, and angels. In different Gnostic systems, these emanations are differently named, classified, and described, but the emanation theory itself is common to all forms of Gnosticism.

The origin of the universe is described as a process of emanation from the Godhead. As a fire does not intend to emanate light, but does so simply because of its nature, so does God emanate and produce. The male and female aspects of the Father, acting in conjunction, manifested themselves in the Son. The Son is depicted by Valentinians as a male-female dyad.

We will see that the Son, the Lord, claimed he is called by many names but God gave him two. These are male and female. But, the female energy or part should not be confused with a female person or being. Jesus tells James that he existed before the feminine. This is because God is unified, God is one, and the "aspects" of God do not exist apart from the oneness of God. Females were produced after the Christ spirit, so says the Son to James. After the Son came into being, he manifested himself in twenty-six spiritual entities or Aeons arranged into male-female pairs. Together they constitute the Fullness (pleroma) of the Godhead.

The Aeons who are manifested by the Son are conceived as having psychological autonomy. They lie within God or the sphere where God resides but are separated from him by a boundary. As a result, they do not know the one who brought them into being. The Aeons sensed that they were incomplete and long to know their origin.

According to Valentinus, all Powers and Aeons were made in pairs. All had a consort that balanced and perfected them. Sophia's consort was Christ. We see how Valentinus may have arrived at this conclusion by looking at the Catholic and Orthodox Bibles and the book of Wisdom, contained in the Apocrypha.

The Book of Wisdom uses personification. The Hebrew word chakmah, like its Greek (sophia) and Latin (sapientia) equivalents, is a noun with feminine gender.

"I will tell you what wisdom is and how she came to be, and I will hide no secrets from you, but I will trace her course from the beginning of creation, and make knowledge of her clear, and I will not pass by the truth" (Wisdom 6:22).

"With you is wisdom, she who knows your works and was present when you made the world; she understands what is pleasing in your sight and what is right according to your commandments" (Wisdom 9:9).

Wisdom is called the "fashioner of all things" (Wisdom 7:22).

She has a spirit that is intelligent, holy, unique, subtle, mobile, clear, unpolluted, distinct, invulnerable, loving the good, keen, irresistible, humane, steadfast, sure, and free from anxiety (Wisdom 7:22–23).

Even in Proverbs 1–9 Wisdom is spoken of as a woman.

Sophia (Wisdom), the youngest of the Aeons, yearned to know the All, the parent of all beings. She attempted to know and understand him. Some stories have her capturing a divine creative spark from God and using it by herself, without her consort. As a result, she became separated from her consort. According to several Gnostic stories, the consort of Sophia was Christ himself. Being separated from him she fell into a state of deficiency and suffering. In such a state, her creation was deficient and monstrous. He is called the Demiurge, the half-maker, and the craftsman.

Sophia's fall into ignorance produced three creations. The first is "Illusion". This is the belief the material world is all there is. But there is always a deeper feeling there is something else lying beyond. Illusion is characterized by a material existence and suffering. The personification of this state is the Devil.

The second creation of the fallen Sophia is the Soul. It originated as ignorance begins to give way to knowledge. It is personified as the Craftsman or Demiurge who formed the material world. He is a creative force but is deficient and is usually seen as ignorant of his position, ignorant of the All, and lacking Gnosis.

The third creation is the "Spiritual Seed", which is born from her knowledge (gnosis) and is personified in the fallen Sophia herself.

Through the power of Limit, Sophia was divided into two parts. Her higher part was returned to her consort but her lower part was separated from the Fullness into a lower realm along with the deficiency and suffering. This lower realm is the material or physical world.

Valentinians envisioned the universe as series of spheres within spheres. The smallest and center sphere is the physical world or deficiency, where the fallen or lower Sophia was exiled. Enclosing this is a larger sphere of the Fullness (pleroma) where the Aeons are. The Aeons are enclosed within the Son, as his sphere is with the Father and encompasses all things. The largest sphere is where the Son resides with the Father (Depth and Silence).

There is a boundary or limit between God and the pleroma. There is a second boundary or limit between the pleroma and the material world. Just as the pleroma is a product of the Godhead and lies within it, so the realm of deficiency, which is the material world, is a product of the pleroma and is contained in a sphere lying within the sphere of the pleroma. The deficiency arose as result of ignorance and it will only be escaped or dissolved through knowledge (gnosis).

In Gnosticism "Limit" is a power or creation. Where the word "Limit or Boundary" are used, it can be an actual creation with the active ability to cleave, cut, separate, or contain.

Through the mediation of the Son, which is the knowledge of the true Father of All and how all beings were created and connected, the Aeons within the pleroma were given rest. All twenty-six of the Aeons then joined together in celebration and were spontaneously integrated back into the personality of the Son. The fully integrated Son is called the Savior. He is destined to be the male partner or bridegroom of the fallen Sophia. He is surrounded by angels who were brought forth in honor of the Aeons.

The fallen Sophia remained in ignorance, trapped in the fallen material sphere. She continued to suffer the emotional pain of grief, fear and confusion. Because of her confusion and ignorance, she was unable to distinguish what was real and what unreal. In her pain, she began to call out for help. She sought the light and she began to plead for help. Her consort responded. The Savior, and his assisting and attending angels descended through the Limit to her. Through his knowledge (gnosis) of the eternal realm he freed the fallen part of Sophia from her illusion and suffering.

Sophia rejoiced because of her Savior and consort and his angels. In her joy she produced spiritual substances or spiritual seeds in his image (some stories have her producing spiritual seeds in the images of the savior and his angels, others have her producing spiritual seeds in the image of the savior). This spiritual substance or seed are the spirits present in every Christian and collectively make up the spiritual Church. The Savior is the bridegroom of Sophia. In the end times his emanations, the angels, will be the bridegrooms of the spiritual seeds, which are the Christians making up the spiritual church.

In the act of salvation, it is Sophia who sows a spiritual seed in all who hear the message of Jesus. Those who accept and gain Gnosis are spiritual Christians.

Despite the fact that the fallen Sophia was no longer ignorant, the ignorance was not fully dissipated. The spiritual seeds were immature and needed training. For this purpose, the creation of the material world was necessary. The fallen Sophia and the Savior secretly influenced the Demiurge to create the material world in the image of the Fullness. The Demiurge is ignorant of his mother and the All. He thinks that he acts alone and is the only creative force, but he unconsciously acts as her agent.

The Demiurge created the material world and human beings. In addition to a physical body, Valentinians believed that people were composed of a demonic part (chous / dirt, dust), a rational soul (psyche / mind), and a spiritual seed (pneuma / spirit).

Because the Demiurge is the deficient, corrupt, and cruel creator of this world, Gnostic theology has answered many nagging questions, such as why there is suffering, why is there disease, and why do bad things happen to good people.

Human beings were divided into three categories, depending on which of the three natures they exhibited. Valentinus belived that the children of Adam and Eve metaphorically represented the three categories of humans. Cain represented the carnal (choic) Abel represented the animate (psychic), and Seth represented the spiritual (pneumatic).

The ultimate pinnacle of world history came in the ministry of Jesus. Jesus is the physical manifestation of the Son or Savior. Prior to his coming, the true God was unknown. Jesus came to bring knowledge (gnosis) to a suffering humanity that was desperately seeking the true God.

This is why the Old Testament God and New Testament God are so different. The Old Testament God, the Demiurge, was vengeful, jealous and cruel, and the New Testament God, who Jesus was sent to reveal to us, is kind and merciful.

By knowledge, the spiritual seed and their consorts or counterpart, the angels are joined. This union was foreshadowed by the reuniting of Sophia and Christ.

In Valentinian Gnosticism there is a distinction between the human Jesus and the divine Jesus. The human Jesus the son of Mary and Joseph. By grace his body was constructed of the same substance as Sophia and her spiritual seed. When Jesus was thirty years old, he was baptized by John and as he went down into the water God sent the "Spirit of the Thought of the Father" in the form of a dove and it descended on him and he was born of the virgin spirit. According to Valentinus, this is the true "virgin birth" and resurrection from the dead.

Jesus taught the people in parables, so that only the matured and spiritually awake would understand. He revealed the full and plain truth about the fall of Sophia and the coming restoration of the Fullness only to his closest followers. According to Valentinus, Mary Magdalene was a member of this inner circle. She is seen as an image of the lower Sophia and is described as Jesus' consort in the Gospel of Philip.

The divine Jesus experienced all of the emotions of human beings including grief, fear and confusion in the Garden of Gethsemane but only the body suffered. The son of Mary and Joseph was crucified but the spiritual Jesus did not physically suffer death, for before the body suffered and died the spiritual Jesus ascended.

Following the crucifixion Jesus appeared and taught his disciples about the Father for eighteen months. After his ascension, he appeared in visions. This is how Paul and Valentinus experienced Jesus.

People who receive the knowledge of Jesus' teaching receive a spiritual seed from Sophia that will bear fruit by awakening them from their stupor to a mystical knowledge (gnosis). They recognize their own spiritual nature. With or because of this knowledge they are joined with their angel consorts who accompany the Savior. This is the true resurrection of the dead. It is the spirit that was dead and now resurrected. Resurrections does not take place after death. It must be experienced in the living present.

First, the person spiritually ascends above the realm of the Demiurge and this material world to join with their consort angel, Sophia and the Savior in the higher realm of the Fullness or pleroma. Then, rejoicing with all of the saved, the person is joined with their angel and enters the Fullness. The person continues to have a physical existence in the material world but they are an awakened spirit and are in the world but not of it. They come to understand this physical existence is an illusion to keep men enslaved and asleep.

We have explored an outline of the doctrine and cosmology of Valentinian Gnosticism so we may better understand the book of the Apocalypse of James. The storyline of James has Jesus teaching James regarding the coming crucifixion of Jesus and how the body of the man Jesus will be killed but the Savior, who is the Son, and the Christ Spirit will leave the body before death. Further, Jesus tells of James' soon coming martyrdom.

The Lord tells James he will be martyred and after he departs his body he will encounter "Powers" that will attempt to block his path back to "the Pre-Existent One". These are called toll-collectors, gate-keepers, and other such designators, according to the translation of the text. These beings wish to capture or control the soul for their own purposes. However, the gate-keepers can be controlled or defeated with the proper words. The proper words, terms, and answers are given by the Lord to James with instructions on their use. Properly performed, the knowledge is meant to confuse and misdirect the Powers so that James may avoid their bondage and ascend to the Pre-Existent One.

The teaching given to James indicates salvation is in fact the liberation of the spirit from the earthly plane and fleshly body and the spirit's return to the place of its origin, the eternal beginning and its union with God.

After the Lord instructs James on how to apply the new teaching and knowledge, he then comments on the place of female disciples. The Lord mentions a dispute between James and the other apostles.

The Apocrypha of James was likely written by a Gnostic scholar with the intent of furthering Gnostic teaching. The rejection of an actual bodily or familial relationship between James and Jesus is used as a way of placing the Lord in a separate state, wherein he does not have to possess a fleshly, human body. The Lord tells James they are only spiritual brothers even though the Bible states that James was the brother of Jesus. This distinction and separation of fallen and inferior flesh not being compatible with pure spirit continues the line of Gnostic teachings.

(New International Version: Galatians 1:19 "I saw none of the other apostles--only James, the Lord's brother.") the Catholic and Orthodox doctrine, as well as some Anglicans and Lutherans, teach the perpetual virginity of Mary. Owning to this belief they teach that James and others that are referred to in the Bible as the brothers and sisters of Jesus were not the biological children of Mary, but were cousins of Jesus or step-brothers and step-sisters of Jesus by way of his mother's husband, Joseph from Joseph's previous marriage.

James died in martyrdom between 62 and 69 A.D., and was an important figure of the Apostolic Age. He was also referred to as James the Just, or James, brother of the Lord.

James is referred to as "James the Just", which was a Christian designation. It indicates the book was written after the title was established by the followers of Jesus. Here we see the influence of the Jewish Christian community.

Besides being a Gnostic gospel, one of the most curious features of the First Apocalypse of James is that the date of writing of the original text indicates it was written after the text of The Second Apocalypse of James, which we will examine later in this book.

Now, let us look into the fascinating text titled, The Apocalypse of James.

The First Apocalypse of James

The Lord himself spoke to me saying: "Look, this is the completion of my redemption. I have given you a sign of all these things, my brother, James. I called you my brother for a reason. For although you are not my earthly brother I know you and I know the things concerning you. Because of this I give you a sign so that you will hear and understand."

"Nothing existed except He Who Is. He cannot be named. He cannot be described. Likewise, I cannot be named, for I am from He Who Is. Yet, I have been given a great number of names, but two names are from He Who Is. And now I stand before you.

(Author's Note: In the beginning, there was nothing but the indescribable God, called "He Who Is" and "The All". Gnostic theology describes God bringing forth from himself a female power. From these two came The Christ Spirit, who was born of both male and female energies.)

You asked me about the feminine so now I will speak to you about that. The feminine does exist, but it was not created first. When it came forth it (Sophia) created powers and gods for itself. Since I am the image of He Who Is, I was first and it did not exist when I came forth.

I brought into being the image of He Who Is so that His sons might know what things are theirs and what is alien to them. Be attentive and I will reveal everything about this mystery to you. They will seize me in two days, but my redemption will be near."

James said, "Teacher, you said, 'they will seize me.' What can I possibly do?" He said to me, "James, do not be afraid. They will capture you too. Leave Jerusalem, because it is she (Jerusalem) who always gives a bitter cup to the sons of light. She is the home to a large number of archons.

(Author's Note: Archons were created by and are servants to the Demiurge, who is the "creator god of this world". The Demiurge and the archons stand between the human race and a transcendent God (He Who Is). God can only be reached through gnosis. The gnosis reveals the fact that there is a higher God than the Demiurge and the path to reach the All, He Who Is. The Demiurge and his servants, the archons strive to keep man separated from and ignorant of He Who Is. They would generally equate to the devil and his demons in an orthodox Christian view.)

Your redemption will be protected from them. Listen and I will teach you so that you might understand who they are and what their nature is.

(Author's Note: Here the codex is corrupted or missing pieces. Some words or phrases cannot be completely read.)

They are not [...] but archons [...]. These twelve [...] down [...] archons [...] upon his own group of seven."

James said, "Teacher, are there really twelve groups of seven and not just seven as there are in the scriptures?" The Lord said, "James, the person who taught regarding this scripture had a limited understanding. However, I am going to reveal to you what was produced from him who is beyond numbers. I will give you a sign for the number that came from Him who cannot be numbered and I will give you a sign for the measurement that came from Him who cannot be measured."

James said, "Teacher, Look, I have received their number. They measure seventy-two!" The Lord said, "These are the seventy-two heavens, but they are under the control of the Archons. These are the Powers of all their strength. The heavens were established by them and they were distributed everywhere (together they inhabit all places here), and the twelve archons have authority over them. The inferior power among them (the Demiurge) produced angels and an innumerable host for itself.

(Author's Note: Yaldaboth, the Demiurge, created twelve Powers or Archons to assist him, giving each a portion of his power, which he took from Sophia.)

Nonetheless, He Who Is, has been given [...] on account of [...] He Who Is [...] they are innumerable. If it is your desire to number them now, you will have to you abandon your blind thought, which comes from the prison of flesh that encases (encircles) you. Only then you will reach He Who Is. Then you will no longer be James but you are (will realize you are) the one who is. And each of those who are innumerable will have been named."

James said, "Teacher, how can I reach He Who Is, since all these powers and the host are armed against me?" He said to me, "These powers are not armed against you personally. They are armed against another specifically. They are armed against me.

They are enforced with other powers. Judgement is their weapon against me. They did not give [...] in it to me [...] through them [...]. In this place [...] my suffering, I shall [...]. He will [...] and I shall not try to stop them. Inside me shall be a silence and a hidden mystery. I shall be timid in the face of their anger."

James said, "Teacher, if they arm themselves against you, then how can you be blamed?" You have come with knowledge, that you might destroy their forgetfulness. You have come with recollection (of where you came from), that you might destroy their ignorance.

I was worry about you because you descended into the great ignorance that is here, but you have not been defiled by anything in it.

You descended into this great mindlessness, but your memories remained.
You walked in this mud, but your clothes were not soiled, and you have not been buried in their filth. You have not been entrapped.

Even though I was not like them, I clothed myself with everything of theirs. Forgetfulness is within me, but still, I remember things that are not from them.

There is in me [....], and I am in their [...]. [...] knowledge [...] not in their sufferings [...]. But I am afraid of them, because they are the rulers here. What will they do (to me)? What will I be able to say (to them)? What word will I be able to say that will allow me to escape from them?"

The Lord said, "James, I admire your understanding and I understand your fear. If you must worry, do not concern yourself about anything other than your own redemption. Watch and see. I will complete my destiny upon this earth as I have announced from the heavens. And I shall show you your redemption."

James said, "Teacher, after they capture you and you complete your destiny you will go up to He Who is, so how will you appear to us again?

The Lord said, "James, after these things have happened I will reveal everything to you, not only for your sake but for the sake of the unbelieving men. I do this so that faith may be in them also. Through this a multitude will attain faith and they will increase in (number / strength?)[...]. After this I shall appear to condemn the archons. And I will show them he who cannot be seized. If they seize him, then he will overpower each one of them.

I shall go now. Remember the things I have spoken to you and let the knowledge precede you." James said,"Lord, I shall hurry to do as you have said." The Lord bade him farewell. And the Lord fulfilled all that was right to do."

When James heard of his suffering he was very distressed. They awaited the sign of his coming and he came several days later.

And James was walking on a mountain called "Gaugelan", with his (the Lord's) disciples. They were listening to James because they were distressed and he was [...] being a comforter, saying, "This is [...] the second [...]" After the crowd dispersed James remained [...] in prayer [...], as was his custom.

(Author's Note: Gaulgelan is probably Golgotha. In Syriac the name of the mount is Gagultha. However, there may be a link with Gaugal, a mountain near Amida, mentioned by Syriac writers. Amida was an ancient city in Mesopotamia located where modern Diyarbakır, Turkey now stands. The Roman writers Ammianus Marcellinus and Procopius consider it a city of Mesopotamia. The city was located on the right bank of the Tigris. The walls were high and substantial, and constructed of the recycled stones from older buildings.)

And the Lord appeared to him. Then he stopped praying and embraced the Lord. He kissed the Lord and said, "Teacher, I have found you. I heard about all the suffering you went through. I have been so distressed. You know my compassion.

(Author's Note: The word "compassion" is made up of two words. Together – Suffer. To have compassion is the suffer together.)

I was thinking and I was wishing that I would not have to see these people. They must be judged for the things they have done (to you). What they have done goes against what is right and proper."

The Lord said, "James, do not be concerned for me or for these people. I am he who was within me. I never suffered in any way. I have not been anxious or in any pain. These people have done me no harm.

(Author's Note: Jesus has shed his body and is now a spiritual being. He is "He Who Is". The spirit left the body before the torment began and the divine Jesus was not harmed or hurt. His death held no great meaning for Gnostic since it was his teaching and not his death that freed people and pointed their way to heaven. This divergence from the view of the crucifixion held by the orthodox church turned the church against Gnostics and in time lead to the murder of thousands of Gnostics by the church, culminating in the Cathar massacre. The Cathars were a Gnostic Christian community living in southern France, between the 12th and 14th centuries. In 1209 the crusaders came, sent by the Pope. The order was to kill every Gnostic in the area. Arnaud-Amaury, the Cistercian abbot-commander, is supposed to have been asked how to tell Cathars from Catholics. His reply, recalled by Caesarius of Heisterbach, a fellow Cistercian, thirty years later was "Caedite eos. Novit enim Dominus qui sunt eius" – "Kill them all, the Lord will recognise His own". The doors of the church of St Mary Magdalene were broken down and the refugees dragged out and slaughtered. At least 7,000 innocent men, women and children were killed there by Catholic forces. In the town Gnostic and Catholics were living together. There was no way to distinguish between the two Christian sects. All were killed. Thousands were mutilated and murdered. Prisoners were blinded, dragged behind horses, and used for target practice. The permanent population of the town at that time was then probably no more than 5,000, but local refugees seeking shelter within the city walls could conceivably have increased the number to 20,000.)

These people existed as a symbol of the archons, and the symbol and type should be destroyed through them.

But [...] the archons, [...] who has [...] since it [...] angry with (you) [...] The just (one) [...] is his servant.

Therefore, now your name will be "James the Just". Did you realize how you became sober when you saw me? (You woke up.) You stopped your prayer. You embraced and kissed me. Now you are a just man of God. Because of these things, you have stirred up great anger and rage against yourself. But (this has happened) so that others might come to be (free)."

But James was afraid and anxious, and he wept. The Lord sat with him on a rock. And the Lord said to him, "James, you will undergo suffering, but do not be sad. The flesh is weak and it will receive what it has been destined to receive, but do not be weak or fearful". Then the Lord stopped speaking.

Then, when James heard these things, he wiped away the bitter tears from his eyes [...] which is [...].

The Lord said to him, "James, listen and I will reveal your redemption to you. When you are seized, and you are suffering, a multitude of arms will be (fight) against you they may seize you. Three arms in particular may capture you. They are the one who sit as gate keepers. Not only do they demand toll, but they also steal souls.

When you come are their captive, the one who is their guard will ask you, 'Who are you and where do you come from?' You are to say to him, 'I am a son, and I am from the Father.' Then he will ask you, 'What kind of son are you, and to what father do you belong?' You must say to him, 'I am from the Pre-existent Father, and I am a son within the Pre-existent One.' When he says to you, [...], you must say to him [...] in the [...] that I might [...]."

(When he asks) "[...] of alien things? You must to him, "They are not entirely alien, but they are from Achamoth, who is the female (fallen Spohia)."

(Author's Note: This section is not complete but the Archons may be asking about the feminine energies, females, and Sophia. In Gnostic tradition, Sophia is a feminine figure, analogous to the human soul but also simultaneously one of the feminine aspects of God. Gnostics held that she was the consort of balancing half of Jesus Christ and the Bride of Christ. She is occasionally referred to by the Hebrew equivalent of Achamoth, ⵎχαμὼθ. James must explain that Sophia is an Aeon and is fallen but not alien. Although the higher Sophia remained in the pleroma, Achamoth is the lower or fallen Sophia, who descended into the physical realm. The name, Achamoth, is not associated with the higher Sophia in Valentinius Gnosticism. Since Achamoth is the fallen Sophia, and was half of Sophia when she was split into two parts when she fell, and the lower Sophia was rescued by Christ. Achamoth is seen as a female brought into being by a female with no male consort. This was done in the same way the Demiurge and the Archons were brought into being by Sophia without the consent or help of her consort, Jesus.)

"And these thing/beings she produced as she brought down the race (of Archons) from the Pre-existent One. Therefore, they are not alien, but they are ours. They belong to us because she who their mother is from the Pre-existent One. Yet, they are alien because the Pre-existent One did not have intercourse with her, when she produced them."

When he asks, 'Where will you go?', you must say to him, 'I shall return to the place I came from.' If you say these things, you will escape their attacks.

"But when you come to those three who would take you captive and steal your soul [...] these. You [...] are a vessel [...] of much more than [...] of the one whom you [...] for [...] her root.

Also, you must be cautious [...]. Then I will call upon the eternal, incorruptible knowledge, which is Sophia, who is in the Father and who is the mother / creator of Achamoth. Achamoth had no father nor was there a male consort who helped create her, but she is female produced from a female (alone).

She (Achamoth) produced you (James) without a male, since she (Achamoth) thought she was alone. She was living in ignorance. She did not know and was unaware of what lives through her mother because she thought that she alone existed. (She did not know that she came to exist through her mother.)

But I shall cry out to Achamoth's mother (the higher Sophia). And then they, the Archons, will become confused and they will blame their origins and the race of their mother (Achamoth). But you, James will ascend to what is yours [...] and you will [...] be with the Pre-existent One."

(Author's Note: According to Valentinus, Aeons were created in pairs, male and female energies, which balanced, completed, and fulfilled each other. Since the fall of Sophia produced the material world, man, and the Archons, as well as splitting Sophia and producing Achamoth, Christ must rescue Achamoth out of the chaos of the lower, material world in order to restore Sophia to wholeness and have his consort in the restored and intact Sophia. Meanwhile, it is the higher Sophia that places the spirit within man as Gnosis occurs and allows for his salvation.)

"They are a type of the twelve disciples and the twelve pairs, [...] (one of these is) Achamoth, which is translated 'Sophia'. I myself am one, (and) so is the imperishable (higher) Sophia. It is she through whom you will be redeemed, and these redeemed are all the sons of He Who Is. These things they have known and have hidden within them.

You also are to hide these things within you, and you are to keep silence. But you are to reveal them to Addai.

(Author's Note: Addai is the apostle Thaddeus, one of the seventy sent out by Jesus.)

When you depart, there will immediately be war in this land. Weep for those who dwells in Jerusalem. But let Addai take these things to heart.

In the tenth year let Addai sit down and record these things. And when he writes them down [...] then the records are to be give to [...] he has the [...] and he is called Levi. Then he is to bring [...] the word [...] from what I said earlier [...] to a woman [...] for Jerusalem is in her [...] and he will begat two sons through her. They are to inherit these things along with the understanding of him who [...] exalts. And they are to inherit [...] his intellect. Now, the younger of them will be greater than the older. These things will remain hidden in him until he is seventeen years old, then [...] beginning [...] through them.

The Archons will intently pursue him, since they are from his [...]

companions. But he will become acknowledged through them, and they will proclaim this word. He will become a seed of [...]."

James said, "I am satisfied [...] and they are [...] my soul, but I have one more question. Who are the seven women who have been your disciples? I have seen that all women bless you. I am amazed at how strong a weak vessel become when they recognize what is contain in them."

The Lord said, "You [...] (see) well [...] (there is) a spirit of [...], a spirit of thought, a spirit of counsel of a [...], a spirit [...] a spirit of knowledge [...] of their fear. [...] when we had passed through the breath of an archon named Adonaios [...] him and [...] he was ignorant [...] when I came forth from him, he remembered that I am one of his sons. Because I am his son he was gracious to me at that time. But before I appeared here, he cast them down among this people. And from the place of heaven the prophets [...]."

(Author's Note: Adonaios is an offspring of Yaldaboth. He helped create the physical world. Jesus may be saying that his body, the material Jesus was created by Adonaios but because the Archon are "asleep" and ignorant, Jesus had to reveal to him that Jesus was his son. Adonaios is also a name referring to the entity and powers of the Father in the Construction of the Sethian-Valentinian creation story. He is part of the divine tripartite powers of Jesus, Father-Mother-Son. The word has Sethian-Mandaean roots and is used as Adonai-Sabaoth. Adonaios or Father is an Archon of the Pleroma. According to Origen's Contra Celsum, a sect called the Ophites posited the existence of seven archons, beginning with Yaldabaoth, who created the six that follow: Yao, Sabaoth, Adonaios, Elaios, Astaphanos, and Horaios. It is unclear as to what this prior text means. Adonaios was ignorant that Jesus was his son. This could refer to the fact that a flame is oblivious to the light it produces since it is the light and would not account for each ray. Yet, seeing a ray the light would know its own.)

James said, "Teacher, [...] I [...] completely [...] in them especially
[...]." The Lord said, "James, I commend you [...] travel on the earth
[...] the words while he [...] on the [...]. You should cast this cup of
bitterness away from you. Some from [...] will set themselves
against you now that you have begun to understand their roots
from beginning to end.

Reject all lawlessness. And beware because they will envy you.
When you communicate your new way of seeing things you
should encourage these four: Salome and Mariam and Martha and
Arsinoe. [...] since he takes some [...] to me he is [...] burnt
offerings and [...]. But I [...] not in this way; but [...] first-fruits of
the [...] upward [...] so that the power of God might appear.

The perishable has ascended to the eternal and the feminine has
attained its male counterpart."

James said, "Teacher, now into these three (things), has their [...]
been cast. They have been hated, and they have been persecuted
[...]. Look [...] everything [...] from everyone [...]. You have
attained [...] of knowledge. And [...] that is what the [...] go [...] you
will discover [...]. Now I will go and will reveal things to those
who believed in you so that they may be content with their
blessing and salvation. In this way, your revelation will come to
pass."

Then he went from there immediately and scolded and
reprimanded the twelve and shocked them out of their
contentment with their (old) knowledge [...].

[...]. The majority of them [...] took in the messenger [...]. The
others [...] said, "[...] wipe him from this earth. He is not worth
living." Others were afraid. They fled saying, "We want no part in

this blood. Is it right that a just man should perish through injustice?"

So, James departed. And they that [...] look [...] for we [...] him.

The Apocalypse of James

Introduction To
The Second Apocalypse of James

Although no Greek manuscript has been found, there is linguistic evidence in the extant Coptic text that the Second Apocalypse of James goes back to a translation from a Greek text. The occasional appearance of a name or a word of Greek origin or influence is an indication of a translation from the Greek. This can prove helpful in our understanding of the Coptic text.

The Coptic translation was likely accomplished as early as the second half of the 3rd century. The Greek text was probably written in middle of the 2nd century, although there is little evidence in the text or in any historical record to be certain.

The Second Apocalypse of James is an apocalyptic text of the Nag Hammadi library. It was placed directly after the First Apocalypse of James of what is now known as Codex V. The text narrates the martyrdom of James the Just.

The gnostic text contains many Jewish-Christian themes, making many scholars think it may be one of the earlier texts and was likely written before The First Apocalypse of James.

The prominent role of James the Lord's brother appears to speak for the geographical area of Syria and Palestine rather than for any other.

The text is clearly gnostic in character but the specific Gnostic system of the writer is uncertain. The author has knowledge of Jewish and Christian traditions, or the traditions of the Jewish converts to the Christian sect, and uses the name of James, who held a position of leadership and special prominence in Jewish-Christian circles, and in the Christian church. In the text, James is given a special revelation from Jesus. In both the First Apocalypse and the Second Apocalypse of James, James is given a role of prominence in the gnostic tradition like that of Peter in the orthodox tradition.

As Peter is supposed to be the rock upon which the church is built and the holder of the keys to the kingdom, according to Catholic tradition, in the Gnostic line James is the person who was given the keys in the Second Apocalypse to guide the Gnostic believers through the traps of the Archons and through the door into the heavenly kingdom.

In the text, the name of James' father and Mary's husband is given not as Joseph but as Theudas. The text reads, 'he (Jesus) is a brother of yours (James'). Unlike the First Apocalypse of James, the writer does not go out of his or her way to reject a bodily, material, or brotherhood relationship between Jesus and James. The text states that James and Jesus were nourished from the same milk. This reference to mother's milk could easily be taken as spiritually metaphorical.

The wife of Theudas is named Mary, but whether this Mary is the same woman as the mother of Jesus is not clear from the text.

The text features a kiss between James and Jesus, on the lips, in the way Jesus kissed Mary Magdalene in other gnostic texts. A kiss is a metaphor for the passing of gnosis and nothing more.

The text ends with the death of James by stoning, possibly reflecting an early oral tradition of what became of James.

The text can be broken down into four sections, having a hymn like quality. In the third section, James is described as performing

414

the function of gnostic redeemer. After James' function is articulated the final section is the prayer of James set just before his death.

There are issues with the flow and clarity of texts, not the least of which is that the resurrected Jesus speaks in several places without being announced and without any sign of transition from one narrator or character to the next. We only pick up on this fact because Jesus is the only voice fitting the context. In these places, he refers to James in the second person (as "you"). The story line then switches back and forth from Jesus speak to James or about James and back to the voice of James preaching to the people. All the while we cannot forget the story of James was witnessed and recorded by Meriem, the priest and told to Theuda, the father of James. Meriem's place in the story is only evident in the first and last paragraphs of the text. Author's notes have been added to assist the reader in the difficult transitions and theological meanings in the text.

The Second Apocalypse of James

This regards the lesson that James the Just preached in Jerusalem, which Mereim, one of the priests, wrote down and told to Theuda, who is the father of (James) the Just One, because he was a relative of James.

He (Meriem) said, "Come quickly! Bring Mary, your wife, and also your relatives [...] the reason is [...] of this [...] to him. He will understand.

You will see that a large group is upset over his [...]. They are very angry at him. [...] and they pray [...]. He is telling them the same thing he often told others.

He (James) used to preach while people were gathered and seated. But this time he came in and did not sit down in the place, as he usually did. Instead he sat above them on the fifth story, which is reserved for honored guest. Then all our people [...] (heard) his words [...]."

"He (James) said, [...]. I am he who received a revelation from the Eternal Pleroma. I am the one who was first summoned by the great one. And I obeyed the Lord as he passed through the worlds [...]. It was he who [...]. He stripped himself and went about naked and he was seen in a transitory state, though he was about to ascend into an eternal state. This same Lord who is with us came as a son who sees, and as a brother was he search for. He will come to [...] that he produced him because [...] and he unites [...] to make him free [...] in [...] and he who came to [...]."

"Once again I am rich in knowledge. I understanding like no other, because this understanding could only be produced from above. The [...] comes from a [...]. I am the [...] the person I knew. The things revealed to me are hidden from everyone and can be revealed only through Him.

These two who see me, they have already proclaimed through the words: He shall be judged with those who are unrighteous. He who has lived without blaspheming died by blasphemy (from others). He who was rejected, they [...]."

[...] in the flesh. But it is by gnosis that I shall come forth from the flesh. I am certainly going to die, but I shall be found in life. I came to this place so that they could judge [...] I shall come out in [...] as judge [...] but I will not lay blame on any of his servants [...].

I hurry to free them. I wish to bring them with me and ascend over the one who wants to rule over them here. I am their secret brother who wants to help them. It is I who prayed to the Father until he [...] in [...] reign [...] eternally [...] first in [...].

(Author's Note: Jesus speaks in the following hymn-like sequence.)

I am the firstborn son. Father will destroy all of them (the Demiurge and archons) and their control and their kingdom.

I am the beloved one. I am the one who is righteous. I am the only son of the Father.

I have spoken what I have heard. I have commanded as I heard the command. I have shown you what I have found.

Listen as I speak so that I may come forth (in you).

417

Be attentive to me so that you may (really) see me.

If I have come manifested, who am I? I did not come here as I (really) am, and I would not have appeared as I (truly) am. I exist (here) for a short period of time [...]."

(Author's Note: James carries on from here.)
"Once when I was sitting and meditating, the one you hated and persecuted (Jesus) came in to me. He opened the door and said to me, "Hello, my brother. My brother, hello." I raised my face and stared at him. Then my mother said to me, "Do not be afraid because he called you 'my brother', my son. Because you both were nourished with the same milk he calls me "My mother". He is no stranger to us. He is your step-brother [...]."

(Author's Note: We assume this milk refers to mother's milk from their earthy mother who suckled both of them, but it is unclear and may refer to a metaphorical spiritual milk. Jesus begins speaking. He refers to James as "you".)

"[...] these words [...] great [...] I will find them, and they will come out. However, I am the stranger, and they have no idea or thought of me in their minds, but they know me in this place. However, it was right that others gain gnosis through you.

" Hear and understand, I say to you. A multitude will hear but they will be slow witted. But you understand what I will be able to tell you. Your father is not my father. But my father has become a father to you.

(Author's Note: James' father can be seen as either his parent or Yaldaboth the Demiurge, who made his world. The father of Jesus is He Who Is, the All. Jesus is saying that through Gnosis the ALL has become James' father.)

"You have heard about this particular virgin. This is how [...] virgin [...] specifically this virgin. [...], how [...] to me for [...] to understand [...] not as [...] whom I [...]. For this man [...] to him, and this will benefit you. You know your Father is rich. He will grant your inheritance, which is all these things that you see.

"Preach these words that I shall now speak to you. When you hear, listen closely and understand, then apply it as it was intended. You are the reason that they (the Archons) come by, and it was initiated by the glorious one.

And if they want to disturb you and take possession [...] he began [...] not, and not those who are coming, who were sent forth by (the Demiurge) him that formed this present creation. After these things happen, he will be ashamed and he will be disturbed that his labor is far inferior (to the Aeons) and amounts to nothing. He will see the inheritance he boasted of as being so great will seem small. His gifts are not blessings. His promises are evil conspiracies. You are not the recipient of his compassion, but he uses you to do violence. He never wants to treat you or I fairly or with justice. He will enforce his rule throughout the time he is given.

"But now understand and become familiar with the Father who is compassionate. He did not receive an inheritance that was unlimited. His inheritance is not limited in duration. It is as the eternal day [...] it is [...] perceive [...]. And he used [...].

(Author's Note: The Demiurge received his power from Sophia. This was his inheritance. The world and all the things he created are transient and unstable, limited in lifespan and duration. The true Father, the ALL did not inherit anything. He is everything and his kingdom in eternal and incorruptible.)

The fact is, he (the Demiurge) did not come from them and he is despised. So, he boasts, because he does not want to be scolded, chastised, or punished. He is superior to those below him, those who looked down on you. He captures ones from the Father and imprisons them and then he molds them into his image and they continue their existence with him.

(Author's Note: James speaks.)

"I saw this all happen as if I was high above, watching. I have explained to you how it all happened. They were in another form when they were visited and while I watched they became familiar with me through those I know."

(Author's Note: Jesus speaks. The "you" I the text now refers to James. Here we see James being assigned the role of guide and a type of spiritual leader. Some go so far as to say this makes James a Gnostic messiah.)

"Before these things come to pass they will make a [...]. I realized how they tried to come down here to get close to [...] the small children, but now I desire to reveal the spirit of power through you so that he might be revealed to those who are yours.

Those who desire to enter in and wish to walk in the path that is before the door will open this blessed door through you. They will follow you inside and you will be their escort when they are inside. And you will allow each that is ready to receive a reward.

Even though you are not THE redeemer or the helper of strangers, you are one who shines a light and A redeemer of those who are mine, and now a redeemer of those who are yours. You will let them see and you will bring good to all of them. Because of all your powerful deeds they will admire you. The heavens bless you. He, (the Demiurge) who calls himself Lord, will envy you. I am the [...] of those who have been taught these things along with you.

For your sake, they will be taught these things so that they can rest.
For your sake, they will become kings and reign.
For your sake, they will have compassion on those they choose to pity.

As you were first to have clothed yourself (taken on this body, been born), you will be the first to strip himself (of his body), and you will become like you were before you were stripped."

(Author's Note: Gnostics believe we are held prisoners in this world by our bodies. The ultimate freedom is to lay down the body in death and thus gain freedom for our spirits. Our spirits, being the real beings, ascend to reunite with the Divine All. Jesus now stops speaking and James describes what happens next.)

"And he (Jesus) kissed my mouth. He held me and said, "My beloved, look and I will reveal to you those things that neither the heavens nor their archons have known.

(Author's Note: A kiss is symbolic of Gnosis passing from teacher to student. Jesus speaks again.)

Watch and I will reveal to you these things. He (the Demiurge), who did not understand but boasted by saying, "[...] there is no other except me. Am I not alive? Because I am a father, do I not have power for everything?"

Look, my beloved, I shall reveal everything to you. Understand and know them, so that you can come forth just as I am. Look and I will reveal to you him who is hidden. Reach out now and hold on to me."

"And then I reached out but he was not there like I thought he would be. Then I heard him saying, "Understand and take hold of me." I understood and I was afraid and filled with joy at the same time.

"Now I say to you judges, you have been judged. You did not spare anyone from your judgement and so you will not be spared either.

Be on guard and watch [...] you did not know. He (Jesus) was that one that he who created the heaven and the earth and dwelled in it (the Demiurge), did not see. (The Demiurge, who created this heaven and earth did not see or know Jesus.) He (Jesus) is the one who is the life. He was the light. He was that one who will come to be. He will be the way for what has begun (here) to end and this end is about to begin. He was the Holy Spirit and the Invisible One who did not descend upon the earth.

He was the virgin (spirit), and the things he intends, happens to him. That which he wills, comes about for him [...]. I saw that he was naked, and no garment (body) clothed him.

Renounce this difficult and unstable way, and walk with me according to the teaching of the one who desires to have you ascend above every dominion to make you free with me. He will not judge you for those things that you did (here). He will have mercy on you. It was not you that did those things. It was your Lord. He (He Who Is) is not wrath, but he is a kind Father."

The reason you remain in bondage is that you have judged yourselves. You oppress yourselves. You will repent and change your mind but (by that time) it will do you no good. You must see the one who speaks and look for the one who is silent. Know the one who came here, and understand the one who went out from this place.

I am the Just One who does not judge. I am not a master. I am a helper. He was cast out before he could reach out his hand (to save you). I [...]. [...] and now he allows me to hear. So, go ahead and play your trumpets, flutes and harps is this place. The Lord (of this place) has taken you captive from the (true) Lord, because he closed your ears, that they may not hear the sound of my word. However, you will still be able to be attentive in your hearts. Because of this you will call me 'the Just One.'"

(Author's Note: Jesus now speaks.)

Look, I have told you I gave you your house, which you say that God has made. It is the house through which he promised you would attain your inheritance. This house I have doomed to be destroyed, because it is contemptable and those in it are ignorant. Look. The judges are now deliberating [...]."

(Author's Note: The house is the physical body. The Demiurge, in the place of God, promises reward or inheritance for following him, but it is a lie. He, his kingdom, and all things physical will end. Jesus ends his speech and Meriem begins to describe the scene.)

At that time, the crowd of people were not convinced and became very upset. So, he got up and left but continues to preach like he had previously. He came again on the same day and spoke for a few hours.

I (Mereim) was with the priests but I did not tell him I was related or knew James since all of them were in agreement, saying, 'Come on, let us stone the Just One.' Then they got up and said, 'Yes, let us kill him and get him out of our midst. He is worthless.'

(Author's Note: It is easy to forget this story was recorded by Mereim the priest and told to Theuda, the father of James. Mereim continues by telling Theuda how James, is son, died.)

They went there and found him standing beside the columns of the temple beside the large corner stone. And they decided to throw him down from that high place, and they threw him down. Then they [...] they [...] and they grabbed him and struck him as they dragged him on the ground. They stretched him out and placed a stone on his stomach. They all stood on him, yelling 'You have sinned!'
But he was still alive so made him stand up and they made him dig a hole. They made him stand in the hole he dug. Then they buried him up to his chest and they stoned him.

Then James raised his hands and said this prayer, which is different from the way he normally prays:
'My God and my father, who saved me while my hope was dead, you enlivened me through the mystery your will. Now, do not let my days in this world be prolonged. The light of your day [...] remains in [...] salvation. Now, deliver me from my sojourn in this place. Do not let your grace be left behind in my body, but let your grace become pure. Save me from a death of defilement and bring me out of my tomb alive. I know your grace and love live in me for the purpose of fulfilling your work. Save me from this sinful flesh. I trust in you with all the strength I have. You are the life in all things living. Do not let the enemy humiliate me. Do not turn me over to a judge who deals with sin so severely. Forgive me all my sins in my life because I live in you and your grace lives in me. I have left everyone and I have confessed (my faith in) you. Save me from this evil sickness! This is the time and the hour. Holy Spirit, bring me salvation [...] the light [...] the light [...] in the power [...].'

"After he spoke (these words), he remained silent [...] word [...] after [...] this discourse [...]."

The History of The Gospel of Philip

The Gospel of Philip is assumed to be one of the sources of Dan Brown's novel, The Da Vinci Code, about Mary Magdalene, Jesus, and their children. The Gospel is one of Gnostic texts found at Nag Hammadi in Egypt in 1945 and belongs to the same collection of Gnostic documents as the more famous Gospel of Thomas.

It has been suggested that the *Gospel of Philip* was written in the second century B.C. If so, it may be one of the earliest documents containing themes that would later be used in apocryphal literature.

A single manuscript of the *Gospel of Philip*, written in Coptic, was found in the Nag Hammadi library. The collection was a library of thirteen papyrus texts discovered near the town of Nag Hammadi in 1945 by a peasant boy. The writings in these codices comprised 52 documents, most of which were Gnostic in nature.

The codices were probably hidden by monks from the nearby monastery of St. Pachomius when the official Christian Church banned all Gnostic literature around the year 390 A.D

It is believe the original texts were written in Greek during the first or second centuries A.D. The copies contained in the discovered clay jar were written in Coptic in the third or fourth centuries A.D.

The *Gospel Of Philip* is a list of sayings focusing on man's redemption and salvation as framed by Gnostic theology.

The *Gospel of Philip* presented here is based on a comparative study of translations from the Nag Hammadi Codex by Wesley W. Isenberg, Willis Barnstone, The Ecumenical Coptic Project, Bart Ehrman, Marvin Meyer, David Cartlidge, David Dungan, and other sources.

Each verse was weighed against the theological and philosophical beliefs held by the Gnostic community at the time in which the document was penned. All attempts were made to render the most accurate meaning based on the available translations and information.

Exact wording was secondary to the conveyance of the overall meaning as understood by contemporary readers.

When the wording of a verse held two possible meanings or needed expanded definitions, optional translations were placed in parentheses.

The Gospel of Philip

1.   A Hebrew makes a Hebrew convert, and they call him a proselyte (novice). A novice does not make another novice. Some are just as they are, and they make others like themselves to receive. It is enough for them that they simply are as they are.

2.   The slave seeks only to be set free. He does not hope to attain the estate of his master. The son acts as a son (heir), but the father gives the inheritance to him.

3. Those who inherit the dead are dead, and they inherit the dead. Those who inherit the living are alive. They inherit both the living and the dead. The dead cannot inherit anything. How can the dead inherit anything? When the dead inherits the (singular) living, he shall not die but the dead shall live instead.

4.   The Gentile (unbeliever) who does not believe does not die, because he has never been alive, so he could not die. He who has trusted the Truth has found life and is in danger of dying, because he is now alive.

5. Since the day that the Christ came. The cosmos was created, the cities are built (adorned), and the dead carried out.

6.   In the days when we were Hebrews we were made orphans, having only our Mother. Yet when we believed in the Messiah (became the ones of Christ), the Mother and Father both came to us.

7. Those who sow in the winter reap in the summer. The winter is this world system. The summer is the other age / dispensation (to come). Let us sow in the world (cosmos) so that we will reap in

the summer. Because of this, it is right for us not to pray in the winter. What comes from (follows) the winter is the summer. If anyone reaps in the winter he will not harvest but rather pull it up by the roots and will not produce fruit. Not only does it not produce in winter, but on the Sabbath his field shall be bare.

8. The Christ has come to fully ransom some, to save (restore and heal) others, and to be the propitiation for others. Those who were estranged he ransomed. He purchases them for himself. He saves, heals, and restores those who come to him. These he desires to pledge (in marriage). When he became manifest he ordained the soul as he desired (set aside his own life), but even before this, in the time of the world's beginning, he had ordained the soul (he had laid down his own life). At his appointed time, he came to bring the soul he pledged himself to back to himself. It had come to be under the control of robbers and they took it captive. Yet he saved it, and he paid the price for both the good and the evil of the world.

9. Light and dark, life and death, right and left are brothers. It is impossible for one to be separated from the other. They are neither good, nor evil. A life is not alive without death. Death is not death if one were not alive. Therefore each individual shall be returned to his origin from the beginning. Those who go beyond the world will live forever and are in the eternal present.

10. The names that are given to worldly things cause great confusion. They contort our perception from the real to the unreal. He who hears "God" does not think of the real, but rather has false, preconceived ideas. It is the same with "Father", "Son", "Holy Spirit", "Life", "Light", "Resurrection" and "church (the called out ones)", and all other words. They do not think of the real, but rather they call to mind preconceived, false ideas. They learned the reality of human death. They who are in the world system made them think of the false idea. If they had been in

eternity, they would not have designated anything as evil, nor would they have placed things within worldly events (time and place). They are destined for eternity.

11. The only name they should never speak into the world is the name the Father gave himself through the Son. This is the Father's name. It exists that he may be exalted over all things. The Son could not become the Father, unless he was given the Father's name. This name exists so that they may have in their thoughts. They should never speak it. Those who do not have it cannot even think it. But the truth created names in the world for our sake. It would not be possible to learn the truth without names.

12. The Truth alone is the truth. It is a single thing and a multitude of things. The truth teaches us love alone through many and varied paths.

13. Those who ruled (lower gods) desired to deceive man because they knew man was related to the truly good ones. They took the designation of good and they gave it to those who were not good. They did this so that by way of words they might deceive man and bind him to those who are not good. When they receive favor, they are taken from those who are not good and placed among the good. These are they who had recognized themselves. The rulers (lower gods) had desired to take the free person, and enslave him to themselves forever. Rulers of power fight against man. The rulers do not want him to be saved (recognize himself), so that men will become their masters. For if there is man is saved there is saved there will be no need for sacrifice.

14. When sacrifice began, animals were offered up to the ruling powers. They were offered up to them while the sacrificial animals were still alive. But as they offered them up they were killed. But the Christ was offered up dead to God (the High God), and yet he lived.

15. Before the Christ came, there had been no bread in the world. In paradise, the place where Adam was, there had been many plants as food for wild animals, but paradise had no wheat for man to eat. Man had to be nourished like animals. But the Christ, the perfect man, was sent. He brought the bread of heaven, so that man could eat as he should.

16. The rulers (lower gods) thought what they did was by their own will and power, but the Holy Spirit worked through them without their knowledge to do her will.

17. The truth, which exists from the beginning, is sown everywhere, and everyone sees it being sown, but only a few see the harvest.

18. Some say that Mary conceived by the Holy Spirit. They are in error. They do not know what they are saying. How can a female impregnate another female? Mary is the virgin whom no power defiled. She is great among the problem and curse for the Hebrew Apostles and for those in charge. The ruler (lower god) who attempts to defile this virgin, is himself defiled. The Lord was not going to say, "my father in heaven", unless he really had another father. He would simply have said, "my father".

19. The Lord says to the Disciples, "Come into the house of the Father, but do not bring anything in or take anything out from the father's house.

20. Jesus (Yeshua) is the secret name; Christ (messiah) is the revealed name. The name "Jesus" (Yeshua) does not occur in any other language. His name is called "Jesus" (Yeshua). In Aramaic his name Messiah, but in Greek it is: Christ (Cristos). In every language he is called the anointed one. The fact that he is Savior (Yeshua) could be fully comprehended only by himself, since it is

431

the Nazarene who reveals the secret things.

21. Christ has within himself all things; man, angel, mystery (sacraments), and the father.

22. Those who say that the Lord first died and then arose are in error. He would have to first arise before he could die. If he is not first resurrected, he would die, but God lives and cannot die.

23. No one will hide something highly valuable in something ostentatious (that would draw attention). More often, one places something of great worth within a number of containers worth nothing. This is how it is with the (human) soul. It is a precious thing placed within a lowly body.

24. Some are fearful that they will arise (from the dead) naked. Therefore they desire to rise in the flesh. They do not understand that those who choose to wear the flesh are naked. Those who choose to strip themselves of the flesh are the ones who are not naked.

25. Flesh and blood will not be able to inherit the kingdom of God. What is this that will not inherit? It is that which is upon each of us (our flesh). But what will inherit the kingdom is that which belongs to Jesus and is of his flesh and blood. Therefore he says: "He who does not eat my flesh and drink my blood, has no life in him." What is his flesh? It is the word. And his blood is the Holy Spirit. He who has received these has food and drink and clothing.

26. I disagree with those who say the flesh will not arise. They are in error. Tell me what will rise so that we may honor you. You say it is the spirit in the flesh and the light contained in the flesh. But you say there is nothing outside of the flesh (material world). It is necessary to arise in this flesh if everything exists within the flesh.

27. In this world those wearing a garment are more valuable than the garment. In the kingdom of the Heavens the garment is more valuable than the one wearing it.

28. By water and fire the entire realm is purified through the revelations by those who reveal them, and by the secrets through those who keep them. Yet, there are things kept secret even within those things revealed. There is water in baptism and there is fire in the oil of anointing.

29. Jesus took them all by surprise. For he did not reveal himself as he originally was, but he revealed himself as they were capable of perceiving him. He revealed himself to all in their own way. To the great, he revealed himself as great. To the small he was small. he revealed himself to the angels as an angel and to mankind he was a man. Some looked at him and saw themselves. But, throughout all of this, he concealed his words from everyone. However when he revealed himself to his Disciples upon the mountain, he appeared glorious. He was not made small. He became great, but he also made the Disciples great so that they would be capable of comprehending his greatness.

30. He said on that day during his thanksgiving (in the Eucharist): "You have combined the perfect light and the holy spirit along with angels and images."

31. Do not hate the Lamb. Without him it is not possible to see the door to the sheepfold. Those who are naked will not come before the King.

32. The Sons of the Heavenly Man are more numerous than those of the earthly man. If the sons of Adam are numerous although they die, think of how many more Sons the Perfect Man has and

these do not die. And they are continually born every instant of time.

33. The Father creates a Son, but it is not possible for the Son to create a son because it is impossible for someone who was just born to have a child. The Son has Brothers, not sons.

34. There is order in things. All those who are born in the world are begotten physically. Some are begotten spiritually, fed by the promise of heaven, which is delivered by the perfect Word from the mouth. The perfect Word is conceived through a kiss and thus they are born. There is unction to kiss one another to receive conception from grace to grace.

35. There were three women named Mary who walked with the Lord all the time. They were his mother, his sister and Mary of Magdala, who was his consort (companion). Thus his mother, his sister and companion (consort) were all named Mary.

36. "Father" and "Son" are single names, "Holy Spirit" is a double name and it is everywhere; above and below, secret and revealed. The Holy Spirit's abode is manifest when she is below. When she is above she is hidden.

37. Saints are served by evil powers (lesser gods). The evil spirits are deceived by the Holy Spirit to think they think they are assisting a common man when they are serving Saints. A follower of the Lord once asked him for a thing from this world. He answered him saying; Ask you Mother, and she will give you something from another realm.

38. The Apostles said to the students: May all of our offering obtain salt! They had called wisdom salt and without it no offering can become acceptable.

39. Wisdom (Sophia) is barren. She has no children but she is called Mother. Other are found (adopted) by the Holy Spirit, and she has many children.

40. That which the Father has belongs to the Son, but he cannot possess it when he is young (small). When he comes of age all his father has will be given to the son.

41. Those who do not follow the path are born of the Spirit, and they stray because of her. By this same spirit (breath / life force), the fire blazes and consumes.

42. Earthly Wisdom is one thing, and death is another. Earthly Wisdom is simply wisdom, but death is the wisdom of death, and death is the one who understands death. Being familiar with death is minor wisdom.

43. There are animals like the bull and donkey that are submissive to man. There are others that live in the wilderness. Man plows the field with submissive animals, and uses the harvest to feed himself as well as all the animals, domesticated or wild. So it is with the Perfect Man. Through submissive powers he plows and provides a for all things to exist. He causes all things to come together into existence, whether good or evil, right or left.

44 The Holy Spirit is the shepherd; guiding everyone and every power (lower ruler / lesser gods) whether they are submissive, rebellious or feral. She controls them, subdues them, and keeps them bridled, whether they wish it or not.

45. Adam was created beautiful. One would expect his children to be noble. If he were not created but rather born, one would expect his children to be noble. But He was both created and born. Is this nobility?

46. Adultery occurred first and then came murder. And Cain was conceived in adultery because he was the serpent's (Satan's) son. He became a murderer just like his father. He killed his brother. When copulation occurs between those who are not alike, this is adultery.

47. God is a dyer. Just as a good and true dye penetrates deep into fabric to dye it permanently from within (not a surface act), so God has baptized what He dyes into an indelible dye, which is water.

48. It is impossible for anyone to see anything in the real world, unless he has become part of it. It is not like at person in this world. When one looks like the sun he can see it without being part of it. He sees the sky and the earth or any other thing without having to be part of it. So it is with this world, but in the other world you must become what you see (see what you become). To see spirit you must be spirit. To see Christ you must be Christ. To see the father you must be the Father. In this way you will see everything but yourself. If you look at yourself you will become what you see.

49. Faith receives, but love gives. No one can receive without faith. No one can love without giving. Believe and you shall receive. Love and you shall give. If you give without love, you shall receive nothing. Whoever has not received the Lord, continues to be a Jew.

50. The Apostles who came before us called him Jesus, The Nazarene, and The Messiah. Of these names, Jesus (Yeshua), The Nazarene (of the rite of the Nazarites), and The Messiah (Christ), the last name is the Christ, the first is Jesus, and the middle name is The Nazarene. Messiah has two meanings; the anointed one and the measured one. Jesus (Yeshua) means The Atonement (Redemption / Payment). 'Nazara' means Truth. Therefore, the

Nazarite is The Truth. The Christ is The Measured One, the Nazarite (Truth) and Jesus (Redemption) have been measured (are the measurement).

51. The pearl which is thrown into the mud is not worth less than it was before. If it is anointed with balsam oil it is valued no higher. It is as valuable as its owner perceives it to be. So it is with the children of God. Whatever becomes of them, they are precious in their Father's eyes.

52. If you say you are a Jew it will not upset anyone.
If you say you are Roman, on no will care. If you claim to be a Greek, foreigner, slave, or a free man no one will be the least bit disturbed. But, if you claim to belong to Christ everyone will take heed (be concerned). I hope to receive this title from him. Those who are worldly would not be able to endure when they hear the name.

53. A god is a cannibal, because men are sacrificed to it. Before men were sacrificed, animals were sacrificed. Those they are sacrificed to are not gods.

54. Vessels of glass and vessels of clay are always made with fire. But if a glass vessel should break it is recast, because it is made in a single breath. If clay vessel breaks it is destroyed, since it came into being without breath.

55. A donkey turning a millstone walked a hundred miles but when it was untied it was in the same place it started. There are those who go on long journeys but do not progress. When evening comes (when the journey ends), they have discovered no city, no village, no construction site, no creature (natural thing), no power (ruler), and no angel. They labored and toiled for nothing (emptiness).

56. The thanksgiving (Eucharist) is Jesus. For in Aramaic they call him farisatha, which means, "to be spread out. This is because Jesus came to crucify the world.

57. The Lord went into the place where Levi worked as a dyer. He took 72 pigments and threw them into a vat. When he drew out the result it was pure white. He said, "This is how the Son of Man has come. He is a dyer."

58. Wisdom, which they call barren, is the mother of the angels. And the companion (Consort) was Mary of Magdala. The Lord loved Mary more than all the other disciples and he kissed her often on her mouth (the text is missing here and the word is assumed). The others saw his love for Mary asked him: "Why do thou love her more than all of us?" The Savior replied, "Why do I not love you in the same way I love her?" While a blind person and a person who sees are both in the dark, there is no difference, but when the light comes, the one who sees shall behold the light, but he who is blind will remain in darkness.

59. The Lord says: "Blessed is he who existed before you came into being, for he is and was and shall (continue to) be.

60. The supremacy of man is not evident, but it is hidden. Because of this he is master of the animals, which are stronger (larger) than him, in ways both evident and not. This allows the animals to survive. But, when man departs from them, they bite and kill and devour each other because they have no food. Now they have food because man cultivated the land.

61. If one goes down into the water (is baptized) and comes up having received nothing, but claims to belong to Christ, he has borrowed against the name at a high interest rate. But if one receives the Holy Spirit, he has been given the name as a gift. He who has received a gift does not have to pay for it or give it back.

If you have borrowed the name you will have to pay it back with interest when it is demanded. This is how the mystery works.

62. Marriage is a sacrament and a mystery. It is grand. For the world is founded upon man, and man founded upon marriage. Consider sex (pure sex), it has great power although its image is defiled.

63. Among the manifestations of unclean spirits there are male and female. The males are those who mate with the souls inhabiting a female form, and the female spirits invite those inhabiting a male form to have sex. Once seized, no one escapes unless they receive both the male and female power that is endued to the Groom with the Bride. The power is seen in the mirrored Bridal-Chamber. When foolish women see a man sitting alone, they want to subdue him, touch and handle him, and defile him. When foolish men see a beautiful woman sitting alone, they wish to seduce her, draw her in with desire and defile her. But, if the spirits see the man sitting together with his woman, the female spirit cannot intrude upon the man and the male spirit cannot intrude upon the woman. When image and angel are mated, no one can come between the man and woman.

64. He who comes out from the world cannot be stopped. Because he was once in the world he is now beyond both yearning (desire) and fear. He has overcome the flesh and has mastered envy and desire. If he does not leave the world there are forces that will come to seize him, strangle him. How can anyone escape? How can he fear them? Many times men will come and say, "We are faithful, and we hid from unclean and demonic spirits." But if they had been given the Holy Spirit, no unclean spirit would have clung to them. Do not fear the flesh, nor love it. If you fear it, the flesh will become your master. If you love it, the flesh will devour you and render you unable to move.

65. One exists either in this world or in the resurrection or in transition between them. Do not be found in transition. In that world there is both good and evil. The good in it is not good and the evil in it is not evil. There is evil after this world, which is truly evil and it is call the transition. This is what is called death. While we are in this world it is best that we be born into the resurrection, so that we take off the flesh and find rest and not wander within the region of the transition. Many go astray along the way. Because of this, it is best to go forth from the world before one has sinned.

66. Some neither wish nor are able to act. Others have the will to act but it is best for them if they do not act, because the act they desire to perform would make them a sinner. By not desiring to do a righteous act justice is withheld (not obvious). However, the will always comes before the act.

67. An Apostle saw in a vision people confined to a blazing house, held fast in bonds of fire, crying out as flames came from their breath. There was water in house, and they cried out, "The waters can truly save us. They were misled by their desire. This is called the outermost darkness.

68. Soul and spirit were born of water and fire. From water, fire, and light the children of the Bridal-Chamber are born. The fire is the spirit (anointing), the light is the fire, but not the kind of fire that has form. I speak of the other kind whose form is white and it rains down beauty and splendor.

69. The truth did not come unto the world naked, but it came in types and symbols. The world would not receive it any other way. There is a rebirth together with its symbols. One cannot be reborn through symbols. What can the symbol of resurrection raise, or the Bridal-Chamber with its symbols? One must it is come into the truth through the imagery. Truth is this Restoration. It is good

for those not born to take on the names of the Father, the Son, and the Holy Spirit. They could not have done so on their own. Whoever is not born of them, will have the name (Christ's ones) removed from him. The one who receives them receives the anointing of the spirit and the unction and power of the cross. This is what the Apostles call having the right with the left. When this happens, you no longer belong to Christ, you will be Christ.

70. The Lord did everything through sacraments (mysteries / symbols): There was Baptism with anointing with thanksgiving (Eucharist) with an Atonement (sacrifice/payment) and Bridal-Chamber.

71. He says: I came to make what is inside the same as the outside and what is below as it is above. I came to bring all of this into one place. He revealed himself through types and symbols. Those who say Christ comes from the place beyond (above) are confused.

72. He who is manifest in heaven is called "one from below." And He who knows the hidden thing is He who is above him. The correct way to say it would be "the inner and the outer or this which is beyond the outer". Because of this, the Lord called destruction "the outer darkness". There is nothing beyond it. He says, "My Father, who is in secret". He says "Go into your inner chamber, shut the door behind you and there pray to your Father who is in secret; He who is deep within. He is within them all is the Fullness. Beyond Him there is nothing deeper within. The deepest place within is called the uppermost place.

73. Before Christ some came forth. They were not able to go back from where they came. They were no longer able to leave from where they went it. Then Christ came. Those who went in he brought out, and those who went out he brought in.

74. When Eve was still within Adam (man), there had been no

death. When she was separated from him, death began. If she were to enter him again and if he were to receive her completely, death would stop.

75. "My God, my God, Oh Lord why did you abandon me?" He spoke these words on the cross. He divided the place and was not there any longer.

76. The Lord arose from the dead. He became as he had been, but his body had been made perfect. He was clothed in true flesh. Our flesh is not true, but rather an image of true flesh, as one beholds in a mirror.

77. The Bridal-Chamber is not for beasts, slaves, or whores. It is for free men and virgins.

78. Through the Holy Spirit we are born again, conceived in Christ, anointed in the spirit, united within us. Only with light can we see ourselves reflected in water or mirror. We are baptized in water and light. It is the light that is the oil of the anointing.

79. There had been three offering vestibules in Jerusalem. One opened to the west called the holy, another opened to the south called the holy of the holy, the third opened to the east called the holy of the holies where the high priest alone was to enter. The Baptism is the holy, the redemption (payment / atonement) is the holy of the holy, and the holy of the holies is the Bridal-Chamber. The Baptism has within it the resurrection and the redemption. Redemption allows entrance into the Bridal-Chamber. The Bridal-Chamber is more exalted than any of these. Nothing compares.

80. Those who pray for Jerusalem love Jerusalem. They are in Jerusalem and they see it now. These are called the holy of the holies.

81. Before the curtain of the Temple was torn we could not see the Bridal-Chamber. All we had was the symbol of the place in heaven. When the curtain was torn from the top to the bottom it made a way for some to ascend.

82. Those who have been clothed in the Perfect Light cannot be seen by the powers, nor can the powers subdue them. Yet one shall be clothed with light in the sacrament (mystery) of sex (being united).

83. If the woman had not been separated from the man, neither would have died. Christ came, to rectify the error of separation that had occurred. He did this by re-uniting them and giving life to those who died. The woman unites with her husband in the bridal-chamber and those who have united in the Bridal-Chamber will not be parted again. Eve separated from Adam because she did not unite with him in the Bridal-Chamber.

84. The soul of man (Adam) was created when breath (spirit) was blown into him. The elements were supplied by his mother. When soul (mind/will) became spirit and were joined together he spoke in word the powers could not understand.

85. Jesus manifested beside the River Jordan with fullness of the kingdom of the Heavens, which existed before the anything. Moreover, he was born as a Son before birth. He was anointed and he anointed. He was atoned and he atoned.

86. If it is right to speak of a mystery. The Father of the all mated with the Virgin who had come down. A fire shone over him on that day. He revealed the power of the Bridal-Chamber. Because of this power his body came into being on that day. He came forth in the Bridal-Chamber in glory because of issued from the Bridegroom to the Bride. This is how Jesus established everything. It was in his heart. In this same way it is right for each one of the

disciples to enter into his rest.

87. Adam came into being from two virgins, from the Spirit and from the virgin earth. Christ was born from a virgin, so that the error which occurred in the beginning would be corrected by him.

88. There were two trees in paradise. One produces beasts, the other produces man. Adam ate from the tree that produced beasts becoming a beast he gave birth to beasts. Because of this, animals were worshipped. God created man and men created gods. This is how the world works; men create gods and they worship their creations. It would have been more appropriate for gods to worship mankind. This would be the way if Adam had eaten from the tree of life, which bore people.

89. The deed of man follow his abilities. These are his strengths and the thing he does with ease. His result is his children who came forth from his times of rest. His work is governed by his work but in his rest he brings forth his sons. This is the sign and symbol, doing works with strength, and producing children in his rest.

90. In this world the slaves are forced to serve the free. In the kingdom of Heaven the free shall serve the slaves and the Bridegroom of the Bridal-Chamber shall serve the guests. Those of the Bridal-Chamber have a single name among them, it is "rest" and they have no need for any other. The contemplation of the symbol brings enlightenment and great glory. Within those in the Chamber (rest) the glories are fulfilled.

91. Go into the water but do not go down into death, because Christ shall atone for him when he who is baptized comes forth. They were called to be fulfilled in his name. For he said, "We must fulfill all righteousness."

92. Those who say they shall die and then arise are confused. If you do not receive the resurrection while you are alive you will not receive anything when you die. This is why it is said that Baptism is great, because those who receive it shall live.

93. Philip the Apostle said: Joseph the Carpenter planted a grove of trees because he needed wood for his work (craft / trade). He himself made the cross from the trees that he had planted, and his heir hung on that which he had planted. His heir was Jesus, and the tree was the cross. But the tree of life in the midst of the garden (paradise) is the olive tree. From the heart of it comes the anointing through the olive oil and from that comes the resurrection.

94. This world consumes corpses. Everything eaten by (in) the world dies. The truth devours life, but if you eat truth you shall never die. Jesus came (from there) bringing food. And to those wishing it (whom he wished) he gave life, so that they not die.

95. God created the garden (paradise). Man lived in the there, but they did not have God in their hearts and so they gave in to desire. This garden is where it will be said to us, " You may eat this but not eat that, according to your desire." This is the place where I shall choose to eat various things such as being there the tree of knowledge, which slew Adam. In this place the tree of knowledge gave life to man. The Torah is the tree. It has the power to impart the knowledge of good and evil. It did not remove him from the evil or deliver him to good. It simply caused those who had eaten it to die. Death began because truth said, " You can eat this, but do not eat that."

96. The anointing (chrism) is made superior to Baptism, because from the word Chrism we are called Christians (Christ's ones) not because of the word Baptism. And because of Chrism he was called Christ. The Father anointed the Son, and the Son anointed the Apostles, and the Apostles anointed us. He who has been anointed has come to possess all things; he has the resurrection,

the light, the cross, and the Holy Spirit. The Father bestowed this upon him in the Bridal-Chamber. The father gave it to the Son who received it freely. The Father was in the Son, and the Son was in the Father. This is the kingdom of Heaven.

97. It was perfectly said by the Lord: Some have attained the kingdom of Heaven laughing. They came forth from the world joyous. Those who belong to Christ who went down into the water immediately came up as lord of everything. He did not laugh because he took things lightly, but because he saw that everything in this world was worthless compared to the kingdom of Heaven. If he scoffs at the world and sees its worthlessness he will come forth laughing.

98. The Bread and cup, and the oil of anointing (Chrism): There is one superior to them all.

99. The world (system) began in a mistake. He who made this world wished to make it perfect and eternal. He failed (fell away / did not follow through) and did not attain his goal. The world is not eternal, but the children of the world are eternal. They were children and obtained eternity. No one can receive eternity except by becoming a child. The more you are unable to receive, the more you will be unable to give.

100. The cup of the communion (prayer) contains wine and water. It is presented as the symbol of the blood. Over it (because of the blood) we give thanks. It is filled by (with) the Holy Spirit. It (the blood) belongs to the Perfect Man. When we drink we consume the Perfect man

101. The Living Water is a body. It is right that we be clothed with a living body (The Living Man). When he goes down into the water he undresses himself so he may be clothed with the living man.

102. A horse naturally gives birth to a horse, a human naturally gives birth to a human, a god naturally gives birth to a god. The Bridegroom within the Bride give birth to children who are born in the Bridal-Chamber. The Jews do not spring forth from Greeks

(Gentiles), and Christians (those belonging to Christ) do not come from Jews. These who gave birth to Christians were called the chosen generation of the Holy Spirit (living God). The True Man, the Son of Mankind, was the seed that brought forth the sons of Man. This generation is the true ones in the world. This is the place where the children of the Bridal-Chamber dwell.

103. Copulation occurs in this world when man and woman mix (mingle / entwine). Strength joins with weakness. In eternity there is a different kind of mingling that occurs. Metaphorically we call it by the same names, but it is exalted beyond any name we may give it. It transcends brute strength. Where there is no force, there are those who are superior to force. Man cannot comprehend this.
104. The one is not, and the other one is, but they are united. This is He who shall not be able to come unto those who have a heart of flesh. (He is not here, but He exists. However, He cannot inhabit a heart of those who are attached to the fleshly world.)

105. Before you possess all knowledge, should you not know yourself? If you do not know yourself, how can you enjoy those things you have. Only those who have understood themselves shall enjoy the things they have come to possess.

106. The perfected person cannot be captured or seen. If they could see him, they could capture him. The path to grace can only come from the perfect light. Unless one is clothed in the perfect light and it shows on and in him he shall not be able to come out from the World as the perfected son of the Bridal-Chamber. We must be perfected before we come out from the world. Whoever has received all before mastering all, will not be able to master the kingdom. He shall go to the transition (death) imperfect. Only Jesus knows his destiny.

107. The holy person is entirely holy, including his body. If one blesses the bread and sanctifies it, or the cup, or everything else he receives, why will he not sanctify the body also?

108. By perfecting the water of Baptism: thus Jesus washed away death. Because of this, we are descent into the water but not into death. We are not poured out into the wind (spirit) of the world.

Whenever that blows, its winter has come. When the Holy Spirit breathes, summer has come.

109. Whoever recognizes the truth is set free. He who is set free does not go back (sin), for the one who goes back (the sinner) is the slave of sin. Truth is the Mother. When we unite with her it is recognition of the truth. Those who are set free from sin (no longer have to sin) are called free by the world. It is the recognition of the truth that exalts the hearts of those who are set free from sin. This is what liberates them and places them over the entire world. Love builds (inspires). He who is has been set free through this recognition is a slaved of love for those who have not yet set free by the truth. Knowledge makes them capable of being set free. Love does not take anything selfishly. How can it when it possesses all thing? It does not say; "This is mine or that is mine", but it says: "All of this belongs to you."

110. Spiritual love is wine with fragrance. All those who are anointed with it enjoy it. Those who are near to the anointed ones enjoy it also. But when the anointed ones depart the bystanders who are not anointed remain in their own stench. The Samaritan gave nothing to the wounded man except wine and oil for anointing. The wounds were healed, for "love covers a multitude of sins."

111. The children of a women resemble the man who loves her. If the man is her husband, they resemble her husband. If the man is her illicit lover, they resemble him. Often, a woman will have sex with her husband out of duty but her heart is with her lover with whom she also has sex. The children of such a union often resemble the lover. You who live with the Son of God and do not also love the world but love the Lord only will have children that look like the Lord and not the world.

112. Humans mate with the humans, horses mate with horses, donkeys mate with donkeys; Like attracts like and they group together. Spirits unite with Spirits, and the thought (Word) mingles with the thought (Word), as Light merges with Light. If you become person then people will love you. If you become a spirit, then the Spirit shall merge with you. If thou become

thought, then the thought (Word) shall unite with you. If you become enlightened, then the Light shall merge with you. If you rise above this world, then that which is from above shall rest upon (in) you. But, if you become like a horse, donkey, bull, dog, sheep, or any other animal, domestic or feral, neither man nor Spirit nor Word (thought) nor the Light nor those from above nor those dwelling within shall be able to love you. They shall not be able to rest in you, and they will have no part in your inheritance to come.

113. He who is enslaved without his consent can be set free. He who has been set free by the grace of his master, but then sells himself back into slavery cannot be set free.

114. The cultivation in this world comes through four elements. Crops are harvested and taken into the barn only if there is first soil, water, wind, and light. God's harvest is also by means of four elements; faith (trust), hope (expectation), love (agape'), and knowledge (recognition of the truth). Our soil is the faith in which we take root. Our water is the hope by which we are nourished. Wind (spirit) is the love through which we grow. Light is the truth, which causes us to ripen. But, it is Grace that causes us to become kings of all heaven. Their souls are among the blessed for they live in Truth.

115. Jesus, the Christ, came to all of us but did not lay any burden on us. This kind of person is perfect and blessed. He is the Word of God. Ask us about him and we will tell you his righteousness is difficult to define or describe. A task so great assures failure.

116. How will he give rest to everyone; great or small, believer or not? He provides rest to all. There are those who attempt to gain by assisting the rich. Those who see themselves as rich are picky. They do not come of their own accord. Do not grieve them or anyone. It is natural to want to do good, but understand that the rich may seek to cause grief and he who seeks to do good could annoy those who think they are rich.

117. A householder had acquired everything. He had children, slaves, cattle, dogs, and pigs. He also had wheat, barley, straw,

hay, meat, oil, and acorns. He was wise and knew what each needed to eat. He fed his children bread and meat. He fed the slaves oil with grain. The cattle were given barley straw and hay. The dogs received bones and the pigs got acorns and bread scraps. This is how it is with the disciple of God. If he is wise, he is understands discipleship. The bodily forms will not deceive him, but he will understand the condition of the souls around him. He will speak to each man on his own level. In the world there are many types of animals in human form. He must recognize each one. If the person is a pig, feed him acorns. If the person is a bull feed him barley with straw and hay; if a dog, throw him bones. If a person is a slave feed them basic food, but to the sons present the perfect and complete food.

118. There is the Son of Man and there is the son of the son of Man. The Lord is the Son of Man, and his son creates through him. God gave the Son of Man the power to create; he also gave him the ability to have children. That which is created is a creature. Those born are a progeny (child / heir). A creature cannot propagate, but children can create. Yet they say that the creature procreates, however, the child is a creature. Therefore the creature's progeny are not his sons, but rather they are creations. He who creates works openly, and is visible. He who procreates does so in secret, and he hides himself from others. He who creates does so in open sight. He who procreates, makes his children (Son) in secret.

119. No one is able to know what day a husband and wife copulate. Only they know, because marriage in this world is a sacrament (mystery) for those who have taken a wife. If the act of an impure (common) marriage is hidden, the pure (immaculate) marriage is a deeper mystery (sacrament) and is hidden even more. It is not carnal (common) but it is pure (undefiled). it is not founded on lust. It is founded on true love (agape'). It is not part of the darkness or night. It is part of the light of. A marriage (act) which is seen (revealed / exposed) becomes vulgarity (common / prostitution), and the bride has played the whore not only if she has sex with another man, but also if she escapes from the bridle-chamber and is seen. She may only be seen (reveal herself to) by her father, her mother, (the friend of the bridegroom,) and the

attendant of the bridegroom, and the bridegroom. Only these have permission go into the bridal-chamber on a daily basis. Others will yearn to hear her voice or enjoy her perfume (fragrance of the anointing oil). Let them be fed like dogs from the scraps that fall from the table. (Those) being from the Bridegroom with the Bride belong in the Bridal-Chamber. No one will be able to see the Bridegroom or the Bride unless he becomes one like (with) them.

120. When Abraham was allowed (rejoiced at seeing what he was) to see, he circumcised the flesh of the foreskin to show us that it was correct (necessary) to renounce (kill) the flesh of this world.

121. As long as the entrails of a person are contained, the person lives and is well. If his entrails are exposed and he is disemboweled, the person will die. It is the same with a tree. If its roots are covered it will live and grow, but if its roots are exposed the tree will wither and die. It is the same with everything born into this world. It is the this way with everything manifest (seen) and covert (unseen). As long as the roots of evil are hidden, it is strong, but once evil it is exposed or recognized it is destroyed and it dies. This is why the Word says; "Already the ax has been laid to the root of the tree." It will not only chop down the tree, because that will permit it to sprout again, the ax will down into the ground and cleave the very root. Jesus uprooted what others had only partially cut down. Let each one of us dig deeply, down to the root of the evil that is within his heart and rip it out by its roots. If we can just recognize evil we can uproot it. However, if evil remains unrecognized, it will take root within us and yield its fruit in our hearts. It will make evil our master and we will be its slaves. Evil takes us captive, and coerces us into doing what we do not want to do. evil compels us into not doing what we should do. While it is unrecognized, it drives us .

122. Ignorance is the mother of all evil. Evil results in confusion and death. Truth is like ignorance. If it is hidden it rests within itself, but when it is revealed it is recognized and it is stronger that ignorance and error. Truth wins and liberates us from confusion. The Word said; "You shall know the truth and the truth shall set

you free." Ignorance seeks to make us its slaves but knowledge is freedom. By recognizing the truth, we shall find the fruits of the truth within our hearts. If we join ourselves with the truth we shall be fulfilled.

123. Now, we have the visible (beings) things of creation and we say that visible things (beings) are the powerful and honorable, but the invisible things are the weak and unworthy of our attention. The nature of truth is different. In it, the visible things (beings) are weak and lowly, but the invisible are the powerful and honorable. The wisdom of the invisible God cannot be made known to us except that he takes visible form in ways we are accustomed to. Yet the mysteries of the truth are revealed, in types and symbols, but the bridle-chamber is hidden as it is with the holy of holies.

124. The veil of the Temple first concealed how God governed creation. Once the veil was torn and the things within (the Holy of Holies) were revealed, the house was to be forsaken, abandoned, and destroyed. Yet the entire Divinity (Godhead) was to depart, not to the holies of the holies, for it was not able to merge with the light nor unite with the complete fullness. It was to be under the wings of the cross, in its open arms. This is the ark which shall be salvation for us when the destruction of water has overwhelmed (overtaken) them.

125. Those in the priestly tribe shall be able to enter within the veil of the Temple along with the High Priest. This was symbolized by the fact that the veil was not torn at the top only, (but was torn from top to the bottom). If it was torn only at the top it would have been opened only for those who are on high (from the higher realm). If it were torn at the bottom only it would have been revealed only to those who are from below (the lower realm). But it was torn from the top to the bottom. Those who are from above made it available to us who are below them, so that we might enter into the secret of the truth. This strengthening of us is most wonderful. Because of this, we can enter in by means of symbols even though they are weak and worthless. They are humble and incomplete when compared to the perfect glory. It is the glory of glories and the power of powers. Through it the perfect is opened

to us and it contains the secrets of the truth. Moreover, the holies of holies have been revealed and opened, and the bridle-chamber has invited us in.

126. As long as evil hidden, and not completely purged from among of the children of the Holy Spirit, it remains a potential threat. The children can be enslaved by the adversary, but when the Perfect Light is seen, it will pour out the oil of anointing upon within it, and the slaves shall be set free and the slaves shall be bought back.

127. Every plant not sown by my heavenly Father shall be pulled up by the root. Those who were estranged shall be united and empty shall be filled.

128. Everyone who enters the bridal-chamber shall ignite (be born in) the Light. This is like a marriages which takes place at night. The fire is ablaze and is seen in the dark but goes out before morning. The mysteries (sacraments) of the marriage are consummated in the light of day, and that light never dies.

129. If someone becomes a child of the Bridal-Chamber, he shall receive the Light. If one does not receive it in this place, he will not be able to receive it in any other place. He who has received that Light shall not be seen, nor captured. No one in the world will be able to disturb him. When he leaves the world he has will have already received the truth in types and symbols. The world has become eternity, because for him the fullness is eternal. It is revealed only to this kind of person. Truth is not hidden in darkness or the night. Truth is hidden in a perfect day and a holy light.

Introduction to the Gospel of Judas

No discovery since the Dead Sea Scrolls has rocked the Christian world like that of the newly translated "Gospel of Judas." The story presented in the short but powerful text reveals a plan in which heavenly ends justified monstrous means. Betrayal became collaboration and murder resembled suicide as Jesus and Judas began a macabre dance into eternity.

Orthodox Christianity has its doctrine, its canon, and its political story, but these are quite different from those exposed in the Gospel of Judas.

As the orthodox political viewpoint would have it, Jesus' demise was sought by the Roman authorities as he gained a following and was declared "King" by the Jewish populace. The Jewish religious leaders were also planning his death, believing that Jesus was attempting to reform Judaism, and wrest their control over the people.

The Gospel of Judas calls into question this accepted view of the political intrigue leading up to Jesus' betrayal and death. Spokesman for the Maecenas Foundation, one of the companies in Basel, Switzerland working on the Judas project, Director Mario Jean Roberty, reports:
"We have just received the results of carbon dating: the text is older than we thought and dates back to a period between the beginning of the third and fourth centuries. We do not want to reveal the exceptional side of what we have, except that the Judas Iscariot text called into question some of the political principles of Christian doctrine."

Imagine Judas, the man all of Christendom has hated for two thousand years, now portrayed as the chosen one, the martyr, the scapegoat, and the man instructed and appointed by Jesus himself to orchestrate and carry out the greatest treachery of all time. But treachery ordered by the one betrayed is not treachery at all, but a loyal and devoted follower carrying out the wishes of his master.

What was Judas' reward for betraying Jesus? According to the Gospel of Judas it was special recognition by God and the blessing of Jesus, the savior of mankind. Strangely, there is evidence in our own Bible to substantiate this claim. Judas may have been promised a position of authority along with the other apostles.

The Gospel of Judas turns us on our heads and forces upon the reader a new and uncomfortable view. Did Judas have special knowledge and instruction from Jesus? Are we to thank him for the death of Jesus? Is lethal treachery appointed by the victim suicide or murder? Is this murderous quisling really a saint?

Who is this man, Judas? What do we know about him? Where did he come from? What did he want? What did he do?

These are just a few of the questions left to reverberate in the mind of the reader.

Theories of Judas abound. He is presented as greedy and selfish as well as sanctified spirit. Some say he was possessed, some say he was a saint, and some believe him to be Satan himself.

Was Judas the impetus of death, burial, and resurrection for Jesus, and thus the daemon who saved us? Will Judas be the Antichrist we will meet in the end of days or will he be ruling and judging the tribes of Israel?

Every story has two sides. Let us examine both sides, beginning with The Gospel of Judas, its history, its theology, and its text.

Understanding the Intent of
The Gospel of Judas

The Gospel of Judas can be understood on a deeper level if its background is explored first.

One may ask the proper questions regarding the text of "who, what, when, where, and why." The question of "who" wrote the Gospel of Judas we might never know. What the author was trying to say will be explored in depth. Science can and has narrowed down the "when" and "where."

Why mankind writes is axiomatic. We write to document, explain, express, or convince. In the end, those are the reasons. Time will tell if the author of Judas has succeeded.

In a time when Gnosticism was struggling for influence in Christendom, the Gospel of Judas was written to challenge the beliefs of the newly emerging church orthodoxy, to explain Gnostic theology, and to propagate the sect. To better understand the gospel, it must be read with these goals in mind.

For centuries the definition of Gnosticism has in itself been a point of confusion and contention within the religious community. This is due in part to the ever-broadening application of the term and the fact that various sects of Gnosticism existed as the theology evolved and began to merge into what became mainstream Christianity.

Even though Gnosticism continued to evolve, it is the theology in place at the time that the Gospel of Judas was written that should be considered and understood before attempting to render or read a translation. To do otherwise would make the translation cloudy and obtuse.

It becomes the duty of both translator and reader to understand the ideas being espoused and the terms conveying those ideas. A grasp of theology, cosmology, and relevant terms is necessary for a clear transmission of the meaning within the text in question.

With this in mind, we will briefly examine Gnostic theology, cosmology, and history. We will focus primarily on Gnostic sects existing in the first through fourth centuries A.D. since it is believed most Gnostic Gospels were written during that time. It was also during that time that reactions within the emerging Christian orthodoxy began to intensify and the Gospel of Judas was written.

The downfall of many books written on the topic of religion is the attempt to somehow remove history and people from the equation. History shapes religion because it shapes the perception and direction of religious leaders. Religion also develops and evolves in an attempt to make sense of the universe as it is seen and understood at the time. Thus, to truly grasp a religious concept it is important to know the history, people, and cosmology of the time. These areas are not separate but are continually interacting.

What is the Gospel of Judas?

What is the Gospel of Judas and why does it differ so greatly from the gospel stories of the Bible?

The Gospel of Judas is considered a Gnostic text. The Gnostics were a sect of Christianity and like any sect or religion, they were fighting to expand and continue under the persecution of the newly emerging orthodoxy of the day. The Gospel of Judas may have been written to help bolster and continue Gnosticism. This may explain its radical departure from the traditional Gospel story, as well as the reason for its creation.

Indeed, one way of looking at any religious book, canon or not, is as an attempt to explain one's beliefs, to persuade others toward those beliefs, and to interpret history and known storylines in the light of one's own theology and cosmology. This is done not only to add weight to one's own belief system but also simply because man sees events as having relevance to what he or she holds as truth.

As previously stated, the Gospel of Judas is, above all things, a Gnostic gospel since it revolves around a special knowledge or Gnosis given to Judas by Jesus. This knowledge represented that which Gnostics held as the universal truth. But what is Gnosticism?

The roots of the Gnosticism may pre-date Christianity. Similarities exist between Gnosticism and the wisdom and mystery cults found in Egypt and Greece. Gnosticism contains the basic terms and motifs of Plato's cosmology as well as the mystical qualities of Pythagorean cosmology and Buddhism. All of this was mixed with the Christianity of the second and third centuries to form the Gnosticism that is offered in the Gospel of Judas.

Plato was steeped in Greek mythology, and the Gnostic creation myth has elements owing to this. Both cosmology and mysticism within Gnosticism present an interpretation of Christ's existence and teachings, thus, Gnostics are considered to be a Christian sect.

Gnostic followers are urged to look within themselves for the truth and the Christ spirit hidden, asleep in their souls. The battle cry can be summed up in the words of the Gnostic Gospel of Thomas, verse 3:

Jesus said: If those who lead you say to you: Look, the Kingdom is in the sky, then the birds of the sky would enter before you. If they say to you: It is in the sea, then the fish of the sea would enter ahead of you. But the Kingdom of God exists within you and it exists outside of you. Those who come to know (recognize) themselves will find it, and when you come to know yourselves you will become known and you will realize that you are the children of the Living Father. Yet if you do not come to know yourselves then you will dwell in poverty and it will be you who are that poverty.

Paganism was a religious, traditional society in the Mediterranean leading up to the time of the Gnostics. Centuries after the conversion of Constantine, mystery cults worshipping various Egyptian and Greco-Roman gods continued. These cults taught that through their secret knowledge worshippers could control or escape the mortal realm. The Gnostic doctrine of inner knowledge and freedom may have part of its roots here. The concept of duality and inner guidance taught in Buddhism added to and enforced Gnostic beliefs, as we will see later.

The belief systems of Plato, Buddha, and paganism melded together, spread, and found a suitable home in the mystical side of the Christian faith as it sought to adapt and adopt certain Judeo-Christian beliefs and symbols.

Like modern Christianity, Gnosticism had various points of view that could be likened to Christian denominations of today. Complex and elaborate creation myths took root in Gnosticism, being derived from those of Plato. Later, the theology evolved and Gnosticism began to shed some of its more unorthodox myths, leaving the central theme of inner knowledge or "gnosis" as the path to enlightenment and salvation. In Gnosticism it is knowledge that saves one from hell fire. This knowledge and its place in man's salvation was their message to propagate. Exactly what the knowledge was and how is was expressed seemed to vary between Gnostic sects.

The existence of various sects of Gnosticism, differing creation stories, along with the lack of historical documentation, has left scholars in a quandary about exactly what Gnostics believed.

Although it appears that there were several sects of Gnosticism, we will attempt to discuss the more universal Gnostic beliefs along with the highlights of the major sects.

Gnostic cosmology, (which is the theory of how the universe is created, constructed, and sustained), is complex and very different from orthodox Christianity cosmology. In many ways Gnosticism may appear to be polytheistic or even pantheistic.

To understand some of the basic beliefs of Gnosticism, let us start with the common ground shared between Gnosticism and modern Christianity. Both believe the world is imperfect, corrupt, and brutal. The blame for this, according to mainstream Christianity, is placed squarely on the shoulders of man himself. With the fall of man (Adam), the world was forever changed to the undesirable and harmful place in which we live today. However, Gnostics reject this view as an incorrect interpretation of the creation myth.

According to Gnostics, the blame is not in us, but in our creator. The creator of this world was himself somewhat less than perfect and in fact, deeply flawed and cruel, making mankind the children of a lesser God. It is in the book, *The Apocryphon of John* that the Gnostic view of creation is presented to us in great detail.

Gnosticism also teaches that in the beginning a Supreme Being called The Father, The Divine All, The Origin, The Supreme God, or The Fullness, emanated the element of existence, both visible and invisible. His intent was not to create but, just as light emanates from a flame, so did creation shine forth from God. This manifested the primal element needed for creation. This was the creation of Barbelo, who is the Thought of God.

The Father's thought performed a deed and she was created from it. It is she who had appeared before him in the shining of his light. This is the first power which was before all of them and which was created from his mind. She is the Thought of the All and her light shines like his light. It is the perfect power which is the visage of the invisible. She is the pure, undefiled Spirit who is perfect. She is the first power, the glory of Barbelo, the perfect glory of the kingdom (kingdoms), the glory revealed. She glorified the pure, undefiled Spirit and it was she who praised him, because thanks to him she had come forth.

  The Apocryphon of John

  It could be said that Barbelo was the creative emanation and, like the Divine All, is both male and female. It was the "agreement" of Barbelo and the Divine All, representing the union of male and female, that created the Christ Spirit and all the Aeons. In some renderings the word "Aeon" is used to designate an ethereal realm or kingdom. In other versions "Aeon" indicates the ruler of the realm. The Aeons of this world are merely reflections of the Aeons of the eternal realm. The reflection is always inferior to real. This idea is of Aeons above and below, the real and reflected, the superior and inferior is brought up in the Gospel of Judas. Barbelo is mentioned by name in Judas. Another of these rulers was called Sophia or Wisdom. Her fall began a chain of events that led to the introduction of evil into the universe.

  Seeing the Divine flame of God, Sophia sought to know its origin. She sought to know the very nature of God. Sophia's passion ended in tragedy when she managed to capture a divine and creative spark, which she attempted to duplicate with her own creative force, without the union of a male counterpart. It was this act that produced the Archons, beings born outside the higher divine realm. In the development of the myth, explanations seem to point to the fact that Sophia carried the divine essence of creation from God within her but chose to attempt creation by using her own powers. It is unclear if this was in an attempt to understand the Supreme God and his power, or an impetuous act that caused evil to enter the cosmos in the form of her creations.

The realm containing the Fullness of the Godhead and Sophia is called the pleroma or Realm of Fullness. This is the Gnostic heaven. The lesser Gods created in Sophia's failed attempt were cast outside the pleroma and away from the presence of God. In essence, she threw away and discarded her flawed creations.

"She cast it away from her, outside the place where no one of the immortals might see it, for she had created it in ignorance. And she surrounded it with a glowing cloud, and she put a throne in the middle of the cloud so that no one could see it except the Holy Spirit who is called the mother of all that has life. And she called his name Yaldaboth."
Apocryphon of John

The beings Sophia created were imperfect and oblivious to the Supreme God. Her creations contained deities even less perfect than herself. They were called the Powers, the Rulers, or the Archons. Their leader was called the Demiurge, but his name was Yaldaboth, also spelled "Yaldabaoth." It was the flawed, imperfect, spiritually blind Demiurge, (Yaldaboth), who became the creator of the material world and all things in it. Gnostics considered Yaldaboth to be the same as Jehovah (Yahweh), who is the Jewish creator God. These beings, the Demiurge and the Archons, would later equate to Satan and his demons, or Jehovah and his angels, depending on which Gnostic sect is telling the story. Both are equally evil.

In one Gnostic creation story, the Archons created Adam but could not bring him to life. In other stories Adam was formed as a type of worm, unable to attain personhood. Thus, man began as an incomplete creation of a flawed, spiritually blind, and malevolent god. In this myth, the Archons were afraid that Adam might be more powerful than the Archons themselves. When they saw Adam was incapable of attaining the human state, their fears were put to rest, thus, they called that day the "Day of Rest."

Sophia saw Adam's horrid state and had compassion, because she knew she was the origin of the Archons and their evil. Sophia descended to help bring Adam out of his hopeless condition. It is this story that set the stage for the emergence of the sacred feminine force in Gnosticism that is not seen in orthodox Christianity. Sophia brought within herself the light and power of the Supreme God. Metaphorically, within the spiritual womb of Sophia was carried the life force of the Supreme God for Adam's salvation.

In the Gnostic text, *The Apocryphon of John*, Sophia is quoted:

"I entered into the midst of the cage which is the prison of the body. And I spoke saying: 'He who hears, let him awake from his deep sleep.' Then Adam wept and shed tears. After he wiped away his bitter tears he asked: 'Who calls my name, and from where has this hope arose in me even while I am in the chains of this prison?' And I (Sophia) answered: 'I am the one who carries the pure light; I am the thought of the undefiled spirit. Arise, remember, and follow your origin, which is I, and beware of the deep sleep.'"

Sophia would later equate to the Holy Spirit as it awakened the comatose soul.

As the myth evolved, Sophia, after animating Adam, became Eve in order to assist Adam in finding the truth. She offered it to him in the form of the fruit of the tree of knowledge. To Gnostics, this was an act of deliverance.

Other stories have Sophia becoming the serpent in order to offer Adam a way to attain the truth. In either case, the apple represented the hard sought truth, which was the knowledge of good and evil, and through that knowledge Adam could become a god. Later, the serpent would become a feminine symbol of wisdom, probably owing to the connection with Sophia. Eve, being Sophia in disguise, would become the mother and sacred feminine of us all. As Gnostic theology began to coalesce, Sophia would come to be considered a force or conduit of the Holy Spirit, in part due to the fact that the Holy Spirit was also considered a feminine and creative force from the Supreme God. The Gospel of Philip echoes this theology in verse six as follows:

In the days when we were Hebrews we were made orphans, having only our Mother. Yet when we believed in the Messiah (and became the ones of Christ), the Mother and Father both came to us. Gospel of Philip

As the emerging orthodox church became more and more oppressive to women, later even labeling them "occasions of sin," the Gnostics countered by raising women to equal status with men, saying Sophia was, in a sense, the handmaiden or wife of the Supreme God, making the soul of Adam her spiritual offspring. But, the placement and purpose of Sophia, Barbelo, Yaldaboth, and other deities vary somewhat from one type of Gnosticism to another.

In several Gnostic cosmologies the "living" world is under the control of entities called Aeons, of which Sophia is head. This means the Aeons influence or control the soul, life force, intelligence, thought, and mind. Control of the mechanical or inorganic world is given to the Archons. They rule the physical aspects of systems, regulation, limits, and order in the world. Both the ineptitude and cruelty of the Archons are reflected in the chaos and pain of the material realm.

The lesser God that created the world, Yaldaboth began his existence in a state that was both detached and remote from the Supreme God in aspects both spiritual and physical. Since Sophia had misused her creative force, which passed from the Supreme God (some say, through Barbelo) to her, Sophia's creation, the Demiurge, or Yaldaboth, contained only part of the original creative spark of the Supreme Being. He was created with an imperfect nature caused by his distance in lineage and in spirit from the Divine All or Supreme God. It is because of his imperfections and limited abilities the lesser God is also called the "Half-Maker."

The Creator God, the Demiurge, and his helpers, the Archons took the stuff of existence produced by the Supreme God and fashioned it into this material world.

Since the Demiurge (Yaldaboth) had no memory of how he came to be alive, he did not realize he was not the true creator. The Demiurge believed he somehow came to create the material world by himself. The Supreme God allowed the Demiurge and Archons to remain deceived.

The Creator God (the Demiurge) intended the material world to be perfect and eternal, but he did not have it in himself to accomplish the feat. What comes forth from a being cannot be greater than the highest part of him, can it? The world was created flawed and transitory and we are part of it. Can we escape? The Demiurge was imperfect and evil. So was the world he created. If it was the Demiurge who created man and man is called upon to escape the Demiurge and find union with the Supreme God, is this not demanding that man becomes greater than his creator? Spiritually this seems impossible, but as many children become greater than their parents, man is expected to become greater than his maker, the Demiurge. This starts with the one fact that the Demiurge denies the existence and supremacy of the Supreme God, but through gnosis man rises above this blindness.

Man was created with a dual nature as the product of the material world of the Demiurge with his imperfect essence, combined with the spark of God that emanated from the Supreme God through Sophia. A version of the creation story has Sophia instructing the Demiurge to breathe into Adam that spiritual power he had taken from Sophia during his creation. It was the spiritual power from Sophia that brought life to Adam.

It is this divine spark in man that calls to its source, the Supreme God, and which causes a "divine discontent," that

465

nagging feeling that keeps us questioning if this is all there is. This spark and the feeling it gives us keeps us searching for the truth.

The Creator God sought to keep man ignorant of his defective state by keeping him enslaved to the material world. By doing so, he continued to receive man's worship and servitude. He did not wish man to recognize or gain knowledge of the true Supreme God. Since he did not know or acknowledge the Supreme God, he views any attempt to worship anything else as spiritual treason.

The opposition of forces set forth in the spiritual battle over the continued enslavement of man and man's spiritual freedom set up the duality of good and evil in Gnostic theology. There was a glaring difference between the orthodox Christian viewpoint and the Gnostic viewpoint. According to Gnostics, the creator of the material world was an evil entity and the Supreme God, who was his source, was the good entity. Christians quote John 1:1 "In the beginning was the Word, and the Word was with God, and the Word was God."

According to Gnostics, only through the realization of man's true state or through death can he escape captivity in the material realm. This means the idea of salvation does not deal with original sin or blood payment. Instead, it focuses on the idea of awakening to the fullness of the truth.

According to Gnostic theology, neither Jesus nor his death can save anyone, but the truth that he came to proclaim can allow a person to save his or her own soul. It is the truth, or realization of the lie of the material world and its God, that sets one on a course of freedom. It cannot be overstated that in the eyes of many Gnostics, the death of Jesus was part of a plan implemented to show men in metaphorical terms the lack of worth and permanence of the physical world as opposed to the spiritual. The physical death of Jesus could not save us in the way orthodox Christianity came to understand it. His death was not a sacrifice to pay for our sins, but instead it was more of a lesson by example of the fight and plight of the temporal world which was at war with the eternal world.

To escape the earthly prison and find one's way back to the pleroma (heaven) and the Supreme God, is the soteriology (salvation doctrine) and eschatology (judgment, reward, and doctrine of heaven) of Gnosticism.

The idea that personal revelation leads to salvation may be what caused the mainline Christian church to declare Gnosticism a heresy. The church could better tolerate alternative theological views if the views did not undermine the authority of the church and its ability to control the people. Gnostic theology placed salvation in the hands of the individual through personal revelations and knowledge, excluding the need for the orthodox church and its clergy to grant salvation or absolution. This fact, along with the divergent interpretation of the creation story, which placed the creator God, Yaldaboth or Jehovah, as the enemy of mankind, was too much for the church to tolerate. Reaction was harsh. Gnosticism was declared to be a dangerous heresy.

Gnosticism may be considered polytheistic because it espoused many "levels" of Gods, beginning with an ultimate, unknowable, Supreme God and descending as he created Sophia, and Sophia created the Demiurge (Creator God); each becoming more inferior and limited.

There is a hint of pantheism in Gnostic theology due to the fact that creation occurs because of a deterioration of the Godhead and the dispersion of the creative essence, which eventually devolves into the creation of man.

In the end, there occurs a universal reconciliation as being after being realizes the existence of the Supreme God and renounces the material world and its inferior creator.

Combined with its Christian influences, the cosmology of the Gnostics may have borrowed from the Greek philosopher, Plato, as well as from Pythagoras and even Buddhism. There are disturbing parallels between the creation myth set forth by Plato and some of those recorded in Gnostic writings.

Pythagoras was born on the island of Samos between 580 and 570 B.C. His father is thought to have been a gem-engraver, and it is likely that the son would have been trained in that same craft.

Some scholars report that he was the first man to call himself and philosopher, or "lover of wisdom." Indeed, many of the accomplishments of such great men as Plato, Aristotle, and even Copernicus were based on the work of Pythagoras.

Pythagoras believed in Orphism, which is a theology that taught the soul and body are united but unequal. The soul is divine, immortal, and eternal. Its original state was one of freedom, before being imprisoned in a body. The body holds it imprisoned but death frees the soul, although only for a while. The soul is destined to be imprisoned again and again as the cycle of birth and death revolves until the end of time.

The soul journeys through its existence alternating from freedom to capture through reincarnations, as it learns lessons through many bodies of men and animals. The earliest Greek we can connect to Orphism is the sixth century thinker, Pherecydes. Pythagoras was his pupil and the individual most responsible for spreading Orphism throughout Greece.

Pythagoras further developed his beliefs while visiting Egypt, Greece, and Tyre in Lebanon. During his visit to Tyre he was initiated for the first time into the 'Ancient Mysteries' of the Phoenicians and studied for about 3 years in the temples of Tyre, Sidon, and Byblos.

It was after years of study that Pythagoras founded the famous Pythagorean School of philosophy, mathematics, and natural sciences. There he taught a simple lifestyle was best. Modesty, austerity, patience, and self-control were stressed. They consumed vegetarian, dried and condensed food, and unleavened bread. They did not cut their hair, beard, and nails.

The Pythagoreans believed that the universe could be understood in terms of whole numbers. This belief stemmed from observations in music, mathematics, and astronomy. He once commented, "Number is the ruler of form and the ideas and cause of gods and demons." We will see that symbolism of number plays a large part in The Gospel of Judas.

The Pythagoreans taught the doctrine of transmigration of souls, which states that after death, a man's soul enters the body of a newborn infant or animal and so lives another life. The soul wanders from the home of the blessed, being born into all kinds of corporeal forms as it travels from one path of life to another.

One of his students wrote, "I am also one of these, an exile and a wanderer from the Gods. Ere now, I too have been a boy, a girl, a bush, a bird, and a scaly fish in the sea." - Empedocles

Their cosmology conceived of a universe made of numbers. There were four major numbers and meanings making up all we see: one for a point, two for a line, three for a surface, and four for a solid. One was the basis, and generated the series of even and odd numbers, and with them the whole universe. Moral qualities were numbers: 4 (2x2 and 2+2) was justice, equal shares all round. A special number was 10, built up of 1+2+3+4, and containing the point, line, plane, and solid. This sequence was known as the *tetractys*. *Followers swore* an oath not to reveal the mysteries of the society 'by Him who reveals Himself to our minds in the Tetractys, which contains the source and roots of everlasting nature'.

Pythagoras had also discovered the mathematical basis of music, and the fact that the relation halves can express an octave. A string stopped at half its length will vibrate to give the sound of the octave above the full length. So music was involved in all life; and even the planets circling in their courses sounded the music of the spheres.

Plato lived from 427 to 347 B.C. He was the son of wealthy Athenians and a student of the philosopher, Socrates, and the mathematician, Pythagoras. Plato himself was the teacher of Aristotle.

In Plato's cosmology, the Demiurge was an artist who imposed form on materials that already existed. The raw materials were in a chaotic and random state. The physical world must have had visible form which was put together in a fashion much like a puzzle is constructed. This later gave way to a philosophy which stated that all things in existence could be broken down into a small subset of geometric shapes.

In the tradition of Greek mythology, Plato's cosmology began with a creation story. The story was narrated by the philosopher Timaeus of Locris, a fictional character of Plato's making. In his account, nature is initiated by a creator deity, called the "Demiurge," a name which may be the Geek word for "craftsman" or "artisan" or, according to how one divides the word, it could also be translated as "half-maker."

The Demiurge sought to create the cosmos modeled on his understanding of the supreme and original truth. In this way he created the visible universe based on invisible truths. He set in place rules of process such as birth, growth, change, death, and dissolution. This was Plato's "Realm of Becoming." It was his Genesis. Plato stated that the internal structure of the cosmos had innate intelligence and was therefore called the World Soul. The cosmic super-structure of the Demiurge was used as the framework on which to hang or fill in the details and parts of the universe. The Demiurge then appointed his underlings to fill in the details, which allowed the universe to remain in a working and balanced state. All phenomena of nature resulted from an interaction and interplay of the two forces of reason and necessity. Plato represented reason as constituting the World Soul. The material world was a necessity in which reason acted out its will in the physical realm. The duality between the will, mind, or reason of the World Soul and the material universe and its inherent flaws set in play the duality of Plato's world and is seen reflected in the beliefs of the Gnostics.

In Plato's world, the human soul was immortal, each soul was assigned to a star. Souls that were just or good were permitted to return to their stars upon their death to rest and dwell there in peace. Unjust souls were reincarnated to try again. Escape of the soul to the freedom of the stars and out of the cycle of reincarnation was best accomplished by following the reason and goodness of the World Soul and not the physical world, which was set in place only as a necessity to manifest the patterns of the World Soul.

Although in Plato's cosmology the Demiurge was not seen as evil, in Gnostic cosmology he was considered not only to be flawed and evil, but he was also the beginning of all evil in the material universe, having created it to reflect his own malice.

Following the path of Pythagoras and Plato's cosmology, some Gnostics left open the possibility of reincarnation if the person had not reached the truth before his death. This idea of the transmigration of the soul may have been linked to influences from the East.

In the year 13 A.D. Roman annals record the visit of an Indian king named Pandya or Porus. He came to see Caesar Augustus carrying a letter of introduction in Greek. He was accompanied by a monk who burned himself alive in the city of Athens to prove his faith in Buddhism. The event was described by Nicolaus of Damascus as, not surprisingly, causing a great stir among the people. It is thought that this was the first transmission of Buddhist teaching to the masses.

In the second century A.D., Clement of Alexandria wrote about Buddha: "Among the Indians are those philosophers also who follow the precepts of Boutta (Buddha), whom they honour as a god on account of his extraordinary sanctity." (Clement of Alexandria, "The Stromata, or Miscellanies" Book I, Chapter XV).

"Thus philosophy, a thing of the highest utility, flourished in antiquity among the barbarians, shedding its light over the nations. And afterwards it came to Greece." Clement of Alexandria, "The Stromata, or Miscellanies".

To clarify what "philosophy" was transmitted from India to Greece, we turn to the historians Hippolytus and Epiphanius who wrote of Scythianus, a man who had visited India around 50 A.D. They report; "He brought 'the doctrine of the Two Principles.'"

According to these writers, Scythianus' pupil Terebinthus called himself a Buddha. Some scholars suggest it was he that traveled to the area of Babylon and transmitted his knowledge to Mani, who later founded Manichaeism.

Adding to the possibility of Eastern influence, we have accounts of the Apostle Thomas' attempt to convert the people of Asia-Minor. If the Gnostic gospel bearing his name was truly written by Thomas, it was penned after his return from India, where he also encountered the Buddhist influences.

Following the transmission of the philosophy of "Two Principals," both Manichaeism and Gnosticism retained a dualistic viewpoint. The black-versus-white dualism of Gnosticism came to rest in the evil of the material world and its maker, versus the goodness of the freed soul and the Supreme God with whom it seeks union.

Oddly, the disdain for the material world and its Creator God drove Gnostic theology to far-flung extremes in attitude, beliefs, and actions. Gnostics idolized the serpent in the "Garden of Eden" story. After all, if your salvation hinges on secret knowledge, the offer of becoming gods through the knowledge of good and evil sounds wonderful. So powerful was the draw of this "knowledge myth" to the Gnostics that the serpent became linked to Sophia by some sects. This can still be seen today in our medical and veterinarian symbols of serpents on poles, conveying the ancient meanings of knowledge and wisdom.

Genesis 3 (King James Version)

1 Now the serpent was more subtil than any beast of the field which the LORD God had made. And he said unto the woman, Yea, hath God said, Ye shall not eat of every tree of the garden?

2 And the woman said unto the serpent, We may eat of the fruit of the trees of the garden:

3 But of the fruit of the tree which is in the midst of the garden, God hath said, Ye shall not eat of it, neither shall ye touch it, lest ye die.

4 And the serpent said unto the woman, Ye shall not surely die:

5 For God doth know that in the day ye eat thereof, then your eyes shall be opened, and ye shall be as Gods, knowing good and evil.

It is because of their vehement struggle against the Creator God and the search for some transcendent truth, that Gnostics held the people of Sodom in high regard. The people of Sodom sought to "corrupt" the messengers sent by their enemy, the Creator God. Anything done to thwart the Demiurge and his minions was considered valiant.

Genesis 19 (King James Version)

1 And there came two angels to Sodom at even; and Lot sat in the gate of Sodom: and Lot seeing them rose up to meet them; and he bowed himself with his face toward the ground;

2 And he said, Behold now, my lords, turn in, I pray you, into your servant's house, and tarry all night, and wash your feet, and ye shall rise up early, and go on your ways. And they said, Nay; but we will abide in the street all night.

3 And he pressed upon them greatly; and they turned in unto him, and entered into his house; and he made them a feast, and did bake unleavened bread, and they did eat.

4 But before they lay down, the men of the city, even the men of Sodom, compassed the house round, both old and young, all the people from every quarter:

5 And they called unto Lot, and said unto him, Where are the men which came in to thee this night? bring them out unto us, that we may know them.

6 And Lot went out at the door unto them, and shut the door after him,

7 And said, I pray you, brethren, do not so wickedly.

8 Behold now, I have two daughters which have not known man; let me, I pray you, bring them out unto you, and do ye to them as is good in your eyes: only unto these men do nothing;

for therefore came they under the shadow of my roof.

9 And they said, Stand back. And they said again, This one fellow came in to sojourn, and he will needs be a judge: now will we deal worse with thee, than with them. And they pressed sore upon the man, even Lot, and came near to break the door.

10 But the men put forth their hand, and pulled Lot into the house to them, and shut to the door.

To modern Christians, the idea of admiring the serpent, which we believe was Satan, may seem unthinkable. Supporting the idea of attacking and molesting the angels sent to Sodom to warn of the coming destruction seems appalling; but to Gnostics the real evil was the malevolent entity, the Creator God of this world. To destroy his messengers, as was the case in Sodom, would impede his mission. To obtain knowledge of good and evil, as was offered by the serpent in the garden, would set the captives free.

The battle and highest call of Gnosticism was to awaken the inner knowledge of the true God. This is the God who is above and beyond that lower and evil god that created the material world. The material world was designed to prevent the awakening by entrapping, confusing, and distracting the spirit of man. The aim of Gnosticism was the spiritual awakening and freedom of man.

Gnostics, in the age of the early church, would preach to converts (novices) about this awakening, saying the novice must awaken the God within himself and see the trap that was the material world. Salvation came from the recognition or knowledge contained in this spiritual awakening. Moreover, it was the knowledge that the "illusion" of the material world existed and should be transcended that was the driving force and saving gnosis (knowledge) that Gnosticism was built upon.

Not all people were ready or willing to accept the Gnosis. Many were bound to the material world and satisfied to be only as and where they were. These have mistaken the Creator God for the Supreme God and do not know there is anything beyond the Creator God or the material existence. These people knew only the lower or earthly wisdom and not the higher wisdom above the Creator God. They were referred to as "dead."

Gnostic sects split primarily into two categories. Both branches held that those who were truly enlightened could no longer be influenced by the material world. Both divisions of Gnosticism believed that their spiritual journey could not be impeded by the material realm since the two were not only separate but in opposition. Such an attitude influenced some Gnostics toward Stoicism, choosing to abstain from the world, and others toward Epicureanism, choosing to indulge and satiate any and all appetites, since they believed the material world could not influence the spiritual world.

Major schools fell into two categories; those who rejected the material world of the Creator God, and those who rejected the laws of the Creator God. For those who rejected the world the Creator God had spawned, overcoming the material world was accomplished by partaking of as little of the world and its pleasures as possible. These followers lived very stark and ascetic lives, abstaining from meat, sex, marriage, and all things that would entice them to remain (or even wish to remain) in the material realm.

Other schools believed it was their duty to simply defy the Creator God and all laws that he had proclaimed. Since the Creator God had been identified as Jehovah, God of the Jews, these followers set about to break every law held dear by Christians and Jews.

As human nature is predisposed to do, many Gnostics took up the more wanton practices, believing that nothing done in their earthly bodies would affect their spiritual lives. Whether it was excesses in sex, alcohol, food, or any other assorted debaucheries, the Gnostics were safe within their faith, believing nothing spiritually bad could come of their earthly adventures.

Early Church leaders mention the actions of the Gnostics. One infamous Gnostic school is actually mentioned in the Bible, as we will read later.

The world was out of balance, inferior, and corrupt. The spirit was perfect and intact. It was up to the Gnostics to tell the story, explain the error, and awaken the world to the light of truth. The Supreme God had provided a vehicle to help in their effort. He had created a teacher of light and truth.

Since the time of Sophia's mistaken creation of the Archons, there was an imbalance in the cosmos. The Supreme God began to re-establish the balance by producing Christ to teach and save man. That left only Sophia, now in a fallen and bound state, along with the Demiurge, and the Archons to upset the cosmic equation. In this theology one might loosely equate the Supreme God to the New Testament Christian God, the Demiurge to Satan, the Archons to demons, the pleroma to heaven, and Sophia to the creative or regenerative force of the Holy Spirit.

This theory holds up well except for one huge problem. If the Jews believed that Jehovah created all things, and the Gnostic believed that the Demiurge created all things, then to the Gnostic mind, the Demiurge must be Old Testament god, Jehovah, and that made Jehovah their enemy. In this twist, the Old Testament God was the evil creator. The New Testament God was the true Supreme God, and Satan was a good and wise deity or savior, since he had offered a way of escape from the creator god when Satan offered the fruit of the tree of knowledge (or the Gnosis) to Eve.

For those who sought that which was beyond the material world and its flawed creator, the Supreme God sent Messengers of Light to awaken the divine spark of the Supreme God within us. This part of us will call to the True God as deep calls to deep. The greatest and most perfect Messenger of Light was the Christ. He is also referred to as The Good, Christ, Messiah, and The Word. He came to reveal the Divine Light to mankind in the form of knowledge.

According to the Gnostics, Christ came to show us our own

divine spark and to awaken us to the illusion of the material world and its flawed maker. He came to show us the way back to the divine Fullness (The Supreme God). The path to enlightenment was the knowledge sleeping within each of us. Christ came to show us the Christ spirit living in each of us. Individual ignorance or the refusal to awaken our internal divine spark was the only original sin. Christ was the only Word spoken by God that could awaken us. Christ was also the embodiment of the Word itself. He was part of the original transmission from the Supreme God that took form on the earth to awaken the soul of man so that man might search beyond the material world.

One Gnostic view of the Incarnation was "docetic," which is an early heretical position that Jesus was never actually present in the flesh, but only appeared to be human. He was a spiritual being and his human appearance was only an illusion. Of course, the title of "heretical" can only be decided by the controlling authority of the time. In this case it was the church that was about to emerge under the rule of the Emperor Constantine.

Most Gnostics held that the Christ spirit indwelt the earthly man, Jesus, at the time of his baptism by John, at which time Jesus received the name, and thus the power, of the Lord or Supreme God.

The Christ spirit departed from Jesus' body before his death. These two viewpoints remove the idea of God sacrificing himself as an atonement for the sins of man. The idea of atonement was not necessary in Gnostic theology since it was knowledge and not sacrifice that set one free.

Since there was a distinction in Gnosticism between the man Jesus and the Light of Christ that came to reside within him, it is not contrary to Gnostic beliefs that Mary Magdalene could have been the consort and wife of Jesus. Neither would it have been blasphemous for them to have had children.

Various sects of Gnosticism stressed certain elements of their basic theology. Each had its head teachers and its special flavor of beliefs. One of the oldest types was the Syrian Gnosticism. It existed around 120 A.D. In contrast to other sects, the Syrian lacked much of the embellished mythology of Aeons, Archons, and angels.

The fight between the Supreme God and the Creator God was not eternal, though there was strong opposition to Jehovah, the Creator God. He was considered to have been the last of the seven angels who created this world out of divine material which emanated from the Supreme God. The Demiurge attempted to create man, but only created a miserable worm which the Supreme God had to save by giving it the spark of divine life. Thus man was born.

According to this sect, Jehovah, the Creator God, must not be worshiped. The Supreme God calls man to his service and presence through Christ his Son. They pursued only the unknowable Supreme God and sought to obey the Supreme Deity by abstaining from eating meat and from marriage and sex, and by leading ascetic lives. The symbol of Christ was the serpent, who attempted to free Adam and Eve from their ignorance and entrapment to the Creator God.

Another Gnostic school was the Hellenistic or Alexandrian School. These systems absorbed the philosophy and concepts of the Greeks, and the Semitic nomenclature was replaced by Greek names. The cosmology and myth had grown out of proportion and appear to our eyes to be unwieldy. Yet, this school produced two great thinkers, Basilides and Valentinus. Though born at Antioch, in Syria, Basilides founded his school in Alexandria around the year A.D. 130, where it survived for several centuries.

Valentinus first taught at Alexandria and then in Rome. He established the largest Gnostic movement around A.D. 160. This movement was founded on an elaborate mythology and a system of sexual duality of male and female interplay, both in its deities and its savior.

Tertullian wrote that between 135 A.D. and 160 A.D. Valentinus, a prominent Gnostic, had great influence in the Christian church. Valentinus ascended in church hierarchy and became a candidate for the office of bishop of Rome, the office that quickly evolved into that of Pope. He lost the election by a narrow margin. Even though Valentinus was outspoken about his Gnostic slant on Christianity, he was a respected member of the Christian community until his death and was probably a practicing bishop in a church of lesser status than the one in Rome.

The main platform of Gnosticism was the ability to transcend the material world through the possession of privileged and directly imparted knowledge. Following this doctrine, Valentinus claimed to have been instructed by a direct disciple of one of Jesus' apostles, a man by the name of Theodas.

Valentinus is considered by many to be the father of modern Gnosticism. His vision of the faith is summarized by G.R.S. Mead in the book "Fragments of a Faith Forgotten."

"The Gnosis in his hands is trying to embrace everything, even the most dogmatic formulation of the traditions of the Rabbi. The great popular movement and its incomprehensibilities were recognized by Valentinus as an integral part of the mighty outpouring; he laboured to weave all together, external and internal, into one piece, devoted his life to the task, and doubtless only at his death perceived that for that age he was attempting the impossible. None but the very few could ever appreciate the ideal of the man, much less understand it."

Fragments of a Faith Forgotten

The main stream of Gnosticism presented in the Gospel of Judas seems to be Sethian Gnosticism. Marvin Meyer, a respected scholar, describes Gospel of Judas as a Sethian Gnostic because it mentions the incorruptible generation of Seth and it shares common ideas with other Sethian Gnostic writings found in the Nag Hammadi. The generation of Seth in Gnostic writings signified those born of the new generation of humanity after the tragic death of Abel and the banishment of Cain.

For Sethian Gnostics, Jesus was a teacher, "not a savior who dies for the sins of the world. For Gnostics, the fundamental problem in human life is not sin, but ignorance, and the best way to address this problem is not through faith, but through knowledge" (Meyer, Introduction to the Gospel of Judas [Washington, DC: National Geographic Society, 2006].

In the time period of the Gospel of Judas at about 180 A.D., Sethian Gnosticism had evolved by absorbing several basic doctrines: Hellenistic-Jewish mythology of Sophia, the divine wisdom; the midrashic interpretation of Genesis 1-6; a particular doctrine of baptism; the developing Christology of the early church; a religiously oriented view of Pythagorean metaphysics; and the teaching and philosophy of Plato including his theology and mythos regarding creation, Sophia, Barbelo, and the Creator God, Yalabaoth.

Sethian doctrines have baptism as a spiritualized ritual. In Sethian baptismal water was understood to be "Living Water" identified with light or enlightenment and therefore salvation.

The history claimed by Sethian Gnosticism is derived from a peculiar exegesis of Genesis from a Jewish stand point. It should be stressed that the Sethian origins are not Christian but it absorbed Christian beliefs later. In their beginning they were looking for a messiah just as the Jews were, however, they believed he would be Seth. This is because they believed the imparted divine knowledge came down from God to Adam and was then transmitted to Seth.

Sethians adopted the rite of baptism often referred to as the Five-Seals. The ritual symbolized the removal of the person from the material world of the flesh and the ascension into the realm of light through the invocation of certain divine beings.

Sethianism began to change by its involvement in Christianity. This took place over time.

Sethianism was a non-Christian baptismal sect of the first centuries B.C.E. and C.E. which believed in enlightenment through knowledge by the divine wisdom which was that same wisdom that was revealed to Adam and Seth. It may be assumed that this was an incomplete passing of knowledge because the

480

culmination was expected in a final visitation of Seth marked by his conferral of a saving baptism.

Baptism represented the descent of Seth as the living word or "Logos", which was bestowed through a holy baptism in the Living Water.

Barbelo, the Father-Mother god, who was a higher form of the Sophia figure, initiates those who were baptized in or by the Logos or Seth.

Barbelo communicated to those who love her by Voice or Word (Logos). This figure of Barbelo was the fountain or spring from which comes the Word like flowing water.

Protennoia is the Word or Logos, which was produced from Thought. The Word descends and enlightened her children.

The last of these entities was Eleleth who produces Sophia in the same way as fire produces light. The re-emission of this light through Sophia produced the demon Yaldaboth who stole the power of creation imparted to Sophia and produced the lower aeons and man.

The Archons thought that Protennoia (Logos) was "their Christ," while actually she is the "Father" of everyone. Protennoia identified herself as the beloved of the Archons, and disguised herself as the child of the Great Creator.

Sethianism gradually Christianized in the latter first century as it began to identify Seth and Adam in terms of the pre-existent Christ.

This means that according to Sethian beliefs the true Son of Man is Adamas (Adam), the Son of the supreme deity who is the only human form in which the deity revealed himself. Seth, the son of Adam or Adamas, is the mediator between man and God's son, Adam. Seth was the Christ image or mediator.

Gnostic theology seemed to vacillate from polytheism to pantheism to dualism to monotheism, depending on the teacher and how he viewed and stressed certain areas of their creation myths.

Marcion, a Gnostic teacher, espoused differences between the

God of the New Testament and the God of the Old Testament, claiming they were two separate entities. According to Marcion, the New Testament God was a good true God while the Old Testament God was an evil angel. Although this may be a heresy, it pulled his school back into monotheism. The church, however, disowned him.

Syneros and Prepon, disciples of Marcion, postulated three different entities, carrying their teachings from monotheism into polytheism in one stroke. In their system the opponent of the good God was not the God of the Jews, but Eternal Matter, which was the source of all evil. Matter, in this system became a principal creative force. Although it was created imperfect, it could also create, having the innate intelligence of the "world soul."

Of all the Gnostic schools or sects the most famous is the Antinomian School. Believing that the Creator God, Jehovah, was evil, they set out to disrupt all things connected to the Jewish God, including his laws. It was considered their duty to break any law of morality, diet, or conduct given by the Jewish God, who they considered the evil Creator God. The leader of the sect was called Nicolaites. The sect existed in Apostolic times and is mentioned in the Bible.

Revelation 2 (King James Version)
5 Remember therefore from whence thou art fallen, and repent, and do the first works; or else I will come unto thee quickly, and will remove thy candlestick out of his place, except thou repent.
6 But this thou hast, that thou hatest the deeds of the Nicolaitanes, which I also hate.

Revelation 2 (King James Version)
14 But I have a few things against thee, because thou hast there them that hold the doctrine of Balaam, who taught Balac to cast a stumbling block before the children of Israel, to eat things sacrificed unto idols, and to commit fornication.
15 So hast thou also them that hold the doctrine of the

Nicolaitanes, which thing I hate.

16 Repent; or else I will come unto thee quickly, and will fight against them with the sword of my mouth.

One of the leaders of the Nocolaitanes, according to Origen, was Carpocrates, whom Tertullian called a magician and a fornicator.

Carpocretes taught that one could only escape the cosmic powers by discharging one's obligations to them and disregarding their laws. The Christian church fathers, St. Justin, Irenaeus, and Eusebius wrote that the reputation of these men (the Nicolaitanes), brought infamy upon the whole race of Christians.

Although Gnostic sects varied, they had certain points in common. These commonalities included salvation through special knowledge, and the fact that the world was corrupt, since it was created by an evil God.

According to Gnostic theology, nothing can come from the material world that is not flawed. Because of this, Gnostics did not believe that Christ could have been a corporeal being. Thus, there must be some separation or distinction between Jesus, as a man, and Christ, as a spiritual being born from the Supreme, unrevealed, and eternal God.

To closer examine this theology, we turn to Valentinus, the driving force of early Gnosticism, for an explanation. Valentinus divided Jesus Christ into two very distinct parts; Jesus, the man, and Christ, the anointed spiritual messenger of God. These two forces met in the moment of Baptism when the Spirit of God came to rest on Jesus and the Christ power entered his body.

Here Gnosticism runs aground on its own theology, for if the spiritual cannot mingle with the material then how can the Christ spirit inhabit a body? The result of the dichotomy was a schism within Gnosticism. Some held to the belief that the specter of Jesus was simply an illusion produced by Christ himself to enable him to do his work on earth. It was not real, not matter, not corporeal, and did not actually exist as a physical body would. Others came to believe that Jesus must have been a specially prepared vessel and was the perfect human body formed by the very essence of the plumora (heaven). It was this path of thought that allowed Jesus to continue as human, lover, and father.

Jesus, the man, became a vessel containing the Light of God, called Christ. In the Gnostic view we all could and should become Christs carrying the Truth and Light of God. We are all potential vehicles of the same Spirit that Jesus held within him when he was awakened to the Truth.

The suffering and death of Jesus then took on much less importance in the Gnostic view, as Jesus was simply part of the corrupt world and was suffering the indignities of this world as any man would.

The Gnostic texts seem to divide man into parts, although at times the divisions are somewhat unclear. The divisions alluded to may include the soul, which is the will of man; the spirit, which is depicted as wind or air (pneuma) and contains the holy spark that is the spirit of God in man; and the material human form, the body. The mind of man sits as a mediator between the soul, or will, and the spirit, which is connected to God.

Without the light of the truth, the spirit is held captive by the Demiurge, which enslaves man. This entrapment is called "sickness." It is this sickness that the Light came to heal and then to set us free. The third part of man, his material form, was considered a weight, an anchor, and a hindrance, keeping man attached to the corrupted earthly realm. The Demiurge proclaimed himself to be God under three separate titles:

"Now the archon (ruler) who is weak has three names. The first name is Yaltabaoth, the second is Saklas ("fool"), and the third is Samael. And he is impious in his arrogance which is in him. For he said, 'I am God and there is no other God beside me,' for he is ignorant of his strength, the place from which he had come." Apocryphon of John

As we read the text, we must realize that Gnosticism

conflicted with traditional Christianity. Overall, theology can rise and fall upon small words and terms. If Jesus was not God, his death and thus his atonement meant nothing. His suffering meant nothing. Even the resurrection meant nothing, if one's view of Jesus was that he was not human to begin with, as was true with some Gnostics.

For the Gnostics, resurrection of the dead was unthinkable since flesh as well as all matter are destined to perish. According to Gnostic theology, there was no resurrection of the flesh, but only of the soul. How the soul would be resurrected was explained differently by various Gnostic groups, but all denied the resurrection of the body. To the enlightened Gnostic the actual person was the spirit who used the body as an instrument to survive in the material world but did not identify with it.

29. Jesus said: If the flesh came into being because of spirit, it is a marvel, but if spirit came into being because of the body, it would be a marvel of marvels. I marvel indeed at how great wealth has taken up residence in this poverty.

   Gospel of Thomas

Owing to the Gnostic belief of such a separation of spirit and body, it was thought that the Christ spirit within the body of Jesus departed the body before the crucifixion. Others said the body was an illusion and the crucifixion was a sham perpetrated by an eternal spirit on the men that sought to kill it. Lastly, some suggested that Jesus deceived the soldiers into thinking he was dead. The resurrection under this circumstance became a lie, which allowed Jesus to escape and live on in anonymity, hiding, living as a married man, and raising a family until his natural death.

Think of the implications to the orthodox Christian world if the spirit of God departed from Jesus as it fled and laughed as the body was crucified. This is the implication of the Gnostic interpretation of the death of Jesus when he cries out, "My power, my power, why have you left me?" as the Christ spirit left his body before his death. What are the ramifications to the modern Christian if the Creator God, the Demiurge, is more evil than his creation? Can a creation rise above its creator? Is it possible for man to find the spark within himself that calls to the Supreme God and free himself of his evil creator?

Although, in time, the creation myth and other Gnostic differences began to be swept under the rug, it was the division between Jesus and the Christ spirit that put them at odds with the emerging orthodox church. At the establishment of the doctrine of the trinity, the mainline church firmly set a divide between themselves and the Gnostics.

To this day there is a battle raging in the Christian world as believers and seekers attempt to reconcile today's Christianity to the sect of the early Christian church called, "Gnosticism."

The History of the Gospel of Judas

The newly discovered Gospel of Judas is very controversial for several reasons. Theologically, it is divisive due to its Gnostic theology. The main controversy in the text revolves around the theory that Jesus asked Judas to betray Him in order to fulfill His destiny and the scriptures. If this is true it would make Judas a saint and not the sinner and traitor as believed by the mainline church.

The text is also interesting simply because it is written in Coptic. Documents from the time period and region where the Coptic language was native are a rare find.

The word Coptic is an Arabic corruption of the Greek word Aigyptos, which in turn comes from the word Hikaptah, one of the names of the city of Memphis, the first capital of ancient Egypt.

There has never been a Coptic state or government per se, however, the word has been used to generally define a culture and language present in the area of Egypt within a particular timeframe.

The known history of the Copts starts with King Mina the first King, who united the northern and southern kingdoms of Egypt circa 3050 B.C. The ancient Egyptian civilization under the rule of the Pharaohs lasted over 3000 years. Saint Mina (named after the king) is one of the major Coptic saints. He was martyred in 309 A.D.

The culture has come to be recognized as one containing distinctive language, art, architecture, and even certain religious systems. There is even a very distinctive Coptic Christian church system with its own canon, which contains several more books than those of the Protestant or Catholic Bibles.

The religious controversy of the Gospel of Judas is compelling, if for no other reason than that of its differing view, which forces us to re-examine the way we read and understand the place, path, and actions of Judas and his act of betrayal.

The Gospels and the Book of Acts tell the story of Judas' betrayal of Jesus and the end to which Judas came. The canonical books refer to Judas as a traitor, betrayer, and as one influenced by the devil. However, the Gospel of Judas turns this idea on its head by claiming the Judas was requested, if not required, to plan and carry out the treachery that would be the impetus for the crucifixion. The plan was to surrender Jesus to the authorities so that scripture and prophecy could be fulfilled, and Jesus was the person devising the plan.

Most scholars agree that the Gospels of Matthew, Mark, Luke, and John were written between the date of Jesus' death and about 90 A.D. The Gospel of Judas was written originally in Greek around A.D. 180 at the earliest. If this is true, Judas could not have been the author. For Judas to have penned this work he would have been about 120 years of age at the time of its writing. Discounting this possibility, the original author is unknown.

Dates of the original texts are based on words and usage common to certain periods of time. This is comparable to how slang and catch phrases pass in and out of vogue in our own language.

Another way of narrowing down the date of the original text is to look for references to it in other writings. This would set the date marking the latest the text could have been written.

Tixeront, translated by Raemers, states: "Besides these Gospels, we know that there once existed a Gospel of Bartholomew, a Gospel of Thaddeus, mentioned in the decree of Pope Gelasius, and a Gospel of Judas Iscariot in use among the Cainites and spoken of by St. Irenaeus."

In Roberts-Donaldson's translation from Irenaeus the church father states, "Others again declare that Cain derived his being from the Power above, and acknowledge that Esau, Korah, the Sodomites, and all such persons, are related to themselves. On this account, they add, they have been assailed by the Creator, yet no one of them has suffered injury. For Sophia was in the habit of carrying off that which belonged to her from them to herself. They declare that Judas the traitor was thoroughly acquainted with these things, and that he alone, knowing the truth as no others did, accomplished the mystery of the betrayal; by him all things, both earthly and heavenly, were thus thrown into confusion. They produce a fictitious history of this kind, which they style the Gospel of Judas."

Irenaeus went on to say that the writings came from what he called a "Cainite" Gnostic sect that jousted with orthodox Christianity. He also accused the Cainites of lauding the biblical murderer Cain, the Sodomites and Judas, whom they regarded as the keeper of secret mysteries.

Knowing the dates of the writings of Irenaeus further clarifies the date to be around or before 180 A.D. Of course, this affects the Gospel of Judas only if we conclude that the text Irenaeus spoke of is the same text we have today. Sadly, there is no way to know with any certainty, but we do have a few clues.

Cain is not mentioned in the version of the Gospel of Judas we have today. Furthermore, the evolution of cosmology tends to be from the simple to the complex and this trend is shown in the current version since Yaldabaoth, who is also called "Nebro" the "rebel", is presented as the creator of Saklas and it is Saklas who is depicted later in the Gospel of Judas as the creator mankind and the physical world. However, in other Gnostic writings, Yaldabaoth is the "demiurge" or fashioner of the world, and is clearly identified as the same deity as Saklas. This means that in the Gospel of Judas there has been a split between Yaldaboth and Saklas, leading to a more complex cosmology. This indicates that the Gospel of Judas we have today was written later than that of which Irenaeus speaks, since in his time these deities were one and the same.

Now the archon who is weak has three names. The first name is Yaltabaoth, the second is Saklas ("fool"), and the third is Samael. And he is impious in his arrogance which is in him. For he said, 'I am God and there is no other God beside me,' for he is ignorant of his strength, the place from which he had come."

Apocryphon of John, ca. 200 AD.

As for the dating of the copy found in Egypt, the formation of certain letters also change with time and the style of the lettering within the texts places the copies within a certain period. The 26-page Judas text is a copy in Coptic of the original Gospel of Judas, which was written in Greek the century before.

Radioactive-carbon-dating tests as well as experts in ancient languages have established that the copy was written between 220 and 340 A.D.

The discovered Gospel was written on papyrus, probably at a Gnostic monastery in Egypt. Although other copies may have been made they were probably lost in St. Athanasius's fourth-century campaign to destroy all heretical texts. All texts not accepted by the newly established church were to be burned. Heresy was not to be tolerated, and Gnosticism was considered at the top of the list. Not only was Gnosticism different from the orthodox theology, it condoned a personal search for God through knowledge and that was something outside the control of the church. To maintain its control, the new church had to crush these beliefs.

In order to protect the text from Athanasius's soldiers it is thought a Gnostic monk or scribe buried copies of certain Gnostic texts in an area of tombs in Egypt. These were not discovered until the late 1970s. The Gospel was one of three texts found that were bound together in a single codex.

The gospel was unearthed in 1978 by a farmer. He found a small container like a tomb box in a cave near El Minya, Egypt. In the small, carved, and sealed box was part of a codex, or collection of devotional texts.

The farmer sold the codex to an antiquities dealer in Cairo. The deal was kept secret but was reported to have taken place in 1983. The antiquities dealer was unaware of the content of the codex when he offered the gospel for sale to the Coptic studies scholar, Stephen Emmel, of Germany's University of Munster and another scholar. The meeting took place in a Geneva, Switzerland hotel room.

It was Emmel who examined the codex and first suspected the papyrus sheets discussed Judas. Although the text more than intrigued Emmel, the asking price was so high at $3 million dollars U.S. that there was no way to afford the purchase.

The seller was offered a price that was an order of magnitude lower than the asking price. This, the seller took as an insult and the deal stalled.

Due to the frustration brought about by not having his greed satisfied, the dealer stored the codex in a safe in a Hicksville, N.Y. bank for 16 years. There, away from the dry desert air, in the box with higher humidity, it deteriorated and crumbled until Zurich-based antiquities dealer Frieda Nussberger-Tchacos purchased it in 2000 for a sum much less than the original asking price. The codex was then acquired by the Maecenas Foundation for Ancient Art in Switzerland in 2001.

The foundation invited National Geographic to help with the restoration in 2004.

Over the next 5 years thousands of pieces of papyrus were placed back together like a jigsaw puzzle. Thousands of pieces, some so small they contained only a letter or two were restored to their position in the text using tweezers and computer imaging.

Once completed, a team of scholars translated the document into English, as best they could, considering the condition of the document and the number of pieces missing. The restored original is now housed in Cairo's Coptic Museum. A rendering of the text in Coptic can be seen at:

http://www.nationalgeographic.com/lostgospel/_pdf/CopticGos pelOfJudas.pdf

Because of the extreme age and ill-treatment of the text much of it is illegible. There are gaps and holes in the codex. Entire lines are missing. Some parts of the translation were done on a "best-guess" basis. If there were letters missing from common words of phrases the translators could assume and replace letters and even words or phrases. When the gaps became larger or the meaning of the phrase was uncertain the translators simple noted the absence of data.

In this rendering we have attempted two bold moves. We wished to present a more engaging interpretation for the public, which necessarily demanded notes and explanations available at the point the ideas were encountered. We also wished to attempt to fill in some of the gaps in the text if possible.

As a matter of a disclaimer, it should be understood that the original translators did a remarkable job with the thousands of slivers and chips of papyrus that made up the codex. Once reconstructed, it became obvious that much of the text was simply missing, having disintegrated into dust and powder, never to be read again.

The text presented here takes the work done by many others and places the Gospel of Judas into a more readable language and format along with in-line commentary. It then expands the text, filling in the gaps as best it could be done, based on an understanding of the Gnostic theology, historical information, textual references, and logical flow of conversation.

All words or phases in parentheses indicate those additions made to the text, either as a matter of filling in the missing letters, words, or lines; or as a matter of clarification of ambiguous wording in the original text or its translation. When a word could be translated in more than one way, a slash "/" was used to note the various choices.

Commentary are marked clearly as "Notes" and are place in italic font within the text.

The reader should keep the probable function of the text in mind. The title gives some hint. It is not "The Gospel According to Judas", but it is instead, "The Gospel of Judas." This indicates that the writer wanted to exalt Judas, his position and contribution according to the theology being espoused and propagated by the text.

Knowing these things, the words and lines missing in the text can be a matter of educated and reasonable assumptions. They are, however, assumptions nonetheless.

The Gospel of Judas

This is the proclamation, which was secretly revealed to Judas Iscariot by Jesus during that eight-day period that included (that was) the three days before he (Jesus) celebrated Passover (one translator has "celebrated his passion / suffering).

Note: The proclamation is not the logos, word or Christ for the orthodox church. The word here is a proclamation of judgment as in a court verdict.

1. Jesus appeared on earth to perform miracles and wondrous acts in order to save humanity.
Because some conducted themselves in a righteous way and others continued in their sins, he decided to call the twelve disciples.

2. He began to talk to them about the mysteries that lay beyond this world and what would happen at this world's end (at the end). He often changed his appearance and was not seen as himself but looked like a child (some translators have apparition or spirit) when he was with his disciples.

3. He came upon his disciples in Judea once when they were sitting together piously (training their piety – training in godliness). As he got closer to the disciples he saw they were sitting together, giving thanks and saying a prayer over the bread (Eucharist / thanksgiving). He laughed.

4. The disciples asked Him, "Rabbi, why are you laughing at our prayer of thanks? Have we not acted appropriately?"
He said, "I am not laughing at you. It is just that you are not doing this because you want to. You are doing this because your god (has to be / will be) praised."

5. They said, "Rabbi, you are the (earthly / only) son of our god."
Jesus answered, "How do you know me? (Do you think you know me?) I say to you truly, no one among you in this generation (in this race) will understand me."

6. His disciples heard this and became enraged and began mumbling profanities and mocking him in their hearts. When Jesus saw their inability (to understand what he said to them (their stupidity), he said,) "Why did you get so upset that you became angry? Your god, who is inside of you, (and your own lack of understanding guides you and) have instigated this anger in your (mind / soul). (I challenge) any man among you to show me who is (understanding enough) to bring out the perfect man and stand and face me."

7. They all said, "We are strong enough."
But in their (true being) spirits none dared to stand in front of him except for Judas Iscariot. Judas was able to stand in front of him, but even he could not look Jesus in the eyes, and he turned his face away.

Note: It is uncertain as to the reason Judas did not look at Jesus. It was a custom of respect not to look a superior in the eyes. Either Judas was unable to look at Jesus or was constrained by the position of Jesus as his Rabbi.

8. Judas said to Him, "I know who you are and where you came from. You are from the everlasting (eternal) aeon (realm or kingdom) of Barbelo (Barbelo's everlasting kingdom). I am not worthy to speak the name of the one who sent you."

9. Jesus knew that Judas was capable of understanding (showing forth / thinking about) something that was glorious, so Jesus said to him, "Walk away (step a distance away) from the others and I will tell you about the mysteries of God (the reign of God / kingdom of God).

10. It is possible for you to get there, but the path will cause you great grief because you will be replaced so that the twelve may be complete with their god again."
Judas asked him, "When will you tell me how the great day of light will dawn for this generation (race)? When will you explain these things?"
But as he asked these things, Jesus left him.

11. At the dawn of the next day after this happened, Jesus appeared to his disciples.

They asked Him, "Rabbi, where did you go and what did you do when you left us?"

Jesus said to them, "I went to another generation (race) that is a greater and holier generation (race)."

12. His disciples asked him, "Lord, what is this great race that is superior to us and holier than us, that is not now in this realm (kingdom)?"

When Jesus heard this, he laughed and said to them, "Why are you thinking in your hearts about the mighty and holy race (generation)? So be it - I will tell you. No one born in this age (realm / aeon) will see that (generation / race), and not even the multitude (army) of angels (controlling) the stars will rule over that generation (race), and no mortal (corruptible) person can associate (belong) with it.

13. That generation does not come from (a realm) which has become (mortal / corrupted). The generation of people among (you) is from the generation of humanity (of inferior / without) power, which (cannot associate with the) other powers (above) by (whom) you rule / are ruled."

When (the /his) disciples heard this, they were all troubled in (their heart / spirit). They were speechless (could not utter a word).

Note: This begins a distinction drawn between the generation or race of mankind, which is inferior, decaying, and unenlightened, and the "great generation or race," which is enlightened, incorruptible, and eternal. There are only two races; those who have gnosis and those who do not. Interestingly, Jesus does not place the disciples in the great generation.

14. On another day Jesus came up to (them). They said to (him), "Rabbi, we have seen you in a (dream), because we all had weighty (dreams about a night you were taken away / arrested)."

(He said), "Why have (you come to me when you have) gone into hiding?"

15. They said, "There was (an imposing building with a great altar in it and twelve men, (which we would say were) the priests, and there was a name, and a crowd of people waiting (enduring because of their perseverance) at that altar, (for) the priest (to come and receive) the offerings. (However) we kept waiting (we were tenacious also)."

(Jesus asked), "What were (the priests) like?"

They said, "Some (of them would fast) for two weeks; (others would) sacrifice their own children, others their wives, (all the while) in praise (offered in) humility with each other; some have sex with other men; some murder; some commit a plethora of sins and acts of crime. And the men who stand in front of the altar call upon your (name / authority), and in all the acts springing from their lack of knowledge (lack of light), the sacrifices are brought to completion (by their hands) (the alter remained full through their handiwork of slaughtering the sacrifices)."

After they said these things they became uneasy and quiet.

16. Jesus asked them, "Why are you bothered? So be it, I tell you that all the priests who have stood before that altar call upon my name. I have told I you many times that my name has been written on the (judgment) of this race (and on) the stars through the human generations. In my name (these people) have planted barren trees, (and have done so) without any honor."

17. Jesus said to them, "You are like those men you have seen conducting the offerings at the altar. That is the god you serve, and the twelve men you have seen represent you. The cattle you saw that were brought for sacrifice represent the many people you have led (will lead) astray before that altar. (You) will stand (lead / represent) and use my name in that way, as will the generations of the pious and you all will remain loyal to "him." (Some translations have- "The lord of chaos will establish his place in this way.") After "him" another man will lead from (the group of fornicators), and another (will lead at the alter from those who) murder children, and another from those who are homosexuals, and (another) those who fast, and (one will stand from) the rest of those who pollution themselves and who are lawlessness and who sin, and (from) those who say, 'We are like the angels'; they are the stars that (make everything happen / bring everything to an

end).

18. It has been said to the human generations, 'Look, God has received your sacrifice from the hands of a priest.' But the priest is a minister of error (minister in error / ministers but is in sin). But it is the Lord, the Lord of all (the fullness of the divine), who commands, 'On the last day (of time) they will be shamed (some have - "at the end of days").'"

Note: Jesus tells the disciples that they are loyal to the wrong god. He goes on to say that they are the ones who murder, fornicate, and sin. Furthermore, Jesus tells them that they will lead people into a spiritual slaughter like the cattle they saw sacrificed in their dream. At this time the 12 included Judas. This, along with other such verses has led many scholars to conclude that the Gospel of Judas was not depicting Judas to be the sanctified person the original translators thought him to be.

19. Jesus (told them), "Stop (sacrificing that which) you have (and stop hovering) over the altar. The priests are over your stars and your angels. They have already come to their end there. So let them (be entrapped / quarrel / fight) before you, and leave them alone. (Do not be tainted by this generation but instead eat the food of knowledge given to you by the great one.)

Note: We will see "stars" referred to often in the text. They are used to symbolize two unique concepts. It was thought that in the creation of the cosmos, luminaries were created which were powers controlling each person's destiny. It was also thought that each person was assigned a star as his or her eternal home or resting place. A good person would ascend to his or her own star to rule and rest. Thus, stars were conscious powers, carrying out orders from God, and also were places of destiny for those who escape the material plane.

20. A baker cannot feed all creation under (heaven). And (they will not give) to them (a food) and (give) to (those of the great generation the same food).
Jesus said to them, "Stop struggling with (against) me. Each of you has his own star, and every (Lines are missing here. Text could read " person has his own destiny." Or possibly, "person who does well will dwell and rest on their star").

(All things happen in their own season and all seasons are appointed. And in (the season) which has come (it is spring) for the tree (of paradise) of this aeon / age (and it will produce) for a time (then wither) but he has come to water God's paradise, and (also water this generation) that will last, because (he) will not corrupt / detour) the (path of life for) that generation, but (will guide it) from eternity to eternity."

21. Judas asked him, "Rabbi, what kind of fruit does this generation produce?"
Jesus answered, "The souls of every human generation will die. However, when these people (of this kingdom) have completed the time in the kingdom and the living breath leaves them, their bodies will die but their souls will continue to be alive, and they will ascended (be lifted up / be taken up)."
Judas asked, "What will the remainder of the human generations do?"
Jesus said, "It is not possible to plant seeds in (rocky soil) and harvest its fruit. (This is also the way (of) the (corrupted) race (generation), (the children of this kingdom) and corruptible Sophia / wisdom) (is / are) not the hand that has created mortal people, so that their souls ascend to the eternal realms above. Amen, I say, (that no) angel (or / of) power will be able to see that (kingdom of) these to whom (belong that) holy generations (above)."
After Jesus said this, he departed.

22. Judas said, "Rabbi, you have listened to all of those others, so now listen to me too. I have seen a great vision."

23. When Jesus heard this, he laughed and said to him, "You (are the) thirteenth spirit (daemon), why are you trying so hard / why do you excite yourself like this? However, speak up, and I will be patient with you."
Judas said to him, "In the vision I saw myself and the twelve disciples were stoning me and persecuting me very badly / severely / strongly. And I (was following you and I) arrived at a place where I saw (a large house in front me), and my eyes could not (take in / comprehend) its size. Many people were surrounding it, and the house had a roof of plants (grass / green

vegetation), and in the middle of the house (there was a crowd) (and I was there with you), saying, 'Rabbi, take me in (the house) along with these people.'"

24. He responded and said, "Judas, your star has misled you. No person of mortal birth is worthy to enter the house you have seen. It is a place reserved for the saints. Not even the sun or the moon or day (light) will rule there. Only the saints will live there, in the eternal kingdom with the holy angels, always (some have the text as – "will be firmly established with the holy angels forever"). Look, I have explained to you the mysteries of the kingdom and I have taught you about the error of the stars; and (I have) sent it (on its path) on the twelve ages (aeons)."

Note: The Lost Book of Enoch tells of stars, which are the guiding forces of man and nature, erring. They become misplaced and out of order. They had to be placed or directed back into their proper paths. See The Lost Book of Enoch, by Joseph Lumpkin.

Note: There are 12 Astrological Ages. The 12 signs of the zodiac make up a 360-degree ecliptic path around the Earth, and takes 25,920 years to make the Precession of the Equinoxes. Each sign is comprised of 30 degrees of celestial longitude. Each degree of the precession is equal to 72 Earth years, and each year is equal to 50 seconds of degrees of arc of celestial longitude. In a 24 hour Earth day, the Earth rotates the entire 360 degrees of the ecliptic, allowing a person to see all 12 signs.

25. Judas said, "Rabbi, could it be that my (spiritual) seed will conquer the rulers of cosmic power (could also be rendered: "is under the control of the archons or rulers of cosmic power"?)"

26. Jesus answered and said to him, "Come (with me so) that I (may show you the kingdom you will receive. I will show you what is to come of you and this generation), but you will be grieved when you see the kingdom and all its race (of people)."
When Judas heard Him he said to him, "What good is it if I have received it seeing that you have set me apart from that race?"
Jesus answered him and said, "You will become the thirteenth, and you will be cursed by the other generations, and you will

come to rule over them. In the last days they will curse your ascent to the holy (race / kingdom)."

Note: I have chosen the word, "daemon" and not "demon" because the meaning of the text is unclear. A daemon is a divinity or supernatural being of a nature between gods and humans. In verse 24 Jesus tells Judas that he will never be worthy to enter the house, which symbolizes the eternal kingdom. Later in verse 26 Jesus seems to indicate that Judas will be cursed by the other disciples but will be raised to enter the holy generation in the last days. It is possible the interim time will be spent in what the Bible calls, "his own place."

27. Jesus said, "(Follow / come with me), so that I may teach you the (secrets) that no person (has) ever seen.

Note: This begins a creation myth based on certain Sethian Gnostic cosmology. The telling of the story appears to be an attempt to link the Gnostic cosmology to the teachings of Jesus in order to add validity and authority to the creation story and entities as well as assisting in the propagation of the sect.

There is a great and limitless kingdom, whose scope no generation of angels has seen (and in it) The Great Invisible (Spirit) is, and no angel's eye has ever seen, no thought of the heart (mind) has ever understood it, and no name can be assigned it (it cannot be named).

28. "And a brightly glowing cloud appeared there. The Great Spirit said, 'Let an angel come into being as my assistant (attendant / helper).'
"A great angel, the enlightened, divine, Self-Generated (Self-Created) one emerged from the cloud. Because of him, four other angelic lights (luminaries), (Harmozel, Oroiael, Daveithai, and Eleleth) began to exist from another cloud, and they became assistants (helpers / attendants) to the Self-Generated angel (messenger). The Self-Created one proclaimed, 'Let (there) come into being (a star / Adam),' and it (he) came into being (at once). He (created) the first star (luminary / bright, shining being) to reign over him.

He said, 'Let angels (messengers) begin existence to adore (worship) (him),' and an innumerable plethora became existent. He said, '(Let there be) an aeon of light,' and he began existence. He created the second star to rule over him, to render service together with the innumerable plethora of angels. That is how he created the rest of the aeons of light. He made them rulers over them, and he created for them an innumerable plethora of angels to assist them.

29. "Adamas (Adam) was in the first luminous cloud (the initial divine expression) that no angel has ever seen, including all those called 'God.' He (was the one) that (created the enlightened aeon and beheld) the image and produced him after the likeness of (this) angel. He made the incorruptible (generation) of Seth appear (from) the twelve (aeons and) the twenty-four (stars / angelic lights / luminaries). He made seventy-two angelic lights appear in the imperishable generation, as the will of the Spirit dictated. The seventy-two angelic lights themselves made three hundred sixty angelic lights appear in the immortal race, by following the will of the Spirit, that their number should be five for each.

Note: Seth is the son of Adam and was considered to be divine as Adam was divine. Seth produced "that incorruptible generation." He was thought to have received the knowledge that would bring freedom from the material realm, and thus, salvation.

30. "The twelve realms (aeons) of the twelve angelic lights make up / appoint their Father, with six heavens for each aeon, so that there are seventy-two heavens for the seventy-two angelic lights, and for each (there are five) skies, (producing all) three hundred sixty (skies for the stars). They were given authority and a innumerable host of angels, for glory and adoration (worship), (and then he gave the) virgin (pure spirits), for glory and worship

of all the aeons and the heavens and their firmaments (skies).

Note: The numbers assigned to the various aeons, angels, and stars have significance in both biblical number symbolism and Pythagorean numerology.

> *One – Unity, sovereign, God, causality.*
> *Two – Duality and / or merging.*
> *Three - Spiritually complete, fullness, creation.*
> *Four – Foundations, systems, order.*
> *Five – Spirit, grace, movement.*
> *Six - Mankind.*
> *Seven – God, wisdom, knowledge, perfection.*
> *Twelve – Law, rule, authority.*
> *Thirteen – Cursed, beyond or without law.*
> *Twenty-four – Heavenly government, elders, a*
> *system. Duality within the system.*
> *Seventy-two – Both elements of two and seven as   well*
> *as the element of completion.*
>
> *Three hundred and sixty – Elements of three and   six as well as the meaning of a full cycle such as a   yearly cycle. An end, and a new start.*

31. The totality (gathering) of those immortals is called the cosmos, that is to say perdition / decay / corruption, by the Father and the seventy-two angelic lights / luminaries who are with the Self-Created one and his seventy-two aeons. In the cosmos the first human appeared with his incorruptible powers.

Note: This first human is Adamas or Adam. It should be noted that the name "Adam" can also be rendered as "Man" in Hebrew.

32. And the aeon that appeared with his generation and the aeon in whom are the cloud of knowledge and the angel, is called El.

Note: El was the name of a Semitic god who was chief among the pantheon of gods affecting nature and society. He is father of the divine family and president of the divine assembly on the 'mount of assembly', the equivalent of Hebrew har mo'ed, which became through the Greek transliteration Armageddon. In Canaanite mythology he is known as 'the Bull', symbolizing his strength and creative force. He is called 'Creator of Created Things' which is how rivers were also metaphorically thought of. In the Biblical Garden of Eden a river flowed to form the four rivers, Tigris, Euphrates, Gihon and Pishon."

El expressed the concept of ordered government, justice and creation. The Bible never stigmatizes the Canaanite worship of El, whose authority in social affairs was recognized by the Patriarchs. His consort was Asherah, the mother goddess, represented in Canaanite sanctuaries by a natural tree (Hebrew ashera) such as the tree of life.

33. (He created the) aeon, (after that) (El) said, 'Let twelve angels come into being (in order to) rule over chaos and the (cosmos / perdition).' And look, from the cloud {called Sophia} there appeared an (angel / aeon) whose face flashed with fire and whose appearance was defiled with blood. His name was Nebro, meaning "rebel." Another angel, Saklas, also came from the cloud. So Nebro created six angels—as well as Saklas—to be assistants, and these produced twelve angels in the heavens, with each one receiving a piece of the heavens.

Note: Nebro may be a female demon who mates with Saklas; others call Nebro by the name "Yaldaboth (child of chaos) Yaldaboth and Saklas are both names given to the insane or deficient deity that created the physical world. Also the reading could be influenced by the fact that in some mythologies Nebro is a head demon and Saklas is a head angel. Nebro has the same meaning as Nimrod, which is "rebel."

The Jews and Greeks of the day were literalists. Each and every word of the scriptures was taken at face value. Therefore, the god who created Adam and Eve was a limited and tangible god. He walked and talked and asked questions, the answers to which he did not seem to know. By building a creation story that includes Saklas the problems were solved. Now the references to multiple gods were answered and when god said let "us" create man, the references could be to Saklas and his helpers. Since the Saklas deity was limited and restricted it left the Supreme God to be "God."

34. "The twelve rulers (aeons) spoke with the twelve angels: 'Let each of you (receive a portion) and let them (that are in this) generation (be ruled by these) angels':

504

The first is Seth, who is called Christ.
The (second) is Harmathoth, who is (head ruler of the underworld).
The (third) is Galila.
The fourth is Yobel.
The fifth (is) Adonaios.
These are the five who ruled all of the underworld, and primarily over chaos.

Note: These five names are probably associated with the five planets known at the time the Gospel of Judas was written. They were placed on their paths and courses to keep order and give light, both real and spiritual.

35. "Then Saklas said to his angels, 'Let us create a human being in the similitude and after the figure / image / representation (of the Supreme God) .' They fashioned Adam and his wife Eve, who is called Zoe / life when she was still in the cloud.

Note: Zoe is another name for Eve in the Septuagint.

36. For it is this name (life) that all the generations seek the man, and each of them calls the woman by these names. Now, Sakla did not command (as he was instructed) but (he commanded) the generations (of man to live so long / for a defined period of time), (but he did created them in his (Saklas') likeness). And the (ruler Saklas) said to Adam, 'You shall live long, with your children.'"

37. Judas said to Jesus, "(What length) is the long span of time that humans will live?"
Jesus said, "Why are you curious about this? Adam and his generation has lived his lifespan in the place where he received his kingdom, with his longevity bestowed by his ruler (as numbered with his ruler)."

38. Judas said to Jesus, "Does the human spirit die?"
Jesus said, "This is why God (the god of this realm) ordered Michael to loan spirits to people so that they would serve (be in servitude), but the Great One commanded Gabriel to give spirits

to the great generation (race) which had no ruler over it (a generation that cannot be dominated). He gave the spirit and the soul. Therefore, the (remainder / mountain) of souls (loaned will come back to the god of this realm in the end).

Note: This passage indicates two lines of creation. For those people created by the god of this world the angel Michael was commanded to temporarily assign souls to his creation. To keep their souls they were enslaved to worship the god of this world. In contrast, the Great One commanded Gabriel to give souls to those of the great generation for eternity.

39. "(There was no) light (in this world to shine) around (the people to) allow (the) spirit (which is) within you all to dwell in this (body) among the generations of angels. But God caused knowledge to be (given) to Adam and those with him, so that the kings of chaos and the underworld might not oppress them with it."

Note: The word rendered as "rule" by most translators has the connotation of oppression.

40. Judas said to Jesus, "So what will those generations do?"
Jesus said, "Truthfully, I tell you all, that for all of them the stars bring matters to completion (heavenly apocalypse). When Saklas completes the span of time assigned for him, their first star will appear with the generations, and they will finish what they said they would do. Then they will (have illicit sex in my name and kill (sacrifice) their children and they will fast, and they will kill their wives in praise offered in humility with each other; some have sex with other men; some will murder, some commit a plethora of sins and acts of crime all in my name, and Saklas will destroy) your star over the thirteenth aeon."

41. After that Jesus (laughed).

Note: Jesus seems to find humor in the misguided judgments or concepts of the disciples. He laughs, as if shaking his head in disbelief of the error, then attempts to give insight and correction.

(Judas asked), "Rabbi, (why do you laugh at us)?"
(He) answered (Judas and said), "I am not laughing (because of you) but at the error of the stars, because these six stars wander about with these five warriors and they all will be destroyed along with their creations."

Note: The six stars were those who, along with Saklas or yaldaboth, created man and the cosmos. The five warriors refer to the five known planets at the time of the writing of the text. These planets were also connected with pagan worship and deities.

42. Judas said to Jesus, "Look at what those who have been baptized in your name do?"
Jesus said, "Truthfully I tell (you), this baptism done in my name (are done by those who do not know me. They sacrifice in vain to the god of this world. I baptized no one, for those baptized here have their hope here and those who follow me need no baptism for they will come) to me. In truth (I) tell you, Judas, (those offering) sacrifices to Saklas (do not offer sacrifice to the Great) God (but instead worship) everything that is evil.
"But you will exceed all of them. For you will sacrifice the man (the body that clothes / bares / contains me)."

Note: Gnostic theology sets up a duality between the material world and the spiritual world. Since the god that created the material world was flawed, cruel, and insane, anything produced in that environment must be corrupted and opposed to the spiritual world. In this belief system the killing of Jesus' body was a good thing since it would free his spirit and unite it with the "Great One." Looked at from this angle, Judas was assisting Jesus in showing mankind the way. This line of reasoning must be taken as metaphorical. Some authors have suggested that Jesus had become entombed in his body and was asking Judas to free him. This cannot be so since Jesus comes and goes from the Holy Race or Generation above at will. Neither is Jesus touting mass suicide. Gnostic lived long lives and propagated their faith. The message here is that to remain detached from the material or corporeal and to strive to receive the knowledge here will free you in the life to come.

Already your horn has been raised, your anger has been ignited, your star has shown brightly, and your heart has (prevailed /

been made strong / pure).

Note: The symbol horn is a phallic symbol but also a symbol of strength in much the way a rhino's horn is a sign of power and might.

Note: Although the lines added to the first half of this verse are tenuous, the information that is available establishes Judas' place according to this story. It does, however, open some questions. What was Judas' anger directed against? Was he sacrificing Jesus because he was angry at the established religion of the day? Was it this anger that made his heart strong or pure? Was anger his motivating force? If so, it harmonizes well with certain readings of the canonical gospels, which may indicate Judas wanted to expedite Jesus' kingdom so he would have a place of authority therein.

43. "Truly (I tell you,) your last (act will become that which will free this race but it will) grieve (you and will anger this generation and) the ruler, since he will be destroyed. (And then the) image of the great race of Adam will be raised high, for before heaven, earth, and the angels, that race from the eternal realms, exists (existed). Look, you have been told everything. Lift up your eyes and look to the cloud and the light within it and the stars around it. The star that leads the way is your star (you are the star)."

44. Then, Judas raised his eyes and saw the radiant cloud, and entered it. Those standing below him heard a voice coming from the cloud, saying, (The return of the) great race (is at hand and the image of the Great One will be established in them because of Judas' sacrifice).

Note: This is the same cloud mentioned in verse 24. By entering the cloud Judas became one with the primal causality or "Great One / Supreme God." The Gnosis was imparted to him and he knew the mysteries. He then had understanding and strength to do what he was asked to do. This amounts to a transfiguration for Judas, much like that of Jesus. In the same manner, a voice from heaven announced his destiny.

45. (But the scribes waited for Judas, hoping to place a price on the head of Jesus.) Their high priests whispered that he had gone into the guest room for his prayer. But some scribes were there

watching closely in order to arrest Jesus during the prayer, for they were afraid of the people, since he was accepted by everyone as a prophet. They approached Judas and said to him, "Why are you here? You are Jesus' disciple." Judas answered them in the way they wished. And he was given an amount of money and he handed Jesus over to them.

Note: We read of Judas' entrance into the radiant cloud and then his transaction with the scribes but there is no transition. It is possible the cloud is a metaphor for divine knowledge of the primal causality or Great God that produced Barbelo. See verse 28.

Note: The actual betrayal of Jesus by Judas is drastically downplayed. Only one paragraph is devoted to the actual act. Within this single paragraph no details are offered.

The gospel is constructed to give the reason for the betrayal. Building the rational of the act becomes far more important than the act itself, given the fact that it was the body that clothed Jesus that was destroyed and not the inner spirit. Shedding the body fulfilled destiny and freed the Christ spirit.

This was done as a demonstration of Jesus' belief in the immortal and eternal realm, which lay beyond human senses. The lesson of the Gospel of Judas and of Gnosticism in general had to do with reaching inside to gain knowledge of the unseen spiritual world. The orthodox church taught that only through martyrdom or the blessing of the church could one pass into the spiritual realm. Jesus was teaching another way. His death was the only way to exemplify his faith and show his disciples there was more than they could see in the material world. According to the Gnostic texts, the death of Jesus did not bring salvation. His life and death taught and provided knowledge, that if understood, would free the human race of its chains and allow it to ascend to the immortal realm.

This ends the Gospel of Judas.

Introduction to the Gnosticism in Eugnostos the Blessed and The Sophia of Jesus

The roots of Gnosticism may pre-date Christianity. Similarities exist between Gnosticism and the wisdom and mystery cults found in Egypt and Greece. Gnosticism contains the basic terms and motifs of Plato's cosmology as well as the mystical qualities of Buddhism. Plato was steeped in Greek mythology, and the Gnostic creation myth has elements owing to this. Both cosmology and mysticism within Gnosticism present an interpretation of Christ's existence and teachings, thus, Gnostics are considered to be a Christian sect. Gnostic followers are urged to look within themselves for the truth and the Christ spirit hidden, asleep in their souls.

The battle cry can be summed up in the words of the Gnostic Gospel of Thomas, verse 3:
Jesus said: If those who lead you say to you: Look, the Kingdom is in the sky, then the birds of the sky would enter before you. If they say to you: It is in the sea, then the fish of the sea would enter ahead of you. But the Kingdom of God exists within you and it exists outside of you. Those who come to know (recognize) themselves will find it, and when you come to know yourselves you will become known and you will realize that you are the children of the Living Father. Yet if you do not come to know yourselves then you will dwell in poverty and it will be you who are that poverty.

Paganism was a religious traditional society in the Mediterranean leading up to the time of the Gnostics. Centuries after the conversion of Constantine, mystery cults worshipping various Egyptian and Greco-Roman gods continued. These cults taught that through their secret knowledge worshippers could control or escape the mortal realm. The Gnostic doctrine of inner

510

knowledge and freedom may have part of its roots here. The concept of duality and inner guidance taught in Buddhism added to and enforced Gnostic beliefs, as we will see later.

The belief systems of Plato, Buddha, and paganism melted together, spread, and found a suitable home in the mystical side of the Christian faith as it sought to adapt and adopt certain Judeo-Christian beliefs and symbols.

Like modern Christianity, Gnosticism had various points of view that could be likened to Christian denominations of today. Complex and elaborate creation myths took root in Gnosticism, being derived from those of Plato. Later, the theology evolved and Gnosticism began to shed some of its more unorthodox myths, leaving the central theme of inner knowledge or gnosis to propagate.

The existence of various sects of Gnosticism, differing creation stories, along with the lack of historical documentation, has left scholars in a quandary about exactly what Gnostics believed. Some have suggested that the Gnostics represented a free thinking and idealistic movement much like that of the "Hippie" movement active in the United States during the 1960's.

Just as the "Hippie" movement in the U.S. influenced political thought, some early sects of Gnostics began to exert direct influence on the Christian church and its leadership.

Although it appears that there were several sects of Gnosticism, we will attempt to discuss the more universal Gnostic beliefs along with the highlights of the major sects.

Gnostic cosmology, (which is the theory of how the universe is created, constructed, and sustained), is complex and very different from orthodox Christian cosmology. In many ways

Gnosticism may appear to be polytheistic or even pantheistic.

To understand some of the basic beliefs of Gnosticism, let us start with the common ground shared between Gnosticism and modern Christianity. Both believe the world is imperfect, corrupt, and brutal. The blame for this, according to mainstream Christianity, is placed squarely on the shoulders of man himself. With the fall of man (Adam), the world was forever changed to the undesirable and harmful place in which we live today. However, Gnostics reject this view as an incorrect interpretation of the creation myth.

According to Gnostics, the blame is not in ourselves, but in our creator. The creator of this world was himself somewhat less than perfect and in fact, deeply flawed and cruel, making mankind the child of a lesser God. It is in the book, *The Apocryphon of John*, that the Gnostic view of creation is presented to us in great detail.

Gnosticism also teaches that in the beginning a Supreme Being called The Father, The Divine All, The Origin, The Supreme God, or The Fullness, emanated the element of existence, both visible and invisible. His intent was not to create but, just as light emanates from a flame, so did creation shine forth from God. This manifested the primal element needed for creation. This was the creation of Barbelo, who is the Thought of God.

The Father's thought performed a deed and she was created from it. It is she who had appeared before him in the shining of his light. This is the first power which was before all of them and which was created from his mind. She is the Thought of the All and her light shines like his light. It is the perfect power which is the visage of the invisible. She is the pure, undefiled Spirit who is perfect. She is the first power, the glory of Barbelo, the perfect glory of the kingdom (kingdoms), the glory revealed. She glorified the pure, undefiled Spirit and it was she who praised him,

because thanks to him she had come forth.
The Apocryphon of John

It could be said that Barbelo is the creative emanation and, like the Divine All, is both male and female. It is the "agreement" of Barbelo and the Divine All, representing the union of male and female, that created the Christ Spirit and all the Aeons. In some renderings the word "Aeon" is used to designate an ethereal realm or kingdom. In other versions "Aeon" indicates the ruler of the realm. One of these rulers was called Sophia or Wisdom. Her fall began a chain of events that led to the introduction of evil into the universe.

Seeing the Divine flame of God, Sophia sought to know its origin. She sought to know the very nature of God. Sophia's passion ended in tragedy when she managed to capture a divine and creative spark, which she attempted to duplicate with her own creative force, without the union of a male counterpart. It was this act that produced the Archons, beings born outside the higher divine realm. In the development of the myth, explanations seem to point to the fact that Sophia carried the divine essence of creation from God within her but chose to attempt creation by using her own powers. It is unclear if this was in an attempt to understand the Supreme God and his power, or an impetuous act that caused evil to enter the cosmos in the form of her creations.

The realm containing the Fullness of the Godhead and Sophia is called the pleroma or Realm of Fullness. This is the Gnostic heaven. The lesser Gods created in Sophia's failed attempt were cast outside the pleroma and away from the presence of God. In essence, she threw away and discarded her flawed creations.

"She cast it away from her, outside the place where no one of the immortals might see it, for she had created it in ignorance. And she surrounded it with a glowing cloud, and she put a throne in the middle

of the cloud so that no one could see it except the Holy Spirit who is called the mother of all that has life. And she called his name Yaldaboth."
Apocryphon of John

The beings Sophia created were imperfect and oblivious to the Supreme God. Her creations contained deities even less perfect than herself. They were called the Powers, the Rulers, or the Archons. Their leader was called the Demiurge, but his name was Yaldaboth. It was the flawed, imperfect, spiritually blind Demiurge, (Yaldaboth), who became the creator of the material world and all things in it. Gnostics considered Yaldaboth to be the same as Jehovah (Yahweh), who is the Jewish creator God. These beings, the Demiurge and the Archons, would later equate to Satan and his demons, or Jehovah and his angels, depending on which Gnostic sect is telling the story. Both are equally evil.

In one Gnostic creation story, the Archons created Adam but could not bring him to life. In other stories Adam was formed as a type of worm, unable to attain personhood. Thus, man began as an incomplete creation of a flawed, spiritually blind, and malevolent god. In this myth, the Archons were afraid that Adam might be more powerful than the Archons themselves. When they saw Adam was incapable of attaining the human state, their fears were put to rest, thus, they called that day the "Day of Rest."

Sophia saw Adam's horrid state and had compassion, because she knew she was the origin of the Archons and their evil. Sophia descended to help bring Adam out of his hopeless condition. It is this story that set the stage for the emergence of the sacred feminine force in Gnosticism that is not seen in orthodox Christianity. Sophia brought within herself the light and power of the Supreme God. Metaphorically, within the spiritual womb of Sophia was carried the life force of the Supreme God for Adam's salvation.

In the Gnostic text called, *The Apocryphon of John*, Sophia is quoted:

"I entered into the midst of the cage which is the prison of the body. And I spoke saying: 'He who hears, let him awake from his deep sleep.' Then Adam wept and shed tears. After he wiped away his bitter tears he asked: 'Who calls my name, and from where has this hope arose in me even while I am in the chains of this prison?' And I (Sophia) answered: 'I am the one who carries the pure light; I am the thought of the undefiled spirit. Arise, remember, and follow your origin, which is I, and beware of the deep sleep.'"

Sophia would later equate to the Holy Spirit as the Spirit awakened the comatose soul. As the myth evolved, Sophia, after animating Adam, became Eve in order to assist Adam in finding the truth. She offered it to him in the form of the fruit of the tree of knowledge. To Gnostics, this was an act of deliverance.

Other stories have Sophia becoming the serpent in order to offer Adam a way to attain the truth. In either case, the fruit represented the hard sought truth, which was the knowledge of good and evil, and through that knowledge Adam could become a god. Later, the serpent would become a feminine symbol of wisdom, probably owing to the connection with Sophia. Eve, being Sophia in disguise, would become the mother and sacred feminine of us all. As Gnostic theology began to coalesce, Sophia would come to be considered a force or conduit of the Holy Spirit, in part due to the fact that the Holy Spirit was also considered a feminine and creative force from the Supreme God. The Gospel of Philip echoes this theology in verse six as follows:

In the days when we were Hebrews we were made orphans, having only our Mother. Yet when we believed in the Messiah (and became the ones of Christ), the Mother and Father both came to us.   Gospel of Philip

As the emerging orthodox church became more and more oppressive to women, later even labeling them "occasions of sin," the Gnostics countered by raising women to equal status with men, saying Sophia was, in a sense, the handmaiden or wife of the Supreme God, making the soul of Adam her spiritual offspring.

In Gnostic cosmology the "living" world is under the control of entities called Aeons, of which Sophia is head. This means the Aeons influence or control the soul, life force, intelligence, thought, and mind. Control of the mechanical or inorganic world is given to the Archons. They rule the physical aspects of systems, regulation, limits, and order in the world. Both the ineptitude and cruelty of the Archons are reflected in the chaos and pain of the material realm.

The lesser God that created the world, Yaldaboth. began his existence in a state that was both detached and remote from the Supreme God in aspects both spiritual and physical. Since Sophia had misused her creative force, which passed from the Supreme God to her, Sophia's creation, the Demiurge, Yaldaboth, contained only part of the original creative spark of the Supreme Being. He was created with an imperfect nature caused by his distance in lineage and in spirit from the Divine All or Supreme God. It is because of his imperfections and limited abilities the lesser God is also called the "Half-Maker".

The Creator God, the Demiurge, and his helpers, the Archons took the stuff of existence produced by the Supreme God and fashioned it into this material world.

Since the Demiurge (Yaldaboth) had no memory of how he came to be alive, he did not realize he was not the true creator. The Demiurge believed he somehow came to create the material world by himself. The Supreme God allowed the Demiurge and Archons to remain deceived.

The Creator God (the Demiurge) intended the material world

to be perfect and eternal, but he did not have it in himself to accomplish the feat. What comes forth from a being cannot be greater than the highest part of him, can it? The world was created flawed and transitory and we are part of it. Can we escape? The Demiurge was imperfect and evil. So was the world he created. If it was the Demiurge who created man and man is called upon to escape the Demiurge and find union with the Supreme God, is this not demanding that man becomes greater than his creator? Spiritually this seems impossible, but as many children become greater than their parents, man is expected to become greater than his maker, the Demiurge. This starts with the one fact that the Demiurge denies: the existence and supremacy of the Supreme God.

Man was created with a dual nature as the product of the material world of the Demiurge with his imperfect essence, combined with the spark of God that emanated from the Supreme God through Sophia. A version of the creation story has Sophia instructing the Demiurge to breath into Adam that spiritual power he had taken from Sophia during his creation. It was the spiritual power from Sophia that brought life to Adam.

It is this divine spark in man that calls to its source, the Supreme God, and which causes a "divine discontent," that nagging feeling that keeps us questioning if this is all there is. This spark and the feeling it gives us keeps us searching for the truth.

The Creator God sought to keep man ignorant of his defective state by keeping him enslaved to the material world. By doing so, he continued to receive man's worship and servitude. He did not wish man to recognize or gain knowledge of the true Supreme God. Since he did not know or acknowledge the Supreme God, he viewed any attempt to worship anything else as spiritual treason.

The opposition of forces set forth in the spiritual battle

over the continued enslavement of man and man's spiritual freedom set up the duality of good and evil in Gnostic theology. There was a glaring difference between the orthodox Christian viewpoint and the Gnostic viewpoint. According to Gnostics, the creator of the material world was an evil entity and the Supreme God, who was his source, was the good entity. Christians quote John 1:1 "In the beginning was the Word, and the Word was with God, and the Word was God."

According to Gnostics, only through the realization of man's true state or through death can he escape captivity in the material realm. This means the idea of salvation does not deal with original sin or blood payment. Instead, it focuses on the idea of awakening to the fullness of the truth.

According to Gnostic theology, neither Jesus nor his death can save anyone, but the truth that he came to proclaim can allow a person to save his or her own soul. It is the truth, or realization of the lie of the material world and its God, that sets one on a course of freedom.

To escape the earthly prison and find one's way back to the pleroma (heaven) and the Supreme God, is the soteriology (salvation doctrine) and eschatology (judgment, reward, and doctrine of heaven) of Gnosticism.

The idea that personal revelation leads to salvation, may be what caused the mainline Christian church to declare Gnosticism a heresy. The church could better tolerate alternative theological views if the views did not undermine the authority of the church and its ability to control the people. Gnostic theology placed salvation in the hands of the individual through personal revelations and knowledge, excluding the need for the orthodox church and its clergy to grant salvation or absolution. This fact, along with the divergent interpretation of the creation story, which placed the creator God, Yaldaboth or Jehovah, as the enemy of mankind, was too much for the church to tolerate. Reaction was harsh. Gnosticism was declared to be a dangerous heresy.

Gnosticism may be considered polytheistic because it espoused many "levels" of Gods, beginning with an ultimate, unknowable, Supreme God and descending as he created Sophia, and Sophia created the Demiurge (Creator God); each becoming more inferior and limited.

There is a hint of pantheism in Gnostic theology due to the fact that creation occurs because of a deterioration of the Godhead and the dispersion of the creative essence, which eventually devolves into the creation of man.

In the end, there occurs a universal reconciliation as being after being realizes the existence of the Supreme God and renounces the material world and its inferior creator.

Combined with its Christian influences, the cosmology of the Gnostics may have borrowed from the Greek philosopher, Plato, as well as from Buddhism. There are disturbing parallels between the creation myth set forth by Plato and some of those recorded in Gnostic writings.

Plato lived from 427 to 347 B.C. He was the son of wealthy Athenians and a student of the philosopher, Socrates, and the mathematician, Pythagoras. Plato himself was the teacher of Aristotle.

In Plato's cosmology, the Demiurge is an artist who imposed form on materials that already existed. The raw materials were in a chaotic and random state. The physical world must have had visible form which was put together much like a puzzle is constructed. This later gave way to a philosophy which stated that all things in existence could be broken down into a small subset of geometric shapes.

In the tradition of Greek mythology, Plato's cosmology began with a creation story. The story was narrated by the philosopher Timaeus of Locris, a fictional character of Plato's making. In his account, nature is initiated by a creator deity, called the "Demiurge," a name which may be the Greek word for "craftsman" or "artisan" or, according to how one divides the word, it could also be translated as "half-maker."

The Demiurge sought to create the cosmos modeled on his understanding of the supreme and original truth. In this way he created the visible universe based on invisible truths. He set in place rules of process such as birth, growth, change, death, and dissolution. This was Plato's "Realm of Becoming." It was his Genesis. Plato stated that the internal structure of the cosmos had innate intelligence and was therefore called the World Soul. The cosmic super-structure of the Demiurge was used as the framework on which to hang or fill in the details and parts of the universe. The Demiurge then appointed his underlings to fill in the details which allowed the universe to remain in a working and balanced state. All phenomena of nature resulted from an interaction and interplay of the two forces of reason and necessity.

Plato represented reason as constituting the World Soul. The material world was a necessity in which reason acted out its will in the physical realm. The duality between the will, mind, or reason of the World Soul and the material universe and its inherent flaws set in play the duality of Plato's world and is seen reflected in the beliefs of the Gnostics.

In Plato's world, the human soul was immortal, each soul was assigned to a star. Souls that were just or good were permitted to return to their stars upon their death. Unjust souls were reincarnated to try again. Escape of the soul to the freedom of the stars and out of the cycle of reincarnation was best accomplished by following the reason and goodness of the World Soul and not the physical world, which was set in place only as a necessity to manifest the patterns of the World Soul.

Although in Plato's cosmology the Demiurge was not seen as evil, in Gnostic cosmology he was considered not only to be flawed and evil, he was also the beginning of all evil in the material universe, having created it to reflect his own malice.

Following the path of Plato's cosmology, some Gnostics left open the possibility of reincarnation if the person had not reached the truth before his death.

This idea appears to be of Buddhists origin. Resurrection was a Jewish and Christian concept, which shows up in surprising ways, such as when the people asked John the Baptist if he was Elijah.
New International Version
John 1:21
They asked him, "Then who are you? Are you Elijah?" He said, "I am not." "Are you the Prophet?" He answered, "No."

Even though the Jews expected the return of Elijah, they did not look for a reincarnated prophet, but someone God would send back from paradise to earth with a perfected body through the same reanimation used to bring Jesus back to life. Reincarnation assumes a person's spirit will inhabit another body from birth. There was a possible transmission of Buddhist ideas early in the first century.

In the year 13 A.D. Roman annals record the visit of an Indian king named Pandya or Porus. He came to see Caesar Augustus carrying a letter of introduction in Greek. He was accompanied by a monk who burned himself alive in the city of Athens to prove his faith in Buddhism. The event was described by Nicolaus of

Damascus as, not surprisingly, causing a great stir among the people. It is thought that this was the first transmission of Buddhist teaching to the masses.

In the second century A.D., Clement of Alexandria wrote about Buddha: "Among the Indians are those philosophers also who follow the precepts of Boutta (Buddha), whom they honour as a god on account of his extraordinary sanctity." (Clement of Alexandria, "The Stromata, or Miscellanies" Book I, Chapter XV). "Thus philosophy, a thing of the highest utility, flourished in antiquity among the barbarians, shedding its light over the nations. And afterwards it came to Greece." (Clement of Alexandria, "The Stromata, or Miscellanies").

To clarify what "philosophy" was transmitted from India to Greece, we turn to the historians Hippolytus and Epiphanius who wrote of Scythianus, "a man who had visited India around 50 A.D. They report; 'He brought 'the doctrine of the Two Principles.'" According to these writers, Scythianus' pupil Terebinthus called himself a Buddha. Some scholars suggest it was he who traveled to the area of Babylon and transmitted his knowledge to Mani, who later founded Manichaeism.

Adding to the possibility of Eastern influence, we have accounts of the Apostle Thomas' attempt to convert the people of Asia-Minor. If the Gnostic gospel bearing his name was truly written by Thomas, it was penned after his return from India, where he also encountered the Buddhist influences.

Ancient church historians mention that Thomas preached to the Parthians in Persia, and it is said he was buried in Edessa. Fourth century chronicles attribute the evangelization of India (Asia-Minor or Central Asia) to Thomas.

The text of the Gospel of Thomas, which some believe predate the four gospels, has a very "Zen-like" or Eastern flavor.

Since it is widely held that the four gospels of Matthew, Mark, Luke, and John have a common reference in the basic text of Mark, it stands to reason that all follow the same general insight and language. If The Gospel of Thomas was written in his absence from the other apostles or if it was the first gospel written, one can assume it was written outside the influences common to the other gospels.

Although the codex found in Egypt is dated to the fourth century, the actual construction of the text of Thomas is placed by most Biblical scholars at about 70–150 A.D. Most agree the time of writing was in the second century A.D.

Following the transmission of the philosophy of "Two Principals," both Manichaeism and Gnosticism retained a dualistic viewpoint. The black-versus-white dualism of Gnosticism came to rest in the evil of the material world and its maker, versus the goodness of the freed soul and the Supreme God with whom it seeks union.

Oddly, the disdain for the material world and its Creator God drove Gnostic theology to far-flung extremes in attitude, beliefs, and actions. Gnostics idolize the serpent in the "Garden of Eden" story. After all, if your salvation hinges on secret knowledge the offer of becoming gods through the knowledge of good and evil sounds wonderful. So powerful was the draw of this "knowledge myth" to the Gnostics that the serpent became linked to Sophia by some sects. This can still be seen today in our medical and veterinarian symbols of serpents on poles, conveying the ancient meanings of knowledge and wisdom.

Genesis 3 (King James Version)
1 Now the serpent was more subtil than any beast of the field which the

LORD God had made. And he said unto the woman, Yea, hath God said,
Ye shall not eat of every tree of the garden?
2 And the woman said unto the serpent, We may eat of the fruit of the
trees of the garden:
3 But of the fruit of the tree which is in the midst of the garden, God
hath said, Ye shall not eat of it, neither shall ye touch it, lest ye die.
4 And the serpent said unto the woman, Ye shall not surely die:
5 For God doth know that in the day ye eat thereof, then your eyes shall
be opened, and ye shall be as Gods, knowing good and evil.

It is because of their vehement struggle against the Creator
God and the search for some transcendent truth, that Gnostics
held the people of Sodom in high regard. The people of Sodom
sought to "corrupt" the messengers sent by their enemy, the
Creator God. Anything done to thwart the Demiurge and his
minions was considered valiant.

Genesis 19 (King James Version)
1 And there came two angels to Sodom at even; and Lot sat in the gate of
Sodom: and Lot seeing them rose up to meet them; and he bowed himself
with his face toward the ground;
2 And he said, Behold now, my lords, turn in, I pray you, into your
servant's house, and tarry all night, and wash your feet, and ye shall rise
up early, and go on your ways. And they said, Nay; but we will abide in
the street all night.
3 And he pressed upon them greatly; and they turned in unto him, and
entered into his house; and he made them a feast, and did bake
unleavened bread, and they did eat.
4 But before they lay down, the men of the city, even the men of Sodom,
compassed the house round, both old and young, all the people from
every quarter:
5 And they called unto Lot, and said unto him, Where are the men
which came in to thee this night? bring them out unto us, that we may
know them.
6 And Lot went out at the door unto them, and shut the door after him,

7 And said, I pray you, brethren, do not so wickedly.

8 Behold now, I have two daughters which have not known man; let me, I pray you, bring them out unto you, and do ye to them as is good in your eyes: only unto these men do nothing; for therefore came they under the shadow of my roof.

9 And they said, Stand back. And they said again, This one fellow came in to sojourn, and he will needs be a judge: now will we deal worse with thee, than with them. And they pressed sore upon the man, even Lot, and came near to break the door.

10 But the men put forth their hand, and pulled Lot into the house to them, and shut to the door.

To modern Christians, the idea of admiring the serpent, which we believe was Satan, may seem unthinkable. Supporting the idea of attacking and molesting the angels sent to Sodom to warn of the coming destruction seems appalling; but to Gnostics the real evil was the malevolent entity, the Creator God of this world. To destroy his messengers, as was the case in Sodom, would impede his mission. To obtain knowledge of good and evil, as was offered by the serpent in the garden, would set the captives free.

To awaken the inner knowledge of the true God was the battle. The material world was designed to prevent the awakening by entrapping, confusing, and distracting the spirit of man. The aim of Gnosticism was the spiritual awakening and freedom of man.

Gnostics, in the age of the early church, would preach to converts (novices) about this awakening, saying the novice must awaken the God within himself and see the trap that was the material world. Salvation came from the recognition or knowledge contained in this spiritual awakening.

Not all people were ready or willing to accept the Gnosis.

Many were bound to the material world and were satisfied to be only as and where they were. These have mistaken the Creator God for the Supreme God and do not know there is anything beyond the Creator God or the material existence. These people know only the lower or earthly wisdom and not the higher wisdom above the Creator God. They were referred to as "dead."

Gnostic sects split primarily into two categories. Both branches held that those who were truly enlightened could no longer be influenced by the material world. Both divisions of Gnosticism believed that their spiritual journey could not be impeded by the material realm since the two were not only separate but in opposition. Such an attitude influenced some Gnostics toward Stoicism, choosing to abstain from the world, and others toward Epicureanism, choosing to indulge.

Major schools fell into two categories; those who rejected the material world of the Creator God, and those who rejected the laws of the Creator God. For those who rejected the world the Creator God had spawned, overcoming the material world was accomplished by partaking of as little of the world and its pleasures as possible. These followers lived very stark and ascetic lives, abstaining from meat, sex, marriage, and all things that would entice them to remain in the material realm.   Other schools believed it was their duty to simply defy the Creator God and all laws that he had proclaimed. Since the Creator God had been identified as Jehovah, God of the Jews, these followers set about to break every law held dear by Christians and Jews.

As human nature is predisposed to do, many Gnostics took up the more wanton practices, believing that nothing done in their earthly bodies would affect their spiritual lives. Whether it was excesses in sex, alcohol, food, or any other assorted debaucheries, the Gnostics were safe within their faith, believing nothing spiritually bad could come of their earthly adventures.

The actions of the Gnostics are mentioned by early Church leaders. One infamous Gnostic school is actually mentioned in the Bible, as we will read later.

The world was out of balance, inferior, and corrupt. The spirit was perfect and intact. It was up to the Gnostics to tell the story, explain the error, and awaken the world to the light of truth. The Supreme God had provided a vehicle to help in their effort. He had created a teacher of light and truth.

Since the time of Sophia's mistaken creation of the Archons, there was an imbalance in the cosmos. The Supreme God began to re-establish the balance by producing Christ to teach and save man. That left only Sophia, now in a fallen and bound state, along with the Demiurge, and the Archons to upset the cosmic equation. In this theology one might loosely equate the Supreme God to the New Testament Christian God, Demiurge to Satan, the Archons to demons, the pleroma to heaven, and Sophia to the creative or regenerative force of the Holy Spirit. This holds up well except for one huge problem. If the Jews believed that Jehovah created all things, and the Gnostic believed that the Demiurge created all things, then to the Gnostic mind, the Demiurge must be Old Testament god, Jehovah, and that made Jehovah their enemy.

For those who seek that which is beyond the material world and its flawed creator, the Supreme God has sent Messengers of Light to awaken the divine spark of the Supreme God within us. This part of us will call to the True God as deep calls to deep. The greatest and most perfect Messenger of Light was the Christ. He is also referred to as The Good, Christ, Messiah, and The Word. He came to reveal the Divine Light to us in the form of knowledge.

According to the Gnostics, Christ came to show us our own divine spark and to awaken us to the illusion of the material world and its flawed maker. He came to show us the way back to the divine Fullness (The Supreme God). The path to enlightenment was the knowledge sleeping within each of us. Christ came to show us the Christ spirit living in each of us. Individual ignorance or the refusal to awaken our internal divine spark was the only original sin. Christ was the only Word spoken by God that could awaken us. Christ was also the embodiment of the Word itself. He was part of the original transmission from the Supreme God that took form on the earth to awaken the soul of man so that man might search beyond the material world.

One Gnostic view of the Incarnation was "docetic," which is an early heretical position that Jesus was never actually present in the flesh, but only appeared to be human. He was a spiritual being and his human appearance was only an illusion. Of course, the title of "heretical" can only be decided by the controlling authority of the time. In this case it was the church that was about to emerge under the rule of the Emperor Constantine.

Most Gnostics held that the Christ spirit indwelt the earthly Jesus at the time of his baptism by John, at which time Jesus received the name, and thus the power, of the Lord or Supreme God.

The Christ spirit departed from Jesus' body before his death. These two viewpoints remove the idea of God sacrificing himself as an atonement for the sins of man. The idea of atonement was not necessary in Gnostic theology since it was knowledge and not sacrifice that set one free.

Since there was a distinction in Gnosticism between the man Jesus and the Light of Christ that came to reside within him, it is not contrary to Gnostic beliefs that Mary Magdalene could have been the consort and wife of Jesus. Neither would it have been blasphemous for them to have had children.

Various sects of Gnosticism stressed certain elements of their basic theology. Each had its head teachers and its special flavor of beliefs. One of the oldest types was the Syrian Gnosticism. It existed around 120 A.D. In contrast to other sects, the Syrian lacked much of the embellished mythology of Aeons, Archons, and Angels.

The fight between the Supreme God and the Creator God was not eternal, though there was strong opposition to Jehovah, the Creator God. He was considered to have been the last of the seven angels who created this world out of divine material which emanated from the Supreme God. The Demiurge attempted to create man, but only created a miserable worm which the Supreme God had to save by giving it the spark of divine life. Thus man was born.

According to this sect, Jehovah, the Creator God, must not be worshiped. The Supreme God calls us to his service and presence through Christ his Son. They pursued only the unknowable Supreme God and sought to obey the Supreme Deity by abstaining from eating meat and from marriage and sex, and by leading an ascetic life. The symbol of Christ was the serpent, who attempted to free Adam and Eve from their ignorance and entrapment to the Creator God.

Another Gnostic school was the Hellenistic or Alexandrian School. This system absorbed the philosophy and concepts of the Greeks. They replace their Jewish or Semitic nomenclature with Greek terms and names. The cosmology and myth had grown out of proportion and appear to our eyes to be unwieldy. Yet, this school produced two great thinkers, Basilides and Valentinus. Though born at Antioch, in Syria, Basilides founded his school in Alexandria around the year A.D. 130, where it survived for several centuries.

Valentinus first taught at Alexandria and then in Rome. He established the largest Gnostic movement around A.D. 160. This movement was founded on an elaborate mythology and a system of sexual duality of male and female interplay, both in its deities and its savior.

Tertullian wrote that between 135 A.D. and 160 A.D. Valentinus, a prominent Gnostic, had great influence in the Christian church. Valentinus ascended in church hierarchy and became a candidate for the office of bishop of Rome, the office that quickly evolved into that of Pope. He lost the election by a narrow margin. Even though Valentinus was outspoken about his Gnostic slant on Christianity, he was a respected member of the Christian community until his death and was probably a practicing bishop in a church of lesser status than the one in Rome.

The main platform of Gnosticism was the ability to transcend the material world through the possession of privileged and directly imparted knowledge. Following this doctrine, Valentinus claimed to have been instructed by a direct disciple of one of Jesus' apostles, a man by the name of Theodas.

Valentinus is considered by many to be the father of modern Gnosticism. His vision of the faith is summarized by G.R.S. Mead in the book "Fragments of a Faith Forgotten."

"The Gnosis in his hands is trying to embrace everything, even the most dogmatic formulation of the traditions of the Master. The great popular movement and its incomprehensibilities were recognized by Valentinus as an integral part of the mighty outpouring; he laboured to weave all together, external and internal, into one piece, devoted his life to the task, and doubtless only at his death perceived that for that age he was attempting the impossible. None but the very few could ever appreciate the ideal of the man, much less understand it. " (Fragments of a Faith

Forgotten, p. 297)

Gnostic theology seemed to vacillate from polytheism to pantheism to dualism to monotheism, depending on the teacher and how he viewed and stressed certain areas of their creation myths.   Marcion, a Gnostic teacher, espoused differences between the God of the New Testament and the God of the Old Testament, claiming they were two separate entities. According to Marcion, the New Testament God was a good true God while the Old Testament God was an evil angel. Although this may be a heresy, it pulled his school back into monotheism. The church, however, disowned him.

Syneros and Prepon, disciples of Marcion, postulated three different entities, carrying their teachings from monotheism into polytheism in one stroke. In their system the opponent of the good God was not the God of the Jews, but Eternal Matter, which was the source of all evil. Matter, in this system became a principal creative force. Although it was created imperfect, it could also create, having the innate intelligence of the "world soul."

Of all the Gnostic schools or sects the most famous is the Antinomian School. Believing that the Creator God, Jehovah, was evil, they sat out to disrupt all things connected to the Jewish God. This included his laws. It was considered their duty to break any law of morality, diet, or conduct given by the Jewish God, who they considered the evil Creator God. The leader of the sect was called Nicolaites. The sect existed in Apostolic times and is mentioned in the Bible.

Revelation 2 (King James Version)
5 Remember therefore from whence thou art fallen, and repent, and do the first works; or else I will come unto thee quickly, and will remove thy candlestick out of his place, except thou repent.
6 But this thou hast, that thou hatest the deeds of the Nicolaitanes, which

531

I also hate.

Revelation 2 (King James Version)
14 But I have a few things against thee, because thou hast there them that hold the doctrine of Balaam, who taught Balac to cast a stumbling block before the children of Israel, to eat things sacrificed unto idols, and to commit fornication.
15 So hast thou also them that hold the doctrine of the Nicolaitanes, which thing I hate.
16 Repent; or else I will come unto thee quickly, and will fight against them with the sword of my mouth.

One of the leaders of the Nocolaitanes, according to Origen, was Carpocrates, whom Tertullian called a magician and a fornicator. Carpocretes taught that one could only escape the cosmic powers by discharging one's obligations to them and disregarding their laws. The Christian church fathers, St. Justin, Irenaeus, and Eusebius wrote that the reputation of these men (the Nicolaitanes), brought infamy upon the whole race of Christians.

Although Gnostic sects varied, they had certain points in common. These commonalities included salvation through special knowledge, and the fact that the world was corrupt as it was created by an evil God.

According to Gnostic theology, nothing can come from the material world that is not flawed. Because of this, Gnostics did not believe that Christ could have been a corporeal being. Thus, there must be some separation or distinction between Jesus, as a man, and Christ, as a spiritual being born from the Supreme, unrevealed, and eternal God.

To closer examine this theology, we turn to Valentinus, the driving force of early Gnosticism, for an explanation. Valentinus divided Jesus Christ into two very distinct parts; Jesus, the man, and Christ, the anointed spiritual messenger of God. These two forces met in the moment of Baptism when the Spirit of God came to rest on Jesus and the Christ power entered his body.

Here Gnosticism runs aground on its own theology, for if the spiritual cannot mingle with the material then how can the Christ spirit inhabit a body? The result of the dichotomy was a schism within Gnosticism. Some held to the belief that the specter of Jesus was simply an illusion produced by Christ himself to enable him to do his work on earth. It was not real, not matter, not corporeal, and did not actually exist as a physical body would. Others came to believe that Jesus must have been a specially prepared vessel and was the perfect human body formed by the very essence of the plumora (heaven). It was this path of thought that allowed Jesus to continue as human, lover, and father.

Jesus, the man, became a vessel containing the Light of God, called Christ. In the Gnostic view we all could and should become Christs, carrying the Truth and Light of God. We are all potential vehicles of the same Spirit that Jesus held within him when he was awakened to the Truth.

The suffering and death of Jesus then took on much less importance in the Gnostic view, as Jesus was simply part of the corrupt world and was suffering the indignities of this world as any man would. Therefore, from their viewpoint, he could have been married and been a father without disturbing Gnostic theology in the least.

The Gnostic texts seem to divide man into parts, although at times the divisions are somewhat unclear. The divisions alluded to may include the soul, which is the will of man; the spirit, which is depicted as wind or air (pneuma) and contains the holy spark that is the spirit of God in man; and the material human form, the body. The mind of man sits as a mediator between the soul, or will, and the spirit, which is connected to God.

Without the light of the truth, the spirit is held captive by the Demiurge, which enslaves man. This entrapment is called "sickness." It is this sickness that the Light came to heal and then to set us free. The third part of man, his material form, was considered a weight, an anchor, and a hindrance, keeping man attached to the corrupted earthly realm.

As we read the text, we must realize that Gnosticism conflicted with traditional Christianity. Overall theology can rise and fall upon small words and terms. If Jesus was not God, his death and thus his atonement meant nothing. His suffering meant nothing. Even the resurrection meant nothing, if one's view of Jesus was that he was not human to begin with, as was true with some Gnostics.

For the Gnostics, resurrection of the dead was unthinkable since flesh as well as all matter is destined to perish. According to Gnostic theology, there was no resurrection of the flesh, but only of the soul. How the soul would be resurrected was explained differently by various Gnostic groups, but all denied the resurrection of the body. To the enlightened Gnostic the actual person was the spirit who used the body as an instrument to survive in the material world but did not identify with it. This belief is echoed in the Gospel of Thomas.

29. Jesus said: If the flesh came into being because of spirit, it is a marvel, but if spirit came into being because of the body, it would be a marvel of marvels. I marvel indeed at how great wealth has taken up residence in this poverty.

Owing to the Gnostic belief of such a separation of spirit and body, it was thought that the Christ spirit within the body of Jesus departed the body before the crucifixion. Others said the body was an illusion and the crucifixion was a sham perpetrated by an eternal spirit on the men that sought to kill it. Lastly, some suggested that Jesus deceived the soldiers into thinking he was dead. The resurrection under this circumstance became a lie which allowed Jesus to escape and live on in anonymity, hiding, living as a married man, and raising a family until his natural death.

Think of the implications to the orthodox Christian world if the spirit of God departed from Jesus as it fled and laughed as the body was crucified. This is the implication of the Gnostic interpretation of the death of Jesus when he cries out, "My power, my power, why have you left me," as the Christ spirit left his body before his death. What are the ramifications to the modern Christian if the Creator God, the Demiurge, is more evil than his creation? Can a Creation rise above its creator? Is it possible for man to find the spark within himself that calls to the Supreme God and free himself of his evil creator?

Although, in time, the creation myth and other Gnostic differences began to be swept under the rug, it was the division between Jesus and the Christ spirit that put them at odds with the emerging orthodox church. At the establishment of the doctrine of the trinity, the mainline church firmly set a divide between themselves and the Gnostics.

To this day there is a battle raging in the Christian world as believers and seekers attempt to reconcile today's Christianity to the sect of the early Christian church called, "Gnosticism."

Feminine Forces in the Old Testament
According to the Old Testament book of Genesis in the Hebrew text, there was a balance of male and female forces within God from the beginning. Neither male nor female, both male and female, God showed the male energy of forming and shaping, as well as the female energy of nurturing and brooding. Although

one may have a difficult time in distinguishing God the Spirit from the Spirit of God, the word for "spirit" is "ruach" and is a female word.

Genesis 1
Amplified Bible

1) In the beginning God (prepared, formed, fashioned, and) created the heavens and the earth.

2) The earth was without form and an empty waste, and darkness was upon the face of the very great deep. The Spirit of God was moving (hovering, brooding) over the face of the waters.

The Holy Spirit is the designated representation of the feminine principle. This idea is supported by the Hebrew word for "spirit". Jerome, the author of the Latin Vulgate knew this when he rendered the passage into Latin. He is quoted as saying:
"In the Gospel of the Hebrews that the Nazarenes read it says, 'Just now my mother, the Holy Spirit, took me.' Now, no one should be offended by this, because "spirit" in Hebrew is feminine, while in our language [Latin] it is masculine, and in Greek it is neuter. In divinity, however, there is no gender."

In Jerome's Commentary on Isaiah 11, an explanation contains a pointed observation. There was a tradition among a sect of Early Christians which believed that the Holy Spirit was our Lord's spiritual mother. Jerome comments that the Hebrew word for "spirit" (ruach or ruak) is feminine, meaning, that for the 1st Century Christians in the Aramaic world, the Holy Spirit was a feminine figure. This was likely because in the beginning, the converts to this new cult of Judaism, called Christianity, were mostly Jews. The gender was lost in the translation from the Hebrew into the Greek, rendering it neuter, and then it was changed to a masculine gender when it was translated from the Greek into the Latin.

536

The Bible in Genesis describes a male/female God with male creating and female brooding. But, man could not hold onto that unfamiliar concept and the primitive Jews chose to take up the Canaanite deities of the God, El and his wife, Asherah. But, she was simply a fertility goddess.

Although the balance of male and female energies were presented in Genesis from the outset, primitive man was not ready to accept or understand the spiritual truth of balance. Instead, mankind had to evolve spiritually over thousands of years until they were ready to resume the search for the Sacred Feminine. This time, it was within their one true God. Monotheism does not easily reveal the dualism of male and female forces.

Even today, the churches continue to struggle with the fact that God is at once male and female. God is neither. God is both. God is all.

Possibly, if we better understood the original language and context of the time, the church would not have gone so far astray. The word used for the station of women in conjunction with men is "helpmeet."

The truth has been there in the Bible all along. Let us look closely at the words used regarding the place of woman in regards to man. The word used is "Helpmeet."

HELP

Strong's # 5828 (**Hebrew - ezer**) aid: - help
Strong's Root # 5826 (Hebrew - azar) azar - prime root: to surround, i.e., protect or aid: help, succor
Heinrich Friedrich Wilhelm Gesenius (1786–1842), noted author of

the first Hebrew lexicon, adds that the primary idea lies in girding, surrounding, hence defending .

MEET

(**Hebrew - *kenegdo***) corresponding to, counterpart to, equal to, matching

The traditional teaching for the woman as help (meet) is that of assistant or helper, subservient to the one being helped. This definition would appear to line up with Strong's definition of the word. However, if you look at the context of every other use of the word *ezer* in the scripture, you will see that *ezer* refers to either God or military allies. In all other cases the one giving the help is superior to the one receiving the help. Adding *kenegdo* (meet) modifies the meaning to that of equal rather than superior status. Let us remember that it was the man was the one who needed help.

Dr. Susan Hyatt gives the following definition from her book *In the Spirit We're Equal:* "Re: Hebrew *ezer kenegdo.* In Genesis 2:18, the word "Helpmeet " does not occur. The Hebrew expression *ezer kenegdo* appears meaning, "one who is the same as the other and who surrounds, protects, aids, helps, supports." There is no indication of inferiority or of a secondary position in a hierarchical separation of the male and female "spheres" of responsibility, authority, or social position.

The word *ezer* is used twice in the Old Testament to refer to the female and 14 times to refer to God. For example, in the Psalms when David says, "The Lord is my Helper," he uses the word *ezer.*"
Usages of '*ezer* in the Old Testament show that in most cases God is an '*ezer* to human beings, which calls to question if the word

"helper" is a valid interpretation of '*ezer* in any instance it is used. "Evidence indicates that the word '*ezer* originally had two roots, each beginning with different guttural sounds. One meant "power" and the other "strength." As time passed, the two guttural sounds merged, but the meanings remained the same. The article below by William Sulik explains this point quite well. He references R. David Freedman and Biblical Archaeology Review 9 [1983]: (56-58).

"She was to be his "helper". At least, that is how most of the translations have interpreted this word. A sample of the translations reads as follows:
'I shall make a helper fit for him' (RSV); 'I will make a fitting helper for him' (New Jewish Publication Society); 'I will make an aid fit for him' (AB); 'I will make him a helpmate' (JB); 'I will make a suitable partner for him' (NAB); 'I will make him a helper comparable to him' (NKJV).

[Source: *Hard Sayings of the Bible* by Walter C. Kaiser, Peter H. Davids, F. F. Bruce, and Manfred Brauch]

However, the customary translation of the two words `*ezer kenegdo* as "helper fit" is almost certainly wrong. Recently R. David Freedman has pointed out that the Hebrew word *ezer* is a combination of two roots: `-z-r, meaning "to rescue, to save," and g-z-r, meaning "to be strong." The difference between the two is the first letter in the Hebrew language.

Today, that letter is silent in the Hebrew; but in ancient times, it was a guttural sound formed in the back of the throat. The "g" was a *ghayyin*, and it came to use the same Hebrew symbol as the other sound, `*ayin*. But the fact that they were pronounced differently is clear from such names of places which preserve the "g" sound, such as Gaza or Gomorrah. Some Semitic languages distinguished between these two signs and others did not. For

example, Ugaritic did make a distinction between the `ayin and the *ghayyin*; Hebrew did not. (R. David Freedman, "*Woman, a Power Equal to a Man*,"
Biblical Archaeology Review 9 [1983]: 56-58).

It would appear that sometime around 1500 BCE, these two signs began to be represented by one sign in Phoenician. Consequently, the two "phonemes" merged into one "grapheme." What had been two different roots merged into one, much as in English the one word "fast" can refer to a person's speed, abstinence from food, his or her slyness in a "fast deal," or the adamant way in which someone holds "fast" to positions. The noun `ezer occurs twenty-one times in the Old Testament. In many of the passages, it is used in parallelism to words that clearly denote strength or power. Some examples of this are: "There is none like the God of Jeshurun, The Rider of the Heavens in your strength (`-z-r), and on the clouds in his majesty."

(Deut.33:26 [source author's translation])
"Blessed are you, O Israel! Who is like you, a people saved by the Lord? He is the shield of your strength (`-z-r) and the sword of your majesty." (Deut. 33:29, [source author's translation]

The case begins to build for the surety that `ezer means "strength" or "power" whenever it is used in parallelism with words for majesty or other words for power such as `oz or `uzzo. In fact, the presence of two names for one king, Azariah and Uzziah, both referring to God's strength, makes it abundantly clear that the root `ezer meaning "strength" was known in Hebrew.

Therefore, we could conclude that Genesis 2:18 be translated as, "I will make a power [or strength] corresponding to man." Freedman even suggests, on the basis of later Hebrew, that the second word in the Hebrew expression found in this verse should be rendered "equal to him." If so, then God makes a woman fully his equal and fully his match for the man.

The same line of reasoning occurs with the apostle Paul, who urged in 1 Corinthians 11:10, "For this reason, a woman must have power [or authority] on her head [that is to say, invested in her]."

This line of reasoning, which stresses full equality, is continued in Genesis 2:23 where Adam says of Eve, "This is now bone of my bones and flesh of my flesh; she shall be called 'woman,' for she was taken out of man." The idiomatic sense of this phrase, "bone of my bones", is a "very close relative" to "one of us" or, in effect, "our equal."

The woman was never meant to be an assistant or "helpmate" to the man. The word "mate" slipped into English since it was so close to the Old English word "meet," which means "fit to" or "corresponding to" the man which comes from the phrase that likely means "equal to."

What God had intended, then, was to make a "power" or "strength" for the man who would in every way "correspond to him", or "be his equal." The closest word connecting the corporeal station of "helpmeet" to the spiritual world within the Godhead is the word that explains the female attributes and energies within God. That word is "Ruach," also spelled "Ruak," since transliteration from Hebrew is not precise. The spirit of God, Ruach, is a female word. Ruach broods and nurtures. She "mothers." To this day, few people, Jew or Christian, have understood this. Others continue to view the deities as two separate entities, just as Yahweh and His consort.

Let us consider a word or two and the various ways the translators have decided to render the words. We will begin with the Hebrew word, "Chayil."

Virtuous = Strong's #2428 (*chayil*) wealth, virtue, valor, strength, might, power.

Before we precede, it must be understood that Hebrew has a reasonably small lexicon. Words are interpreted according to context. The same form may be used as a noun, a verb, an adjective, or an adverb.

Chayil occurs 242 times in the Old Testament. It is translated "army" and "war" 58 times; "host" and "forces" 43 times; "might" or "power" 16 times; "goods," "riches," "substance" and "wealth" in all 31 times; "band of soldiers," "band of men," "company," and "train" once each"; "activity" once; "valor" 28 times; "strength" 11 times: these are all noun forms. The word is often translated as an adjective or adverb.

It is translated "valiant" and "valiantly" 35 times; "strong" 6 times; "able" 4 times; "worthily" once, and "worthy" once. One can see a pattern to the translations of the word. All choices connote power, war, ability, and substance. However, these are the translations of the word only when the translators saw that the word applied to a male, or the actions or results of actions enacted by a man or by men.

In the four instances in which the word is used in describing a woman, the word seems to be rendered as if it were not the same word. In the four cases relating to women, the word is translated differently, and the choices of the words used to rendered *Chayil* into English shows a gender bias.

Ruth, the Moabitess, was a woman of courage, loyalty, and decisiveness. In her loyalty to her dead husband's mother, she refused to leave her mother-in-law and re-marry in her own land, but was inalterably determined to accompany her mother-in-law to a foreign land. There, in an unknown city she committed herself to the task of keeping them both from starvation. She labored tirelessly. Boaz, recognizing her traits would later say to her: "All the city of my people doth know that thou art a woman of *cha-yil*," (Ruth 3:11). The Septuagint rendered the Hebrew word, *Chayil*, into Greek as follows, "Thou art a woman of power" (dunamis).

In the last chapter of Proverbs, there is a description of an ideal wife, whose "price is far above rubies." Here are some of her characteristics: "She is like the merchants' ships, she brings her food from afar." "She considers a field and buys it." "She girds her loins with strength, and strengthens her arms." "Strength and honor are her clothing." The is obviously a woman of determination, strength, and will. This is the kind of woman a mother would choose to marry her son. The translators wrote: "Who can find a virtuous woman? "Virtue" is a moral quality, but does not capture the impressive strength of a women who works day and night in many areas of life and is a success in them all, as the Proverb indicated about this woman. The word used for "Virtue" is the Hebrew word, "*Chayil*." She is a "Mighty" woman.

The ideal woman is summed up in the 29th verse, in the words: "Many daughters have done *cha-yil*, but thou excel them all." "Worthily," "valiantly," are the only translations that we have in any other part of the Bible for this word where it is applied to a man, but here, the word is translated "virtuously" to the female. This pressed the medieval concept of sexual purity into the text where it was not necessarily intended.

In Proverbs 12:4, the Hebrew text reads, "A woman of *cha-yil* is a crown to her husband." The translators render the English text as, "A virtuous woman is a crown to her husband." Again, Septuagint translates the word as a word for strength, power, might, valor, ability, uprightness, integrity.

To sum up the difference in word choices of the translation of "*Chayil*", let us look at the grouping of the examples below:

Ruth 3:11 And now my daughter, fear not, I will do to thee all that thou require; for all the city of my people know that thou art a virtuous *[chayil]* woman.

Proverbs 12:4 A virtuous *[chayil]* woman is a crown to her husband; but she that makes ashamed is as rottenness in his bones.

Proverbs 31:10 Who can find a virtuous *[chayil]* woman? For her price is far above rubies.

Proverbs 31:29 Many daughters have done virtuously *[chayil]* , but thou excel them all.

In **Ps. 18:32 and 39** the word *Chayil* is translated as strength.

Ps.18:32 It is God that girds me with strength *[chayil]*, and makes my way perfect.
vs. 39   For thou hast girded me with strength *[chayil]* unto the battle: thou hast subdued under me those that rose up against me.

The Torah Study for Reform Jews says, "From the time of creation, relationships between spouses have at times been adversarial."

In Genesis 2:18, God calls woman an *ezer kenegdo,* a "helper against him." The great commentator, Rashi, takes the term literally to make a wonderful point: "If he [Adam] is worthy, [she will be] a help *[ezer]*. If he is not worthy [she will be] against him *[kenegdo]* for strife." This Jewish study also described man and woman facing each other with arms raised holding an arch between them, giving a beautiful picture of equal responsibility.

Although a small number of Christian denominations have managed to re-capture some type of balance between male and female energy within the godhead, most have not.

An official publication of the LDS (Mormon) Church states:
"Our Father in heaven was once a man as we are now, capable of physical death. By obedience to eternal gospel principles, he progressed from one stage of life to another until he attained the state that we call exaltation or godhood. In such a condition, he and our mother in heaven were empowered to give birth to spirit children whose potential was equal to that of their heavenly parents. We are those spirit children." (Achieving a Celestial Marriage p 132)

The LDS (Mormon) Church offers courses in religion and supplies books and manuals from which to teach. In the 3rd chapter of the manual for a course entitled, *Doctrines of the Gospel,* that is part of an advanced course for the Religion 231 and 232, we find the church addresses the nature of God. Joseph Smith's "King Follett" sermon is cited as authoritative by this official Church publication along with a statement from Spencer W. Kimball, one of the earlier church prophets:
God made man in his own image and certainly he made woman in the image of his wife-partner (Spencer W. Kimball, The Teachings of Spencer W. Kimball, p.25).

Again we encounter the concept of the heavenly Mother, God's wife in heaven, and have the interesting assertion that women are made, not in the image of God, but in the image of God's wife-partner.

In the above quotes, we see the Church of Jesus Christ of Latter day Saints sought to fill the void of the divine or Sacred Feminine with an entity, who was the wife of God.

It is within the Christian Science Church, also called the Church of Christ Scientists, that the balance of a singular God containing all attributes of both male and female is encountered again after thousands of years.

In the church of Christ Scientists (Christian Science), God is hailed as "The Mother-Father God," vocalizing their held belief of the existence of attributes and energies of both male and female within the spirit of God.

Mary Baker Eddy defined God as "the all-knowing, all-seeing, all-acting, all-wise, all-loving, and eternal; Principle; Mind; Soul; Spirit; Truth; Love; all substance; intelligence" (Eddy 587). Very importantly, Mrs. Eddy throughout her writing also refers to God as the Father-Mother God.

Mary Baker Eddy was not the first one to perceive God as being both Father and Mother (Peel 91). Mother Ann Lee, a Shaker woman, was part of just one of many faiths that spoke of God as Mother. She wrote:
"As Father, God is the infinite Fountain of intelligence, and the Source of all power, "the Almighty and terrible in majesty"; "the high and lofty one, that inhabiteth eternity, whose name is Holy, dwelling in the high and holy place"; and "a consuming fire." But as, Mother, "God is Love" and tenderness. If all the maternal affections of all the female or bearing spirits in animated nature were combined together, and then concentrated in one individual human female, that person would be put as the type or image of our Eternal Heavenly Mother." (Peel 28).

This matches the Christian Science understanding of God's motherly aspects and serves as a helpful illustration of the maternal nature of God as Mother. God as Father is a powerful being that offers intelligence and strength; yet there is something untouchable about Him. God as Mother can be seen as our earthly mothers, tender, nurturing, maternal, and approachable, although it must be stated that neither "ezer" or "chyil" convey the attitude of "motherliness" as we commonly regard it.

Mary Baker Eddy produced an interpretation of the Lord's Prayer based on her understanding of the balance of male and female elements within the Godhead.

Lord's Prayer with Spiritual Interpretation by Mary Baker Eddy
Our Father which art in heaven,
Our Father-Mother God, all-harmonious,
Hallowed be Thy name.
Adorable One.
Thy kingdom come.
Thy kingdom is come; Thou art ever-present.
Thy will be done in earth, as it is in heaven.
Enable us to know – as in heaven, so on earth – God is omnipotent, supreme.
Give us this day our daily bread;
Give us grace for today; feed the famished affections;
And forgive us our debts, as we forgive our
debtors.
And Love is reflected in love;
And lead us not into temptation, but deliver us
from evil;
And God leadeth us not into temptation, but delivereth us from sin, disease, and death.
For Thine is the kingdom, and the power, and the
glory, forever.
For God is infinite, all-power, all Life, Truth, Love, over all, and All.

Defining The Divine Feminine

Having seen some of the attempts of the modern churches to understand and rectify the lack of recognition or understanding of the Divine Feminine, it is necessary to ask, "What happened to the Divine Feminine of Genesis? What initiated the lack of recognition or denial of the female side of God?"

The feminine side of God was erased with the change of language from the Hebrew feminine word "Ruak" into the Greek word "Pneuma" and into the Latin word "Spiritus". Both words, Spiritus and Pneuma mean "breath", but the word used in Latin is a masculine word and in Greek the word has no gender at all. Thus the feminine side of God simply disappeared into a linguistic void and was forgotten; never to be recognized for her nurturing and brooding nature until centuries later. Since the church was almost completely controlled by men at the time, they either did not notice or they did not care that the feminine spirit of God vanished and was replaced with a translation that rendered the spirit of God either neuter or masculine.

Although it is understood that God is a singular being, our psyches still call out for some manifestation of the female force. We long for a mother as well as a father. We search the Bible for the Sacred Feminine. In its pages we find no less than three distinct feminine archetypal forms within God: Ruak, Shikina, and Sophia (Wisdom).

In the pages of the New Testament and the teaching of the Catholic Church, we find the Divine Feminine, also called the Sacred Feminine, exemplified in the persons of Mary Magdalene and Mary, the mother of Jesus.

Let us first look at the feminine forces of Ruak, Shikhinah, and Sophia (Wisdom).

Ruak, Ruach, or Rawach:

We have already seen that Ruak was the spirit that hovered and brooded over the earth like a mother hen broods over her chicks. In the Ten Commandments, we are taught to "honor your father and your mother" and that doing so would make "your days long upon the land which Yahweh your God is giving you." There seems to be no obvious connection in the temporal sense, except that by not honoring your parents you could be stoned. However, if Yahweh is actually speaking of our spiritual father and mother, that is Yahweh and His Holy Spirit, then it all makes sense. Yahweh is the Creator, Provider, Protector, and ultimate Authority. These are all "male" traits. Ruak Qodesh or Holy Spirit is the maternal aspect of God. She is the Caregiver, Counselor, and Comforter.

Shekinah , Shechinah, Shekhina, or Shechina.

In the Hebrew language this word means the glory or radiance of God. The Glory of God rests or resides in his house or Tabernacle amongst his people. Thus, the word is derived from the Hebrew word 'sakan', which means 'to dwell'.

The Shekhina is defined, in traditional Jewish writings, as the "female aspect of God." It is part of the feminine "presence" of the infinite God in the world. She is introduced in early rabbinical commentaries as the "immanence" or "indwelling" of the living God. Her purpose is to animate or impart life force. She is certainly not the 'Canaanite' Mother Goddess, Asherah. Around 622 BCE, King Josiah removed the Asherah from the Jerusalem temple and destroyed the shrines.

While she does not appear by name in the five books of Moses, her presence is seen in interpreting the text. For example, when Moses encounters the burning bush, he is told to remove his shoes and prepare himself to receive the Shekhina.

A Talmudic verse said: "Let them make Me a sanctuary that I may dwell (*ve'shakhanti*) among them." In a later version, the translation said, "Let them make Me a Sanctuary so that My Shekhina will dwell among them."

A Talmudic quotation from the end of the 1st century BCE: " ...while the Children of Israel were still in Egypt, the Holy One, blessed be He, stipulated that He would liberate them from Egypt only in order that they built him a Sanctuary so that He can let His Shekhina dwell among them ... As soon as the Tabernacle was erected, the Shekhina descended and dwelt among them."

Another quotation from early 3rd century says: "On that day a thing came about which had never existed since the creation of the world. From the creation of the world and up to that hour, the Shekhina had never dwelt among the lower beings. But from the time that the Tabernacle was erected, she did dwell among them."

Although the language of the text may lead us to view "her" as a separate entity, the Shekhina is a specific way the Spirit of God is manifesting. She gives life. This is the most powerful of female attributes.

Another tradition claimed that she had always dwelt among her people, but their sins drove her, from time to time, into heaven. However, she was drawn back to her children and tried to save them, over and over. This viewpoint is more in line with the New Testament idea of the Holy Spirit.

Keeping with the idea of the Shekhina returning to the people, when the Jews were exiled to Babylonia, she transferred her seat there, and appeared alternately in two major synagogues.

Jewish tradition and teaching tells us that as the Jews dispersed throughout the world, the Shekhina comforted the poor and the suffering. She drew the sinner back to God by enlivening their spirit and conscience. She caused sinners to repent and then accepted and comforted them as if they had never sinned. Spiritually, she carried aloft the suffering and those whose hearts were broken and whose spirit was low. They were seated next to the Shekhina.. "When their spirits were healed, the Shekhina walked with them every day...."

Since we are limited in our understanding, the idea of a single entity, even a spirit, being in two places at once was disconcerting for the people. The paradox of dwelling in one place, and being other places with many people at the same time, had to be resolved.

The Talmud attempted to explain the paradox within a simple and well-known anecdote. "The Emperor said to Raban Gamaliel: 'You say that wherever ten men are assembled, the Shekhina dwells among them'."

Still, we continued to worry over the fact that God was at once in heaven and on the earth, manifesting as Shekhina. An interesting Medieval story and teaching shows the Shekhina as a total separate entity, in her most important role - interceding on behalf of her children.

Another story shows her being equated to an intercessor. "The Shekhina comes to the defense of sinful Israel by saying first to Israel: 'Be not a witness against thy neighbor without a cause' and then thereafter saying to God: 'Say not: I will do to him as he hath done to me..' "

This is obviously a conversation taking place among three distinct entities - Israel, God, and the Shekhina.

Another significant passage from the 11th century, describes Rabbi Akiva (a second century sage) saying: "When the Holy One, blessed be He, considered the deeds of the generation of Enoch and that they were spoiled and evil, *He removed Himself and His Shekhina* from their midst and ascended into the heights with blasts of trumpets..."

The Talmud reports that the Shekhina is what caused prophets to prophesy and King David to compose his Psalms. The Shekhina manifests herself as a form of joy, connected with prophecy and creativity. (Talmud Pesachim 117a)

The Shekhina is associated with the transformational spirit of God regarded as the source of prophecy:
"After that thou shalt come to the hill of God, where is the garrison of the Philistines; and it shall come to pass, when thou art come thither to the city, that thou shalt meet a band of prophets coming down from the high place with a psaltery, and a timbrel, and a pipe, and a harp, before them; and they will be prophesying.
And the spirit of the LORD will come mightily upon thee, and thou shalt prophesy with them, and shalt be turned into another man." (1 Samuel 10:5-6 JPS).

The 16th century mystic, Rabbi Isaac Luria, wrote a famous Shabbat hymn about the Shekhina or Glory of God. In it we see how this part of God is directly equated with a bride:
"I sing in hymns to enter the gates of the Field of holy apples.
A new table we prepare for Her, a lovely candelabrum sheds its light upon us.
Between right and left the Bride approaches, in holy jewels and festive garments..."

Zohar states: "One must prepare a comfortable seat with several cushions and embroidered covers, from all that is found in the house, like one who prepares a canopy for a bride. For the Shabbat is a queen and a bride. This is why the masters of the Mishna used to go out on the eve of Shabbat to receive her on the road, and used to say: 'Come, O bride, come, O bride!' And one must sing and rejoice at the table in her honor ... one must receive the Lady with many lighted candles, many enjoyments, beautiful clothes, and a house embellished with many fine appointments ..."

The tradition of the Shekhina as the Shabbat Bride continues to this day as a powerful and moving symbol of the Sacred or Divine Feminine.

Wisdom or Sophia:
We must also look in the Old Testament, the Hebrew Bible, and consider Sophia. Her name means "Wisdom," and she is found repeatedly in scripture as the wife or consort of God.

Proverbs 8
Wisdom's Call
 1) Does not wisdom call out?
  Does not understanding raise her voice?
2) At the highest point along the way,
  where the paths meet, she takes her stand;
3) beside the gate leading into the city,
  at the entrance, she cries aloud:
4) "To you, O people, I call out;
  I raise my voice to all mankind.
5) You who are simple, gain prudence;
  you who are foolish, set your hearts on it (Wisdom).
6) Listen, for I have trustworthy things to say;
  I open my lips to speak what is right.
7) My mouth speaks what is true,

for my lips detest wickedness.

8) All the words of my mouth are just;
   none of them are crooked or perverse.

9) To the discerning all of them are right;
   they are upright to those who have found knowledge.

10) Choose my instruction instead of silver,
   knowledge rather than choice gold,

11) for wisdom is more precious than rubies,
   and nothing you desire can compare with her.

12) I, wisdom, dwell together with prudence; I possess
knowledge and discretion.

13) To fear the LORD is to hate evil; I hate pride and arrogance,
evil behavior and perverse speech.

14) Counsel and sound judgment are mine; I have insight, I have
power.

15) By me kings reign and rulers issue decrees that are just;

16) by me princes govern, and nobles — all who rule on earth.

17) I love those who love me, and those who seek me find me.

18) With me are riches and honor, enduring wealth and
prosperity.

19) My fruit is better than fine gold; what I yield surpasses choice
silver.

20) I walk in the way of righteousness, along the paths of justice,

21) bestowing a rich inheritance on those who love me and
making their treasuries full.

22) The LORD brought me forth as the first of his works, before
his deeds of old;

23) I was formed long ages ago, at the very beginning, when the
world came to be.

24) When there were no watery depths, I was
given birth, when there were no springs
overflowing with water;

25) before the mountains were settled in place, before the hills, I
was given birth,

26) before he made the world or its fields or any of the dust of the earth.

27) I was there when he set the heavens in place, when he marked out the horizon on the face of the deep,

28) when he established the clouds above and fixed securely the fountains of the deep,

29) when he gave the sea its boundary so the waters would not overstep his command, and when he marked out the foundations of the earth.

30) Then I was constantly at his side. I was filled with delight day after day, rejoicing always in his presence,

31) rejoicing in his whole world and delighting in mankind.

32) "Now then, my children, listen to me; blessed are those who keep my ways.

33) Listen to my instruction and be wise; do not disregard it.

34) Blessed are those who listen to me, watching daily at my doors, waiting at my doorway.

35) For those who find me find life and receive favor from the LORD.

36) But those who fail to find me harm themselves; all who hate me love death."

Although the mainstream Christian church would forget about Sophia, the Gnostic Christians would not. In their unorthodox theology, they fought to understand the duality of the world and the Sacred Feminine. The Gnostic movement started before second century A.D., but was condemned by the emerging powers of the orthodox church and newly established church fathers. They could not control the people through Gnostic theology, which taught there was an individual transmission of knowledge from God to the individual without the help or interference of priests or church.

Most Gnostics were suppressed or killed. The last great Gnostic movement came from the Cathars. Catharism represented total opposition to the Catholic church, which they basically viewed as a large, pompous, and fraudulent organization which had lost its integrity and "sold out" for power and money in this world, a world which the Gnostics viewed as evil.

As time went on and the mainstream church became established in its power base, they could more effectively fight their enemies. The Inquisition was proof of this.

In an attempt to cleanse the world of the Gnostics once and for all, whole villages and cities were annihilated, including women and children, and even Catholics, with the justification by the church that this serious heresy must be eliminated no matter what the consequences. Arnold Aimery, the Papal Legate at the siege of Beziers, ordered his men: "Show mercy neither to order, nor to age, nor to sex....Cathar or Catholic, Kill them all... God will know his own....".

Catharism, one of the last great sects of Gnosticism, vanished from the stage of history by the end of the 14th century due to that final, fateful siege of Monsegur in 1244.

Gnostic texts were preserved and many were found in 1945 in Nag Hammadi, Egypt.

In the Gnostic text called, *The Apocryphon of John,* Sophia is quoted:
"I entered into the midst of the cage which is the prison of the body. And I spoke saying: 'He who hears, let him awake from his deep sleep.' Then Adam wept and shed tears. After he wiped away his bitter tears he asked: 'Who calls my name, and from where has this hope arose in me even while I am in the chains of this prison?' And I (Sophia) answered: 'I am the one who carries the pure light; I am the thought of the undefiled spirit. Arise, remember, and follow your origin, which is I, and beware of the deep sleep.'"

As the myth evolved, Sophia, after animating Adam, became Eve in order to assist Adam in finding the truth. She offered it to him in the form of the fruit of the tree of knowledge. To Gnostics, this was an act of deliverance.

Other stories have Sophia becoming the serpent in order to offer Adam a way to attain the truth.
Since in the Gnostic sect of Christianity truth leads to salvation, it was Sophia, offering the knowledge of truth to Adam that symbolized salvation.

In either case, the fruit represented the hard sought truth, which was the knowledge of good and evil, and through that knowledge, Adam could become a god. Later, the serpent would become a feminine symbol of wisdom, probably owing to the connection with Sophia.

Eve, being Sophia in disguise, would become the mother and Sacred Feminine of us all. As Gnostic theology began to coalesce, Sophia would come to be considered a force or conduit of the Holy Spirit, in part due to the fact that the Holy Spirit was also considered a feminine and creative force from the Supreme God. The Gospel of Philip echoes this theology in verse six as follows:

"In the days when we were Hebrews, we were made orphans, having only our Mother. Yet when we believed in the Messiah (and became the ones of Christ), the Mother and Father both came to us. "

Sophia would later equate to the Holy Spirit as she awakened the comatose soul.

So it is that within these three: Ruak – the spirit, Shikinah – the glory, and Sophia- the wisdom, that the Sacred Feminine of God is expressed.

Understanding The Divine Feminine

A dynamic tension between the psychological need of a feminine energy, and a hesitancy to confer or concede any control to a female exists in modern Judeo-Christian religion and culture.

Carl Jung sums up the archetypes of the female as related to the stages or evolution of man's views toward women in general. To be very clear, Jung's four stages of women are the distinct stages of evolution or maturity within the male psyche and how the man views women.

Jung believed anima or life force development has four distinct levels, which he named *Eve, Helen (who we also identify with Mary Magdalene), Mary, the mother of Jesus, and Sophia or Wisdom*. In broad terms, the entire process of life force development in a male is about the male subject opening up to emotionality. In doing so, he obtains a broader spirituality by creating a new conscious paradigm that includes the intuitive processes, creativity, and imagination and psychic sensitivity towards himself and others where it might not have existed previously. Since religion is a reflection of the collective psyche, it is very important to examine these stages and how they each influence, or have influenced, religious thought in regards to women and the place of the Sacred Feminine in Christianity.

Eve

The first is *Eve*, named after the Genesis account of Adam and Eve. It deals with the emergence of a male's object of desire. This coincides with Asherah and her place as a goddess of fertility and procreation.

Helen – Mary Magdalene

The second is *Helen or Mary Magdalene*. Helen is in allusion to Helen of Troy in Greek mythology. In this phase, women are viewed as capable of worldly success and of being self-reliant, intelligent, and insightful, even if not altogether virtuous. This second phase is meant to show a strong schism in external talents (cultivated business and conventional skills) with lacking internal qualities (inability for virtue, lacking faith or imagination). Although Mary Magdalene was not the prostitute in the biblical account, (that person was never given a name), she did have seven demons and was not considered totally virtuous, as the apostles pointed out when they sought to dissuade Jesus from being seen with her. Speculation is that Mary Magdalene was wealthy, being from a village that was know for wealthy ship owners and fishermen, and supplied funds for Jesus' ministry. Luke 8: 1–4 states plainly that Jesus was supported by women, including Mary Magdalene, who "were helping to support Jesus and the Twelve with their own money." (NIRV)

Mary, The Mother

The third phase is *Mary*, named after the Christian theological understanding of the Virgin Mary (Jesus' mother). At this level, females can now seem to possess virtue by the perceiving male (even if in an esoteric and dogmatic way), in so much as certain activities deemed consciously non-virtuous cannot be applied to her. We will see later how the Catholic church has elevated Mary through all phases of Jungian feminine archetypes.

Sophia

The fourth and final phase of anima development is *Sophia*, named after the Greek word for wisdom. Complete integration has now occurred, which allows females to be seen and related to as particular individuals who possess both positive and negative qualities. The most important aspect of this final level is that, as the personification "Wisdom" suggests, the anima is now developed enough that no single object can fully and permanently contain the images to which it is related. Sophia means wisdom. The name of Wisdom shows up in the Old Testament as a persona, and the consort of God. In Gnostic works, Sophia was the creative force that formed the spirit of man and Sophia was Eve, who came down to offer knowledge to Adam.

When we look at these stages in detail, we notice that within each of these archetypes the church has created evolutionary stages as the body works its way back to a balance of male and female forces.

Eve

Eve – her name means "Mother of All Living, Restorer, Reviver." From Eve all human life descends. She is thus the symbol of fertility and procreation. Throughout the life of the church, women have been equated with Eve and her part in the fall of mankind in the garden. In general, the state of Eve in the male psyche has been one of deep ambivalence. There is an old saying that men hate women as a lame man hates his crutch. Following are a few quotes from church fathers regarding women and their place in society and religion:

"Rather should the words of the Torah be burned than entrusted to a woman...Whoever teaches his daughter the Torah is like one who teaches her obscenity." *Rabbi Eliezer*

"Do you not know that you are each an Eve? The sentence of God on this sex of yours lives in this age: the guilt must of necessity live too. You are the Devil's gateway: You are the unsealer of the forbidden tree: You are the first deserter of the divine law: You are she who persuaded him whom the devil was not valiant enough to attack. You destroyed so easily God's image, man. On account of your desertion, even the Son of God had to die." *St.*

Tertullian

"What is the difference whether it is in a wife or a mother, it is still Eve, the temptress that we must beware of in any woman......I fail to see what use woman can be to man, if one excludes the function of bearing children." *St. Augustine of Hippo*

"As regards the individual nature, woman is defective and misbegotten, for the active force in the male seed tends to the production of a perfect likeness in the masculine sex; while the production of woman comes from a defect in the active force or from some material indisposition, or even from some external influence." *St. Thomas Aquinas*

"If they [women] become tired or even die, that does not matter. Let them die in childbirth, that's why they are there." *Martin Luther*

The status of women in the Bible, is disputed. Beginning with Eve herself, there is a dynamic split of position and place, owing to the fact that there are two separate accounts of her creation. The traditional church has seen the role of Eve as mother of Cain and Abel, as well as the person who was deceived into sin by Satan.

Message Bible - Genesis 1:26-28
God spoke: "Let us make human beings in our image, make them reflecting our nature so they can be responsible for the fish in the sea, the birds in the air, the cattle, and, yes, Earth itself, and every animal that moves on the face of Earth."
God created human beings; he created them godlike, reflecting God's nature. He created them male and female. God blessed them: "Prosper! Reproduce! Fill Earth! Take charge!
Be responsible for fish in the sea and birds in the air, for every living thing that moves on the face of Earth."

Genesis 2: 21-22

God put the Man into a deep sleep. As he slept he removed one of his ribs and replaced it with flesh. God then used the rib that he had taken from the Man to make Woman and presented her to the Man. **(23-25)** The Man said, "Finally! Bone of my bone, flesh of my flesh! Name her Woman for she was made from Man." Therefore a man leaves his father and mother and embraces his wife. They become one flesh. The two of them, the Man and his Wife, were naked, but they felt no shame.

In the first account, in Genesis 1:26, woman was made at the same time man was created. In the second account, in Genesis 2: 21, woman was made from man's rib. In the first account, because man and woman were created at the same time, woman was given equal status, but the prevailing ideas of the time would not allow this to stand. It was due to this dual storyline and the fact that women were thought to be inferior to man that the myth of Lilith was born. In this myth, Adam's first wife, Lilith sought to be his equal. The story shows this mindset was thought to be evil.

God created all things living, and then he created man. He created a man and a woman and gave them dominion over all things. God named the man Adam, and the woman He named Lilith. Both were formed from the dust of the earth and in both God breathed the breath of life. They became human souls and God endowed them with the power of speech.

Created at the same time, in the same way, there was no master, no leader, and only bickering between them. Lilith said, "I will not be below you, in life or during sex. I want the superior position". But Adam would not relent and insisted God had created him to be the head of the family and in the affairs of earth. Lilith was enraged and would not submit.

Then God communed with Adam in the cool of the evening and as he entered into His presence, Adam appealed to God. As God fellowshipped with them, they reasoned together, Adam, Lilith, and the living God. But Lilith would not listen to God or Adam. Seeing that with two people of equal authority there could be no solution, Lilith became frustrated, angry, and intractable. Finally, enraged and defiant, she pronounced the holy and indescribable name of God. Corrupting the power of the name, she flew into the air, changing form, and disappeared, soaring out of sight.

Adam stood alone, confused, praying. "Lord of the universe," he said, "The woman you gave me has run away." At once, three holy angels were dispatched to bring her back to Adam. The angels overtook Lilith as she passed over the sea, in the area where Moses would later pass through. The angels ordered Lilith to come with them in the name and by the authority of the most high God, but she refused. As her rebellion increased, she changed, becoming more and more ugly and demonic.

God spoke into Lilith's heart, saying, "You have chosen this evil path, and so shall you become evil. You are cursed from now until the end of days." Lilith spoke to the angels and said, "I have become this, created to cause sickness, to kill children, which I will never have, and to torment men." With these words, she completed her demonic transformation. Her form was that of a succubus.
Confined to the night, she was destined to roam the earth, seeking newborn babes, stealing their lives, and strangling them in their sleep. She torments men even now, causing lust and evil dreams. Her rebellious and evil spirit forever traps her. Bound in the darkness of her own heart, Lilith became the mistress and lover to legions of demons. And Adam's countenance fell and he mourned, for he had loved Lilith, and he was again alone and lonely.

God said, "It is not good for man to be alone." And the Lord God caused a deep sleep to fall on him, and he slept, and He took from Adam a rib from among his ribs for the woman, and this rib was the origin of the woman. And He built up the flesh in its place, and created the woman. He awakened Adam out of his sleep. On awakening Adam rose on the sixth day, and God brought her to Adam, and he knew her, and said to her, "This is now bone of my bones and flesh of my flesh; she shall be called woman for she was taken from man, and she shall be called my wife; because she was taken from her husband."

Mary Magdalene

Mary Magdalene was the woman delivered from demons by Jesus. She was a woman who was seen as deeply flawed by demonic possession. Being set free by the man, Jesus, she followed him to the end. She was a strong, committed, and determined woman, but she was a woman nonetheless. The apostles challenged Jesus because they believed he would be judged harshly by the masses for being to close to Mary. Recent discoveries have led scholars to believe Magdala, the city that Mary came from and whose name is derived from the place-name, was likely a woman of means. The city was known for its ships and fishing industry. Mary was probably part of the fishing industry and could have owned ships. Mary Magdalene was most likely bankrolling part of he ministry of Jesus.

She was a woman who followed Jesus as he ministered and preached.

Luke 8:1-3: Afterward, Jesus journeyed from one town and village to another, preaching and proclaiming the good news of the kingdom of God. Accompanying him were the Twelve and some women who had been cured of evil spirits and infirmities, Mary, called Magdalene, from whom seven demons had gone out, Joanna, the wife of Herod's steward Chuza, Susanna, and many others who provided for them out of their resources.

She was there when Jesus was crucified.

Mark 15:40: There were also some women looking on from a distance, among whom were Mary Magdalene, and Mary, the mother of James the Less and Joses, and Salome.

Matthew 27:56: Among them was Mary Magdalene, and Mary, the mother of James and Joseph, and the mother of the sons of Zebedee.

John 19:25: *But standing by the cross of Jesus were His mother, and His mother's sister, Mary, the wife of Clopas, and Mary Magdalene.*

She continued to believe in Jesus after he was killed.

Mark 15:47: *Mary Magdalene and Mary, the mother of Joses, were looking on to see where He was laid.*

Matthew 27:61: *And Mary Magdalene was there, and the other Mary, sitting opposite the grave.*

Matthew 28:1: *Now after the Sabbath, as it began to dawn toward the first day of the week, Mary Magdalene and the other Mary came to look at the grave.*

Mark 16:1: *When the Sabbath was over, Mary Magdalene, and Mary, the mother of James, and Salome, bought spices, so that they might come and anoint Him.*

She was the first to realize and announce the resurrection of Jesus.

John 20:1: *Now, on the first day of the week, Mary Magdalene came early to the tomb, while it was still dark, and saw the stone already taken away from the tomb.*

Mark 16:9: *Now after He had risen early on the first day of the week, He first appeared to Mary Magdalene, from whom He had cast out seven demons.*

John 20:18: *Mary Magdalene came, announcing to the disciples, "I have seen the Lord," and that He had said these things to her.*

Luke 24: But at daybreak on the first day of the week [the women] took the spices they had prepared and went to the tomb. They found the stone rolled away from the tomb; but when they entered, they did not find the body of the Lord Jesus. While they were puzzling over this, behold, two men in dazzling garments appeared to them. They were terrified and bowed their faces to the ground. They said to them, "Why do you seek the living one among the dead?

He is not here, but he has been raised. Remember what he said to you while he was still in Galilee, that the Son of Man must be handed over to sinners and be crucified, and rise on the third day." And they remembered his words.

Then they returned from the tomb and announced all these things to the eleven and to all the others.

The women were Mary Magdalene, Joanna, and Mary, the mother of James; the others who accompanied them also told this to the apostles, but their story seemed like nonsense and they did not believe them.

Most Gnostic Christians held to the idea of the duality of sexes playing out in multiple layers. The feminine force of Sophia becomes the feminine force of the Holy Spirit and is made the bride of God. The gender duality continues when the feminine force of the Holy Spirit inhabits the perfect man, Jesus, making him the Messiah. The gender context is ripe for the story to be continued in the persons of Jesus and Mary Magdalene, physically shadowing the spiritual relationship of the Holy Spirit and the Supreme God, as well as Jesus and the Holy Spirit.

The concept of a married Jesus is revealed in several verses of The Gospel of Philip, such as verse 118.

"There is the Son of Man and there is the son of the son of Man. The Lord is the Son of Man, and his son creates through him. God gave the

Son of Man the power to create; he also gave him the ability to have children."

If one were to examine the writings of Solomon, the play on words between the masculine and feminine, and the spiritual aspects can be seen clearly. The Gnostics simply expanded on the theme.

Song of Solomon 1 (King James Version)
1 *The song of songs, which is Solomon's.*
2 *Let him kiss me with the kisses of his mouth: for thy love is better than wine.*
3 *Because of the savour of thy good ointments thy name is as ointment poured forth, therefore do the virgins love thee.*
4 *Draw me, we will run after thee: the king hath brought me into his chambers: we will be glad and rejoice in thee, we will remember thy love more than wine.*

Song of Solomon 2
16 *My beloved is mine, and I am his: he feedeth among the lilies.*
17 *Until the day break, and the shadows flee away, turn, my beloved, and be thou like a roe or a young hart upon the mountains of Bether.*

Song of Solomon 3
1 *By night on my bed I sought him whom my soul loveth: I sought him, but I found him not.*
2 *I will rise now, and go about the city in the streets, and in the broad ways I will seek him whom my soul loveth: I sought him, but I found him not...*

Song of Solomon 5
1 *I am come into my garden, my sister, my spouse: I have gathered my myrrh with my spice; I have eaten my honeycomb with my honey; I have drunk my wine with my milk: eat, O friends; drink, yea, drink*

abundantly, O beloved.

2 I sleep, but my heart waketh: it is the voice of my beloved that knocketh, saying, Open to me, my sister, my love, my dove, my undefiled: for my head is filled with dew, and my locks with the drops of the night.

3 I have put off my coat; how shall I put it on? I have washed my feet; how shall I defile them?

4 My beloved put in his hand by the hole of the door, and my bowels were moved for him.

5 I rose up to open to my beloved; and my hands dropped with myrrh, and my fingers with sweet smelling myrrh, upon the handles of the lock.

Song of Solomon 7

1 How beautiful are thy feet with shoes, O prince's daughter! the joints of thy thighs are like jewels, the work of the hands of a cunning workman.

2 Thy navel is like a round goblet, which wanteth not liquor: thy belly is like an heap of wheat set about with lilies.

3 Thy two breasts are like two young roes that are twins.

Due to the inherent dualism of Gnosticism, sex was a symbol, and at times, a portal to a mystical experience. This is one reason the Aeons were said to be created in pairs on male and female. It is also why the texts of The Sophia of Jesus Christ and Eugnostos the Blessed refers to the Aeon and to Jesus as "androgynous" which indicates the existence of both make and female energies. Within the contexts we find in Jesus both male and female powers. Gnosticism seeks a balance of energies, both in the spiritual realm and the physical world. For this reason the Aeons were made in pairs.

The balance or compliment to Jesus is Sophia. Even the supreme and indescribable God had his counterpart in Barbelo. Barbelo is often depicted as a supreme female principle, the single passive antecedent of creation in its infinite forms. She is called the

'Mother-Father', again hinting at androgyny. She is called 'First Human Being', and 'Eternal Aeon'. So prominent was her place amongst some Gnostics that some schools were designated as Barbeliotae, or Barbelognostics.

Keeping in mind that Gnosticism is an amalgam of Plato's cosmology and Christian theology, it is interesting to note Plato's "Split Apart Theory." Plato's theory was that each human being is part of one soul, having both male and female parts, in which they only have half. The idea is that the soul was "split-apart" and separated from each other at the time the soul left heavenly realm. The two halves have been forever searching for one another in order to join together and regain their sense of original created wholeness. Thus, we, in our wholeness, exhibit the same androgyny as the Aeons when we are in our completed state with our "split apart." For this and other reasons, many Gnostic schools believed sex was a portal to a mystical experience.

The idea of completeness in sex and the need for a gender balance in religion was a well-established concept in Gnosticism and their influence on the sects of Christianity that became mainline should not be overlooked. Many religions are replete with sexual allegories, as is Gnosticism. Proceeding from the point of view that people, like aeons, need a complement and balance of male and female energies in Gnostic literature and the likelihood of marriage among the population of Jewish men, controversy arose as to whether Jesus could have married, or should have been married to achieve his "fullness". The flames of argument roared into inferno proportions when the translation of the books of Philip and Mary Magdalene were published.

"And the companion (Consort) was Mary of Magdala (Mary Magdalene). The Lord loved Mary more than all the other disciples and he kissed her often on her mouth (the text is missing here and the word "mouth" is assumed). The others saw his love for Mary and asked him:

"Why do you love her more than all of us?" The Savior replied, "Why do I not love you in the same way I love her?"
  The Gospel of Philip

Peter said to Mary; "Sister we know that the Savior loved you more than all other women. Tell us the words of the Savior that you remember and know, but we have not heard and do not know. Mary answered him and said; "I will tell you what He hid from you."
  The Gospel of Mary Magdalene

Mary was a sinful, damaged, redeemed, powerful person. It is the myth woven into the story of Mary Magdalene that empowers her to us. To many, she is the captive. Possessed, enslaved, caught in the midst of crime and tragedy, but at once redeemed, set free, and loved by God himself. (Mary was connected to the story of a prostitute, but this is not the case.) She is hope and triumph. She represents the power of truth and love to change the life of the lowest and most powerless of us. She is you and me in search of God.

Mary, The Mother of Jesus

The evolution of the status of Mary, the mother of Jesus, is the attempt by the collective psyche of the church to find the correct place for the feminine energies of God. However, since the church leaders have not reconciled the balance of masculine and feminine parts of God, Mary was chosen as a surrogate to be endowed with some of these qualities.

Rising to another level of the Sacred Feminine, *Ruak* becomes the female part of the Godhead that impregnated Mary to produce Jesus. The same spirit empowered Jesus by coming down in the visage of a dove. Mary was visited and carried this spirit within her womb. It is natural that she would come to be equated with the same mothering, nurturing, Sacred Feminine.

The Catholic Church was diminishing the status of women at the same time as they struggled to make sense of their own female redeemer. They began to elevate Mother Mary by announcing the doctrine of the Immaculate Conception, so errors in logic were exposed. If Mother Mary was conceived without sin in order to carry Jesus, who was conceived without sin, one must ask why wasn't it necessary for the mother of Mary to also be conceived without sin. This logic continues backward ad infinitum until Eve herself and all female offspring must be sinless. Of course, the church flatly refuses this line of reasoning, saying only that certain things must be taken on faith. This is the same tactic taken regarding the "Ever-Virginity" of Mother Mary, even in the face of scriptures proclaiming that the mother, sister, and brothers of Jesus had come to have audience with him.

It was the Greek Orthodox Church that already had the answer to this dilemma. Original sin is not in their doctrine. They state only that humans are born with a pre-disposition toward sinning. This makes the problem of sinless birth from the beginning, null.

Even though the theological events of doctrine concerning Mother Mary occurred over time, they serve as an undeniable pattern of the Catholic Church as it endeavored to "purify" women and rid them of sexuality. It is within Mary that we find the complete evolution of the Sacred Feminine, but with sexuality systematically muted and removed.

Beginning as a teenage girl, dismissed by society as a lowly female, she has, over time, been elevated to a position wherein the Catholic Church has placed her alongside, although not quite equal to, the savior himself. Some of the positions of the Catholic Church regarding Mary were not officially accepted until the mid to late nineteenth century.

In the writings of the early church fathers (Justin Martyr 165 A.D. and Irenaeus 202 A.D.), Mother Mary was seldom mentioned and only to contrast Mary's obedience with Eve's disobedience.

The doctrine of Mary as Theotokos (God-bearer) probably originated in Alexandria and was first introduced by Origen. It became common in the fourth century and accepted at the Council of Ephesus in 431 A.D.

Since the accepted Christian church continued to slip farther and farther toward the belief that sex was evil, the doctrine of the "Ever-Virginity" of Mary was established. This was the belief that Mary conceived as a virgin, but also remained a virgin even after giving birth to Jesus and thereafter, for the rest of her life. The Catholic Church rejects the idea that Mary had other children, although the Bible speaks of the brothers and sisters of Jesus. The doctrine of "virginity" was established around 359 A.D.

The doctrine of the bodily Assumption of Mary was formally developed by St. Gregory of Tours around 594 A.D. This doctrine stated that Mary, the mother of Jesus, was taken up into heaven to be seated at the side of Jesus. The idea has been present in apocryphal texts since the late fourth century. The Feast of the Assumption became widespread in the sixth century, and sermons on that occasion tended to emphasize Mary's power in heaven.

Of all the doctrines regarding Mary, the doctrine of the Immaculate Conception widened the divide between the Catholic churches and other Christian churches. This doctrine took the position that Mother Mary was born without the stain of original sin. Both Catholics and Orthodox Christians accept this doctrine, but only the Roman Catholic Church has named it "The Immaculate Conception" and articulated it as doctrine.

Eastern Orthodox Christians reject the western doctrine of original sin, preferring instead to speak of a tendency towards sin. They believe Mary was born without sin, but so was everyone else. Mary simply never gave in to sin.

As we see in the following statement, the doctrine was not formally accepted until 1854 A.D. "The Most Blessed Virgin Mary was, from the first moment of her conception, by a singular grace and privilege of almighty God and by virtue of the merits of Jesus Christ, Savior of the human race, preserved immune from all stain of original sin."
Pope Pius IX, Ineffabilis Deus (1854)

We will examine the four Marian dogmas, among a large number of other teachings about Mary, and how they mirror the evolution of the Scared Feminine.

Perpetual Virginity – Established in the Third Century – Proclaims that Mary was a virgin before, during, and after the birth of Jesus.

Mother of God – First Council of Ephesus in 431 A.D. - Mary is truly the mother of God, because of her unity with Christ, the Son of God.

Immaculate Conception – Pope Pius IX (1854) Mary, at her conception, was preserved immaculate from the original sin.

Assumption into Heaven – Pope Pius XII (1950) - Mary, having completed the course of her earthly life, was assumed body and soul into heavenly glory.

'Perpetual Virginity of Mary', means that Mary was a virgin before, during and after giving birth.

Mary was a teenage unwed mother in a world where such things brought shame and death by stoning. Beginning in the general status as Eve, stressing only her lowly station as a younger woman married to an older man for the purpose of procreation and service, she is raised by the doctrine of "Ever-Virginity" to one that is a step above the norm, being without sin when it comes to her primary purpose of procreation.

This oldest Marian dogma from the Roman Catholic, Eastern Orthodox, and Oriental Orthodox Churches affirms in their doctrine that the virginity of Mary, mother of Jesus is "real and perpetual even in the act of giving birth to the Son of God made Man." According to this doctrine, Jesus was her only biological son, whose incarnation and nativity are miraculous.

In the year 107 A.D. Ignatius of Antioch described the virginity of Mary as "hidden from the prince of this world ... loudly proclaimed, but wrought in the silence of God." The Gospel of James, a text written around 120-150 A.D., was concerned with the character and purity of Mary. The text claims that Joseph had children from a marriage previous to Mary. However, the text does not explicitly assert the doctrine of perpetual virginity. The earliest such surviving reference is Origen's *Commentary on Matthew*, where he cites the *Protoevangelium* in support.

By the fourth century, the doctrine was generally accepted. Athanasius described Mary as "Ever-Virgin".

In Thomas Aquinas' teaching, (*Summa Theologiae* III.28.2), Mary gave birth painlessly in miraculous fashion without opening of the womb and without injury to the hymen. *"From the first formulations of her faith, the Church has confessed that Jesus was conceived solely by the power of the Holy Spirit in the womb of the Virgin Mary, affirming also the corporeal aspect of this event: Jesus was conceived "by the Holy Spirit without human seed."*

Her corporal integrity was not affected by giving birth. The Church does not teach how this occurred physically, but insists that virginity during child birth is different from virginity of conception. *Pope Pius XII*

Mystici Corporis: "Within her virginal womb she brought into life Christ our Lord in a marvelous birth." This indicated the miraculous nature of the Virgin birth. In fact, this was the first act that would remove the stain of sex from Mary, making her a virgin forever. She is now a woman removed from the natural cause and effect of her sexuality.

Mary is truly the *Mother of God*.
Even though Mary was clear of adultery, as Joseph first thought when she announced her pregnancy, and the sin of coitus was removed from her by declaring her a perpetual virgin, when it comes to procreation, she remains a woman in service to men, being different from other women, but not reverenced. In this proclamation, the church elevates Mary to the heights of womanhood, announcing that she is "Theotokos", Mother-of-God, where she begins to be honored.

After the Church fathers found common ground on Mary's virginity before, during, and after giving birth, this was the first specifically Marian doctrine to be formally defined by the Church. The definition *Mother of God* (in Greek: Theotokos) was formally affirmed at the held at Third Ecumenical Council in Ephesus in 431 A.D. The competing view, advocated by the Patriarch of Constantinople, Nestorius of Constantinople, was that Mary should be called *Christotokos*, meaning, "Birth-giver of Christ," to restrict her role to the mother of Christ's humanity only and not his divine nature.

The holy virgin gave birth in the flesh to God united with the flesh according to hypostasis, and for that reason, we call her *Theotokos*... If anyone does not confess that Emmanuel is, in truth, God, and, therefore, that the holy virgin is *Theotokos* (for she bore, in a fleshly manner, the Word from God become flesh), let him be anathema (banned, exiled, excommunicated)."
  (Cyril's third letter to Nestorius)

Immaculate Conception of Mary
Mary was conceived without original sin.
For Mary to be so different from other women, there must have been a divine intervention from the beginning. The answer was a miracle that kept Mary from the sin of being fully human, for to be fully human, according to the church, one would be born as a sinful creature. This is the first doctrine to hint that the most righteous woman could be as sinless as the most righteous man, Jesus. Both were conceived without sin.

According to the Roman Catholic Church, Immaculate Conception is the conception of a child without any stain of original sin in her mother's womb: the dogma states that, from the first moment of her existence, she (Mary) was preserved by God from the sin that afflicts mankind, and that she was instead filled with Divine Grace.

It is further believed that she lived a life completely free from sin. Her immaculate conception in the womb of her mother, by normal coitus (Christian tradition identifies her parents as Joachim and Anne), should not be confused with the doctrine of the virginal conception of her son, Jesus.

The feast of the Immaculate Conception, celebrated on December 8, was established in 1476 by Pope Sixtus IV. Pope Pius IX, in his

constitution *Ineffabilis Deus*, on December 8, 1854, solemnly
defined the Immaculate Conception as a dogma, a truth, not
merely an implied condition, by the deposit of faith, and
discerned by the Church under the infallible guidance of the Holy
Spirit. However, the dogma is specifically and explicitly
contained as an object of supernatural faith in the Public
Revelation of the Deposit of Faith.

Mary is Mother of all Christians – 1579 A.D.
Obedience to God, perfect faith, and the church's position, which
removed Mary from the sin that besets all who are "born of
woman" has positioned Mary as the perfect mother. God has
been born from her sinless body. She has raised and mothered
God himself. In doing so, she has given birth to the church. Now
she is given the status of the greatest mother in the world and is
crowned as "Mother of all Christians." Still, Mary is identified
only as a woman and a mother, but she is now the zenith and
apex of these things.

The Catholic Church teaches that the Virgin Mary is mother of the
Church and of all its members, namely all Christians. The
Catechism of the Catholic Church states:

*"The Virgin Mary . . . is acknowledged and honoured as being truly the
Mother of God and of the redeemer.... She is 'clearly the mother of the
members of Christ' . . . since she has by her charity joined in bringing
about the birth of believers in the Church, who are members of its head."
"Mary, Mother of Christ, Mother of the Church."*

Mary is seen as mother of all Christians because Christians are
said in scripture to become spiritually part of the body of Christ
and Mary bore Christ in her body. Christians are adopted by Jesus
as his "brothers". They therefore share with Him the Fatherhood
of God and also the motherhood of Mary. To back up this stance,
in the Book of John, Jesus, gives the Apostle John to Mary as her

son, and gives Mary to John as his mother as he is about to die. John here, as the sole remaining Apostle remaining steadfast with Jesus, is taken to represent all loyal followers of Jesus from that time on.

Pope John Paul II , in his work, "Totus Tuus" was inspired by the writings of Saint Louis de Montfort on total consecration to the Virgin Mary, which he quoted:.

"Now, since Mary is of all creatures the one most conformed to Jesus Christ, it follows that among all devotions that which most consecrates and conforms a soul to our Lord is devotion to Mary, his Holy Mother, and that the more a soul is consecrated to her the more will it be consecrated to Jesus Christ."

Assumption of Mary
Mary was assumed into heaven with body and soul.
As time went on, the church removed women from positions of authority and spiritual leadership. The assumption of Mary in 1950 places a woman at the throne of God, beside her son, Jesus. She has surpassed being a mother and is now bodily in heaven, placing her in the company of only three others: Jesus, Elijah, and Enoch, who were also taken up to heaven in physical form.

Mary, the ever virgin, mother of God was free of original sin. The Immaculate Conception is one basis for the 1950 dogma. Another was the century old Church-wide veneration of the Virgin Mary as being assumed into heaven, which Pope Pius XII referred to in *Deiparae Virginis Mariae*. Although the assumption of Mary was only recently defined as dogma, accounts of the bodily assumption of Mary into heaven have circulated, at least, since the 5th century. The Catholic Church itself interprets chapter 12 of the Book of Revelation as referring to it. The story appears in "The Passing of the Virgin Mary", a late 5th century work ascribed to

Melito of Sardis and tells the story of the apostles being transported by white clouds to the death-bed of Mary, each from the town where he was preaching at the hour.

Theological debate about the Assumption continued until 1950 when, in the Apostolic Constitution, Munificentissimus Deus, it was defined as definitive doctrine by Pope Pius XII.

"We pronounce, declare, and define it to be a divinely revealed dogma: that the Immaculate Mother of God, the ever Virgin Mary, having completed the course of her earthly life, was assumed body and soul into heavenly glory."

Since the 1870 solemn declaration of Papal Infallibility by the Vatican I, this declaration by Pope Pius XII has been the only use of Papal Infallibility. While Pope Pius XII deliberately left open the question of whether Mary died before her Assumption, the more common teaching of the early Fathers is that she did. "

After the proclamation of the assumption of Mary, Carl Jung wrote:

"The promulgation of the new dogma of the Assumption of the Virgin Mary could, in itself, have been sufficient reason for examining the psychological background. It is interesting to note that, among the many articles published in the Catholic and Protestant press on the declaration of the dogma, there was not one, so far as I could see, which laid anything like proper emphasis on what was undoubtedly the most powerful motive: namely the popular movement and the psychological need behind it."

Essentially, the writers of the articles were satisfied with learned considerations, dogmatic and historical, which have no bearing on the living religious process. But anyone who has followed with attention the visions of Mary which have been increasing in number over the last few decades, and has taken their psychological significance into account, might have known what was brewing.

The fact, especially, that it was largely children who had the visions might have given pause for thought, for in such cases, the collective unconscious is always at work ...One could have known for a long time that there was a deep longing in the masses for an intercessor and mediatrix who would at last take her place alongside the Holy Trinity and be received as the 'Queen of heaven and Bride at the heavenly court.' For more than a thousand years it has been taken for granted that the Mother of God dwelt there.

I consider it to be the most important religious event since the Reformation. It is a petra scandali for the unpsycholgical mind: how can such an unfounded assertion as the bodily reception of the Virgin into heaven be put forward as worthy of belief? But the method which the Pope uses in order to demonstrate the truth of the dogma makes sense to the psychological mind, because it bases itself firstly on the necessary prefigurations, and secondly on a tradition of religious assertions reaching back for more than a thousand years.

What outrages the Protestant standpoint in particular is the boundless approximation of the Deipara to the Godhead and, in consequence, the endangered supremacy of Christ, from which Protestantism will not budge. In sticking to this point it has obviously failed to consider that its hymnology is full of references to the 'heavenly bridegroom,' who is now suddenly supposed not to have a bride with equal rights. Or has, perchance, the 'bridegroom,' in true psychologistic manner, been understood as a mere metaphor?

The dogmatizing of the Assumption does not, however, according to the dogmatic view, mean that Mary has attained the status of goddess, although, as mistress of heaven and a mediator, she is functionally on a par with Christ, the King and mediator. At any rate her position satisfies a renewed hope for the fulfillment of that yearning for peace

580

which stirs deep down in the soul, and for a resolution of the threatening tension between opposites. Everyone shares this tension and everyone experiences it in his individual form of unrest. The more unrest he has, the less he sees any possibility of getting rid of it by rational means. It is no wonder, therefore, that the hope, indeed, the expectation of divine intervention arises in the collective unconscious and, at the same time, in the masses. The papal declaration has given comforting expression to that yearning. "How could Protestantism so completely miss the point?" ("The Answer to Job" by Carl Jung)

Mary as Mediatrix

Although this position does not make her equal to God or his son, it does acknowledge that there is now a feminine influence and energy in Heaven. With compassion and caring, the church has her whispering her counsel and wisdom into the ear of her son, the Savior.

In Catholic teachings, Jesus Christ is the only mediator between God and man, although priests may intercede. He alone reconciled, through his death on the cross, creator and creation. But this does not exclude a secondary mediating role for Mary. The teaching that Mary intercedes for all believers, especially those who request her intercession through prayer, has been held in the Church since early times, for example by Ephraim, the Syrian "after the mediator, a mediatrix for the whole world." Intercession is something that may be done by all the heavenly saints, but Mary is seen as having the greatest intercessory power. The earliest surviving recorded prayer to Mary is the *Subtuum Praesidium*, written in Greek around 250 A.D.

Mary has increasingly been seen as a principal dispenser of God's graces and an advocate for the people of God. She is mentioned as such in several official Church documents. Pope Pius IX used the title in the *Ineffabilis Deus Supremi Apostolatus*. In the first of his so called *Rosary Encyclicals*, (1883), Pope Leo XIII calls Our

Lady, *The guardian of our peace and the dispensatrix of heavenly graces.*
In his 1954 Encyclical, *Ad Caeli Reginam,* Pope Pius XII calls Mary
the Mediatrix of peace.

Co-Redemptrix
This position is not doctrine, but is held as a position by many in
the church. The idea was once again submitted for consideration
as dogma in the late 1990's. The idea submitted by the church that
Mary is Co-Redemptrix places her above all men, save one. She is
now raised above those others with bodily form in heaven, except
Jesus himself. At this point, Mary has been promoted.

Co-Redemptrix refers to the participation of Mary in the salvation
process. Already, Irenaeus, the Church Father (Died 200 A.D.),
referred to Mary as "causa salutis" [cause of our salvation],
acknowledging her authority formally. It is teaching, which has
been considered since the 15th century but never declared a
dogma. The Roman Catholic view of Co-Redemptrix does not
imply that Mary participates as equal part in the redemption of
the human race, since Christ is the only redeemer. Mary herself
needed redemption and was redeemed by Jesus Christ her son.
Being redeemed by Christ, implies that she cannot be his equal in
the redemption process. (It seems that in this part of the doctrine
Mary was born without original sin, but must have later sinned in
some way in order to need redemption.)

Co-redemptrix refers to an indirect or unequal but important
participation by Mary in the redemption process. She gave free
consent to give life to the redeemer, to share his life, to suffer with
him under the cross and to sacrifice him for the sake of the
redemption of mankind. Co-redemption is not something new.

Queen of Heaven
The doctrine that the Virgin Mary has been crowned Queen of

Heaven, "the Mother of the King of the universe," and the "Virgin Mother who brought forth the King of the whole world" goes back to St. Gregory Nazianzen. The Catholic Church often sees Mary as queen in heaven, bearing a crown of twelve stars in the Book of Revelation.

The evolution of the status of Mary, the Mother of Jesus has taken eighteen-hundred years to become what it is today. The king of glory now has a queen and the balance is restored in the mind of the church. But this balance is a false one and does not fulfill the reunification of the vital male and female energies in the one and only God. With Mary, there is still duality, and duality is not an acceptable answer to the unity found within one God and spirit.

Wisdom – Sophia
Sophia has a double meaning within Christian theology owing to the split within the early church between orthodoxy and Gnosticism. Wisdom within orthodox (mainstream) Christianity is presented as a spirit entity and consort of God. The book of Proverbs is a well known book of the Bible. The book of Wisdom is found in the Bibles of the Catholic Church and Orthodox Church. The verses here reflect the reverence of wisdom within the church, but they did not view her as a entity or the consort of God, even though the texts state that she is. Wisdom became directly connected with the Logos of the New Testament. Later, we will discuss the place of Sophia within lesser known sects such as the Gnostic Church.

Proverbs 8
22) The Lord created me first of all, the first of his works, long ago.
23) I was made in the very beginning, at the first, before the world began.
24) I was born before the oceans, when there were no springs of water.

25) I was born before the mountains, before the hills were set in place,

26) before God made the earth and its fields or even the first handful of soil.

27) I was there when he set the sky in place, when he stretched the horizon across the ocean,

28) when he placed the clouds in the sky, when he opened the springs of the ocean

29) and ordered the waters of the sea to rise no further than he said. I was there when he laid the earth's foundations.

30) I was beside him like an architect. I was his daily source of joy, always happy in his presence,

31) happy with the world and pleased with the human race.

32) Now, young people, listen to me. Do as I say, and you will be happy.

33) Listen to what you are taught. Be wise; do not neglect it.

34) Those who listen to me will be happy, those who stay at my door every day, waiting at the entrance to my home.

35) Those who find me find life, and the Lord will be pleased with them.

36) Those who do not find me hurt themselves; anyone who hates me loves death.

The Book of Wisdom 7
(Apocrypha and Orthodox Bible)

21) I learned things that were well known and things that had never been known before,

22) because Wisdom, who gave shape to everything that exists, was my teacher.

The Nature of Wisdom

23) The spirit of Wisdom is intelligent and holy. It is of one nature, but reveals itself in many ways. It is not made of any material substance, and it moves about freely. It is clear, clean,

and confident; it cannot be harmed. It loves what is good. It is sharp and unconquerable, kind, and a friend of humanity. It is dependable and sure, and has no worries. It has power over everything, and sees everything. It penetrates every spirit that is intelligent and pure, no matter how delicate its substance may be.
24) Wisdom moves more easily than motion itself; she is so pure that she penetrates everything.
25) She is a breath of God's power a pure and radiant stream of glory from the Almighty. Nothing that is defiled can ever steal its way into Wisdom.
26) She is a reflection of eternal light, a perfect mirror of God's activity and goodness.
27) Even though Wisdom acts alone, she can do anything. She makes everything new, although she herself never changes. From generation to generation she enters the souls of holy people, and makes them God's friends and prophets.
28) There is nothing that God loves more than people who are at home with Wisdom.
29) Wisdom is more beautiful than the sun and all the constellations. She is better than light itself,
30) because night always follows day, but evil never overcomes Wisdom.

Wisdom 8
1) Her great power reaches into every part of the world, and she sets everything in useful order.

Solomon's Love for Wisdom
2) Wisdom has been my love. I courted her when I was young and wanted to make her my bride. I fell in love with her beauty.
3) She glorifies her noble origin by living with God, the Lord of all, who loves her.
4) She is familiar with God's mysteries and helps determine his course of action.
5) Is it good to have riches in this life? Nothing can make you

richer than Wisdom, who makes everything function.

6) Is knowledge a useful thing to have? Nothing is better than Wisdom, who has given shape to everything that exists.

7) Do you love justice? All the virtues are the result of Wisdom's work: justice and courage, self-control and understanding. Life can offer us nothing more valuable than these.

8) Do you want to have wide experience? Wisdom knows the lessons of history and can anticipate the future. She knows how to interpret what people say and how to solve problems. She knows the miracles that God will perform, and how the movements of history will develop.

Wisdom 9

Solomon Prays for Wisdom

1) God of my ancestors, merciful Lord, by your word you created everything.

2) By your Wisdom you made us humans to rule all creation,

3) to govern the world with holiness and righteousness, to administer justice with integrity.

4) Give me the Wisdom that sits beside your throne; give me a place among your children.

5) I am your slave, as was my mother before me. I am only human. I am not strong, and my life will be short. I have little understanding of the Law or of how to apply it.

6) Even if someone is perfect, he will be thought of as nothing without the Wisdom that comes from you.

7) You chose me over everyone else to be the king of your own people, to judge your sons and daughters.

8) You told me to build a temple on your sacred mountain, an altar in Jerusalem, the city you chose as your home. It is a copy of that temple in heaven, which you prepared at the beginning.

9) Wisdom is with you and knows your actions; she was present

when you made the world. She knows what pleases you, what is right and in accordance with your commands.

10) Send her from the holy heavens, down from your glorious throne, so that she may work at my side, and I may learn what pleases you.

11) She knows and understands everything, and will guide me intelligently in what I do. Her glory will protect me.

12) Then I will judge your people fairly, and be worthy of my father's throne. My actions will be acceptable.

13) Who can ever learn the will of God?

14) Human reason is not adequate for the task, and our philosophies tend to mislead us,

15) because our mortal bodies weigh our souls down. The body is a temporary structure made of earth, a burden to the active mind.

16) All we can do is make guesses about things on earth; we must struggle to learn about things that are close to us. Who, then, can ever hope to understand heavenly things?

17) No one has ever learned your will, unless you first gave him Wisdom, and sent your holy spirit down to him.

18) In this way, people on earth have been set on the right path, have learned what pleases you, and have been kept safe by Wisdom.

Proverbs 1

Wisdom Calls

20) Listen! Wisdom is calling out in the streets and marketplaces,

21) calling loudly at the city gates and wherever people come together:

22) Foolish people! How long do you want to be foolish? How long will you enjoy making fun of knowledge? Will you never learn?

23) Listen when I reprimand you; I will give you good advice and share my knowledge with you.

24) I have been calling you, inviting you to come, but you would not listen. You paid no attention to me.

25) You have ignored all my advice and have not been willing to let me correct you.

26) So when you get into trouble, I will laugh at you. I will make fun of you when terror strikes

27) when it comes on you like a storm, bringing fierce winds of trouble, and you are in pain and misery.

28) Then you will call for wisdom, but I will not answer. You may look for me everywhere, but you will not find me.

29) You have never had any use for knowledge and have always refused to obey the Lord.

30) You have never wanted my advice or paid any attention when I corrected you.

31) So then, you will get what you deserve, and your own actions will make you sick.

32) Inexperienced people die because they reject wisdom. Stupid people are destroyed by their own lack of concern.

33) But whoever listens to me will have security. He will be safe, with no reason to be afraid.

Sophia, in Gnostic theology, is a creative, spiritual person. In one Gnostic creation story, the Archons (lesser angels) created Adam, but could not bring him to life. In other stories, Adam was formed as a type of worm, unable to attain personhood. Thus, man began as an incomplete creation. In this myth, the Archons were afraid that if Adam were fully formed, he might be more powerful than the Archons themselves. When they saw Adam was incapable of attaining the human state, their fears were put to rest, thus, they called that day the "Day of Rest."

Sophia saw Adam's horrid state and had compassion. Sophia descended to help bring Adam out of his hopeless condition. It is this story that set the stage for the emergence of the Sacred Feminine force in Gnosticism that is not seen in orthodox Christianity. Sophia brought within herself the light and power of the Supreme God. Metaphorically, within the spiritual womb of

Sophia was carried the life force of the Supreme God for Adam's salvation as seen in the Gnostic text, "*The Apocryphon of John.*"

As the emerging orthodox church became more and more oppressive to women, later even labeling them "occasions of sin," the Gnostics countered by raising women to equal status with men, saying that Sophia was, in a sense, the handmaiden or wife of the Supreme God, making the soul of Adam her spiritual offspring.

Sophia represents the highest and purest attributes of the feminine energies. Sophia is intelligent, independent, powerful, creative, caring, nurturing, and a goddess in her own right. She is the consort of God.

Who is She?
Sophia (fem. Gk. for "wisdom") is a complex biblical figure described variously as a divine attribute, a distinct hypostasis of God, a goddess-like co-partner with God, and sometimes even as synonymous with God. She arises in the later texts of the Jewish tradition, first simply as wisdom with a capital "W," and then, in the Book of Proverbs, personified in a female form. The writings of early Christianity frequently draw on Sophia as a metaphor for Christ. The texts that include references to Sophia have only been canonized in Roman Catholicism and Eastern Orthodoxy, but many contemporary feminists have turned to her as a general model for feminist spirituality.

Her personality is riddled with contradictions. She is at once creator and created; teacher and that which is to be taught; divine presence and elusive knowledge; tempting harlot and faithful wife; sister, lover, and mother; both human and divine. Her very existence thus deconstructs all traditional binary relationships, as if she were the creation of Hélène Cixous, Luce Irigaray or some other modern feminist theorist. Frequently Sophia defies the feminine norm established by society. As Virginia Mollenkott writes in The Divine Feminine, Sophia "is a woman but no lady." (Mollenkott 98). We see her crying aloud at street corners, raising her voice in the public squares, offering her saving counsel to anybody who will listen to her. Wisdom's behavior runs directly counter to the socialization of a proper lady, who is taught to be rarely seen and even more rarely heard in the sphere of public activity. (Mollenkott 98)

Her Origins

Just as Sophia defies definition, her origins seem impossible to trace. Scholars have suggested Semitic sources (the goddess of love and fertility, Ishtar), Egyptian sources (Maat, the goddess of conception), and Hellenistic sources (the goddesses Demeter, Persephone, Hecate, and Isis), and yet they have found no source for Sophia within the Hebrew tradition. Thus, it is still unclear whether she was borrowed from a nearby civilization or invented by the Hebrew writings. Scholars have dated Sophia's textual sources at least 500 years after most of the Hebrew tradition was developed. Sophia can be found in The Book of Proverbs, Wisdom of Solomon, Ecclesiasticus (Ben Sirach), and in the Christian Gospels and epistles.

Her Development

According to the authors of Wisdom's Feast, only God, Job, Moses and David are treated in greater depth in the Hebrew Scriptures than Sophia. (Cady et. al. 15). She grows in power throughout these texts, until, as Christian feminist Joan Chamberlain Engelsman suggests, Sophia comes to rival God's power, promising salvation for those who choose to follow her.

However, the extent of Sophia's divinity in this period has been widely debated. Both Engelsman and Rosemary Radford Ruether insist that the strictly monotheistic texts of Roman-era Judaism never portray Sophia as an autonomous female divine figure. Others have argued that some passages actually describe Sophia as a co-partner with God.

Early Christians seeking to understand Jesus as savior within the context of their Jewish origins searched the Hebrew Scriptures for related figures. Jesus did not completely match the traditional Jewish conception of the messiah who was to be a human king who would establish a new reign of justice and peace in Israel. Jesus actually seemed to have much more in common with Sophia who was part divine and part human, sent by God to change society. And, as the authors of Wisdom's Feast argue, both Christ and Sophia ultimately failed to completely transform society: Sophia's cries to humanity were in vain and Jesus was crucified. Thus, early Christians adopted Sophia as a model for their portrayals of Christ while continuing to refer to him as the messiah.

Paul makes the following associations between Christ and Sophia: Christ is the Wisdom of God; like Sophia, he is a creator, first born of all creation, the radiance of God's glory and the image of the invisible God. Luke describes Jesus as Sophia's son who communicates her wisdom to humanity. In Matthew's writings, Jesus is explicitly described as personified Wisdom. Perhaps John's Gospel draws the strongest connection between the two figures, relating the story of Sophia as the pre-history of Jesus.

The Disappearance of Sophia

Eventually Sophia was completely fused with Christ. Wisdom became Logos, and explicit associations between Sophia and Jesus disappeared from Christianity. Many Christian feminists describe her disappearance in the psychological language of repression. In her essay, "Wisdom Was Made Flesh," Elizabeth Johnson argues that the feminine Wisdom was replaced by the masculine Logos "as it became unseemly, given the developing patriarchal tendencies in the church, to interpret the male Jesus with a female symbol of God" (Johnson 105). The authors of Wisdom's Feast offer a very different theory. They suggest that in order to recognize Jesus as equal to God the Father, all explicit associations between Jesus and the weaker Sophia had to be abandoned.

Wisdom's Feast also traces Sophia's disappearance to the tensions at this time between the Gnostics and the mainstream Christians. The Gnostics tended to downplay Jesus' humanity, and many rejected the notion that he was human. They adopted the association between Jesus and Sophia in order to de-emphasize Christ's bodily pain and suffering and focus more on the wisdom he imparted. Mainstream Christians, eager to separate themselves from the Gnostics, thus avoided reference to Sophia.

Sophia and Feminist Spirituality
Following in the line of feminist theorists like Hélène Cixous and Luce Irigaray, the author's of Wisdom's Feast argue that in order to develop feminist spirituality we need to deconstruct traditional hierarchical binaries (i.e. sacred/profane, good/bad, male/female) and create a unity that celebrates the differentiation of its parts. Sophia, they insist, embodies this unity.

The orthodox or mainline church fight against this idea with such verses as Galatians 3:28, although that verse could also be seen as indicating the need for the balance they oppose.
New International Version
There is neither Jew nor Gentile, neither slave nor free, nor is there male and female, for you are all one in Christ Jesus.

It was the drive to keep things connected that was at the heart of the wisdom tradition. In the face of threats to Israel's national consciousness and to its provincial view of the world, the wisdom tradition sought to create a new more connected frame of reference. While groups within the priestly tradition in Israel and Judaism sought to separate and re-isolate the Hebrew faith, the wisdom tradition was trying to integrate the Hebrew perspective into the larger picture. (Cady et. al. 54)

Sophia was not only a force for unity within Judaism. She also established continuity between Judaism and Christianity. And her fusion with Christ offers contemporary Christians a way to understand their Savior as a union of male and female. As Mollenkott explains, "the combination of Wisdom/Christ leads to a healthy blend of male and female imagery that empowers everyone and works beautifully to symbolize the One God who is neither male nor female yet both male and female" (Mollenkott 104).

Similarly Johnson writes that through the filter of the Sophia metaphor, "new ways of appreciating Christ can be formed, less associated with patriarchal control and more in tune with women's daily life and collective wisdom, so often discounted as a source of insight" (Johnson 106). In light of this feminist revival of the Sophia figure, some Christian women have begun to speak of the "Sophia-God of Jesus" and of "Jesus Sophia."

Mollenkott also suggests that Sophia can replace the Virgin Mary as a positive role model for Catholic women. Mary, she insists, is an impossible model to follow, for no woman can be both virgin and mother. In addition, she argues that the strong, independent women of today cannot identify with Mary, for the Virgin Mother is a passive figure submissive to a masculine God. Sophia, however, may be a much more viable role model: "Dame Wisdom is an especially important symbol for contemporary women because she gets us beyond the concept that femaleness finds its primary fulfillment in motherhood. Wisdom is busy in the public sphere; she is no shrinking violet, no vessel waiting to be given her significance by someone else" (Mollenkott 102). Sophia supports a two-way flow of energy--both give and take--and thus she is an especially important figure for women who need to learn to restrain themselves from giving excessively.

However, like the Virgin Mary, Sophia too was shaped by a highly patriarchal society. In fact, some biblical portrayals of Dame Wisdom are clearly sexist. Some depictions of Sophia seem to reveal concerns that her growing power threatens patriarchal society. Proverbs 7 thus picks up on the traditional "bad girl" stereotype, describing Sophia as an evil harlot who threatens the patriarchally dominated institution of marriage.

Ultimately, the authors of Wisdom's Feast have to admit that much of the treatment of Sophia in the Bible and in the Christian tradition reinforces patriarchal values, making Sophia a potentially dangerous symbol of the divine. Too often she has played a mediating role, pointing toward God rather than to herself, and thus upholding male power. Because Sophia did not develop co-equal status with Yahweh, because her voice is not identified in the Christian scriptures, it has been easy to keep her secondary and derivative. (Cady et. al. 13)

In more modern Gnostic groups, Sophia is talked about in relation to Eve, Mary, and Mary Magdalene. She is compared to Eve because both women experienced a "fall from grace" which resulted in the creation of the material world into the form it is today. In the myth she gives birth to a defective creature who she casts away, but who still retains power due to her holiness. In the end, most sources agree that Sophia can be developed into a positive figure for feminist spirituality.

Conclusion:
In more ways than one the Sophia figure suggests that the gender stratification of Judaism and Christianity is centered in the body.

Most revealing is the name of this extremely powerful female figure of Judaism and Christianity. Her name "Wisdom" seems to lend her the power to transcend the "impurities" of her female body. Sophia's role in the Gnostic community also suggests that her power was rooted in her wisdom. Here, more divine than flesh and blood, she was capable of transcending any impurities that might have been associated with her female body. Although she was sometimes described as a mother of mankind and a lover of God, these were only metaphorical depictions of Sophia. Clearly her wisdom was manifested for mankind in the physical world.

The similarity continues with the way both texts describe the Supreme Being as "indescribable ." Jesus says the word in response, however, to a question from Matthew. And so the two texts move along, with the Eugnostos the Blessed revealing how the universe emerged out of the "indescribable " Father. A series of Aeons (male and female) emanated from him. They, in turn, along with their assorted attendants, fill various heavenly realms. Eventually humans emerge. Their realm is called the realm of Immortal Man. In the Sophia of Jesus Christ, much of the same information unfolds in Jesus' answers to his disciples' questions. The Father of the Universe, according to Eugnostos the Blessed, is more correctly referred to **not** as Father but as Forefather. The text discusses how that which comes from the imperishable will never perish but that which emerges from the perishable will die. These sections of the two texts are almost identical. Both texts conclude with the revelation that the Son of Man and his consort Sophia together show forth a light that is both great and androgynous — this light is the Savior. His masculine name is Savior, Father of All Things; his feminine name is Sophia, All Begetress (or Mother). The Syrian and Egyptian schools of Gnosticism often featured in their doctrines an unknowable Supreme Being who emanated lesser beings called Aeons in pairs (male and female). These

Aeons came forth in sequential order with the lowest of them being the Christ and Sophia pair. All together, they were seen as symbolizing the abstract nature of the Divine.

History of The Gospel Of Mary Magdalene

While traveling and researching is Cairo in 1896, German scholar, Dr. Carl Reinhardt, acquired a papyrus containing Coptic texts entitled the Revelation of John, the Wisdom of Jesus Christ, and the Gospel of Mary.

Before setting about to translate his exciting find two world wars ensued, delaying publication until 1955. By then the Nag Hammadi collection had also been discovered.

Two of the texts in his codex, the Revelation of John, and the Wisdom of Jesus Christ, were included there. Importantly, the codex preserves the most complete surviving copy of the Gospel of Mary, named for its supposed author, Mary of Magdala.

Two other fragments of the Gospel of Mary written in Greek were later unearthed in archaelogical digs at Oxyrhynchus in Northern Egypt.

All of the various fragments were brought together to form the translation presented here. However, even with all of the fragments assembled, the manuscript of the Gospel of Mary is missing pages 1 to 6 and pages 11 to 14. These pages included sections of the text up to chapter 4, and portions of chapter 5 to 8.

Although the text of the Gospel of Mary is incomplete, the text presented below serves to shake the very concept of our assumptions of early Christianity as well as Christ's possible relationship to Mary of Magdala, whom we call Mary Magdalene.

The Gospel of Mary Magdalene

(Pages 1 to 6 of the manuscript, containing chapters 1 - 3, are lost. The extant text starts on page 7...)

Chapter 4

21 (And they asked Jesus), "Will matter then be destroyed or not?"

22) The Savior said; "All nature, all things formed, and all creatures exist in and with one another, and they will be desolved again into their own elements (origins).

23) This is because it is the nature of matter to return to its original elements.

24) If you have an ear to hear, listen to this.

25) Peter said to him; "Since you have explained all things to us, tell us this also: What sin did the world commit (what sin is in the world)?

26) The Savior said; "There is no sin (of the world). Each person makes his own sin when he does things like adultery (in the same nature as adultery). This is called sin.

27) That is why the Good came to be among you. He came to restore every nature to its basic root.

28) Then He continued; "You become sick and die because you did not have access to He who can heal you."

29) If you have any sense, you must understand this.

30) The material world produced a great passion (desire / suffering) without equal. This was contrary to the natural balance. The entire body was disturbed by it.

31) That is why I said to you; "Be encouraged, and if you are discouraged be encouraged when you see the different forms nature has taken.

32) He who has ears to hear, let him hear.

33) When the Blessed One had said this, He greeted them all of them and said; "Peace be with you. Take my peace into you.

34) Beware that no one deceives you by saying Look (he is) here or look (he is) there. The Son of Man is within you.

35) Follow Him there.

36) Those who seek Him will find Him.

37) Go now and preach the gospel of the Kingdom.

38) Do not lay down any rules beyond what I appointed you, and do not give a law like the lawgivers (Pharisee) or you will be held to account for the same laws.

39) When He said this He departed.

Chapter 5

1) Then they were troubled and wept out loud, saying, How shall we go to the Gentiles and preach the gospel of the Kingdom of the Son of Man? If they did not spare Him, how can we expect that

they will spare us?

2) Then Mary stood up, greeted them all, and said to her follow believers, "Do not weep and do not be troubled and do not waver, because His grace will be with you completely and it will protect you.

3) Instead, let us praise His greatness, because He has prepared us and made us into mature (finished / complete) people.

4) Mary's words turned their hearts to the Good, and they began to discuss the words of the Savior.

5) Peter said to Mary; "Sister we know that the Savior loved you more than all other woman.

6) Tell us the words of the Savior that you remember and know, but have we heard and do not know.

7) Mary answered him and said; "I will tell you what He hid from you."

8) And she began to speak these words to them; "She said, I saw the Lord in a vision and I said to Him, 'Lord I saw you today in a vision.'

9) He answered and said to me; "You will be happy that you did not waver at the sight of Me. Where the mind is there is the treasure.

10) I said to Him; "Lord, does one see visions through the soul or through the spirit?"

11) The Savior answered and said; "He sees visions through neither the soul nor the spirit. It is through the mind that is

between the two. That is what sees the vision and it is (there the vision exists.)

(pages 11 - 14 are missing from the manuscript)

Chapter 8:

10) And desire (a lesser god) said; "Before, I did not see you descending, but now I see you ascending. Why do you lie since you belong to me?"

11) The soul answered and said; "I saw you but you did not see me nor recognize me. I covered you like a garment and you did not know me.

12) When it said this, the soul went away greatly rejoicing.

13) Again it came to the third power (lesser god), which is called ignorance.

14) The power questioned the soul, saying, Where are you going? You are enslaved (captured) in wickedness. Since you are its captive you cannot judge (have no judgment).

15) And the soul said: "Why do you judge me, when I have not judged?

16) I was captured, although I have not captured anyone.

17) I was not recognized. But I have recognized that God (the All) is in (being dissolved), both the earthly things and the heavenly.

18) When the soul had overcome the third power, it ascended and saw the fourth power, which took seven forms.

19) The first form is darkness, the second desire, the third ignorance, the fourth is the lust of death, the fifth is the dominion of the flesh, the sixth is the empty useless wisdom of flesh, the seventh is the wisdom of vengeance and anger. These are the seven powers of wrath.

20) They asked the soul; "Where do you come from, slayer of men, where are you going, conqueror of space?"

21) The soul answered and said; "What has trapped me has been slain, and what kept me caged has been overcome,

22) My desire has been ended, and ignorance has died.

23) In an age (dispensation) I was released from the world in a symbolic image, and I was released from the chains of oblivion, which were only temporary (in this transient world).

24) From this time on will I attain the rest of the ages and seasons of silence.

Chapter 9

1) When Mary had said this, she fell silent, since she had shared all the Savior had told her.

2) But Andrew said to the other believers; "Say what you want about what she has said, but I do not believe that the Savior said this. These teachings are very strange ideas.

3) Peter answered him and spoke concerning these things.

4) He questioned them about the Savior and asked; "Did He really speak privately with a woman and not openly to us? Are we to turn around and all listen to her? Did He prefer her to us?"

5) Then Mary sobbed and said to Peter; "My brother Peter, what do you think? Do you think that I have made all of this up in my heart by myself? Do you think that I am lying about the Savior?"

6) Levi said to Peter; "Peter you have always had a hot temper."

7) Now I see you fighting against this woman like she was your enemy.

8) If the Savior made her worthy, who are you to reject her? What do you think you are doing? Surely the Savior knows her well?

9) That is why He loved her more than us. Let us be ashamed out this and let us put on the perfect Man. Let us separate from each other as He commanded us to do so we can preach the gospel, not laying down any other rule or other law beyond what the Savior told us.'

10) And when they heard this they began to go out and proclaim and preach.

Introduction to Eugnostos the Blessed

The treatise of *Eugnostos the Blessed* (50-150 A.D.) and the gospel called, *The Sophia of Jesus Christ*, (50-200 A.D.) are presented together in a single volume, due to their close and undeniable connection. In fact, one borrowed heavily from the other. *The Sophia of Jesus Christ*, also called The **Wisdom of Jesus Christ**, seems to be a later and Christianized version of *Eugnostos the Blessed*, a non-Christian Gnostic text. Separate audiences were being targeted with the two related texts and thus they use different modes of presentation, however the words and ideas remain the same.

Eugnostos the Blessed was written to a Gnostic audience that may not have been Christian, whereas *The Sophia of Jesus Christ* was written to Christian Gnostics or the Gnostics the writer wished to sway toward Gnostic Christianity. One of the modes of persuasion was to place the words from *Eugnostos the Blessed* on the lips of Jesus in a dialog explaining the nature of God and the heavenly creations. The Gnostic cosmology, (as well as the path and plan of divine power and manifestation), is complex and deserves explanation in order to better understand the texts of *Eugnostos the Blessed* and *The Sophia of Jesus Christ*.

First, let us look at some simple definitions.

"**Gnosticism**: A system of religion mixed with Greek and Oriental philosophy of the 1st through 6th centuries A.D. Intermediate between Christianity and paganism, Gnosticism taught that knowledge rather than faith was the greatest good and that through knowledge alone could salvation be attained."
Webster's Dictionary

Tractate

noun formal

a treatise.

• a book of the Talmud.

ORIGIN late 15th cent.: from Latin tractatus, from tractare 'to handle,' frequentative of trahere.

Dictionary

"**Sophia** (σοφία, Greek for "wisdom") is a central idea in Hellenistic philosophy and religion, Platonism, Gnosticism, Orthodox Christianity, Esoteric Christianity, as well as Christian mysticism. Sophiology is a philosophical concept regarding wisdom, as well as a theological concept regarding the wisdom of the biblical God.

Sophia is honored as a goddess of wisdom by Gnostics, as well as by some Neo-pagan, New Age, and feminist-inspired Goddess spirituality groups. In Orthodox and Roman Catholic Christianity, Sophia, or rather Hagia Sophia (Holy Wisdom), is an expression of understanding for the second person of the Holy Trinity, (as in the dedication of the church of Hagia Sophia in Istanbul) as well as in the Old Testament, as seen in the Book of Proverbs 9:1, but not an angel or goddess.

Sophia (Greek Σοφία, meaning "wisdom," Coptic τcοφια tsophia) is a major theme, along with Knowledge (Greek γν⬚σις gnosis, Coptic sooun), among many of the early Christian knowledge-theologies grouped by the heresiologist Irenaeus as gnostikos, "learned." Gnosticism is a 17th-century term expanding the definition of Irenaeus' groups to include other syncretic and mystery religions.

In Gnostic tradition, Sophia is a feminine figure, analogous to the human soul but also simultaneously one of the feminine aspects of God. Gnostics held that she was the syzygy of Jesus Christ (i.e. the Bride of Christ), and Holy Spirit of the Trinity. She is occasionally referred to by the Hebrew equivalent of Achamōth (Ⓧχαμώθ, Hebrew chokhmah) and as Prunikos (Προύνικος). In the Nag Hammadi texts, Sophia is the lowest Aeon, or anthropic expression of the emanation of the light of God. She is considered to have fallen from grace when she created another being of some kind, without God's approval, in so doing creating or helping to create the material world."

Wikipedia 2014

The word Gnostic is based on the Greek word "Gnosis," which means "knowledge." The "Gnosis" is the knowledge of the ultimate, supreme God and his spirit, which is contained within us all. It is this knowledge that allows one to transcend this material world with its falsities and spiritual entrapments and ascend into heaven to be one with God.

For centuries the definition of Gnosticism has in itself been a point of confusion and contention within the religious community. This is due in part to the ever-broadening application of the term and the fact that various sects of Gnosticism existed as the theology evolved and began to merge into what became mainstream Christianity.

Even though Gnosticism continued to evolve, it is the theology in place at the time that the Gnostic Gospels were written that should be considered and understood before attempting to render or read a translation. To do otherwise would make the translation cloudy and obtuse.

It becomes the duty of both translator and reader to understand the ideas being espoused and the terms conveying those ideas. A grasp of theology, cosmology, and relevant terms is necessary for a clear transmission of the meaning within the text in question.

With this in mind, we will briefly examine Gnostic theology, cosmology, and history. We will focus primarily on Gnostic sects existing in the first through fourth centuries A.D. since it is believed most Gnostic Gospels were written during that time. It was also during that time that reactions within the emerging Christian orthodoxy began to intensify.

The downfall of many books written on the topic of religion is the attempt to somehow remove history and people from the equation. History shapes religion because it shapes the perception and direction of religious leaders. Religion also develops and evolves in an attempt to make sense of the universe as it is seen and understood at the time. Thus, to truly grasp a religious concept it is important to know the history, people, and cosmology of the time. These areas are not separate but are continually interacting. This is how the information in this book will be presented to the reader.

The translations of The Sophia of Jesus Christ and Eugnostos the Blessed presented in this volume are loosely based on the work of Douglas M. Parrott, who has done extensive scholarly work on both texts. It was thought Parrott's work may appeal to highly trained theologians but was not suitable for the general public due to a style of translation which assumed a deeper knowledge of various forms of Gnosticism, as well as obscure terms and theologies. The translation herein attempts to be more clear, self-explanatory and, when needed, elucidated through commentary.

In the Nag Hammadi library, two separate versions of Eugnostos The Blessed were found. Codex III and Codex V contained the tractate Eugnostos the Blessed and the two versions show some differences.

Codex III contains Eugnostos in its third document, occupying pages 70 -90. The first two lines of the text read, 'Eugnostos the blessed, to those who are his,' and the title at the end of the tractate is given as 'Eugnostos the Blessed.' For that reason the tractate is generally referred to as Eugnostos the Blessed. The opening of the version of the text in Codex V pages1-17 cannot be reconstructed in the same way, and the title at the conclusion of the document is merely 'Eugnostos.

The two versions are quite different from one another, and probably represent independent Coptic translations of a Greek original. The version in Codex III is usually taken to be an earlier version than the one in Codex V. In *The Nag Hammadi Library in English* the version in Codex III is the one chosen for translation, with missing or damaged portions supplemented by the version in Codex V.

Eugnostos is an interesting name. In Greek, *eugnostos* is an adjective composed of *eu*, 'good' or 'well,' and *gnostos*, 'known,' and so Eugnostos means 'well known,' but could also mean 'easy to understand.' One should not interpret it as "easy to understand" without acknowledging the irony in the name, since the Gnostic concepts contained within the work are difficult to follow for the modern reader, unfamiliar with the subtleties of ancient Gnosticism.

The opposite of this term is *agnostos*, 'unknown,' a term commonly used in philosophy to indicate the supreme God. This adjective also has an active meaning, 'the one who can know,' 'the one capable of knowing' and is a play on the word and a synonym of the term *gnostes, meaning* 'the one who knows,' *Acts*26:3). Those who are Gnostic are gnostes. The link between *gnostos* and *gnostes* makes the name Eugnostos highly symbolic.

The name Eugnostos also appears in another Nag Hammadi document titled, *Holy Book of the Great Invisible Spirit*. In the final portion of this text the author introduces himself with his two names: Eugnostos, his spiritual name, and Gongessos, the name he would go by in his everyday life.

Eugnostos the Blessed is a philosophical treatise, if one could call Gnosticism a philosophy, rather than a theological treatise. It is presented in a letter written by Eugnostos to the readers as an explanation of the creation of gods in their realms and man.

The letter includes greetings to the recipients, and a formal conclusion.
Eugnostos follows a clear train of thought in its attempt to explain its doctrine. It employs techniques of explanation and argument found in the philosophical schools of the time.

The letter contains a variety of material and doctrine, which may indicate the letter was changed or expanded in stages through time.

The author of *Eugnostos* opens with a criticism of philosophical theories (an allusion to Stoics, Epicureans, and Babylonian scholars) and proceeds to focus on truth as a divine revelation, not a human construction.

The author describes the divine realm inhabited by five beings, each having his own aeon and heavenly followers, angels, and deities. The exact names will vary depending on the way they are translated. These five beings are the (1) unborn, unbegotten or unconceived Father, (2) the Human Father by himself, (3) the Immortal Human or Immortal Man, (4) the Son of Humanity or the Son of Man, and (5) the Savior.

According to the author, *Eugnostos,* these beings were not produced through emanations, as is described in other Gnostic texts, but rather, they came into being as a continuous chain. The highest God, the unborn or unbegotten Father, is described by means of both negative theology with words and terms as "he cannot be described, indescribable , without name, infinite, incomprehensible, cannot be known, unchanging, imperishable, immortal, untraceable, and so on. He also uses positive theology, with words and phrases such as, he surpasses everything, and he is blessed, perfect, and the like. This way of approaching the notion of God was common in Middle Platonic schools and is employed in other Nag Hammadi texts. The *Secret Book of John* and *Allogenes the Stranger* also use this technique.

 Eugnostosis was heavily influenced by Greek philosophical speculation and technique, but he also focuses on mystical Jewish elements. There is a deep interest in angelology but no particular preoccupation with angelic names and their pronunciation, as is generally seen in other Jewish pseudepigrapha, letters of Jewish mysticism, or other Nag Hammadi treatises.

Michel Tardieu concludes that *Eugnostos* "is a text which represents, for the history of thought, the first (in a temporal sense) expository treatise of revelation where metaphysics serves angelology and where angelology changes constantly into metaphysics."

Scopello states, "The original Greek text of *Eugnostos the Blessed* was probably composed in Egypt as early as the end of the first century. From Egypt this tractate circulated in Syria, and it was known in the school of Bardaisan in the beginning of the third century." (*The Nag Hammadi Scriptures*, p. 274)

Eugnostos the Blessed was most likely used to construct The Sophia of Jesus and when we look at Eugnostos we are likely seeing a Gnostic document, generally lacking in Christian theology and components, which was altered and expanded by the author of the Sophia of Jesus to render a book directed to the Gnostic

Christian community. Thus, in Eugnostos we are able to go back one generation and see how the theology was altered and expanded.

To the readers of today, the main idea espoused within most Gnostic texts regarding creation may seem absurd and very tedious, as a "unbegotten" or "unborn" god spontaneously creates a being or beings via an unexplained emanation, only to have that creation then create others, who in turn also create, and on literally ad nauseam. To our scientific and critical minds, this action is best understood if one examines radio or sound waves.

As a frequency is radiated, or emanated, the frequency produces harmonics, which are an integer multiple of the fundamental frequency. In turn the harmonics produce more harmonics, each one becoming less powerful as it is produced from the one before. The forth harmonic is usually less powerful than the second, as each is in turn farther away from the "source" or fundamental frequency. Each harmonic has the property of being a periodic of the fundamental frequency.

In the same way the source of light and life in the Gnostic belief system produced beings, which in turn produced beings, each having less power as the creations are progressively farther removed from the source. Even though this insight will not mitigate the redundant creation patterns in the text, it will bring about a clearer understanding of the aim and purpose of the Gnostic explanation of creation.

Eugnostos the Blessed

Eugnostos, the Blessed, to those who are in his care.
Rejoice in the fact that you know (you have gnosis).
Greetings!

I have taught you that all men born from the beginning of the
world until now are dust. While they have searched and
questioned about God, and wanted to know who he is and what
he is like, they have not found him.

The wisest among them have speculated about the truth regarding
how the world was formed and how it runs but their speculation
has not brought them to the truth.

Three separate philosophers have opinions and have speculated
about this and none agree. Some of them say the world runs by
itself. Others say God directs it. Others, that it is fate and it is
random. But none of these are correct.

Again, of three voices that I have just mentioned, none is true. For
whatever is born from itself is an empty life; it is self-made.

The thought of providence is foolish.

(Since "providence can mean god or nature this could be a
statement that the "god of this world is foolish" or "leaving things
to a natural outcome yields foolishness.")

Fate does not discern between people.

Whoever is able to break free of these three voices and listen to another voice and thus confess the God of truth and know (agree with) everything about him, that person will be an immortal dwelling in the midst of mortal men.

"He-Who-Is" is beyond description. No important person knew him, no authority or those subject to them, nor any creature from the beginning of the world knew him. Only he alone knew himself.

 For he is immortal and eternal, having no birth; for everyone who is born will perish, but he was never born. He is unbegotten, having no beginning; for everyone who has a beginning has an end. No one rules over him. He has no name; for whoever has a name is the creation of another. He is unnameable. He has no human form; for whoever has human form is the creation of another. He has his own semblance - not like anything we have perceived or seen, but he has a strange, unfamiliar semblance that surpasses all things and is beyond anything and everything ever seen. (He is beyond infinity, thus) he looks to every side and sees himself from himself. He is infinite; he is incomprehensible. He is ever eternal and is unlike anything. He is unchanging good. He is faultless. He is everlasting. He is blessed. He is unknowable and only he knows himself. He is immeasurable. He is untraceable. He is perfect and flawless. He is eternally blessed. He is called 'Father of the Universe'.

Before anything was visible among those that are visible, the majesty and the authorities were in him and he embraces the wholeness and totality of everything, and nothing embraces him. He is all mind, thought and reflection, consideration, rationality and power.

All these elements are equal powers. They are the sources of the totalities. And their whole race from first to last was in the foreknowledge of the Unbegotten, but they had not yet come to

613

visible manifestation.

Now a difference existed among the immortal aeons. We know that everything that comes from something or someone perishable (mortal) will perish, since it came from something that will perish. Whatever came from immortal will not perish but will become immortal, since it came from immortality. Many men went astray because they did not known this difference, and thus they died.

(Note: The above text is an explanation of the Gnostic idea of salvation. A person must "denounce this world and all connections to the mortal, perishable world and realize his/her connection and path to the immortal, eternal, universal Father, from where we all originated. By doing so we achieve his same immortality in spirit.)

This is all that needs to be said, since it is impossible for anyone to dispute the nature of my words about the blessed, immortal, true God.

Now, if anyone desires to have faith in the words I have set down here, let him go from here to the end of what is visible an discover what is hidden and invisible, and "Thought" will instruct him in how faith in those things that are not visible was found in what is visible. This is a principle of knowledge.

The Lord of the Universe is incorrectly called 'Father' but he is the 'Forefather'. For the Father is the beginning and real source of what is visible. For the Lord is without beginning and is the Forefather. He sees himself within himself, like a mirror, having appeared in his likeness as Self-Father, that is, Self-Father, and as he who stands before himself, since he is the Unborn (Unbegotten) First Existent one who stands before himself. He is indeed of equal age with the one who is before him, but he is not equal to him in power.

(Note: Set up two mirrors so an image seen in the first is reflected into both infinitively. All images are equal, but only the source image has the power.)

Afterward he revealed many self-begotten ones standing before him, equal in age and power, being in glory and without number, and they are called 'The Generation of Kingdoms over Whom There Is No Kingdom'. And the whole multitude of that place, over which there is no kingdom, is called 'Sons of Unborn (Unbegotten) Father.'

Now the Unknowable One is forever full of immortal and indescribable joy. They all rest in him, rejoicing eternally in indescribable, unchanging measureless joy voiced in ceaseless jubilation that was never heard or known among all the aeons and their worlds. But, we should stop here, for we could go no forever describing the wondrous principles of the Father.

The first who appeared before the universe in infinity is the Self-created, Self-made Father, and he is full of shining, indescribable light. In the beginning, he decided his likeness should become a great power. Immediately, the source of light appeared as the Immortal Man, who had both male and female energies. His male name is 'Begotten, Perfect Mind'. And his female name is 'Mother Sophia', the all-wise one. It is said that she resembles her brother and her consort. She is uncontested truth. Yet, here, in the world below her world, error exists but her truth fights against it.

Through the Immortal Man appeared the first divisions of his choice, which were divinity and kingdom. This was because the Father, who is called 'The Self-Fathered Man' (self-begotten man) revealed this.

He created a great aeon for his own majesty. He gave him great authority, and he ruled over all creations. He created gods and archangels and angels, myriads without number to attend him.

Now through that Man originated divinity and kingdom. Therefore he was called 'God of gods', 'King of kings'.

The "First Man" is 'Faith' ('pistis' is the Greek word for faith) for those who will come after him. Within him is a unique mind and thought. He is thought, reflection, consideration, rationality, and power. All the attributes that exist are perfect and immortal.

Certainly, they are equally immortal, but they are not equal in power, just as there is a difference in authority between a father and son. The son is the thought of the father, which remains.

I taught you earlier that of all the things that were created the "Unity," (indivisible, totality and oneness) was first and the (division) duality followed it, and after that, the triad followed it and divisions continued up to the tenth divisions and beyond. Those from the tenths rule the hundredths; the hundredths rule the thousandths; the thousands rule the ten thousands. This is the pattern of the immortals.

This is the pattern that exists among the immortals. The indivisible and the "Thought" are those things that belong to "the Immortal Man." The things that precede from thought belong to the tenths, and the teachings belong to the hundreds. Counsel belongs to the thousands. Power belongs to the ten thousands.

In the beginning, the mind produced thought and the things that came from thinking. Teaching came from these things and counsels came from teachings, and power came from counsels. Power manifested all the attributes; all that was manifested appeared from his powers, and everything created had form which was manifested from the attributes of power.

And what was formed appeared from what was created. What was named appeared from what was formed. This is when differences arose among begotten things, which appeared from what was named from the first to the last, by power of all the aeons. Now " The Immortal Man" is full of every eternal and indescribable glory and all joy. His whole kingdom rejoices in everlasting joy like no one ever heard or known in any aeon or world that came after them.

Afterward another principle came from "The Immortal Man," who is called 'The Self-perfected Father.' When he and his consort, Great Sophia were in agreement he revealed that first-begotten man, who had both male and female energies, who is called, 'The First-begotten Son of God'.

His female aspect is 'The First Born,' called Sophia, Mother of the Universe, and some call her 'Love'. The First-begotten, was given authority from his father to create countless angels to accompany and assist him. The entire gathering of those angels is called 'The Assembly of the Holy Ones," and the Lights without shadow.' When they greet one another their embraces become like the angels themselves.

The First Father is called 'Adam of the Light.' The kingdom of "The Son of Man" is full of indescribable joy and perpetual jubilation, and they rejoice forever in great joy for their eternal glory, which no aeon has heard, nor has it been revealed to any aeons that has ever existed.

Then Son of Man was in agreement with Sophia, his consort, and manifested a great Light, which is both male and female. His masculine name is called 'Savior, Father of All things'. His feminine name is called 'Sophia, The Mother of All' and some call her "Faith" (or Pistis in Greek).

Then the Savior was in agreement with his consort, Pistis Sophia, and revealed six spiritual beings, who were the type of those preceding them, having both male and female energies. Their male names are these:
The first, 'Unborn' (unbegotten); the second, 'Self-created' (self-begotten)'; the third, 'Father'; the fourth, 'First Father'; the fifth, 'All-Father'; and the sixth, 'Arch-Father'.

Also the names of the females are these; the first, 'All-wise Sophia'; the second, 'Mother of All - Sophia'; the third, 'All Wise Mother' (Mother of all Wisdom); the fourth, 'First Mother Sophia'; the fifth, 'Love Sophia'; and the sixth, 'Pistis Sophia (Faith – Wisdom)'.

Those I have just mentioned were in agreement and thoughts appeared in the aeons that exist. From thoughts came reflections (remembering); from reflections came considerations; from considerations came reason, from reason came will, and from will came words.

Then the twelve powers, whom I have just discussed, were in agreement with each other, males and females were revealed. Because of this, there are seventy-two powers. Each one of the seventy-two revealed five spiritual powers, which are the three hundred and sixty powers. When these all came together there was will.

These aeon came into existence as the type of Immortal Man. Now, time is a reflection of the types and came from the First Father, his son. The year is a type of Savior. The twelve months is the type of the twelve powers. The three hundred and sixty days is the type of the three hundred and sixty powers who appeared from Savior. Their hours are the type of the angels who came from them and moments are the type of the powers, who are without

618

number.

When all of these appeared, All-Father, their father, soon created twelve aeons to accompany the twelve angels. And in each aeon there were six heavens, producing a total of seventy-two heavens, for the seventy-two powers who appeared from him. Each heaven contained five firmaments, totaling three hundred sixty firmaments from the three hundred sixty powers that appeared from them. When the firmaments were completed, they were called 'The Three Hundred Sixty Heavens', because these were the name of the heavens that were before them. And all these are perfect, flawless and good. But this was the way the defect of separate female energy appeared.

The first aeon is "The Immortal Man". The second aeon is the "Son of Man", who is also called '"The First Father". It is he who is called "Savior". The one encompassing these is the aeon over which there is no kingdom. He is the Eternal Infinite God, the aeon of the aeon, and all immortals who are in the aeon above the Eighth that appeared in chaos.

The Immortal Man revealed aeons, powers and kingdoms and gave authority to everyone who appeared from him, so that they could make whatever they desire until the days of chaos come.

And these were in agreement with each other and manifested a multitude of splendid things from spirit and light and it was glorious. These received names in the beginning, that is, the first, the middle, the complete (perfect), which were the first aeon and the second and the third.

The first was called Unity and the second is Rest, since each one has its own name, and the third aeon is called 'Assembly'. A great multitude appeared in the one and in him there was a multitude. Therefore, when the multitude gathers in unity they are called

'Assembly', from the Assembly that is above heaven. Therefore, the Assembly of the Eighth was manifested both male and female energies and was named partly as male and partly as female. The male was called 'Assembly', the female was called 'Life'. This was to show that the female produced life in all the aeons. Then from the beginning all the names were received.

He agreed with his thought and the powers appeared who were called 'gods'; and from careful thoughts the gods revealed the divine gods; and from their deep thought the gods manifested lords; and the lords of the lords were formed from their words; and the lords from their powers produced archangels; the archangels made angels; from them, the likenesses appeared, with structure and form for naming all the aeons and their worlds.

All the immortals have authority from the power of Immortal Man and Sophia, his consort, who was also called 'Silence', because by reflecting without speech she perfected her own majesty. Since the immortals had the authority, and each produced a number of great kingdoms in all the eternal heavens and their firmaments, thrones and temples, to demonstrate their own majesty.

Some are in buildings and chariots, which were indescribable in their glory so that no creature could attain them. And hosts of angels without number were made by these aeons in order to accompany them in glory and the angels were spirits of unimaginable light, perpetual in their virginity. They are pure will, having no sickness nor weakness, and they come into being instantaneously. In this way the aeons with their heavens and firmaments for the glory of Immortal Man and Sophia, his consort came into being.

The pattern of every aeon and their worlds and those that came afterward are herein contained in order to provide the types. And from the chaos of the world their likenesses were revealed in the heavens.

From the Immortal One, who is Unbegotten, to the revelation of chaos, everything is in the light that shines without shadow in indescribable joy and jubilation without words. They are eternally delighted because of their glory that does not change, and the complete rest, which cannot be described. No aeons that came to be nor any of their powers can conceive of the depth of glory or rest. But this much is enough, that you might accept these things until the one who does not need be taught appears among you. Then he will speak all these things to you with zeal and in purity of knowledge.

History of the Sophia of Jesus

The Sophia of Jesus Christ is dependent on and derived from the text called *Eugnostos the Blessed*, both of which were unearthed at Nag Hammadi. In the caves the archeologists found two copies for each book, but the copies differed somewhat.

The Sophia of Jesus Christ took the information and theology within *Eugnostos* and converted it into a dialogue with Jesus, placing the teachings of Eugnostos in the teaching of Jesus, spoken by him to his followers.

Scholars have referred to Eugnostos the Blessed and the Sophia of Jesus Christ as a revelation discourse in which the risen Christ answers his disciples' questions. Eugnostos the Blessed may have been composed during Jesus' lifetime or shortly thereafter and the Sophia of Jesus Christ seems to be near the end of the first century.

Eugnostos the Blessed opens as a letter with a formal greeting and goes on to proclaim that even the wisest philosophers have not understood the truth about the "ordering" of the world and that they have spoken three opinions, not agreeing. The Sophia of Jesus Christ opens after Jesus has risen and his twelve disciples and some women go up on a mountain called Divination and Joy. There the Savior appears and tells them that their speculation about the world order has not reached the truth, nor has it been reached by the three ways the philosophers have put forth.

Douglas M. Parrott, in his translation for the book, *The Nag Hammadi Library in English*, edited by Robinson writes: "The notion of three divine men in the heavenly hierarchy appears to be based on Genesis 1-3 (Immortal Man = God; Son of Man = Adam [81,12]; Son of Son of Man, Savior = Seth). Because of the presence of Seth, although unnamed in the tractate, *Eugnostos* must be thought of as Sethian, in some sense. However, since it is not

622

classically Gnostic and lacks other elements of developed Sethian thought, it can only be characterized as proto-Sethian. Egyptian religious thought also appears to have influenced its picture of the supercelestial realm. The probable place of origin for *Eugnostos*, then, is Egypt. A very early date is suggested by the fact that Stoics, Epicureans and astrologers are called "all the philosophers." That characterization would have been appropriate in the first century B.C.E., but not later.

Eugnostos and *Soph. Jes. Chr.* may have influenced the Sethian-Ophites, as described by Irenaeus. Some have proposed an influence by *Eugnostos* on Valentinianism. Because of the dating of *Eugnostos*, it would not be surprising if *Soph. Jes. Chr.* had been composed soon after the advent of Christianity in Egypt - the latter half of the first century C.E. That possibility is supported by the tractate's relatively nonpolemical tone."

The translation of "The Sophia of Jesus Christ," also called "The Wisdom of Jesus Christ," is derived from two separately preserved copies of the text. The first copy is in Nag Hammadi Codex III (NHC III); a second copy of this text was preserved in the Berlin Gnostic Codex. A third fragment of the text in Greek was also found among the Oxyrhynchus papyrus documents. Thus we have three distinct copies of this scripture attested from three separate ancient sources, two in Coptic, one in Greek.

The mythologies preserved in the Nag Hammadi documents are dated to about the second century A.D. and are built on the assumptions and concepts of Plato and the philosophers who followed him. They elaborated on the creation of the universe in Plato's *Timaeus*.

The Sophia's main sources, *Eugnostos the Blessed*, is replete with Platonisms. The cosmology and theology of Plato, combined with Christian ideas gave us Christian Gnosticism and the degree of Platoisms within the Gnostic system gave rise to various Gnostic "denominations." Generally Gnosticism is considered a type of Christianity but there were Gnostics that were not Christians. These held to the belief that one had to receive knowledge or gnosis to see the true nature of the world and thus escape but they did not hold to the belief that Jesus or Jesus alone was sent to impart that gnosis. The revelation could come from a teacher or from the indescribable God directly. This seems to be the type of Gnosticism presented in Eugnostos the Blessed. One could see how this, by adding the exclusive conduit of Jesus, could become a Christian Gnostic text.

Both *Eugnostos* and *The Sophia* list the main emanations or beings that came to constitute the perfect, spiritual realm along with the Forefather. These beings include the "Self-Father" (the image of the Forefather as if viewed in a mirror), the "Immortal Man" who had the balance of male and female power. It is this entity who emerges in the beam of light as the Forefather views his/her image, the "Son of Man," who is the first-*begotten*, meaning the others were not begotten, and the "Savior," who is "revealed" by the Son of Man as a "great light," having both male and female energies. Each of these figures are endowed with both male and female energies and have their corresponding "female" portion, usually called "Sophia" or Wisdom.

The Sophia of Jesus Christ places the whole letter of instruction with Eugnostos the Blessed into the form of a dialogue between "the Saviour", Jesus the Christ, and his disciple *Eugnostos*, who at the time of the teaching from Jesus showed no signs of being "Christian."

Most Gnostic systems in and around Syria or Egypt taught that the universe began with an original, unknowable God, referred to as the Indescribable God, Parent God, Bythos, the Monad, the Unity or the One. God is looked at as a divine light and from light souls are formed. The One spontaneously emanated and created Aeons. These are beings we would consider angels or demons. They were created in pairs and as the light shown, it traveled forth and as it diminished it begat or produced through its emanation progressively 'lesser' beings in sequence as it went forth. Each being was farther away from the source and was less in some way as the one before.

624

As the beings were created, so was their abode with the creator in the midst. The place, which we would view as heaven, is called the Pleroma, or fullness of God. Since God is in the Pleroma it is symbolic of being in or with the divine nature.

According to some Gnostic texts, Sophia, one of the first and most powerful Aeons, wished to know or unite with the indescribable God. Depending on the mythos, she either tried to emulate God and attempted to create on her own, without help or consent, or she attempted to breach the barrier between herself and the unknowable One. After failing, she was ejected from the Pleroma and was then in a fallen state.

Sophia's misplaced desires gave rise to matter and soul. The first-born and most powerful result of her disaster is the Demiurge whose name is Yaldabaoth, "Son of Chaos." Sophia saw the grotesqueness of her mistake and flung her creation away from her. The Demiurge, being alone, perceived himself to be his own creator and the ultimate power. He then began to create Aeons of his own.

He and his Aeons created the physical universe in which we live, including man. Man was created imperfect from the imperfect god. The Demiurge did not have the power, or possess enough of the divine spark of life to fully complete the task. Man was produced in the form of a worm. Sophia looked on man and had pity, feeling responsible for him since it was her mistake that brought the pitiful creature to life. Sophia infused some of her divine spark or pneuma into man.

In another Gnostic text. The Pistis Sophia, Christ is sent from the Godhead in order to bring Sophia back into the fullness (Pleroma). Christ enables her to again see the light, bringing her knowledge of the spirit. Christ is then sent to earth in the form of the man

Jesus to give men the Gnosis needed to rescue themselves from the physical world and return to the spiritual world. In Gnosticism, the Gospel story of Jesus itself is an allegory. It is considered the Outer Mystery or first mystery and is used as an introduction to Gnosis.

For the Gnostics, the drama of the redemption of the Sophia through Christ must be repeated in all of us. The word of God must call out to the wisdom in all of us and enable us to see the truth and find our way back to the one true God. The Sophia resides in all of us as the Divine Spark to be fanned to flame with the truth Christ delivers.

Jews in Alexandria, being heavily influenced by Greek philosophy, were occupied with the concept of the Divine Sophia, as the revelation of God's wisdom and feminine voice or force. They believed she was involved in the formation and running of the natural universe. She was responsible for communicating divine insight and knowledge to mankind. It was easy and natural for the fascination and reverence for Sophia to influence new Christians in the area, since they made up the majority of the new Jesus sect of Judaism.

In Proverbs 8, Sophia or Wisdom is described as God's Counselor and Work-mistress. The Revised Version has it as "Workmen" but the noun is feminine. She dwelt beside Him before the Creation of the world and was with Him.

Proverbs 8
Douay-Rheims 1899 American Edition (DRA)
8 Doth not wisdom cry aloud, and prudence put forth her voice?
2 Standing in the top of the highest places by the way, in the midst of the paths.
3 Beside the gates of the city, in the very doors she speaketh, saying:
4 O ye men, to you I call, and my voice is to the sons of men.

5 O little ones, understand subtilty, and ye unwise, take notice.

6 Hear, for I will speak of great things: and my lips shall be opened to preach right things.

7 My mouth shall meditate truth, and my lips shall hate wickedness.

8 All my words are just, there is nothing wicked nor perverse in them.

9 They are right to them that understand, and just to them that find knowledge.

10 Receive my instruction, and not money: choose knowledge rather than gold.

11 For wisdom is better than all the most precious things: and whatsoever may be desired cannot be compared to it.

12 I wisdom dwell in counsel, and am present in learned thoughts.

13 The fear of the Lord hateth evil: I hate arrogance, and pride, and every wicked way, and a mouth with a double tongue.

14 Counsel and equity is mine, prudence is mine, strength is mine.

15 By me kings reign, and lawgivers decree just things,

16 By me princes rule, and the mighty decree justice.

17 I love them that love me: and they that in the morning early watch for me, shall find me.

18 With me are riches and glory, glorious riches and justice.

19 For my fruit is better than gold and the precious stone, and my blossoms than choice silver.

20 I walk in the way of justice, in the midst of the paths of judgment,

21 That I may enrich them that love me, and may fill their treasures.

22 The Lord possessed me in the beginning of his ways, before he made any thing from the beginning.

23 I was set up from eternity, and of old before the earth was made.

24 The depths were not as yet, and I was already conceived. neither had the fountains of waters as yet sprung out:

25 The mountains with their huge bulk had not as yet been established: before the hills I was brought forth:

26 He had not yet made the earth, nor the rivers, nor the poles of the world.

27 When he prepared the heavens, I was present: when with a certain law and compass he enclosed the depths:

28 When he established the sky above, and poised the fountains of waters:
29 When he compassed the sea with its bounds, and set a law to the waters that they should not pass their limits: when be balanced the foundations of the earth;
30 I was with him forming all things: and was delighted every day, playing before him at all times;
31 Playing in the world: and my delights were to be with the children of men.

Based on the above verse, and other sources, Gnostics gave a special place to Sophia, and her relation to the physical world.

In the time of the Gnostics only seven planets were known. They were thought of as seven circles rising one above another, and dominated by the seven Archons. These constituted the (Gnostic) Hebdomad. The Hebdomad is the seven "world-creating" archons in most Gnostic systems. Above the highest of them, and over-vaulting it, was the Ogdoad, the sphere of immutability, which was next to the spiritual.

Sophia's position is further defined in Proverbs 9.

Proverbs 9
Douay-Rheims 1899 American Edition (DRA)

9 Wisdom hath built herself a house, she hath hewn her out seven pillars.
2 She hath slain her victims, mingled her wine, and set forth her table.
3 She hath sent her maids to invite to the tower, and to the walls of the city:
4 Whosoever is a little one, let him come to me. And to the unwise she said:
5 Come, eat my bread, and drink the wine which I have mingled for you.
6 Forsake childishness, and live, and walk by the ways of prudence.
7 He that teacheth a scorner, doth an injury to himself: and he that rebuketh a wicked man, getteth himself a blot.

8 Rebuke not a scorner lest he hate thee. Rebuke a wise man, and he will love thee.

9 Give an occasion to a wise man, and wisdom shall be added to him. Teach a just man, and he shall make haste to receive it.

10 The fear of the Lord is the beginning of wisdom: and the knowledge of the holy is prudence.

11 For by me shall thy days be multiplied, and years of life shall be added to thee.

12 If thou be wise, thou shalt be so to thyself: and if a scorner, thou alone shalt bear the evil.

13 A foolish woman and clamorous, and full of allurements, and knowing nothing at all,

14 Sat at the door of her house, upon a seat, in a high place of the city,

15 To call them that pass by the way, and go on their journey:

16 He that is a little one, let him turn to me. And to the fool she said:

17 Stolen waters are sweeter, and hid den bread is more pleasant.

18 And he did not know that giants are there, and that her guests are in the depths of hell.

Based on the above verse, Gnostic believed Sophia had her house above the created universe, in the place of the midst, between the upper and lower world. She sits at "the gates of the mighty," at the realms of the seven Archons, and at the "entrances" to the upper realm of light her praise is sung. Sophia is therefore the highest ruler over the visible universe, and at the same time the mediatrix between the upper and the lower realms. She is "the mother of the living," from which all souls draw their beginning and creation. By her the light is brought down from the pleroma in order to light the darkness of the physical world.

Sophia was with God and lost her first estate. She lost her memory of God and had to be restored to her rightful place by Jesus, who came to "re-teach" her the things she once knew. The fate of Sophia is the prototype of what is repeated in the history of all individual souls, which, being of a heavenly origin, have fallen from the upper world of light, which was their original home. Souls should have remembered their origins because they have the divine spark from God in them, which came through Sophia, but they came under the influence of evil powers, from whom they must endure suffering until they return to the upper world once more.

Sophia needed the redemption through Christ, by whom she is delivered from her ignorance and was then brought back to her original home in the Upper Pleroma. The souls of all her children must follow her example and be returned to heaven. There, in the heavenly bridal chamber, they will all celebrate the marriage feast of eternity.

Being armed with a surface knowledge of Gnosticism we can proceed to the texts, which we are now equipped to better understand.

The Sophia of Jesus Christ
Also Called
The Wisdom of Jesus Christ

Following the resurrection of Jesus, the twelve, along with seven women, continued to be his disciples, and went to Galilee to the mountain called "Seeking Knowledge and Joy".

When they gathered together they were baffled and had questions concerning the nature and structure of the universe, the intended plan of redemption, God's protection and intention, and the power of the spiritual rulers. The disciples had questions about the mysteries the Savior had taught them in secret.

It was at this point the Savior appeared. He did not appear in his previous form, but in the form of an invisible spirit. And his likeness was like an immense angel of light. But what he looked like I must not describe. No earthly flesh could endure it, but only pure and perfect flesh, the nature of which he taught us about on the Mount of Olives, in Galilee.

And he said: "Peace be to you, My peace I give you!" They were amazed and frightened but the Savior laughed and said to them: "What are you thinking about? What are the questions perplexing you?"

Philip said: "We do not understand the underlying reality of the universe, the plan of redemption, or the meaning of the mysteries."

The Savior replied to them: "I want you to understand that every person born on earth from the beginning of the world until now

631

were mortal (dust / animal). They sought God and had questions about who he is and about his nature, but none found him.

The wisest among these types of men have speculated about the way the world works and about its movement. But their speculations have not brought them to the truth. All this speculation has culminated into three philosophies and their philosophers do not agree.

Some say the world directs itself. Others say that it is the hand of God that directs it. Others say that it is fate. But none of these three views are close to being the truth. They are mere speculation and are in error.

(Note: Of the three philosophies, some think the world runs like a clock, once wound up or created, it runs itself without guidance from man or god. Some believe god controls each situation and event. Some believe it is not controlled at all, but life is simply a series of random events.)

I know "He who is Infinite Light" and I have come from him to teach you about the nature of life and to teach you the truth.

Mortal life which comes from mortal life is unclean. Fate and randomness have no wisdom and do not discern between people. But you have been chosen to know the truth and if you are worthy of this knowledge you will receive it and understand it. Whoever has not been conceived and born from the act of carnal sex (literally: whoever has not been sown by the act of rubbing flesh together in uncleanness) but instead has been begotten by the First Born who was sent, he will be an immortal being in the midst of mortal men."

Matthew said to him: "Lord, no one can find the truth except through you. So, we ask you to teach us the truth (so we can know your source)."

The Savior said: "He Who Is indescribable cannot be known by anything or anyone made. Nothing created can know him. No idea can fathom him. From the beginning of the world until now, he has not been revealed or understood by anyone except himself alone and those to whom he wishes to reveal himself, and that revelation comes through "He Who is From the Source of Light."

From this point forward, it is I who am the Great Savior, and I will teach you about the source of light. He is immortal and eternal. He is eternal because he was not born, for everyone was was born or shall be born will perish. He was not conceived and has no beginning. All who have a beginning will have an end.

He has no name. All creatures (things created or born) have a name and are the creation of some other person or creature. He comes from no one and no one rules over him.

He cannot be named. You cannot know his nature. He has no body, for whoever has human form is the creation of another person."

"He resembles no one but himself. He is unlike anything or anyone you have ever seen or perceived. His visage exceeds anything in the universe.

He is infinite and is the only thing in the universe that can see all aspects of himself. No mind can grasp him. He is immortal and looks like nothing anyone has ever seen. He is unchanging good, perfect and eternal. He is holy. Even though he cannot be known, he knows himself and he is omniscient. He cannot be quantified or measured. He is blessed, sacred, timeless, flawless, eternal and he is called 'Father of the Universe'".

Philip said: "Lord, how did god reveal himself to the perfect ones?"

The perfect Savior answered: "Before all that is seen became visible, the power and authority were his. He contained the unity and entirety of all things, and there was nothing outside of him. He is mind and thought, consideration, memory, rationality and power. All of these parts had equal authority and value since they were all from the source of his total mind. Before the beginning the eternal Father knew the entire race of the perfect ones, from first one to last one."

(Note: The reader must keep in mind that even though we are socially comfortable in referring to god as "he" the Gnostics gave god both male and female attributes equally. These attributes or energies are expressed in the following dialog.)

Thomas asked him: "Master and Savior, why were they created, and why were they revealed?"

The perfect Savior responded: "I came to you from infinity so that I can explain all things to you. The Existent Spirit was the father, who had the power to beget (like a father) and also had the nature to give form to creation (like a mother). He did this because he wished to reveal the vast wealth that was hidden within him. Because of his mercy and love, he wished to bring forth fruit by himself, so he did not have to experience goodness alone.

He wished other perpetual spirits to bring forth flesh and fruit in a glorious and upright way, in order to show his eternal and infinite grace so that the treasures of Self-Created God, the father of every eternal thing, might be revealed by those that came into existence afterward. But they had not yet been made visible and great differences existed among the eternal beings."

He cried out, announcing: "Whoever has ears to hear about the things of infinity, let him hear! I speak to you who are awake."

He continued and said: "Everything that came from that which will perish will itself perish. Like begets like. But whatever came from that which will not perish will not perish but it will be eternal. Many men went missed their aim because they did not know the difference before they died."

Mary asked him: "Lord, how can we really know what you have taught us?"
The perfect Savior said: "You originated from the place of invisible things and came into the realm of visibility. Those who belong to Unbegotten Father, The emanation of pure thought, will understand through his revelation how faith in the invisible realm is found in those that are visible. Whoever has ears to hear, let him hear!

(Note: Gnostics believe that the creator of the visible realm is not the Lord of the universe. The creator of the visible realm was the Demiurge. Thus if the Demiurge was the "father" of the physical realm the Lord of the Universe would be called the forefather, since the forefather created Sophia and Sophia created the Demiurge. This means both Sophia and the Demiurge have a beginning and creator, but the Lord of the Universe is without a beginning.)

And he continued: "The Lord of the Universe should not be called 'Father', but he should be called 'Forefather', because he is the beginning of those that will appear. The Lord has no beginning, so he is called the Forefather. "

(Note: The following paragraphs are difficult to understand if one is not a Gnostic of the first century. They seem convoluted but represent an attempt to explain how the "Prime Causality" or the "Forefather" became both Forefather and Son of God by producing his own image.)

He continued, saying: "Seeing himself within himself as in a mirror, he resembled no one but himself, and his appearance was as the Holy Father for he is the father of himself. He is watcher who is viewing the watched one, and he was the First in Existence and the Father who was never begotten. He is equal to himself in age, for he is the Light facing the same Light, but he is not equal to him in power."

Then an entire multitude begot themselves and they were equal in age, power, and glory, and they were innumerable, and the race was called 'The Generation Ruled By No Kingdom.'

It was from one of these that mankind appeared. Those in that multitude over which there is no kingdom are called 'Sons of Unbegotten Father, God, Savior, and Son of God.'

You have his likeness. He is the unknowable, and full of eternal ever-lasting glory and indescribable joy. All are at rest in him, rejoicing in indescribable joy forever in his eternal glory and they celebrate greatly such as was never heard or known among any of the aeons or their worlds until now."

Matthew said to him: "Master and Savior, how was Man manifested?"

The perfect Savior responded: "I taught you that he who came into being existed before the universe. He is infinite. He made and grew from himself because he is full of light, bright and indescribable. From the beginning he decided to have his image become a great power. When he decided this, immediately The Source of Light appeared as an Immortal Man, having both male and female attributes and energies. It is through that Immortal Androgynous Man people might attain their salvation and awaken from their forgetfulness. The one who was sent to teach you and explain this to you is now with you until the end of the poverty, which the robbers have brought upon you.

And his consort is the Great Sophia, who was created from the beginning in him and for him to be united with him. The immortal, self-created divine king and father revealed this. And he created a great aeon, whose name is 'Ogdoad', for his own majesty."

(Note: Valentinius was a prominent second century Gnostic leader. He used the term Ogdoad to describe eight emanations - grouped in pairs of male/female, active/passive principles - by which Creation was effected. Initially there was the masculine principle of Bythos (the Abyss or Depth which was boundless and unqualified) from which came the feminine Silence, Grace or Thought. The uniting of these two produced Mind (masculine) and Truth (feminine). These four principles are the root of everything. The powers brought forth further powers called Aeons, which were produced in masculine/feminine pairs. The union of Mind and Truth brought forth Word (logos), which was masculine, and Life, which was feminine. Together they created Man (masculine) and the Church (feminine). This group of eight principles formed the Ogdoad, which in turn produced further Aeons. The thirtieth of these was Sophia. Her desire for wisdom drove her attempt to know god in ways she was not capable of. The error of Sophia in not comprehending her limits. Her error that caused the Fall that made our Universe, according to Valentinian myth. Later, some Gnostic would apply the term to Jesus. According to the Gnostics, most people are asleep and do not realize that there exists a higher spiritual reality. They sleepwalk, seeing only the lower manifestations and assume there is nothing more. Through gnosis brought about by Jesus it is possible for the higher Mind (logos) to discern the true nature of reality. Jesus would be the Ogdoad, and the expression of this higher knowledge.)

"He was given full authority to rule over the creation of poverty. He created gods and angels, archangels, and innumerable myriads of creatures, and they accompanied him. From that Light and the tri-male Spirit, which is that of Sophia, his consort they were made. But God was the source of divinity and the kingdom, and therefore he was called 'God of gods' and 'King of kings'.

This "First Man" has God's unique mind. He is like God within and in his thought. This is because he is the thought, consideration, reflection, rationality, and power of God. All the attributes that exist are perfect and immortal. As God is eternal, so is the First man and they are equal in mind and immortality but not in power. In power (authority) they are different, like the difference between father and son. As I said earlier, among the things that were created, the monad is first."

(Note: When the texts indicates the "First Son" is not equal to God in power we must consider this, not as power of creation or destruction, but more in the area of authority. A son may be as strong as the father but the father will have more authority than the son. Think about the difference in degree of authority between a king and a prince.)

"And at the conclusion everything was manifested from his power. And from that which was created everything was fashioned, from what was fashioned everything was formed, and from everything that was formed everything was named. And this how there arose differences among the unbegotten ones from beginning to end."

Then Bartholomew said to him: " In the Gospel 'Man' and 'Son of Man' are mentioned? To which of them is this Son related?"

The Holy One said to him: "I taught you The First Man is called

638

'The One Who Begets`, and `Self-perfected Mind'. He and the Great Sophia, his consort, reflected together and manifested his first-begotten son who contains both male and female energies. His male name is 'First Father, and Son of God', his female name is 'First Woman who Begat, Sophia, Mother of the Universe'. Some call her 'Love'. Now First-begotten is called 'Christ'. Since he has authority from his father, he created an innumerable multitude of angels who accompany the Spirit and Light."

His disciples said to him: "Lord, teach us about the one called 'Man', that we also may completely know his glory."

The perfect Savior said: "Whoever has ears to hear, let him hear. First Father is called 'Adam, Eye of Light.' He is called this because he came from shining Light. The Light's holy angels have no shadow and are beyond description, and they rejoice with joy forever as they reflect what they received from their Father.

The entire Kingdom of "Son of Man", who is called 'Son of God,' is indescribably joyous and constant jubilation. It is without shadow and in it there is rejoicing forever over His eternal glory. The likes of such a celebration has never been heard until now, nor have the aeons that came afterward or any of their worlds experienced anything like it. I came to you from self-created one who is the first and infinite light, that I might reveal everything to you."

Once again, his disciples questioned him, saying: "Explain to us how they came down from the invisible, immortal world to the mortal world."
The perfect Savior said: "Son of Man consented with Sophia, his consort, and manifested a great light, having both male and female components. His male name is called 'Savior, Father of All Things'. His female name is called 'Mother of All, Sophia (wisdom)'. Some call her 'Faith'.

"All who come into the world are like a single drop from the Light. They are sent to the world of the Almighty Light in order to be guarded by the Light. The Almighty Light bound the drops with forgetfulness through the power he retained from Sophia's will during her creation of him. He did this so that the matter might be spread through the whole world in poverty, and "Almighty" may continue in his arrogance and blindness and ignorance, which befit his real name (Yaldaboth).

But I came from the realms above by the will of the great Light. I escaped from his bond. I have brought the work of the robbers to a halt. I have awakened those drops that were sent from Sophia, so that they might bear much fruit through me.
 They can now be perfected and never again go back to their defective state.

Through me, the Great Savior, the glory of the true god will be revealed, so that Sophia might regain her state from the defective state she initiated, and her sons might not again become defective but might attain honor and glory and be able to go to their Father, and know the words of the masculine Light.

And you were sent by the Son, and the Son was sent so that you might receive Light, and remove yourselves from the induced state of forgetfulness brought about by the rulers here. And I am here so that the condition might not overtake you again or be manifested again because when you have sex that comes from the fire and fear that came from the flesh it produces distorted malicious intent, and this is the intent of the rulers."

Then Thomas said to him: "Lord, Savior, how many aeons are in the realms above the heavens (sky)?"
The perfect Savior said: "I am proud of all of you because you asked me about the great aeons. It shows me that your roots are in

640

the infinite. When those whom I have discussed with you earlier were revealed, Self-created Father very soon created twelve aeons to accompany the twelve angels. All these are perfect and good, but the defect (imbalance) in the female appeared."

And Thomas said to him: "How many immortal aeons came from the infinite?"

The perfect Savior said: "Whoever has ears to hear, let him hear. The first aeon is the Son of Man, who is called 'First Father' and he is called 'Savior' and he has appeared. The second aeon is Man, who is called 'Adam, Eye of Light'. The aeon covering him has no kingdom. He is the aeon of the Eternal Infinite God, the Self-created aeon and is over the aeons. He is the aeon of the immortals, whom I described earlier. He is the aeon above the Seventh, which appeared from Sophia, which is the first aeon.

"Now Immortal Man manifested aeons and powers and kingdoms, and gave authority to all who appear in him, that they might exercise their desires until the last things that are above chaos. For these come together with each other and manifest everything considered magnificent. They brought about the light of spirit in a multitude of glorious manifestations and they are without number. These were called forth in the beginning by the first aeon who was first called 'Unity and Rest'.

Each Aeon has its own name but together they were called 'Assembly' because from the great multitude appeared in one aeon and in one aeon a multitude revealed themselves. Now because the multitudes gather and come to a unity we call them 'Assembly of the Eighth. They appeared with both male and female energies and attributes and were named partly as male and partly as female. The male is called 'Assembly', while the female is called 'Life', that it might be shown that from a female came the life for all the aeons. And from the beginning they were so named.

From the agreement of his thought, the powers appeared quickly and they were called 'gods'. And the gods of the gods from their wisdom manifested gods. From their wisdom they manifested masters and the masters of the masters through the power of their thoughts manifested archangels. Then archangels from their words revealed angels and from angles the outward appearances of reality manifested, with structure and form and name for all the aeons and their worlds."

"And the immortals, whom I have just described, all have authority passed to them from 'Immortal Man', who is called 'Silence', because through thought without speech all her own majesty was perfected. The immortals had power for each to create a great kingdom in the Eighth, and also thrones and temples and firmaments for their own majesties. For these all came into being through the will of the Mother of the Universe."

Then the Holy Apostles said to him: "Lord and Savior, it is necessary that we know, so please tell us about those who are in the aeons."

The perfect Savior said: "I will tell you about anything you ask. They created hosts of angels, myriads without number, for their accompaniment and for their glory. They created virgin spirits, the indescribable and unalterable lights. And through the strength of their will they have no sickness nor weakness."

"In this fashion the aeons were created rapidly in the heavens and the firmaments and contained the glory of "Immortal Man" and "Sophia," his consort. Their creation was patterned after the heavens of chaos and their worlds. This was their template. All natures, from the manifestation of chaos on are all in the Light that shines without shadow, and it contains joy that cannot be described, and unspeakable jubilation. They delight themselves forever because they have unchanging glory, all power, and rest without end. Even among the aeons this cannot be described. I have revealed this to you, I teach you this so you might shine in Light more than these."

Mary said to him: "Holy master, where did your disciples come from, and where are they going, and what is their purpose here?" The Perfect Savior said to them: "I taught you that Sophia, the Mother of the Universe and the consort, desired to bring these into existence by herself and without her male consort. She wanted to use the will of the Father of the Universe, (a part of which she contained) that his unfathomable goodness might be revealed. But he created that barrier between the immortals and those that came afterward, so that the consequence might follow.

Every aeon and chaos would show the defect of the female power alone, and the result would be that she would struggle with the error. And this error became the barrier of (for) spirit.

As I have taught you, it is from aeons above the emanations of Light that a drop from Light and Spirit came down to the lower regions of "Almighty" into chaos, that their fashioned forms might appear from that drop. The result is a judgment on him who is called "Arch-Father," and whose name is Yaldabaoth.

That drop manifested a fashioned form through the breath, as a living soul. But it was withered, misshapen and slept, as in a coma, and was ignorant of the soul. When it was heated from the breath of the Great Light of the Male it began to be able to think. Only then were names given by all who are in the world of chaos. All things in that realm of the soul came through that Immortal One when he breathed into him.

But when this came about by the will of "Mother Sophia", "Immortal Man" pieced together the garments by way of his breath, for a judgment on the robbers. But since he was like a soul himself, he was not able to take that power for himself until the number of the aeons of chaos was completed and the time determined by the great angel was fulfilled.

I have taught you about "Immortal Man" and in doing so I have freed you from the bonds of the robbers. I have done this for him. I have broken the gates of the cruel ones as they looked on. I have humiliated them and revealed their malicious intent. I have shamed them and forced them to face their ignorance.

I came here to do these things so that they have the opportunity to join with that Spirit and Breath and that they may be brought into unity and the two may become one, just as from the first. In this state of unity you will be fruitful and you will ascend to "Him Who Is from the Beginning", in unspeakable joy and glory and honor and grace of the Father of the Universe.

Whoever knows the Father in pure gnosis will ascend to the Father and rest in unborn Father. But whoever does not know him or has faulty error in their knowledge will go to the dwell in a defective state with those rejected from the Eighth. Now whoever knows "Immortal Spirit of Light in silence", through their thoughts and in their welcoming of the truth will show me proof they know of the Invisible One, and he will become a light in the Spirit of Silence. Whoever knows Son of Man in gnosis and love will bring me a sign of "Son of Man," and he will go to the dwelling-places with those in the Eighth.

Then he said: Behold, I have revealed to you the name of the "Perfect One" and the entire will of the Mother of the Holy Angels. I have shown you how the masculine multitude was completed. You have been told how the aeons appeared in the infinity and came to be in the unfathomable wealth of the Great Invisible Spirit and how they all took from his goodness, which

644

was the treasure house of rest, which has no kingdom over it.

I came from First Who Was Sent, that I might reveal to you "Him Who Is from the Beginning." In their arrogance, "Arch-Father" and his angels thought they were gods. And I came to remove them from their blindness, that I might tell everyone about the God who is above the universe. I will stomp upon their graves, humiliate them, expose their malicious intent, and break their yoke. I will awaken my own. I have given you authority over all things as Sons of Light, that you might tread upon their power with your feet."

After the blessed Savior said these things he disappeared from them. Then all the disciples were greatly overjoyed in their spirit from that day on. And his disciples began to preach the Gospel of God, the eternal, immortal Spirit. Amen.

Printed in Great Britain
by Amazon